SOMETHING ABOUT THE AUTHOR®

Something about
the Author *was named
an "**Outstanding
Reference Source**,"
the highest honor given
by the American
Library Association
Reference and Adult
Services Division.*

ISSN 0276-816X

something ABOUT THE AUTHOR®

Facts and Pictures about Authors and Illustrators of Books for Young People

volume 131

GALE®

THOMSON

GALE

Detroit • New York • San Diego • San Francisco • Cleveland • New Haven, Conn. • Waterville, Maine • London • Munich

THOMSON
GALE

Something about the Author, Volume 131

Project Editor
Scot Peacock

Editorial
Karen V. Abbott, Katy Balcer, Frank Castronova, Sara Constantakis, Anna Marie Dahn, Alana Joli Foster, Madeline Harris, Arlene M. Johnson, Michelle Kazensky, Julie Keppen, Jennifer Kilian, Joshua Kondek, Lisa Kumar, Marie Lazzari, Thomas McMahon, Jenai Mynatt, Judith L. Pyko, Mary Ruby, Anita Sundaresan, Maikue Vang, Denay L. Wilding, Thomas Wiloch

Research
Michelle Campbell, Nicodemus Ford, Sarah Genik, Barbara McNeil, Tamara C. Nott, Gary J. Oudersluys, Tracie A. Richardson, Cheryl L. Warnock

Permissions
Debra Freitas, Lori Hines

Imaging and Multimedia
Dean Dauphinais, Robert Duncan, Leitha Etheridge-Sims, Mary K. Grimes, Lezlie Light, Michael Logusz, Dan Newell, David G. Oblender, Christine O'Bryan, Kelly A. Quin, Luke Rademacher

Manufacturing
Stacy L. Melson

LIBRARY OF CONGRESS CATALOG CARD NUMBER 72-27107

ISBN 0-7876-4719-5
ISSN 0276-816X

Contents

Authors in Forthcoming Volumes

Below are some of the authors and illustrators that will be featured in upcoming volumes of *SATA*. These include new entries on the swiftly rising stars of the field, as well as completely revised and updated entries (indicated with *) on some of the most notable and best-loved creators of books for children.

*Laurie Halse Anderson: Anderson writes for children and young adults, in work ranging from lighthearted folktales such as *Ndito Runs,* to earnest morality tales for the publishers of the "American Girl" series, and taut dramas for older teens, such as *Speak* and the historical thriller *Fever 1793. Speak,* a first-person narrative written in the voice of a young rape victim, was a Michael L. Printz Award Honor Book the first year the prize was awarded.

Barbara Bash: Bash is known for creating picture books on nature topics that capture the imagination of older and younger children alike. In her self-illustrated books, simple texts that explain the wonders of nature are accompanied by meticulously detailed paintings. Her 2001 work *Dig, Wait, Listen: A Desert Toad's Tale* was "an Outstanding Science Trade Book for Children" selection.

*Lynley Dodd: Dodd is a New Zealand author and illustrator who has been widely praised for her books for children. Her self-illustrated stories for young children often feature animals, most often of the domesticated variety. In Dodd's popular "Hairy Maclary" books, a small, scruffy black terrier engages in adventures with a host of four-legged friends. Dodd was awarded the Distinguished Companion of the New Zealand Order of Merit in 2002 for "services to children's literature and book illustration."

*Walter Farley: A popular, prolific American writer of fiction and nonfiction for children and young adults, Farley is considered a major contributor to juvenile literature as well as a prominent author of animal stories. He is best known as the creator of the "Black Stallion" series, twenty-one tales that feature a magnificent, half-wild Arabian horse and his offspring. The series has been a favorite of young readers for more than sixty years and has sold over a hundred million copies.

*Hilary Knight: Knight is a well-respected author and multitalented illustrator with a worldwide reputation for creating unique and delightful characters in both words and pictures. Knight has written and illustrated nine books for children, illustrated nearly sixty other books for both children and adults, breathed new life into a number of classic folktales with his illustrations, and designed theater posters promoting several very popular Broadway plays. Knight is probably most identified as the illustrator of Kay Thompson's enormously popular "Eloise" books.

*Beatrix Potter: English author and illustrator Potter was a beloved children's storyteller and artist. Her classic, enduring series featuring woodland animals began with the publication of *The Tale of Peter Rabbit* in 1901 and continued over the next two decades as she produced over twenty self-illustrated works that have entertained young and old readers for nearly a century.

*José Maria Sánchez-Silva: One of the most renowned Spanish children's writers whose works have been translated into English, Sánchez-Silva is known in the United States as the author of *Marcelino: A Story from Parents to Children, The Boy and the Whale, Ladis and the Ant,* and *Second Summer with Ladis,* all books that were first published in his native language. Sánchez-Silva's children's books have won praise for their poetic fusion of the magical and the real in themes centering on family, religion, and death through portrayals of relationships between children and animals.

William Stout: Stout has illustrated picture books, comic strips, movie posters, and record albums. He has also worked as a designer on such films as Disney's *Dinosaurs.* In 2002 he published *The New Dinosaurs,* and in 2002 he illustrated Richard Matheson's fable *Aby and the Seven Miracles.*

Terry Trueman: In 2000 Trueman burst onto the literary scene with the young adult novel *Stuck in Neutral,* which earned popular and critical acclaim. In this novel, he portrayed the interior life of Shawn, a boy with cerebral palsy who appears outwardly to be severely impaired, yet has a rich mental existence. Trueman found inspiration for the work in the life of his own son Sheehan, who was injured at birth and suffers from severe cerebral palsy.

*Douglas Wood: Wood--a folk singer, wilderness guide, and naturalist-- became an overnight sensation in the world of children's books with the 1992 publication of *Old Turtle,* a gently didactic book that reminds readers of the unity of all living things. Wood continued to stretch the limits of the picture book genre with *Grandad's Prayers of the Earth,* which received the Christopher Award in 1999. Wood is also the author of three popular, humorous picture books featuring dinosaurs as main characters: *What Dads Can't Do,* published in 2000; *What Moms Can't Do,* published in 2001; and *What Teachers Can't Do,* published in 2002.

Introduction

Something about the Author (*SATA*) is an ongoing reference series that examines the lives and works of authors and illustrators of books for children. *SATA* includes not only well-known writers and artists but also less prominent individuals whose works are just coming to be recognized. This series is often the only readily available information source on emerging authors and illustrators. You'll find *SATA* informative and entertaining, whether you are a student, a librarian, an English teacher, a parent, or simply an adult who enjoys children's literature.

What's Inside SATA

SATA provides detailed information about authors and illustrators who span the full time range of children's literature, from early figures like John Newbery and L. Frank Baum to contemporary figures like Judy Blume and Richard Peck. Authors in the series represent primarily English-speaking countries, particularly the United States, Canada, and the United Kingdom. Also included, however, are authors from around the world whose works are available in English translation. The writings represented in *SATA* include those created intentionally for children and young adults as well as those written for a general audience and known to interest younger readers. These writings cover the entire spectrum of children's literature, including picture books, humor, folk and fairy tales, animal stories, mystery and adventure, science fiction and fantasy, historical fiction, poetry and nonsense verse, drama, biography, and nonfiction.

Obituaries are also included in *SATA* and are intended not only as death notices but also as concise overviews of people's lives and work. Additionally, each edition features newly revised and updated entries for a selection of *SATA* listees who remain of interest to today's readers and who have been active enough to require extensive revisions of their earlier biographies.

New Autobiography Feature

Beginning with Volume 103, *SATA* features two or more specially commissioned autobiographical essays in each volume. These unique essays, averaging about ten thousand words in length and illustrated with an abundance of personal photos, present an entertaining and informative first-person perspective on the lives and careers of prominent authors and illustrators profiled in *SATA*.

Two Convenient Indexes

In response to suggestions from librarians, *SATA* indexes no longer appear in every volume but are included in alternate (odd-numbered) volumes of the series, beginning with Volume 57.

SATA continues to include two indexes that cumulate with each alternate volume: the Illustrations Index, arranged by the name of the illustrator, gives the number of the volume and page where the illustrator's work appears in the current volume as well as all preceding volumes in the series; the Author Index gives the number of the volume in which a person's biographical sketch, autobiographical essay, or obituary appears in the current volume as well as all preceding volumes in the series.

These indexes also include references to authors and illustrators who appear in Gale's *Yesterday's Authors of Books for Children, Children's Literature Review,* and *Something about the Author Autobiography Series.*

Easy-to-Use Entry Format

Whether you're already familiar with the *SATA* series or just getting acquainted, you will want to be aware of the kind of information that an entry provides. In every *SATA* entry the editors attempt to give as complete a picture of the person's life and work as possible. A typical entry in *SATA* includes the following clearly labeled information sections:

- *PERSONAL:* date and place of birth and death, parents' names and occupations, name of spouse, date of marriage, names of children, educational institutions attended, degrees received, religious and political affiliations, hobbies and other interests.

- *ADDRESSES:* complete home, office, electronic mail, and agent addresses, whenever available.

- *CAREER:* name of employer, position, and dates for each career post; art exhibitions; military service; memberships and offices held in professional and civic organizations.

- *AWARDS, HONORS:* literary and professional awards received.

- *WRITINGS:* title-by-title chronological bibliography of books written and/or illustrated, listed by genre when known; lists of other notable publications, such as plays, screenplays, and periodical contributions.

- *ADAPTATIONS:* a list of films, television programs, plays, CD-ROMs, recordings, and other media presentations that have been adapted from the author's work.

- *WORK IN PROGRESS:* description of projects in progress.

- *SIDELIGHTS:* a biographical portrait of the author or illustrator's development, either directly from the biographee—and often written specifically for the *SATA* entry—or gathered from diaries, letters, interviews, or other published sources.

- *BIOGRAPHICAL AND CRITICAL SOURCES:* cites sources quoted in "Sidelights" along with references for further reading.

- *EXTENSIVE ILLUSTRATIONS:* photographs, movie stills, book illustrations, and other interesting visual materials supplement the text.

How a SATA Entry Is Compiled

A *SATA* entry progresses through a series of steps. If the biographee is living, the *SATA* editors try to secure information directly from him or her through a questionnaire. From the information that the biographee supplies, the editors prepare an entry, filling in any essential missing details with research and/or telephone interviews. If possible, the author or illustrator is sent a copy of the entry to check for accuracy and completeness.

If the biographee is deceased or cannot be reached by questionnaire, the *SATA* editors examine a wide variety of published sources to gather information for an entry. Biographical and bibliographic sources are consulted, as are book reviews, feature articles, published interviews, and material sometimes obtained from the biographee's family, publishers, agent, or other associates.

Entries that have not been verified by the biographees or their representatives are marked with an asterisk (*).

Contact the Editor

We encourage our readers to examine the entire *SATA* series. Please write and tell us if we can make *SATA* even more helpful to you. Give your comments and suggestions to the editor:

BY MAIL: Editor, *Something about the Author,* The Gale Group, 27500 Drake Rd., Farmington Hills, MI 48331-3535.

BY TELEPHONE: (800) 877-GALE

BY FAX: (248) 699-8054

Something about the Author Product Advisory Board

The editors of *Something about the Author* are dedicated to maintaining a high standard of excellence by publishing comprehensive, accurate, and highly readable entries on a wide array of writers for children and young adults. In addition to the quality of the content, the editors take pride in the graphic design of the series, which is intended to be orderly yet inviting, allowing readers to utilize the pages of *SATA* easily and with efficiency. Despite the longevity of the *SATA* print series, and the success of its format, we are mindful that the vitality of a literary reference product is dependent on its ability to serve its users over time. As literature, and attitudes about literature, constantly evolve, so do the reference needs of students, teachers, scholars, journalists, researchers, and book club members. To be certain that we continue to keep pace with the expectations of our customers, the editors of *SATA* listen carefully to their comments regarding the value, utility, and quality of the series. Librarians, who have firsthand knowledge of the needs of library users, are a valuable resource for us. The *Something about the Author* Product Advisory Board, made up of school, public, and academic librarians, is a forum to promote focused feedback about *SATA* on a regular basis. The five-member advisory board includes the following individuals, whom the editors wish to thank for sharing their expertise:

- **Eva M. Davis,** Teen Services Librarian, Plymouth District Library, Plymouth, Michigan

- **Joan B. Eisenberg,** Lower School Librarian, Milton Academy, Milton, Massachusetts

- **Francisca Goldsmith,** Teen Services Librarian, Berkeley Public Library, Berkeley, California

- **Harriet Hagenbruch,** Curriculum Materials Center/Education Librarian, Axinn Library, Hofstra University, Hempstead, New York

- **Monica F. Irlbacher,** Young Adult Librarian, Middletown Thrall Library, Middletown, New York

- **Robyn Lupa,** Head of Children's Services, Jefferson County Public Library, Lakewood, Colorado

- **Eric Norton,** Head of Children's Services, McMillan Memorial Library, Wisconsin Rapids, Wisconsin

- **Victor L. Schill,** Assistant Branch Librarian/Children's Librarian, Harris County Public Library/Fairbanks Branch, Houston, Texas

- **Caryn Sipos,** Community Librarian, Three Creeks Community Library, Vancouver, Washington

Acknowledgments

Grateful acknowledgment is made to the following publishers, authors, and artists whose works appear in this volume.

ALLEN, JONATHAN B. Allen, Jonathan B., illustrator. From an illustration in *Chicken Licken,* by Jonathan B. Allen. Transworld Publishers Ltd., 1996. © 1996 Jonathan B. Allen. Reproduced by permission of Harcourt, Inc. First published in Great Britain in 1996 by Transworld Publishers Ltd./ Allen, Jonathan B., illustrator. From an illustration in *Don't Wake the Baby!,* by Jonathan B. Allen. Tango Books, 2000. Text and illustrations © 2000 by Jonathan Allen. Reproduced by permission.

ANHOLT, CATHERINE. Anholt, Catherine, illustrator. From an illustration in *Catherine and Laurence Anholt's Big Book of Families,* by Laurence Anholt. Candlewick Press, 1998. Illustrations © 1998 Catherine Anholt and Laurence Anholt. Reproduced by permission of the publisher Walker Books Limited, London.

ARNOLD, CAROLINE. Arnold, Caroline, photograph by Arthur Arnold. Reproduced by permission of Caroline Arnold./ Arnold, Caroline, photographer. From a photograph in *Easter Island: Giant Stone Statues Tell of a Rich and Tragic Past,* by Caroline Arnold. Clarion Books, 2000. © 2000 by Caroline Arnold. Reproduced by permission./ From a photograph in *El Nino: Stormy Weather for People and Wildlife,* by Caroline Arnold. Clarion Books, 1998. Reproduced by permission of Houghton Mifflin Company./ Trachok, Cathy, illustrator. From an illustration in *Did You Hear That?: Animals with Super Hearing* by Caroline Arnold. Charlesbridge, 2001. Text copyright © 2001 by Caroline Arnold. Illustrations © 2001 by Cathy Trachok. Reproduced by permission of Charlesbridge Publishing, Inc. All rights reserved.

AXELROD, AMY. McGinley-Nally, Sharon, illustrator. From an illustration in *Pigs Go to Market: Fun with Math and Shopping,* by Amy Axelrod. Aladdin, 1999. Illustrations copyright © 1997 by Sharon McGinley-Nally. Reproduced by permission of Simon & Schuster Books for Young Readers, an imprint of Simon & Schuster Children's Publishing Division.

BATT, TANYA ROBYN. Griffin, Rachel, illustrator. From an illustration in *The Fabrics of Fairytale: Stories Spun from Far and Wide,* collected and retold by Tanya Robyn Batt. Barefoot Books, 2000. Illustrations © 2000 by Rachel Griffin. Reproduced by permission.

BRIGGS, RAYMOND (REDVERS). Briggs, Raymond (Redvers), photograph by Allen Daniels. © Allen Daniels. Courtesy of Hamish Hamilton, Ltd. Reproduced by permission of Penguin Books Ltd./ Briggs, Raymond, illustrator. From an illustration in his *Ethel and Ernest.* Jonathan Cape, 1998. Copyright © 1998 by Raymond Briggs. Reproduced by permission of Random House Group, Limited and Alfred A. Knopf, a division of Random House, Inc./ Briggs, Raymond, illustrator. From an illustration in his *The Snowman.* Random House. 1978. Copyright © 1978 by Raymond Briggs. Reproduced by permission of Random House Children's Books, a division of Random House, Inc.

BRUCHAC, JOSEPH (III). Bruchac, Joseph, photograph by Michael Greenlar. Reproduced by permission of Joseph Bruchac./ Nelson, S. D., illustrator. From an illustration in *Crazy Horse's Vision,* by Joseph Bruchac. Lee & Low, 2000. Illustrations copyright © 2000 by S. D. Nelson. Reproduced by permission of Lee & Low Books, Inc./ Johnson, Stephen T., illustrators. From a jacket of *Sacajawea: The Story of Bird Woman and the Lewis and Clark Expedition,* by Joseph Bruchac. Silver Whistle, 2000. Jacket illustration copyright © 2000 by Stephen T. Johnson. Reproduced by permission of Harcourt, Inc. This material may not be reproduced in any form or by any means without the prior written permission of the publisher.

CLARKE, PAULINE. Bryson, Bernarda, illustrator. From an illustration in *The Return of the Twelves,* by Pauline Clarke. The Akadine Press, 1990. Copyright © 1962, 1990 by Pauline Clarke. Reproduced by permission.

COBB, VICKI. Cobb, Vicki, photograph by Michael Gold. Reproduced by Permission of Vicki Cobb.

CRAATS, RENNAY. Cover of *Living Science: The Science of Fire,* by Rennay Craats. Gareth Stevens Publishing, 2000. Copyright © 2000 by Weigl Educational Publishers Limited. Reproduced by permission.

CURLEY, MARIANNE. Curley, Marianne, photograph. Copyright Amanda Curley, 2001. Reproduced by permission.

DECLEMENTS, BARTHE (FAITH). DeClements, Barthe, photograph. Reproduced by permission./ Illustration by Tom Newsom from a cover of *Sixth Grade Can Really Kill You,* by Barthe DeClements. An Apple Paperback published by Scholastic Inc. Cover Illustration copyright © 1996 by Scholastic Inc. Reprinted by permission.

something ABOUT THE AUTHOR

ALLEN, Jonathan B. 1957-
(Jonathan Dean Allen)

Personal

Born February 17, 1957, in Luton, England; children: two. *Ethnicity:* "British." *Education:* Attended Impington Village College, and Cambridge College of Arts and Technology; St. Martin's College of Art, B.A.

Addresses

Home and office—Acorn Cottage, South Street, Lillington, NR Royston, Hertfordshire SG8 0QR, England.

Career

Children's book author and illustrator.

Awards, Honors

Virginia Young Readers Award, 1989, for illustrations in *The Great White Man-Eating Shark* by Margaret Mahy.

Writings

A Bad Case of Animal Nonsense (poems), Godine (Boston, MA), 1981.
A Pocketful of Painful Puns and Poems, Dent (London, England), 1983.
Guthrie Comes Clean, Dent (London, England), 1984.
My Cat, Dial (New York, NY), 1986.

My Dog, Macmillan (London, England), 1987, Gareth Stevens (Milwaukee, WI), 1989.
Mucky Moose, Macmillan (New York, NY), 1990.
Keep Fit Canaries, Doubleday (New York, NY), 1992.
Who's at the Door?, Tambourine Books (New York, NY), 1993.
Two by Two by Two, Orion Children's Books (London, England), 1994, Dial (New York, NY), 1995.
Sweetie, Macmillan (London, England), 1994.
Chicken Licken, Golden (New York, NY), 1996.
Fowl Play, Orion Children's Books (London, England), 1996.
Wake Up, Sleeping Beauty!, Dial (New York, NY), 1997.
Wolf Academy, Orchard Books (London, England), 1997.
Jonathan Allen Picture Book, Orchard Books (London, England), 1997.
Flying Squad, Yearling (London, England), 1998.
Don't Wake the Baby!, Candlewick Press (Cambridge, MA), 2000.

"WIZARD GRIMWEED" SERIES

B. I. G. Trouble, Orchard Books (London, England), 1993.
Potion Commotion, Orchard Books (London, England), 1993.
The Funniest Man in the World, Orchard Books (London, England), 1994.
Nose Grows, Orchard Books (London, England), 1994.
The Witch Who Couldn't Spell, Orchard Books (London, England), 1996.
Dragon Dramatics, Orchard Books (London, England), 1996.

"FRED CAT BOARD BOOKS" SERIES

Dressing Up, Orchard Books (London, England), 1997.

My Noisy Toys, Orchard Books (London, England), 1997.

Weather and Me, Orchard Books (London, England), 1997.

What My Friends Say, Orchard Books (London, England), 1997.

"JONATHAN ALLEN BOARD BOOKS" SERIES

Purple Sock, Pink Sock, Orchard Books (London, England), Tambourine Books (New York, NY), 1992.

Big Owl, Little Towel, Orchard Books (London, England), Tambourine Books (New York, NY), 1992.

One with a Bun, Orchard Books (London, England), Tambourine Books (New York, NY), 1992.

Up the Steps, Down the Slide, Orchard Books (London, England), Tambourine Books (New York, NY), 1992.

ILLUSTRATOR

Jeremy Strong, *Trouble with Animals,* Crowell (New York, NY), 1980.

(Illustrator, with John Carter) Gyles Brandreth, *The Big Book of Silly Riddles,* Sterling (New York, NY), 1985.

David Henry Wilson, *There's a Wolf in My Pudding,* Dent (London, England), 1986.

David Henry Wilson, *Yucky Ducky,* Dent (London, England), 1988.

David Henry Wilson, *Gander of the Yard,* Dent (London, England), 1989.

Margaret Mahy, *The Great White Man-Eating Shark,* Dial (New York, NY), 1990.

Gillian Osband, *Boysie's Kitten,* Carolrhoda Books (Minneapolis, MN), 1990.

Gillian Osband, *Boysie's First Birthday,* Carolrhoda Books (Minneapolis, MN), 1990.

David Henry Wilson, *Gideon Gander Solves the World's Greatest Mysteries,* Piper (London, England), 1993.

Margaret Mahy, *The Three-Legged Cat,* Viking (New York, NY), 1993.

Frank O'Rourke, *Burton and Stanley,* Godine (Boston, MA), 1993.

Edward Lear, *Nonsense Songs,* Henry Holt (New York, NY), 1993.

Stephen Wyllie, *Red Dragon,* Dial (New York, NY), 1993.

Corinne Mellor, *Clark the Toothless Shark,* Western (New York, NY), 1994.

Rose Impey, *Monster and Frog Get Fit,* Collins (London, England), 1994.

Rose Impey, *Monster's Terrible Toothache,* Collins (London, England), 1994.

Rose Impey, *Monster and Frog,* Collins (London, England), 1994.

Rose Impey, *Monster and Frog Mind the Baby,* Collins (London, England), 1994.

Rose Impey, *Monster and Frog at Sea,* Collins (London, England), 1994.

Stephen Wyllie, *Bear Buys a Car,* Dial (New York, NY), 1995.

Corinne Mellor, *Bruce the Balding Moose,* Dial (New York, NY), 1996.

Bill Grossman, *The Bear Whose Bones Were Jezebel Jones,* Dial (New York, NY), 1997.

Margaret Mahy, *Beaten by a Balloon,* Viking (New York, NY), 1998.

Margaret Mahy, *Simply Delicious!,* Orchard (New York, NY), 1999.

Kara May, *Joe Lion's Big Boots,* Kingfisher (New York, NY), 2000.

Sidelights

British children's book illustrator Jonathan B. Allen lives and works in a Hertfordshire house called Acorn Cottage. Born in 1957 in Luton, England, Allen earned a graphic-arts degree from St. Martin's College of Art, and his first illustrations for a children's book appeared in 1980 in Jeremy Strong's *Trouble with Animals.* In a career since that has encompassed dozens of titles, either written and illustrated by him, or in collaborative efforts with other authors, Allen has achieved a reputation for his winsome illustrations. "Allen ... specializes in quirky characters," remarked *School Library Journal* writer Dorothy Houlihan, "whose entertaining expressions extend and expand the humor of the story."

Early in his career Allen authored two books of rhyme on his own, *A Bad Case of Animal Nonsense,* which took place in an imagined "Alphabet Game Park" of animals, replete with oddities like a "panda in the bath" and a "stoat on a bicycle," to help young readers identify sounds and letters. "Allen's sense of humor is uninhibited," noted a *Publishers Weekly* reviewer of this title. Allen continued in the same vein with *A Pocketful of Painful Puns and Poems,* which appeared in 1983. This work featured enticing word-play images for children, such as a "hot-air baboon."

From there Allen ventured into creating board books and stories for children just beginning to read on their own. Works such as *My Cat,* published in 1986, offered simple but appealing images. This work depicts a little boy and his tabby, and tells the story of how she came to live with his family. The narrator recounts his pet's feline quirks and how the two play together. "Allen's primitively drawn ... tabby has a certain endearing charm," noted Ilene Cooper in *Booklist.* Allen also created a series of board books for very young readers to teach basic skills. *Purple Sock, Pink Sock* helps children identify colors by name, while *Big Owl, Little Towel* and *Up the Steps, Down the Slide* teach the concept of opposites. "Allen's bright watercolors focus attention on the concepts," opined Marge Loch-Wouters in a *School Library Journal* review of several titles from this series.

Allen's *Mucky Moose* story was well liked by children at reading hours, reported several librarian-critics. The title character is a moose who prefers the foulest part of his forest's swamp, and therefore emits quite a terrible smell. One day, his stench averts a hungry wolf, and the determined predator's attempts to re-attack make up the bulk of the story. The wolf pinches his nose shut with a clothespin and dons a gas mask, among other strategies, but is always overpowered by Mucky Moose's pungency; in the end, the wolf leaves the forest for good. Cooper, reviewing the title for *Booklist,* praised *Mucky Moose*'s chronicle of a "goofy looking moose," a "razor-toothed wolf," "and accounts of some pretty bad smells. What's not to like?"

Allen's illustrations for others have also earned praise. He drew the images for Frank O'Rourke's *Burton and Stanley,* a title, not about the famed African explorers, but about two marabou storks the wind carried from their native Kenya to a dusty railroad station in Nebraska in 1935. The town's children love the exotic birds, but the coming Plains winter threatens their delicate health. Moreover, some government wildlife officials are on their way to Nebraska after hearing the rumors about the two exotic storks. Fortunately, Burton and Stanley know Morse code and use it to communicate with the local telegraph operator. He helps them make it to New Orleans, where they then stow away on a ship bound for home. A *Publishers Weekly* reviewer commended Allen's creatures, describing them as "lugubrious, slightly untidy birds with curiously human features" that help make *Burton and Stanley* "a thoroughly warmhearted and rather touching entertainment."

That same year Allen also published *Who's at the Door?,* a retelling of the *Three Little Pigs* story. In this version the fabled door takes up most of page spreads, and readers see the worried trio of pigs on one side and the crafty wolf in a variety of disguises on the other. The wolf tries various means to gain entry, including impersonating a police officer and then wearing a pig disguise. In response, the pigs evade the potential intrusion by various means, including dressing in a wolf costume, which scares their dim-witted tormentor. "The split-page device guarantees a lively pace, while Allen's puckish, cartoon-like pictures heighten the humor still further," noted a *Publishers Weekly* reviewer. *Five Owls* critic Mary Lou Voigt noted that the Three Pigs and the fearsome wolf had become a favorite subject for children's books of late, but commended Allen's interpretation for "the appealing porkers on the jacket. You can almost see the ideas forming in their heads as they plan new ways to outwit the wolf."

Allen's illustrations for Margaret Mahy's *The Three-Legged Cat* won enthusiastic reviews. Tom, the feline of the title, is missing a leg, and lives quietly with a very

Preschool readers lift the flaps to help Chicken Licken find the king in Jonathan B. Allen's **Chicken Licken.**

The quieter Dad tries to be, the noisier he gets in Allen's **Don't Wake the Baby!,** *an interactive book.*

nearsighted older woman, Mrs. Gimble, who prides herself on living a respectable and uneventful life. Tom, however, longs for adventure and unseen vistas. One day Mrs. Gimble's brother Danny, whom she calls "a drifter," comes to visit. He arrives wearing a molting Russian fur hat, and leaves instead with Tom curled up on his head. Mrs. Gimble mistakes the forgotten hat for Tom, and praises his newly docile demeanor. She is also pleased that he does not seem to eat very much. Tom, as expected, gets to see the world. A critique in *Publishers Weekly* found that the book's "cartoony illustrations serve up a deliciously bizarre, out-of-kilter world peopled by flat, pop-eyed characters." *Horn Book* reviewer Mary M. Burns commended Allen and Mahy's collaboration, noting that the artist's "flair for farce equals hers, as demonstrated by his agile line and sense for telling detail."

Allen expressed a similarly zany sense of humor in *The Keep-Fit Canaries,* the story of seven pet-shop birds who leave for a home of their own, but find that they dislike the boredom of a household as much as they did that of the pet-shop window. The birds—ranging in name from Horace to Doris, Alice to Clarice—discover a stash of aerobics tapes and work hard to become physically fit. They break out of their cage and begin a rampage that culminates with harassing neighbors and stealing food. In the end, they find a happy medium with a steady job as bodyguards to the Lord Mayor's pet parrot. "The up-to-the-minute dialogue sparkles with wit," noted *School Librarian* contributor Elizabeth Finlayson, who also liked the way in which "minor human characters emerge brilliantly in thumbnail

sketches." Allen returned to his fearsome birds in a sequel, *Flying Squad,* in 1998.

In 1995 Allen wrote and illustrated *Two by Two by Two,* a retelling of the biblical tale of Noah and his ark for readers aged four to eight. The story tells about Noah and his giant vessel, on which he brought two of each species of animal to wait out a massive flood. But Allen's story imagines how Noah struggled to keep peace aboard the ship, and thus devised games and even cabaret shows to relieve the tension. His "Ark is a festive floating jungle, with breezy but accurate gouache-and-ink cartoons of exotic animals," noted a *Publishers Weekly* critic.

Imaginative young readers were also the intended audience for *Bear Buys a Car,* a work that Allen illustrated for author Stephen Wyllie. Bear is excited about his new vehicle, purchased from the somewhat shady business owner Wolf at Wolf Motors. Bear believes the dealer when he is told that it runs on potatoes and carrots instead of gasoline. The vegetables are not fuel, however, but rather food for the enslaved pig inside the car, who powers the car with his own feet. Allen's paper engineering allows readers to move across the pages of scenery with Bear and his car. "Expressive, lighthearted illustrations cheerfully complement this jolly tale," noted a *Publishers Weekly* reviewer, who also praised Allen's depictions of "a gullible Bear and a pleasingly detestable, smirking Wolf" as sure to appeal to children.

Beleaguered farm animals are the subject of two more books from Allen that appeared in 1996—*Fowl Play,* in which Detective Hubert Hound tries to discover the whereabouts of six missing chickens—and *Chicken Licken,* a reworking of the oft-told story about the creature who cried, "the sky is falling!" Here Allen brings in new characters to round out the cast, including Funny Bunny and Foxy Loxy. "Beginning readers are sure to enjoy reading this for themselves," predicted *Magpies* critic Annette Dale-Meiklejohn in a review of *Chicken Licken.*

Allen revisited the lupine mind in greater detail with his humorous *Wolf Academy* in 1997. The story begins when two wolves adopt an abandoned cub they find in the forest, believing it to be one of their own. As little Phillip grows, however, he displays increasingly strange behavior that is anything but wolflike. The school of the title is recommended, and here Phillip performs even more abysmally, snarling at his classmates, until one day when the teacher instructs them to disguise themselves as sheep. Phillip turns out to be not a wolf at all, but rather a sheepdog skilled in herding sheep and keeping the wolves at bay.

Allen and Mahy have collaborated on a number of other titles, including *Simply Delicious!* from 1999. The story features Mr. Minky, who buys his son an ice cream cone, then realizes he must speed home on his bicycle before it melts. He takes the short cut through the jungle, and has to evade a series of hungry creatures, including a toucan, a tiger, and a crocodile. "Readers and listeners alike will get into the swing of things, cheering Mr. Minky on over each lumpy bump, all the way home," predicted a *Horn Book* reviewer, while *Booklist*'s Michael Cart noted that Allen "captures the rhythm of the text and adds to the fun with droll depictions" of all the jungle animals.

Allen also illustrated his first work for author Kara May with *Joe Lion's Big Boots* in 2000. The title character is a diminutive lion cub who worries that he's the smallest in his family and at school as well. To feel larger, he takes to wearing a pair of extra-large boots, but these make it impossible to play soccer, which he loves, and he is surprised to learn that being larger has its drawbacks, for now he can reach the sink and must help with the dinner dishes. *School Library Journal* reviewer Maura Bresnahan commended the "colorful, cartoonlike illustrations that add to the child-friendly appeal."

Biographical and Critical Sources

BOOKS

St. James Guide to Children's Writers, 5th edition, St. James Press (Detroit, MI), 1999.

PERIODICALS

Booklist, March 15, 1986, Ilene Cooper, review of *My Cat,* p. 1078; March 1, 1991, Ilene Cooper, review of *Mucky Moose,* p. 1396; September 1, 1993, Carolyn Phelan, review of *Big Owl, Little Towel* and *Up the Steps, Down the Slide,* p. 807; July, 1995, Janice Del Negro, review of *Two by Two by Two,* p. 1882; March 15, 1998, Hazel Rochman, review of *Beaten by a Balloon,* p. 1250; September 1, 1999, Michael Cart, review of *Simply Delicious!,* p. 141; December 1, 2000, Ilene Cooper, review of *Don't Wake the Baby!,* p. 728.

Books for Keeps, May, 1988, Liz Waterland, review of *Guthrie Comes Clean,* p. 9; September, 1988, Moira Small, review of *My Cat,* p. 6; July, 1993, George Hunt, review of *The Keep-Fit Canaries,* p. 14; September, 1994, Peter Hollindale, review of *A Bad Case of Animal Nonsense,* p. 10; May, 1997, Judith Sharman, review of *Chicken Licken,* p. 20; November, 1997, Jill Bennett, review of *Wolf Academy,* pp. 21-22; March, 1998, George Hunt, review of *Fowl Play,* p. 19.

Five Owls, May-June, 1993, Mary Lou Voigt, review of *Who's at the Door?,* p. 111.

Growing Point, September, 1984, review of *Guthrie Comes Clean,* p. 4319.

Horn Book, July-August, 1993, Mary M. Burns, review of *The Three-Legged Cat,* p. 446; September, 1999, review of *Simply Delicious!,* p. 596.

Junior Bookshelf, August, 1992, review of *The Keep-Fit Canaries,* p. 145.

Magpies, November, 1991, Melanie Guile, review of *Mucky Moose,* p. 28; July, 1996, Annette Dale-Meiklejohn, review of *Chicken Licken,* pp. 24-25.

New Statesman, December 2, 1983, Michael Rosen, "Rhymeo Nasties," p. 27.

Publishers Weekly, October 16, 1981, review of *A Bad Case of Animal Nonsense,* p. 78; October 12, 1992, review of *One with a Bun, Big Owl, Little Towel,* and *Purple Sock, Pink Sock,* p. 76; February 1, 1993, review of *Burton and Stanley,* p. 96; April 12, 1993, review of *Who's at the Door?,* p. 61; May 17, 1993, review of *The Three-Legged Cat,* p. 79; April 4, 1994, review of *Clark the Toothless Shark,* p. 77; May 22, 1995, review of *Two by Two by Two,* p. 59; September 25, 1995, review of *Bear Buys a Car,* p. 56; July 21, 1997, review of *The Bear Whose Bones Were Jezebel Jones,* p. 201.

School Librarian, September, 1983, review of *A Pocketful of Painful Puns and Poems,* p. 231; August, 1992, Elizabeth Finlayson, review of *The Keep-Fit Canaries,* p. 99; August, 1993, Janet Sims, review of *Potion Commotion,* p. 109; May, 1994, Jean Needham, review of *B.I.G. Trouble,* p. 59; May, 1996, Elizabeth J. King, review of *Chicken Licken,* p. 56; February, 1997, Catriona Nicholson, review of *Fowl Play,* p. 17; November, 1997, Julia Marriage, review of *Wolf Academy,* p. 184; summer, 1998, Marie Imeson, review of *Flying Squad,* p. 76.

School Library Journal, January, 1982, Margaret Bush, review of *A Bad Case of Animal Nonsense;* August, 1986, Lorraine Douglas, review of *My Cat,* p. 78; March, 1990, Nancy A. Gifford, review of *My Dog,* p. 184; August, 1991, Dorothy Houlihan, review of *Mucky Moose,* p. 142; March, 1993, Marge Loch-Wouters, review of *Pink Sock, Purple Sock, Up the Steps, Down the Slide, Big Owl, Little Towel* and *One with a Bun,* p. 170; June, 1995, Kathy Piehl, review of *Two by Two by Two,* p. 76; December, 2000, Martha Topol, review of *Don't Wake the Baby!,* p. 94; February, 2001, Maura Bresnahan, review of *Joe Lion's Big Boots,* p. 100.*

*   *   *

ANHOLT, Catherine 1958-

Personal

Born January 18, 1958, in London, England; daughter of Daniel (an artist) and Diana (a nurse) Hogarty; married Laurence Anholt (a writer and teacher), July, 1984; children: Claire, Tom and Madeline (twins). *Education:* John Radcliffe College, Oxford, training as state registered nurse, 1976; Oxford Falmouth School of Art, B.A. (honors), 1982; Royal College of Art, M.A., 1985.

Addresses

Home and office—Old Woodhouse, Woodhouse Hill, Uplyme, Lyme Regis, Dorset DT7 3SQ, England. *E-mail*—info@anholt.co.uk.

Career

Freelance illustrator of children's books, 1984—.

Awards, Honors

Children's Book Foundation Book of the Year designation, 1991, for *What I Like;* named among top sixteen books of the year, Smithsonian Institute, 1999, for *Billy and the Big New School.*

Writings

FOR CHILDREN; SELF-ILLUSTRATED

Good Days, Bad Days, Putnam (New York, NY), 1990.
Animal Friends, Orchard Books (London, England), 1991.
Bedtime, Orchard Books (London, England), 1991.
Helping, Orchard Books (London, England), 1991.
Playing, Orchard Books (London, England), 1991.
Baby's Things (board book), Candlewick Press (Cambridge, MA), 2000.
Clothes (board book), Candlewick Press (Cambridge, MA), 2000.
First Words (board book), Candlewick Press (Cambridge, MA), 2000.
Colors (board book), Candlewick Press (Cambridge, MA), 2000.

ILLUSTRATOR; BY HUSBAND, LAURENCE ANHOLT

Truffles' Day in Bed, Methuen (London, England), 1987, published as *Truffles Is Sick,* Little, Brown (Boston, MA), 1987.
Truffles in Trouble, Joy Street Books (Boston, MA), 1987.
Chaos at Cold Custard Farm, Methuen (London, England), 1988.
When I Was a Baby, Joy Street Books (Boston, MA), 1988.
Tom's Rainbow Walk, Heinemann (London, England), 1989.
The Snow Fairy and the Spaceman, Dell (New York, NY), 1990.
Aren't You Lucky!, Little, Brown (Boston, MA), 1990.
Going to the Playground, Orchard Books (London, England), 1991.
The Twins, Two by Two, Candlewick Press (Cambridge, MA), 1992.
The Forgotten Forest, Sierra Club Books for Children (San Francisco, CA), 1992.
Can You Guess?, Frances Lincoln (England), 1992.
All about You, Viking (New York, NY), 1992.
Kids, Candlewick Press (Cambridge, MA), 1992.
What I Like, Walker (London, England), 1993, Candlewick Press (Cambridge, MA), 1998.
Toddlers, Candlewick Press (Cambridge, MA), 1993.
Here Come the Babies, Candlewick Press (Cambridge, MA), 1993.
Bear and Baby (board book), Candlewick Press (Cambridge, MA), 1993.
One, Two, Three, Count with Me, Heinemann (London, England), 1994, Viking (New York, NY), 1994.
Come Back, Jack!, Candlewick Press (Cambridge, MA), 1994.
What Makes Me Happy?, Walker (London, England), 1994, Candlewick Press (Cambridge, MA), 1995.
The New Puppy, Western Artists & Writers (New York, NY), 1995.
Shopping Bag, Candlewick Press (Cambridge, MA), 1995.
Toy Bag, Candlewick Press (Cambridge, MA), 1995.

Sun, Snow, Stars, Sky, Viking (New York, NY), 1995.
First Words and Pictures, Candlewick Press (Cambridge, MA), 1996.
Going to Playgroup, Orchard (London, England), 1997.
A Kiss Like This, Barron's Educational (Hauppauge, NY), 1997.
Catherine and Laurence Anholt's Big Book of Families, Candlewick Press (Cambridge, MA), 1998.
Billy and the Big New School, Albert Whitman (Morton Grove, IL), 1999.
Sophie and the New Baby, Albert Whitman (Morton Grove, IL), 2000.
Harry's Home, Farrar, Straus (New York, NY), 2000.
Chimp and Zee, Phyllis Fogelman Books (New York, NY), 2001.
Chimp and Zee and the Big Storm, Phyllis Fogelman Books (New York, NY), 2002.
Chimp and Zee's Noisy Book, Phyllis Fogelman Books (New York, NY), 2002.
Monkey around with Chimp and Zee, Penguin Putnam (New York, NY), 2002.

Also author of *Little Copy Cub,* Hamish Hamilton (London, England); *Animal Friends,* Orchard (London, England); *Busy Day,* Orchard (London, England); *Animals, Animals All Around,* Mammoth (London, England); *Look What I Can Do; Good Night,* Orchard (London, England); and *Playtime,* Orchard (London, England).

Sidelights

As the artistic half of one of Great Britain's most popular picture book-making teams, Catherine Anholt contributes colorful illustrations to texts penned by her husband, Laurence Anholt. In addition to providing whimsical pen-and-ink and watercolor drawings for her husband's stories, Catherine has also written several stories of her own, among them *Good Days, Bad Days, Animal Friends,* and a series of board books designed to help toddlers learn basic concepts. Reflecting the praise typically accorded her illustrations by critics, Anholt's work for the 1994 picture book *Come Back, Jack!* was described by Roger Sutton, writing in *Bulletin of the Center for Children's Books,* as "springtime-colored pen-and-watercolor illustrations [that] are breezy and affectionate."

Born in 1958, Anholt was one of eight children in her family, and grew up in "a small village in the Cotswold Hills in England," she once told *SATA,* "where my father was a potter and artist. Part of our rambling house was given over to this." While her father worked at home in his studio, Anholt's mother served as a pediatric nurse at a local hospital. "I have vivid memories of being brought up in a creative household—drawing and making things with clay," the illustrator added. Still, she first trained to follow her mother into nursing, and, as she described it, "worked as a nurse myself before turning to a career in art which seemed better suited to my temperament."

In **Catherine and Laurence Anholt's Big Book of Families,** *the pair celebrate families, from brothers and sisters to grandmothers, with verse and watercolors.*

Married to teacher Laurence Anholt in 1984, she returned to school and earned her M.A. at the Royal College of Art. "After the birth of our first child, ... I decided to try to find some way of continuing my interest in art while at the same time being around to see the children grow up," she recalled. Under those circumstances, illustrating children's picture books seemed the perfect career choice. "Although I had been trained in fine art, illustration was new to me and at first came very slowly," Anholt explained, adding that her drawings are done from memory rather than from life.

Since 1987, Anholt has worked in collaboration with her husband, matching her illustrations to his texts. The first book they created together was *Truffles' Day in Bed,* published in the United States as *Truffles Is Sick.* In *Come Back, Jack!,* a gentle story about two siblings and their adventures inside a picture book that reads as a patchwork of traditional fairy tales and nursery rhymes, Laurence's text is highlighted by Catherine's "light-hearted, bright watercolor-and-ink illustrations," according to *School Library Journal* contributor Judy Constantinides. The antics of toddlers figure prominently in the couple's storybooks, as in *The Twins, Two by Two,* which depicts a pair of youngsters preparing for bedtime by acting out the story of Noah's Ark. Despite its title, *Here Come the Babies* also focuses on toddlers, providing expectant parents with a rhyming book containing short verses that reflect the perspective of an "affectionate older brother or sister who's upbeat about having babies around the house," noted *Booklist*'s Carolyn Phelan.

The New Puppy is a story for children who love animals as much as its main character, Anna. In addition to collecting dogs of all shapes, sizes, and substances—from tiny china dogs to big stuffed dogs—Anna is lucky enough to get a real puppy named Tess. Unlike her stuffed dogs, Tess proves to be a bit of work, and when Tess chews the ears of Anna's fuzzy puppy slippers, the young dog-lover decides that a real dog is too much. However, Tess's cries of loneliness in the dark soon rekindle the young girl's affection, as she realizes that living dogs require a special kind of affection. Describing *The New Puppy* as "gently instructive without preachiness," *Booklist*'s Leone McDermott praised Anholt's illustrations as "droll" and "delicately drawn."

In the Anholts' 2000 picture book, *Harry's Home,* a child's anxiety at leaving home for an extended visit to someplace new is depicted. Harry lives in a city apartment, and when he visits his grandfather's farm in the country he cannot believe how dark it gets at night or how quiet it is. After a week Harry comes to love caring for grandfather's animals, but although he enjoys the country life, he looks forward to the comforting noise and bustle of the city. Readers of *Harry's Home* will particularly enjoy "the loving particulars of place, the complexity of feelings, and the rhythm of the telling," observed Hazel Rochman in *Booklist,* while *School Library Journal* reviewer Miriam Lang Budin had special praise for Anholt's illustrations. Praising them as "detail-packed," Budin noted that the watercolor and pen-and-ink renderings "have a friendly look and plenty of child appeal."

In addition to story books, the Anholts have also produced a number of concept books for younger children. In *What I Like,* six children express their favorite and least favorite things: in the "like" column are playing with toys, holidays, and curly hair, while "not like's" include having to share. Similar in format, *What Makes Me Happy?* deals with emotions such as joy, sadness, fear, and anger. The rhyming text used in both books matches each object, emotion, or activity to one of Anholt's humorous illustrations, making the books useful for even the youngest lap-sitter, noted critics. *Toddlers* focuses on the many things that young children do during a typical day, particularly their feelings, and the text has a rollicking rhythm that works perfectly with what Liza Bliss described in a *School Library Journal* review as "pleasant watercolor illustrations ... typical of the Anholts' previous efforts." Number concepts are covered by the Anholts in their upbeat *One, Two Three, Count with Me,* which features "bright, whimsical illustrations with lots of detail," according to *School Library Journal*'s Sally R. Dow.

Anholt and her husband and family live in Lyme Regis, in an old house that overlooks the sea. "I never forget how fortunate I am to be able to work from home at something I really enjoy," the artist-illustrator maintained. "We are looking for universal themes—the daily ups and downs of family life and the development of young children—which is not all that easy," Anholt explained of the books she and her husband produce. "We aim to give a realistic and unsentimental account. We want children to identify with our books and we want them to laugh. Our ultimate aim is to produce that elusive thing—a classic children's story."

Biographical and Critical Sources

PERIODICALS

Booklist, February 1, 1992, Hazel Rochman, review of *The Twins, Two by Two,* p. 1034; October 15, 1993, Carolyn Phelan, review of *Here Come the Babies,* p. 444; November 1, 1993, Hazel Rochman, review of *Bear and Baby* and *Toddlers,* p. 526; June 1, 1994, Hazel Rochman, review of *Come Back Jack!,* p. 1835; June 1, 1994, Hazel Rochman, review of *One, Two, Three, Count with Me,* p. 1824; May 1, 1995, Hazel Rochman, review of *What Makes Me Happy?,* p. 1578; May 15, 1995, Janice Del Negro, review of *Sun, Snow, Stars, Sky,* p. 1650; August, 1995, Leone McDermott, review of *The New Puppy,* p. 1954; December 15, 1998, Hazel Rochman, review of *Catherine and Laurence Anholt's Big Book of Families,* p. 753; March, 1999, Hazel Rochman, review of *Billy and the Big New School,* p. 1218; May 1, 2000, Hazel Rochman, review of *Harry's Home,* p. 1675; September 15, 2000, Connie Fletcher, review of *Sophie and the New Baby,* p. 247.

Books for Keeps, May, 1993, Moira Small, review of *What I Like,* p. 7; May, 1994, Trevor Dickinson, review of *One, Two, Three, Count with Me,* p. 33; May, 1994,

Moira Small, review of *The Twins, Two by Two,* p. 11; March, 1995, Judith Sharman, review of *Here Come the Babies,* p. 10.

Books for Your Children, spring, 1994, M. Maran, review of *Tom's Rainbow Walk,* p. 9.

Bulletin of the Center for Children's Books, March, 1994, Roger Sutton, review of *Come Back, Jack!,* p. 214.

Horn Book, July-August, 1991, Maeve Visser Knoth, review of *Good Days, Bad Days,* p. 443; July-August, 1992, Margaret A. Bush, review of *All about You,* p. 444; September-October, 1992, Margaret A. Bush, review of *Kids,* p. 571; July-August, 1995, Margaret A. Bush, review of *What Makes Me Happy?,* p. 447.

Publishers Weekly, May 29, 1987, review of *Truffles Is Sick,* p. 75; June 10, 1988, review of *Chaos at Cold Custard Farm,* p. 78; August 31, 1992, review of *Kids,* p. 78; November 23, 1998, review of *Catherine and Laurence Anholt's Big Book of Families,* p. 65; November 23, 1998, review of *What I Like,* p. 70; May 8, 2000, review of *Harry's Home,* p. 220; October 23, 2000, review of *Sophie and the New Baby,* p. 74; July 30, 2001, review of *Chimp and Zee,* p. 83.

School Library Journal, June-July, 1987, Carolyn Noah, review of *Truffles Is Sick,* p. 75; June-July, 1988, Jane Gardner Connor, review of *Chaos at Cold Custard Farm,* p. 83; July, 1990, Susannah Price, review of *Tom's Rainbow Walk,* p. 55; July, 1991, Lucy Young Clem, review of *Aren't You Lucky!,* p. 52; September, 1991, Mary Lou Budd, review of *Good Days, Bad Days,* p. 226; February, 1992, Nancy Seiner, review of *The Snow Fairy and the Spaceman,* p. 70; January, 1994, Liza Bliss, review of *Toddlers,* p. 80; July, 1994, Judy Constantinides, review of *Come Back, Jack!,* p. 73; August, 1994, Sally R. Dow, review of *One, Two, Three, Count with Me,* p. 126; July, 1995, Jacqueline Elsner, review of *Sun, Snow, Stars, Sky,* p. 54; July, 1995, Patricia Dole, review of *What Makes Me Happy?,* p. 54; December, 1998, Maura Bresnahan, review of *Catherine and Laurence Anholt's Big Book of Families,* p. 99; March, 1999, Shelley Woods, *Billy and the Big New School,* p. 162; April, 2000, Miriam Lang Budin, review of *Harry's Home,* p. 90; November, 2000, Martha Topol, review of *Sophie and the New Baby,* p. 110; October, 2001, Rachel Fox, review of *Chimp and Zee,* p. 104.

OTHER

Anholt Web Site, http://www.anholt.co.uk/ (January 28, 2002).

Puffin Books Web Site, http://www.puffin.co.uk/ (January 28, 2002), "Catherine Anholt."*

*   *   *

ARNOLD, Caroline 1944-

Personal

Born May 16, 1944, in Pittsburgh, PA; daughter of Lester L. (a social worker) and Catherine (a social worker; maiden name, Young) Scheaffer; married Arthur Arnold (a neuroscientist), June 24, 1967; children: Jennifer Elizabeth, Matthew William. *Education:* Grinnell College, B.A., 1966; attended Hunter College, 1967-68, and Art Students League of New York, 1967-70; University of Iowa, M.A., 1968; attended Central State University, 1968-69, and University of California—Los Angeles extension, 1977-78. *Hobbies and other interests:* Tennis, gardening, cooking, traveling.

Addresses

Home and office—2700 Selby Ave., Los Angeles, CA 90064. *Agent*—Andrea Brown, P.O. Box 1027, Montara, CA 94037.

Career

Freelance writer, 1979—. Art instructor in IA, OH, and NY, 1966-76; substitute teacher in OH, NY, and CA, 1968-78; freelance artist, 1968-78; New York Hospital, New York, NY, secretary, 1969-70; Rockefeller University, New York, NY, laboratory technician, 1971-72, 1972-76; University of California—Los Angeles, laboratory technician, 1976-79, extension course writing teacher, 1982—. Speaker at conferences of teachers and librarians, and at schools and libraries nationwide. *Exhibitions:* Exhibitor of paintings and drawings at juried shows, including Dayton Art Institute (Dayton, OH), Museum of Fine Arts (Springfield, MA), and New Mexico State University. *Member:* Authors Guild, Authors League of America, PEN, Society of Children's Book Writers and Illustrators, Southern California Council on Literature for Children and Young People.

Caroline Arnold

Awards, Honors

Honorable mention, Children's Science Book awards, New York Academy of Science, 1983, for *Animals That Migrate,* and 1987, for *Trapped in Tar: Fossils from the Ice Age;* Golden Kite Nonfiction Honor Award, Society of Children's Book Writers and Illustrators, 1983, for *Pets without Homes;* Notable Work of Nonfiction citation, Southern California Council on Literature for Children and Young Adults, 1985, for *Too Fat? Too Thin? Do You Have a Choice?; Booklist* Children's Editors' Choice, *School Library Journal* Best Book selection, and American Library Association (ALA) Notable Book selection, all 1985, and PEN, Los Angeles Center, Special Achievement Award, 1986, all for *Saving the Peregrine Falcon;* Best Children's Books and Films selection, American Academy of Arts and Sciences (AAAS), and Junior Library Guild Book selection, both 1987, both for *Trapped in Tar;* Junior Library Guild selection, 1987-88, for *Juggler;* John Burroughs Nature Book Award, and Best Children's Books and Films selection, AAAS, both for *A Walk on the Great Barrier Reef;* BSC/CSCBC List, for *A Walk in the Woods;* ALA Notable Book selection, and International Best selection, Society of School Librarians, 1989, both for *Dinosaur Mountain;* Orbis Pictus Award for Outstanding Nonfiction, National Council of Teachers of English (NCTE), for *Cheetah* and *Hippo;* Pick of the Lists, American Booksellers Association, Best Children's Books and Films selection, AAAS, and Best Children's Science Book list, *Science Books and Films,*

all for *Orangutan;* Pick of the Lists, American Booksellers Association, and Best Children's Books and Films selection, AAAS, for *Wild Goat;* Junior Library Guild selection, 1992, and Best Books of the Year selection, *School Library Journal,* both for *The Ancient Cliff Dwellers of Mesa Verde;* award for outstanding body of work, Southern California Council on Literature for Children and Young People, 1994; Best Children's Books and Films selection, AAAS, and Favorite Paperbacks selection, International Reading Association/Children's Book Council, 1994, for *Koala;* Nonfiction Honor List, *Voice of Youth Advocates,* 1998, for *Hawk Highway in the Sky: Watching the Raptor Migration;* Best Children's Books of the Year list, Bank Street College, 1999, for *Bobcats;* Certificate of Excellence, Cat Writer's Association, 1999, for *Cats;* Notable Book in the Field of Social Studies designations, National Council for the Social Studies/Children's Book Council, 1999, for *Children of the Settlement Houses,* and 2001, for *Easter Island: Giant Stone Statues Tell of a Rich and Tragic Past.* Honorary D.H.L., Grinnell College, Grinnell, IA, 2001.

Outstanding Science Trade Book citations, National Science Teachers Association/Children's Book Council, for *Electric Fish, Five Nests, Pets without Homes, Saving the Peregrine Falcon, The Biggest Living Thing, Genetics, Trapped in Tar, Koala, Kangaroo, Giraffe, Zebra, Llama, Penguin, A Walk on the Great Barrier Reef, Hippo, Cheetah, Tule Elk, Dinosaur Mountain,*

Flamingo, Snake, Dinosaurs Down Under, House Sparrows Everywhere, Rhino, Lion, Bat, Fox, and *Hawk Highway in the Sky: Watching the Raptor Migration;* California Literature for Science and Mathematics citation, for *Genetics, Trapped in Tar, Kangaroo, Llama, Penguin, Hippo, Cheetah, A Walk on the Great Barrier Reef, Dinosaur Mountain, Tule Elk,* and *A Walk in the Woods;* Maine Student Book Award, for *The Ancient Cliff Dwellers of Mesa Verde;* Children's Choice, Averill School, Michigan, for *Watch out for Sharks.*

Writings

NONFICTION; FOR CHILDREN

Electric Fish, illustrated by George Gershinowitz, Morrow (New York, NY), 1980.

Five Nests, illustrated by Ruth Sanderson, Dutton (New York, NY), 1980.

(And illustrator) *Sun Fun,* F. Watts (New York, NY), 1981.

Sex Hormones: Why Males and Females Are Different, illustrated by Jean Zallinger, Morrow (New York, NY), 1981.

Animals That Migrate, illustrated by Michele Zylman, Carolrhoda (Minneapolis, MN), 1982.

(And illustrator) *The Biggest Living Thing,* Carolrhoda (Minneapolis, MN), 1983.

Pets without Homes, photographs by Richard Hewett, Houghton (Boston, MA), 1983.

Summer Olympics, F. Watts (New York, NY), 1983, 2nd updated edition, 1988.

Winter Olympics, F. Watts (New York, NY), 1983.

Too Fat? Too Thin? Do You Have a Choice?, Morrow (New York, NY), 1984.

Music Lessons for Alex, photographs by Richard Hewett, Houghton (Boston, MA), 1985.

(With Herma Silverstein) *Anti-Semitism,* Messner (New York, NY), 1985.

(With Herma Silverstein) *Hoaxes That Made Headlines,* Messner (New York, NY), 1986.

The Golden Gate Bridge, F. Watts (New York, NY), 1986.

Pain: What Is It? How Do We Deal with It?, illustrated by Frank Schwarz, Morrow (New York, NY), 1986.

Genetics: From Mendel to Gene Splicing, F. Watts (New York, NY), 1986.

Australia Today, F. Watts (New York, NY), 1987.

Everybody Has a Birthday ("Ceremonies and Celebrations" series), F. Watts (New York, NY), 1987.

How People Get Married, F. Watts (New York, NY), 1987.

Trapped in Tar: Fossils from the Ice Age ("Social Studies Bookshelf" series), Houghton (Boston, MA), 1987.

***Arnold describes the causes of El Niño weather and its effect on people and wildlife in* El Niño.** *(Photo by the American Red Cross.)*

What We Do When Someone Dies ("Ceremonies and Celebrations" series), illustrated by Helen Davie, F. Watts (New York, NY), 1987.

Coping with Natural Disasters, Walker (New York, NY), 1988.

Juggler, photographs by Richard Hewett, Clarion (New York, NY), 1988.

Dinosaur Mountain: Graveyard of the Past, photographs by Richard Hewett, Clarion (New York, NY), 1989.

Animals, Ladybird, 1990.

Dinosaurs Down Under: And Other Fossils from Australia, photographs by Richard Hewett, Clarion (New York, NY), 1990.

The Earth, Ladybird, 1990.

Heart Disease, F. Watts (New York, NY), 1990.

The Human Body, Ladybird, 1990.

My Body, Ladybird, 1990.

Space, Ladybird, 1990.

A Walk in the Desert ("Natural Science" series), illustrated by Freya Tanz, Silver Burdett Press (Parsippany, NY), 1990.

A Walk up the Mountain ("Natural Science" series), illustrated by Freya Tanz, Silver Burdett Press (Parsippany, NY), 1990.

A Walk by the Seashore ("Natural Science" series), illustrated by Freya Tanz, Silver Burdett Press (Parsippany, NY), 1990.

A Walk in the Woods ("Natural Science" series), illustrated by Freya Tanz, Silver Burdett Press (Parsippany, NY), 1990.

Weather, Ladybird, 1990.

A Guide Dog Puppy Grows Up, photographs by Richard Hewett, Harcourt (San Diego, CA), 1991.

The Olympic Summer Games, F. Watts (New York, NY), 1991.

The Olympic Winter Games, F. Watts (New York, NY), 1991.

Soccer: From Neighborhood Play to the World Cup, F. Watts (New York, NY), 1991.

Watch out for Sharks!, photographs by Richard Hewett, Clarion (New York, NY), 1991.

The Ancient Cliff Dwellers of Mesa Verde, photographs by Richard Hewett, Houghton (Boston, MA), 1992.

Pele: The King of Soccer, F. Watts (New York, NY), 1992.

Cats: In from the Wild ("Understanding Animals" series), photographs by Richard Hewett, Carolrhoda (Minneapolis, MN), 1993.

Dinosaurs All Around: An Artist's View of the Prehistoric World, photographs by Richard Hewett, Houghton (Boston, MA), 1993.

On the Brink of Extinction: The California Condor ("Gulliver Green" series), photographs by Michael Wallace, Harcourt (San Diego, CA), 1993.

Prairie Dogs, illustrations by Jean Cassels, Scholastic (New York, NY), 1993.

Reindeer, illustrations by Pamela Johnson, Scholastic (New York, NY), 1993.

City of the Gods: Mexico's Ancient City of Teotihuacan, photographs by Richard Hewett, Houghton (Boston, MA), 1994.

Fireflies, illustrated by Pamela Johnson, Scholastic (New York, NY), 1994.

Arnold explains how archaeological finds, history, and legend reveal the mysteries of the people who carved the giant stone statues, called moai, on Easter Island. (From Easter Island, *text and photographs by Arnold.)*

Sea Turtles, illustrated by Marshall Peck, Scholastic (New York, NY), 1994.

Stories in Stone: Rock Art Pictures by Early Americans, photographs by Richard Hewett, Clarion (New York, NY), 1996.

African Animals, Morrow (New York, NY), 1997.

Stone Age Farmers beside the Sea: Scotland's Prehistoric Village of Skara Brae, photographs by Arthur P. Arnold, Clarion (New York, NY), 1997.

Hawk Highway in the Sky: Watching Raptor Migration, photographs by Robert Kruidenier, Harcourt (New York, NY), 1997.

Bobcats, photographs by Richard Hewett, Lerner (Minneapolis, MN), 1997.

Children of the Settlement Houses, Carolrhoda (Minneapolis, MN), 1998.

El Niño: Stormy Weather for People and Wildlife, Clarion (New York, NY), 1998.

(With Richard Hewett) *Baby Whale Rescue: The True Story of J.J.,* Bridgewater Books (Mahwah, NJ), 1999.

Cats, photographs by Richard Hewett, Lerner Publications (Minneapolis, MN), 1999.

South American Animals, Morrow (New York, NY), 1999.

Shockers of the Sea, and Other Electric Animals, illustrated by Crista Forest, Charlesbridge (Watertown, MA), 1999.

Easter Island: Giant Stone Statues Tell of a Rich and Tragic Past, Clarion (New York, NY), 2000.

Australian Animals, Morrow (New York, NY), 2000.

Giant Shark: Megalodon, Prehistoric Super Predator, illustrated by Laurie Caple, Clarion (New York, NY), 2000.

Ostriches, photographs by Richard Hewett, Lerner (Minneapolis, MN), 2000.

The Geography Book: Activities for Exploring, Mapping, and Enjoying Your World, John Wiley & Sons (New York, NY), 2001.

Did You Hear That?: Animals with Super Hearing, illustrations by Cathy Trachok, Charlesbridge (Watertown, MA), 2001.

Dinosaurs with Feathers: The Ancestors of Modern Birds, illustrated by Laurie Caple, Clarion (New York, NY), 2001.

When Mammoths Walked the Earth, illustrated by Laurie Caple, Clarion (New York, NY), 2002.

(With Madeleine Comora) *Taj Mahal,* illustrated by Rahul Bhushan, Millbrook Press (Brookfield, CT), 2003.

"NATURE WATCH" SERIES; FOR CHILDREN

Saving the Peregrine Falcon, Carolrhoda (Minneapolis, MN), 1985.

A Walk on the Great Barrier Reef, photographs by Arthur Arnold and Marty Snyderman, Carolrhoda (Minneapolis, MN), 1987.

Tule Elk, photographs by Richard Hewett, Carolrhoda (Minneapolis, MN), 1988.

Ostriches and Other Flightless Birds, photographs by Richard Hewett, Carolrhoda (Minneapolis, MN), 1990.

House Sparrows Everywhere, photographs by Richard Hewett, Carolrhoda (Minneapolis, MN), 1992.

Watching Desert Wildlife, photographs by Arthur Arnold, Carolrhoda (Minneapolis, MN), 1994.

"ANIMAL FAVORITES" SERIES; FOR CHILDREN

Giraffe, photographs by Richard Hewett, Morrow Junior Books (New York, NY), 1987.

Kangaroo, photographs by Richard Hewett, Morrow Junior Books (New York, NY), 1987.

Koala, photographs by Richard Hewett, Morrow Junior Books (New York, NY), 1987.

Zebra, photographs by Richard Hewett, Morrow Junior Books (New York, NY), 1987.

Llama, photographs by Richard Hewett, Morrow Junior Books (New York, NY), 1988.

Penguin, photographs by Richard Hewett, Morrow Junior Books (New York, NY), 1988.

Cheetah, photographs by Richard Hewett, Morrow Junior Books (New York, NY), 1989.

Hippo, photographs by Richard Hewett, Morrow Junior Books (New York, NY), 1989.

Orangutan, photographs by Richard Hewett, Morrow Junior Books (New York, NY), 1990.

Wild Goat, photographs by Richard Hewett, Morrow Junior Books (New York, NY), 1990.

Flamingo, photographs by Richard Hewett, Morrow Junior Books (New York, NY), 1991.

Snake, photographs by Richard Hewett, Morrow Junior Books (New York, NY), 1991.

Camel, photographs by Richard Hewett, Morrow Junior Books (New York, NY), 1992.

Panda, photographs by Richard Hewett, Morrow Junior Books (New York, NY), 1992.

Elephant, photographs by Richard Hewett, Morrow Junior Books (New York, NY), 1993.

Monkey, photographs by Richard Hewett, Morrow Junior Books (New York, NY), 1993.

Killer Whale, photographs by Richard Hewett, Morrow Junior Books (New York, NY), 1994.

Sea Lion, photographs by Richard Hewett, Morrow Junior Books (New York, NY), 1994.

Lion, photographs by Richard Hewett, Morrow Junior Books (New York, NY), 1995.

Rhino, photographs by Richard Hewett, Morrow Junior Books (New York, NY), 1995.

Bat, photographs by Richard Hewett, Morrow Junior Books (New York, NY), 1996.

Fox, photographs by Richard Hewett, Morrow Junior Books (New York, NY), 1996.

"COMMUNITY" SERIES

What Is a Community?, illustrated by Carole Bertol, F. Watts (New York, NY), 1982.

Where Do You Go to School?, illustrated by Carole Bertol, F. Watts (New York, NY), 1982.

Who Works Here?, illustrated by Carole Bertol, F. Watts (New York, NY), 1982.

Who Keeps Us Healthy?, illustrated by Carole Bertol, F. Watts (New York, NY), 1982.

Who Keeps Us Safe?, illustrated by Carole Bertol, F. Watts (New York, NY), 1982.

Why Do We Have Rules?, illustrated by Ginger Giles, F. Watts (New York, NY), 1983.

What Will We Buy?, illustrated by Ginger Giles, F. Watts (New York, NY), 1983.

How Do We Have Fun?, illustrated by Ginger Giles, F. Watts (New York, NY), 1983.

How Do We Travel?, illustrated by Ginger Giles, F. Watts (New York, NY), 1983.

How Do We Communicate?, illustrated by Ginger Giles, F. Watts (New York, NY), 1983.

"EASY-READ GEOGRAPHY ACTIVITY BOOK" SERIES

Charts and Graphs: Fun, Facts, and Activities, illustrated by Penny Carter, F. Watts (New York, NY), 1984.

Maps and Globes: Fun, Facts, and Activities, illustrated by Lynn Sweat, F. Watts (New York, NY), 1984.

Measurements: Fun, Facts, and Activities, illustrated by Pam Johnson, F. Watts (New York, NY), 1984.

Bodies of Water, illustrated by Lynn Sweat, F. Watts (New York, NY), 1985.

Land Masses, illustrated by Lynn Sweat, F. Watts (New York, NY), 1985.

Natural Resources: Fun, Facts, and Activities, illustrated by Penny Carter, F. Watts (New York, NY), 1985.

"ZOO ANIMALS" SERIES

Splashtime for Zoo Animals, photographs by Richard Hewett, Carolrhoda (Minneapolis, MN), 1999.

Sleepytime for Zoo Animals, photographs by Richard Hewett, Carolrhoda (Minneapolis, MN), 1999.

Noisytime for Zoo Animals, photographs by Richard Hewett, Carolrhoda (Minneapolis, MN), 1999.

Playtime for Zoo Animals, photographs by Richard Hewett, Carolrhoda (Minneapolis, MN), 1999.

Mother and Baby Zoo Animals, photographs by Richard Hewett, Carolrhoda (Minneapolis, MN), 1999.

Mealtime for Zoo Animals, photographs by Richard Hewett, Carolrhoda (Minneapolis, MN), 1999.

All of the titles in the "Zoo Animals" series have been adapted as electronic books by iPictureBooks, 2002.

OTHER

My Friend from Outer Space (picture book), illustrated by Carol Nicklaus, F. Watts (New York, NY), 1981.

(Illustrator) Elizabeth Bremner and John Pusey, *Children's Gardens: A Field Guide for Teachers, Parents, and Volunteers,* Cooperative Extension, University of California, Los Angeles (Los Angeles, CA), 1982.

The Terrible Hodag (fiction), illustrated by Lambert Davis, Harcourt (San Diego, CA), 1989.

Excerpts from Arnold's books have been included in *Noble Pursuits,* Macmillan, 1988; *Garden Gates,* Silver Burdett, 1989; *Going Places,* Silver Burdett, 1989; and *Tail of a Kite,* Silver Burdett, 1994. Contributor to periodicals, including *Cricket, Dolphin Log,* and *Highlights for Children.* Also author of "Fire for Hire," *K-I-D-S* (television series), KCET, 1984; and contributor of text to *Globocop* (CD-ROM), Newsweek Interactive, 1994.

Adaptations

My Friend from Outer Space was adapted as a filmstrip and tape, Westport Communications Group, 1981.

Sidelights

The author of well over one hundred children's books, Caroline Arnold has addressed a plethora of subjects, including geography, geology, sociology, biology, archaeology, anthropology, paleontology, and even meteorology. In her award-winning titles, Arnold has proven herself to be an incredibly versatile and ever-curious writer, dissecting and explaining complex social and scientific themes for young readers. Although she has penned a few works of fiction, she is best known for her science and nature books. With photographer Richard Hewett and others, Arnold has created works that allow children to gain close-up perspectives of some of nature's most fascinating animals while learning about their life cycles, habitats, and histories. Many of these books, such as *Saving the Peregrine Falcon, Panda,* and *On the Brink of Extinction: The California Condor*—the last with photographs by condor expert Michael Wallace—discuss the effect of humans upon animal habitats and explain conservation attempts. In the popular "Animal Favorites" series, Arnold and Hewett teamed up on over two dozen titles that focus on individual animals, providing middle graders with a zoological library. Other lauded works, like *Trapped in Tar: Fossils from the Ice Age, The Ancient Cliff Dwellers of Mesa Verde,* and *Easter Island: Giant Stone Statues Tell of a Rich and Tragic Past,* emphasize the attempts by scientists to understand animals, plants, and humans that lived long ago.

Arnold once told *SATA* that her "fascination with scientific subjects is reinforced" by her "own and other children's eagerness to know more about the world around them." She enjoys "the challenge of writing about complicated subjects in language that even a very young child can understand." Arnold's dedication and enthusiasm are reflected in her texts, which convey a sense of wonder along with well-organized, carefully researched, and clearly explained information. To her credit, Arnold provides her curious readers with a look at the work of those scientists, biologists, paleontologists, and artists who continuously shape our understanding of nature. She hints that the reader, too, can transform her or his interest in nature into a satisfying career.

As a young girl growing up in Minneapolis, Minnesota, Arnold learned to love books. "Among my earliest memories," she related, "are trips to the library with my parents and three younger brothers on Saturday mornings. When I grew older I was allowed to go to the library by myself, riding my bicycle and filling my basket with as many books as would fit. In fifth grade I met a girl who loved to read as much as I did. We often spent whole days reading and talking about books, especially during the long, lazy days of summer when we lay on blankets under the apple tree in my backyard or took our books and a picnic lunch to one of the lakes nearby."

Arnold revealed that she also learned to appreciate nature at an early age. "Part of each summer was spent in northern Wisconsin at a camp that was owned by the settlement house that my father directed. I learned to love nature in those north woods." Arnold's father always extended the three-hour drive to the camp with excursions through the wilderness along the side of the road. There, the family searched for wild flowers, butterflies, and birds. "When my cousins, who were rock hounds, came with us, we also stopped to hunt for agates and other kinds of stones." Arnold remembers the "excitement that we shared when we spied a deer or uncovered the fossil of an ancient sea creature.... As I write about animals, dinosaur bones and other scientific subjects, my goal is to convey that same sense of discovery."

As she once recalled for *SATA,* Arnold had "no idea" that she would be a writer when she grew up. "I liked to draw and at Grinnell College and the University of Iowa I studied art, intending to become a professional artist and art teacher." For a dozen years Arnold pursued a career as art instructor and substitute teacher, freelancing as an artist on the side. The she made a momentous decision. "Beginning in 1976, I decided to use my training in art to try book illustration. My favorite subjects were plants and animals, and as I wrote stories to provide the text for my drawings, I found myself becoming a science writer." Arnold's career as a writer took off with *Five Nests* and *Electric Fish,* both published in 1980. She did not illustrate her own work until she wrote *Sun Fun,* her fifth book, published in 1981. "I discovered that for every page I had to do a separate drawing for each color. Techniques have changed since then but after illustrating three books I decided to stop drawing and devote all of my energy to writing."

Arnold has been lucky in her collaborative efforts, as her books created with photographer Richard Hewett have enriched both her work and reputation. In a review of *Koala* and *Kangaroo,* for example, *Horn Book* writer Karen Jameyson observed that Arnold's "vivid descriptions ... enhance the writing, as do the copious photographs." According to Margaret A. Bush in a *Horn Book* review of *Camel* and *Panda,* Arnold and Hewett "display mastery at collaboration" and provide "seamless, interesting presentations." Arnold once explained her working relationship with Hewett for *SATA.* "I function both as a writer and as a photographer's assistant. The firsthand experience of seeing animals close-up, going behind the scenes in a museum, or climbing up ancient ruins also helps me to bring my subjects to life when I write my manuscript. I also hold film, adjust lights, and when necessary, act as a model. All of our projects are true collaborative efforts with my text providing a guide for the photos and the photos exerting an influence over my final text."

Each of Arnold's books for Morrow's "Animal Favorites" series, with photographs by Hewett, focuses on a wild animal. Arnold had seen some of these animals in their natural habitats soon after her marriage, while her husband Art conducted a research project in western Uganda. For four months, she recalled, "we lived literally in the midst of lions, elephants, zebras, hippos, and other African wildlife." Although Arnold and Hewett traveled to Australia to research and photograph koalas and kangaroos, they often were not able to observe and photograph animals in their natural habitats. Instead, they visited them in zoos and wild animal parks where the animals live in settings similar to their natural habitats, like the Wildlife Safari Park in Oregon, Sea World in California, and the Chapultepec Zoo in Mexico City, Mexico. According to Myra R. Oleynik in *School Library Journal,* Arnold and Hewett have "a way of guiding readers to unusual places where they can get to know animals with unusual faces."

Arnold and Hewett's books in the Morrow series give general information about each animal's history, anatomy, species variation, diet, stages of growth, behavior, reproduction, care of young, and habitat. As some critics have noted, Arnold's texts do not just briefly explain the photographs, they provide useful and intriguing facts and statistics. Most of the books, such as *Camel, Flamingo,* and *Giraffe,* follow a baby animal's birth and development. Again, Bush observed in a *Horn Book* review of *Giraffe* and *Zebra* that Arnold "smoothly [integrates] explanations of how the species lives in the wild and how the animals behave and live in captivity."

The texts in some of the books, like *Panda, Zebra,* and *Wild Goat,* relate how conservation efforts may save the animals from extinction.

Overall, the books in the series have won critical praise as well as approval from awards committees. In a *Horn Book* review of *Elephant* and *Monkey,* for example, Elizabeth S. Watson dubbed Arnold and Hewett an "expert team ... rooting text and photographs in the life of one particular animal." *Sea Lion,* likewise, according to *Booklist* contributor Carolyn Phelan, is one of many "excellent books" in the series. In each title, Phelan noted, "the clear, full-color photography provides a good visual counterpoint to the lucid, well-organized text." Reviewing their *Killer Whale,* Bush remarked in *Horn Book,* "Once again Caroline Arnold and Richard Hewett achieve a very high standard of nonfiction." Similarly, Phelan, writing in *Booklist,* felt that *Rhino* and *Lion* "feature clear writing" and "excellent photographs," and provide "dependable resources for research or browsing." *Fox* and *Bat,* the last titles in the series, once again employ the winning Arnold-Hewett formula of clear text and vibrant color photographs. Phelan praised Arnold's "succinct, readable" text, while Susan S. Verner, reviewing both titles in the *Bulletin of the Center for Children's Books,* noted that Arnold "forthrightly defends her predator subjects by explaining how they help control pests such as rodents and insects." Verner also referred to Arnold's "jam-packed text" which offers "intriguing information." Lisa Wu Stowe, in a *School Library Journal* review of both *Bat* and *Fox,* felt that these titles "share the good organization, clear writing, and beautiful full-color photographs that made [Arnold and Hewett's] previous collaborations successful."

Working in other series and in stand-alone titles, Arnold has also authored books focusing on individual animals. Her 1998 *Bobcats,* for example, blends cogent text with photographs. Reviewing the title in *School Library Journal,* Susan Oliver found it to be "exceptionally good, written with energy and full of lively, full-color photographs." Animal specialists are featured in other books from Arnold. In *Shockers of the Sea and Other Electrical Animals,* she presents a "fascinating look," as *Booklist* contributor Shelley Townsend-Hudson noted, at fish which can feel and produce electricity. Such fish use this extra sense for defense, communication, and for getting food. Similarly, in *Did You Hear That?: Animals with Super Hearing,* Arnold focuses on creatures with an acutely developed aural sense, such as bats, dolphins, and even rhinos. "The book," wrote Margaret Bush in *School Library Journal,* "should be useful in science classes, and the presentation encourages some reflective thinking." *Booklist* reviewer Carolyn Phelan also praised the title, calling *Did You Hear That?* an "attractive introductory book on ultrasound and infrasound in the animal kingdom."

Since she wrote *Animals That Migrate,* and wrote and illustrated *The Biggest Living Thing,* Arnold's books for Carolrhoda have received acclaim. *Tule Elk,* according to Margaret C. Howell in *School Library Journal,* is an "informative" as well as "appealing" discussion of

America's smallest elk that includes a discussion of elk habitat and life cycle. *Ostriches and Other Flightless Birds,* as Amy Adler noted in *School Library Journal,* contains "fascinating tidbits" of information about flightless birds, called *ratites. House Sparrows Everywhere* tells how the little bird, which was introduced to the United States from Europe due to its ability to kill leaf-eating inchworms, produced unplanned natural consequences. She also describes the birds' habitat, communication, and reproduction.

In *Saving the Peregrine Falcon* Arnold relates how a species of falcon came close to extinction and how scientists have struggled to save it. These scientists take eggs from the birds, hatch the chicks, and finally release the young birds when they are strong. According to *School Library Journal* contributor Ellen Fader, Hewett's "spectacular" and "arresting" photographs are "well integrated with the text" and the book is "an excellent introduction to the peregrine falcon." Like *Saving the Peregrine Falcon, On the Brink of Extinction: The California Condor* is about an endangered species of bird. Arnold describes the condor's appearance, size, and diet, and tells how this species, which has existed for 40,000 years, was almost devastated by modern society in the span of just one century. The California condor barely escaped extinction in 1986, when it was estimated that just one pair of condors still lived in the California wilderness.

Arnold traces the programs designed by the Los Angeles and San Diego zoos to save the condor in *On the Brink of Extinction.* By incubating eggs in laboratories, feeding baby birds with puppet replicas of their parents, and releasing the maturing bird into the wild, the programs have increased the condor's population. Nevertheless, as Arnold demonstrates, no one knows for sure whether the condor will avoid extinction. *Horn Book* critic Bush described *On the Brink of Extinction* as a "tantalizing account" that "leaves the reader wanting to know more." After describing Arnold's text as "clear" and "engaging," Amy Nunley concluded in *School Library Journal* that the book is "a treasure-trove for the eye and for the heart."

Other books by Arnold dealing with preservation topics include *Hawk Highway in the Sky: Watching Raptor Migration* and *Baby Whale Rescue: The True Story of J.J.* In the former title, Arnold details the work of Hawk Watch International whose volunteers track hawks, eagles, and falcons near Nevada's Goshute Mountains. Susan Scheps, writing in *School Library Journal,* found this "short, informative book" both "attractive and interesting," while *Booklist* contributor Candace Smith noted that Arnold's "clear, well-organized text" helps readers imagine "the fierce beauty of the birds as well as the scientists' painstaking work." In *Baby Whale Rescue,* Arnold teamed up once again with Hewett to tell the true story of the rescue of a baby whale who had become separated from its mother on the coast of California. Lauren Peterson called this real-life adventure "fascinating" in a *Booklist* review, while Patricia Manning,

writing in *School Library Journal,* concluded that it is a "heartwarming story with an excellent scientific focus."

Several of Arnold's books provide children with information about natural life in various regions and, in the process, demonstrate where to find wildlife. *A Walk on the Great Barrier Reef,* with photographs by Arnold's husband, explains "relationships within the habitat of the reef community" according to *School Library Journal* critic Ellen Fader, and includes maps and diagrams. Written for younger children, *A Walk by the Seashore* and *A Walk up the Mountain* are books that, in the words of *School Library Journal* contributor Diane Nunn, "establish a sense of place in the natural world." With *African Animals* Arnold and Hewett take "a lucid look at twenty African animals," according to *Booklist* reviewer Julie Corsaro, who found the book to be "surprisingly informative." Geared for the very young reader, *African Animals* is "a standout," according to Susan Oliver, who lauded the book's "[s]uperb full-color photography, simple but intelligent language, and excellent organization" in her *School Library Journal* review. "This is a book that youngsters will want to return to again and again," concluded Oliver. Arnold does the same for the Western Hemisphere with *South American Animals,* an "attractive, high-quality companion" to *African Animals,* as *Booklist* contributor Peterson noted. Frances E. Millhouser, reviewing *South American Animals* for *School Library Journal,* felt that it was an "attractive browsing book," while Erica L. Stahler, writing in *Horn Book Guide,* called it a "brief but informative overview."

Animals in their environment take a new twist with Arnold's series of "Zoo Animals" books. Here the "natural" environment becomes the confines of zoo in board books geared for the very young. A reviewer for *Publishers Weekly* noted that the series "immerses readers in the daily routines at the zoo." Each title deals with a separate activity, as in *Mealtime for Zoo Animals, Sleepytime for Zoo Animals,* or *Splashtime for Zoo Animals.* Reviewing *Mealtime for Zoo Animals,* a contributor for *Kirkus Reviews* noted that the book "makes for a perfect visual outing on those days when the zoo is closed." Dawn Amsberry, reviewing *Sleepytime for Zoo Animals* and *Splashtime for Zoo Animals,* wrote that "these books are bound to please." *Sleepytime* "captures the quieter side of zoo life," according to Amsberry, while *Splashtime* "captures animals in more playful moments." In a *Booklist* review of *Noisytime for Zoo Animals,* Susan Dove Lempke remarked that the series "makes a fine choice for reading to preschoolers."

In other books, Arnold focuses on dinosaurs and those who study them. *Trapped in Tar: Fossils from the Ice Age,* with black-and-white photographs by Hewett, features the models and skeletons in the collection of the George C. Page Museum of La Brea Discoveries in Los Angeles. Arnold explains how the fossils are found and excavated, as well as how scientists attempt to reconstruct the bodies and lives of ancient creatures with these fossils for exhibits. In addition, as Betsy Hearne noted in *Bulletin of the Center for Children's Books, Trapped in Tar* also provides information about "animal and plant life in the Ice Age." With Arnold's text and Hewett's full-color photographs, *Dinosaurs All Around: An Artist's View of the Prehistoric World* illuminates a specific process of recreating dinosaurs for exhibits. Arnold discusses the work of sculptors like artists Stephen and Sylvia Czerkas, who conduct research on each dinosaur's anatomy and skin texture, patterns, and colors before beginning to create their realistic models. As in *Trapped in Tar,* Arnold also provides information about the types of dinosaurs being recreated. Cathryn A. Camper, writing in *School Library Journal,* concluded that *Dinosaurs All Around* "will probably foster career possibilities beyond paleontology for dinosaur fans."

The fossils found at the Dinosaur Mountain National Monument in Utah are just one topic of interest in *Dinosaur Mountain: Graveyard of the Past.* Hewett's color photographs show the quarry where the fossils were found and are displayed, models of dinosaurs (with people in the photos to call attention to size), and paleontologists working. Ellen Fader wrote in *Horn Book* that "Arnold seamlessly blends" information about paleontology with information "about specific finds" on

the site and "offers intriguing descriptions of ongoing work." Arnold introduces fossils exhibited in "Kadimakara: Fossils of the Australian Dreamtime" in *Dinosaurs Down Under: And Other Fossils from Australia.* The exhibit features the fossils of fish, reptiles, birds, and mammals as well as dinosaurs found in Australia. In the 2001 title *Dinosaurs with Feathers: The Ancestors of the Modern Birds,* Arnold provides an introduction to the modern research which traces birds back to their ancient progenitors. *Booklist* contributor John Peters thought that Arnold's brief survey "will excite children unaware of some startling developments in our understanding of prehistoric life."

Like Arnold's dinosaur books, *The Ancient Cliff Dwellers of Mesa Verde* discusses the work of those who meticulously try to reconstruct the past as well as the objects of their study. Yet the scientists featured in this book are archaeologists attempting to learn about the ancient Anasazi people who lived in the Southwestern United States long ago in high cliff dwellings. The Anasazi people left their homes and many artifacts at the Mesa Verde site, but scientists still wonder about the

In **Did You Hear That?,** *Arnold profiles bats, dolphins, rodents, insects, and other creatures with super hearing.* (Illustrated by Cathy Trachok.)

development of the society and its demise. More archaeology is served up in *Stone Age Farmers beside the Sea: Scotland's Prehistoric Village of Skara Brae.* Here Arnold traces the origins of one of Europe's oldest villages, located on Scotland's Orkney Islands and inhabited from about 3100 to 2500 B.C., predating the Egyptian pyramids. A contributor for *Kirkus Reviews* noted that the author's narrative "deftly recounts" not only the design of the stone houses, but also the daily life of the farming inhabitants.

Arnold's award-winning *Easter Island: Giant Stone Statues Tell of a Rich and Tragic Past* focuses on another archaeological puzzle, the remote Easter Island in the Pacific Ocean and the huge stone statues which dot its landscape. "As usual," wrote *Booklist* reviewer Ilene Cooper, "Arnold provides a solid, cogent text," dealing with both a chronological and engineering description of the stones and their placement. The author also explores variant theories to explain the ultimate disappearance of the island's population. "Arnold provides a clear and concise look at the many mysteries that surround it," commented Jeanette Larson in a *School Library Journal* review, while a reviewer for *Horn Book* noted that Arnold "avoids theatrical speculation in this straightforward account."

Arnold proves her versatility as both a fiction and nonfiction author with three other books, *The Terrible Hodag, Children of the Settlement Houses,* and *El Niño: Stormy Weather for People and Wildlife.* In these titles, Arnold moves away from her usual animal or anthropological focus to deal with tall tales, urban history, and meteorology. Those summers in Wisconsin that provided Arnold with an appreciation for nature and a sense of discovery also inspired her to try her hand at story telling. Sitting around a campfire at night, Arnold heard tales which became the basis for *The Terrible Hodag.* The terrible, talking Hodag, with an ox head, a dinosaur back, an alligator tail, bear paws, and red glowing eyes towers forty feet high. Although the lumberjacks in the Wisconsin woods fear him, Ole Swenson finds him more accommodating than his tyrannical boss, who refuses to pay his men until they clear a hillside of trees. With his giant tail, the Hodag helps Ole and the other lumberjacks get their job done. When the boss refuses to pay the lumberjacks anyway, the Hodag chases him away, leaving the forest and the trees to the lumberjacks, who vow to take no more than they need from the forest. As Susan Scheps wrote in *School Library Journal,* "Tales of this beast do not appear in collections of American lore and legend"; this Wisconsin tale "has its place in children's literature."

In *Children of the Settlement Houses,* Arnold details the history of settlement houses in early twentieth-century America. Such community centers provided learning centers as well as playgrounds and baths for urban poor and new immigrants. Anne Chapman, writing in *School Library Journal,* called this title a "fascinating look," while *Booklist* reviewer Shelle Rosenfeld dubbed it an "excellent introduction to an important aspect of urban American history." In *El Niño,* Arnold deals with turbulent weather patterns, investigating the effects of ocean warming on the world's weather. Drawing on modern research technologies that correlate ocean temperatures with weather patterns, she presents a "picture of the atmospheric and ecological import of such shifts in ocean temperatures" through a "readable, informative text," according to Patricia Manning writing in *School Library Journal.* Reviewing the title in *Appraisal,* Kathleen Dummer "highly recommended" *El Niño* for students ages ten to thirteen. In *Booklist,* Chris Sherman added to the praise, noting, "Science teachers and students will appreciate this very readable introduction to the El Niño current."

Arnold once told *SATA* that she enjoys "the opportunity to explore different formats" in her writing. "Each new book is a challenge to find the best way to present the information I have collected in my research. I like writing because I like to find out things and with every new book I discover things I never knew before."

Biographical and Critical Sources

PERIODICALS

Appraisal, spring, 1999, Kathleen Dummer, review of *El Niño: Stormy Weather for People and Wildlife,* p. 7.
Booklist, November 1, 1984, p. 358; November 1, 1988, p. 476; October 1, 1992, p. 323; September 15, 1994, Carolyn Phelan, review of *Sea Lion* and *Killer Whale,* p. 128; December 1, 1994, pp. 670-671; December 15, 1994, p. 747; September 15, 1995, Carolyn Phelan, review of *Lion* and *Rhino,* p. 154; August, 1996, Carolyn Phelan, review of *Bat* and *Fox,* p. 1897; p. 1897; December 15, 1996, p. 722; March 15, 1997, Julie Corsaro, review of *African Animals,* p. 1236; April 15, 1997, p. 1424; June 1, 1997, Candace Smith, review of *Hawk Highway in the Sky,* p. 1687; September 15, 1998, Shelle Rosenfeld, review of *Children of the Settlement Houses,* p. 221; October 1, 1998, Chris Sherman, review of *El Niño,* p. 326; March 1, 1999, Lauren Peterson, review of *Baby Whale Rescue,* p. 1204; June 1, 1999, Susan Dove Lempke, review of *Noisytime for Zoo Animals,* p. 1832; July, 1999, Lauren Peterson, review of *South American Animals,* p. 1939; October 15, 1999, Shelley Townsend-Hudson, review of *Shockers of the Sea and Other Electrical Animals,* p. 448; March 15, 2000, Ilene Cooper, review of *Easter Island,* p. 1371; November 1, 2000, p. 528; October 1, 2001, John Peters, review of *Dinosaurs with Feathers,* p. 313; December 1, 2001, Carolyn Phelan, review of *Did You Hear That?: Animals with Super Hearing,* p. 654; February 15, 2002, Carolyn Phelan, review of *The Geography Book: Activities for Exploring, Mapping, and Enjoying Your World,* p. 1011.
Bulletin of the Center for Children's Books, March, 1986, p. 121; June, 1987, Betsy Hearne, review of *Trapped in Tar: Fossils from the Ice Age,* p. 181; October, 1996, Susan S. Verner, review of *Fox* and *Bat,* p. 47.
Highlights for Children, October, 1988, p. 3; October, 1996, Susan S. Verner, review of *Fox,* p. 47.

Horn Book, May-June, 1987, Karen Jameyson, review of *Kangaroo* and *Koala,* pp. 354-355; January-February, 1988, Margaret A. Bush, review of *Giraffe* and *Zebra,* p. 80; September-October, 1989, Ellen Fader, review of *Dinosaur Mountain: Graveyard of the Past,* p. 635; May-June, 1991, p. 345; November-December, 1992, Margaret A. Bush, review of *Panda* and *Camel,* p. 735; May-June, 1993, Margaret A. Bush, review of *On the Brink of Extinction: The California Condor,* pp. 343-344; November-December, 1993, Margaret A. Bush, review of *Monkey* and *Elephant,* p. 759; November-December, 1994, Margaret A. Bush, review of *Killer Whale* and *Sea Lion,* p. 742; March-April, 1995, p. 218; May-June, 2000, review of *Easter Island,* p. 329.

Horn Book Guide, spring, 1997, pp. 126, 136; fall, 1999, Erica L. Stahler, review of *South American Animals,* p. 337; fall, 1998, p. 385; spring, 1999, p. 150; fall, 1999, pp. 228, 350.

Kirkus Reviews, June 15, 1989, p. 911; February 15, 1997, review of *Stone Age Farmers beside the Sea,* p. 296; April 1, 1997, p. 548; February 15, 1999, p. 296; April 15, 1999, review of *Mealtime for Zoo Animals,* p. 638.

Publishers Weekly, April 19, 1999, review of *Mother and Baby Zoo Animals,* p. 75.

School Library Journal, March, 1985, Ellen Fader, review of *Saving the Peregrine Falcon,* p. 160; December, 1985, p. 66; January, 1987, p. 70; June, 1987, p. 76; December, 1987, p. 90; June-July, 1988, p. 120; August, 1988, Ellen Fader, review of *A Walk on the Great Barrier Reef,* pp. 99-100; June, 1989, Susan Scheps, review of *The Terrible Hodag,* p. 82; September, 1989, Margaret C. Howell, review of *Tule Elk,* p. 258; July, 1990, Amy Adler, review of *Ostriches and Other Flightless Birds,* p. 80; November, 1990, p. 102; March, 1991, p. 220; April, 1991, Diane Nunn, review of *A Walk by the Seashore* and *A Walk up the Mountain,* pp. 108-109; November, 1992, Myra R. Oleynik, review of *Camel,* pp. 100, 102; May, 1993, Cathryn A. Camper, review of *Dinosaurs All Around: An Artist's View of the Prehistoric World,* p. 112; June, 1993, Amy Nunley, review of *On the Brink of Extinction: The California Condor,* p. 113; September, 1996, Lisa Wu Stowe, review of *Bat* and *Fox,* p. 210; March, 1997, Susan Oliver, review of *African Animals,* p. 170; June, 1997, Susan Scheps, review of *Hawk Highway in the Sky,* p. 130; March, 1998, Susan Oliver, review of *Bobcats,* pp. 191-192; December, 1998, Patricia Manning, review of *El Niño,* pp. 132-133; January, 1999, Anne Chapman, review of *Children of the Settlement House,* p. 109; March, 1999, Patricia Manning, review of *Baby Whale Rescue,* p. 216; August, 1999, Dawn Amsberry, review of *Sleepytime for Zoo Animals* and *Splashtime for Zoo Animals,* pp. 143-144; September, 1999, Frances E. Millhouser, review of *South American Animals,* p. 210; January, 2000, pp. 115-116; April, 2000, Jeanette Larson, review of *Easter Island,* p. 144; October, 2000, p. 144; November, 2000, p. 167; December, 2000, p. 52; August, 2001, Margaret Bush, review of *Did You Hear That?,* p. 166.

Science Books and Films, May, 1998, p. 113.

Voice of Youth Advocates, December, 1984, p. 271.

OTHER

Caroline Arnold Home Page, http://www.geocities.com/Athens/1264 (February 19, 2002).*

* * *

AUSTIN, R. G.
See GELMAN, Rita Golden

* * *

AXELROD, Amy

Personal

Born in MA; married, husband's name Michael; children: two sons. *Education:* Brandeis University, B.A.; graduate degree from Columbia University; additional course work in elementary education.

Addresses

Home—New York. *Office*—c/o Author Mail, Simon and Schuster, 1230 Avenue of the Americas, New York, NY 10020.

Career

Author.

Writings

The News Hounds in the Great Balloon Race: A Geography Adventure, illustrated by Tim Bowers, Simon & Schuster (New York, NY), 2000.

The News Hounds Catch a Wave: A Geography Adventure, illustrated by Tim Bowers, Simon & Schuster (New York, NY), 2001.

My Last Chance Brother, illustrated by Jack E. Davis, Penguin (New York, NY), 2002.

"PIGS WILL BE PIGS" SERIES

Pigs Will Be Pigs, illustrated by Sharon McGinley-Nally, Simon & Schuster (New York, NY), 1994.

Pigs on a Blanket, illustrated by Sharon McGinley-Nally, Simon & Schuster (New York, NY), 1996.

Pigs Go to Market: Fun with Math and Shopping, illustrated by Sharon McGinley-Nally, Simon & Schuster (New York, NY), 1997.

Pigs in the Pantry: Fun with Math and Cooking, illustrated by Sharon McGinley-Nally, Simon & Schuster (New York, NY), 1997.

Pigs on the Ball: Fun with Math and Sports, illustrated by Sharon McGinley-Nally, Simon & Schuster (New York, NY), 1998.

Pigs on the Move: Fun with Math and Travel, illustrated by Sharon McGinley-Nally, Simon & Schuster (New York, NY), 1999.

Pigs at Odds: Fun with Math and Games, illustrated by Sharon McGinley-Nally, Simon & Schuster (New York, NY), 2000.

The Pigs have fun with math as they shop for treats for their Halloween party in Amy Axelrod's **Pigs Go to Market.**
(Illustrated by Sharon McGinley-Nally.)

Pigs in the Corner: Fun with Math and Dance, illustrated by Sharon McGinley-Nally, Simon & Schuster (New York, NY), 2001.

Sidelights

Children's author Amy Axelrod is the creator of the "Pigs Will Be Pigs" series of math books. Her aim is to introduce math concepts to younger children in an entertaining way. In the first book in the series, *Pigs Will Be Pigs,* Mr. and Mrs. Pig discover that both their refrigerator and their wallets are empty. But instead of going to an automated teller, the Pig family decides to go on a money-hunt around their home, looking for loose coins and bills. The younger Pigs join in the chase too, emptying their toy box for change, while Mr. and Mrs. Pig find errant bills in toolboxes and laundry rooms. After they have turned the house upside down, the family sits down and counts out their booty, enough for dinner at the "Enchanted Enchilada." Writing in

Booklist, Mary Harris Veeder predicted that the "Pigs' spirit will suit young listeners." While noting a small distraction with extra numbers embedded in the illustrations, *Arithmetic Teacher* critic David J. Whitin nonetheless suggested that "children will enjoy counting the money along the way," going on to say that *Pigs Will Be Pigs* "presents a good problem-solving story for readers."

The Pig family's adventures continue in additional books, including *The Pigs Go to Market: Fun with Math and Shopping, Pigs on the Ball: Fun with Math and Sports,* and *Pigs at Odds: Fun with Math and Games.* In *The Pigs Go to Market,* the Pig family has been true to their name by eating up all of the Halloween candy before the trick or treaters arrive. During a last-minute dash to the store, Mrs. Pig wins a shopping spree and fills her cart with more candy to be counted by readers. Writing in *School Library Journal,* contributor Pamela K. Bomboy considered *The Pigs Go to Market* "perfect for integrating math into the curriculum at Halloween time." *Pigs on the Ball* tackles the subject of geometry as the Pigs celebrate Mr. Pig's birthday with a round of miniature golf. The Pig family visits the carnival in *Pigs at Odds,* and readers help the porcine family calculate the odds of winning prizes at the fair. According to *School Library Journal* critic Lisa Gangemi, "The odds are high that this title will be another piggy hit."

Biographical and Critical Sources

PERIODICALS

Arithmetic Teacher, May, 1994, David J. Whitin, review of *Pigs Will Be Pigs,* p. 563.

Booklist, February 15, 1994, Mary Harris Veeder, review of *Pigs Will Be Pigs,* p. 1091; March 1, 1997, Carolyn Phelan, review of *Pigs in the Pantry: Fun with Math and Cooking,* p. 1168.

Bulletin of the Center for Children's Books, May, 1997, Elizabeth Bush, review of *Pigs in the Pantry,* p. 312.

New York Times Book Review, November 16, 1997, Ruth Reichl, review of *Pigs in the Pantry,* p. 38.

Publishers Weekly, December 20, 1993, review of *Pigs Will Be Pigs,* p. 72; May 13, 1996, review of *Pigs on a Blanket,* p. 75; October 6, 1997, review of *Pigs Go to Market: Fun with Math and Shopping,* p. 49; February 7, 2000, review of *The News Hounds in the Great Balloon Race: A Geography Adventure,* p. 86; October 29, 2001, "Math Matters," p. 66.

School Library Journal, May, 1994, Lucinda Snyder Whitehurst, review of *Pigs Will Be Pigs,* p. 84; June, 1996, John Peters, review of *Pigs on a Blanket,* p. 92; April, 1997, Rosie Peasley, review of *Pigs in the Pantry,* p. 90; September, 1997, Pamela K. Bomboy, review of *Pigs Go to Market,* p. 172; October, 1998, Alicia Eames, review of *Pigs on the Ball: Fun with Math and Sports,* p. 86; October, 1999, Tracy Taylor, review of *Pigs on the Move: Fun with Math and Travel,* p. 65; April, 2000, Jill O'Farrell, review of *The News Hounds in the Great Balloon Race,* p. 90; January, 2001, Lisa Gangemi, review of *Pigs at Odds: Fun with Math and Games,* p. 91.

OTHER

Amy Axelrod Web Site, http://www.amyaxelrod.com (April 20, 2002).*

B

BACON, Betty
See BACON, Elizabeth

* * *

BACON, Elizabeth 1914-2001
(Betty Bacon, Betty Morrow)

OBITUARY NOTICE—See index for SATA sketch: Born September 15, 1914, in Los Angeles, CA; died of respiratory failure, June 6, 2001, in Berkeley, CA. Librarian, educator, and author. Elizabeth Bacon worked as a children's librarian in California for twenty years, beginning in 1958. She also taught children's literature classes at the University of California at Berkeley and at other colleges and universities. Bacon was the founder of the Bay Area Storytelling Festival, and she published children's books under her maiden name, Betty Morrow. She wrote about subjects of particular interest to her: the Jewish faith in *Jewish Holidays* (1967) and *The Story of Hanukkah* (1968), and nature and the environment in *See through the Sea* (1955) and *See up the Mountain* (1958). As Betty Bacon, the author was also a community activist in the San Francisco Bay area, focusing on human rights and civil rights activities, and a self-described "armchair anthropologist" with an interest in the lifestyle and history of the Native Americans of the Bay area. Prior to her move to California in 1958, Bacon worked for publishing firms in New York City for nearly twenty years. While there, she contributed poetry to the *New Yorker* and reviews to the *New York Times Book Review*.

OBITUARIES AND OTHER SOURCES:

PERIODICALS

San Francisco Chronicle, June 27, 2001, obituary by Eric Brazil, p. D14.

BALGASSI, Haemi 1967-

Personal

Born July 2, 1967, in Korea; immigrated to the United States at age seven; daughter of Hyun Suk Rowe; married Joseph Balgassi, 1987; children: Adria, Louisa. *Hobbies and other interests:* "Reading, photographing my family, working on my Web site."

Addresses

Home—Westfield, MA. *Agent*—c/o Author Mail, Clarion Books, 215 Park Ave., S., New York, NY 10003.

Career

Author.

Awards, Honors

Notable Children's Book selection, *Smithsonian* magazine, and Best Books of 1996 selection, *San Francisco Chronicle,* both 1996, both for *Peacebound Trains;* Notable Children's Trade Book in the Field of Social Studies, Children's Book Council/National Council for the Social Studies, 1998, Maine Student Book Award nominee, 1999, and Lamplighter Classic Award, National Christian Schools Association, 2000, all for *Tae's Sonata.*

Writings

Peacebound Trains, illustrated by Chris K. Soentpiet, Clarion Books (New York, NY), 1996.
Tae's Sonata, Clarion Books (New York, NY), 1997.

Contributor of poems, articles, and stories to magazines and literary journals, including *Cicada.*

Work in Progress

A middle-grade novel and magazine stories.

Sidelights

Haemi Balgassi's first books address her cultural heritage, the experiences of Korean people in Korea and as immigrants in the United States. Her debut book, *Peacebound Trains,* was based directly on the experiences of her mother and grandmother while they lived in Korea. "When I was a young girl, my grandmother shared with me the story of her (and her daughters') harrowing rooftop train ride during the first harsh winter of the Korean War. My grandmother passed away when I was eleven, but her story stayed with me," Balgassi wrote on her personal Web site. "When I was in high school, I asked my mother to tell me what she remembered of that rooftop train ride. My mother added another layer to my grandmother's story—the memories she'd carried since she rode the train as a five year old." This short, illustrated novel, also called a chapter book, came about after several attempts. "I considered telling the story directly from the time of the war, without the present-day characters," Balgassi told Cynthia Leitch-Smith of *Children's Literature Resources.* "After a couple drafts, I realized that the story would work best if I introduced it to young readers the way I myself first heard it." So Balgassi had the grandmother character of the story tell her granddaughter of a fearful ride atop a train that would lead refugees away from war. *Peacebound Trains* was featured on the U.S. government's Korean War Fiftieth Anniversary Web site and earned praise from critics. Although *Booklist* reviewer Stephanie Zvirin found the link between past and present in the story to be unclear, she applauded the "wonderfully individualized" characters. So too, writing in *Reading Teacher,* Yvonne Siu-Runyan and Elaine Vilscek determined that "detailed illustrations" and "eloquent language combine for a strong understanding of Korean culture."

Like *Peacebound Trains, Tae's Sonata,* a middle-grade novel, was based on family history, this time Balgassi's experiences of growing up in the United States as an immigrant. "*Tae's Sonata* is inspired by my own middle-grade years. Like Tae, I struggled to find a balance between my Korean (home) and American (school) identities," she told Leitch-Smith. "In writing *Tae's Sonata,* I drew from my childhood memories of taking piano lessons, and attending a Korean church here in the United States. Many of the characters are based on people I really knew." Told in the first person by eighth-grader Taeyoung Kim, the plot revolves around the narrator's struggle to overcome hers and others' premature assumptions—about popularity, about ethnicity, and about relationships. Writing the novel proved to be a learning experience for Balgassi, as well. "Tae was very possessive of my time. Her voice consumed me. . . . I felt that I couldn't rest until I wrote her story," she explained to Leitch-Smith. "It wasn't always easy, though. Tae brought back some painful memories of my adolescence that I thought I'd buried years earlier."

Reviewers found much to like about *Tae's Sonata.* Calling the characters "familiar and believable," Nina Lindsay described the novel as "well written and appealing" in her *School Library Journal* review. It provides "insight into the struggles" Tae's family undergo, a *Publishers Weekly* contributor concluded.

Biographical and Critical Sources

PERIODICALS

Book Links, January, 1998, Stanley F. Steiner, and Lane Cobiskey, "Refugees and Homeless: Nomads of the World," pp. 55-62.

Booklist, September 15, 1996, Stephanie Zvirin, review of *Peacebound Trains,* pp. 236-237; October 10, 1997, Ilene Cooper, review of *Tae's Sonata,* p. 404.

Book Report, May-June, 1998, Diana Jackson, review of *Tae's Sonata,* p. 32.

Bulletin of the Center for Children's Books, October, 1996, review of *Peacebound Trains,* p. 48; December, 1997, review of *Tae's Sonata,* p. 80.

Children's Book Review Service, November, 1996, review of *Peacebound Trains,* p. 29; December, 1997, review of *Tae's Sonata,* p. 45.

Kirkus Reviews, July, 1997, review of *Tae's Sonata,* p. 1026.

New York Times Book Review, March 30, 1997, review of *Peacebound Trains,* p. 18.

Publishers Weekly, January, 1997, Cynthia K. Richey, review of *Peacebound Trains,* p. 75; June 30, 1997, review of *Tae's Sonata,* p. 76.

Reading Teacher, December, 1997, Evelyn B. Freeman and Barbara A. Lehman, "Children's Books: Memorable Journeys," pp. 5-9; Yvonne Siu-Runyan and Elaine Vilscek, review of *Peacebound Trains,* p. 309.

School Library Journal, January, 1997, Cynthia K. Richey and Trevelyn E. Jones, review of *Peacebound Trains,* p. 75; September, 1997, Nina Lindsay, review of *Tae's Sonata,* p. 210.

Smithsonian, November, 1996, review of *Peacebound Trains,* p. 171.

Social Education, April, 1997, review of *Peacebound Trains,* p. 6.

Stone Soup, May-June, 1998, Emma Ward, review of *Tae's Sonata,* pp. 28-29.

OTHER

Children's Literature Resources, http://www.cynthialeitichsmith.com/ (February 20, 2002), Cynthia Leitch-Smith, "Interview with Children's Book Author Haemi Balgassi."

Haemi Balgassi, http://www.haemibalgassi.com/ (January 22, 2002).

*   *   *

BATT, Tanya Robyn 1970-

Personal

Born November 27, 1970, in Auckland, New Zealand; daughter of Warren David (a geologist) and Diane (a teacher; maiden name, Hawkes) Schmidt. *Education:* Auckland College of Education, diploma of teaching; Auckland University, B.Ed.; earned certificate in community dance.

Addresses

Home and office—Imagined Worlds, P.O. Box 8223, Symonds St., Auckland, New Zealand. *Agent*—Ray Richards Literary Agency, P.O. Box 31240, Milford, Auckland, New Zealand. *E-mail*—trbatt@ihug.ro.nz.

Career

Storyteller, author, and early childhood specialist. Imagined Worlds, Auckland, New Zealand, owner, 1995—. Facilitator at workshops for teachers and caregivers; teacher of creative dance and drama to children. *Member:* New Zealand Association for Drama in Education, Society for Storytelling (England), Guild of Storytellers, Organization Mondiale pour l'Education Préscolaire, Dance and the Child, Magdalena, Children's Literature Foundation of New Zealand, New Zealand Storytelling Guild.

Awards, Honors

Welsh Arts Council bursary, for writing; has been awarded places in literary competitions in Great Britain and New Zealand for her poetry.

Writings

Faery Favourites (audio recording), New Frontier, 2000.
(Reteller) *The Fabrics of Fairytale: Stories Spun from Far and Wide* (with audio recording), illustrated by Rachel Griffin, Barefoot Books (Bristol, England), 2000.
Mermaid Tales (audio recording), New Frontier, 2001.
The Terrible Queue, illustrated by Trevor Pye, Scholastic (Auckland, New Zealand), 2001.
Imagined Worlds: A Journey through Expressive Arts in Early Childhood, illustrated by Lea-Anne Sheather, Playcenter Publications (Auckland, New Zealand), 2001.
A Child's Book of Fairies, Barefoot Books (Bristol, England), 2002.
The Fairy's Gift, Barefoot Books (Bristol, England), 2002.

Contributor of poetry to periodicals. Author and creator of "We Can Keep Safe" child protection program.

Work in Progress

Plant Cudd (Welsh for "Hidden Children"), "a fictional tale based on the life of my great-grandmother."

Sidelights

An accomplished storyteller, Tanya Robyn Batt has also written several books for young readers, including the well-received *The Fabrics of Fairytale: Stories Spun from Far and Wide.* Collected and retold by Batt, *The Fabrics of Fairytale* features seven folktales collected from diverse locales, among them China, Hawaii, and Sweden. While each story is unique in that it reflects a specific culture's folklore, all of the retellings contain a common focal point: fabric. For example, in "Clever Anaeet," an Armenian king uses the skills his wife

Tanya Robyn Batt retells tales of magical garments and fabrics from around the world in The Fabrics of Fairytale. *(Illustrated by Rachel Griffin.)*

taught him to weave a carpet with a secret message, while in "The Patchwork Coat," a Jewish man loses a coat in which he has secretly sewn his money, until a bit of clever thinking returns his missing garment back to him. Batt prefaces each of her tales with information about the textile featured in the story, a feature that "add[s] further luster to this unusual theme collection," according to *Booklist* contributor John Peters. Other reviewers found Batt's work an effective way to introduce children to folklore. A critic in *Publishers Weekly* called *The Fabrics of Fairytale* "an intriguing way to introduce lesser-known folktales and the cultures from which the derive," while *School Library Journal* contributor Nancy Call commented that in Batt's "captivating collection" the author "skillfully weaves together folktales from around the world with fascinating information."

Batt told *SATA:* "I was born in Auckland, New Zealand, in November of 1970. My mother had just finished the last of her teaching exams. So near term was she that she was placed in a small room to one side of the examination hall, lest she 'pop' and disrupt, morally or otherwise, the remaining students. After all, she was supposed to be teaching children, not birthing them!

"Soon after I was born, my family—that is, my mum, dad, and I—moved to the South Island of New Zealand.

We lived in a [trailer] on the side of a mountain, just out of a small town called Glenorchy, which is very near a place that was sign-posted Paradise. Paradise! I think that's the nearest I've ever gotten to it, and I am still trying to get back there!

In 1972, Michael, the first of my five brothers, was born, and in 1974, the four of us left the lush, green folds of New Zealand and headed for the dry outback of central New South Wales, Australia.

"It was very hot, very red, and very dusty.

"Cobar—the name of the small town we hovered about—although difficult to find on a map, proved to be of great significance to me. I saw my first fifty snakes, learnt how to swim (not bad for a dry spot several hundred kilometers from the sea) and read, fell in love with the dentist's son and my mother's homemade bread, and had my first memorable encounter with God and story. It was also where my parent's marriage ended. So there you have it—fear, joy, love, loss, and sorrow. . . . All I ever needed to know, I learnt in the middle of nowhere.

"But more about story. . . . From the dry out-reaches of the outback came ... the giant devil dingo! An Aboriginal legend of cannibalism, hunting, and death. I loved it. That and the story of Narri killer boar ... a family tall tale that predated the Australian film *Razorback*. Driving at home at night along the long, lonely straight roads, the headlights clouded by a feathery haze of moths, our eyes peeled, waiting for the killer pig to leap from the scrub that hedged the road and charge the Land Rover.

"In a land so arid and dry, my imagination bloomed.

"I have always loved story. In turn it has pervaded every part of my life.

"From a very young age, I loved creative writing. Initially, I chose poetry over prose. My Nana holds the early records of these poetic endeavors—a short piece, the subject being my pop and his tractor. Despite having pieces published in the newspapers and journals and receiving awards for my writing when I was younger, I never really had a strong desire to be a 'writer,' though the magic of books fascinated me, and they were always my first chosen companions. Writing for me was a highly personal form of expression. It was my primary vehicle for meaning-making.

"It wasn't until my late twenties that I ever considered 'publishing.' I think this is because I worked with story so much in oral form as a performance storyteller. To commit a story to print, to lock it into the hard edges of written text, seemed not too dissimilar from caging a living thing. Writing for publication began with the invitation from a publishing house to adapt the concept of a performance storytelling piece, "The Fabric of Fairytales," into a picture-book collection."

Batt finds that her teaching and storytelling have provided added inspiration for her writing. "I have my own business called Imagined Worlds. This title encompasses the teaching, writing, and performing that I do. Still, writing is only a vehicle of expression. The stories I tell, the stories children tell me, the stories that come from the very story that I live, all feed the stories that I write."

Biographical and Critical Sources

PERIODICALS

Booklist, November 15, 2000, John Peters, review of *The Fabrics of Fairytale: Stories Spun from Far and Wide,* p. 640.
Publishers Weekly, September 4, 2000, review of *The Fabrics of Fairytale,* p. 108.
School Library Journal, November, 2000, Nancy Call, review of *The Fabrics of Fairytale,* p. 139.

OTHER

Imagined Worlds Web site, http://www.imagined-worlds.net (March 20, 2002).

* * *

BATTLE-LAVERT, Gwendolyn
See LAVERT, Gwendolyn Battle

* * *

BLAIR, Pauline Hunter
See CLARKE, Pauline

* * *

BLISS, Corinne Demas
See DEMAS, Corinne

* * *

BRIDGES, Ruby 1954-

Personal

Born 1954, in Tylerton, MS; daughter of Abon (a service station attendant) and Lucille (a domestic worker) Bridges; married Malcolm Hall; children: four sons.

Addresses

Home—New Orleans, LA. *Office*—c/o Ruby Bridges Foundation, P.O. Box 6, Rockville Centre, NY 11571-0006.

Career

Travel agent. Lecturer. Founded the Ruby Bridges Foundation.

Awards, Honors

Recipient of two honorary college degrees.

Writings

Through My Eyes: The Autobiography of Ruby Bridges, Scholastic (New York, NY), 1999.

Adaptations

Through My Eyes was adapted for television by Disney and aired as *The Ruby Bridges Story.*

Sidelights

As a child Ruby Bridges made history as the first African-American student to attend the previously all-white William Frantz Elementary School in New Orleans, Louisiana, an ordeal she recounted in the children's book *Through My Eyes: The Autobiography of Ruby Bridges.* In this book, illustrated with photographs and sidebars, Bridges put in perspective the events that she hardly understood as a first-grader.

Ruby was the eldest of eight children born to Abon and Lucille Bridges, Mississippi sharecroppers. She left the farm when she was four years old, moving to an all-black neighborhood in New Orleans, where her father worked as a service station attendant and her mother at various jobs, including cleaning and casket-making. Because of a federal order to desegregate the public schools, Ruby had the opportunity to attend a previously all-white school. Although her parents disagreed about what to do when Ruby was accepted to attend the William Frantz Elementary School, they wanted to offer her the best in life. On November 16, 1960, Ruby and her mother, escorted by federal marshals to protect them from the threatening crowd outside the school, entered and made history. "My father heard about the trouble at school," Ruby recalled in her book. "That night when he came home from work, he said I was his 'brave little Ruby.'"

Ruby was taught by Barbara Henry, a teacher newly arrived from Boston, who did not know that she and Ruby would end up one-on-one in the classroom for all the other parents of first-graders boycotted the school. "Being Mrs. Henry's only student wasn't a chore," she recalled in the autobiography. "It was fun and felt sort of special. She was more like my best friend than just an ordinary teacher. She was a loving person, and I knew she cared about me." Henry thought Ruby was pretty special as well. "Ruby was a smart, sensitive person," she is quoted as saying in *Through My Eyes.* "It was a joy to go to school each day and to have her as—well—my child. I was newly married and had no children of my own at that time, and I think Ruby became 'my child'! She was so sweet, beautiful, and so brave. It was such an anxious time, and I often wondered how that little girl could come to school each day and be as relaxed and trusting as she was."

Ruby and Barbara Henry spent each day alone. For a long time, Ruby did not even know there were any other children in the school. "Mrs. Henry and I always had fun. We did everything together, reading and word puzzles, spelling and math. We sang songs and played games," she wrote. "Since I couldn't go outside, we pushed desks out of the way and did jumping jack exercises." The reason for staying inside was that for months crowds of people shouting obscenities continued to gather outside the school. Ruby's family suffered as well, her father losing his job because of the publicity. People from other areas, who had learned about Ruby from the news media, sent the family money and gifts. After some months, the owner of a painting company hired her father as a painter.

Ruby finished that first year as a pioneer and then desegregation became more accepted. Her parents divorced when she was in seventh grade, and she went on to graduate from an integrated high school in New Orleans, where she has lived ever since. Bridges studied tourism and became a travel agent, working as one of the first African Americans employed by American Express in New Orleans.

Ruby Bridges came to a turning point in her life in the early 1990s, when her younger brother Milton was killed in a drug-related shooting in the New Orleans housing project in which he lived. Her brother's young children attended the William Frantz Elementary School, and Bridges began to volunteer there. She also reflected and gained new insight into the role she had played as a child in the civil rights movement. She founded the Ruby Bridges Foundation to help strengthen the William Franz Elementary School, which like many inner-city schools, was not up to current standards. Originally the foundation was funded by the proceeds from the sale of a picture book titled *The Story of Ruby Bridges,* written by Robert Coles, a child psychologist who had worked with her during the early desegregation years.

Bridges, thus, wrote *Through My Eyes* not only to inspire other children, but also so that the proceeds from its sale could benefit her foundation. The work was well received by critics. "Bridges needs no intermediaries to cloud the lens of her story; she relates it far more powerfully than anyone else to date," lauded a critic in *Horn Book.* "Bridges's words," wrote a *Publishers Weekly* contributor, "are more vivid than even the best of the photos. Like poetry or prayer, they melt the heart."

Bridges eventually became an advocate for civil rights and a public speaker, making public appearances throughout the United States. "In all of this, I feel my part is just to trust in the Lord and step out of the way," she wrote in her autobiography. "For many years, I wasn't ready to be who I am today, but I've always tried not to lose my faith. Now I feel I'm being led by just that—faith—and now I'm closer to being at peace with myself than I ever have been." At schools she does talks and signs books, as does Barbara Henry, with whom she was reunited in 1996, a year after the book's publication.

Henry found Bridges by contacting the book's publisher. In *Through My Eyes,* Bridges concluded, "I now know that experience comes to us for a purpose, and if we follow the guidance of the spirit within us, we will probably find that the purpose is a good one."

Biographical and Critical Sources

BOOKS

Bridges, Ruby, *Through My Eyes: The Autobiography of Ruby Bridges,* Scholastic (New York, NY), 1999.

Coles, Robert, *The Story of Ruby Bridges,* Scholastic (New York, NY), 1995.

PERIODICALS

Booklist, November 15, 1999, Hazel Rochman, review of *Through My Eyes: The Autobiography of Ruby Bridges,* p. 622; March 1, 2000, Stephanie Zvirin, review of *Through My Eyes,* p. 1248; March 15, 2000, review of *Through My Eyes,* p. 1359.

Canada and the World Backgrounder, September, 1996, "Making Things Better," p. 30.

Christianity Today, August 9, 1985, Robert Coles, "The Inexplicable Prayers of Ruby Bridges," pp. 17-20.

Horn Book, January, 2000, review of *Through My Eyes,* p. 92.

Instructor, August, 2001, Lucille Renwick, "The Courage To Learn," p. 35.

Jet, October 16, 2000, Simeon Booker, "Ticker Tape," p. 10.

National Geographic World, Lynda DeWitt, "The Courage of Ruby," pp. 22-25.

Publishers Weekly, October 18, 1999, review of *Through My Eyes,* p. 84; November 1, 1999, review of *Through My Eyes,* p. 58.

School Library Journal, December, 1999, Daryl Grabarek, review of *Through My Eyes,* p. 146.

Social Education, May, 2001, Brenda B. Smith, review of *Through My Eyes,* p. 217.*

*   *   *

BRIGGS, Raymond (Redvers) 1934-

Personal

Born January 18, 1934, in London, England; son of Ernest Redvers (in milk delivery) and Ethel (Bowyer) Briggs; married Jean Taprell Clark (a painter), 1963 (died, 1973). *Education:* Attended Wimbledon School of Art, 1949-53; received National Diploma in Design, 1953; attended Slade School of Fine Art, 1955-57; University of London, D.F.A., 1957. *Politics:* "Green." *Religion:* "None—atheist." *Hobbies and other interests:* Reading, gardening, growing fruit, modern jazz, second-hand bookshops.

Addresses

Home—Weston, Underhill Lane, Westmeston, Hassocks, Sussex BN6 8XG, England.

Career

Illustrator and author of books for children, 1957—. Brighton Polytechnic, Sussex, England, part-time lecturer in illustration, 1961-87; teacher at Slade School of Fine Art and Central Art School. Set designer and playwright. Member of British Campaign for Nuclear Disarmament, beginning 1982. *Military service:* British Army, 1953-55. *Member:* Chartered Society of Designers (fellow), Society of Industrial Artists, Dairy Farmer's Association, Groucho Club.

Awards, Honors

British Library Association Kate Greenaway Medal, commendation, 1964, for *Fee Fi Fo Fum,* winner, 1966, for *Mother Goose Treasury,* and 1973, for *Father Christmas,* and high commendation, 1978, for *The Snowman;* Spring Book Festival Picture Book honor, *Book World,* 1970, for *The Elephant and the Bad Baby;* Children's Book Showcase, Children's Book Council, 1974, for *Father Christmas;* Art Books for Children Citations, Brooklyn Museum and Brooklyn Public Library, 1975, for *Father Christmas,* and 1979, for *The Snowman;* Francis Williams Illustration Awards, Book Trust, 1977, for *Father Christmas,* and 1982, for *The Snowman; Boston Globe-Horn Book* Award for Illustration, Premio Critici in Erba from Bologna Book Fair, Lewis Carroll Shelf Award, and Dutch Silver Pen Award, all 1979, and *Redbook* Award, 1986, all for *The Snowman;* Other Award, Children's Rights Workshop, 1982, for *When the Wind Blows;* British Academy Award for best children's program—Drama, 1982, and Academy Award ("Oscar") nomination for best animated short film, 1982, both for *The Snowman;* most outstanding radio program, Broadcasting Press Guild, 1983, for *When the Wind Blows.*

Writings

SELF-ILLUSTRATED

The Strange House, Hamish Hamilton (London, England), 1961.

Midnight Adventure, Hamish Hamilton (London, England), 1961.

Ring-a-Ring o' Roses (verse), Coward (New York, NY), 1962.

Sledges to the Rescue, Hamish Hamilton (London, England), 1963.

(Editor) *The White Land: A Picture Book of Traditional Rhymes and Verses,* Coward (New York, NY), 1963.

(Editor) *Fee Fi Fo Fum: A Picture Book of Nursery Rhymes,* Coward (New York, NY), 1964.

(Editor) *The Mother Goose Treasury,* Coward (New York, NY), 1966.

Jim and the Beanstalk, Coward (New York, NY), 1970.

Father Christmas, Coward (New York, NY), 1973.

Father Christmas Goes on Holiday, Coward (New York, NY), 1975.

Fungus the Bogeyman, Hamish Hamilton (London, England), 1977.

Gentleman Jim, Hamish Hamilton (London, England), 1980.

When the Wind Blows, Schocken, 1982.

Fungus the Bogeyman Plop-up Book, Hamish Hamilton (London, England), 1982.

The Tin-Pot Foreign General and the Old Iron Woman, Little, Brown (New York, NY), 1984.

Unlucky Wally, Hamish Hamilton (London, England), 1987.

The Bear, Random House (New York, NY), 1994.

The Man, Random House (New York, NY), 1995.

Ethel and Ernest, Knopf (New York, NY), 1999.

"SNOWMAN" SERIES

The Snowman, Random House (New York, NY), 1978.

Building the Snowman, Little, Brown (New York, NY), 1985.

Dressing Up, Little, Brown (New York, NY), 1985.

Walking in the Air, Little, Brown (New York, NY), 1985.

The Party, Little, Brown (New York, NY), 1985.

The Snowman Pop-up, Hamish Hamilton (London, England), 1986.

The Snowman Storybook, Random House (New York, NY), 1990.

The Snowman Flap Book, Random House (New York, NY), 1991.

The Snowman Tell-the-Time Book, Hamish Hamilton (London, England), 1991.

The Snowman: Things to Touch and Feel, See and Sniff, Random House (New York, NY), 1994.

ILLUSTRATOR

(With others) Julian Sorell Huxley, *Wonderful World of Life,* Doubleday, 1958.

Ruth Manning-Sanders, *Peter and the Piskies,* Oxford University Press, 1958, Roy, 1966.

Alfred Leo Duggan, *Look at Castles,* Hamish Hamilton (London, England), 1960, published as *The Castle Book,* Pantheon, 1961.

Alfred Leo Duggan, *Arches and Spires,* Hamish Hamilton (London, England), 1961; Pantheon, 1962.

Jacynth Hope-Simpson, editor, *The Hamish Hamilton Book of Myths and Legends,* Hamish Hamilton, 1964.

William Mayne, *Whistling Rufus,* Hamish Hamilton (London, England), 1964; Dutton, 1965.

Elfrida Vipont, *Stevie,* Hamish Hamilton (London, England), 1965.

Manning-Sanders, editor, *Hamish Hamilton Book of Magical Beasts,* Hamish Hamilton (London, England), 1965, published as *A Book of Magical Beasts,* T. Nelson, 1970.

James Aldridge, *The Flying 19,* Hamish Hamilton (London, England), 1966.

Mabel Esther Allan, *The Way over Windle,* Methuen, 1966.

Bruce Carter (pseudonym of Richard Alexander Hough), *Jimmy Murphy and the White Duesenberg,* Coward (New York, NY), 1968.

Bruce Carter, *Nuvolari and the Alfa Romeo,* Coward (New York, NY), 1968.

Nicholas Fisk, *Lindbergh: The Lone Flier,* Coward (New York, NY), 1968.

Fisk, *Richthofen: The Red Baron,* Coward (New York, NY), 1968.

William Mayne, editor, *The Hamish Hamilton Book of Giants,* Hamish Hamilton (London, England), 1968,

Raymond Briggs

published as *William Mayne's Book of Giants,* Dutton (New York, NY), 1969.

Michael Brown, *Shackelton's Epic Voyage,* Coward (New York, NY), 1969.

Elfrida Vipont, *The Elephant and the Bad Baby,* Coward (New York, NY), 1969.

Showell Styles, *First up Everest,* Coward (New York, NY), 1969.

James Reeves, *Christmas Book,* Dutton (New York, NY), 1970.

Ian Serraillier, *The Tale of Three Landlubbers,* Hamish Hamilton (London, England), 1970, Coward (New York, NY), 1971.

Virginia Haviland, editor, *The Fairy Tale Treasury,* Coward (New York, NY), 1972.

Manning-Sanders, editor, *Festivals,* Heinemann, 1972, Dutton, 1973.

James Reeves, *The Forbidden Forest,* Heinemann, 1973.

(With Mitsumasa Anno) *All in a Day,* Philomel, 1986.

Also illustrator of a book of Cornish fairy stories for Oxford University Press, 1957, *The Wonderful Cornet,* by Barbara Ker Wilson, 1958, *Peter's Busy Day,* by A. Stephen Tring, 1959, and *William's Wild Day Out,* by Meriol Trevor, 1963.

OTHER

The Snowman (animated film), TV Cartoons, 1982.

When the Wind Blows (stage play; produced in London, England, 1983, Washington, DC, 1984, and New York, NY, 1988), Samuel French, 1983.

When the Wind Blows (radio play), British Broadcasting Corp., 1983.

Gentleman Jim (stage play), produced at Nottingham Playhouse, 1985.

When the Wind Blows (animated film), TV Cartoons/ Meltdown Productions, 1987.

Sidelights

Raymond Briggs is an award-winning author and illustrator of popular books for children as well as dark, satirical works for adults. He has drawn hundreds of pictures for collections of traditional nursery rhymes and fairy tales, revisited old favorites like "Jack and the Beanstalk," and written his own stories. Briggs's *Fungus the Bogeyman* is a cartoon-style look at a repulsive yet humane imaginary world, full of filth and wordplay; *The Snowman* is a wordless story, poignant and more softly illustrated. *When the Wind Blows,* a devastating, understated cartoon-style work basically for adults, portrays a middle-aged working-class couple before, during, and after a nuclear war. The characters and settings in the books often reflect elements of Briggs's past.

Briggs had "an uneventful but happy childhood and home life," he told Lee Bennett Hopkins in *Books Are by People.* "My parents were happily married. Their faces turn up constantly in my illustrations but quite unconsciously. I hated school for there was too much emphasis on teamwork, competition, sports, science, and mathematics—all the opposite interests of an 'arty' type." Briggs was always drawing and as an only child was somewhat spoiled, so when at fifteen he said he'd like to study art, his parents "weren't fussed that I didn't want to learn a useful trade," he recalled in a *Publishers Weekly* interview. The principal of the school he wanted to attend, however, was dismayed that Briggs wanted to be a cartoonist. "He said: 'Good God, boy, is that *all* you want to do?'" Briggs revealed in *Designer.* "He told me it wasn't an occupation for gentlemen. It was a great shock to realise that these things weren't respectable. So I changed to painting."

In his painting courses Briggs did a lot of figure drawing, which he said was "absolutely perfect training for an illustrator, in that you learnt about tone and colour, and figure composition in general." It was a very traditional art education, like that of Renaissance painters. Abstract art was not taught. Cartooning and illustration were scorned as "commercial." In *Designer,* Briggs described what happened when his tutor found one of his

A young boy's snowman comes to life and takes him on a wonderful flight in Briggs's wordless **The Snowman.**

In comic-strip style, Briggs tells the true story of his English working-class parents' lives from their first meeting in the 1920s until their deaths fifty years later. (From Ethel and Ernest.*)*

illustrations: "He said, horrified: 'You're *not* doing this in school time, are you?'—almost as if I was spitting in church. 'No sir, certainly not. Good Lord.'" Briggs continued to practice illustration in his spare time anyway. Finally he decided that painting was not really his strength and was unprofitable as well, so he started accepting illustration assignments from publishers and advertising agencies.

"Out of all the work I did, I must have suited the children's book world best," Briggs remarked in *Designer,* "because that was the sort of work that increasingly came in. I didn't choose it; it chose me. I entered the field at a very good time, when there were some marvellous books being written and I was lucky enough to get some to illustrate." *The Mother Goose Treasury,* for which Briggs did nearly nine hundred pictures, was one example. Reviewers praised it for its completeness and for Briggs's exuberant illustrations, and he received the Kate Greenaway Medal for his work. But he found other books "appalling," he continued, "and it was this that made me start writing. I could see simple grammatical faults even, and felt that if publishers were willing to publish tripe like that, I couldn't do worse. I wrote two or three little stories, and showed the first one to the

editor just to get his advice—to see if he thought I might ever write anything. To my absolute amazement he said he'd publish it. To me, that just showed the standard. I thought it was staggering that someone who knew nothing about writing could make a first attempt and have it published, just like that."

Father Christmas was one of Briggs's first original books to become widely popular. Instead of the usual jolly or saintly image of Saint Nick, Briggs presents a grumbling but dutiful old fellow with very human foibles. Not fond of winter, Father Christmas dreams of a beach holiday and complains about "blooming chimneys" and "blooming soot." As Briggs observed in *Junior Bookshelf,* "I think the character of Father Christmas is very much based on my father," who delivered milk early each morning. "The jobs are similar and they both grumble a lot in a fairly humorous way." Briggs also drew on his own past for details of Father Christmas's house and other aspects of his life—sometimes unconsciously. Often when Briggs draws something, he says, "I recognise it when it appears on the paper and think 'Gosh, yes! That's how it was.'"

A few years after *Father Christmas* came *Fungus the Bogeyman,* Briggs's story about and descriptive guide to the mucky lives of Bogeys, who revel in filth and rise each night to frighten humans. Fungus is a happily married Bogey who wonders about the meaning of his life and wistfully dreams of a day when Bogeys and humans can get along with each other. Oddly enough, this story also bears some resemblance to Briggs's life. Observed Suzanne Rahn in *The Lion and the Unicorn,* "Briggs ... came from a working-class family, and one can see a similarity between his milkman-father and Fungus: both have a 'round' of houses to which they deliver their stock-in-trade while most of their customers are still sleeping." Briggs has suggested a more direct link between Fungus and himself. When Elaine Moss in *Signal* asked him whether the character was real, Briggs answered, "I'm noticing all my characters now are sad old men or, rather, sad middle-aged men, which is what I am probably."

The Snowman, published the year after *Fungus the Bogeyman,* is a very different book, but like the earlier story it also draws on Briggs's life. The artist used his own house and garden as the setting for his gentle, loving tale. Unlike *Fungus the Bogeyman,* it is a wholesome story, describing how a snowman comes to life and befriends the boy who made him. During a magical night, the snowman shares the human world and the world of snow people with the boy. In the morning the boy sadly discovers that his friend has mostly melted away. Briggs conveyed the story completely without words, and for the first time he set aside the black pen and watercolor of cartoon-style work. Noting that people often said they liked his original pencil drawings better than his ink work, Briggs decided to use colored pencils for the book. "I wanted to avoid the abrupt change that takes place when a brutal black pen line is scratched on top of a quiet pencil drawing," he said when he accepted the *Boston Globe-Horn Book* Award for the book.

Originally published as a book for adults, *When the Wind Blows* is Briggs's cartoon-style comment on how unprepared ordinary people are to deal with nuclear war. Its two characters are a retired British husband and wife living in the country. They survived the bombing of England during World War II, and they ignorantly expect the next war to be much the same. They build a useless bomb shelter, following government guidelines, and cheerily go on with life after the bomb drops, wondering why the water is shut off and why nothing is on the radio. Briggs got the idea for the book when he saw a documentary on the effects of nuclear war. "I imagined what would actually happen if some ordinary people were told there would be war in three days' time," he told Bart Mills in a *Los Angeles Times* interview. "I used to think the main threat facing us was the Russian menace. Now I think the main threat is nuclear weapons themselves." Several critics judged *When the Wind Blows* too grim for young readers, and Briggs agreed. "But we found it went into the children's bookshops and started selling there too, to my surprise," he said in a *Times Educational Supplement* interview with Richard North. It has also been recommended

reading for high schools and junior high schools that have courses dealing with nuclear war.

Briggs does not aim his books specifically at children or at adults. "I just write and draw to please myself and feel it ought to please others," he said in *Publishers Weekly.* His work appeals to all ages, in fact. His more adult-oriented books reach younger readers with their cartoon style, and the so-called children's books often discuss adult issues. Even nursery rhymes have adult aspects, Briggs observed. Many are actually "quite rude, quite tough, adult gutsy material about money and marriage and work and laziness and theft—not sweet innocent pink and blue baby stuff," he said in *Signal.* His own books fit this description in many ways. *Father Christmas* shows adult attitudes toward work and features a character who swears constantly, if mildly. *Fungus the Bogeyman* looks at human intolerance and philosophical ideas. *The Snowman* squarely faces the sorrow of losing a friend. "Each one I do is different," said Briggs in *Designer.* Despite his doubts about how they would be received, he remarked, "they've all sold like hot cakes."

Biographical and Critical Sources

BOOKS

Children's Literature Review, Volume 10, Gale (Detroit, MI), 1986.

Hopkins, Lee Bennett, *Books Are by People,* Citation Press, 1969.

Kilborn, Richard, *The Multi-Media Melting Pot: Marketing "When the Wind Blows,"* Comedia, 1986.

Rahn, Suzanne, "Beneath the Surface with *Fungus the Bogeyman,*" *The Lion and the Unicorn,* Volume 7-8, 1983-84.

Twentieth-Century Children's Writers, St. Martin's (Detroit, MI), 1983.

PERIODICALS

Animation, Spring, 1988; Winter, 1989.

Designer, October, 1982, "Best Children's Book: Raymond Briggs 'The Snowman,'" pp. 8-9.

Films and Filming, February, 1987.

Junior Bookshelf, August, 1974, Raymond Briggs, "That Blooming Book," pp. 195-96.

Horn Book Magazine, December, 1966; February, 1980, Raymond Briggs, "For Illustration: *The Snowman*" (acceptance speech for *Boston Globe-Horn Book* Award), p. 96.

Los Angeles Times, November 10, 1982, Bart Mills, "Author! Author! Wind Blowing Raymond Briggs' Way," Part V, p. 12.

New York Times, September 14, 1982.

Observer (London), February 8, 1987.

Plays and Players, July, 1983.

Publishers Weekly, November 5, 1973, Jean P. Mercier, "PW Interviews: Raymond Briggs," p. 12; May 14, 1982.

Signal, January, 1979, Elaine Moss, "Raymond Briggs: On British Attitudes to the Strip Cartoon and Children's-Book Illustration," p. 28.

Times (London), September 20, 1984; May 8, 1985; November 17, 1986; February 6, 1987.

Times Educational Supplement, November 18, 1977; June 11, 1982, Richard North, "Cartoon Apocalypse," p. 41.
Times Literary Supplement, December 2, 1977; October 5, 1984.
Undercurrents, April, 1982.
Variety, April 27, 1983.
Washington Post, March 6, 1984.*

* * *

BRUCHAC, Joseph (III) 1942-

Personal

Surname is pronounced "*brew*-shack"; born October 16, 1942, in Saratoga Springs, NY; son of Joseph E. (a taxidermist) and Flora (Bowman) Bruchac; married Carol Worthen, June 13, 1964; children: James Edward, Jesse Bowman. *Education:* Cornell University, A.B., 1965; Syracuse University, M.A., 1966; graduate study at State University of New York—Albany, 1971-73; Union Institute (Ohio), Ph.D., 1975.

Addresses

Office—P.O. Box 308, Greenfield Center, NY 12833. *Agent*—Barbara Kouts, P.O. Box 558, Bellport, NY 11713.

Career

Fiction writer, poet, and storyteller. Keta Secondary School, Keta, Ghana, teacher of English and literature, 1966-69; Greenfield Review Press, Greenfield Center, NY, publisher and editor of *Greenfield Review,* 1969-90; Skidmore College, Saratoga Springs, NY, instructor in creative writing and in African and black literatures, 1969-73; Great Meadows Institute, Comstock Prison, teacher of creative writing, 1972-74; Greenfield Review Literary Center, director, 1981—. Musician with Dawn Land Singers. *Member:* Poetry Society of America, PEN, Wordcraft Circle of Native Writers and Storytellers.

Awards, Honors

New York State Arts Council grant, 1972; Vermont Arts Council grant, 1972; poetry prize, Poetry Society of America, 1972; New York State CAPS poetry fellowships, 1973, 1982; Coordinating Council of Literary Magazines poetry fellowship, 1980; Rockefeller Foundation humanities fellowship, 1982-83; American Book Award, Before Columbus Foundation, 1984, for *Breaking Silence: An Anthology of Contemporary Asian American Poets;* Cherokee Nation Prose Award; Hope S. Dean Award for Notable Achievement in Children's Literature, Foundation for Children's Literature; Benjamin Franklin Person of the Year award, Publisher's Marketing Association, 1993; Notable Children's Book in the Language Arts, and International Reading Association Young Adults and Teachers Choice, both 1993, both for *Thirteen Moons on Turtle's Back: A Native*

American Year of Moons; Young Readers Book Award, *Scientific American,* 1995, for *The Story of the Milky Way;* Parents' Choice Honor Award, 1995, for *Dog People: Native Dog Stories;* Notable Children's Book, American Library Association (ALA), and Mountains & Plains Booksellers Association Regional Book Award, 1996, for *A Boy Called Slow;* Paterson Prize for Books for Young People, 1996, for *Dog People: Native Dog Stories;* Knickerbocker Award for Juvenile Literature, New York State Library Association, 1996; Nonfiction Honor, *Boston Globe-Horn Book,* and Notable Children's Book designation, ALA, both 1996, both for *The Boy Who Lived with the Bears: And Other Iroquois Stories;* Woodcraft Circle Writer of the Year autobiography award, 1998, for *Bowman's Store;* Woodcraft Circle Storyteller of the Year award for traditional Native stories, 1998.

Writings

FICTION

Turkey Brother and Other Tales (folktales), illustrated by Kahonhes, Crossing Press (Santa Cruz, CA), 1975.
The Dreams of Jesse Brown (novel), Cold Mountain Press (Austin, TX), 1977.
Stone Giants and Flying Heads: More Iroquois Folk Tales, illustrated by Kahonhes and Brascoupe, Crossing Press (Santa Cruz, CA), 1978, published as *Stone Giants and Flying Heads: Adventure Stories of the Iroquois,* 1979.
The Wind Eagle and Other Abenaki Stories, Bowman Books, 1984.
Iroquois Stories: Heroes, Heroines, Monsters and Magic, Crossing Press (Santa Cruz, CA), 1985.
The Faithful Hunter: Abenaki Stories, Greenfield Review Press (Greenfield Center, NY), 1988.
Return of the Sun: Native American Tales from the Northeast Woodlands, Crossing Press (Santa Cruz, CA), 1989.
Hoop Snakes, Hide Behinds, and Side-Hill Winders: Tall Tales from the Adirondacks, Crossing Press (Santa Cruz, CA), 1991.
Turtle Meat and Other Stories, Holy Cow! Press (Duluth, MN), 1992.
Dawn Land (novel), Fulcrum (Golden, CO), 1993.
The First Strawberries: A Cherokee Story, illustrated by Anna Vojtech, Dial (New York, NY), 1993.
Flying with the Eagle, Racing the Great Bear: Stories from Native North America, illustrated by Murv Jacob, BridgeWater (Mahwah, NJ), 1993.
Fox Song (for children), illustrated by Paul Morin, Philomel (New York, NY), 1993.
(With Gayle Ross) *The Girl Who Married the Moon: Stories from Native North America,* illustrated by S. S. Burrus, BridgeWater (Mahwah, NJ), 1994.
Gluskabe and the Four Wishes (stories), illustrated by Christine Nyburg Shrader, Cobblehill Books/Dutton (New York, NY), 1994.
The Great Ball Game: A Muskogee Story, illustrated by Susan L. Roth, Dial (New York, NY), 1994.
The Boy Who Lived with the Bears and Other Iroquois Stories, illustrated by Murv Jacob, HarperCollins (New York, NY), 1995.

A Boy Called Slow (juvenile), illustrated by Rocco Baviera, Philomel (New York, NY), 1995.

Native Plant Stories, Fulcrum (Golden, CO), 1995.

(With Gayle Ross) *The Story of the Milky Way,* illustrated by Virginia A. Stroud, Dial (New York, NY), 1995.

Dog People: Native Dog Stories, illustrated by Murv Jacob, Fulcrum (Golden, CO), 1995.

Long River (novel), Fulcrum (Golden, CO), 1995.

Children of the Longhouse (novel for young readers), Dial (New York, NY), 1996.

Between Earth and Sky: Legends of Native American Sacred Places, illustrated by Thomas Locker, Harcourt Brace (New York, NY), 1996.

Four Ancestors: Stories, Songs, and Poems from Native North America, BridgeWater (Mahwah, NJ), 1996.

Eagle Song, illustrated by Dan Andreasen, Dial (New York, NY), 1997.

(With Melissa Jayne Fawcett) *Makiawisug: The Gift of the Little People,* illustrated by David Wagner, Little People Publications (Uncasville, CT), 1997.

The Arrow over the Door, Dial (New York, NY), 1998.

When the Chenoo Howls: Native American Tales of Terror, Walker (New York, NY), 1998.

The Heart of a Chief (children's novel), Dial (New York, NY), 1998.

The Waters Between: A Novel of the Dawn Land, University Press of New England (Hanover, NH), 1998.

Sacajawea: The Story of Bird Woman and the Lewis and Clark Expedition, Harcourt (San Diego, CA), 2000.

Crazy Horse's Vision, illustrated by S. D. Nelson, Lee & Low Books (New York, NY), 2000.

Skeleton Man, illustrated by Sally Wern Comport, Harper-Collins (New York, NY), 2001.

Squanto's Journey: The Story of the First Thanksgiving, illustrated by Greg Shed, Silver Whistle (San Diego, CA), 2001.

The Journal of Jesse Smoke: A Cherokee Boy, Scholastic (New York, NY), 2001.

(With James Bruchac) *How Chipmunk Got His Stripes: A Tale of Bragging and Teasing,* illustrated by José Aruego and Ariane Dewey, Dial (New York, NY), 2001.

Foot of the Mountain and Other Stories, Holy Cow! Press (Duluth, MN), 2002.

POETRY

Indian Mountain and Other Poems, Ithaca House (Ithaca, NY), 1971.

Flow, Cold Mountain Press (Austin, TX), 1975.

The Road to Black Mountain, Thorp Springs Press (Austin, TX), 1977.

This Earth Is a Drum, Cold Mountain Press (Austin, TX), 1977.

Entering Onondaga, Cold Mountain Press (Austin, TX), 1978.

There Are No Trees inside the Prison, Unicorn Press (Greensboro, NC), 1979.

Ancestry, Great Raven (Fort Kent, ME), 1980.

Translator's Son, Cross-Cultural Communications (Merrick, NY), 1981.

Remembering the Dawn, Blue Cloud (Marvin, SD), 1983.

Tracking, Ion Books (Memphis, TN), 1986.

Walking with My Sons, and Other Poems, Landlocked Press (Madison, WI), 1987.

Near the Mountains: New and Selected Poems, White Pine Press (Buffalo, NY), 1987.

Long Memory, and Other Poems, Wurf, 1989.

(With Jonathan London) *Thirteen Moons on Turtle's Back: A Native American Year of Moons,* illustrated by Thomas Locker, Philomel (New York, NY), 1992.

The Earth under Sky Bear's Feet: Native American Poems of the Land, illustrated by Thomas Locker, Philomel (New York, NY), 1995.

The Circle of Thanks: Native American Poems and Songs of Thanksgiving, BridgeWater (Mahwah, NJ), 1996.

No Borders: Poems, Holy Cow Press (Duluth, MN), 1999.

OTHER

The Poetry of Pop (essays), Dustbooks, 1973.

How to Start and Sustain a Literary Magazine: Practical Strategies for Publications of Lasting Value, Provision House Press, 1980.

Survival This Way: Interviews with Native American Poets, University of Arizona Press (Tucson, AZ), 1987.

(With Michael Caduto) *Keepers of the Earth: Native American Stories and Environmental Activities for Children,* Fulcrum (Golden, CO), 1988, excerpts published as *Native American Animal Stories,* 1988.

(With Michael Caduto) *Keepers of the Animals: Native American Stories and Wildlife Activities for Children,* Fulcrum (Golden, CO), 1991.

Native American Sweat Lodge: History and Legends, Crossing Press (Santa Cruz, CA), 1993.

(With Michael Caduto) *Keepers of Life: Discovering Plants through Native American Stories and Earth Activities for Children,* Fulcrum (Golden, CO), 1994.

(With Michael Caduto) *Keepers of the Night: Native American Stories and Nocturnal Activities for Children,* Fulcrum (Golden, CO), 1994.

Native Wisdom, HarperCollins (New York, NY), 1995.

(With Michael Caduto) *Native American Gardening,* Fulcrum (Golden, CO), 1996.

Roots of Survival (essays), Fulcrum (Golden, CO), 1996.

Many Nations: An Alphabet of Native America, illustrated by Robert Goetzel, BridgeWater (Mahwah, NJ), 1997.

Lasting Echoes: An Oral History of Native American People, illustrated by Paul Morin, Silver Whistle (San Diego, CA), 1997.

Tell Me a Tale: A Book about Storytelling, Harcourt (San Diego, CA), 1997.

Bowman's Store (autobiography), Dial (New York, NY), 1997.

Seeing the Circle (autobiography), illustrated by John Christopher Fine, R. C. Owen (Katonah, NY), 1999.

Trail of Tears, illustrated by Diana Magnuson, Random House (New York, NY), 1999.

Trails of Tears, Paths of Beauty, National Geographic Society (Washington, DC), 2000.

(With James Bruchac) *Native American Games and Stories,* Fulcrum (Golden, CO), 2000.

Pushing up the Sky: Seven Native American Plays for Children, illustrated by Teresa Flavin, Dial (New York, NY), 2000.

Navajo Long Walk, illustrated by Shanto Begay, National Geographic Society (Washington, DC), 2002.

Bruchac's work is widely anthologized; poetry and articles by Bruchac have appeared in numerous periodicals, including *Akwesasne Notes, American Poetry Review, Hudson Review, National Geographic, New Letters, Parabola, Paris Review,* and *Smithsonian* magazine. With Dawn Land Singers, recorder of stories and music on *Abenaki Cultural Heritage* and *Alnobak,* Good Mind Records.

EDITOR

(With William Witherup) *Words from the House of the Dead: An Anthology of Prison Writings from Soledad,* Greenfield Review Press (Greenfield Center, NY), 1972.

The Last Stop: Writings from Comstock Prison, Greenfield Review Press (Greenfield Center, NY), 1974.

(With Roger Weaver) *Aftermath: An Anthology of Poems in English from Africa, Asia, and the Caribbean,* Greenfield Review Press (Greenfield Center, NY), 1977.

The Next World: Poems by Thirty-two Third-World Americans, Crossing Press (Santa Cruz, CA), 1978.

Songs from This Earth on Turtle's Back: Contemporary American Indian Poetry, Greenfield Review Press (Greenfield Center, NY), 1983.

Breaking Silence: An Anthology of Contemporary Asian American Poets, Greenfield Review Press (Greenfield Center, NY), 1984.

The Light from Another Country: Poetry from American Prisons, Greenfield Review Press (Greenfield Center, NY), 1984.

(With others) *North Country: An Anthology of Contemporary Writing from the Adirondacks and Upper Hudson Valley,* Greenfield Review Press (Greenfield Center, NY), 1985.

New Voices from the Longhouse: An Anthology of Contemporary Iroquois Writing, Greenfield Review Press (Greenfield Center, NY), 1989.

Returning the Gift: Poetry and Prose from the First North American Native Writers Festival, University of Arizona Press (Tucson, AZ), 1994.

Smoke Rising: The Native North American Literary Companion, Visible Ink Press (Detroit, MI), 1995.

Assistant editor, *Epoch,* 1964-65; contributing editor, *Nickel Review,* 1967-71; contemporary music editor, *Kite,* 1971-73; editor, *Prison Writing Review,* 1976-82, and *Studies in American Indian Literatures,* 1983—.

Adaptations

Many of Bruchac's stories have been recorded on audio cassette, including *The Boy Who Lived with the Bears,* Caedmon/Parabola; *Gluskabe Stories,* Yellow Moon Press; *Iroquois Stories,* Good Mind Records; and *Dawn Land, Keepers of the Earth: Native American Stories and Environmental Activities for Children, Keepers of the Animals: Native American Stories and Wildlife Activities for Children,* and *Keepers of Life: Discovering Plants through Native American Stories and Earth Activities for Children,* all from Fulcrum.

Joseph Bruchac

Sidelights

"It is important to recognize that Native people are not locked into the past," remarked storyteller, poet, novelist, and children's author Joseph Bruchac in an interview with Eliza T. Dresang in *CCBC-Net.* "That those called American Indian have long traditions. We need to recognize the fact that there is tremendous diversity from one tribal nation to the next as well as diversity between individuals." In addition to diversity, Bruchac recognizes commonalities among Native Americans: "The strength of oral traditions, an informed awareness of the process which is now called ecology, and the place that human beings play within the circle of life." In his over one hundred published works, Bruchac celebrates the varied landscape of Native American culture through genres that range from retellings of folktales and myths, to nonfiction works examining the history—both natural and man-made—of Native America, to original novels and poems illustrating the world of the American Indian in the countryside, on the reservation, and even in the gray streets of urban American.

Bruchac, part Native American and a member of the Abenaki tribe of upper New York State, draws on personal experience and Native American legends for many of his books for young readers. In volumes such as the award-winning *Thirteen Moons on Turtle's Back: A Native American Year of Moons* and its sequel, *The*

Moon under Sky Bear's Feet: Native American Poems of the Land; in retellings such as *Dog People: Native Dog Stories, The Story of the Milky Way, When the Chenoo Howls: Native American Tales of Terror,* and *How Chipmunk Got His Stripes: A Tale of Bragging and Teasing;* in narrative histories such as *A Boy Called Slow* and *Crazy Horse's Vision;* and in original novels such as *Eagle Song, The Arrow over the Door, Heart of a Chief,* and *Skeleton Man,* Bruchac portrays a culture he finds very much alive, a culture with much wisdom and practical knowledge to add to today's world.

Bruchac grew up in New York's Adirondack Mountain region, raised by his maternal grandparents. Of Slovak heritage on his father's side, Bruchac was, on his mother's, a mixture of English and Native American. There was, however, little talk of Abenaki culture when Bruchac was growing up. "Everybody in the county knew he was Indian," Bruchac said of his grandfather in an interview with Susan Stan in *Five Owls.* "It was taken for granted—but he would not talk about it because there was a lot of shame connected with being dark-skinned, being native." That feeling of shame is one of the reasons Bruchac has devoted a large portion of his life to writing, storytelling, and working with children in order to make different cultures understood and respected.

Bruchac tells the story of the young Lakota Indian boy whose vision transforms him into the warrior Crazy Horse. (*From* Crazy Horse's Vision, *illustrated by S. D. Nelson.*)

Despite his neglected heritage, Bruchac still felt drawn to his Native American roots. As a teenager he began to meet other Native Americans and to take an interest in Abenaki culture and language. His first poems while a student at Cornell University were about "American Indian themes," he noted in an interview with Kit Alderdice in *Publishers Weekly.* But a deep immersion into such themes did not happen until after he had completed a master's degree at Syracuse State University and done three years of teaching in Africa with his wife. Returning to the United States, Bruchac settled in the home where he had grown up, and he eventually had two sons of his own. He ultimately converted the former house and gas station/general store of his grandparents into a home and the office that now houses the Greenfield Review Press, an independent publishing house his wife and he founded. Their literary magazine, *Greenfield Review,* published multicultural poetry and stories for over twenty years, and its publishing arm brought out dozens of titles by Bruchac and many others. Bruchac has gone on to lead a busy life: husband, father, poet, publisher, editor, and instructor of creative writing at a college program inside a prison.

With the 1975 publication of *Turkey Brother and Other Tales,* Bruchac's work took a new turn. Recalling several Iroquois legends and stories from his childhood, he had started to collect them in earnest to tell to his own sons, with whom he has a close relationship. He searched out such stories from books and from tribal elders, and many of these found a retelling in *Turkey Brother and Other Tales.* The first three stories feature Turtle, a trickster character similar to the Anansi figure of Ashanti folklore, and in these stories he is both a crafty winner and is himself undone. "All the legends are fascinating and well told," commented a reviewer in *Publishers Weekly,* and a *Booklist* critic noted that "the prose is smooth, simple and written to be read aloud." Bruchac did exactly that at one bookstore signing, but halfway through reading the first tale, he stopped and simply began telling the tales from memory, enchanting his audience, and thus starting another career for himself as a storyteller. Further Iroquois legends and adventure stories were collected in *Stone Giants and Flying Heads: Adventure Stories of the Iroquois,* which introduces readers to the trickster Skunny-Wundy among other characters, in stories highlighting virtues such as "bravery, obedience or goodness rewarded," according to a critic in *Booklist.* Gale Eaton in *School Library Journal* noted that the stories "should be quite accessible to reluctant readers." Bruchac's interest in his heritage paid off close to home. "My own sons have grown up taking such things as sweat lodges and powwows and pride in Indian ancestry for granted. The small amount I have learned I've tried, when right to do so, to share with others," he once wrote in *Native North American Literature.*

Such retellings, most of them in the picture-book format, have continued to be a staple for Bruchac, and he does not concentrate solely on Abenaki and Iroquois legends for his stories. A Cherokee tale explaining the origin of strawberries was the inspiration for *The First Strawber-*

ries: A Cherokee Story, which Carolyn Phelan in *Booklist* called a "delectable story for reading aloud." Despite his broad focus, Bruchac does not claim to be a voice for all Native Americans. With over 400 different cultures in North America, no one could know them all. But as he told *Publishers Weekly,* "What I can say is that I know a bit, to some detail, about a couple of them." In *The Great Ball Game: A Muskogee Story,* Bruchac tells a traditional Muskogee story about a sport that resembles modern lacrosse, and in *Flying with the Eagle, Racing the Great Bear: Stories from Native North America,* he recounts sixteen rite-of-passage stories from a variety of North American Indian cultures, creating a "volume that will be useful to students of multicultural folklore as well as to those interested in good storytelling," according to Yvonne Frey in *School Library Journal.* Additionally, girls and women get their day in *The Girl Who Married the Moon,* sixteen stories celebrating the passage from adolescence to womanhood.

Turtle Meat and Other Stories draws on Bruchac's Abenaki heritage to tell seventeen stories about Indian and white relations in the Adirondacks over many centuries—from Viking times to World War II. Bruchac also incorporates ideas from the Native Americans' ever-present eco-consciousness. "Style, humor and grace enliven familiar themes; atypical for folklore writing, most characters emerge three-dimensional and real," stated a contributor in *Kirkus Reviews.* A *Publishers Weekly* reviewer noted that Bruchac is "perhaps the best-known contemporary Native American storyteller," and that his stories in this volume are "often poignant, funny, ironic—and sometimes all three at once." Yvonne Frey, writing in *School Library Journal,* called the collection "thought-provoking," and a "good blend of well-crafted stories that are deserving of careful analysis," and Carl L. Blankston III, writing in the *Bloomsbury Review,* noted the plethora of styles and forms in the writing. "Bruchac is one of the true storytellers," Blankston commented. "He finds the mythical in the real, the survival of the past in the present, and an indigenous soul in a land conquered by Europeans. This is a voice we will want to hear again."

Dog People includes five stories of Abenaki children and their dogs, recreating the period setting so thoroughly that "readers will identify with the people," commented Kathleen McCabe in *School Library Journal.* And with *The Story of the Milky Way,* coauthored with Gayle Ross, Bruchac returned to Cherokee legend to explain the origin of the Milky Way, while at the same time "stressing the merits of communal labor," according to a *Publishers Weekly* contributor. Donna L. Scanlon, writing in *School Library Journal,* noted that the tale is accessible to a variety of readers: "It will hold the attention of young listeners, yet remain interesting to older readers."

In *Gluskabe and the Four Wishes,* Bruchac retells an ancestral legend of the Abenaki people with "graceful insight," according to *Booklist* reviewer Julie Walton. When a magical figure gives four men a wish each, it is

Told in alternating points of view by Sacajawea and William Clark, Bruchac's novel offers a personal look at the story of the sixteen-year-old Shoshone guide who made the Lewis and Clark expedition possible. (Cover illustration by Stephen T. Johnson.)

only the one who wishes to become a good enough hunter to feed his people who ultimately survives. Walton felt that this story "is highly moral" and tells an allegory of the pitfalls of greed and selfishness with "no loss of entertainment value." *Horn Book* contributor Martha V. Parravano called the same picture book "impeccably sourced" and "well-told." More Iroquois stories are served up in *The Boy Who Lived with the Bears,* tales "threaded through with bits of humor and wisdom," according toe *Horn Book* reviewer Margaret A. Bush. In two similar retellings Bruchac has teamed up with his son James Bruchac. In *When the Chenoo Howls,* father and son present a dozen tales of terror and monsters from the northeast woodland Native American communities. These books provide an "interesting alternative for children who love horror stories," thought Darcy Schild in a *School Library Journal* review, and make a "successful, accessible collection," according to Janice M. Del Negro in the *Bulletin of the Center for Children's Books.* In the 2001 title, *How Chipmunk Got His Stripes: A Tale of Bragging and Teasing,* the

Bruchacs teamed up with noted illustrators Ariane Dewey and José Aruego to present a "polished, cohesive, and energetic" book, as Grace Oliff described it in *School Library Journal.*

With *Thirteen Moons on Turtle's Back: A Native American Year of Moons,* illustrated by Thomas Locker, Bruchac turned to poetry to tell moon legends from various tribes from Cree to Huron that "show respect for Native-American culture and traditions," according to Barbara Barstow in *Horn Book Guide.* "This unusual and intelligent book is an exemplary introduction to Native American culture with its emphasis on the importance of nature," added a reviewer for *Publishers Weekly.* In *The Earth under Sky Bear's Feet,* Bruchac once again teamed up with illustrator Locker in a companion volume to *Thirteen Moons.* Twelve brief story-poems describe the nighttime world as witnessed by Sky Bear or the Big Dipper. "The poems provide an imaginative introduction to American Indian folklore," wrote *Horn Book* reviewer Ellen Fader. Legends of Native American sacred places are presented in *Between Earth and Sky,* once again illustrated by Locker. Fader, in a *Horn Book* review, felt that it was an "excellent choice that will provoke both introspection and discussion." *Four Ancestors* delivers more native American poems, as well as stories and songs, while *Circle of Thanks* presents Native American poems and songs of Thanksgiving.

With *Keepers of the Earth: Native American Stories and Environmental Activities,* coauthored with Michael Caduto, Bruchac hit on another winning combination: a blend of folktales with classroom teaching materials. Though the book was rejected by forty publishers before finding a home with Fulcrum Press, it has proved a tremendous success both in content and in sales. Bruchac has teamed up with Caduto on several other similar titles: *Keepers of the Night: Native American Stories and Nocturnal Activities for Children, Keepers of the Animals: Native American Stories and Wildlife Activities for Children,* and *Keepers of Life: Discovering Plants through Native American Stories and Earth Activities for Children,* all still in print. Each of the books, suitable for use in the classroom, provides traditional narratives and activities that "highlight the delicate balance between people and nature," according to Cyndi Giorgis and Janelle Mathis in *New Advocate.* Specifically referring to *Keepers of Life,* Giorgis and Mathis noted that "this valuable resource brings traditional stories and humanity's relationship with the environment full circle." In a review of *Native American Animal Stories,* a volume adapted from *Keepers of the Animals,* Charles Solomon in the *Los Angeles Times Book Review* concluded that "the unfamiliar but moving tales in this collection offer wonderful read-aloud material for parents who want to teach their children to revere the Earth."

The versatile and prolific Bruchac has also produced novels for adult and young adult readers. With *Dawn Land,* Bruchac tells a lyrical story set some 10,000 years ago, in what is now New England and the Canadian maritime provinces. Called the Dawn Land, or the first place the rising sun hits the North American continent, this ancient territory is home to the Abenaki, who live a peaceful existence in thirteen villages, with dogs so in tune with their human keepers that animals and humans can communicate with each other using a form of telepathy. Then comes a threat to the people: it is feared the Cannibal Giants have returned and the brave Young Hunter is sent to meet the enemy. He carries with him a secret weapon—the bow. A reviewer in *Publishers Weekly* concluded that Bruchac's simple yet elegant prose lends to his story "the deceptive weight of legend," and Judy Sokoll, writing in *School Library Journal,* noted that Bruchac "writes in a rich, precise, gentle, yet powerful descriptive style" in this novel that incorporates myth and the belief in the sacred interrelatedness of all living things. The tale of Dawn Land is carried forward in *Long River,* set two years after the end of *Dawn Land.* Young Hunter must once again save his people, this time from Walking Hill, a wounded mammoth, and from renewed threats from the Ancient Ones. "The story is at its best," commented a reviewer for *Publishers Weekly,* "when it incorporates actual myths from the oral tradition of the Abenaki." In *The Waters Between,* Bruchac continues the saga of Young Hunter and his family. In this installment, Young Hunter and his dog discover a Loch Ness-like monster which has been trapped in the waters of their lake after the ocean receded. The youth must defeat this giant serpent which has cut off his people from a major source of their food. A contributor for *Publishers Weekly* felt that Bruchac "leavens his premodern story with retellings of myths from the Abenaki oral traditions, and he unquestionably knows his subject matter." Reviewing the same novel in *World Literature Today,* Howard Meredith noted that Young Hunter "offers the best elements of Abenaki society. He is the personification of community and nature, in harmony with each other."

Other novels from Bruchac are aimed at a younger audience. His *Children of the Longhouse* tells of one young Mohawk boy's challenge from a tribal bully and how he finally resolves his problems on the lacrosse field. A *Publishers Weekly* critic felt that in the novel Bruchac "eloquently conveys how democracy, respect and justice are integral components of the Native Americans' religion and government." In *Eagle Song,* a fourth-grade boy has to move to Brooklyn from the reservation and faces discrimination at school until his father helps pave the son's way by eloquently speaking at school about Native America. "With so many Native American stories set in the misty past," wrote *Booklist* contributor Hazel Rochman, "it's great to read about an Iroquois boy who lives in the city now." A reviewer for *Publishers Weekly* noted that Bruchac's "appealing portrayal of a strong family offers an unromanticized view of Native American culture."

Actual events from 1777 inspired *The Arrow over the Door,* a novel told from the viewpoints of a white and an Indian boy who learn to live in harmony. *Booklist* reviewer Karen Hutt called the book a "quietly compelling story" and a "truly excellent example of historical fiction for the middle-grade/junior-high audience." Bruchac explores the modern Native American world with *The Heart of a Chief* in which eleven-year-old Chris must deal with the alcoholism of his father, casino gambling on his reservation, and racism as it is found in the naming of sports teams. A critic for *Publishers Weekly* found the book to be a "perceptive first-person narrative" with "universal" themes. "Bruchac," the same reviewer concluded, "succeeds in allowing readers to see into the heart of this burgeoning chief." With *Skeleton Man,* Bruchac features a strong sixth-grade girl as the narrator of "an incredibly scary story," as Carol A. Edwards described the novel in *School Library Journal.* When young Molly's parents suddenly disappear, a man claiming to be her uncle takes guardianship of her, locking her into her room at night but allowing her to attend school during the day. Molly uses her Mohawk heritage and the decipherment of her dreams to finally solve this mystery and rescue her parents. A critic for *Kirkus Reviews* called the novel a "nail-biter," and a "natural for under-the-blanket reading." Edwards concluded, "In the classic horror tradition, Bruchac offers a timely tale that will make hearts beat and brows sweat, and it has the bonus of a resourceful heroine to put the world right again."

Both in picture book format and in longer texts, Bruchac has also contributed narrative history titles examining various aspects of Native America. *A Boy Called Slow,* an ALA Notable Book, is a Lakota tale about a young Sioux who longs for the inspiration to capture an adult name better than his juvenile one. When the time comes for him to prove himself in a battle against the Crow, he performs heroically and earns the title of Sitting Bull, the name by which he went down in history. A critic in *Publishers Weekly* felt that the story was not only satisfying in its attention to history but was also "stirring in its consummate storytelling." Reviewing the tale in *Horn Book,* Fader noted that this "picture book coming-of-age story's important message—that success comes through hard work and determination rather than as a right of one's birth—comes through clearly." Bruchac does the same for another famous Native American in *Crazy Horse's Vision,* which covers the early years of Tashunka Witco, also known as Crazy Horse. *Booklist*'s Hutt felt that Bruchac created "a memorable tale ... capturing the spirit of one of the most dedicated and daring leaders of the Lakota." More fictionalized history comes in the novel-length *Sacajawea: The Story of Bird Woman and the Lewis and Clark Expedition.* Told from the points of view of Sacajawea, Clark, and their Shoshone interpreter, the author creates characters "who are both lifelike and compelling, at a fascinating juncture in history," as a reviewer for *Publishers Weekly* commented. William McLoughlin, reviewing the historical novel in *School Library Journal,* likewise called it "intelligent" and "elegantly written."

Turning to nonfiction history, Bruchac presents Native Americans in their own words with *Lasting Echoes: An Oral History of the Native American People. Horn Book*'s Bush praised the book as a "reference resource, a literary anthology, and a history" detailing the seven generations since the arrival of Europeans in America. "By summoning the voices Bruchac so admires, he creates a powerful testament to the endurance of a people," noted a contributor for *Publishers Weekly.* The Trail of Tears, the story of the Cherokee removal, finds a place in several titles from Bruchac, including the fictionalized diary *The Journal of Jesse Smoke,* an easy reader, *Trail of Tears,* and *Trails of Tears, Paths of Beauty.* Likewise the trials of the Navajo are presented in the 2001 title *Navajo Long Walk.*

In his *Publishers Weekly* interview with Alderdice, Bruchac explained what he felt the purpose of writing should be—that for him it involves at least a dual purpose. "The first is to entertain," Bruchac said. "Because if it entertains, then people will pay attention to it. The second is to teach. To provide lessons. And not to do so in an overly preachy way." The omnipresent lesson of Bruchac's work is a reverence for nature and the idea that mankind must become part of nature, part of the land. For Bruchac, much of the current popularity of Native American literature can be explained by the themes found in such books: the value placed on family, environment, and community. "But these are basic human values," the writer told Alderdice. "And you do not have to be an Indian, or even interested, per se, in American Indian culture," for such books to be meaningful, to find a message in them. Concluding his interview with Dresang in *CCBC-Net,* Bruchac said that he hopes to be thought of and remembered "as a voice for the people rather than as one who spoke for himself. Whatever gifts I've been given have been given to me for a reason. No matter how much I give back, it could never be enough."

Biographical and Critical Sources

BOOKS

Authors and Artists for Young Adults, Volume 19, Gale (Detroit, MI), 1997.
Native North American Literature, Gale (Detroit, MI), 1994.
Silvey, Anita, editor, *Children's Books and Their Creators,* Houghton Mifflin (Boston, MA), 1995.

PERIODICALS

Bloomsbury Review, May-June, 1993, Carl L. Blankston, III, review of *Turtle Meat and Other Stories,* p. 5.
Booklist, March 1, 1976, review of *Turkey Brother and Other Tales,* p. 974; April 1, 1979, review of *Stone Giants and Flying Heads: Adventure Stories of the Iroquois,* p. 1217; July, 1993, Carolyn Phelan, review of *The First Strawberries: A Cherokee Story,* p. 1969; December 1, 1994, p. 96; December 15, 1994, Julie Walton, review of *Gluskabe and the Four Wishes,* p. 756; February 1, 1996, p. 927; May 1, 1996, p. 1506; November 15, 1996, p. 581; February 1, 1997, Hazel Rochman, review of *Eagle Song,* p. 939; September 15, 1997, pp. 234-235; December 15, 1997, p. 687; February 15, 1998, Karen Hutt, review of *The Arrow over the Door,* p. 1007; November 1, 1998, p. 518; December 1, 1999, p. 715; March 1, 2000, p. 1238; May 15, 2000, Karen Hutt, review of *Crazy*

Horse's Vision, p. 1747; February 1, 2001, p. 1054; July, 2001, Karen Hutt, review of *The Journal of Jesse Smoke,* p. 2005; September 1, 2001, p. 96.

Bulletin of the Center for Children's Books, September, 1993, p. 6; October, 1993, p. 40; September, 1994, p. 7; January, 1995, p. 160; July-August, 1996, pp. 364-365; September, 1998, Janice M. Del Negro, review of *When the Chenoo Howls,* p. 8; December, 1998, p. 126.

Five Owls, February, 1993, Susan Stan, "Joseph Bruchac: Poet, Storyteller, Publisher, Activist," pp. 57-58.

Horn Book, November, 1993, p. 77; January, 1994, p. 60; March, 1994, p. 209; November, 1994, p. 738; March-April, 1995, Martha V. Parravano, review of *Gluskabe and the Four Wishes,* pp. 203-204; September-October, 1995, Ellen Fader, review of *A Boy Called Slow,* pp. 616-617; November-December, 1995, Margaret A. Bush, review of *The Boy Who Lived with Bears,* pp. 750-751; January-February, 1996, Ellen Fader, review of *The Earth under Sky Bear's Feet,* p. 85; May-June, 1996, Ellen Fader, review of *Between Earth and Sky,* pp. 341-342; January-February, 1998, Margaret A. Bush, review of *Lasting Echoes,* p. 90; September-October, 1998, pp. 638-639; July-August, 2000, p. 433.

Horn Book Guide, January-June, 1992, Barbara Barstow, review of *Thirteen Moons on Turtle's Back,* p. 322; spring, 1997, p. 151; fall, 1997, p. 366; spring, 1998, p. 188.

Kirkus Reviews, October 1, 1992, review of *Turtle Meat and Other Stories,* p. 1201; December 15, 1997, p. 1833; August 1, 2001, review of *Skeleton Man,* p. 1118.

Kliatt, January, 1993, pp. 25-26; March, 1993, p. 21; November, 1993, p. 52; September, 1995, p. 30.

Los Angeles Times Book Review, November 1, 1992, Charles Solomon, review of *Native American Animal Stories,* p. 11.

New Advocate, spring, 1995, Cyndi Giorgis and Janelle Mathis, "Visions and Voices of American Indians in Children's Literature," pp. 127-128.

Publishers Weekly, April 26, 1976, review of *Turkey Brother and Other Tales,* p. 60; February 10, 1992, review of *Thirteen Moons on Turtle's Back,* pp. 80-81; October 19, 1992, review of *Turtle Meat and Other Stories,* p. 73; March 15, 1993, review of *Dawn Land,* p. 68; January 9, 1995, review of *A Boy Called Slow,* p. 64; July 31, 1995, review of *Long River,* p. 68; October 2, 1995, review of *The Story of the Milky Way,* p. 74; February 19, 1996, Kit Alderdice, "Joseph Bruchac: Sharing a Native-American Heritage," pp. 191-192; April 15, 1996, p. 67; June 10, 1996, review of *Children of the Longhouse,* p. 100; December 30, 1996, review of *Eagle Song,* p. 67; March 10, 1997, p. 69; November 24, 1997, review of *Lasting Echoes,* p. 75; August 17, 1998, review of *The Waters Between,* p. 50; November 16, 1998, review of *The Heart of a Chief,* p. 75; February 14, 2000, review of *Sacajawea,* p. 201; May 29, 2000, p. 83; September 25, 2000, p. 65; August 13, 2001, review of *Skeleton Man,* p. 313; January 15, 2001, review of *How Chipmunk Got His Stripes,* p. 76; November 12, 2001, pp. 62-63.

School Library Journal, April, 1979, Gale Eaton, review of *Stone Giants and Flying Heads: Adventure Stories of the Iroquois,* p. 53; December, 1992, Yvonne Frey, review of *Turtle Meat and Other Stories,* p. 137; August, 1993, Judy Sokoll, review of *Dawn Land,* p. 205; September, 1993, Yvonne Frey, review of *Flying with the Eagle, Racing the Great Bear,* p. 238; September, 1995, Donna L. Scanlon, review of *The Story of the Milky Way,* p. 192; January, 1996, Kathleen McCabe, review of *Dog People: Native Dog Stories,* pp. 114-115; May, 1996, pp. 120-121; July, 1996, pp. 82, 88; March, 1997, p. 149; December, 1997, p. 75; April, 1998, p. 128; December, 1998, Darcy Schild, review of *When the Chenoo Howls,* p. 134; November, 1999, pp. 133-134; March, 2000, p. 222; May, 2000, William McLoughlin, review of *Sacajawea,* p. 170; November, 2000, p. 110; February, 2001, Grace Oliff, review of *How Chipmunk Got His Stripes,* p. 109l; August, 2001, Carol A. Edwards, review of *Skeleton Man,* p. 176.

Voice of Youth Advocates, February, 1995, p. 354; February, 1998, p. 398; October, 1998, pp. 292, 294.

World Literature Today, summer, 1999, Howard Meredith, review of *The Waters Between,* pp. 572-573.

Writer's Digest, June, 1995, Ann Hauprich, "Traveling between Two Worlds," p. 6.

OTHER

CCBC-Net, http://www.education.wise.edu/ccbc/ (October 22, 1999), Eliza T. Dresang, "An Interview with Joseph Bruchac."

Internet Public Library, http://www.ipl.org/ (February 18, 2002), "Native American Authors: Joseph Bruchac."

Scholastic Web Site, http://teacher.scholastic.com/ (February 18, 2002).

Wordsmith.org, http://www.wordsmith.org/ (January 10, 2001), "Online Chat with Joseph Bruchac."

C

CLARE, Helen
See CLARKE, Pauline

* * *

CLARKE, Pauline 1921-
(Pauline Hunter Blair, Helen Clare)

Personal

Born May 19, 1921, in Kirkby-in-Ashfield, Nottingham-shire, England; daughter of Charles Leopold (a minister of religion) and Dorothy Kathleen (Milum) Clarke; married Peter Hunter Blair (a historian), 1969 (died, 1982). *Education:* Somerville College, Oxford, England, B.A. (with honors), 1943. *Hobbies and other interests:* Music, theatre, films, history, archaeology, gardening, walking, travel.

Addresses

Home—Church Farm House, 69 High Street, Bottisham, Cambridgeshire CB5 9BA, England. *Agent*—Curtis Brown, Ltd., Fourth Floor, Haymarket House, 28/29 Haymarket, London, SW1Y 4SP.

Career

Writer of fiction and verse for children, editor, lecturer, adapter of own stories for the British Broadcasting Corporation. *Member:* British Society of Authors.

Awards, Honors

Carnegie Medal from British Library Association, 1963, International Board on Books for Young People (IBBY) Honor List, Great Britain, Hans Christian Andersen Award Honor List, and *New York Herald Tribune* Children's Spring Book Festival Honor Book, all 1964, all for *The Twelve and the Genii* (U.S. title, *The Return of the Twelves);* Deutsche Jugendbuch Preis (Germany), Lewis Carroll Shelf Award, both 1968, both for *The Return of the Twelves.*

Writings

FICTION FOR CHILDREN

The Pekinese Princess, illustrated by Cecil Leslie, J. Cape (London, England), 1948.

The Great Can, illustrated by Cecil Leslie, Faber (London, England), 1952.

The White Elephant, illustrated by Richard Kennedy, Faber (London, England), 1952, Abelard-Schuman (New York, NY), 1957.

Smith's Hoard, illustrated by Cecil Leslie, Faber (London, England), 1955, published as *Hidden Gold,* Abelard-Schuman (New York, NY), 1957, published as *The Golden Collar,* Faber (London, England), 1967.

Sandy the Sailor, illustrated by Cecil Leslie, Hamish Hamilton (London, England), 1956.

The Boy with the Erpingham Hood, illustrated by Cecil Leslie, Faber (London, England), 1956.

James the Policeman, illustrated by Cecil Leslie, Hamish Hamilton (London, England), 1957.

James and the Robbers, illustrated by Cecil Leslie, Hamish Hamilton (London, England), 1959.

Torolv the Fatherless, illustrated by Cecil Leslie, Faber (London, England), 1959.

The Lord of the Castle, illustrated by Cecil Leslie, Hamish Hamilton (London, England), 1960.

The Robin Hooders, illustrated by Cecil Leslie, Faber (London, England), 1960.

Keep the Pot Boiling, illustrated by Cecil Leslie, Faber (London, England), 1961.

James and the Smugglers, illustrated by Cecil Leslie, Hamish Hamilton (London, England), 1961.

The Twelve and the Genii, illustrated by Cecil Leslie, Faber (London, England), 1962, published as *The Return of the Twelves,* illustrated by Bernarda Bryson, Coward, McCann (New York, NY), 1964, reprinted, Gregg Press (Boston, MA), 1981.

James and the Black Van, illustrated by Cecil Leslie, Hamish Hamilton (London, England), 1963.

Pauline Clarke mixes fiction and literary history in **The Return of the Twelves,** *illustrated by Bernarda Bryson.*

The Bonfire Party, illustrated by Cecil Leslie, Hamish Hamilton (London, England), 1966.

The Two Faces of Silenus, Coward, McCann (New York, NY), 1972.

UNDER PSEUDONYM HELEN CLARE

Five Dolls in a House, illustrated by Cecil Leslie, Lane (London, England), 1953, illustrated by Aliki, Prentice Hall (Englewood Cliffs, NJ), 1965.

Merlin's Magic, illustrated by Cecil Leslie, Lane (London, England), 1953.

Bel the Giant and Other Stories, illustrated by Peggy Fortnum, Bodley Head (London, England), 1956, published as *The Cat and the Fiddle and Other Stories,* illustrated by Ida Pellei, Prentice Hall (Englewood Cliffs, NJ), 1968.

Five Dolls and the Monkey, illustrated by Cecil Leslie, Bodley Head (London, England), 1956, illustrated by Aliki, Prentice Hall (Englewood Cliffs, NJ), 1967.

Five Dolls in the Snow, illustrated by Cecil Leslie, Bodley Head (London, England), 1957, illustrated by Aliki, Prentice Hall (Englewood Cliffs, NJ), 1967.

Five Dolls and Their Friends, illustrated by Cecil Leslie, Bodley Head (London, England), 1959, illustrated by Aliki, Prentice Hall (Englewood Cliffs, NJ), 1968.

Seven White Pebbles, illustrated by Cynthia Abbott, Bodley Head (London, England), 1960.

Five Dolls and the Duke, illustrated by Cecil Leslie, Bodley Head (London, England), 1963, illustrated by Aliki, Prentice Hall (Englewood Cliffs, NJ), 1968.

OTHER

Silver Bells and Cockle Shells (verse), illustrated by Sally Ducksbury, Abelard-Schuman (New York, NY), 1962.

Crowds of Creatures, illustrated by Cecil Leslie, Faber (London, England), 1964.

(Editor under name Pauline Hunter Blair, with Michael Lapidge) Peter Hunter Blair, *Anglo-Saxon Northumbria,* Variorum (London, England), 1984.

Contributor of essays and review to periodicals, including *Times Literary Supplement, Eastern Daily News* (Norwich), and *Junior Bookshelf.*

Sidelights

Pauline Clarke is notable as the author of imaginative, magical stories for children, and particularly of her fantasy *The Return of the Twelves,* for which she won the prestigious Carnegie Medal from the British Library Association as well as other honors in the United States.

Born in Nottinghamshire, Clarke lived for many years in Norfolk (the background for *The Boy with the Erpingham Hood* and several other books) and attended schools in London and Essex before she became a student of English literature at Somerville College, Oxford. Somerville was one of the all-women colleges that granted women full academic privileges during the 1920s. As Clarke once stated, both of her parents "in different ways encouraged a love of the English language and a delight in using it. [My] mother's ardent love of poetry, and a true gift for storytelling, led to hundreds of short stories for magazines which paid her three daughter's school fees; while [my] father's biting command of English in sermons, arguments, everyday polemics and books on theology, was (though often very scary) notable."

After a few years working on a children's magazine and as a journalist, Clarke turned to writing. Her first book came about while she shared a home with several Pekinese dogs and their owner, artist Cecil Leslie, who illustrated Clarke's first book, *The Pekinese Princess,* and many later ones. Clarke explained how this book came about: "[Leslie] was never without a drawing book, and the antics, faces and figures of these dogs frequently appeared. Looking for an unusual setting, [I, then an] aspiring author thought 'China!' The London Library, a life-saving institution for the English country-dwelling author, sent books about everything Chinese, the social framework, the court life, religions and ancient customs. It appeared that the 'little lion dogs' were immensely important: one of the Empresses wrote a piece about them which tells how they were taught to 'bite the foreign devil' instantly, how they should be reared, how they were regarded not only as friends but accorded imperial respect. Out of this arose a complete kingdom of Pekinese, a princess stolen on the eve of her wedding by a race of envious monkeys from the forest and carried off in a basket by an eagle to the high peaks, whence her valiant bridegroom must bring her back. No human beings impinged on this story."

In 1953 *Five Dolls in a House* appeared; it was the first of Clarke's books under the pseudonym Helen Clare. The ensuing *Five Dolls* series for younger readers was also illustrated by Cecil Leslie and had five dolls as main characters. Clarke relayed how this book came to be written: "An imposing Georgian-looking dolls' house had been enlarged and beautified for a little girl, Christina, [whom I adopted] following World War II. In it lived various small dolls, old-fashioned and Edwardian. When Christina invited the doctor's daughter over to play, [I] would overhear their talk, as they took on the rolls of mother, father, or one of the dolls: a mixture of grown-up assertions, childish comment, wrong-meanings and pronunciations (reflected in the speech of Vanessa, the boss doll) and inconsequential sentences (which it would be hard for an adult to invent). From this arose the *Five Dolls* books, in which a small girl enters her own dolls' house."

The *Five Dolls* stories found favor with American children and were published in the United States as well as in England. In the *Five Dolls* books no grown-ups appear in person; they are only talked about. As Clarke explained to Cornelia Jones and Olivia R. Way in an interview for *British Children's Authors,* "Elizabeth is the little girl who can get small enough to go into her doll's house. All the action takes place amongst toys— toy trains, toy castles, a toy zoo. It's a toy world. . . . The real world is always there for Elizabeth to come from and go back to, but it doesn't come into the stories." Yet the dolls do what children do in real life: they go to weddings, they have picnics, they help in the house or the garden. "It's just life from a doll's-eye view," Clarke emphasized.

When *The Twelve and the Genii* was published in England in 1962, it won instant recognition with the English public because of its captivating style and characters and its connection with the famous Bronte family of Haworth. After winning several honors, including the Carnegie Medal, it was published in the United States in 1964 as *The Return of the Twelves* and again was a prize-winner. The story is based on the adventures of twelve toy soldiers that were given to Branwell Brönte, younger brother of Charlotte, Emily, and Ann, in 1826. The soldiers were called "the Twelves," and the children "worked a very special game with these Twelves," as Clarke explained in *British Children's Authors.* The children were their guardian angels or genii, and each child had a special soldier that was hers or his. "Branwell was the ringleader, imagining battles and adventures and sea voyages," Clarke elaborated. These games continued until about 1830, when Branwell was twelve years old.

The children's imaginative games were kept secret from the grown-ups. Their father, a clergyman, was determined to maintain a quiet household where he could write his sermons in peace. So, much like the Brönte children themselves, the soldiers in the stories "freeze," or look lifeless, when an outsider or grown-up appears. All four Brönte children took part in writing down the soldiers' adventures, and their narrative became known as *The History of the Young Men.* These tiny books containing the stories of the Twelves (written in tiny black letters) attracted Clarke's attention when she visited the Brönte Museum, and she became absorbed in the idea of bringing the Twelves to life in her next book.

Clarke and her illustrator did a great deal of research on the Bröntes and the story's setting. Clarke described their efforts to recreate the climax of the story in *British Children's Authors:* "I did the march back to Haworth from maps, photos, and imagination, and from memory. I had been there in 1953 ... but the artist ... wanted very much to go to Haworth to get the feeling of the countryside ... and see Branwell's own paintings and drawings of his soldiers.... So while she was at Haworth, she actually walked out that march ... and in one particular she corrected it. When she saw Branwell's drawings, very faded watercolors of the soldiers, she noticed that some of the soldiers were wearing feathers in their caps and carrying a flag in battle." So Clarke added these details, completing a most unusual collaboration between artist and author and between artists living more than a century apart.

"In historical stories I get great pleasure and satisfaction from building up a picture of a past time with countless tiny details—about clothes and kitchens, and cooking and daily life," Clarke continued in her *British Children's Authors* interview. "Of course you never really know how close your picture is to the real one.... You can only aim at making it a total and convincing picture, after doing your research as widely as you can." Clarke did express satisfaction with *Torolv the Fatherless* and *The Boy with the Erpingham Hood,* two of her best-known books for young people based on English history. *The Boy with the Erpingham Hood* is an action-packed book that describes the Battle of Agincourt.

Torolv's hero is rescued from a mishap at sea by a Viking warrior crew (who are referred to as traders, but are really pirates). Then, after one of their raids, Torolv is accidentally left ashore in England. He is taken into the Christian household of the earl of the East Saxons at Heybridge on the Essex coast. Torolv is eager to learn and eventually grows to love the earl's family and the life at Heybridge, so that when he has to make a choice at the Battle of Maldon, he remains loyal to the English.

In a later work, *The Two Faces of Silenus,* Clarke turns to fantasy and sets her characters, an English family, in a small hill town of Italy. As Clarke told *MAICYA,* "While [my] husband attended a conference in Spoleto [Italy], [I] had many happy hours of explore the enchanting little town and its surroundings. [I] was captivated by the stone face of Silenus, presiding over a spring with a water bowl, in a small square; the water flowed through his open mouth, where a small tusk showed at each side; his nose was soft and wrinkled like a horse." The statue of Silenus, described in the book as "the wild god who knows wisdom, can sing the ultimate secret of life, if you can but catch him," comes to life for the children—and magical, dramatic events lead to a tremendous climax before Silenus turns to stone again.

Biographical and Critical Sources

BOOKS

Cameron, Eleanor, *The Green and Burning Tree: On the Writing and Enjoyment of Children's Books,* Little, Brown (Boston, MA), 1962.
Crouch, Marcus, *The Nesbit Tradition: The Children's Novel in England, 1945-1970,* Rowman & Littlefield (Totowa, NJ), 1972.
Crouch, Marcus, and Alec Ellis, editors, *Chosen for Children: An Account of the Books Which Have Been Awarded the Library Association Carnegie Medal,* 3rd edition, Library Association (London, England), 1977.
Eyre, Frank, *British Children's Books in the Twentieth Century,* revised edition, Longman (London, England), 1971.
Fisher, Margery, *Intent upon Reading: A Critical Appraisal of Modern Fiction for Children,* Brockhampton Press (Leicester, England), 1961.
Hunt, Caroline, editor, *Dictionary of Literary Biography,* Volume 161: *British Children's Writers since 1960,* Gale (Detroit, MI), 1996.
Jones, Cornelia and Olivia R. Way, editors, *British Children's Authors: Interviews at Home,* American Library Association (Chicago, IL), 1976.
Kuznets, Lois Rostow, *When Toys Come Alive: Narratives of Animation, Metamorphosis, and Development,* Yale University Press (New Haven, CT), 1994.
St. James Guide to Children's Writers, 5th edition, St. James Press (Detroit, MI), 1999.

PERIODICALS

Children's Book Council Calendar, March-August, 1975, Pauline Clarke, "Books Remembered."
Horn Book, April, 1970, Ravenna Helson, "Fantasy and Discovery," pp. 121-133; December, 1972, Virginia Haviland, review of *The Two Faces of Silenus,* pp. 594-595; February, 1983, Eleanor Cameron, "The Inmost Secret," pp. 17-24.
Junior Bookshelf, July, 1953, review of *Merlin's Magic,* pp. 111-112.

*   *   *

COBB, Vicki 1938-

Personal

Born August 19, 1938, in Brooklyn, NY; daughter of Benjamin Harold (a labor arbitrator) and Paula (Davis) Wolf; married Edward Scribner Cobb (a psychology professor), January 31, 1960 (divorced 1983); children: Theodore Davis, Joshua Monroe. *Education:* Attended University of Wisconsin, 1954-57; Barnard College, B.A. (zoology), 1958; Columbia University Teachers College, M.A. (secondary school science education), 1960.

Addresses

Agent—c/o HarperCollins Publishers, 10 East 53rd St., New York, NY 10022.

Career

Writer and lecturer. Sloan-Kettering Institute and Pfizer & Company, Rye, NY, scientific researcher, 1953-61; high school science teacher, Rye, NY, 1961-64; Teleprompter Corp., New York, NY, hostess and principal writer of television series *The Science Game,* beginning 1972; American Broadcasting Company, New York, NY, writer for *Good Morning America,* 1976; Scott Publishing Company, public relations director, 1978-83; Pinwheel Publishers, vice president. *Member:* Authors Guild, Authors League of America, Writers Guild, Society of Children's Book Writers and Illustrators.

Awards, Honors

Cable television award for best educational series, 1973, for *The Science Game;* Outstanding Science Trade Books for Children Award, Children's Book Council-National Science Teachers Association, 1975, for *Supersuits,* 1980, for *Bet You Can't!: Science Impossibilities to Fool You,* 1981, for *Lots of Rot,* and 1982, for *The Secret Life of Hardware;* Book of the Year Award, Child Study Children's Book Committee, 1979, for *Truth on Trial: The Story of Galileo Galilei;* Children's Book Selections, Library of Congress, 1979, for *More Science You Can Eat,* 1981, for *How to Really Fool Yourself: Illusions for All Your Senses,* and 1983, for *The Monsters Who Died: A Mystery About Dinosaurs;* Children's Choice Selection, International Reading Association-Children's Book Council, 1980, for *More Science You Can Eat;* Children's Science Book Award, New York Academy of Sciences, 1981, for *Bet You Can't!;* Notable Book Citation, American Library Association, 1982, for *How to Really Fool Yourself;* Washington Irving Children's Book Choice Award for nonfiction, Westchester Library Association, 1984, for *The Secret Life of School Supplies: A Science Experiment Book;* Eva L. Gordon Award, American Nature Study Society, 1985.

Writings

FOR CHILDREN; NONFICTION

Science Experiments You Can Eat, illustrated by Peter Lippman, Lippincott (Philadelphia, PA), 1972, revised and updated edition, illustrated by David Cain, Harper-Collins (New York, NY), 1994.
How the Doctor Knows You're Fine, illustrated by Anthony Ravielli, Lippincott (Philadelphia, PA), 1973.
Arts and Crafts You Can Eat, illustrated by Peter Lippman, Lippincott (Philadelphia, PA), 1974.
Supersuits, illustrated by Peter Lippman, Lippincott (Philadelphia, PA), 1975.
More Science Experiments You Can Eat, illustrated by Giulio Maestro, Lippincott (Philadelphia, PA), 1979.
Magic . . . Naturally!: Science Entertainments and Amusements, illustrated by Lance R. Miyamoto, Lippincott (Philadelphia, PA), 1979, revised edition, illustrated by Lionel Kalish, HarperCollins (New York, NY), 1993.
Truth on Trial: The Story of Galileo Galilei, illustrated by George Ulrich, Coward (New York, NY), 1979.

Vicki Cobb

(With Kathy Darling) *Bet You Can't!: Science Impossibilities to Fool You,* illustrated by Martha Weston, Lothrop (New York, NY), 1980.
How to Really Fool Yourself: Illusions for All Your Senses, illustrated by Leslie Morrill, Lippincott (New York, NY), 1981, revised edition, illustrated by Jessica Wolk-Stanley, Wiley (New York, NY), 1999.
Lots of Rot, illustrated by Brian Schatell, Lippincott (New York, NY), 1981.
The Secret Life of School Supplies, illustrated by Bill Morrison, Lippincott (New York, NY), 1981.
The Secret Life of Hardware: A Science Experiment Book, illustrated by Bill Morrison, Lippincott (New York, NY), 1982.
Fuzz Does It!, illustrated by Brian Schatell, Lippincott (New York, NY), 1982.
(With Kathy Darling) *Bet You Can!: Science Possibilities to Fool You,* illustrated by Stella Ormai, Avon (New York, NY), 1983, hardcover edition, Lothrop (New York, NY), 1990.
Gobs of Goo, illustrated by Brian Schatell, Lippincott (New York, NY), 1983.
The Monsters Who Died: A Mystery About Dinosaurs, illustrated by Greg Wenzel, Coward (New York, NY), 1983.
Chemically Active!: Experiments You Can Do at Home, illustrated by Theo Cobb, Lippincott (New York, NY), 1983.

The Secret Life of Cosmetics: A Science Experiment Book, illustrated by Theo Cobb, Lippincott (New York, NY), 1985.

Inspector Bodyguard Patrols the Land of U, illustrated by John Sanford, Simon & Schuster (New York, NY), 1986.

Skyscraper Going Up!: A Pop-Up Book, design and paper engineering by John Strejan, Crowell (New York, NY), 1987.

Why Doesn't the Earth Fall Up?: And Other Not Such Dumb Questions About Motion, illustrated by Ted Enik, Lodestar Books (New York, NY), 1988.

Getting Dressed, illustrated by Marylin Hafner, Lippincott (New York, NY), 1989.

Keeping Clean, illustrated by Marylin Hafner, Lippincott (New York, NY), 1989.

Writing It Down, illustrated by Marylin Hafner, Lippincott (New York, NY), 1989.

Feeding Yourself, illustrated by Marylin Hafner, Lippincott (New York, NY), 1989.

For Your Own Protection: Stories Science Photos Tell, Lothrop (New York, NY), 1989.

Natural Wonders: Stories Science Photos Tell, Lothrop (New York, NY), 1990.

Why Doesn't the Sun Burn Out?: And Other Not Such Dumb Questions About Energy, illustrated by Ted Enik, Lodestar Books (New York, NY), 1990.

Why Can't You Unscramble an Egg?: And Other Not Such Dumb Questions About Matter, illustrated by Ted Enik, Lodestar Books (New York, NY), 1990.

Fun and Games: Stories Science Photos Tell, Lothrop (New York, NY), 1991.

(With Josh Cobb) *Light Action!: Amazing Experiments with Optics,* illustrated by Theo Cobb, HarperCollins (New York, NY), 1993.

(With Kathy Darling) *Wanna Bet?: Science Challenges to Fool You,* illustrated by Meredith Johnson, Lothrop (New York, NY), 1993.

Why Can't I Live Forever?: And Other Not Such Dumb Questions About Life, illustrated by Mena Dolobowsky, Lodestar Books (New York, NY), 1997.

Blood and Gore Like You've Never Seen, Scholastic (New York, NY), 1997.

Dirt and Grime Like You've Never Seen, Scholastic (New York, NY), 1998.

(With Kathy Darling) *Don't Try This at Home!: Science Fun for Kids on the Go,* illustrated by True Kelley, Morrow (New York, NY), 1998.

You Gotta Try This!: Absolutely Irresistible Science, illustrated by True Kelley, Morrow (New York, NY), 1999.

Bangs and Twangs: Science Fun with Sound, illustrated by Steve Haefele, Millbrook Press (Brookfield, CT), 2000.

Squirts and Spurts: Science Fun with Water, illustrated by Steve Haefele, Millbrook Press (Brookfield, CT), 2000.

Whirlers and Twirlers: Science Fun with Spinning, illustrated by Steve Haefele, Millbrook Press (Brookfield, CT), 2001.

See for Yourself: More Than 100 Experiments for Science Fairs and Projects, illustrated by Dave Klug, Scholastic (New York, NY), 2001.

I Get Wet, illustrated by Julia Gorton, HarperCollins (New York, NY), 2001.

I See Myself, illustrated by Julia Gorton, HarperCollins (New York, NY), 2002.

Sources of Forces: Science Fun with Force Fields, illustrated by Steve Haefele, Millbrook Press (Brookfield, CT), 2002.

I Face the Wind, illustrated by Julia Gorton, HarperCollins (New York, NY), 2003.

"FIRST BOOK" SERIES

Logic, illustrated by Ellie Haines, Franklin Watts (New York, NY), 1969.

Cells: The Basic Structure of Life, illustrated by Leonard Dank, Franklin Watts (New York, NY), 1970.

Gases, illustrated by Ellie Haines, Franklin Watts (New York, NY), 1970.

Heat, illustrated by Robert Byrd, Franklin Watts (New York, NY), 1973.

"STEPPING-STONE" SERIES

Making Sense of Money, illustrated by Olivia H. H. Cole, Parents' Magazine Press (New York, NY), 1971.

Sense of Direction: Up, Down, and All Around, illustrated by Carol Nicklaus, Parents' Magazine Press (New York, NY), 1972.

The Long and Short of Measurements, illustrated by Carol Nicklaus, Parents' Magazine Press (New York, NY), 1973.

"HOW THE WORLD WORKS" SERIES

The Scoop on Ice Cream, illustrated by G. Brian Karas, Little, Brown (Boston, MA), 1985.

Sneakers Meet Your Feet, illustrated by Theo Cobb, Little, Brown (Boston, MA), 1985.

More Power to You!, illustrated by Bill Ogden, Little, Brown (Boston, MA), 1986.

The Trip of a Drip, illustrated by Eliot Kreloff, Little, Brown (Boston, MA), 1986.

"IMAGINE LIVING HERE" SERIES; ILLUSTRATED BY BARBARA LAVALLEE

This Place Is Cold, Walker (New York, NY), 1989.

This Place Is Dry, Walker (New York, NY), 1989.

This Place Is Wet, Walker (New York, NY), 1989.

This Place Is High, Walker (New York, NY), 1989.

This Place Is Lonely, Walker (New York, NY), 1991.

This Place Is Crowded: Japan, Walker (New York, NY), 1992.

This Place Is Wild: East Africa, Walker (New York, NY), 1998.

"THE FIVE SENSES" SERIES; ILLUSTRATED BY CYNTHIA C. LEWIS

Follow Your Nose: Discover Your Sense of Smell, Millbrook Press (Brookfield, CT), 2000.

Your Tongue Can Tell: Discover Your Sense of Taste, Millbrook Press (Brookfield, CT), 2000.

Feeling Your Way: Discover Your Sense of Touch, Millbrook Press (Brookfield, CT), 2001.

Perk Up Your Ears: Discover Your Sense of Hearing, Millbrook Press (Brookfield, CT), 2001.

Open Your Eyes: Discover Your Sense of Sight, Millbrook Press (Brookfield, CT), 2002.

OTHER

Brave in the Attempt: The Special Olympics Experience (adult nonfiction), photographs by Rosemarie Hausherr, Pinwheel, 1983.

Also editor of *Biology Study Prints,* 1970, and author of *Scraps of Wraps,* 1988. The author's papers and manuscripts are held in the de Grummond Collection at the University of Southern Mississippi.

Sidelights

Vicki Cobb, author of science books for children, once commented: "When you think about the great teachers who influenced you, who they were as human beings was at least as important as what they taught you. The passion and energy they brought to their teaching—their humanity—somehow touched their students. I believe that revealed humanity is the bridge to authentic and powerful communication, both oral and written. Students and readers learn best when they are moved—when feelings are associated with concepts. The feelings and personalities of top fiction writers are part of their 'voice' as storytellers. Personal voices are beginning to be heard in children's nonfiction, but such writing is a break with tradition. There is an underlying assumption that nonfiction gains authority by being dispassionate and straightforward, although the result may be dry and perhaps boring. But is the word from 'on high' any more than the word communicated with wit or enthusiasm? Why can't the real world be presented in lively prose as fictional worlds are? I consider myself to be a storyteller of the real world. It is my job to present that world in a manner that is engaging to my readers."

In an essay for the *Something About the Author Autobiography Series* (*SAAS*), Cobb credited her childhood experiences for her hands-on approach to science and her interest in books. "The importance of being a doer obviously came from my home," the author commented. "I painted and did woodwork with my father. I cooked and sewed and knitted with my mother. I had four years as an only child, four years as the sole apple of my parents' eyes before my sister Elly was born. All that exclusive adult attention helped me become a reader at age four. Reading became my most important form of entertainment." Another early influence on the author was her experience at The Little Red School House, a private school in Greenwich Village. "At 'Little Red,' it was strongly believed that children learned by doing things," Cobb explained. "When we studied the Indians, we built a tepee in the classroom and we ground corn to make cornmeal the way the Indians did. When we studied the early American colonists, we made candles and soap. We wrote stories and did arts-and-crafts projects. We wrote plays and performed them for each other." Cobb was also influenced by her experience as a counselor-in-training at Buck's Rock Work Camp, where campers and counselors designed and produced crafts for sale to the public. "In those days

I was interested in being an artist," the author commented. "I created all kinds of designs for production.... No other camper or CIT had as many items in production as I. I loved thinking up products that the public might enjoy having and then creating them. My success this last summer, before entering college, played an important part in my becoming what I am today."

At age sixteen, under an early enrollment program for promising high school students, Cobb entered the University of Wisconsin. The author said that 1954, the first year of her college studies, was a time when "girls went to college to find husbands." While at Wisconsin, Cobb found that she liked to study the sciences, and she also became engaged to a student from New York. She later transferred to Barnard College in Manhattan in order to stay with her fiancé, but the engagement ended soon after the transfer. After graduating, Cobb worked for several years as a researcher testing anti-cancer drugs on mice. During that time she married Edward Cobb.

Two years after her marriage, the author became a junior high school teacher and discovered that she liked explaining basic concepts to her students. While pregnant with her first child, Cobb left her job and turned her attention to writing science texts. However, her first few manuscripts were not printed because the publishers with whom she had contracted went out of business. In 1969 *Logic* became Cobb's first published work. The author commented in *SAAS:* "The day I remember best was the day the galleys arrived and I first saw 'by Vicki Cobb' in type. I must have spent hours gazing at those three words. Suddenly, it was real. After five years, three unpublished books, and countless small writing jobs, I would finally be an author." However, Cobb's first books were series titles for which the writing style was strictly regulated. "When you write for a series," she explained, "your job as author is to sound like all the other authors in the series. My editors made sure of it. When I look back on these early books now, I cringe. The writing is so flat and dull! I'm glad these books are out of print."

Cobb has cited *Science Experiments You Can Eat,* published in 1972, as the first book in which she could be creative. Commenting on her research for the book, the author stated: "In the morning I got the boys off to day camp and then went prowling through the supermarket aisles looking for ideas. I tried out all kinds of experiments, which often failed. Nevertheless, my family was game about eating them." A *Scientific American* review called *Science Experiments You Can Eat* "a first-rate introduction to the sciences of matter for boys and girls old enough to work by themselves." At the time Cobb was working on *Science Experiments You Can Eat,* her husband was developing a problem with alcoholism, and they were divorced a few years later.

Some of Cobb's earlier books have occasionally been criticized for inaccuracies or oversimplifications. For example, an *Appraisal* reviewer found that *Heat* is "well conceived and planned, but carelessly executed in too many spots." The reviewer was particularly disturbed by

Cobb's assertion that "dust particles increase the motion of the air, which causes the temperature to drop." However, a more recent work, *Lots of Rot,* was judged by another *Appraisal* reviewer to be "a wonderful introduction to the subject of decay and the agents and condition that cause it." Cobb's writings have also won several awards, including the Children's Science Book Award in 1981 for *Bet You Can't!: Science Impossibilities to Fool You* and the Eva L. Gordon Award for children's literature in science in 1985.

In the early and mid-1970s, Cobb worked as a writer for television programs. "When I was a child," she explained, "I became a reader because it was the best form of entertainment. We didn't get a television until I was twelve. But my children were brought up on television. I was fascinated and sometimes appalled at the impact it had on them.... As a writer for children, the medium fascinated me. I thought it could be used to teach all kinds of things because there was no question that children learned from it." In 1972 Cobb wrote and hosted *The Science Game,* which featured experiments that could be reproduced at home, for a cable television company in New York. In 1976 Cobb became a writer for *Good Morning America,* the ABC-TV talk show, but she lost her job when a new executive producer brought in his own staff. The author then resumed her career as a writer of science books for children.

In addition to writing, Cobb conducts science demonstrations based on her writings, and she also holds science workshops for teachers. She asserted in her *SAAS* essay: "Doing in-service programs for teachers all over the country has made me think hard, again, about education. I am more firmly convinced than ever that the 'Little Red' educational philosophy was right. I look back over my life and see that my fulfillment in my work comes from repeating the same kinds of activities I enjoyed as a child. I recall sixth grade as a magic year of self-discovery and discovery of the world around me. In some ways, I now re-create sixth grade for myself through my work. When I think of new ideas for books, I am re-creating that summer at Buck's Rock when I was dreaming up products to sell to the public."

Among Cobb's most recent titles are several books in a series that explores the five senses with her hallmark combination of fun and learning: *Follow Your Nose, Your Tongue Can Tell, Feeling Your Way, Perk Up Your Ears,* and *Open Your Eyes.* Reviewer Lauren P. Gattilia, on the *Education World* Web site, commended Cobb's collection of experiments, demonstrations, and craft projects in *Follow Your Nose* and *Your Tongue Can Tell* for a "kid-friendly, casual style that never talks down to readers" as well as for "solid explanations of the way the senses work." Gillian Engberg, in a *Booklist* review, pointed out the "hip collage and lively text" in the "Five Senses" volumes. Engberg noted that "the text weaves basic concepts into anecdotes and suggestions for easy experiments, which are illustrated with kitchy, irreverent collages contributed by Cynthia Lewis."

Cobb introduces young readers to some of the basics of physics in a recent series that includes *Bangs and Twangs: Science Fun with Sound, Squirts and Spurts: Science Fun with Water, Whirlers and Twirlers: Science Fun with Spinning, Sources of Forces: Science Fun with Force Fields. Booklist* reviewer Gillian Engberg, commenting on the "lively cartoon format" and "rowdy fun" of *Bangs and Twangs* and *Squirts and Spurts,* found that "both titles hook the reader from the start." Noting that the books "will encourage enthusiastic learning," Engberg felt that the books successfully "[convey] sophisticated concepts" and credited Cobb's "accessible language" and "Steve Haefele's drawings of an exuberant, grinning narrator and her robot sidekick."

Commenting on her departure from the traditional approach to writing about science, Cobb once noted that "traditional written treatment of information often requires that the reader have an agenda, such as a school assignment, before coming to the material. Thus, the reasons a reader wants access to information may have nothing to do with the intrinsic nature of the material or the reader's basic curiosity. When something is required reading, dry, impersonal writing is likely to stifle further inquiry, rather than nurture and support it. My books are a departure from the traditional. I've used a slightly irreverent tone—'science is not the mysterious process for eggheads it's cracked up to be.'"

Biographical and Critical Sources

BOOKS

Children's Literature Review, Volume 2, Gale (Detroit, MI), 1976.
McElroy, Lisa Tucker, *Meet My Grandmother: She's a Children's Book Author,* photographs by Joel Benjamin, Millbrook Press (Brookfield, CT), 2001.
Silvey, Anita, editor, *Children's Books and Their Creators,* Houghton Mifflin (Boston, MA), 1995.
Something About the Author Autobiography Series, Volume 6, Gale (Detroit, MI), 1988.
Wyatt, Flora R., and others, *Popular Nonfiction Authors for Children,* Libraries Unlimited (Englewood, CO), 1998.

PERIODICALS

Appraisal, fall, 1974, review of *Heat;* winter, 1982, review of *Lots of Rot,* p. 22.
Booklist, December 1, 1995, Carolyn Phelan, reviews of *Light Action: Amazing Experiments with Optics* and *Why Doesn't the Sun Burn Out?: And Other Not Such Dumb Questions About Energy,* p. 632; April, 1998, Carolyn Phelan, *Don't Try This at Home!: Science Fun for Kids on the Go,* p. 1316, and Shelley Townsend-Hudson, review of *This Place Is Wild: East Africa,* p. 1316; August, 1999, Carolyn Phelan, review of *You Gotta Try This!: Absolutely Irresistible Science,* p. 2048; October 15, 2000, Gillian Engberg, reviews of *Squirts and Spurts: Science Fun with Water* and *Bangs and Twangs: Science Fun with Sound,* p. 432; November 15, 2000, Gillian Engberg, reviews of *Your Tongue Can Tell: Discover Your Sense of Taste* and *Follow Your Nose: Discover Your Sense of Smell,* p. 636.

Horn Book, April, 1977, p. 197.

School Library Journal, May, 1997, Carolyn Angus, review of *Why Can't I Live Forever?: And Other Not Such Dumb Questions About Life,* p. 118; May, 1998, Anne Chapman, review of *This Place Is Wild: East Africa,* p. 130; July, 1998, Kathryn Kosiorek, *Don't Try This at Home!,* p. 104; August, 1999, Marion F. Gallivan, review of *You Gotta Try This!,* p. 167; March, 2001, Eunice Weech, review of *Bangs and Twangs,* p. 232; May, 2001, Wendy S. Carroll, review of *Feeling Your Way: Discover Your Sense of Touch,* p. 140.

Scientific American, December, 1972, review of *Science Experiments You Can Eat,* p. 119.

OTHER

AuthorsDen, http://www.authorsden.com/ (September 12, 2001).

Education World, http://education-world.com/ (May 26, 2000), Lauren P. Gattilia, reviews of *Follow Your Nose, Your Tongue Can Tell,* and *How to Really Fool Yourself.*

Vicki Cobb's Kid's Science Page, http://www.vickicobb.com/ (September 12, 2001), author's Web site.

*   *   *

CRAATS, Rennay 1973-

Personal

Born March 10, 1973, in Regina, Saskatchewan, Canada; daughter of Klaas (a musician) and Arlene (an office manager; maiden name, Schuh) Craats; married Bryce McLean (a draftsman), May 26, 2001. *Education:* University of Calgary, B.A. (communication studies), 1995; Ryerson Polytechnic University, B.A. (journalism), 1998.

Addresses

Home and office—331 Citadel Hills Place, NW, Calgary, Alberta T3G 2X1 Canada. *E-mail*—boomerang-com@shaw.ca.

Career

Freelance writer and editor for various institutions, including the Calgary Board of Education and Calgary Catholic School Board. *Member:* Editor's Association of Canada.

Writings

Canada Through the Decades: The 1970s, Weigl Educational Publishers (Calgary, Canada), 2000.

Canada Through the Decades: The 1940s, Weigl Educational Publishers (Calgary, Canada), 2000.

Canada Through the Decades: The 1910s, Weigl Educational Publishers (Calgary, Canada), 2000.

Living Science: The Science of Fire, Weigl Educational Publishers (Calgary, Canada), 2000.

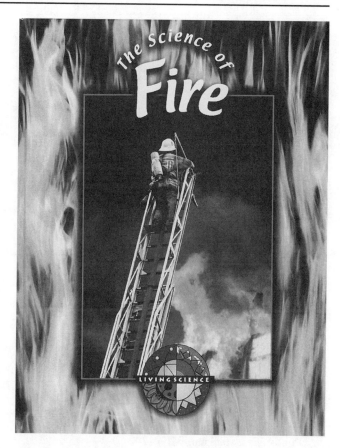

Rennay Craats's "Living Science" series book includes many different aspects on the topic of fire. (Cover photo by Corbis.)

Living Science: The Science of Sound, Weigl Educational Publishers (Calgary Canada), 2000.

Great Canadian Prime Ministers, Weigl Educational Publishers (Calgary Canada), 2000.

20th Century U.S.A.: History of the 1900s, Weigl Educational Publishers (Mankato, MN), 2002.

Canadian Provinces: Quebec, Weigl Educational Publishers (Calgary, Canada), 2002.

Canadian Cities: Toronto, Weigl Educational Publishers (Calgary, Canada), 2002.

E. B. White ("My Favorite Writer" series), Weigl Educational Publishers (Calgary, Canada), 2002.

Roald Dahl ("My Favorite Writer" series), Weigl Educational Publishers (Calgary, Canada), 2002.

Canadian History: Canada in the Global Age, Weigl Educational Publishers (Calgary, Canada), 2003.

American Cities: New Orleans, Weigl Educational Publishers (Calgary, Canada), 2003.

War and Peace: The American Civil War, Weigl Educational Publishers (Calgary, Canada), 2003.

Contributor to periodicals, including *Sposa, Ryerson Review of Journalism, SAIT Alumni Newsletter, Canadian Fire Chief Magazine, Club Managers Quarterly, Avenue, American Health and Fitness, Arch: The University of Calgary Alumni Magazine, Trade and Commerce,* and *Realm.*

"FOR THE LOVE OF" SERIES

For the Love of Baseball, Weigl Educational Publishers (Mankato, MN), 2001.

For the Love of Basketball, Weigl Educational Publishers (Mankato, MN), 2001.

For the Love of Karate, Weigl Educational Publishers (Mankato, MN), 2002.

For the Love of Judo, Weigl Educational Publishers (Mankato, MN), 2002.

For the Love of Skateboarding, Weigl Educational Publishers (Mankato, MN), 2002.

For the Love of Snowboarding, Weigl Educational Publishers (Mankato, MN), 2002.

For the Love of Cycling, Weigl Educational Publishers (Mankato, MN), 2002.

For the Love of In-line Skating, Weigl Educational Publishers (Mankato, MN), 2002.

"AMERICAN STATES" SERIES

American States: Indiana, Weigl Educational Publishers (Mankato, MN), 2001.

American States: Arizona, Weigl Educational Publishers (Mankato, MN), 2002.

American States: Illinois, Weigl Educational Publishers (Mankato, MN), 2002.

American States: New Mexico, Weigl Educational Publishers (Mankato, MN), 2002.

American States: New Hampshire, Weigl Educational Publishers (Mankato, MN), 2002.

American States: Maryland, Weigl Educational Publishers (Mankato, MN), 2002.

American States: Michigan, Weigl Educational Publishers (Mankato, MN), 2002.

Work in Progress

Researching a novel involving Alzheimer's disease and the Holocaust.

Sidelights

Rennay Craats told *SATA:* "Ever since I was a young girl, I have been interested in writing. Through the years, it has been my therapy, my way of expressing myself, and finally my livelihood. For me, the appeal of writing is the opportunity to constantly learn new things and meet new people—things and people I would otherwise not have the chance to encounter. Through words, I can slip into another time or dive into fascinating subjects, and invite readers along for the ride. Most often, I learn as much writing for children as they do reading my work—and it gives me an advantage in trivia games!

"I have always been an avid reader, so writing was an obvious next step. Children's educational writing has given me the opportunity to pass my love for words and reading on to young people, and maybe teach them something in the process. When I'm writing, I try to think of what an elementary or junior high student would want to know and try to fashion my work accordingly. In the history books I write about Canada and the United States, I tried to find strange tidbits of information to draw readers into the material. If they are intrigued

enough to turn the page, I've done my job. Writing is more than what I do—it's who I am, and I look forward to doing it for the rest of my life."

Biographical and Critical Sources

PERIODICALS

School Library Journal, March, 2001, Marilyn Long Graham, review of *The Science of Sound,* p. 232; March, 2002, Steven Engelfried, review of *The Science of Fire,* p. 232.

*   *   *

CURLEY, Marianne 1959-

Personal

Born May 20, 1959, in Windsor, New South Wales, Australia; daughter of Joseph Michael (a caretaker) and Mary Violet (a dressmaker; maiden name, Rizzo) Mizzi; married John Joseph Curley (a horticulturist) on May 24, 1980; children: Amanda, Danielle, Christopher. *Education:* Blacktown Secretarial College, Day Secretarial Certificate, 1975; Coffs Harbour TAFE College, Certificate in Word Processing, 1991, Basic Methods of Instruction Course, 1992; Sydney Open College, Typewriting Teaching Certificate, 1991, Advanced Shorthand Teaching Certificate, 1991. *Religion:* Catholic.

Marianne Curley

Addresses

Home—43 Nariah Crescent, Toormina, New South Wales 2452, Australia. *Agent*—Anthony A. Williams, P.O. Box 1379, Darlinghurst, New South Wales 1300, Australia. *E-mail*—mtcurley@australis.net.

Career

Author. The Electricity Commission of New South Wales, New South Wales, Australia, senior legal stenographer, 1976-81; Benchmark Frames and Trusses, secretary/receptionist, 1991; Skillshare Coffs Harbour, part-time trainer, 1992; part-time teacher, 1992-96; word processing operator, 1997; private computer instructor, 1997. *Member:* Australian Society of Authors, Federation of Australian Writers, New South Wales Writers' Centre.

Writings

Old Magic, Bloomsbury Children's Books (London, England), 2000.
The Named, Bloomsbury Children's Books (London, England), 2002.

Old Magic has been translated into other languages, including Danish, Norwegian, Dutch, and German.

Work in Progress

Currently working on a sequel to *The Named*.

Sidelights

Marianne Curley told *SATA:* "Writing is an extension of my love for reading. When I first started writing, I was surprised at how natural it felt. My first attempt was a romance novel (for adults). And even though it was terrible, I knew writing was what I wanted to do with my life from that moment on. So I worked at learning the craft. I took several writing courses and for a long time struggled to find my 'voice.' I started writing young adult literature after a conversation with my daughters, aged thirteen and fourteen, at the dinner table one night. Both avid readers, they were complaining about not having enough good books to read and urged me to write something for their age group. I tossed around an idea I'd been thinking about and they encouraged me to write it.

"It took many attempts (and many rejections) before my writing was of a publishable standard. While learning to write I taught office studies and computers at the Coffs Harbour TAFE College. I gave myself five years to make a go of my writing, and during my fourth year my first book, *Old Magic,* a young adult fantasy, was sold to a UK publisher, Bloomsbury Children's Books. It was released there in October 2000, and subsequently in Australia in December 2000. *Old Magic* is currently being translated into ten foreign languages. It has been released in Denmark, the Netherlands, Norway, Spain, and in Germany, where it is currently in its third printing in hardback. France, Italy, Finland, Greece and Japan are to follow. . . .

"Writing for young adults is very satisfying. My primary objective is to create a story that will sweep the reader away, to give them time out from everyday life, with all its difficulties, even if it is only for a few hours. To accomplish this, the story needs to be fast-paced, with characters so real they could be the girl or boy next door.

"I do my writing on a computer, typing straight to the screen. It helps having previous typing skills—eighty odd words a minute, so when I'm on a roll, I can type anything up to four of five thousand words a day. Of course this is rare! I would probably manage to average two thousand words a day on the first draft. It's this first draft, which I call the 'skeleton,' that is the bones to the story. It takes about six weeks to complete, then I go back and re-write it all over again, fleshing in the characters now that I know them better.

"The best advice I can give an aspiring writer is to persist and keep working at improving your craft. It helps to be attuned to the market, having a sense of what is going to be popular in the future. Otherwise keep trying and don't be afraid to put your work out there with publishers you might have never thought of, as long as they deal in your kind of literature. To me, success came only after my agent decided to try a market outside my homeland Australia."

Biographical and Critical Sources

PERIODICALS

Publishers Weekly, February 4, 2002, review of *Old Magic,* p. 77.
Times Educational Supplement, February 2, 2001, Fergus Crow, review of *Old Magic*.

D

DeCLEMENTS, Barthe (Faith) 1920-

Personal

Born October 8, 1920, in Seattle, WA; daughter of Ralph Clinton (in sales) and Doris (a homemaker; maiden name, Hutton) DeClements; married Don Macri, 1939 (marriage ended, 1940); married Gordon Greimes, October 24, 1947 (divorced, 1983); children: Nicole Southard, Mari, Christopher, Roger. *Education:* Western Washington College, teaching certificate, 1942; University of Washington, B.A. (English composition), 1942, M.Ed. (educational psychology), 1970. *Politics:* Independent.

Addresses

Home—1511 Russell Rd., Snohomish, WA 98290-5624. *Agent*—William Reiss, John Hawkins and Associates, 71 West 23rd Street, Suite 1600, New York, NY, 10010.

Career

Teacher and author. Medical-Dental Building Psychiatric Clinic, Seattle, WA, psychologist, 1947-48; Seattle school district, Seattle, part-time school psychologist, 1950-55; Kirkland/Edmonds school district, junior high school teacher in Kirkland, 1944-46, teacher of grades 4-8, 1960-67, and 1974-78, high school teacher of English, creative writing, and psychology, 1967-74, guidance counselor in Edmonds, 1977-83; freelance writer, 1979—. Volunteer counselor at Open Door Clinic, 1969-73, 1977. *Member:* Authors Guild, Authors League of America, Society of Children's Book Writers and Illustrators, PEN Center USA-West.

Awards, Honors

Children's Choice Book designation, International Reading Association/Children's Book Council, 1981, for *Nothing's Fair in Fifth Grade,* 1983, for *How Do You Lose Those Ninth Grade Blues?,* 1985, for *Sixth Grade Can Really Kill You,* 1986, for *I Never Asked You to Understand Me,* 1987 (with coauthor Christopher Greimes), for *Double Trouble,* and 1988, for *The Fourth Grade Wizards;* Alabama Young Reader's Choice Award, California Young Reader's Medal, Georgia Children's Book Award, Hawaii's Nene Award, Iowa Children's Choice Award, Kansas Golden Archer Award, Massachusetts Children's Choice Award, Minnesota's Maud Hart Lovelace Award, Nebraska Golden Sower Award, New Mexico Land of Enchantment Children's Book Award, Ohio Buckeye Award, Texas Bluebonnet Award, and Wisconsin Golden Archer Award, all for *Nothing's Fair in Fifth Grade;* Florida Sunshine State Young Reader's Award, Nebraska Golden Sower Award, New Mexico Land of Enchantment Award, Nevada Young Reader's Award, Ohio Buckeye Children's Book Award, and Pacific Northwest Young Reader's Choice Award, all for *Sixth Grade Can Really Kill You;* Pen Center USA West literary award, 1989, for *Five-Finger Discount;* Milner Award, Children's Favorite Author Series, 1992.

Writings

Nothing's Fair in Fifth Grade, Viking Penguin (New York, NY), 1981.

How Do You Lose Those Ninth Grade Blues?, Viking Penguin (New York, NY), 1983.

(With son, Christopher Greimes) *Seventeen and In-Between,* Viking Penguin (New York, NY), 1984.

Sixth Grade Can Really Kill You, Viking Penguin (New York, NY), 1985.

I Never Asked You to Understand Me, Viking Penguin (New York, NY), 1986.

(With son, Christopher Greimes) *Double Trouble,* Viking Penguin (New York, NY), 1987.

No Place for Me, Viking Penguin (New York, NY), 1987.

The Fourth Grade Wizards, Viking Penguin (New York, NY), 1988.

Five-Finger Discount, Delacorte (New York, NY), 1989.

Monkey See, Monkey Do, Delacorte (New York, NY), 1990.

Breaking Out, Delacorte (New York, NY), 1991.

Barthe DeClements

Wake Me at Midnight, Viking Penguin (New York, NY), 1991.

The Bite of the Gold Bug, Viking Penguin (New York, NY), 1992.

The Pickle Song, Viking Penguin (New York, NY), 1993.

The Red Chow, the Doctor, and Me, Scholastic (New York, NY), 1994.

Tough Loser, Viking Penguin (New York, NY), 1994.

Spoiled Rotten, illustrated by Jennifer Plecas, Hyperion (New York, NY), 1996.

Liar, Liar, Marshall Cavendish (New York, NY), 1998.

Contributor to periodicals, including *Washington Educational Journal, Mount Madison Park Mirror,* and *Storyworks.*

Work in Progress

A young-adult novel about a seventeen-year-old baseball pitcher.

Sidelights

Reading any of the popular books by Barthe DeClements is like overhearing a conversation in a middle-school hallway between classes or eavesdropping on a

huddle of girls or boys talking excitedly about the events of their day on the playground during recess. DeClements has been repeatedly praised by reviewers for her realistic, engaging characters and the vivid dialogue that characterizes her writing for young adults. DeClements's novels, which include the multi-award-winning *Nothing's Fair in Fifth Grade, Sixth Grade Can Really Kill You,* and *Five-Finger Discount,* hold a strong appeal for young readers who can hear the echo of their own concerns amid the pages.

Born in 1920, DeClements grew up in Seattle, Washington, the only girl among three children born to her parents, Ralph and Doris DeClements, and memories of her childhood there have been incorporated into much of the writing she has done for children. In an interview, DeClements once reminisced: "There were no girls in the neighborhood. . . . and when I was about twelve a girl moved in and I came running home to my mother to tell her. I was so happy to have somebody to play with besides boys!" She credits the time spent with her two brothers, as well as that spent raising two sons of her own, for her ability to create realistic boy characters and narratives in her books. Indeed, one of her most likeable characters is fifth grader Jerry Johnson, who readers meet in *Five-Finger Discount* as he is trying to deal with the stigma of having a father in prison. In *Monkey See, Monkey Do* DeClements's readers follow Jerry into the sixth grade, as his new challenges include his parents' divorce and accepting the reality that his dad is not going to change his ways. Jerry moves on to junior high school in *Breaking Out,* where he gains a new stepfather, learns to emotionally separate himself from his real father, and establishes a resilient sense of self through an acting role in a locally produced television commercial. Throughout all three books, the conversations between Jerry Johnson, his neighbor and schoolmate Grace, and the many other characters introduced to the reader ring true through DeClements's critically acclaimed ear for dialogue.

As a young girl, DeClements loved to read, so much so that it sometimes got her into trouble. Her parents went out to dinner several nights a week, leaving their daughter in charge of dinner. "My mother would tell me just what I was supposed to do—macaroni and cheese; when to put it in the oven and how to make a salad—and I would invariably be reading a book while she was telling this to me, and then I would finish my book and I would try to remember: 'What did she say? What was I supposed to make for dinner?'" Although it did result in some late meals, her brothers managed to survive and reading persisted in being one of DeClements's main weaknesses, her favorite books including *Lassie Come Home, Black Beauty, Heidi,* and *Pollyanna.* Each of these books incorporated an element of poignancy within its plot, and DeClements has tried to incorporate this same aspect of plotting into her own books, drawing her readers into a broader range of feelings than just "fun and games."

Although she remained an avid reader through her childhood and into college, DeClements never had any childhood aspirations of becoming an author in her own right. Not that she didn't write, of course. "I remember following my mother around in the house and reading a story to her when I must have been about ten years old and my brother was laughing in the living room because I had my hero in a terrible wreck one day and had him well the next day," she once recalled in an interview. In grade school she wrote plays that her class acted out; in high school she wrote stories in study hall when she should have been studying; "of course when the report cards came up that was the end of that," she remembered. "It never occurred to me to show the stories to my English teacher or do anything with them other than write them. I didn't think of myself as a writer. I just wrote stories."

Although DeClements didn't think of herself as a "writer," she was publishing a column in a local newspaper by the time she was sixteen and went on to write for her school humor magazine when she became a student at the University of Washington. In college, she decided to train for a career in teaching because it was felt that she didn't have the skills necessary to work in an office. For one thing, she couldn't spell. "Because I excelled in other subjects, my parents regarded my failures in spelling ... as idiosyncracies of my personali-

ty," DeClements explained, "to be duly noted but not to be fussed over." After a short, unhappy marriage following her first year of college, she went to her family for advice. "I remember sitting on the floor in my parents' living room while they and my older brother discussed my future. 'She spells poorly and she types poorly. She'll never succeed in an office,' I remember my mother saying. Her opinion was respected on this matter because she had taught business school. It was decided that I should return to college to prepare for a career in teaching. Fortunately for the children and me, I found teaching exhilarating."

DeClements's first stint in front of the classroom was at a junior high school in Kirkland, Washington, "a raucous adventure," as she recalled it. Although her rapport with her students was great, her deficiency at spelling continued to haunt her. "When I ... wrote on the blackboard I would keep a dictionary on my desk behind me and I would have to turn and refer to it. One time when I was teaching a new boy came into the room and when they were doing a composition he asked me how to spell a word. There was a very bright boy in the class—his name was Jim Walker—and when the boy asked me how to spell a word one kid piped up, 'Don't

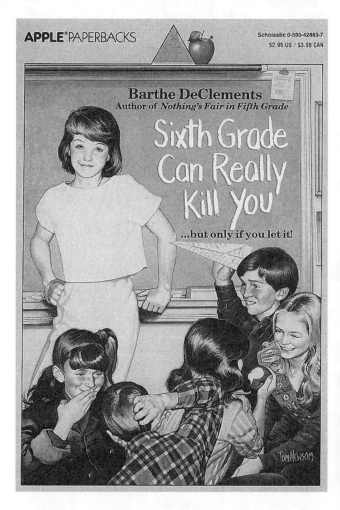

Helen's poor reading skills threaten to keep her from passing sixth grade, so she decides to enter a special education class.

ask her, she don't know, ask Jim Walker—he can spell.'"

DeClements continued teaching while raising her own four children from a second marriage in 1947, and when her youngest was old enough she went back to school and got her master's degree in psychology. From 1977 to 1983 she worked as a guidance counselor in the Edmonds, Washington, school district, a position that would keep her in touch with young people and the issues that confronted them. In 1979 she found the time to begin writing seriously, and her first book, *Nothing's Fair in Fifth Grade,* was published two years later, to great critical acclaim.

Nothing's Fair in Fifth Grade introduces readers to Elsie Edwards, the "new girl in school." Elsie not only has to find new friends in her new town; she also has to overcome the immediate dislike of her classmates caused by her weight problem. Constantly threatened with boarding school by her impatient mother and thwarted by a series of mishaps, Elsie nonetheless finds some new friends who help her learn to control her eating and get along with her schoolmates. Underlying tensions between Elsie and her mother are not resolved, and continue through the book *How Do You Lose Those Ninth Grade Blues?* Elsie continues to suffer from her mother's rejection of her through *Seventeen and In-Between,* when mother and daughter learn to manage their relationship with one another. Through their evolving relationships with other people—Elsie with a boy named Craddoc and Mrs. Edwards with a man named Sam—their interpersonal difficulties are brought out into the open and Elsie's mother begins to take responsibility for her behavior.

The difficulties of middle-school friendships are revisited by DeClements in 1998's *Liar, Liar,* as another "new kid in town" makes an appearance that quickly transforms Gretchen's sixth-grade experience into chaos. Marybelle has a way of getting involved in things and then messing them up by telling lies. When the little lies escalate into accusations of shoplifting, parents get involved and ultimately, thanks to Marybelle's older brother, she is revealed as the source of a string of problems that had pitted friend against friend. "DeClements knows this world well," commented Roger Sutton in a *Horn Book* review of *Liar, Liar,* "and her readers will recognize it as their own." Unlike many children's authors, DeClements shows the true effect of behavior like Marybelle's: while excuses such as a difficult family life may be acknowledged as reasons, as *Booklist* contributor Carolyn Phelan pointed out, *Liar, Liar* illustrates "the painful realization that the damage caused by lies and rumors can't be completely undone."

During her decades working with young people, De-Clements has gained an awareness of the changes in the issues and challenges confronting teens, some of which society—and many parents—would rather not confront. The subject matter she focuses on in her books has occasionally been deemed too controversial for young-adult readers. One of her greatest disappointments as an author was the published version of 1986's *I Never Asked You to Understand Me.* Recalling her original manuscript, DeClements once explained: "When I wrote it I was counseling in an alternative school and I felt very strongly toward the girls who had suffered from sexual abuse. They are very damaged and they blame it on themselves. They think it was something that they did and they think their family is weird and that it only happens to them. I wrote that book for those girls and unfortunately [publishers] weren't ready for it—it went through eight editors and five years. . . . it never got to [those girls] until it was too late."

In addition to the praise from readers and critics, DeClements's own family enthusiastically supported her writing career: Her daughters critique her manuscripts and catch the odd misspelled word that DeClements continues to overlook. The epistolary novel *Seventeen and In-Between* marked a rewarding collaboration between DeClements and her son, Christopher Greimes. "He wrote the letters that Jack wrote in that book. I thought it would be more realistic to have him write them than for me to write them. It was fun and it worked out." Mother and son went on to collaborate on 1987's *Double Trouble,* another novel written as a sequence of letters, this time between twins able to communicate with each other telepathically when events force them to live apart.

DeClements always has words of encouragement for budding writers. "The first thing [kids] need to do is learn to write about what they know about. Sometimes children think they should write about movie-stars or astronauts, and what they need to do is also keep a journal and write about their feelings—not only what happens to them but how they feel about what happens to them—because that's what's going to be precious to them later. I kept a journal when I was seventeen and when I was in my twenties I read it over and I thought, 'Oh, this is so stupid,' and I threw it in the fireplace, and I would have given anything to have that journal when I was writing *Seventeen and In-Between.* . . . I don't think you can stop singers from singing and I don't think you can stop artists from drawing or dancers from dancing. And if they're going to be a writer, they're going to be writing."

Biographical and Critical Sources

BOOKS

Children's Literature Review, Volume 23, Gale (Detroit, MI), 1991.

PERIODICALS

Booklist, August, 1998, Carolyn Phelan, review of *Liar, Liar,* p. 2001.
Horn Book, July-August, 1998, Roger Sutton, review of *Liar, Liar,* p. 485.
New York Times Book Review, November 13, 1988, p. 44.
Publishers Weekly, February 9, 1998, review of *Liar, Liar,* p. 96.

School Library Journal, April, 1989, p. 101; August, 1991, p. 164; July, 1996, William C. Heckman, review of *Spoiled Rotten,* p. 58.

* * *

DEMAS, Corinne 1947-
(Corinne Demas Bliss)

Personal

Born May 14, 1947, in New York, NY; daughter of Nicholas Constantine (a dentist) and Electra (a biology teacher; maiden name, Guizot) Demas; children: Austin Constantine Bliss. *Education:* Tufts University, A.B. (magna cum laude), 1968; Columbia University, M.A. (highest honors), 1969, M.Phil., 1978, Ph.D. (English and comparative literature), 1980. *Hobbies and other interests:* Travel in Greece, music, cross-country skiing.

Addresses

Home—Western Massachusetts. *Office*—Department of English, Mount Holyoke College, South Hadley, MA 10175. *Agent*—McIntosh & Otis, 353 Lexington Ave., New York, NY 10016.

Career

Educator and author. University of Pittsburgh, Pittsburgh, PA, instructor in English, 1970-78; Mount Holyoke College, South Hadley, MA, assistant professor, 1978-84, associate professor, 1984-98, professor of English, 1998—. Lecturer at Chatham College, 1977-78; guest writer at Westfield State College, 1979; visiting writer at Goddard College, 1981; does readings and presentations at schools and colleges. Founder and director, Valley Writers; editor of Author's Registry (literary agency), 1967-68. Fiction editor, *Massachusetts Review. Member:* PEN, Authors Guild, Authors League, Modern Language Association, Society of Children's Book Writers and Illustrators, Bay State Writers Association.

Awards, Honors

National Endowment for the Arts fellowships, 1978, 1983; Andrew W. Mellon Foundation fellowship, 1982; Breakthrough contest winner, University of Missouri Press, 1983, for *Daffodil;* Lawrence Foundation Prize, for story in *Michigan Quarterly;* winner of PEN Syndicated Fiction competition.

Writings

FOR CHILDREN

(And photographer, as Corinne Demas Bliss; with son, Austin Bliss) *That Dog Melly!,* Hastings House (Fern Park, FL), 1981.

(As Corinne Demas Bliss) *Matthew's Meadow,* illustrated by Ted Lewin, Harcourt, Brace (San Diego, CA), 1992.

Over the course of seven summers, a red-tailed hawk teaches Matthew how to appreciate nature in Corinne Demas Bliss's **Matthew's Meadow.** *(Illustrated by Ted Lewin.)*

(As Corinne Demas Bliss) *The Shortest Kid in the World* (book 1 of "Step into Reading" series), illustrated by Nancy Poydar, Random House (New York, NY), 1994.

(As Corinne Demas Bliss) *Electra and the Charlotte Russe,* illustrated by Michael Garland, Boyds Mills Press (Honesdale, PA), 1997.

(As Corinne Demas Bliss) *Snow Day* (book 2 of "Step into Reading" series), illustrated by Nancy Poydar, Random House (New York, NY), 1998.

(As Corinne Demas Bliss) *The Littlest Matryoshka,* illustrated by Katherine Brown, Hyperion (New York, NY), 1999.

Hurricane!, illustrated by Lenice Strohmeier, Marshall Cavendish (New York, NY), 1999.

The Disappearing Island, illustrated by Ted Lewin, Simon & Schuster (New York, NY), 2000.

If Ever I Return Again (middle-grade novel), HarperCollins (New York, NY), 2000.

Nina's Waltz, illustrated by Deborah Lanino, Orchard Books (New York, NY), 2000.

The Perfect Pony (reader), illustrated by Jacqueline Rogers, Random House (New York, NY), 2000.

The Boy Who Was Generous with Salt, illustrated by Michael Hays, Marshall Cavendish (New York, NY), 2001.

The Magic Apple, illustrated by Alexi Natchev, Golden Books (New York, NY), 2001.

OTHER

(As Corinne Demas Bliss) *The Same River Twice* (novel), Atheneum (New York, NY), 1982.

(As Corinne Demas Bliss) *Daffodils; or, The Death of Love: Short Fiction,* University of Missouri Press (Columbia, MO), 1983.

(As Corinne Demas Bliss) *What We Save for Last: Stories,* Milkweed Editions (Minneapolis, MN), 1992.

Eleven Stories High: Growing up in Stuyvesant Town, 1948-1968 (memoir), State University of New York Press (Albany, NY), 2000.

Work represented in anthologies, including *Secrets and Other Stories by Women,* 1979. Contributor of short stories, poems, and reviews to periodicals, including *American Literary Review, Harvard Review, Images,*

Electra attempts to disguise three pastries that were accidentally dropped in **Electra and the Charlotte Russe,** *written by Bliss and illustrated by Michael Garland.*

Mademoiselle, Massachusetts Review, Michigan Review, Pittsburgh Review, Ploughshares, Kansas Quarterly Kenyon Review, Southern Review, Shenandoah, Transatlantic Review, Virginia Quarterly, McCall's, Fiction Monthly, Boston Review, and *Esquire.*

Adaptations

Matthew's Meadow was adapted for the stage by the Regional Touring Company of Western Illinois and produced in 1994.

Sidelights

Although Corinne Demas has written several works of fiction for adults, most of her writing is for younger readers. A professor of English at Mount Holyoke College during the school year, Demas spends her summers on the New England coast. This region and its history have inspired several of her children's books, including the picture books *The Boy Who Was Generous with Salt* and *The Disappearing Island* as well as the middle-grade novel *If Ever I See You Again.* In addition to her book-length works, Demas has published dozens of short stories in magazines and journals, and she also serves as a fiction editor for the *Massachusetts Review.* Prior to 2000 she published under the name Corinne Demas Bliss.

Demas was born in 1947, and grew up in a pleasant, eighteen-square-block, middle-class housing project in New York City called Stuyvesant Town. Her parents were both of Greek heritage: her father was a dentist, while her mother went to work as a high school biology teacher once Corinne reached her teens. In her memoir *Eleven Stories High: Growing up in Stuyvesant Town, 1948-1968,* Demas recalls her youth spent in a world of elevators, concrete sidewalks, pigeons, and subways. She began writing when she was very small, her first book—self-illustrated in crayon—a story about a king, a prince, and a witchlike woman, penned at the age of six in a composition book. After graduating from New York's Hunter High School, she enrolled at Tufts University and graduated magna cum laude in 1968. After obtaining her master's degree in English from Columbia University, Demas entered academia, and accepted a position at Mount Holyoke College in 1978. "The subject of my doctoral dissertation was the short story—an inquiry into how writers make readers respond the way they want them to and a study of what makes certain short stories work," noted Demas, adding that, while she has grown increasingly comfortable with the longer novel format, "I am most naturally a short story writer."

The job of being a college English professor, "writing about literature and teaching it, influences my own writing," Demas once explained to *SATA,* "just as being a writer influences my teaching of literature and writing." Another major influence on her writing was becoming a mother to son Austin. "My children's books have been written for my own child and his friends," she explained, noting that the age level of her books adjusted

as he grew older. "My first published book, *That Dog Melly,* was coauthored with my son, Austin," Demas noted on her Web site. "I had him re-tell me the story [of how Melly ran away and was found] in his own words so that the narrator would sound like a real kid. The illustrations are photographs I took of Austin and our standard poodle, Melly."

Among Demas's picture books for young readers is *Matthew's Meadow,* published in 1992. The ecological story, originally written for young Austin and inspired by the setting near the author's family home, finds nine-year-old Matthew learning to understand the quiet voice of nature through the changes in the meadow and its creatures during the passing seasons. A hawk that appears yearly in this meadow "instructs the boy about his special kinship with life," wrote a *Publishers Weekly* contributor.

Electra and the Charlotte Russe was inspired by a story told to Demas by her mother, the Electra of the story. Taking place in the Bronx during the 1920s, the story finds young Electra sent off to the bakery to purchase some special pastries for her mother to serve at tea. For some reason, the pastries arrive home for tea without the whipped cream that was on them when Electra picked them up. Although the whereabouts of the missing whipped cream is soon confessed by the guilty Electra, the girl's mother deals with the incident with love, and the exotic pastries make it to the tea table despite all. Also featuring a young protagonist and a close-knit, loving family, *Nina's Waltz* brings readers to the modern era, as Nina has high hopes that her father will win the much-needed cash prize at the annual state fiddle championship. When he is stung by wasps before going on stage, shy Nina takes the fiddle and, overcoming her fear of public performance, plays the song her father wrote for her, in a "quiet" story that *School Library Journal* contributor Kathleen Whalin praised as a "hymn to the transforming power of music."

In addition to picture books for young readers, Demas has penned several works of adult fiction as well as a middle-grade novel. Her 2000 historical novel *If Ever I Return Again,* features a twelve-year-old protagonist named Celia Snow who must fight for survival on the high seas in the nineteenth century. Demas's fictional story was inspired by real-life captain's wife Augusta Penniman, who accompanied her husband on several lengthy voyages, sometimes bringing her daughter Bessie. In *If Ever I Return Again,* Celia's father, captain of the whaling ship *Jupiter,* dies during the family's voyage from New Bedford, Massachusetts, to the Pacific islands in 1856. Celia and her mother are then forced to wrest control of the ship from the hands of a greedy first mate and sail for home using Celia's navigation skills. Celia's two-year-long adventure, told through a series of letters to cousin Abigail, is "very effective in portraying Celia's character," noted *Booklist*'s Carolyn Phelan. Calling Celia "courageous and intelligent," a *Publishers Weekly* contributor noted that the effectiveness of Demas's story is the result of "the evolution of the relationship between Celia and her mother, who,"

Jamie thinks she has found just the right horse for herself, but another girl may have first claim in this early reader, **The Perfect Pony.** *(Illustrated by Jacqueline Rogers.)*

though not as adventurous as her daughter, "proves to have hidden strengths." Joining other critics in praise of narrator Celia, *School Library Journal* reviewer Valerie Diamond added that the narrator's "fresh, bright perspective is starkly juxtaposed with the harshness of whaling life and a conniving crew," making *If I Ever Return Again* a realistic portrayal of life at sea in the 1800s.

Another story that takes place on the high seas during the 1800s is Demas's *The Boy Who Was Generous with Salt,* published in 2001. In this picture book, eight-year-old Ned, the son of a Cape Cod fisherman, is unhappy about being at sea on the *Adeline* and working as a cook. Learning about the importance of nutrition among seabound sailors, particularly the importance of things like salt, Ned works hard to prepare his specialties—bean soup, fish chowder, and biscuits—until the lengthy voyage finds him contemplating a meal plan that would have the ship put for home in time for his ninth birthday party. Demas's *The Disappearing Island* also takes place

near the Cape Cod coast and profiles within the story of Carrie and her grandmother the slow deterioration of a fragment of land known as Billingsgate Island.

Demas writes for a while every morning before work. "Sometimes I even eat my breakfast at my desk," she admitted on her Web site. "On days that I'm not teaching, I write all day. For a break I go for a walk with the dog or [my pet miniature] donkey (they both have red raincoats for rainy days) or I dig in the garden." Demas's third pet, a rabbit, prefers to remain indoors even in good weather.

Biographical and Critical Sources

PERIODICALS

Booklist, March 15, 1992, Deborah Abbott, review of *Matthew's Meadow,* p. 1356; March 15, 1999, Stephanie Zvirin, review of *Snow Day,* p. 1336; September 15, 1999, Carolyn Phelan, review of *The Littlest Matryoshka,* p. 258; March 1, 2000, Connie Fletcher, review of *Hurricane!,* p. 1250; April 1, 2000, Carolyn Phelan, review of *If Ever I Return Again,* p. 1477; May 1, 2000, Stephanie Zvirin, review of *Hurricane!,* p. 1677; June 1, 2000, Gillian Engberg, review of *The Disappearing Island,* p. 1907.

Glamour, December, 1982, Nancy Evans, review of *The Same River Twice,* p. 100.

Library Journal, October 1, 1982, review of *The Same River Twice,* p. 1893; May 1, 1992, Ann H. Fisher, review of *What We Save for Last,* p. 121; July, 2000, Patricia A. Beaber, review of *Eleven Stories High: Growing up in Stuyvesant Town, 1948-1968,* p. 107.

Publishers Weekly, August 27, 1982, review of *The Same River Twice,* p. 348; March 16, 1992, review of *What We Save for Last,* p. 74; March 30, 1992, review of *Matthew's Meadow,* p. 105; August 23, 1999, review of *The Littlest Matryoshka,* p. 58; June 19, 2000, review of *If I Ever Return Again,* p. 81; June 19, 2000, review of *The Disappearing Island,* p. 79; July 24, 2000, review of *Eleven Stories High,* p. 80.

School Library Journal, April 15, 1992, review of *That Dog Melly!,* p. 56; August, 1992, Susan Scheps, review of *Matthew's Meadow,* p. 132; October, 1997, Carolyn Jenks, review of *Electra and the Charlotte Russe,* p. 88; March, 1999, Blair Christolon, review of *Snow Day,* p. 164; December, 1999, Denise Anton Wright, review of *The Littlest Matryoshka,* p. 87; April, 2000, Sally R. Dow, review of *Hurricane!,* p. 103; July, 2000, Kate McClelland, review of *The Disappearing Island,* p. 70; August, 2000, Valerie Diamond, review of *If Ever I Return Again,* p. 180; November, 2000, Kathleen Whalin, review of *Nina's Waltz,* p. 113.

OTHER

Corrine Demas Web site, http://www.corinnedemas.com (December 10, 2001).*

DUFFEY, Betsy (Byars) 1953-

Personal

Born February 6, 1953, in Anderson, SC; daughter of Edward Ford (an engineer) and Betsy (a children's book author) Byars; married William Simon Duffey, Jr. (a lawyer); children: Charles, Scott. *Education:* Clemson University, B.S., 1975. *Hobbies and other interests:* Reading, gardening, quilting.

Addresses

Home—4825 Franklin Pond Rd., Atlanta, GA 30342.

Career

Writer. *Member:* Society of Children's Book Writers and Illustrators.

Awards, Honors

Pick of the Lists citation, American Booksellers Association, 1991, and Children's Crown Award, National Christian Schools Association, 1992, both for *A Boy in the Doghouse;* Pick of the Lists citation, American Booksellers Association, 1992, for *Lucky in Left Field;* Pick of the Year citation, Federation of Children's Book Groups, 1992, Sunshine State Young Reader's Award master list finalist, 1993, and West Virginia Children's Book Award master list nominee, 1993-94, all for *The Math Wiz;* Kentucky Bluegrass Award master list nominee, 1993, for *The Gadget War;* Parents' and Children's Choice Award, 1994, for *How to Be Cool in the Third Grade.*

Writings

The Math Wiz, illustrated by Janet Wilson, Viking (New York, NY), 1990.

A Boy in the Doghouse, illustrated by Leslie Morrill, Simon & Schuster (New York, NY), 1991.

The Gadget War, illustrated by Janet Wilson, Viking (New York, NY), 1991.

Lucky in Left Field, illustrated by Leslie Morrill, Simon & Schuster (New York, NY), 1992.

Puppy Love ("Pet Patrol" series), illustrated by Susanna Natti, Viking (New York, NY), 1992.

How to Be Cool in the Third Grade, illustrated by Janet Wilson, Viking (New York, NY), 1993, published as *How to Be Cool in Junior School,* illustrated by J. Douglas, Viking (London, England), 1996.

Lucky on the Loose, illustrated by Leslie Morrill, Simon & Schuster (New York, NY), 1993.

Wild Things ("Pet Patrol" series), illustrated by Susanna Natti, Viking (New York, NY), 1993.

Throw-Away Pets ("Pet Patrol" series), illustrated by Susanna Natti, Viking (New York, NY), 1993.

Lucky Christmas, illustrated by Leslie Morrill, Simon & Schuster (New York, NY), 1994.

Coaster, Viking (New York, NY), 1994.

Utterly Yours, Booker Jones, Viking (New York, NY), 1995, published as *Buster and the Black Hole,* Viking (London, England), 1996.

Hey, New Kid!, illustrated by Ellen Thompson, Viking (New York, NY), 1996.

Camp Knock Knock, illustrated by Fiona Dunbar, Delacorte Press (New York, NY), 1996.

The Camp Knock Knock Mystery, illustrated by Fiona Dunbar, Doubleday (New York, NY), 1997.

Virtual Cody, illustrated by Ellen Thompson, Viking (New York, NY), 1997.

Cody's Secret Admirer, illustrated by Ellen Thompson, Viking (New York, NY), 1998.

Spotlight on Cody, illustrated by Ellen Thompson, Viking (New York, NY), 1998.

Alien for Rent, Delacorte Press (New York, NY), 1999.

Cody Unplugged, illustrated by Ellen Thompson, Viking (New York, NY), 1999.

(With mother, Betsy Byars, and Laurie Myers) *My Dog, My Hero,* illustrated by Loren Long, Holt (New York, NY), 2000.

Fur-Ever Yours, Booker Jones, Viking (New York, NY), 2001.

Adaptations

Audiobooks based on Duffey's books include *Virtual Cody* and *Hey, New Kid!,* both produced by Recorded Books, 2000.

Sidelights

Like her mother, noted children's author Betsy Byars, Betsy Duffey has devoted her career to writing books for young readers. Noting that her mother's work as an author "was part of my childhood," Duffey retains "early memories of watching my mother at the typewriter, of reading her manuscripts, of sharing the excitement of her acceptances and of seeing her manuscripts become books," as she once told *SATA.* Although she did not know it at the time, the same would be true for her; among her popular books for children are *How to Be Cool in the Third Grade, Lucky on the Loose,* and a series of chapter books featuring a likeable third-grader named Cody Michaels who stumbles in and out of adventures in *Spotlight on Cody, Virtual Cody,* and other titles. Praising in particular her "Cody" series, *Horn Book* contributor Marilyn Bousquin noted in a review of *Spotlight on Cody* that "Duffy's subtle sense of humor, coupled with a deep empathy for the highs and lows of an ordinary third grader," give this series value.

Born in 1953 in Anderson, South Carolina, and raised in Morgantown, West Virginia, Duffey grew up surrounded by books and quickly gained a love of reading. Even so, after graduating from high school, she did not go to college for an English or writing degree. Instead, she graduated from Clemson University in 1975 with a bachelor of science degree, then married and began to raise her two sons. "In 1989 some things came together in my life that made me want to write," Duffey once explained to *SATA.* "First, my older son, Charles, who had always loved books, reached the end of first grade and stopped reading. I combed the library searching for the right book for him. All the books I found that he would like were too difficult for him to read. In my mind I knew the book that he needed—a book with the look of a novel, driven with action but with a simple vocabulary and sentence style. I wanted to write a book for him."

Out of this search for the perfect book for her son, Duffey came up with an original idea for a book. "I was teaching a fourth-grade class as a PTA volunteer in my son's school. The class was called Peer Proof and was developed by Rainbow Girls. We taught the kids things like six ways to say no, how to deflect teasing, how to start a conversation. We talked about problems and how to solve them." Among the problems was one common to many students, voiced by a fourth-grade girl and shared by Duffey herself as a child: "'Every time my class goes outside for free time they choose teams for soccer and nobody picks me.'" Duffey recalled the feeling of being unwanted "like it had happened yesterday," and set to work writing the book that would become *The Math Wiz.* "That was the beginning of my career as a writer."

Marty Malone, the main character in *The Math Wiz,* can solve any math problem. As smart as he is, Marty cannot figure out how to get picked to play in team sports, that is, until one of his teachers offers a solution that *Booklist* critic Leone McDermott termed "both hopeful and realistic." "*The Math Wiz* and all the books that followed started with a feeling that I remembered from my childhood," Duffey related to *SATA.* "I take those feelings and give it to a contemporary child and the book begins."

Duffey's *A Boy in the Doghouse* developed the feeling "of having a pet and having to make that pet behave," the author remembered. "I was trying unsuccessfully to housebreak my dog, Chester. My husband, Bill, had never had a dog in his life. He kept saying things like 'What is this puddle on the floor?' 'What happened to the corner of my briefcase?' 'Was that barking I heard last night?' I created the character Lucky based on Chester and all the other dogs that I have had in my life." *A Boy in the Doghouse* pits Lucky, a dog so smart he does not want to be trained, against George, the boy who is supposed to train him, in alternating chapters.

Lucky the dog returns in Duffey's 1992 book *Lucky in Left Field,* inspired, according to the author, by "watching fifteen hours of Little League baseball practices a week one spring. I knew I had two choices—write a baseball book or lose my mind. I started taking a notebook to practices and writing as I sat in the bleachers. I wrote down everything. When the coach said 'Choke up,' I wrote it down. I looked under the bleachers and saw empty popcorn boxes and hot dog wrappers and wrote that down. When someone slid in to home I asked, 'How did it feel?'" Again using alternating dog and boy perspectives on the events of the story, Duffey tells of George and Lucky as they endure a new baseball coach who, among other things, has his players try chewing tobacco. *School Library Journal* contributor

Blair Christolon termed *Lucky in Left Field* "one of Duffey's best efforts to date." The dog and his boy have since returned in *Lucky on the Loose* and *Lucky Christmas.*

Several of Duffey's books have been inspired by her sons. "When Charles attended Young Inventor's Camp I was delighted and proud when he came home with his first invention," Duffey recalled. "My delight turned to horror when I realized that it was a food fight catapult. My horror turned back to delight when I realized what a wonderful story it would make. Three months later *The Gadget War* was finished." In this tale, Duffey centers on the issue of rivalry as two children with a knack for inventing gadgets use their talents against each other until they discover a reason to join forces. Carolyn Phelan, writing in a *Booklist* review, praised the book's "strong sense of the drama and comedy of the third-grade classroom milieu."

When her sons began to protest the fact that they could not wear jeans to school, *How to Be Cool in the Third Grade* was the result. In this story, Robbie York is mortified; his mother still walks him to the bus stop, calls him "Robbie" and not the more mature "Rob", and will not let him wear jeans and a T-shirt like the other kids. As if he did not already have these strikes against him, Robbie accidentally trips and falls into the class bully's lap during a school bus ride, earning himself an embarrassing new nickname. While *Bulletin of the Center for Children's Books* critic Roger Sutton dubbed the book's ending "pat but satisfying," Dot Minzer wrote in *School Library Journal* that "Duffey shows real empathy for her beginning-to-be-independent character."

In another book for elementary school-aged readers, Duffey plays in the realm of science fiction. *Alien for Rent* finds third graders Lexie and friend J. P. in a quandary after an unseen alien named Bork grants Lexie's offhanded wish that the school bully be turned into a big baby in exchange for part of Lexie's lunch. With the fifth-grade bully now reduced to an oversized and untoilet-trained toddler, the two girls have to figure out how to set the world right before the school bell rings at the end of the day. "Newly independent readers will appreciate this lighthearted tale of wishes, aliens, and bully-gets-his-due," according to *Bulletin of the Center for Children's Books* contributor Elaine A. Bearden, while Stephanie Zvirin noted in *Booklist* that *Alien for Rent* is "lots of slapstick fun."

In *Hey, New Kid!,* readers meet third grader Cody Michaels, the reluctant new kid in school, through the pages of large-print chapter books featuring simple vocabularies and engaging characters. Unsuccessful at his efforts to stay home on the first day, Cody braves the introductions to his new class by adopting a new persona: super-smart Super Cody. Unfortunately, both his classmates and his teacher quickly realize that he is no genius, leaving Cody to attempt to make friends as himself. Noting the realistic situation, *Horn Book* contributor Maeve Visser Knoth praised Duffey for her ability to "convey ... the vulnerabilities of her characters" and noted that "Cody is all the more likeable for his foibles." In *Virtual Cody,* the third grader's ego takes a major hit when he discovers that he was named after a family dog, and *Cody's Secret Admirer* finds the ultra-imaginative nine year old flummoxed following the arrival of a super-sentimental Valentine's Day card and fearful that he is being manipulated into an early marriage by his parents.

"The strongest element of Duffey's books is her characters and she's right on target here," noted *School Library Journal* contributor Christina Dorr regarding 1998's *Spotlight on Cody.* In this installment in the ongoing series, Cody becomes discouraged over his lack of ability to participate in the school's end-of-the-year talent show, until his teachers discover he has an artistic bent and he makes signs for all the performers. With school over, summer camp looms, and in *Cody Unplugged* that means weeks away from home with no television and no computer. Instead, Cody and his new friend Arthur tackle a succession of challenges at Camp Bear, including the food, fishing, and the dreaded swimming test. "Duffey develops the story line with a sure and light touch," commented *Booklist* contributor Shelley Townsend-Hudson, adding that readers will be aware that Cody's accomplishments at Camp Bear relate well with his growing self-confidence.

In addition to her "Cody" novels, Duffey has written three books in the "Pet Patrol" series, about children who help animals. In the first installment, *Puppy Love,* Evie and Megan start a new business based on their love of pets, and their first client asks them to find homes for four puppies. A contributor to *Publishers Weekly* praised Duffey's heroines for their "ingenuity, persistence and sincerity," and remarked positively on the realistic, humorous friendship between the two girls. *The Wild Things* involves a mysterious marauder who disrupts a neighborhood's trash cans, leaving it to Evie to discover whether it is a dog or a possum. *Throw-Away Pets* finds the girls and their friends learning about the responsibility of owning a pet when they accidentally discover a temporary shelter for abandoned pets.

In addition to penning books for beginning readers, Duffey has written several more challenging chapter books. In *Coaster* she focuses on twelve-year-old Hartwell, whose dad has divorced his mom and has rarely visited since. Because their only time spent together is riding roller coasters, Hart becomes obsessed with the activity and is helped by his friend Frankie in building one. Only after his homemade coaster, *The Termite,* is discovered to be unsafe during a dangerous ride does Hart begin to separate out his feelings for his dad from his confused ideas about bravery and maturity. In her *Horn Book* review, Elizabeth S. Watson praised *Coaster* as "a realistic coming-of-age novel with a fresh twist," while in *Voice of Youth Advocates,* contributor Jill Western praised Duffey for providing readers with "flashes of humor, insightful glimpses into the struggles of adolescence, and exhilarating descriptions of roller coaster rides."

"It's challenging to write for children today," Duffey once commented to *SATA.* "They are growing up in a different world than I did. They have grown up in the TV age and are used to sophisticated plots and characters. Their books must be on target and realistic. I am always looking for ways to make my books real. No child in my neighborhood is surprised anymore when I say, 'May I try that?' 'How do you do that?' or 'What did you just say? Say it again please, *slowly.*' Ideas are everywhere."

Biographical and Critical Sources

PERIODICALS

Booklist, September 15, 1990, Leone McDermott, review of *The Math Wiz;* October 1, 1991, Carolyn Phelan, review of *The Gadget War,* p. 328; October 1, 1992, Kay Weisman, review of *Puppy Love,* p. 326; February 1, 1993, Stephanie Zvirin, review of *Lucky in Left Field,* p. 984; March 1, 1993, Carolyn Phelan, review of *The Wild Things,* p. 1229; July, 1993, Deborah Abbott, review of *Throw-Away Pets,* p. 1966; September 1, 1993, Stephanie Zvirin, review of *How to Be Cool in the Third Grade,* p. 60; August, 1994, Mary Harris Veeder, review of *Coaster,* p. 2042; June 1, 1997, Stephanie Zvirin, review of *Virtual Cody,* p. 1702; February 1, 1998, Hazel Rochman, review of *Cody's Secret Admirer,* p. 918; October 1, 1998, Chris Sherman, review of *Spotlight on Cody,* p. 330; January 1, 1999, Stephanie Zvirin, review of *Alien for Rent,* p. 876; June 1, 1999, Shelley Townsend-Hudson, review of *Cody Unplugged,* p. 1828; June 1, 2001, Carolyn Phelan, review of *Fur-Ever Yours, Booker Jones,* p. 1882.

Books for Keeps, March, 1995, George Hunt, review of *Puppy Love,* p. 12.

Bulletin of the Center for Children's Books, October, 1993, Roger Sutton, review of *How to Be Cool in the Third Grade,* p. 42; September 15, 1995, Lauren Peterson, review of *Utterly Yours, Booker Jones,* p. 162; June, 1997, Susan S. Verner, review of *Virtual Cody,* p. 355; May, 1998, Deborah Stevenson, review of *Cody's Secret Admirer,* p. 319; February, 1999, Elaine A. Bearden, review of *Alien for Rent,* p. 199.

Horn Book, January-February, 1995, Elizabeth S. Watson, review of *Coaster,* pp. 58-59; November-December, 1995, Maeve Visser Knoth, review of *Utterly Yours, Booker Jones,* p. 740; July, 1996, Maeve Visser Knoth, review of *Hey, New Kid!,* pp. 461-463; July-August, 1997, Marilyn Bousquin, review of *Virtual Cody,* p. 453; November, 1998, review of *Spotlight on Cody,* pp. 726-727; January, 1999, Marilyn Bousquin, review of *Alien for Rent,* p. 58; May, 1999, Marilyn Bousquin, review of *Cody Unplugged,* p. 328.

Junior Bookshelf, December, 1996, review of *How to Be Cool in Junior School,* p. 251.

Junior Literary Guild, October, 1991-March, 1992, p. 30.

Kirkus Reviews, July 15, 1995, review of *Utterly Yours, Booker Jones,* p. 1022; February 15, 1996, review of *Hey, New Kid!,* p. 294; June 15, 1997, review of *The Camp Knock Knock Mystery,* p. 948; December 15, 1998, review of *Alien for Rent,* p. 1796.

Library Journal, February, 1993, Blair Christolon, review of *Lucky in Left Field,* p. 72; September, 1993, Jana R. Fine, review of *Throw-Away Pets,* p. 206.

Publishers Weekly, July 13, 1992, review of *Puppy Love,* p. 56.

School Librarian, February, 1997, Jennifer Taylor, review of *Buster and the Black Hole,* p. 24.

School Library Journal, September, 1991, Maggie McEwen, review of *A Boy in the Doghouse,* p. 232; November, 1991, Blair Christolon, review of *The Gadget War,* p. 116; September, 1992, Carol Kolb Phillips, review of *Puppy Love,* p. 202; February, 1993, Blair Christolon, review of *Lucky in Left Field,* p. 72; April, 1993, Margaret C. Howell, review of *The Wild Things,* p. 96; September, 1993, Dot Minzer, review of *How to Be Cool in the Third Grade,* p. 206; March, 1994, Denise Furgione, review of *Lucky on the Loose,* p. 222; September, 1994, Carol Schene, review of *Coaster,* p. 214; April, 1996, Christina Dorr, review of *Hey, New Kid!,* p. 132; November, 1998, Christina Dorr, review of *Spotlight on Cody,* p. 83; March, 1999, Kate Kohlbeck, review of *Alien for Rent,* pp. 173-174; January, 2001, Pat Leach, review of *My Dog, My Hero,* p. 92; July, 2001, Ashley Larsen, review of *Fur-Ever Yours, Booker Jones,* p. 106.

Voice of Youth Advocates, April, 1995, Jill Western, review of *Coaster,* p. 22.

OTHER

Betsy Duffey Web Site, http://www.betsyduffey.com (April 20, 2002).

E–F

ELLIS, Sarah 1952-

Personal

Born May 19, 1952, in Vancouver, British Columbia, Canada; daughter of Joseph Walter (a clergyman) and Ruth Elizabeth (a nurse; maiden name, Steabner) Ellis. *Education:* University of British Columbia, B.A. (with honors), 1973, M.L.S., 1975; Simmons College, M.A. (children's literature), 1980.

Addresses

Home—4432 Walden St., Vancouver, British Columbia V5V 3S3, Canada. *E-mail*—sarah@nvdpl.north-van.bc.ca.

Career

Toronto Public Library, librarian, about 1975; Vancouver Public Library, Vancouver, British Columbia, children's librarian, 1976-81; North Vancouver District Library, North Vancouver, British Columbia, librarian, 1981—. Writer-in-residence, Massey College, University of Toronto, 1999. Speaker at schools, colleges, conferences, and workshops. *Member:* Canadian Society of Children's Authors, Illustrators, and Performers, Writers Union of Canada, Vancouver Society of Story-telling.

Awards, Honors

Sheila A. Egoff awards, 1987, for *The Baby Project,* and 1997, for *Back of Beyond;* Governor-General's Award for Children's Literature, 1991, for *Pick-up Sticks;* Mr. Christie's Book Award, and Violet Downy Award, I.O.D.E., both 1994, both for *Out of the Blue;* Vicky Metcalf Award, Canadian Authors' Association, 1995, for body of work.

Sarah Ellis

Writings

The Baby Project, Groundwood Books (Toronto, Ontario, Canada), 1986, published as *A Family Project,* Macmillan (New York, NY), 1988.

Claire helps the bus driver by announcing stops all the way to the last one—home—in Next Stop!, *Ellis's picture book for very young readers. (Illustrated by Ruth Ohi.)*

Next-Door Neighbours, Groundwood Books (Toronto, Ontario, Canada), 1989, published as *Next-Door Neighbors,* Macmillan (New York, NY), 1990.

Putting up with Mitchell, illustrated by Barbara Wood, Brighouse Press, 1989.

Pick-up Sticks, Groundwood Books (Toronto, Ontario, Canada), 1991, Macmillan (New York, NY), 1992.

Out of the Blue, Groundwood Books (Toronto, Ontario, Canada), 1994, Simon & Schuster (New York, NY), 1995.

Back of Beyond: Stories of the Supernatural, Groundwood Books (Toronto, Ontario, Canada), 1996, Margaret K. McElderry Books (New York, NY), 1997.

The Young Writer's Companion, Douglas & McIntyre (Toronto, Ontario, Canada), 1999.

Next Stop! (picture book), illustrated by Ruth Ohi, Fitzhenry & Whiteside (Niagara Falls, NY), 2000.

From Reader to Writer: Teaching Writing through Classic Children's Books, Groundwood Press (Toronto, Ontario, Canada), 2000.

A Prairie as Wide as the Sea: The Immigrant Diary of Ivy Weatherall, Scholastic Canada (Markham, Ontario, Canada), 2001.

Big Ben, illustrated by Kim LaFave, Groundwood Press (Toronto, Ontario, Canada), 2001.

Also author of column "News from the North," published in *Horn Book Magazine,* 1984-98. Humor editor for *The Looking Glass* (Internet magazine).

Sidelights

Writer, columnist, and librarian Sarah Ellis has become one of the best known children's authors in her native Canada with titles such as *The Baby Project, Pick-up Sticks,* and *Back of Beyond: Stories of the Supernatural.* With *The Baby Project,* Ellis created "one of the most appealing and moving family stories to come along in ages," according to *Horn Book Magazine* contributor Hanna B. Zeiger, and her subsequent novels have received numerous awards. In addition to young adult novels, Ellis has also written for younger children and has authored several books about the craft of writing. Praised by *Booklist* contributor Hazel Rochman as "one of the best children's literature critics," Ellis "writes without condescension or pedantry.... Her prose is a delight: plain, witty, practical, wise."

Ellis was born in Vancouver, British Columbia, Canada, in 1952, the youngest of three children in her family. As she once noted, "[My] joy in embroidering the truth probably comes from my own childhood. My father was a rich mine of anecdotes and jokes. He knew more variations on the 'once there were three men in a rowboat' joke than anyone I've encountered since. My mother was always willing to stop what she was doing to tell me about growing up on the prairies, stories of making doughnuts for the harvesters or how Aunt Florence threw eggs at the horses. I have one brother who collects tales of the absurd and another who is a born exaggerator. As youngest in the family I had to become a good storyteller just to hold my own at the dinner table."

Reading and tale-telling were important in Ellis's family while she was growing up. Books were also always close at hand. "The first books I remember were a set of little yellow and black paper-bound fairy tales, sent by Great-Aunt Lou in a Christmas parcel from England. My favorite was *The Wolf and the Seven Little Kids,*" she said. "I found the idea of hiding in a grandfather clock very comforting. Read-alouds in our house were picked to appeal to my older brothers, and that is how I first heard *Tom Sawyer,* in an edition with lovely pictures by Louis Slobodkin. (Later, in memory of those pictures, I gave one of my characters the last name of Slobodkin. Writers get to play these games.)

"When I got to school I discovered that you were allowed to take home one book a day from the library. So I did, every day. If it was raining (and it nearly always was in rainy Vancouver) the librarian would wrap the book in brown paper. It was like carrying home a present.

"Some of the books I read are still around—the 'Little House' books, *The Secret Garden, Half Magic.* I had *Peter Pan* read to me during a long stay in the hospital. I received *The Wizard of Oz* for Christmas when I was eight, and I read it all on Christmas afternoon. One summer I found a damp old copy of *Little Women* in the holiday cabin and for three days I lay on a top bunk,

reading and weeping and happy, while the adults said, 'Wouldn't you like to go outside in the sun and play?'"

After graduating from high school, Ellis enrolled at the University of British Columbia, then went on to earn her degree in library science. After working for several years as children's librarian in North Vancouver, she traveled to Boston and earned an advanced degree in children's literature from Simmons College. While studying this curriculum as an enhancement to her work as a librarian, Ellis also did some of her first writing for children. However, it would be four more years before she would seriously undertake writing a children's book. In 1984 she took a leave from her job at the library and wrote, first articles, then short fiction, and finally a picture book. Although the picture book was rejected when she submitted it to a publisher, the publisher encouraged her to continue her efforts. Her next undertaking became *The Baby Project,* Ellis's first published work and the winner of the Sheila K. Egoff Award in 1987.

The Baby Project—published in the United States as *A Family Project*—is the story of how a young girl and her family deal with the expectation and ultimate loss of a new baby. Eleven-year-old Jessica eagerly awaits her new sister, and even prepares a school project around the expected arrival. After the baby dies of crib death, Jessica must deal not only with her own feelings, but her family's grief as well. Ellis creates a realistic and moving picture of a family in crisis, according to many critics. "She successfully focuses on the details of change, and in so doing creates an honest portrayal of family life," David Gale wrote in *School Library Journal.* The result, Gale added, is "a credible depiction of important family events, in turn funny and sad."

Much of the success of *The Baby Project* is due to the lifelike characters of Jessica and her family. Her parents and brothers are portrayed as quirky, lovable people with a sense of humor. And "although Jessica's point of view is consistently maintained, each complex character develops in a different way," Betsy Hearne observed in *Bulletin of the Center for Children's Books.* Overall, she added, "the cast is subtly portrayed." *Voice of Youth Advocates* contributor Mary Hedge also found the characters believable, and praised "Jessica's courageous and cooperative attitude" in particular as "inspiring."

Ellis's second novel, *Next-Door Neighbors,* is also distinguished by "plausible characters in real life situations," according to Maria B. Salvadore in a review for *School Library Journal.* The story takes place in 1957, when Peggy, the daughter of a minister, has just moved from the country to the city with her family. There she slowly makes friends with George, the son of a refugee, and with the Chinese gardener of a wealthy, prejudiced neighbor. In telling the story of how Peggy learns about racism and responsibility, Ellis "has a deft descriptive touch, a way with a quirky phrase, and a convincing child's-eye view of hypocritical adults," Joan McGrath commented in *Quill and Quire.* The author "etches personalities that are likable amid their strengths and weaknesses and creates family dynamics that fit smoothly and believably into the plot," Barbara Elleman likewise wrote in *Booklist,* making her "ever in touch with her theme, her characters, her plot, and her audience."

Ellis's third novel, *Pick-up Sticks,* was inspired by a radio interview she heard in which a homeless woman expressed her fear and frustration at not being able to care for her family. In the story, thirteen-year-old Polly must leave her single mom and go live with a financially secure uncle while her mother searches for proper housing in between holding down a job. In her new circumstances, Polly is confronted with the life she wished she could have had: a stable, comfortable home, in a nice neighborhood, where opportunities for friends and after-school activities are provided. Through her spoiled cousin and her new friends, she comes to learn that people of all walks of life experience discontent of some type, and that even her financially impoverished life with her mom is rich in many things.

In a change of pace, Ellis incorporates elements of fantasy into her 1997 book *Back of Beyond,* which contains twelve stories written for older teens. Although her stories are based on traditional British folk tales, Ellis garbs them in modern dress, with the Internet, Mr. Potato Head, cults and gangs, and chat rooms figuring prominently. As John Burns noted in an article in *Canadian Materials,* in *Back of Beyond* "mundane and magical worlds overlap. Ellis's protagonists have one foot in childhood and the other in adulthood; their transitional role means that anything can happen, and does." Praising the narrative voice as, by turns "funny, cheeky, or probing," *Horn Book* contributor Marilyn Bousquin added that *Back of Beyond* is about "contemporary kids with ... ordinary problems [who] realize new dimensions of themselves through their bone-chilling, sometimes heartwarming encounters with the other-world."

Picture books by Ellis include *Next Stop!,* about a young girl named Claire and her weekly Saturday trip on the town bus. During her trip, the outgoing and imaginative Claire helps the driver, calling out the stops one by one, and greeting other regular riders. Ellis's text evokes the soothing regularity of a daily bus route; as *School Library Journal* contributor Steven Engelfried noted, "the repetitive pattern of the text suits the stop, start rhythm of a bus ride." In *Big Ben,* a little brother's frustration over being too little to do all the things older siblings Joe and Robin can is intensified by report-card day—"Ben is a little kid in preschool. There are no subjects in pre-school"—until he gets a homemade report card of his own in which Joe and Robin show how good he is at being a little brother. Joe and Robin's "affirmation is meaningful but not patronizing, and their delight in the remedy is as apparent as Ben's," noted a *Horn Book* reviewer.

Ellis devotes seven hours a day to her writing, and each of her young-adult novels takes about a year to complete. "When I was young I never once thought of becoming a writer," Ellis once noted. "Now, when I'm digging in the vegetable patch and I realize that I'm making up phrases for my gardening journal, or when I'm traveling and I find myself composing postcards at every new place, I wonder how I could ever not be a writer. Maybe I do want to record the events of my ordinary life, after all." To aid other budding writers, she has published *The Young Writer's Companion,* which contains a host of suggestions about starting a clipping file and a writing notebook, and also contains a number of exercises for writers-to-be.

Biographical and Critical Sources

BOOKS

Children's Literature Review, Vol. 42, Gale (Detroit, MI), 1997.
St. James Guide to Young Adult Writers, 2nd edition, St. James Press (Detroit, MI), 1999.
Seventh Book of Junior Authors and Illustrators, H. W. Wilson (Bronx, NY), 1996.

PERIODICALS

Booklist, March 1, 1990, Barbara Elleman, review of *Next-Door Neighbors,* p. 1340; January 1, 1998, Chris Sherman, review of *Back of Beyond,* p. 794; October 15, 2000, Hazel Rochman, review of *From Reader to Writer: Teaching Writing through Classic Children's Books,* p. 449; December 1, 2000, Hazel Rochman, review of *Next Stop!,* p. 718.
Bulletin of the Center for Children's Books, April, 1988, Betsy Hearne, review of *A Family Project,* p. 154.
Canadian Materials, March 28, 1997, John Burns, "Sarah Ellis."
Horn Book Magazine, May-June, 1988, Hanna B. Zeiger, review of *A Family Project,* p. 350; November-December, 1997, Marilyn Bousquin, review of *Back of Beyond,* p. 680; May, 2001, Cathryn Mercer, review of *From Reader to Writer,* p. 289; March-April, 2002, review of *Big Ben.*
National Post, November 3, 2000, Elizabeth MacCallum, review of *Next Stop!,* p. B9.
Quill and Quire, September, 1989, Joan McGrath, review of *Next-Door Neighbors,* p. 23; December, 2001, Joanne Findon, review of *Big Ben.*
School Library Journal, March, 1988, David Gale, review of *A Family Project,* p. 188; March, 1990, Maria B. Salvadore, review of *Next-Door Neighbors,* p. 217; January, 2001, Steven Engelfried, review of *Next Stop!,* p. 93; September, 2001, Mary Lankford, review of *From Reader to Writer,* p. 262.
Voice of Youth Advocates, June, 1988, Mary Hedge, review of *A Family Project,* p. 85.

OTHER

Canadian Children's Book Centre Web site, http://collections.ic.gc.ca/ (November 29, 2001), "Sarah Ellis."
Friends of the CCBC Web site, http://www.education. wic.edu/ccbc/friends/ (1999), Tana Elia, "Update from the North: An Interview with Sarah Ellis."

FRASCONI, Antonio 1919-

Personal

Born April 28, 1919, in Buenos Aires, Argentina; immigrated to the United States, 1945; son of Franco (a chef) and Armida (a restauranteur; maiden name, Carbonai) Frasconi; married Leona Pierce (an artist), July 18, 1951; children: Pablo, Miguel. *Education:* Attended Circulo de Bellas Artes (Montevideo, Uruguay); studied at Art Students League, New York, NY, 1945-46; studied mural painting at New School for Social Research (now New School University), 1947-48.

Addresses

Home—26 Dock Rd., South Norwalk, CT 06854. *Office*—Visual Arts Dept., State University of New York at Purchase, Purchase, NY 10577. *Agent*—Terry Dintenfass, Inc. Gallery, 50 West 57th St., New York, NY 10019; Weyhe Gallery, 794 Lexington Ave., New York, NY 10021; and Jane Haslem Gallery, 406 7th St. N.W., Washington, DC 20004.

Career

Graphic artist and illustrator. *Marcha* and *La Linea Maginot* (weeklies), Montevideo, Uruguay, political cartoonist, 1940; New School for Social Research, New York, NY, member of art faculty, 1951-57; State University of New York, College at Purchase, adjunct associate professor, 1973-77, associate professor, 1977-79; professor of visual arts, beginning 1979. Instructor at Vassar College, Brooklyn Museum, California State College at Hayward, University of California at Berkeley, and Carnegie-Mellon University; artist-in-residence, Yaddo, 1954, University of Hawaii, Honolulu, 1964, Dartmouth College, 1984, and Arizona State University, 1985; lecturer. Member of Mayor's Committee for Art in Public Places, Norwalk, CT, 1978, and of Arts Review Committee, Westchester County, NY, 1980. *Exhibitions:* Exhibitor at galleries, museums, and universities throughout the world, including Whitney Museum of American Art; Museum of Modern Art; Weyhe Gallery, New York, NY; Brooklyn Museum of Arts and Sciences; San Francisco Museum of Art; Baltimore Museum of Art; Cleveland Museum of Art; Los Angeles County Museum; Detroit Institute of Arts; Smithsonian Institute; Minneapolis Institute of Arts; Atlanta Art Institute; Carnegie College of Fine Arts; Penelope Galeria d'Arte, Rome; Museo de Arte Moderno, Cali, Colombia; Museum of Art, Fribourg, Switzerland; American Institute of Graphic Arts; National Academy of Design, New York; National Gallery of Art, Washington, DC; Pratt Graphic Center, NY; Taipei Museum of Fine Arts, Taiwan, China; Parson's School Art Gallery; and Museum of Contemporary Arts. Traveling exhibit "The Books of Antonio Frasconi" toured U.S. museums and college campuses, 1992-93. Work housed in permanent collections at Museum of Fine Arts, Boston; Fogg Art Museum, Harvard University, Cambridge; Bibliothèque Nationale, Paris, France; Library of Congress, Washington, DC; Museum of Modern Art;

Metropolitan Museum of Art; Art Institute of Chicago; San Diego Museum of Art; Brooklyn Museum; St. Louis Museum; Casa Americas, Havana, Cuba; Museo Nacional de Bellas Artes, Montevideo, Uruguay; Museo Municipal Juan M. Blanes, Montevideo; Newark Museum; Philadelphia Museum of Art; Honolulu Academy of Arts; Akron Art Institute, OH; University of Notre Dame; Joslyn Art Museum, Omaha, NE; Graphic Arts Collection, Princeton University; Seattle Art Museum; University of Puerto Rico; Cincinnati Art Museum; J. B. Speed Art Museum, Louisville, KY; New York Public Library; Wadsworth Atheneum, Hartford, CT; Baltimore Museum of Art; Arts Council of Great Britain, London; National Portrait Gallery, Washington, DC; and Grunwald Center for the Graphic Arts, University of California, Los Angeles.

Awards, Honors

Purchase prizes, Brooklyn Museum, 1946, University of Nebraska, 1951, and American Academy and the Institute of Arts and Letters, 1986; Philadelphia Print Club Prize, 1951; Guggenheim Inter-American Fellowship in graphic arts, 1952; Erickson Award, Society of American Graphic Artists, 1952; Yaddo scholarship, 1952; Joseph Pennell Memorial Medal, Pennsylvania Academy of the Fine Arts, 1953; National Institute of Arts and Letters grant, 1954; First Prize for Book Illustration, Limited Editions Club/Society of American Graphic Artists, 1956; Grand Prix, Venice Film Festival, 1960, for *The Neighboring Shore;* Tamarind Lithography Workshop grant, 1962; winner of competition to design postage stamp honoring National Academy of Science, 1963; Joseph H. Hirshorn Foundation Prize, Society of American Graphic Artists, 1963; W. H. Walker Prize, Philadelphia Print Club, 1964; Le Prix du President du Comité National de la Region de la Moravie at the Biennale d'Art Graphique, Brno, Czechoslovakia, 1966; Salon Nacional de Bellas Artes prize, Montevideo, 1967; Gran Premio, Exposition de la Habana, Cuba, 1968; named National Academician by the National Academy of Design, NY, 1969; commissioned by the Metropolitan Museum of Art, NY, for a series of Christmas ornaments "Snow Flakes," 1972; Connecticut Commission on the Arts grant, 1974; prize of Ninth International Biennial of Arts, Tokyo, Japan, 1975; Xerox Corporation grant, 1978, for color copier experimentation; Cannon Prize, National Academy of Design, NY, 1979; Ralph Fabri Prize, National Academy of Design, 1983; Chancellor's Award, State University of New York, 1983, for excellence in teaching; Bienal de la Habana-Comision Nacional Cubana de la UNESCO award, 1984; Meissner Prize, National Academy of Design, 1985; named Distinguished Teaching Professor, State University of New York, Purchase, 1986.

Fifty Best Books of the Year citations, American Institute of Graphic Arts, 1955, for *Twelve Fables of Aesop,* 1958, for *Birds from My Homeland,* 1959, for *The Face of Edgar Allan Poe,* 1964, for *Known Fables,* and 1965, for *The Cantilever Rainbow;* Best Illustrated Books of the Year citations, *New York Times,* 1955, for

See and Say, 1958, for *The House That Jack Built,* 1961, for *The Snow and the Sun,* and 1985, for *Monkey Puzzle and Other Poems;* American Institute of Graphic Arts Children's Books citations, 1958-60, for *The House That Jack Built,* and 1970, for *Unstill Life* and *Overhead the Sun;* Caldecott honor book citation, 1959, for *The House That Jack Built;* American Institute of Graphic Arts Children's Book Show, 1973-74, for *Crickets and Frogs,* and 1985, for *Monkey Puzzle and Other Poems;* Child Study Association's Children's Books of the Year citation, 1974, for *The Elephant and His Secret;* American Library Association Notable Book citations, for *See and Say, The House That Jack Built, The Snow and the Sun/La nieve y el sol,* and *Overhead the Sun; Horn Book* honor list citation, for *The Snow and the Sun/ La nieve y el sol.*

Writings

SELF-ILLUSTRATED

See and Say: A Picture Book in Four Languages, Harcourt (New York, NY), 1955.

The House That Jack Built: A Picture Book in Two Languages, Harcourt (New York, NY), 1958.

The Snow and the Sun/La nieve y el sol: A South American Folk Rhyme in Two Languages, Harcourt (New York, NY), 1961.

A Sunday in Monterey, Harcourt (New York, NY), 1964.

See Again, Say Again: A Picture Book in Four Languages, Harcourt (New York, NY), 1964.

Kaleidoscope in Woodcuts, Harcourt (New York, NY), 1968.

(Editor) Walt Whitman, *Overhead the Sun: Lines from Walt Whitman,* Farrar, Straus (New York, NY), 1969.

(Editor) Herman Melville, *On the Slain Collegians: Selections from Poems,* Farrar, Straus (New York, NY), 1971.

Antonio Frasconi's World, Macmillan (New York, NY), 1974.

Frasconi against the Grain: The Woodcuts of Antonio Frasconi, introduction by Nat Hentoff, Macmillan (New York, NY), 1974.

ILLUSTRATOR

Glenway Wescott, reteller, *Twelve Fables of Aesop,* Museum of Modern Art (New York, NY), 1954, revised edition, 1964.

Jorge Luis Borges, *Dreamtigers,* University of Texas Press (Austin, TX), 1964.

Ruth Krauss, *The Cantilever Rainbow,* Pantheon (New York, NY), 1965.

Pablo Neruda, *Bestiary/Bestiario* (verse), translated by Elsa Neuberger, Harcourt (New York, NY), 1965.

Louis Untermeyer, editor, *Love Lyrics,* Odyssey, 1965.

Mario Benedetti, editor, *Unstill Life: An Introduction to the Spanish Poetry of Latin America,* Harcourt (New York, NY), 1969.

Isaac Bashevis Singer, *Elijah the Slave: A Hebrew Legend Retold,* Farrar, Straus (New York, NY), 1970.

Gabriela Mistral, *Selected Poems of Gabriela Mistral,* Johns Hopkins University Press (Baltimore, MD), 1970.

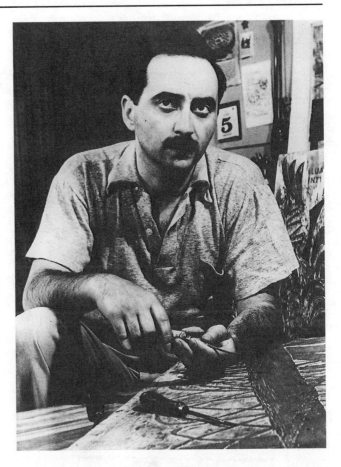

Antonio Frasconi

Gabriela Mistral, *Crickets and Frogs: A Fable in Spanish and English,* translated by Doris Dana, Atheneum (New York, NY), 1972.

Gabriela Mistral, *The Elephant and His Secret,* translated by Doris Dana, Atheneum (New York, NY), 1974.

Myra Cohn Livingston, editor, *One Little Room, an Everywhere: Poems of Love,* Atheneum (New York, NY), 1975.

Penelope Farmer, compiler, *Beginnings: Creation Myths of the World,* Chatto & Windus (London, England), 1978, Atheneum (New York, NY), 1979.

Norma Faber, *How the Left-behind Beasts Built Ararat,* Walker (New York, NY), 1978.

Jan Wahl, *The Little Blind Goat,* Stemmer House (Owing Mills, MD), 1981.

Merce Rodereda, *The Salamander,* Red Ozier Press, 1982.

Isaac Bashevis Singer, *Yentl the Yeshiva Boy,* translated by Marion Magid and Elizabeth Pollet, Farrar Straus (New York, NY), 1983.

Myra Cohn Livingston, *Monkey Puzzle and Other Poems,* Atheneum (New York, NY), 1984.

Muso Soseki, *Sun at Midnight* (poems), translated from Japanese by W. S. Merwin, Nadja, 1986.

Carlos Oquendo de Amat, *Five Meters of Poems,* Turkey Press, 1986.

Myra Cohn Livingston, *If the Owl Calls Again: A Collection of Owl Poems,* Macmillan (New York, NY), 1990.

Valerie Worth, *At Christmastime* (poetry), HarperCollins (New York, NY), 1992.

Juan Ramón Jiménez, *Platero y yo = Platero and I,* adapted and translated by Myra Cohn Livingston and Joseph F. Domínguez, Clarion (New York, NY), 1994.

Martha Robinson, *The Zoo at Night,* Margaret K. McElderry (New York, NY), 1995.

Barbara Wersba, *The Wings of Courage,* Braziller (New York, NY), 1998.

LIMITED EDITIONS; ILLUSTRATED WITH WOODCUTS

Aesop, *Some Well-Known Fables,* privately printed, 1950.

A Book of Vegetable Plants, privately printed, 1951.

Foothill Dairy, privately printed, 1951-52.

The World upside Down, privately printed, 1952.

The Fulton Fish Market, privately printed, 1953.

Federico Garcia Lorca, *Dos Poemas de Federico Garcia Lorca: Romance de la luna, luna; Romance de la guardia civil española,* privately printed, 1953.

Outdoors, privately printed, 1953.

Plants, Ants, and Other Insects, privately printed, 1953.

Santa Barbara, privately printed, 1953.

The Acrobats, privately printed, 1954.

THE WINGS OF COURAGE

By George Sand · Retold by Barbara Wersba

WOODCUTS BY ANTONIO FRASCONI

Frasconi's woodcuts illustrate the power of the individual and the beauty of nature in the timeless story of a lame French boy who lives among the seabirds and grows his own wings of courage.

El camino real, privately printed, 1954.

Lettuce Country, privately printed, 1954.

Printing with Dough, privately printed, 1954.

A Book of Many Suns, privately printed, 1955.

Fire Island Dunes, privately printed, 1955.

High Tide, privately printed, 1955.

Abraham Lincoln, *The Fundamental Creed of Abraham Lincoln: A Selection from His Writings and Speeches,* edited by Earl Schenk Miers, privately printed, 1956.

An Old Czech Carol, Murray Printers, 1956.

Woodcuts 1957, Spiral Press (New York, NY), 1957, published as *Woodcuts: With Comments by Antonio Frasconi,* Weyhe Gallery (New York, NY), 1957.

Homage to Thelonious Monk, privately printed, 1958.

Birds from My Homeland: Ten Hand-Colored Woodcuts with Notes from W. H. Hudson's "Birds of La Plata", Roodenko, 1958.

A Calendar for 1960, privately printed, 1959.

The Face of Edgar Allan Poe: With a Note on Poe by Charles Baudelaire, Roodenko, 1959.

Walt Whitman, *A Whitman Portrait,* Spiral Press (New York, NY), 1960.

Six Spanish Nursery Rhymes, privately printed, 1960.

American Wild Flowers, privately printed, 1961.

Berthold Brecht, *Das Lied vom Sa-mann,* Spiral Press (New York, NY), 1961.

Oda a Lorca, privately printed, 1962.

Known Fables, Spiral Press (New York, NY), 1964.

Six South American Folk Rhymes about Love: With Woodcuts, Spiral Press (New York, NY), 1964.

An Appointment Calendar for 1966, Baltimore Museum of Art (Baltimore, MD), 1965.

Henry David Thoreau, *A Vision of Thoreau,* Spiral Press (New York, NY), 1965.

Federico Garcia Lorca, *Llanto por Ignacio Sanches Mejias,* privately printed, 1967.

The Portrait, privately printed, 1967.

Quattro facciate, privately printed, 1967.

Viet Nam!, privately printed, 1967.

Benedetti, selector, *19 Poems de Hispano America,* privately printed, 1969.

Vedute di Venezia, Spiral Press (New York, NY), 1969.

Fourteen Americans, privately printed, 1974.

Venice Remembered, privately printed, 1974.

A View of Tuscany, privately printed, 1974.

Cantos a Garcia Lorca, privately printed, 1974-75.

The Seasons on the Sound, privately printed, 1974-75.

The Sound, privately printed, 1974-75.

Frasconi's Composite Side Show, privately printed, 1978.

Frasconi's Night Creatures, privately printed, 1978.

The Tides at Village Creek, privately printed, 1979.

Monet Gardens, Giverny, privately printed, 1980.

The USA from the San Francisco-Oakland Bay Bridge, California to the George Washington Bridge, New York, Every Six Miles, privately printed, 1982.

Ten Views of Rome, privately printed, 1983.

Theodore Low de Vinne, *The First Editor: Aldus Pius Manutius,* privately printed, 1983.

Los Desaparecidos, privately printed, 1984.

Italo Calvino, *Prima che tu dica "Pronto,"* translated by William Weaver, Plain Wrapper Press, 1985.

Travels through Tuscany, privately printed, 1985.

Views of Venice by Day and Night, privately printed, 1986.

Ralph Waldo Emerson, *Friendship: An Emerson Homage in Remembrance of Joseph Blumenthal,* Kelly-Winterton Press (New York, NY), 1993.

OTHER

The Neighboring Shore (film), Sextant, 1960.
The Woodcuts of Antonio Frasconi (film), American Federation of Arts, 1985.
Los Desaparecidos (film), Darino Films, 1989.

Contributor of illustrations to *New Republic* and *Fortune.*

Adaptations

See and Say (sound filmstrip), Weston Woods, 1964; *Los Desaparecidos,* Darino Films, 1989. *Crickets and Frogs* is available in Braille.

Sidelights

Dubbed a "champion of the common man, enemy of elitism, printmaker, and teacher" by *Americas* essayist Caleb Bach, Argentina-born artist Antonio Frasconi has long been recognized as one of the foremost woodcut artists living and working in the United States. Frasconi's work, which is well represented in the nation's museums and galleries and has toured the United States during 1992 and 1993, has also found a wide audience through book and magazine illustrations, book cover art, and even Christmas cards. Using simple tools and an ancient technique, Frasconi has created a diverse body of work that addresses politics, American and European literature, American scenes, and lighthearted pictures for children. "If artists want to be a part of society, they have to be aware of society," Frasconi explained to Jane Sterrett in *Print Review.* "They should not only paint for it, they should *think* about it. One reason the graphic-art media have been so influential is that they can reach more people. The role of art is not just to end up on a museum wall. How is it possible to ask people who work all day long to go to a museum and see masterpieces? It's a big demand. An artist should be aware that there are people out there."

Frasconi's own social awareness stems from his multicultural background and travels. The son of Italian parents who immigrated to South America during World War I, he was born in Buenos Aires, Argentina in 1919. Within weeks of his birth the family moved on to Uruguay. Frasconi grew up in Montevideo, where his mother managed a restaurant and took in work as a seamstress in order to support Antonio and his two sisters while his father remained employed only intermittently. Speaking heavily accented Spanish in public and Italian at home, Frasconi felt like an outsider in his new home. "I was what I guess Americans would call a loner," the artist remembered in his introduction to *Frasconi against the Grain: The Woodcuts of Antonio Frasconi.* His refuge became art; he loved to draw and to decorate his homework, and some of his teachers encouraged him to develop his talent. His mother, on the other hand, discouraged him from pursuing a career as an artist because "she felt that if I had the divine gift, I wouldn't be where I was—part of a working-class family that was in the restaurant business."

Despite such discouragement, Frasconi continued to draw, paint, and read. He also began taking art lessons at night, and studied at the Circulo de Bellas Artes for almost a year before dropping out. At age twelve he became a printer's apprentice, an experience he recalls with pleasure. "I was truly happy working [in the printing shop]," he told *Something about the Author Autobiography Series* (*SAAS*). "It was my first contact with printers' ink, and I loved it."

As a teenager Frasconi began to publish anti-Fascist cartoons and caricatures of people like Italian dictator Franco and German chancellor Hitler in some of Uruguay's satirical newspapers. "There was a great deal of social awareness in Uruguay when I was growing up," he said in *Frasconi against the Grain.* "We had a good popular press, and we read about everything that was going on in the world. The Spanish Civil War, for instance, affected us the way the Vietnam War affected many Americans during the 1960s. You had to take a position. If you were an artist you still had to take a position."

In the early 1940s the French government sent a selection of art works to Latin America for an extended exhibition. For the first time Frasconi got a chance to see paintings by Cezanne, Van Gogh, Matisse, and Picasso. He was particularly moved by the woodcuts of Gauguin, since he was already experimenting with woodcuts himself. He was also in the process of becoming seduced by U.S. culture; as he told interviewer Carol Goldenberg: "I became familiar with the United States by listening to jazz on the radio and by reading nineteenth- and twentieth-century writers such as Dreiser and Whitman, Thoreau and Sinclair Lewis, Richard Wright, and Dos Passos." This introduction to U.S. culture was "liberating" to the young Frasconi: "Our high school was based in more European culture—all of our records were Italian operas, which I hated. Jazz meant freedom, a cultural revolution to me." In 1943 the young artist applied for a scholarship to the Art Students' League in New York City, and was astounded—but supremely happy—when he was accepted. He moved to the United States in 1945.

While living in New York, Frasconi studied with Japanese artist Yasuo Kuniyoshi at the Art Students' League, where he met fellow artist Leona Pierce, whom he would marry in 1951. First concentrating on painting, he gradually returned to the woodcut and the lithograph as his primary media. The couple lived in California during 1948, and Frasconi took odd jobs while continuing to work on his prints. His first solo exhibits were held at the Santa Barbara Museum of Art in 1948 and the Brooklyn Museum of Art in 1949. A trip to Mexico in 1949 scored an introduction to noted muralist Diego Rivera and a showing of Frasconi's work in Mexico City. By the mid-1950s his work was selling well at several New York galleries, major museums were mounting exhibits of his prints, and he had achieved success as a graphic artist with several magazine covers and book designs to his credit.

In the mid-1950s Frasconi's young son Pablo gave him the idea for what would become his first published book for children, *See and Say: A Picture Book in Four Languages.* By this time Frasconi was already illustrating books as a sideline, but he could not find the kind of book he wanted to use with his own child. "I was looking not for a book to teach a child a foreign language, but one that would show that there are different ways to say the same thing, that there is more than one nation in our world, that there are many other countries where people speak different languages," Frasconi remarked in *SAAS.* "*See and Say* was what I was looking for."

One of several bilingual books Frasconi has contributed to over the years, *See and Say* shows pictures of familiar objects and gives names and pronunciations in several languages. Well received by critics and educators even before the advancement of "multicultural" books for children, the book filled a void and remained in print decades after its first printing. Frasconi was pleased by the book's reception, noting in *SAAS* his excitement that "my work could, in some ways, introduce a young mind to an understanding of our vast cultures." Other bilingual books by Frasconi include *See Again, Say Again, The House That Jack Built,* and *Bestiary/Bestiario,* the text of the last penned by Chilean Nobel laureate Pablo Neruda.

Frasconi's work adorns the halls of prestigious museums in America and abroad, but it is also found on book dust wrappers, on record album covers, and even—in one case—on a postage stamp that was reprinted 120 million times. "I don't think the artist's role in society is to decorate the walls of corporations or museums," he explained to interviewer Jane Sterrett in *Print Review.* "That doesn't make any sense to me. I love to do record covers and book covers—anything that can be viewed by a large audience. Is it art? I really don't care. It's up to the viewer to judge. Judging is not my job."

During his long career Frasconi has addressed a wide variety of themes, from the joyous to the terrible, and some of his best-known pieces offer poignant commentary on economic and social inequities and political events in the United States and in his native South America. "Frasconi's message is not exclusively pessimistic," noted Bach in *America,* "but more a wake-up call, a nudge to listen to that goodness he believes still dwells within us all. He has said his work 'celebrated the joy of living,' and in that sense its message contains a measure of optimism." However, racism, materialism, the plight of the South American *desaparecidos* or "disappeared," and the unjust politics of many countries around the world continued to figure prominently in his images. "I don't really try to make art," Frasconi maintained in his interview for *Print Review.* "I try to communicate something that bothers me. It may not interest you, but I don't care—I still have to tell you. If you want to understand me and know me, just look at my work."

Biographical and Critical Sources

BOOKS

Frasconi, Antonio, *Frasconi against the Grain: The Woodcuts of Antonio Frasconi,* Macmillan (New York, NY), 1974.

The Illustrator's Notebook, Horn Book (Boston, MA), 1978.

Klemin, Diana, *The Illustrated Book: Its Art and Craft,* C. N. Potter (New York, NY), 1970.

Something about the Author Autobiography Series, Volume 11, Gale (Detroit, MI), 1991.

PERIODICALS

Americas, May-June, 1994, Caleb Bach, "Going against the Grain," pp. 38-44.

ARTnews, December, 1988, Ruth Bass, "Antonio Frasconi," p. 158.

Life, October 18, 1954.

Horn Book, November-December, 1994, Carol Goldenberg, "An Interview with Antonio Frasconi," pp. 693-702.

Newsweek, March 17, 1952; April 5, 1954.

Print Review, no. 16-17, Jane Sterrett, "Interview with Antonio Frasconi," 1982.

Time, June 15, 1953; December 20, 1963.*

G

GELMAN, Rita Golden 1937-
(R. G. Austin, a joint pseudonym)

Personal

Born July 2, 1937, in Bridgeport, CT; daughter of Albert (a pharmacist) and Frances (an artist and community activist; maiden name, Friedman) Golden; married Steve Gelman (an editor and writer), December 11, 1960 (divorced, 1987); children: Mitchell, Jan. *Education:* Brandeis University, B.A., 1958; University of California, Los Angeles, M.A., 1984; Ph.D. candidate; additional study at Northeastern University, Yeshiva University, and New York University.

Addresses

Home—Los Angeles, CA. *Agent*—Marilyn Marlow, Curtis Brown Ltd., 575 Madison Ave., New York, NY 10022.

Career

Young Americans magazine, New York, NY, staff writer, 1958-60; Crowell-Collier Publishing Co., New York, NY, editor, 1961-62; Book-of-the-Month Club, New York, NY, juvenile consultant, 1972-76; Macmillan Publishing Co., New York, NY, editor, 1973-74; freelance writer, 1974—. Guest lecturer, University of California—Los Angeles, 1976-78; faculty member, Sixth Annual Writers' Conference in Children's Literature, 1977; faculty member in extension program, California State University—Northridge, 1978-79; lecturer, Association of Southeast Asian Nations (ASEAN) Publisher's Conference, Singapore, 1993. *Member:* PEN, Society of Children's Book Writers and Illustrators.

Awards, Honors

Best Science Book for Children designation, American Institute of Physics, 1987, and Science-Writing award, 1988, both for *Splash! All about Baths;* American Library Association award, 1988, for *Inside Nicaragua: Young People's Dreams and Fears;* John Burroughs Association commendation for Outstanding Nature Book for children, 1991, for *Dawn to Dusk in the Galapagos: Flightless Birds, Swimming Lizards, and Other Fascinating Creatures.*

Writings

FOR CHILDREN

Dumb Joey, illustrated by Cheryl Pelavin, Holt (New York, NY), 1973.

The Can, illustrated by John Trotta, Macmillan (New York, NY), 1975.

Comits: A Book of Comic Skits, illustrated by Robert Dennis, Macmillan (New York, NY), 1975.

The Me I Am, photographs by Michal Heron, Macmillan (New York, NY), 1975.

Fun City, illustrated by Tom Herbert, Macmillan (New York, NY), 1975.

(With Steve Gelman) *Great Quarterbacks of Pro Football,* Scholastic (New York, NY), 1975.

Why Can't I Fly?, illustrated by Jack Kent, Scholastic (New York, NY), 1976.

Hey, Kid!, illustrated by Carol Nicklaus, F. Watts (New York, NY), 1977.

More Spaghetti, I Say!, illustrated by Jack Kent, Scholastic (New York, NY), 1977, illustrated by Mort Gerberg, 1992.

(With Susan Kovacs Buxbaum) *OUCH!: All about Cuts and Other Hurts,* illustrated by Jan Pyk, Harcourt (San Diego, CA), 1977.

(With Joan Richter) *Professor Coconut and the Thief,* illustrated by Emily McCully, Holt (New York, NY), 1977.

(With Steve Gelman), *America's Favorite Sports Stars,* Scholastic (New York, NY), 1978.

Cats and Mice, illustrated by Eric Gurney, Scholastic (New York, NY), 1978.

(With Marcia Seligson) *UFO Encounters,* Scholastic (New York, NY), 1978.

(With Warner Friedman) *Uncle Hugh: A Fishing Story,* illustrated by Eros Keith, Harcourt (San Diego, CA), 1978.

Hello Cat, You Need a Hat, illustrated by Eric Gurney, Scholastic (New York, NY), 1979, illustrated by Dana Regan, Scholastic (New York, NY), 1998.

The Biggest Sandwich Ever, illustrated by Mort Gerberg, Scholastic (New York, NY), 1980.

The Incredible Dinosaurs, illustrated by Christopher Santoro, Random House (New York, NY), 1980.

Favorite Riddles, Knock Knocks, and Nonsense, illustrated by Mort Gerberg, Scholastic (New York, NY), 1980.

Great Moments in Sports, Scholastic (New York, NY), 1980.

Benji at Work, Scholastic (New York, NY), 1980.

(With Susan Kovacs Buxbaum) *Boats That Float,* illustrated by Marilyn MacGregor, F. Watts (New York, NY), 1981.

Fabulous Animal Facts That Hardly Anybody Knows, illustrated by Margaret Hartelius, Scholastic (New York, NY), 1981.

Mount St. Helens, the Big Blast, Scholastic (New York, NY), 1981.

ESP and Other Strange Happenings, Scholastic (New York, NY), 1981.

Mortimer K Saves the Day, illustrated by Bernie Gruver, Scholastic (New York, NY), 1982.

Benji Takes a Dive, Scholastic (New York, NY), 1982.

(With Susan Kovacs Buxbaum) *Body Noises,* illustrated by Angie Lloyd, Knopf (New York, NY), 1983.

Wet Cats, illustrated by Eric Gurney, Scholastic (New York, NY), 1985.

Listen and Look: A Safety Book, illustrated by Cathy Beylon, Marvel Books, 1986.

Care and Share: A Book about Manners, illustrated by Cathy Beylon, Marvel Books, 1986.

A Koala Grows Up, illustrated by Gioia Fiammenghi, Scholastic (New York, NY), 1986.

Pets for Sale, illustrated by Fredrick Winkowski, 1986.

(With Susan Kovacs Buxbaum) *Splash! All about Baths,* illustrated by Maryann Cocca-Leffler, Little, Brown (Boston, MA), 1987.

Leave It to Minnie, illustrated by Mort Gerberg, Scholastic (New York, NY), 1987.

Inside Nicaragua: Young People's Dreams and Fears, F. Watts (New York, NY), 1988.

Stop Those Painters, illustrated by Mort Gerberg, Scholastic (New York, NY), 1989.

Monkeys and Apes of the World, F. Watts (New York, NY), 1990.

Monsters of the Sea, illustrated by Jean Day Zallinger, Little, Brown (Boston, MA), 1990.

Dawn to Dusk in the Galapagos: Flightless Birds, Swimming Lizards, and Other Fascinating Creatures, photographs by Tui De Roy, Little, Brown (Boston, MA), 1991.

A Monkey Grows Up, illustrated by Gioia Fiammenghi, Scholastic (New York, NY), 1991.

What Are Scientists? What Do They Do? Let's Find Out, illustrated by Mark Teague, Scholastic (New York, NY), 1991.

Vampires and Other Creatures of the Night, illustrated by C. B. Mordan, Scholastic (New York, NY), 1991.

Body Battles, illustrated by Elroy Freem, Scholastic (New York, NY), 1992.

I Went to the Zoo, illustrated by Maryann Kovalski, Scholastic (New York, NY), 1993.

A Panda Grows Up, illustrated by Mary Morgan, Scholastic (New York, NY), 1993.

Body Detectives: A Book about the Senses, illustrated by Elroy Freem, Scholastic (New York, NY), 1994.

Queen Esther Saves Her People, illustrated by Frane Lessac, Scholastic (New York, NY), 1998.

Pizza Pat, illustrated by Will Terry, Random House (New York, NY), 1999.

Rice Is Life, illustrated by Yangsook Choi, Holt (New York, NY), 2000.

Mole in a Hole, illustrated by Holly Hannon, Random House (New York, NY), 2000.

Gelman's works have been translated into other languages, including Dutch, Spanish, Japanese, Danish, Swedish, German, and French.

"WHICH WAY" SERIES; WITH NANCY AUSTIN; UNDER JOINT PSEUDONYM R. G. AUSTIN

The Castle of No Return, illustrated by Mike Eagle, Archway (New York, NY), 1982.

Vampires, Spies, and Alien Beings, illustrated by Anthony Kramer, Archway (New York, NY), 1982.

The Spell of the Black Raven, illustrated by Anthony Kramer, Archway (New York, NY), 1982.

Famous and Rich, illustrated by Mike Eagle, Archway (New York, NY), 1982.

Lost in a Strange Land, illustrated by Lorna Tomei, Archway (New York, NY), 1982.

Curse of the Sunken Treasure, illustrated by Lorna Tomei, Archway (New York, NY), 1982.

Cosmic Encounters, illustrated by Doug Jamieson, Archway (New York, NY), 1982.

Creatures of the Dark, illustrated by Gordon Tomei, Archway (New York, NY), 1982.

Invasion of the Black Slime, illustrated by Joseph A. Smith, Archway (New York, NY), 1983.

Trapped in the Black Box, illustrated by Doug Jamieson, Archway (New York, NY), 1983.

Poltergeists, Ghosts, and Psychic Encounters, illustrated by Joseph A. Smith, 1984.

Islands of Terror, illustrated by Gordon Tomei, Archway (New York, NY), 1984.

Several books in the "Which Way" series were published in Portuguese.

"SECRET DOOR" SERIES; WITH NANCY AUSTIN; UNDER JOINT PSEUDONYM R. G. AUSTIN

Wow! You Can Fly!, illustrated by Joseph A. Smith, Archway (New York, NY), 1983.

Giants, Elves and Scary Monsters, illustrated by Ed Parker, Archway (New York, NY), 1983.

The Haunted Castle, illustrated by Winslow Pels, Archway (New York, NY), 1983.

The Secret Life of Toys, illustrated by Sal Murdocca, Archway (New York, NY), 1983.

The Visitors from Outer Space, illustrated by Blanche Sims, Archway (New York, NY), 1983.

The Inch-High Kid, illustrated by Dennis Hockerman, Archway (New York, NY), 1983.

The Magic Carpet, illustrated by Winslow Pels, Archway (New York, NY), 1983.

Happy Birthday to You, illustrated by Joseph A. Smith, Archway (New York, NY), 1983.

The Monster Family, illustrated by Blanche Sims, Archway (New York, NY), 1984.

Brontosaurus Moves In, illustrated by Joseph A. Smith, Archway (New York, NY), 1984.

The Enchanted Forest, illustrated by Winslow Pels, Archway (New York, NY), 1984.

Crazy Computers, illustrated by Joseph A. Smith, Archway (New York, NY), 1984.

OTHER

Tales of a Female Nomad: Living at Large in the World (autobiography), Crown Publishers (New York, NY), 2001.

Work in Progress

Bali Tales, a long saga that tells of a hawk and a mouse who live in Bali and the friendship that develops between them.

Sidelights

The author of over seventy books for children, Rita Golden Gelman is equally at home writing slap-happy, rhythmic, and often rhyming texts for her picture-book creations as she is dealing with science subjects, geography, or travel for older readers. Her writings include tales of saucy little monkeys as well as poems to celebrate rice and retellings for Purim. Gelman is also the author of the adult title, *Tales of a Female Nomad: Living at Large in the World,* which documents her unorthodox lifestyle since the late 1980s, when she left an affluent life in California to live among common people in locations around the world, from Borneo to the Galapagos Islands.

Born in 1937, Gelman grew up in Bridgeport, Connecticut, where her parents ran a local drugstore. "I never would have become a writer if I hadn't had Miss Curnias in the eighth grade," she once told *SATA.* "Our class put out a school newspaper called the Beardsley Press. We collected stories and poems and news items from all the other classes in the school. Miss Curnias typed them onto mimeograph stencils, and we decorated the stencils with a pin-pointed thing called a stylus. (That was before computers.) I wasn't very good at the decorating, but Miss Curnias said I wrote good stories and poems. So, whenever we needed to fill up a page, I wrote something. That was the year I became a writer.

"When I talk to other writers, they often tell me that when they were children, they wrote a lot and read all the time. I wish I had. But the truth is that I played a lot. I lived in a two-family house, just down the street from Beardsley Park. That park was a major character in my childhood. In the summer in the park, we swam in the lake and waded in the brook; we caught grasshoppers to feed to the praying mantises we had caught the day before; we rolled down the grassy hills and we trapped lightning bugs in bottles at night. There was a zoo in the park, and I collected peacock feathers by putting chewing gum on the end of a long stick, sliding the stick though the square holes in the wire fence, and then pressing the gummed tip onto the molted feathers. That was the summer.

"In the fall we piled up the leaves into giant mounds and dived into them until we were buried. In the winter we sledded, built snowmen and forts, and had spectacular snowball fights in the park. And in the spring, we roller-skated, played hide-and-seek, and climbed trees. Today, when I'm writing books for children, the girl who leaped into piles of leaves, scared her parents by presenting them with frogs, and stomped in puddles just because they were there, is still very much a part of me.... I love the smell, the crackle, and all the memories that come to me when I'm over my head in autumn leaves."

Gelman attended Brandeis University, graduating in 1958. For the next four years, she worked as a writer and editor in New York City. Married in 1960, she had two children, and in 1976 she moved to California. Her writing career began in 1973 with publication of *Dumb Joey.* Other picture books followed, and in 1976 she created one of her most popular picture book characters, Minnie the monkey. "My favorite book, *Why Can't I Fly?,* comes from the part of me that used to lie in the

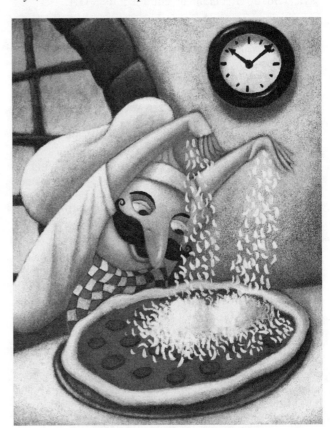

Rita Golden Gelman's rhyming Pizza Pat *describes the making of a pizza ultimately eaten by dozens of mice. (Illustrated by Will Terry.)*

grass as a child and watch the birds," Gelman once told *SATA.* "I still dream about flying, soaring, riding the wind. The main character in *Why Can't I Fly?* is a monkey named Minnie who wants more than anything to fly. She keeps trying and trying, until finally, with the help of her friends, she does the impossible.

"The book, *Why Can't I Fly?* inspired the most touching letter I ever received. It was from a woman in Florida. She wrote that a six-year-old friend of hers named Jessica had just died of a terrible genetic disease. When Jessica was four, someone had given her a copy of *Why Can't I Fly?* Jessica learned how to read from that book, and she carried it with her wherever she went. Every day she read it to her family, her friends, her nurses. Every time she read it, she would laugh, and everyone would laugh with her. When Jessica died, a friend of the family read the book at Jessica's funeral. The last scene in *Why Can't I Fly?* shows Minnie sitting on a sheet and being carried off into the sky by her friends. There's a big grin on her face as she waves goodbye. Minnie's story had become Jessica's story as well, trying and trying and finally flying away."

Gelman returned to her favorite monkey in *More Spaghetti, I Say!* and in *Leave It to Minnie,* which she dedicated to Jessica's family, "so others may laugh because Jessica did." In *More Spaghetti,* Minnie can't stop eating spaghetti "I love it, I love, I love it, I do," she says. "So do I," Gelman admitted to *SATA.*

In fact, food is something of a theme for Gelman. In *The Biggest Sandwich Ever,* she explores life between two crusts of bread. "I never know when I'm going to meet an idea that will become a book," Gelman explained. "One day I received a call from a friend who owned a Swensen's ice cream store. She was in a panic because all her workers had called in sick. Could I help? Absolutely. I was very excited. When I was a teenager, I had worked at the soda fountain in my father's drugstore—making sundaes and ice cream sodas, serving up milkshakes and banana splits. I couldn't wait to once again scoop and squirt and dribble syrups over ice cream. But it turned out that my friend wanted me in the kitchen.

"She stood me at a long counter that was covered with stacks of turkey and chicken and tomatoes and lettuce and tuna fish salad. The stacks were divided by pieces of waxed paper so that the sandwich maker, me, would give just the right amount of filling. On the wall above the counter were the lists of sandwiches and their ingredients. I spent the next five hours staring at the piles and letting my imagination wander. The next day I began writing *The Biggest Sandwich Ever,* about a sandwich the size of a house. I wanted to get more and more ridiculous as the sandwich got higher and higher. I remember sitting one day with my editor and seriously discussing which was more ridiculous: squirting catsup out of a fire hose, or dropping pickles from an airplane. I love the discussions I get to have when I write silly books."

In the 1999 title, *Pizza Pat,* Gelman deals with that perennial favorite food. Set to the rhythm of "This Is the House That Jack Built," the picture book describes the construction of a famous pizza by chef Pat. "Children will be carried along by the rhythm" of the text," wrote Kristina Aaronson in a *School Library Journal* review. In the book Gelman plays with repeated sounds, such as floppy, sloppy, and gloppy. With the year 2000 title, *Rice Is Life,* Gelman draws upon the many years she lived in Bali, developing poems about the animals who live in the rice fields and the people who depend on the crop for sustenance. Each illustration is accompanied by a poem and a paragraph which explains a different aspect of the planting and cultivation of rice. A reviewer for *Publishers Weekly* found the poems to be "inconsistent," but had praise for Gelman's "graceful" prose, "whether explaining how rice plants sprout or how children roast dragonflies for snacks." Likewise, Diane S. Marton, reviewing *Rice Is Life* in *School Library Journal,* found the combination of picture, poetry, and prose "pleasing when one element reinforces the other, but sometimes the text bears little or no connection to the art or the rhythmic poem." However, *Booklist* contributor Connie Fletcher had no reservations about the title, noting that Gelman, with a "light, poetic touch," "shows the drama of the planting season, conveying the rhythm of the planting, the richness of the natural environment." Fletcher dubbed *Rice Is Life* a "delight that will fascinate young readers."

"When I'm not writing, what I like most to do is to learn about other people's lives, people I meet on buses, on trains and in planes, people in line with me at the supermarket, old people, children, people in wheel chairs, people on the street," Gelman once explained. "I have always been interested in learning about how people live their lives. And I have always had a fascination with other cultures. This passion for learning about other people's experiences lured me into studying anthropology in graduate school at UCLA (in 1980), where I spent endless hours reading about how people live and thinking about how they become what they become.

"The characters that I write about have a lot of me in them. *I Went to the Zoo* is about a boy who takes all the zoo animals home with him, elephants, lions, koalas, pandas, and peacocks, among others. As a child, I got to know the animals in the Beardsley Park Zoo, and I often wished that I could take them home with me. I once put an injured squirrel on my mother's bed when she was sick; she was not interested in sharing her bed with a rodent. I frequently smuggled frogs into the house and spent hours searching for them under couches and radiators. *I Went to the Zoo* carries those experiences into the absurd." Reviewing that picture book, a *Publishers Weekly* contributor called it a "sure kidpleaser" with a "slap-happy story, a sot of fantasy version of 'Old MacDonald.'" The same reviewer felt that the book "will earn children's devotions."

"I wrote another book called *Hey, Kid!* after taking a five-hour bus trip with my six-year-old daughter,"

Gelman explained to *SATA*. "For the entire trip she sang and talked, talked and sang. It was as though she was running on one of those never-ending batteries; there wasn't a silent moment. By the end of the trip, I was ready to give her away. Instead, I wrote about Sam, a lovable, friendly, wispy character who is probably still dropping in on unsuspecting people who adore him until they discover that he can't stop talking and singing. Then they give him away."

The prolific Gelman has also written heavily in other genres. "I've written a lot of nonfiction books, usually about things I want to study," she told *SATA*. "Writing a nonfiction book about a subject is a lot like taking a minicourse. You have to read tons of books, talk to experts, and develop your own opinions." Gelman's nonfiction books have covered a wide assortment of topics and themes. She has written about UFO's and ESP, about the country of Nicaragua, and the islands and animals of the Galapagos. She has also written a lot of books about animals: pandas, koalas, monkeys, sea creatures, and dinosaurs. "I wrote one book called, *Fabulous Animal Facts That Hardly Anybody Knows.* What a lot of fun I had doing that one. I just sat in the library on the floor in front of the animal shelves and read. Every time I found myself saying, 'I didn't know that!,' I wrote it down. I filled several notebooks. When I was ready to do a thirty-two-page picture book, I chose the facts that were the most fun."

Additionally, many of Gelman's books have also been written in collaboration. "I like what happens when two heads work together," Gelman told *SATA*. "I worked on most of my science books with my friend, Susan Buxbaum, among them *OUCH!: All about Cuts and Other Hurts; Body Noises; Splash! All about Baths;* and *What Are Scientists? What Do They Do? Let's Find Out.* We have fun doing it. Susan does the research and explains everything to me. Then, I do the writing. I wrote the 'Which Way' series with another friend, Nancy Lamb Austin. And I've worked with others as well. I like collaborating. When Nancy and I wrote together, we laughed a lot; and we always began our working sessions with about a half hour of talking, discussing world events, family problems, and friends. Only then were we ready to work."

By the late 1980s, Gelman's career took an unforeseen turn. "After I received my master's degree, but before I finished the work for a Ph.D., I realized something else about myself: I needed to see and touch and smell and hear the sounds of other cultures, to live with the people, to eat in their homes, to talk to them in their languages. Reading about them was too far away from the real thing." With her children out of the home and her marriage failing, she decided to make the rest of her life an adventure. "So I sold or gave away all my possessions and set off to discover what it was like to live in other worlds. For three and a half years I lived in Mexico, Guatemala, Nicaragua, and the Galapagos Islands of Ecuador. I learned to speak Spanish and to cook Mexican food, and I learned how to weave from the Indian population of Guatemala. In Nicaragua I discovered what it was like to live in a country under siege. And in the Galapagos, I lived on a boat and visited islands populated by sea lions, iguanas, frigate birds, and blue-footed boobies.

"In 1989, I went to Indonesia. I lived with the Dayak people in the Indonesian province of Kalimantan on the island of Borneo, and I studied orangutans in the rain forest there. I stayed for three years with a royal family on the island of Bali. I have climbed the mountains of Irian Jaya (the Indonesian half of the island of New Guinea) and sat around the cooking fires with the tribal families who live there; I have traveled in a dugout boat through the rivers of the Asmat area in the south, learning from the natives about their woodcarving skills and attending their ancestral ceremonies.

"Since 1989, I have been living primarily on the Indonesian island of Bali, where I stay with families, join them in their special ceremonies, and learn (in both English and Indonesian) about their lives and how they think and feel about the world. Wherever I live, I continue to write books for young people, sometimes about the countries I visit and sometimes about universal subjects. I also try to contribute something to the people I live with, by teaching English, by sharing my own culture with them, by reading them my books, and even by cooking Western foods now and then for my friends to try. Sometimes I ask questions, but mostly I learn about people by making friends, living with families, and sharing their lives. My travels have taught me something very important: there is no right or wrong way to 'do' life. The options are infinite."

Since taking to the road, Gelman has written about her travels in books such as *Inside Nicaragua, Monkeys and Apes of the World,* and *Dawn to Dusk in the Galapagos.* With *Queen Esther Saves Her People,* she tells the story of Purim, the Jewish festival commemorating the defeat of Haman's plot to massacre the Jews that is observed around the first of March. "Gelman's pacing is measured as she places her tale in historical context," wrote a critic for *Publishers Weekly,* "but the story picks up steam as Haman gets his comeuppance." The same reviewer felt that young readers would "enjoy this colorful interpretation." *Booklist*'s Ilene Cooper noted that Gelman "personalizes the story with details," concluding that the book is a "solid, attractive choice." In *Bulletin of the Center for Children's Books,* Betsy Hearne remarked that Gelman "[s]moothly incorporated ... the complex plot twists" in this "skillful retelling."

More fanciful fare is served up in the picture books *Hello Cat, You Need a Hat* and *Mole in a Hole.* In the former title, a mouse tries to convince a grumpy cat to wear a rather bizarre assortment of hats, such as a bee hat, a helmet, and a monkey hat. But the stubborn cat refuses to wear them. In *Mole in a Hole,* a mole is lonely because his friends do not like his small, dark hole, but he finally finds the perfect companion in Ms. Mole who, like him, does not like the sun.

Writing for readers of all ages, Gelman chronicles her odyssey since 1987 in *Tales of a Female Nomad.* Reviewing the memoir-travel story in *Booklist,* Carolyn Kubisz thought that Gelman "describes in rich detail how she travels—moving to different countries, staying with locals, observing their customs and learning their language." But Gelman is not simply a tourist, objectively observing. She becomes, as Kubisz noted, "emotionally involved" in the lives of the people with whom she comes into contact. "This attachment comes through in this amazing travelogue," concluded Kubisz. Linda M. Kaufmann, writing in *Library Journal,* felt that Gelman's "enthusiasm for the people she meets and her ability to overcome the challenges faced by a woman traveling alone make for an engrossing and inspirational read." Reviewing the book in the *Washington Post,* Nina King noted that Gelman "is a good storyteller" and that "she has great material."

Through all the changes and adventures in her life, and whether living in a palace or one-room hut, Gelman has continued to write. As she noted in *SATA:* "Because most people don't know that writers are ordinary people, being one gets you 'Oh, really!,' which is a lot better than 'Oh, how nice.' The main problem with being a writer is that you have to write. That means, most of the time, sitting in a room by yourself and putting words into a computer or onto paper. Every once in a while, when I'm writing, I feel as though I'm flying or dancing or skiing down a mountain. The words just keep flowing out, and I fill with music and joy and passion."

Biographical and Critical Sources

BOOKS

Gelman, Rita Golden, *More Spaghetti, I Say,* illustrated by Mort Gerberg, Scholastic (New York, NY), 1992.

Gelman, Rita Golden, *Tales of a Female Nomad: Living at Large in the World,* Crown Publishers (New York, NY), 2001.

PERIODICALS

Booklist, December 15, 1981, p. 553; May 1, 1998, Ilene Cooper, review of *Queen Esther Saves Her People,* p. 1138; May 15, 2000, Connie Fletcher, review of *Rice Is Life,* p. 1745; May 15, 2001, Carolyn Kubisz, review of *Tales of a Female Nomad,* p. 1724.

Bulletin of the Center for Children's Books, February, 1974, p. 94; March, 1998, Betsy Hearne, review of *Queen Esther Saves Her People,* p. 241.

Horn Book, July-August, 1991, pp. 477-478.

Kirkus Reviews, August 15, 1973, p. 882; April 1, 1977, p. 355; May 1, 1991, p. 612.

Library Journal, May 15, 2001, Linda M. Kaufmann, review of *Tales of a Female Nomad,* p. 150.

Los Angeles Times, April 22, 2001, p. L7.

New York Times Book Review, November 13, 1983.

Publishers Weekly, October 8, 1973, p. 97; December 11, 1987, p. 63; July 12, 1993, review of *I Went to the Zoo,* p. 77; December 22, 1997, review of *Queen Esther Saves Her People,* p. 54; June 5, 2000, review of *Rice Is Life,* p. 94.

School Library Journal, May, 1977, p. 76; October, 1977, p. 102; February, 1979, p. 42; December, 1981, pp. 79-80; December, 1981, p. 85; July, 1991, pp. 79-80; November, 1993, p. 79; February, 1998, p. 98; September, 1999, Kristina Aaronson, review of *Pizza Pat,* p. 182; June, 2000, Diane S. Marton, review of *Rice Is Life,* p. 130.

Washington Post, December 4, 2001, Nina King, "The Deliberate Tourist," p. C3.

OTHER

Rita Golden Gelman Web Site, http://www.ritagoldengelman.com (February 22, 2002).*

*   *   *

GOBLE, Paul 1933-

Personal

Born September 27, 1933, in Haslemere, Surrey, England; became U.S. citizen, 1984; son of Robert John (a harpsichord maker) and Marion Elizabeth (a painter and musician; maiden name, Brown) Goble; married Dorothy Lee (an author and industrial designer), 1960 (divorced 1978); married Janet A. Tiller, June 2, 1978; children: (first marriage) Richard, Julia; (second marriage) Robert George. *Education:* Central School of Arts and Crafts, London, England, Diploma (with honors), National Diploma in Design, 1959.

Addresses

Home—Rapid City, South Dakota.

Career

Illustrator, author, and painter. Freelance industrial designer, 1960-68; Ravensbourne College of Art and Design, London, England, senior lecturer in three-dimensional design, 1968-77; illustrator and author of children's books, 1969—. Central School of Arts and Crafts, visiting lecturer, 1960-68. *Exhibitions:* Dahl Fine Art Museum, Rapid City, SD. *Military service:* British Army, 1951-53: served in Germany. *Member:* Society of Industrial Artists and Designers (fellow), Royal Society of Art (fellow).

Awards, Honors

Horn Book Honor List, 1969, for *Red Hawk's Account of Custer's Last Battle;* American Library Association Notable Book awards, 1970, for *Red Hawk's Account of Custer's Last Battle,* 1979, for *The Girl Who Loved Wild Horses,* and 1984, for *Buffalo Woman;* Art Books for Children awards, 1974, for *The Friendly Wolf,* and 1979, for *The Girl Who Loved Wild Horses;* Caldecott Medal, 1979, for *The Girl Who Loved Wild Horses;* Ambassador of Honor/Books across the Sea awards, English-Speaking Union, for *The Gift of the Sacred Dog, Star Boy,* and *Buffalo Woman;* Children's Book of the Year citation, Library of Congress, and International Youth Library Choice designation, both for *Star Boy;* Aesop

Award, 1992, for *Love Flute;* recipient of prizes in industrial design competitions.

Writings

FOR CHILDREN; SELF-ILLUSTRATED

(With Dorothy Goble) *Red Hawk's Account of Custer's Last Battle,* Pantheon (New York, NY), 1969, reprinted, University of Nebraska Press (Lincoln, NE), 1992.

(With Dorothy Goble) *Brave Eagle's Account of the Fetterman Fight, 21 December 1866,* Pantheon (New York, NY), 1972, reprinted, University of Nebraska Press (Lincoln, NE), 1992, published as *The Hundred in the Hands,* Macmillan (London, England), 1972.

(With Dorothy Goble) *Lone Bull's Horse Raid,* Macmillan (London, England), 1973.

(With Dorothy Goble) *The Friendly Wolf,* Bradbury Press (New York, NY), 1974, revised edition published as *Dream Wolf,* 1990.

The Girl Who Loved Wild Horses (also see below), Bradbury Press (New York, NY), 1978, reprinted, Aladdin Books (New York, NY), 1993.

The Gift of the Sacred Dog (also see below), Bradbury Press (New York, NY), 1980.

Star Boy, Bradbury Press (New York, NY), 1980.

Buffalo Woman, Bradbury Press (New York, NY), 1984.

The Great Race of the Birds and Animals, Bradbury Press (New York, NY), 1985.

Paul Goble

Death of the Iron Horse, Bradbury Press (New York, NY), 1987.

Her Seven Brothers (also see below), Bradbury Press (New York, NY), 1988.

Iktomi and the Boulder: A Plains Indian Story, Orchard Books (New York, NY), 1988.

Beyond the Ridge, Bradbury Press (New York, NY), 1989.

Iktomi and the Berries: A Plains Indian Story, Orchard Books (New York, NY), 1989.

Iktomi and the Ducks: A Plains Indian Story, Orchard Books (New York, NY), 1990.

Iktomi and the Buffalo Skull: A Plains Indian Story, Orchard Books (New York, NY), 1991.

I Sing for the Animals, Bradbury Press (New York, NY), 1991.

Crow Chief: A Plains Indian Story, Orchard Books (New York, NY), 1992.

Love Flute, Bradbury Press (New York, NY), 1992.

The Lost Children: The Boys Who Were Neglected, Bradbury Press (New York, NY), 1993.

Iktomi and the Buzzard: A Plains Indian Story, Orchard Books (New York, NY), 1994.

Adopted by the Eagles: A Plains Indian Story of Friendship and Treachery, Bradbury Press (New York, NY), 1994.

The Return of the Buffaloes: A Plains Indian Story about Famine and Renewal of the Earth, National Geographic Society (Washington, DC), 1996.

The Legend of the White Buffalo Woman, National Geographic Society (Washington, DC), 1998.

Iktomi and the Coyote: A Plains Indian Story, Orchard Books (New York, NY), 1998.

Remaking the Earth: A Creation Story from the Great Plains of North America, Orchard Books (New York, NY), 1996.

Iktomi Loses His Eyes: A Plains Indian Story, Orchard Books (New York, NY), 1999.

Paul Goble Gallery: Three Native American Stories (includes *Her Seven Brothers, The Gift of the Sacred Dog,* and *The Girl Who Loved Wild Horses*), Simon & Schuster (New York, NY), 1999.

Snow Maker's Tipi, Atheneum (New York, NY), 2001.

OTHER

(Illustrator) Richard Erdoes, editor, *The Sound of Flutes, and Other Indian Legends,* Pantheon (New York, NY), 1976.

Hau Kola = Hello, Friend ("Meet the Author" series), photographs by Gerry Perrin, R. C. Owen (Katonah, NY), 1994.

Goble's illustrations are collected at the South Dakota Art Museum, Brookings, SD.

Adaptations

Red Hawk's Account of Custer's Last Battle was read by Arthur S. Junaluska, Caedmon Records, 1972.

Work in Progress

Based on a Pawnee story, *Mystic Horse,* HarperCollins, due in 2003; currently working on the canticle of the young men saved from the furnace in the Book of David.

Sidelights

Through his retelling of Plains Indian myths and legends, British-born illustrator Paul Goble is one of the foremost interpreters of Native American folklore for young children. Coupled with the stylized watercolor-and-ink illustrations reflecting the author/artist's deep love of nature and knowledge of native symbols, books such as *The Girl Who Loved Horses, Dream Wolf,* and the trickster tale *Iktomi and the Buzzard* introduce young readers to Sioux, Blackfoot, and Cheyenne tribal cultures through texts that reflect the tradition of Native American storytelling.

"I have been interested in everything Indian since I can remember," Goble noted during his speech—published in *Horn Book*—accepting the 1979 Caldecott Medal for *The Girl Who Loved Horses.* "Before television days my mother read the complete works of [Grey Owl and Ernest Thompson Seton] to my brother and me.... The world they wrote about was so different from the crowded island where I lived." As a boy growing up in England during the 1930s, Goble accompanied his family searching for the stone-age flint instruments still found in certain locations within Great Britain. Goble pictured the makers of these tools as similar in some ways to the American Indians of the Great Plains who had captured his imagination. Throughout his youth, he collected pictures from magazines and books of everything relating to North America's native people.

One Christmas the young Goble received a gift, a copy of George Catlin's *Notes on the North American Indian,* which elevated his study of Indian lore to a more advanced level. He began compiling what has since become a comprehensive library of noteworthy books on Native American culture. Two such books, *The Sacred Pipe* and *Black Elk Speaks,* both by Lakota holy man Black Elk, aided Goble in determining his life's orientation: he went on to integrate Black Elk's insights into both his personal philosophy and his unique style of illustration.

While continuing his independent study of Native Americans, Goble pursued a career in industrial design as both a teacher and designer, believing that his love of nature and Indian culture would not foster a means to support his family. In the summer of 1959, after completing his degree at London's Central School of Arts and Crafts, Goble toured Sioux and Crow reservations in South Dakota and Montana. During his visit he was adopted into the Yakima and Sioux tribes and was given the name Wakinyan Chikala, or "Little Thunder," by Chief Edgar Red Cloud, a great grandson of a famous Sioux war chief.

Although returning to England and his job as a teacher, Goble took several summer trips to the United States, accompanied by his son, Richard, where he would rent a car and, with a small tent and few belongings, spend the summer among the Sioux in South Dakota and their Crow friends in Montana. "I was privileged to take part in ceremonies, to be present at their sacred Sun Dances. I have taken part in building the Sun Dance lodge and have helped to pitch tipis," commented Goble. His time devoted to painting and writing expanded from school vacations in 1977, when Goble moved to the Black Hills of South Dakota and became a full-time author/illustrator. His decision was prompted by the success of his first four previously published children's books. One of those first successful publications, *The Friendly Wolf,* was eventually revised by Goble and reprinted as *Dream Wolf* in 1990.

As an interpreter of the myths and legends of the Great Plains, Goble evaluates several different versions of the same story before writing the text for his books. "I try to go back to the oldest sources when researching a story," he told a *Publishers Weekly* interviewer, explaining that it was not until about 1890 that native stories were first recorded by ethnologists. Goble presents these traditional myths in the formal poetic style characteristic of Indian oral tradition. Many times songs or prayers relating to the subject are included, as well as bibliographies and informative notes on different aspects of tribal culture.

Books featuring the character Iktomi (pronounced Eek-toe-me, a Lakota word for "spider") encourage reader participation through italicized running commentary. Iktomi is a show-off and a trickster whose clever plans to avoid work constantly backfire with humorous consequences. Goble's setting of these traditional tales in the late twentieth century and his insertions of periodic questions both invite reader participation in the traditional storytelling process. The tales also demonstrate that tales about Iktomi are continually evolving and timeless in their appeal. In *Iktomi and the Buzzard,* for example, the lazy and calculating Iktomi, clad in his typical T-shirt and sneakers and bound for a powwow, convinces a buzzard to help him cross a river but gets tossed into a hollow tree when he makes rude gestures behind the airborne bird's back. Calling Goble's illustrations "striking" due to their "vivid colors, distinctive lines, and authentic design," *Booklist* contributor Julie Corsaro added that "It's hard to resist Iktomi—he's so vain and brash." Corsaro praised Gobel on his scholarship, referring to it as "impeccable" and his tales as "enlightening."

In all his books, Goble emphasizes the harmonious relationship between man and nature that underlays Native American spiritualism. He mentioned in his Caldecott acceptance speech that he wrote *The Friendly Wolf* because he was concerned about the threatened extinction of Alaskan wolves by the practice of hunting such animals by helicopter. He believes children have an inborn love of the natural world that is often blunted by exposure to the conventional worlds of cartoons and

A young native American girl spends all her free time with horses in the award-winning The Girl Who Loved Wild Horses, *written and illustrated by Goble.*

picture books, where bears are "cuddly," wolves and tomcats "vicious," and spiders and snakes "evil." Goble's versions of the Native American legends relate the belief that animals are deserving of man's respect and inspiration rather than fear or ridicule in an effort for young readers become aware of how other cultures viewed "the environment."

Goble's *Death of the Iron Horse* counteracts the "movie myth" that Native Americans regularly destroyed railroad trains and robbed and murdered their helpless passengers. The story is based on the only substantiated account of a train wrecked as a result of an Indian attack: the Union Pacific freight train derailed by Cheyennes on August 7, 1867. Goble portrays the attack as a justifiable defense of the Cheyennes' camp by the encroaching "iron horse" and its "iron road." Looting of the train's cargo is depicted as a just reward after a battle won. The story takes on an almost humorous element when Goble shows Indians gathering up small coins contained in the train's strongbox while throwing great quantities of "useless" paper money away, to be carried off by the prairie winds.

Goble's *Beyond the Ridge* sensitively recounts native beliefs about death and dying. Mortality is one of many stages within the "great circle of life" rather than something to be feared due to its threatening finality: as he writes in *Beyond the Ridge,* "Dying is like climbing up a long and difficult slope towards a high, pine-covered ridge on the Great Plains. From the top we shall see, beyond the ridge, the Spirit World, the Land of Many Tipis, the place from which we came, and the place to which we shall return.... We shall live there without fatigue or sorrow or illness."

In his Caldecott acceptance speech, Goble described *The Girl Who Loved Horses* as a synthesis of many legends which focus on the Indian's rapport with his natural surroundings. "The Indian does not feel afraid or alone in the forests and prairies," Goble pointed out; "he knows many stories about ancestors who turned into the seven stars of the Big Dipper and others who became the Pleiades.... Knowledge of this relationship with the universe gives [him] confidence. [He has] no thought to reorganize nature in a way other than that in which the Great Spirit made it."

Storm Maker's Tipi is a Blackfoot legend that comes "grandly to life" under Goble's care, according to a *Publishers Weekly* contributor. A tale of how tipis came to be designed, the story tells of the Storm Maker, who saves a man and his son from a severe blizzard by passing on his design for a buffalo-hide shelter. The illustrations "reveal Goble at his finest," the critic added, "intermingling texture, form and color" as he explains how tipis are constructed and even includes directions that help readers make a model tipi of their own.

Although some of Goble's texts were criticized by a *Bulletin of the Center for Children's Books* reviewer for being "a bit stiff," Eleanor K. MacDonald of *School Library Journal* credited Goble for his reserve. "He

In Her Seven Brothers, *Goble retells and illustrates the Cheyenne legend of the girl and her seven brothers who become the Big Dipper.*

resists the temptation to dramatize the tale," MacDonald maintained, "choosing instead the quiet, matter-of-fact voice of the traditional Indian storyteller." In his 1996 picture book *The Return of the Buffaloes: A Plains Indian Story about Famine and Renewal,* his "retelling of this Lakota myth is respectful and dignified," according to *Horn Book* contributor Maria B. Salvadore. As a restrained narrative is characteristic of Goble's work, his artwork is similarly stylized. His illustrations contain many symbols from tribal culture, including the circle motif signifying unity, and wavy lines depicting lightning bolts and power. His art is also greatly influenced by research into the paintings earlier Native Americans did in ledger books obtained from white traders. In these books they recorded their tribal history with brightly colored, two-dimensional pictures. In his books, Goble combines the spirit of these historic drawings with his knowledge of design and technique. A *Publishers Weekly* reviewer praised Goble for his "fluid" and "compelling" retelling of *The Legend of the White Buffalo Woman,* largely because he was able to handle the history "succinctly and assuredly" through his artwork and message.

Goble's long-standing respect for the Great Plains Indians has not diminished over the years since he and his wife Janet first made their home in the Black Hills of South Dakota, and he remains one of the major contemporary chroniclers of Native American legends and myths. Through his writing and illustration he has promoted a greater understanding of other cultures, as well as encouraging American Indian children to value their cultural heritage. "We're in need of differences," Goble told *Publishers Weekly,* "*and* to not be afraid of those differences." While occasionally criticism has been leveled at Goble's position as a non-native author telling Native American stories, as an essayist in *St. James Guide to Children's Writers* noted: "the largest number of readers have praised his work.... Using illustrations that are physically and symbolically accurate, he has produced narratives that embody the many elements of traditional Plains life and reveal their importance for all readers."

Biographical and Critical Sources

BOOKS

Children's Literature Review, Volume 21, Gale (Detroit, MI), 1990.

de Montreville, Doris, and Elizabeth D. Crawford, editors, *Fourth Book of Junior Authors and Illustrators,* H. W. Wilson (New York, NY), 1978.

Goble, Paul, *Beyond the Ridge,* Bradbury (New York, NY), 1989.

St. James Guide to Children's Writers, 5th edition, St. James Press (Detroit, MI), 1999.

PERIODICALS

American Indian Quarterly, spring, 1984, pp. 117-125; summer, 1992, Clifford E. Trafzer, review of *The Great Race of the Birds and Animals,* p. 381.

Booklist, May 1, 1990, p. 1714; November 1, 1990, p. 523; February 1, 1991, p. 1129; February 15, 1992, Carolyn Phelan, review of *Crow Chief,* p. 1108; March 15, 1993, Carolyn Phelan, review of *The Lost Children,* p. 1351; March 1, 1994, Julie Corsaro, review of *Iktomi and the Buzzard,* p. 1264; November 1, 1994, Mary Harris Veeder, review of *Adopted by the Eagles,* p. 494; June 1, 1996, Carolyn Phelan, review of *The Return of the Buffaloes,* p. 1725; September 15, 1996, Karen Morgan, review of *Remaking the Earth,* p. 235; March 15, 1998, Karen Morgan, review of *The Legend of the White Buffalo Woman,* p. 1237; August, 1999, GraceAnne A. DeCandido, review of *Iktomi Loses His Eyes,* p. 2060; October 1, 2001, Catherine Andronik, review of *Storm Maker's Tipi,* p. 316.

Bulletin of the Center for Children's Books, March, 1981, pp. 133-134; March, 1983; September, 1985; April, 1987; April, 1988; March, 1989.

Horn Book, December, 1972, pp. 605-606; February, 1977; December, 1978, pp. 631-632; April, 1979, pp. 399-401; August, 1979, pp. 396-401; February, 1981; May, 1989, p. 355; March-April, 1993, Ann A. Flowers, review of *Love Flute,* p. 226; September-October, 1993, Ellen Fader, review of *The Lost Children,* p. 608; March-April, 1995, Ellen Fader, review of *Adopted by the Eagles,* p. 206; July-August, 1996, Maria B. Salvadore, review of *The Return of the Buffaloes,* p. 470.

Language Arts, December, 1984, pp. 867-873.

Los Angeles Times Book Review, June 4, 1989, p. 11; September 24, 1989, p. 12.

New York Times Book Review, November 9, 1970; September 24, 1972, p. 8; November 11, 1973, p. 8; November 22, 1987; December 10, 1989, p. 34; June 17, 1990, p. 21.

Publishers Weekly, February 26, 1988, p. 114; February 23, 1990, p. 215; January 27, 1992, review of *Crow Chief,* p. 95; September 28, 1992, review of *Love Flute,* p. 77; March 22, 1993, review of *The Lost Children,* p. 77; April 29, 1996, review of *The Return of the Buffaloes,* p. 70; April 27, 1998, review of *The Legend of the White Buffalo Woman,* p. 65; October 22, 2001, review of *Storm Maker's Tipi,* p. 76.

School Library Journal, June-July, 1988, p. 97; January, 1995, George Delalis, review of *Adopted by the Eagles,* p. 102; October, 2001, Dona J. Helmer, review of *Storm Maker's Tipi,* p. 139.

Wilson Library Bulletin, September, 1984; November, 1988.

OTHER

Canku Ota, http://www.turtletrack.org/ (February 26, 2000), Vicki Lochard, "Featured Artist: Paul Goble."

*   *   *

GREENE, Jacqueline Dembar 1946-

Personal

Born May 21, 1946, in Hartford, CT; married Malcolm R. Greene (an optometrist), 1967; children: Matthew, Kenneth. *Education:* University of Connecticut, B.A. (with honors), 1967; Central Missouri University, M.A. (with special distinction), 1970. *Hobbies and other interests:* Gardening, cross-country skiing, travel, photography.

Addresses

Home and office—21 Sunnyside Ave., Wellesley, MA 02482. *E-mail*—jacquelinegreene@aol.com.

Career

French teacher in and near Boston, MA, 1967-71; worked variously as a reporter, columnist, and feature writer for newspapers, including *Middlesex News,* Framingham, MA, and *Wellesley Townsman,* Wellesley, MA, 1971-80; writer, 1980—. *Member:* Society of Children's Book Writers and Illustrators.

Awards, Honors

Pick of the List citation, *American Bookseller,* 1984, for *The Leveller;* National Jewish Book Award finalist, 1984, for *Butchers and Bakers, Rabbis and Kings;* Sidney Taylor Honor Book citation, Association of Jewish Libraries, and Books for the Teen Age citation, New York Public Library, both 1988, both for *Out of Many Waters;* Sidney Taylor Honor Book for *One Foot Ashore.*

Writings

A Classroom Hanukah, illustrated by Debra G. Butler, Pascal Publishers, 1980.

The Hanukah Tooth, illustrated by Pauline A. Ouellet, Pascal Publishers, 1980.

Butchers and Bakers, Rabbis and Kings, Kar-Ben Copies (Rockville, MD), 1984.

The Leveller, Walker (New York, NY), 1984.

Nathan's Hanukah Bargain, illustrated by Steffi Karen Rubin, Kar-Ben Copies (Rockville, MD), 1986.

Out of Many Waters, Walker (New York, NY), 1988.

The Maya (nonfiction), edited by Iris Rosoff, Franklin Watts (New York, NY), 1992.

What His Father Did, illustrated by John O'Brien, Houghton Mifflin (Boston, MA), 1992.

The Chippewa (nonfiction), edited by Russell Primm, Franklin Watts (New York, NY), 1993.

One Foot Ashore, Walker (New York, NY), 1994.

Manabozho's Gifts: Three Chippewa Tales, Houghton Mifflin (Boston, MA), 1994.

Marie: Mystery at the Paris Ballet, Paris, 1775 ("Girlhood Journeys" series), illustrated by Lyn Durham, Aladdin (New York, NY), 1997.

Marie: Summer in the Country, France, 1775 ("Girlhood Journeys" series), illustrated by Lyn Durham, Aladdin (New York, NY), 1997.

The Tohono O'Odham (nonfiction), Franklin Watts (New York, NY), 1998.

(And photographer) *Powwow: A Good Day to Dance* (nonfiction), Franklin Watts (New York, NY), 1998.

Slavery in Greece and Rome (nonfiction), Franklin Watts (New York, NY), 1999.

Slavery in Egypt and Mesopotamia (nonfiction), Franklin Watts (New York, NY), 2000.

The Emperor's Teacup, and other Tales from Near and Far, Rigby (Crystal Lake, IL), 2002.

Contributor to periodicals, including *Boston Globe, Day Care, Highlights for Children, Lollipops, Ladybugs and Lucky Stars, Nitty Gritty City, Parenting, Parents' Choice, Small Talk,* and *Wellesley.*

Work in Progress

Miguel, Son of Abraham, historical novel.

Sidelights

Jacqueline Dembar Greene came to writing for children as a result of a college course in children's literature. After changing careers from a French teacher to a journalist, the publication of her first book, *A Classroom Hanukah,* allowed her to "leave the bustle of the news office for the quiet of my own imagination," she once remarked. "I have continued to use the research skills from my former career to find the facts and history that I feel make a story relevant and alive." Among Greene's books are the historical novel *Out of Many Waters* and its sequel, *One Foot Ashore,* as well as a number of books on the history and customs of Native American tribes.

Historical facts are woven into many of Greene's books for children. *Butchers and Bakers, Rabbis and Kings* tells of the seemingly all-powerful King Alfonson the Warrior, who strides into Tudela, Spain, in 1114 thinking he needs no help from anyone in establishing his rule. Concerned about their safety in the new kingdom, the Jews of the city devise a plan to convince the king that without his subjects he is just an ordinary man. Tom Cook, the real-life protagonist of *The Leveller,* was shunned by his eighteenth-century Massachusetts neighbors because they thought he was in league with the devil. Using the people's superstition to avoid capture, Tom set out to secretly "level" the fortunes of the poor farmers with those who had an abundance of food and wealth, all the while trying to outwit the devil, who coveted his soul. In *Marie: Mystery at the Paris Ballet, Paris, 1775* and *Marie: Summer in the Country, France, 1775*—two installments in the "Girlhood Journeys" series—Greene opens a window for modern readers onto the daily life, clothes, and living situation of girls growing up in pre-Revolutionary France.

Jacqueline Dembar Greene portrays the events and dances at a Wampanoag powwow in Powwow, *written and photographed by Greene.*

Greene's historical novels *Out of Many Waters* and *One Foot Ashore* relate the story of sisters Isobel and Maria Ben Lazar, who, during the Inquisition, are taken from their parents in Portugal and shipped as slaves to a monastery in Brazil. Escaping in 1654, they attempt to rejoin their parents, but become separated during their flight. *Out of Many Waters* is twelve-year-old Isobel's story. Forced to stow away on a ship, Isobel is rescued by a small group of Jewish colonists who founded the first Jewish settlement in America. Storms, pirates, kidnapping, first love, landing in New Amsterdam, and Isobel's hopes of finding her family move the plot along. Susan Levine, writing for the *Voice of Youth Advocates,* noted that Greene's characterization of Isobel helps the reader "sympathize with her and be interested in her success." Praising *Out of Many Waters* as "a good story with a memorable character," Levine added that the book is "an easy way to learn a little history." Eli N. Evans noted in the *New York Times Book Review* that Greene "has done a relatively smooth job of weaving history, drama and narrative into an arresting story."

In the companion volume, *One Foot Ashore,* sixteen-year-old Maria also stows away on a ship headed for the Netherlands, and survives the brutal voyage. In Amsterdam, she meets the artist Rembrandt van Rijn, gets a job working as his housemaid, and is aided in her search for her parents by a series of helpful people. While noting that "there is much that is contrived" in the plot, *School Library Journal* contributor Renee Steinberg praised *One Foot Ashore* as "an absorbing read." In *Booklist,* reviewer Carolyn Phelan called it an "intriguing historical novel that will lead to requests for sequels," and praised Greene for creating a "concrete, convincing sense of ... time and place."

Greene's 1992 picture book *What His Father Did* is a humorous story of the trickster Herschel, who figures prominently in Jewish folklore. Traveling on a long journey with little money, Herschel stops at an isolated inn and tricks the innkeeper into giving him supper by vaguely threatening to "do what his father did" if he is left hungry. The frightened innkeeper gathers food from nearby merchants, imagining all manner of horrible things the father could have done, and gets a surprise when Herschel reveals what his father REALLY did. A *Kirkus Reviews* contributor noted that Greene's writing is "lively and economical, fine for sharing aloud," while a *Publishers Weekly* critic dubbed the work "dexterously written [and] exquisitely illustrated."

In addition to fiction, Greene has authored several works of nonfiction for young students. The realities of slavery in the ancient world are brought to light in *Slavery in Ancient Egypt and Mesopotamia* and *Slavery in Ancient Greece and Rome,* both published in 2000. Including a discussion of the daily life of slaves in northern Africa, the first volume moves forward in time to the beginnings of slave trading with Europeans, then with merchants in the Americas. In Greene's second book, the role slaves played in allowing for the flowering of Greek culture is discussed; both books feature what *School Library Journal* contributor Eunice Weech characterized as a

"straightforward, factual text [that] does not gloss over the brutality of this institution."

The Chippewa or Ojibway people are the focus of two books by Greene, including 1994's *The Chippewa,* which presents an overview of tribal culture, history, and religion through to modern times. Shape-shifter legends are collected in *Manabozho's Gifts: Three Chippewa Tales,* which includes the story of how the tribe first harvested wild rice to help them survive the winter, how Manabozho gave his people the gift of fire by stealing the substance from an aged sorcerer, and a third tale, "How Manabozho Saved the Rose," which focuses on native ecology. Praising Greene's retellings for their "quiet dignity," *School Library Journal* contributor Jacqueline Elsner also commented on the inclusion of a foreword by Greene that grounds "readers in the Manabozho archetype," a tradition that also is known under the names Nanabozho, Hiawatha, and Manabush. Noting the environmental underpinnings of the collection, Elizabeth Bush commented in *Bulletin of the Center for Children's Books* on the "deep respect for nature [that] emerges from the Manabozho legend."

In *Powwow: A Good Day to Dance,* Greene follows a ten-year-old Abenaki boy to a twentieth-century tribal gathering, providing a history and background of the day of dance. Focusing on one boy's experiences at a Wampanoag powwow in eastern Massachusetts, Greene "is able to relate many details and describe the event in a personal way," noted Darcy Schild in *School Library Journal.* In addition to a discussion of the boy and his activities, Greene includes sidebars that focus on clothing, music, dance, food, drumming, and powwow "etiquette."

"I always remember that we are never far from childhood," Greene once commented to *SATA* in reflecting on her role as a writer. "All the things we have done, the friends we have made, the embarrassments and successes we felt, are part of us and make us the people we are. When I write a book, it is not just written with children in mind. It reflects my feelings and should strike a responsive chord in every reader, regardless of age. I hope my characters speak to everyone expressing the ageless and human emotions we all share, and making readers feel as if they have met someone they never knew before, and will remember for a long time."

Biographical and Critical Sources

PERIODICALS

Booklist, July, 1984; February 1, 1987, p. 843; March 15, 1992, Hazel Rochman, review of *What His Father Did,* p. 1282; June 15, 1992, Karen Hutt, review of *The Maya,* pp. 1829-1830; February 15, 1994, Ilene Cooper, review of *The Chippewa,* p. 1078; April 1, 1994, Carolyn Phelan, review of *One Foot Ashore,* p. 1446; March 15, 1995, Linda Ward-Callaghan, review of *Manabozho's Gifts: Three Chippewa Tales,* p. 1324; April, 1998, Denia Hester, review of *Marie: Summer in the Country, France, 1775,* p. 1319; January, 1999,

Karen Hutt, review of *Powwow: A Good Day to Dance,* p. 865.

Boston Globe, July 8, 1984.

Bulletin of the Center for Children's Books, April, 1984, p. 146; January, 1989, p. 121; February, 1995, Elizabeth Bush, review of *Manabozho's Gifts,* p. 198.

Horn Book, August, 1984, Mary M. Burns, review of *The Leveller,* p. 474; May-June, 1992, Hanna B. Zeiger, review of *What His Father Did,* p. 346; July-August, 1994, Elizabeth S. Watson, review of *One Foot Ashore,* p. 451.

Kirkus Reviews, August 15, 1988, pp. 1240-1241; February 1, 1992, review of *What His Father Did,* p. 183.

New York Times Book Review, March 19, 1989, Eli N. Evans, review of *Out of Many Waters,* p. 24.

Publishers Weekly, February 10, 1992, review of *What His Father Did,* p. 81.

School Library Journal, April, 1984, Deborah M. Locke, review of *The Leveller,* pp. 114-115; November, 1984,

Micki S. Nevett, review of *Butchers and Bakers, Rabbis and Kings,* p. 108; October, 1988, p. 144; August, 1992, Marcia Posner, review of *What His Father Did,* pp. 151-152, 164; June, 1994, Renee Steinberg, review of *One Foot Ashore,* p. 128; January, 1995, Jacqueline Elsner, review of *Manabozho's Gifts,* p. 118; August, 1997, Nancy Menaldi-Scanlan, review of *Marie: Mystery at the Paris Ballet, Paris, 1775,* p. 135; April, 1998, Anne Knickerbocker, review of *Marie: Summer in the Country, France, 1775,* p. 131; February, 1999, Darcy Schild, review of *Powwow,* p. 97; March, 2001, Eunice Weech, review of *Slavery in Ancient Egypt and Mesopotamia;* March, 2001, Ann Welton, *Slavery in Ancient Greece and Rome,* p. 266.

Voice of Youth Advocates, August, 1992, p. 187.

OTHER

Jacqueline Greene Web Site, http://mgjg.dynip.com/jgreene (April 28, 2002).

H

HALLS, Kelly Milner 1957-

Personal

Born December 6, 1957, in Amarillo, TX; daughter of Gene and Georgia (Ketchum) Milner; divorced; children: Vanessa, Kerry. *Education:* Attended Brigham Young University. *Politics:* Democrat. *Religion:* "Be kind." *Hobbies and other interests:* Tennis, skiing, painting, paleontology, animals.

Addresses

Home and office—Spokane, WA. *E-mail*—KellyMilnerH@aol.com.

Career

Author and freelance journalist. *Member:* Society of Children's Book Writers and Illustrators, American Library Association, Young Adult Library Services Association.

Awards, Honors

American Bookseller "Pick of the List" science book, 1995, for *Dino-Trekking: The Ultimate Dinosaur Lover's Travel Guide;* Ed Press honorable mention, 2000, for "Materialism Bug."

Writings

Dino-Trekking: The Ultimate Dinosaur Lover's Travel Guide, illustrated by Rick Spears, Wiley (New York, NY), 1996.

Baby Chick, Boyds Mills Press (Honesdale, PA), 1999.

Kids Go! Denver: A Fun-Filled, Fact-Packed, Travel and Activity Book, John Muir Publications (Santa Fe, NM), 1999.

(With Maria Birmingham and Karen E. Bledsoe) *365 Outdoor Activities,* Publications International (Lincolnwood, IL), 2000.

I Bought a Baby Chicken, illustrated by Karen Stormer Brooks, Boyds Mills Press (Honesdale, PA), 2000.

(With Suzanne Lieurance and Jamie Gabriel) *School Projects for Pennies,* illustrated by George Ulrich, Publications International (Lincolnwood, IL), 2000.

Look What You Can Make with Craft Sticks, Boyds Mills Press (Honesdale, PA), 2002.

Contributor to *Stress Fractures,* edited by Terry Trueman, HarperCollins (New York, NY), 2003. Contributor to periodicals, including *Teen People, Writer's Digest, Highlights for Children, Chicago Tribune, Denver Post, Washington Post, Atlanta Journal Constitution, Fort Worth Star-Telegram, Guidepost for Teens, Parenting Teens, Boy's Life, Fox Kids, Booklist, Voice of Youth Advocates, Book Magazine, Family Fun, U.S. Kids, Child Life, Dig, New Jersey Monthly, Wyoming Magazine, Jurassic Park Institute.*

Work in Progress

My Mummy's a Kid; My Mummy's an Animal; "Dinosaur" series; *Sea Monsters around the World;* (with others) *Girl Meets Boy: An Anthology; Atypical Girl: A Novel* (for young adults).

Sidelights

Kelly Milner Halls told *SATA:* "Though I work full-time as a freelance writer, I am fast becoming a YA literature advocate, determined to broaden the reach of these outstanding coming-of-age stories and authors."

Biographical and Critical Sources

PERIODICALS

Booklist, April 1, 2000, Lauren Peterson, review of *I Bought a Baby Chicken,* p. 1468.

Publishers Weekly, January 17, 2000, review of *I Bought a Baby Chicken,* p. 55.

School Library Journal, July, 2000, Karen James, review of *I Bought a Baby Chicken,* p. 79.

HARNESS, Cheryl 1951-

Personal

Born July 6, 1951, in CA; daughter of Raymond and Elaine Harness. *Education:* Central Missouri State University, B.A. (art education), 1973; attended Uri Shulevitz' summer study, 1984. *Politics:* Democrat. *Religion:* "Optimistic agnostic." *Hobbies and other interests:* Books, pets, movie theaters, sewing, sculpting.

Addresses

Home—2000 N. Farview Drive, Independence, MO. *Agent*—c/o Author Mail, 7th Floor, HarperCollins, 10 East 53rd St., New York, NY 10022.

Career

Author and illustrator. Worked variously as a student teacher, waitress, short order cook, portrait artist, and needlework designer. Greeting card artist for Hallmark Cards and Current. Makes numerous school visits.

Awards, Honors

Republic of San Marino postage stamp painting prize; *Fudge,* by Charlotte Graeber, was awarded the West Virginia Children's award and KC Three award, both 1988-90, the Nene Award, Young Hoosier commendation, and Sequoyah Children's award, all 1990, and the Iowa Children's Choice designation, and Sunshine State award, both 1992; Notable Book designation in the Social Studies, Center for Children's Books, 1998, for *Mark Twain and the Queens of the Mississippi;* Missouri Association of School Librarians Award for *Ghosts of the White House;* Friend of the School Libraries Award, 2001; Colorado Children's Book Award, 2002.

Writings

FOR CHILDREN; SELF-ILLUSTRATED UNLESS OTHERWISE NOTED

(Adaptor) *The Night-Light Mother Goose,* Random House (New York, NY), 1988.

The Windchild, Holt (New York, NY), 1991.

Three Young Pilgrims, Bradbury Press (New York, NY), 1992.

The Queen with Bees in Her Hair, Holt (New York, NY), 1993.

Young John Quincy, Bradbury Press (New York, NY), 1994.

Papa's Christmas Gift: Around the World on the Night before Christmas, Simon & Schuster (New York, NY), 1995.

The Amazing Impossible Erie Canal, Simon & Schuster (New York, NY), 1995.

Young Abe Lincoln: The Frontier Days, 1809-1837, National Geographic Society (Washington, DC), 1996.

They're Off! The Story of the Pony Express, Simon & Schuster (New York, NY), 1996.

Abe Lincoln Goes to Washington, 1837-1865, National Geographic Society (Washington, DC), 1996.

Young Teddy Roosevelt, National Geographic Society (Washington, DC), 1998.

Mark Twain and the Queens of the Mississippi, Simon & Schuster (New York, NY), 1998.

Ghosts of the White House, Simon & Schuster (New York, NY), 1998.

Midnight in the Cemetery: A Spooky Search-and-Find Alphabet Book, illustrated by Robin Brickman, Simon & Schuster (New York, NY), 1999.

Ghosts of the Twentieth Century, Simon & Schuster (New York, NY), 2000.

George Washington, National Geographic Society (Washington, DC), 2000.

Remember the Ladies: One Hundred Great American Women, HarperCollins (New York, NY), 2001.

Ghosts of the Civil War, Simon & Schuster (New York, NY), 2001.

ILLUSTRATOR

Deborah Gould, *Grandpa's Slide Show,* Lothrop, Lee & Shepard (New York, NY), 1987.

Charlotte Towner Graeber, *Fudge,* Lothrop, Lee & Shepard (New York, NY), 1987.

George Shannon, *Oh, I Love!,* Bradbury Press (New York, NY), 1988.

Alice Schertle, *Gus Wanders Off,* Lothrop, Lee & Shepard (New York, NY), 1988.

Deborah Gould, *Aaron's Shirt,* Bradbury Press (New York, NY), 1989.

Joanne Ryder, *Under the Moon,* Random House (New York, NY), 1989.

Clement C. Moore, *The Night before Christmas,* Random House (New York, NY), 1989.

Carolyn Magner, reteller, *Little Red Riding Hood,* Book Club of America (Fort Salonga, NY), 1993.

Work in Progress

The Revolutionary John Adams, Ghosts of the Nile, and *Thomas Jefferson.*

Sidelights

Since her start as a picture-book author/illustrator with 1992's *The Windchild,* artist Cheryl Harness has gone on to specialize in crafting a compelling—and sometimes haunting—mix of fact and fiction. Through her books she brings to life fascinating episodes in the ongoing American drama, from the life stories of great U.S. presidents to the historical overviews contained in such intriguing works as *Ghosts of the Twentieth Century* and *Mark Twain and the Queens of the Mississippi* to more straightforward nonfiction such as *They're Off! The Story of the Pony Express* and *The Amazing Impossible Erie Canal.* Critics have praised Harness's originality in framing her histories and her ability to imaginatively "present a large amount of information succinctly and clearly," according to a *Publishers Weekly* contributor. In *Ghosts of the Twentieth Century* and *Ghosts of the White House,* for instance, a student on a school field trip to an historic locale meets up with a loquacious member of the spirit world who serves as a guide through history. Harness's artistic talents are also consistently praised by critics. In a review of Harness's 1993 picture book *The Queen with Bees in Her Hair,* a *Publishers Weekly* contributor cited the "meticulously wrought scenes" in this "visually captivating tale," and concluded: "the artwork impresses."

Born in 1951 in California, Harness has since made the Midwest her home. As she recalled on her Web site, she was raised in a house full of books. "My favorite books when I was growing up were all of those by Laura Ingalls Wilder. They were wonderful stories that just happened to have happened in the past. I like imagining other times. If you can't have a real time-machine, books make a swell consolation prize. Besides, the past you

visit in your imagination can be just as lively and not nearly so sweaty and dangerous as the real deal."

Although Harness graduated from Central Missouri State University with the intention of becoming an art teacher, she became aware that teaching was not for her after surviving her first student teaching experience. Instead, she decided to become a working artist, and began illustrating greeting cards for several national companies. In the mid-1980s she decided to branch out into book illustration. Assembling her best paintings into a portfolio, she traveled to New York City and made the rounds of publishers. She returned home successful, and was soon busy at work in her home studio, creating book

The ghost of George Washington gives Sara a personal tour of the White House and introduces her to the ghosts of thirty-five other presidents in this work, written and illustrated by Cheryl Harness.

illustrations for Bradbury Press at night and drawing card art during the day. In 1984 she went to Oneonta, New York, and attended a workshop on children's books led by noted illustrator Uri Shulevitz. This workshop inspired her to not only illustrate but write stories for young readers.

In 1992 Harness published her first original picture book, *The Windchild,* which tells a fanciful tale of a boy who accidentally wounds the wind with his arrow so that no breeze will blow through his small village. Praising both text and illustrations, *School Library Journal* contributor Marianne Pilla dubbed the book "an imaginative and touching tale, just right for a hot summer's day." *The Windchild* was followed by another fanciful tale, *The Queen with Bees in Her Hair,* which tells the story of a vain monarch whose massive hairdo creates problems when it is confused by her winged subjects with a beehive.

Three Young Pilgrims was the first book by Harness that was based on historical facts. Taking place in the Plymouth colony, the story recounts the experiences of the three Allerton children—Mary, Bartholomew, and Remember—who traveled with their parents to the New World aboard the *Mayflower.* The 363-mile-long waterway dug from Albany to Buffalo, New York, and finished in the fall of 1825 after eight years of construction is the subject of *The Amazing Impossible Erie Canal,* as Harness presents text and detailed illustrations that recreate this monumental undertaking, done before the days of backhoes, dynamite, and jackhammers.

The Erie Canal was one of several methods Americans devised in order to trade and communicate with one another during the expansion westward in the early years of the nineteenth century. Communication from coast to coast was an even greater problem, one explored by Harness in *They're Off! The Story of the Pony Express.* Recounting the short but dramatic history of the Pony Express from the first relay from St. Joseph, Missouri, to San Francisco, California, in the spring of 1860, the author/illustrator includes "busy and elaborate illustrations [that] ... create a panorama of the age," according to *School Library Journal* contributor Louise L. Sherman. A bibliography and a list of the 182 riders who risked their lives in the ten-day gallop across sometimes dangerous territory are included, alongside a text that focuses on "the youth and instincts of the riders, who battled weather and fatigue," according to a critic writing in *Kirkus Reviews.*

Beginning with her biography of the early years of John Quincy Adams in 1994, Harness has also created several engaging books that allow young readers to gain an appreciation of several great U.S. presidents as people of character and vision. In *Young John Quincy,* the childhood of the sixth president of the United States is depicted, from his childhood spent on a farm in Massachusetts to his experiences during the Revolutionary War as a lad of nine. As the son of Samuel and Abigail Adams, John Quincy witnesses the formation of

Ghosts scare away two children in Harness's search-and-find alphabet book, **Midnight in the Cemetery.** *(Illustrated by Robin Brickman.)*

the nation he would eventually serve as a diplomat and congressman as well as lead as president. *Young Teddy Roosevelt* takes readers on a similar tour of Roosevelt's life before he became the twenty-sixth president, and includes coverage of his stint in the Spanish-American War and his term as governor of New York State. While noting that Harness's text is sometimes uneven, *School Library Journal* contributor Alicia Eames praised *Young Teddy Roosevelt* for its "spirited full-color illustrations that offer a sense of excitement" and noted that the illustrator's design "packs instant visual success" in recounting the early life of one of the most intriguing presidents of the twentieth century. Equally enthusiastic over the book's format, *Booklist* contributor Lauren Peterson praised the diversity of page design, in particular Harness's decisions to "mix several scenes and use a variety of elements, such as borders, maps, and captions."

President Abraham Lincoln is such a pivotal figure in U.S. history that Harness has devoted two books to his life. Readers can begin with *Young Abe Lincoln: The Frontier Days, 1809-1837,* as Lincoln grows up in rural Kentucky with a thirst for learning. Calling the book a "credible, highly personal portrait" of the sixteenth president of the United States, a *Publishers Weekly* contributor praised the book's "realistic, vividly colored illustrations." The companion to *Young Abe Lincoln* is Harness's 1997 picture book *Abe Lincoln Goes to Washington, 1837-1965,* which begins by showing readers the wet-behind-the-ears Kentucky-born lawyer and newly elected state legislator arriving in Springfield, Illinois, to make his mark. Painting a realistic portrait of a man who has become an American myth, Harness's "informal style lends a familiarity to the narrative, interspersing quotes, excerpts, anecdotes, and speeches" into her text, according to a *Kirkus Reviews* critic. Commending the illustrations in particular for their ability to "convey Lincoln's private and public personalities," a *Publishers Weekly* reviewer concluded of *Abe Lincoln Goes to Washington:* "Solid storytelling meets sound history."

Harness's favorite mediums include watercolor, colored pencil, and pastel, giving her illustrations a soft, gentle look. She divides her time as an author/illustrator between traveling to various sites around the country to research her books and working in her home studio. She shares her small, book-filled house in Independence, Missouri, with a cat named Irene and a Scottie dog named Maudie.

Biographical and Critical Sources

PERIODICALS

Booklist, September 1, 1992, Carolyn Phelan, review of *Three Young Pilgrims,* p. 56; March 1, 1993, Deborah Abbott, review of *The Queen with Bees in Her Hair,* p. 1235; March 1, 1994, Carolyn Phelan, review of *Young John Quincy,* p. 1257; May 15, 1995, Carolyn Phelan, *The Amazing Impossible Erie Canal,* p. 1643; September 15, 1995, Kathy Broderick, review of *Papa's Christmas Gift: Around the World on the Night before Christmas,* p. 170; January 1, 1997, Carolyn Phelan, review of *Abe Lincoln Goes to Washington,* p. 863; March 1, 1998, Susan Dove Lempke, review of *Ghosts of the White House,* p. 1128; March 15, 1998, Lauren Peterson, review of *Young Teddy Roosevelt,* p. 1238; January 1, 1999, Carolyn Phelan, review of *Mark Twain and the Queens of the Mississippi,* p. 865; November 15, 1999, John Peters, review of *Midnight in the Cemetery,* p. 626; November 15, 1999, Carolyn Phelan, review of *Ghosts of the Twentieth Century,* p. 620; March 1, 2000, Carolyn Phelan, review of *George Washington,* p. 1239; April 15, 2001, Ilene Cooper, review of *Remember the Ladies: One Hundred Great American Women,* p. 1548; January 1, 2002, Carolyn Phelan, review of *Ghosts of the Civil War,* p. 857.

Bulletin of the Center for Children's Books, September 1, 1996, Kay Weisman, review of *Young Abe Lincoln: The Frontier Days, 1809-1837,* p. 139; November 15, 1996, Lauren Peterson, review of *They're Off! The Story of the Pony Express,* p. 582; January, 1999, Deborah Stevenson, review of *Mark Twain and the Queens of the Mississippi,* p. 168.

Children's Book Review Service, winter, 1992, review of *The Windchild,* p. 63.

Instructor, October, 1997, Judy Freeman, review of *Abe Lincoln Goes to Washington,* p. 26.

Kirkus Reviews, August 15, 1992, review of *Three Young Pilgrims,* p. 1061; February 1, 1994, review of *Young John Quincy,* p. 144; October 15, 1995, review of *Papa's Christmas Gift,* p. 1492; November 15, 1996, review of *They're Off!,* p. 1669; January 1, 1997, review of *Abe Lincoln Goes to Washington, 1837-1865,* p. 58; November 1, 1998, review of *Mark Twain and the Queens of the Mississippi,* p. 1600; December 1, 1999, review of *Ghosts of the Twentieth Century,* p. 1885; November 15, 2001, review of *Ghosts of the Civil War,* p. 1161.

Publishers Weekly, August 31, 1992, review of *Three Young Pilgrims,* p. 204; February 8, 1993, review of *The Queen with Bees in Her Hair,* p. 86; January 10, 1994, review of *Young John Quincy,* p. 62; September 18, 1995, review of *Papa's Christmas Gift,* p. 103; May 20, 1996, review of *Young Abe Lincoln,* p. 259; January 6, 1997, review of *Abe Lincoln Goes to Washington,* p. 73; December 15, 1997, review of *Ghosts of the White House,* p. 58; November 23, 1998, review of *Mark Twain and the Queens of the Mississippi,* p. 67; September 27, 1999, review of *Midnight in the Cemetery,* p. 48; January 3, 2000, "Back in Time," p. 78; January 29, 2001, review of *Remember the Ladies,* p. 91.

School Library Journal, March, 1992, Marianne Pilla, review of *The Windchild,* p. 215; September, 1992, Alexandra Marris, review of *Three Young Pilgrims,* p. 204; June, 1993, Anna Biagioni Hart, review of *The Queen with Bees in Her Hair,* p. 76; April, 1994, Cyrisse Jaffee, review of *Young John Quincy,* p. 120; August, 1995, Kate Hegarty Bouman, review of *The Amazing Impossible Erie Canal,* p. 134; October, 1995, Jane Marino, review of *Papa's Christmas Gift,* p. 38; June, 1996, Rosie Peasley, review of *Young Abe Lincoln,* p. 141; December, 1996, Louise L. Sherman, review of *They're Off!,* pp. 113-114; March, 1997, Shirley Wilton, review of *Abe Lincoln Goes to Washington,* p. 175; April, 1998, Alicia Eames, review of *Ghosts of the White House,* p. 117; July, 1998, Alice Eames, review of *Young Teddy Roosevelt,* p. 88; December, 1998, Barbara Elleman, review of *Mark Twain and the Queens of the Mississippi,* p. 104; November, 1999, Marian Drabkin, review of *Midnight in the Cemetery,* p. 118; February, 2000, Steven Engelfried, review of *Ghosts of the Twentieth Century,* p. 111; April, 2000, Edith Ching, review of *George Washington,* p. 120; February, 2001, Anne Chapman Callaghan, review of *Remember the Ladies,* p. 111; January, 2002, Rita Hunt Smith, review of *Ghosts of the Civil War,* p. 100.

OTHER

Cheryl Harness Web Site, http://www.cherylharness.com (January 22, 2002).

HAYES, Joe 1945-

Personal

Born November 12, 1945, in Ross Township, PA; son of James E. and Marie J. (a teacher) Hayes; children: Kathleen, Adam. *Education:* University of Arizona, B.A., 1968. *Politics:* Democrat. *Religion:* "All."

Addresses

Home—1113 Leaping Powder Rd., Santa Fe, NM 87508.

Career

Storyteller and writer.

Awards, Honors

New Mexico Eminent Scholar, 1989; Southwest Book Award, 1995, for *Watch Out for Clever Women/Cuidado con las mujeres astutas;* New Mexico Governor's Award for Excellence in the Arts, 1995; Arizona Young Readers Award for *Soft Chill,* 1996; Land of Enchantment Children's Book Award for *A Spoon for Every Bite,* 2001.

Joe Hayes

Writings

The Day It Snowed Tortillas: Tales from Spanish New Mexico, illustrated by Lucy Jelinek, Mariposa Publishing (Santa Fe, NM), 1982.

Coyote and . . . : Native American Folktales, illustrated by Lucy Jelinek, Mariposa Publishing (Santa Fe, NM), 1983.

The Checker Playing Hound Dog: Tall Tales from a Southwestern Storyteller, illustrated by Lucy Jelinek, Mariposa Publishing (Santa Fe, NM), 1986.

No Way, Jose!/De Ninguna Manera, Jose!, illustrated by Lucy Jelinek, Trails West (Santa Fe, NM), 1986.

La Llorona/The Weeping Woman, illustrated by Vicki Trego-Hill, Cinco Puntos Press (El Paso, TX), 1987.

Monday, Tuesday, Wednesday, Oh!/Lunes, Martes, Miercoles, O!, illustrated by Lucy Jelinek, Trails West (Santa Fe, NM), 1987.

A Heart Full of Turquoise: Pueblo Indian Tales, Mariposa Publishing (Santa Fe, NM), 1988.

Mariposa, Mariposa, illustrated by Lucy Jelinek, Trails West (Santa Fe, NM), 1988.

The Wise Little Burro, illustrated by Lucy Jelinek, Trails West (Santa Fe, NM), 1990.

That's Not Fair! Earth Friendly Tales, Trails West (Santa Fe, NM), 1991.

Everyone Knows Gato Pinto: More Tales from Spanish New Mexico, illustrated by Lucy Jelinek, Mariposa Publishing (Santa Fe, NM), 1992.

Soft Child: How Rattlesnake Got Its Fangs, illustrated by Kay Sather, Harbinger House (Boulder, CO), 1993.

Antonio's Lucky Day, Scholastic (New York, NY), 1993.

The Butterflies Trick Coyote, Scholastic (New York, NY), 1993.

Watch Out for Clever Women/Cuidado con las Mujeres Astutas, illustrated by Vicki T. Hill, Cinco Puntos Press (El Paso, TX), 1994.

Where There's a Will, There's a Way/Donde hay ganas hay manas, illustrated by Lucy Jelinek, Trails West (Santa Fe, NM), 1995.

A Spoon for Every Bite, illustrated by Rebecca Leer, Scholastic (New York, NY), 1996.

Here Comes the Storyteller, photographs by Richard Barron, Cinco Puntos Press (El Paso, TX), 1996.

La Llorona/The Weeping Woman, illustrated by Vicki Trego-Hill, Cinco Puntos Press (El Paso, TX), 1997.

(With Josbe Ortega) *Grandfather Horned Toad,* Pearson Learning (Parsippany, NJ), 1997.

(Translator) Luis E. Reyes, *Modelo Antiguo: A Novel of Mexico City,* Cinco Puntos Press (El Paso, TX), 1997.

(Editor) J. Manuel Espinosa, compiler, *Cuentos de cuanto hay/Tales from Spanish New Mexico,* illustrated by William Rotsaert, University of New Mexico Press (Albuquerque, NM), 1998.

Tell Me a Cuento/Cuèntame un story, illustrated by Geronimo Garcia, Cinco Puntos Press (El Paso, TX), 1998.

(With Susannah Byrd) *Using a Bilingual Storybook in the Classroom,* Cinco Puntos Press (El Paso, TX), 1998.

A Spoon for Every Bite, illustrated by Rebecca Leer, Scholastic (New York, NY), 1999.

Little Gold Star: A Cinderella Cuento/Estrellita de oro, illustrated by Gloria Osun Perez and Lucia Angela Perez, Cinco Puntos Press (El Paso, TX), 2000.
(Reteller) *El Cucuy!: A Bogeyman Cuento,* illustrated by Honorio Robledo, Cinco Puntos Press (El Paso, TX), 2001.
(Reteller) *Juan Verdades: The Man Who Couldn't Tell a Lie,* illustrated by Joseph Daniel Fielder, Orchard Books (New York, NY), 2001.
Pájaro Verde/The Green Bird, illustrated by Antonio Castro, Jr., Cinco Puntos Press (El Paso, TX), 2002.

Contributor of essays to anthologies, including "The Day after It Snowed Tortillas," in *Sitting at the Feet of the Past: Retelling the North American Folktale for Children,* edited by Gary D. Schmidt and Donald R. Hettinga. Several of Hayes's works have been recorded on audiotape, including *No Way, Jose!*

Sidelights

Folklorist Joe Hayes's more than two dozens picture books testify to his love of the American Southwest. Many of his books have been published in bilingual English-Spanish editions and feature artwork that captures the feel of the Southwest and its various cultures. *Little Gold Star: A Cinderella Cuento/Estrellita de oro* is an adaptation of the Cinderella story that includes some novel plot developments that, according to *Booklist* reviewer Ilene Cooper, "add depth to the story" and thus improve upon the original. For example, Arciá's nasty stepsisters get punished magically for their jealousy and greediness. As one would expect from a seasoned story teller, "the telling ... is crisp, lively and individual," observed Ann Welton of *School Library Journal.*

In *El Cucuy!: A Bogeyman Cuento* Hayes takes up the legend of a monster who snatches naughty children. In Spanish folklore this bogeyman is a gigantic humped back man with a huge, red ear that can hear everyone who lives in the mountains. When a father, who is upset by his two eldest daughters' misbehavior, calls out that el Cucuy ought to take them, he is in for a surprise. The monster carries them off, leaving the father and youngest sister to search for them. Eventually they are rescued by a goat herd and ready to mend their ways. Praising the work as a "masterfully told story," *Booklist* critic Annie Ayres judged the appropriate audience to be those "scoffing, hard-case customers" looking for a "really scary story." Likewise, a *Publishers Weekly* reviewer proposed that this "chilling cautionary tale [is] best enjoyed during the daylight hours."

Juan Verdades: The Man Who Couldn't Tell a Lie is a "smooth retelling" of a traditional story whose "flowing plot [is] enlivened by several wry twists" wrote a *Publishers Weekly* contributor. The plot revolves around a wager by two ranch owners over the honesty of Juan Verdades, a servant of one of the ranchers. Both the illustrations and intermittent use of Spanish phrases add to the work's authentic northern New Mexico flavor and give it a "strong sense of time and place," remarked a

Kirkus Reviews critic, who added, "Though the text is long, the telling is captivating."

"I have lived in this region for forty years and enjoy its people and landscapes immensely," Hayes once told *SATA.* "I see the stories and the land as inseparably bound together. I share stories based on traditional Southwestern folklore because they express my own attachment to this sunny land. The stories reflect diverse cultural traditions—Hispanic, Pueblo Indian, Navajo, Tohono O'odham, etc.—but I really have no lofty educational motive or social purpose in telling them.

"My writing has grown directly out of my storytelling. In fact, most of the stories I've published were worked out orally long before I ever sat down to write them. Kids will ask me, 'How long did it take you to write that book?' And I have to tell them, 'Well, I had been telling those stories for about four years before I wrote them down. So you could say it took four years. On the other hand, since I already had the stories in my head, it only took me about four hours to type them into my computer. So you could say it took four hours.' I like working that way. I think the style ends up more natural, with the ring of the spoken word resounding in the printed stories.

"And, of course, the listeners help shape the stories through their reactions. On the occasions that I've written stories without first telling them, I find that they go through some rapid changes as soon as I start sharing them aloud. I try to parallel the spoken word as I write, but telling the stories sometimes shows me that my style has become somewhat artificial. I also discover that some parts of the story need amplification, and others condensation, to make them really work with an audience. When I write without telling, I almost always find myself wishing I had taken the time to get audience feedback before I let the story become frozen in print."

Biographical and Critical Sources

PERIODICALS

Booklist, March 15, 1996, Ilene Cooper, review of *A Spoon for Every Bite,* p. 1268; May 15, 2000, Ilene Cooper, review of *Little Gold Star: A Cinderella Cuento/ Estrellita de oro,* p. 1756; July, 2001, Annie Ayres, review of *El Cucuy! A Bogeyman Cuento in English and Spanish,* p. 2013; December 1, 2001, Shelle Rosenfeld, review of *Juan Verdades: The Man Who Couldn't Gell a Lie,* p. 646.
Bulletin of the Center for Children's Books, December, 1994, p. 130; March, 1997, Janice M. Del Negro, review of *Here Comes the Storyteller,* p. 263.
Children's Book Review Service, February, 1999, review of *Tell Me a Cuento,* p. 79.
Kirkus Reviews, November 1, 2001, review of *Juan Verdades,* p. 1550.
Publishers Weekly, March 4, 1996, review of *A Spoon for Every Bite,* p. 64; May 21, 2001, review of *El Cucuy!,* p. 107; November 12, 2001, review of *Juan Verdades,* p. 59.

School Library Journal, March, 1985, Priscilla Bennett, review of *Tales of the Southwest,* p. 142; April, 1987, Kevin Booe, review of *No Way, Jose!,* p. 76; August, 1992, Penny Peck, review of *Best-Loved Stories Told at the National Storytelling Festival,* p. 123; April, 1996, Ruth Semrau, review of *A Spoon for Every Bite,* p. 110; October, 1998, Denise E. Agosto, review of *Tell Me a Cuento,* pp. 123-124; November 1, 1998, JoAnn Balingit, review of *La Llorana/The Weeping Woman,* pp. 61-62; June, 2000, Ann Welton, review of *Little Gold Star,* p. 132; July, 2001, Diane Olivo-Posner, review of *El Cucuy!,* p. 94.

*   *   *

HERZOG, Brad 1968-

Personal

Born 1968; son of Myron and Hazel Herzog; married Amy (a marketing executive), 1993; children: Luke. *Education:* Cornell University, B.A., 1990.

Addresses

Home—316 9th St., Pacific Grove, CA 93940. *Agent*—Robert Preskill, Lit West Group, LLC, 1763 Golden Gate Ave., #10, San Francisco, CA 94115. *E-mail*—brad@bradherzog.com.

Career

Ithaca Journal, Ithaca, NY, journalist, 1990-92. Freelance writer, 1992—.

Awards, Honors

Grand Gold Medal, Council for Advancement and Support of Education, 1999, Cornell University, for feature writing in *Cornell Magazine;* Best of Gannett Award, for a six-part series on Native American nicknames and institutionalized racism in sports, 1991; his screenplay *Spin Art* was chosen as a finalist in the Monterey County Film Commission Screen writing Contest, 2000.

Writings

NOVELS

The Hero in the Mirror, Rigby Education (Barrington, IL), 2000.
The Monster's New Friend, Rigby Education (Barrington, IL), 2000.
The Runaway Ball, Rigby Education (Barrington, IL), 2000.
Freddy in the Fridge, Rigby Education (Barrington, IL), 2002.

NONFICTION

The Everything You Want to Know about Sports Encyclopedia, Sports Illustrated for Kids Books (New York, NY), 1994.

Heads Up! Sports Illustrated for Kids Books (New York, NY), 1994.
Seventh-Inning Stretch: Time-out for Baseball Trivia, Sports Illustrated for Kids Books (New York, NY), 1994.
MVP Sports Puzzles, Sports Illustrated for Kids Books (New York, NY), 1995.
Hoopmania!: The Jam-Packed Book of Basketball Trivia, Sports Illustrated for Kids Books (New York, NY), 1995.
Soccer, Celebration Press (Columbus, OH), 1996.
Hot Summer Stars, Sports Illustrated for Kids Books (New York, NY), 1997.
The Fifty Greatest Athletes of Today, Sports Illustrated for Kids Books (New York, NY), 1998.
2000: A Celebration of Sports, Sports Illustrated for Kids Books (New York, NY), 1999.
Olympics 2000: Stars and Stats, Sports Illustrated for Kids Books (New York, NY), 2000.
The Twenty Greatest Athletes of the Twentieth Century, Rosen Publishing Group (New York, NY), 2000.
Laugh Locker, Sports Illustrated Books for Kids (New York, NY), 2000.
Dare to Be Different: Athletes Who Changed Sports, Rosen Publishing Group (New York, NY), 2003.

FOR ADULTS

The Sports One Hundred: The One Hundred Most Important People in American Sports History, Macmillan (New York, NY), 1995.
States of Mind: A Search for Faith, Hope, Inspiration, Harmony, Unity, Friendship, Love, Pride, Wisdom, Honor, Comfort, Joy, Bliss, Freedom, Justice, Glory, Triumph, and Truth or Consequences in America, J. F. Blair (Winston-Salem, NC), 1999.

OTHER

Also author of *Spin Art* (screenplay). Contributor of articles to magazines, including *Sports Illustrated, Sports Illustrated for Kids, Writer's Digest, Basketball Digest, Outdoor Explorer, Via, Sky Magazine,* and *Attaché.*

Sidelights

A prolific writer of books and articles, Brad Herzog does not wait for inspiration to come to him. He finds it—in sports, in places, in people. Over an eight-year period he wrote dozens of articles for *Sports Illustrated for Kids* and the adult version *Sports Illustrated,* with topics ranging from biographical sketches of famous athletes to reviews of sports teaching aids. His books on sports, geared to nine- to twelve-year-old sports enthusiasts, also demonstrate his skill as a sports generalist. They include biographical profiles, a sports encyclopedia, and trivia and game books about athletes in all sports, including Olympic events.

In 1999, Brad and his wife, Amy, then living in Chicago, decided to give up their urban lifestyle for a taste of life on the road. They bought a large recreational vehicle, which they made their home for the next year as they traveled across the United States, looking for interesting, off-the-beaten-path places and their inhabitants. As they covered 21,000 miles in ten months, Brad wrote reflective essays and Amy took photographs about the trip. *States of Mind,* with the subtitle *A Search for Faith, Hope, Inspiration, Harmony, Unity, Friendship, Love, Pride, Wisdom, Honor, Comfort, Joy, Bliss, Freedom, Justice, Glory, Triumph, and Truth or Consequences in America,* rolled off the presses in 1999. Its initial reception was mixed, but a fortuitous event turned *States of Mind* into a best seller. When Herzog appeared on the *Who Wants To Be a Millionaire* television game show, not only did he win $64,000, the show's host mentioned Herzog's *States of Mind.* Then sales skyrocketed and Herzog made the talk-show circuit, discussing his adventure across America.

Biographical and Critical Sources

PERIODICALS

Book World, June 6, 1999, James Conaway, review of *States of Mind: A Search for Faith, Hope, Inspiration, Harmony, Unity, Friendship, Love, Pride, Wisdom, Honor, Comfort, Joy, Bliss, Freedom, Justice, Glory, Triumph, and Truth or Consequences in America,* p. 3.

Columbus Dispatch, June 24, 2001, Elizabeth M. Barovian, "Writer Discovers America in Small Towns."

Library Journal, June 1, 1999, John J. McCormick, review of *States of Mind,* p. 148.

Publishers Weekly, January 15, 1996, review of *The Sports One Hundred: The One Hundred Most Important People in American Sports History,* p. 459; April 10, 2000, Steven M. Zeitchk, "Regis Gives Boost to Small Press Title," p. 18.

OTHER

Brad Herzog, http://www.bradherzog.com/ (January 22, 2002), "About Brad Herzog."

Recreational Vehicle Industry Association, http://www.riva.org/media/ (February 12, 2002), "Meet Brad and Amy Herzog."

*   *   *

HOLBROOK, Sara

Personal

Children: Katie, Kelly. *Education:* Mount Union College (Alliance, OH), B.A. (English).

Addresses

Home—7326 Presley Ave., Mentor, OH 44060.

Career

Writer and performance poet. Worked as part-time teacher; worked in public relations, in law, public housing, and drug prevention fields. Presents poetry and writing workshops at schools and teacher meetings.

Sara Holbrook's collection of poems about school for teen readers includes "Getting Graded," "Gym," and "Spellbound." (Cover photo by The Reuben Group.)

Writings

POETRY; FOR CHILDREN

The Dog Ate My Homework, privately published (Bay Village, OH), 1990, revised edition, Boyds Mills Press (Honesdale, PA), 1996.

Kid Poems for the Not-So-Bad, privately published (Bay Village, OH), 1992, republished as *I Never Said I Wasn't Difficult,* Boyds Mills Press (Honesdale, PA), 1997.

Nothing's the End of the World, illustrated by J. J. Smith-Moore, Boyds Mills Press (Honesdale, PA), 1995.

Am I Naturally This Crazy?, Boyds Mills Press (Honesdale, PA), 1996.

Which Way to the Dragon! Poems for the Coming-on-Strong, Boyds Mills Press (Honesdale, PA), 1996.

Walking on the Boundaries of Change: Poems of Transition, Boyds Mills Press (Honesdale, PA), 1998.

OTHER

Feelings Make Me Real, privately published (Bay Village, OH), 1990.

Some Families, privately published (Bay Village, OH), 1990.

What's So Big about Cleveland, Ohio? (picture book), illustrated by Ennis McNulty, Gray & Co. (Cleveland, OH), 1997.

Chicks up Front (poetry; for adults), Cleveland State University Poetry Center (Cleveland, OH), 1998.

Wham! It's a Poetry Jam: Discovering Performance Poetry (for children), Boyds Mills Press (Honesdale, PA) 2002.

Isn't She Ladylike (for children), Collinwood Media (Mentor, OH), 2002.

Contributor to periodicals, including *Journal of Children's Literature.*

Sidelights

Poet and part-time teacher Sara Holbrook does not think poetry should be confined to the printed page. Referring to herself as a "performance poet," Holbrook dedicates much of her time to reading her works before audiences of children and teachers, as well as in writing workshop and other creative settings. "I write about two things, mostly," Holbrook noted on her Web site, "what I know and what I wonder about. Reading and writing poetry helps me understand my life, the world, and the people I care about. Whether I am writing funny or serious poems, writing poetry helps me see what's true." She added, "I don't really think a poem really comes to life until it is read aloud."

In addition to a poetry collection for adults titled *Chicks up Front,* Holbrook has authored several collections of verse focusing on the things that almost all school-aged kids can relate to: forgetting homework assignments, frustration with parents, living with a bad haircut, or glasses, or braces, annoying babysitters, getting along with friends, and making important choices. As Holbrook noted on her Web site, even the simplest of her poems, such as those in *Which Way to the Dragon! Poems for the Coming-on-Strong* are relevant to kids of all ages, even older high school students: "Just remember for a moment how scary it was to get stuck in the port-a-potty at a T ball game and it will all come back to you."

Several of Holbrook's collections, such as *Nothing's the End of the World* and *Walking on the Boundaries of Change: Poems of Transition,* are geared toward middle-grade readers, who are just beginning adolescence. Calling the latter collection of over fifty short verses "energetic," *Voice of Youth Advocates* contributor Debra Lynn Adams praised in particular the poems "My Plan," "The Runaway," and "On the Verge." "Holbrook's poems have universal appeal," Adams added, "and readers who discover her book will find themselves within its pages." *Am I Naturally This Crazy?,* which focuses on the interests of younger, elementary-aged students, takes a light-hearted approach to such topics as pets, school, divorcing parents, and school issues. According to *School Library Journal* contributor Marjorie Lewis, Holbrook's "inventive wordplay and bouncy

rhythms give some of the short pieces a surprising punch."

Biographical and Critical Sources

PERIODICALS

Horn Book Guide, fall, 1995, Patricia Riley, review of *Nothing's the End of the World,* p. 377.

Publishers Weekly, October 12, 1998, review of *Walking on the Boundaries of Change,* p. 79.

School Library Journal, February, 1995, Sally R. Dow, review of *Nothing's the End of the World,* p. 107; April, 1997, Marjorie Lewis, review of *Am I Naturally This Crazy?* and *Which Way to the Dragon!,* p. 126.

Voice of Youth Advocates, February, 1999, Debra Lynn Adams, review of *Walking on the Boundaries of Change,* pp. 454-455.

Holbrook explores the range of young adult emotions in twenty-two poems such as "Happy All Around," "I Hate My Body," and "Kind?" (Cover photo by The Reuben Group.)

OTHER

Sara Holbrook Web Site, http://www.saraholbrook.com (January 22, 2002).*

*　　*　　*

HOWLAND, Ethan 1963-

Personal

Born December 8, 1963, in Brunswick, ME; son of John (a professor) and Cynthia Howland; married Daphne Robert; children: Esmé, Phoebe. *Education:* Attended University of Geneva and Graduate School for International Studies, Geneva, Switzerland, 1984-85; Hamilton College, B.A., 1986; Northwestern University, M.S., 1991.

Addresses

Home—28 Mayland St., Portland, ME 04103. *E-mail*—ethanhowland@aol.com.

Career

U.S. Peace Corps, Washington, DC, high school English teacher in Morocco, 1987-89; U.S. Embassy Press Office, Rabat, Morocco, reporter, 1989; *Central New Jersey Home News,* New Brunswick, NJ, Washington correspondent, 1991; National Wildlife Federation, Washington, DC, assistant editor, 1992; *Inside EPA's Environmental Policy Alert,* Arlington, VA, associate editor, 1992-94, managing editor, 1994-95; Children's Hospital, Boston, MA, publications editor at Brazelton Institute, 1996-97; Maine Hospital Association, Augusta, ME, communications manager, 1997—.

Writings

The Lobster War, Front Street/Cricket Books (Chicago, IL), 2001.

Assistant editor, *EnviroAction,* 1992.

Sidelights

Ethan Howland told *SATA:* "Along the coast of Maine, where I grew up, the ocean meets a rocky shoreline, the sun glints off the water in the late summer, the fir trees cling to scraps of topsoil on islands. For a writer it was a great place to grow up, with sharp images, tastes, and smells embedding themselves in the memory.

"Ideas for *The Lobster War* came in bits and pieces, floating on the tides of recollection: skating on the ocean in winter, getting a rope knotted around a propeller, smelling the dry, dusty air of a chicken barn. I pictured a kid, Dain Harrington, seventeen years old with a serious problem. Someone is cutting his lobster traps.

"I knew kids like Dain in the town where I grew up. They worked hard at lobstering and came from families who had done it for generations. In the winter, you see lobster traps stacked in the yard alongside lobster boats covered in snow, and in the summer those traps and boats are in the water. These kids, like farm kids, grow up fast. They work, they earn money, and they are responsible for boats, gear, and equipment.

"While lobstering can be dangerous—boats sink and people drown—in *The Lobster War,* lobstering was a refuge for Dain. He is shaken up when his traps get cut, his older brother Eddie pushes him away, and his mother pushes him to go to college. Dain battles with himself, not always successfully, as he works his way through the problems and decides how to act.

"In the end, Dain finds that he's a brave kid, not because he pulls someone from a sinking boat, but because of the way he tackles his everyday, normal problems with his family and finds his place in the world."

J–K

JOBLING, Curtis

Personal

Born in Blackpool, England; children: Andrew.

Addresses

Agent—Rod Hall Agency Ltd., 3 Charlotte Mews, London W1T 4DZ, England.

Career

Author. HOT Animation, model maker and animator for "Bob the Builder." Has worked on various other animated shows and movies, including *A Close Shave, Mars Attacks,* and *Curious Cows.*

Writings

(Self-illustrated) *Frankenstein's Cat,* Simon & Schuster (New York, NY), 2001.
(Illustrator) Jonathan Emmett, *Dinosaurs after Dark,* Golden Books (New York, NY), 2002.

Biographical and Critical Sources

PERIODICALS

Publishers Weekly, September 24, 2001, review of *Frankenstein's Cat,* p. 92; December 24, 2001, review of *Dinosaurs after Dark,* p. 62.*

*   *   *

KESEY, Ken (Elton) 1935-2001

OBITUARY NOTICE—See index for *SATA* sketch. Born September 17, 1935, in La Junta, CO; died of complications from surgery for liver cancer, November 10, 2001, in Eugene, OR. Author. Kesey is the acclaimed author of *One Flew Over the Cuckoo's Nest.* His adventures traveling cross country with friends the Merry Pranksters were recounted by author Tom Wolfe in his book *The Electric Kool-Aid Acid Test.* On the surface, Kesey didn't look like he would become a counter-culture icon. He grew up the son of a dairy farmer and was a successful athlete who played football, wrestled and was voted "most likely to succeed" by his high school class. He won a scholarship for being the outstanding wrestler in the Northwest and attended the University of Oregon, from which he graduated in 1957. Kesey received a scholarship to study writing at Stanford University and enrolled there. While at Stanford he was tipped off by a fellow student to a government drug-testing program that paid $75, and he signed up. Around that time he also was working in the mental ward of a veteran's hospital and his experience there formed the basis of *Cuckoo's Nest.* The book was published in 1962, received strong reviews and became a Broadway play starring Kirk Douglas as Randle Patrick McMurphy, a new inmate who pretends to be crazy to avoid a prison sentence. The book was made into a movie starring Jack Nicholson as McMurphy and Louise Fletcher as Nurse Ratched, and swept the Oscars in 1976, winning for best film, best director, best actor and best actress. Kesey made very little money for the rights to the movie and his screenplay adaptation wasn't used. He took issue with the narrator being changed from Bromden to McMurphy and swore he'd never watch the film. Kesey's second novel, 1964's *Sometimes a Great Notion,* also was made into a film, this time starring Henry Fonda and Paul Newman. But then Kesey took off on his cross-country bus trip and staged "happenings" across the nation, urging the use of LSD and mescaline. He was arrested for marijuana possession and fled to Mexico, although he eventually returned to California and did five months in a county jail. Kesey wrote sporadically and taught writing at the University of Oregon. *Kesey's Garage Sale* contained some of his essays and *The Further Inquiry* was his accounting of the bus trip with the Merry Pranksters. Kesey completed two children's books, *Little Trickler the Squirrel Meets Big Double the Bear,* and *The Sea Lion: A Story of the Sea Cliff People,* but he didn't publish another novel until *Sailor Song* in 1992. *Last Go Round: A Dime Western* was published in 1994.

OBITUARIES AND OTHER SOURCES:

PERIODICALS

Los Angeles Times, November 11, 2001, p. A1.
New York Times, November 11, 2001, p. A34.
Times (London), November 12, 2001, p. 19.
Washington Post, November 11, 2001, p. C6.

*   *   *

KOERTGE, Ron(ald) 1940-

Personal

Surname is pronounced "*kur*-chee"; born April 22, 1940, in Olney, IL; son of William Henry (an owner of an ice-cream store and school janitor) and Bulis Olive (a homemaker; maiden name, Fiscus) Koertge; married Cheryl Vasconcellos (marriage ended); married Bianca Richards (a counselor), November 4, 1992. *Education:* University of Illinois, B.A., 1962; University of Arizona, M.A., 1965.

Addresses

Home—1115 Oxley St., South Pasadena, CA 91030. *Agent*—William Reiss, John Hawkins and Associates, 71 West 23rd St., No. 1600, New York, NY 10010. *E-mail*—RONKOE@earthlink.net.

Career

Writer, 1962—. Pasadena City College, Pasadena, CA, professor of English, 1965-2002.

Awards, Honors

American Library Association (ALA) Best Book citation and ALA Book for Reluctant Readers designation, both for *Where the Kissing Never Stops;* ALA Best Book citation, *Booklist* Books of the Decade, and Young Adult School Library Association (YASLA) 100 Best of the Best, all for *Arizona Kid;* Maine Student Book Award choice, for *Mariposa Blues;* National Endowment for the Arts fellowship, 1990; ALA Best Book citation, and Friends of American Writers award, 1991, both for *The Boy in the Moon;* California Arts Council grant, 1993, ALA Best Book and Notable Book citations, and New York Public Library Books for the Teen-Age designation, all for *The Harmony Arms;* ALA Best Book citation, New York Library 100 Best Children's Books list, *Bulletin of the Center for Children's Books* Blue Ribbon Book, Bank Street Child Study Children's Book Committee Book-of-the-Year choice, Judy Lopez Memorial Award Honor Book, and YASLA Best Books for Young Adults list, all 1994, all for *Tiger, Tiger, Burning Bright; School Library Journal* Best Books citation, 1996, for *Confess-O-Rama;* ALA Best Book citation and Quick Pick citation, both for *The Brimstone Journals.*

Writings

FOR YOUNG ADULTS

Where the Kissing Never Stops, Atlantic Monthly Press (Boston, MA), 1986.
The Arizona Kid, Joy Street Books (Boston, MA), 1988.
The Boy in the Moon, Joy Street Books (Boston, MA), 1990.
Mariposa Blues, Joy Street Books (Boston, MA), 1991.
The Harmony Arms, Joy Street Books (Boston, MA), 1992.
Tiger, Tiger Burning Bright: A Novel, Orchard Books (New York, NY), 1994.
Confess-O-Rama, Orchard Books (New York, NY), 1996.
The Heart of the City, Orchard Books (New York, NY), 1998.
The Brimstone Journals, Candlewick Press (Cambridge, MA), 2001.
Stoner and Spaz, Candlewick Press (Cambridge, MA), 2002.

POETRY; FOR ADULTS

The Father-Poems, Sumac Press, 1973.
Meat: Cheryl's Market-Diary, MAG Press, 1973.
The Hired Nose, MAG Press, 1974.
My Summer Vacation, Venice Poetry, 1975.
Sex Object, Country Press, 1975, revised edition, Little Caesar, 1979.
(With Charles Stetler and Gerald Locklin) *Tarzan and Shane Meet the Toad,* Haas, 1975.
Cheap Thrills, Wormwood Review, 1976.
Men under Fire, Duck Down, 1976.
Twelve Photographs of Yellowstone, Red Hill, 1976.
How to Live on Five Dollars a Week, Etc., Venice Poetry, 1977.
The Jockey Poems, Maelstrom, 1980.
Diary Cows, Little Caesar, 1981.
Fresh Meat, Kenmore, 1981.
Life on the Edge of the Continent: Selected Poems of Ronald Koertge, University of Arkansas Press (Fayetteville, AR), 1982.
High School Dirty Poems, Red Wind (Los Angeles, CA), 1991.
Making Love to Roget's Wife: Poems New and Selected, University of Arkansas Press (Fayetteville, AR), 1997.
Geography of the Forehead, University of Arkansas Press (Fayetteville, AR), 2000.

Contributor to *The Maverick Poets: An Anthology,* edited by Steve Kowit, Gorilla Press, 1988.

OTHER

The Boogeyman (adult novel), Norton (New York, NY), 1980.
One Hundred Things to Write About (college textbook), Holt (New York, NY), 1990.

Contributor to periodicals, including the *Los Angeles Times Book Review.*

Sidelights

Despite a long career as a college English professor, Ron Koertge has not forgotten what it was like to ride the

Ron Koertge

emotional roller-coaster through adolescence into adulthood. The protagonists in his young adult novels suffer the universal anxieties suffered by teen boys over acne pimples, and bemoan the fact that they are shorter than their classmates. They ponder their futures and quarrel with eccentric or domineering parents. In Koertge's novels particularly, they learn to deal with the sexual longings that become tangled up with romantic impulses when they become seriously involved with girls they care about. While Koertge often uses humor in his stories, he never downplays the seriousness of these adolescent concerns. In an essay for the *Dictionary of Literary Biography,* Jane Hoogestraat maintained that Koertge's books are "remarkable for the realism with which they present tough and not-so-tough teenage characters coming of age in a world of AIDS and widespread divorce, but often in a world in which tenderness and love are not absent." Michael Cart, writing in *School Library Journal* felt that Koertge is "a brilliant writer" who has positioned himself among "America's finest authors for young adults."

Koertge was born in 1940, in Olney, Illinois, where his parents worked at a large dairy farm. While Koertge was still young, the family left farm country and moved to Collinsville, Illinois, to open an ice-cream business. The store flourished until the town's first supermarket opened, forcing it and several other specialty stores out of business. Koertge's father became a janitor in the public school system while his mother stayed at home to raise Ron. They were comfortable financially and, as Koertge recalled, "fairly happy."

An only child, Koertge enjoyed sports and school, and as a teen he discovered that he had a knack for writing. "I discovered I was more glib than most of my friends," he once noted, "but I also somehow sensed that my gift wouldn't be really valuable until I was older. Very early on, words seemed to have lives of their own. Still today, the way the words fit together and the way they lie on the music they generate is more interesting to me than the so-called arc of the story." He also discovered that he had a flair for drama, and enjoyed saying and doing outrageous things. "I would say out loud things that other kids seemed reluctant to say," he once admitted. "I liked to shock people—to leave them lurching, not laughing." Koertge's sense of life's quirks was heightened when he suffered a serious bout of rheumatic fever as a young teen. The illness—which might have left him with a weakened heart for the rest of his life, or even killed him—left the fortunate young man with a "sense of the insubstantiality of my body and made me alternately tentative and foolishly bold."

Koertge began writing in high school, "something I was drawn to, partly because it was something I could do," he remembered. He pursued his interest at the University of Illinois, where he earned his bachelor's degree in 1962, and then at the University of Arizona, where he received a master's degree in 1965 and began writing poetry. After graduation, Koertge took a position as a professor of English at Pasadena City College, where he continued to teach until 2002. He began publishing poems in magazines as early as 1970, and a few years after that released the first of many chapbooks of verse. In 1980 he published his only novel for adults, *The Boogeyman.* "But the two novels after that were pitiful. Embarrassing," Koertge later admitted. "Then a friend suggested that I try young adults since I'm a chronic smart ass. I went to the library, read a couple, and figured I could do at least that well. Sure enough: the two failed grown-up novels became *Where the Kissing Never Stops* and *The Arizona Kid.*"

Published in 1986 and 1988 respectively, Koertge's first two young-adult novels, although humorous and touching coming-of-age stories, ignited controversy due to their frank and realistic depiction of sexual encounters and alternative lifestyles. "It might have been naive of me to think that straight talk about sex would be universally welcomed in the secret garden of children's books or that a gay character in a YA would be treated like any other character," Koertge admitted in the *Los Angeles Times Book Review.* "But I was simply looking for something interesting to write." *Where the Kissing Never Stops* finds seventeen-year-old Walker plagued with problems. His cravings for junk food run unchecked, his girlfriend has left town, and worst of all, his mother has taken a job as a stripper in a nearby burlesque parlor. At his lowest ebb, Walker meets Rachel, a mall-loving, cosmopolitan teen. Different as they are, Walker and Rachel begin a romance and ultimately learn to trust one another. *School Library Journal* contributor Marjorie Lewis noted that "Walker's attempts to keep his mother's occupation a secret and make his romance with Rachel a rich, fulfilling one are believable and engrossing." In *The Arizona Kid,* sixteen-year-old Billy faces a summer of change and discovery as he experiences firsthand the colorful world of horse racing, falling in love, losing his virginity, and learning about the gay lifestyle of his Uncle Wes, with whom he is spending the summer in Tucson. "Billy's relationship with his feisty, understanding girlfriend Cara Mae boosts his shaky self-confidence," explained an essayist in *St. James Guide to Young Adult Writers,* while "warm, witty, and generous Uncle Wes fosters Billy's growing sense of independence" despite an initial period of discomfort between the two men.

These first two novels set the standard for much of Koertge's more recent books for teens, humorous tales featuring young men coming of age amid sometimes frustrating, sometimes humorous circumstances. In *The Harmony Arms,* Gabriel McKay moves temporarily with his divorced and eccentric father to Los Angeles, where in the Harmony Arms apartment complex he becomes acquainted with a host of individuals with equally eccentric personalities—including his new friend Tess, an aspiring young film maker who carries a camcorder with her everywhere in order to document her life. "Koertge's brash, outrageous characters give new meaning to the word *diversity,*" noted *Horn Book* critic Nancy Vasilakis, adding that the author "offers a lively defense of the West Coast's let-it-all-hang-out spirit in his funniest novel to date." *Voice of Youth Advocates* contributor John Lord maintained that the "strength" of *The Harmony Arms* "lies in its ... well-drawn and believable" characters. In the 1994 novel *Tiger, Tiger, Burning Bright,* Koertge introduces readers to life in rural central California, where Jesse's grandfather Pappy, a retired cowboy with long hair and a love of the Western desert, now lives. As Pappy becomes more forgetful and begins to get lost during walks in the nearby hill country, Jesse tries to conceal these lapses of memory to keep his mother from taking Pappy away from the place he loves and putting him in a nursing home. A reviewer for *Publishers Weekly* appreciated Koertge's "imaginative characterizations, wacky humor and crackling, authentically adolescent dialogue," while *Booklist* contributor Hazel Rochman maintained that "what carries the story ... is the perfect pitch of Jesse's voice, somewhere between farce and melancholy parody and grief."

In *Confess-O-Rama,* fifteen-year-old Tony meets up with an unusual circle of friends when he and his mother move to a new town after his fourth stepfather dies. Stressed by the constant moves, worried about his widowed mom, and suffering from typical teen angst, he resorts to a confessional hotline: just say your problem out loud and then hang up. Finding out that fellow classmate and potential crush Jordan is on the other end of the hotline comes as a surprise to the unsuspecting Tony, and creates a novel in which the "narrative, characterization, setting, and pacing are realistic, humorous, and insightful," according to *Booklist*'s Karen Simonetti. Deborah Stevenson added in her review of *Confess-O-Rama* for the *Bulletin of the Center for Children's Books* that Koertge "blend[s] humor and

genuine emotion in a way many YA authors essay but fail: Tony's quips and the outrageousness of the plot are genuinely funny but never superficial."

The perspectives of fifteen modern teens are the focus of Koertge's 2001 novel, *The Brimstone Journals.* Branston High School suffers the same acts of violence as many urban schools in the United States, and the anger and frustration of several of its students have given the school the nickname "Brimstone" High. Within the school walls are individual high school seniors dealing with a variety of issues: Kitty has an eating disorder, Sheila is confronting the fact of her homosexuality, Tran is pressured by his Vietnamese father toward a way of life he does not wish to share, while Boyd is fueled by his racist heritage and his father's alcoholism into planning a school shooting. Koertge expresses the thoughts of each of his fifteen students through verses reading like diary entries. *School Library Journal* contributor Sharon Korbeck noted that his "sometimes raw voices provide poignant, honest, and fresh insights into today's teens." While Hazel Rochman in *Booklist* maintained that the end of Koertge's book sees too many

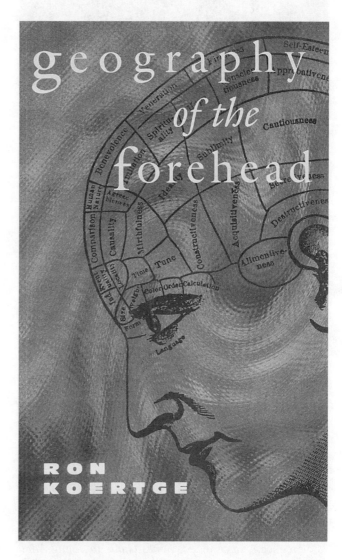

More than fifty entertaining poems are included in this collection published in 2000.

A journal of interconnected poems reveals the growing violence in the lives of students at a high school nicknamed Brimstone. (Cover illustration by Timothy Basil Ering.)

problems solved, she nonetheless noted that he "avoids simplistic therapy, and the dramatic monologues are spare, poetic, and immediate," as well as effective ways to open "group discussion."

About writing for young adults, Koertge once explained to *SATA:* "I never think of myself as writing for children; I never think I know anything special about young people. I don't have children and am not much interested in them as such. But I like to write. And writing YA's is obviously what I'm up to at the moment. I'm as surprised as anyone else at the success I've had. Maybe more." For teen readers, Koertge's continued success and enjoyment of writing is good news. "As readers navigate the perilous realms of their own adolescence," noted the *St. James Guide to Young Adult Writers* contributor, "they will surely want Koertge's books along to help ease their way."

Biographical and Critical Sources

BOOKS

Dictionary of Literary Biography, Volume 105: *American Poets since World War II,* Gale (Detroit, MI), 1992.

Gallo, Donald R., editor, *Speaking for Ourselves, Too,* National Council of Teachers of English (Urbana, IL), 1993.

St. James Guide to Young Adult Writers, St. James Press (Detroit, MI), 1999.

PERIODICALS

Booklist, October 15, 1992, Stephanie Zvirin, review of *The Harmony Arms,* p. 418; February 15, 1994, Hazel Rochman, review of *Tiger, Tiger, Burning Bright,* p. 1075; October 1, 1996, Karen Simonetti, review of *Confess-O-Rama,* p. 342; April, 1998, Linda Perkins, review of *The Heart of the City,* p. 1320; April 15, 2001, Hazel Rochman, review of *The Brimstone Journals,* p. 1548.

Book Report, September-October, 1994, Lynne Hofflund, review of *Tiger, Tiger, Burning Bright,* p. 40; March-April, 1997, Rosie Peasley, review of *Confess-O-Rama,* p. 37.

Buffalo News (Buffalo, NY), July 21, 1998, review of *The Heart of the City,* p. N7.

Bulletin of the Center for Children's Books, November, 1996, Deborah Stevenson, review of *Confess-O-Rama,* p. 102.

English Journal, December, 1993, Alleen Pace Nilsen, review of *The Harmony Arms,* p. 73.

Horn Book, July-August, 1990, p. 462; July-August, 1991, p. 464; November-December, 1992, Nancy Vasilakis, review of *The Harmony Arms,* p. 727; September-October, 1994, Nancy Vasilakis, review of *Tiger, Tiger, Burning Bright,* p. 600.

Kirkus Reviews, October 1, 1992, p. 1256; February 15, 1994, p. 228.

New York Times Book Review, August 21, 1998, p. 25; May 20, 2001, Robin Tzannes, "Arms and the Boy."

Los Angeles Times Book Review, March 21, 1993, Ron Koertge, "Sex and the Single Kid."

Publishers Weekly, April 13, 1990, review of *The Boy in the Moon,* p. 67; May 10, 1991, review of *Mariposa Blues,* p. 284; September 14, 1992, review of *The Harmony Arms,* p. 126; April 18, 1994, review of *Tiger, Tiger, Burning Bright,* p. 63; April 20, 1998, review of *The Heart of the City,* p. 67; February 12, 2001, review of *The Brimstone Journals,* p. 213.

School Library Journal, December, 1986, Marjorie Lewis, review of *Where the Kissing Never Stops,* p. 119; May, 1990, p. 122; May, 1991, p. 111; August, 1992, p. 178; March, 1994, Michael Cart, review of *Tiger, Tiger, Burning Bright,* p. 236; September, 1996, Susan R. Farber, review of *Confess-O-Rama,* p. 227; March, 1998, Kathleen Isaacs, review of *The Heart of the City,* p. 214; March, 2001, Sharon Korbeck, review of *The Brimstone Journals,* p. 270.

Voice of Youth Advocates, October, 1992, John Lord, review of *The Harmony Arms,* pp. 224-225; June, 1994; December, 1996, pp. 271-272.

Wilson Library Bulletin, April, 1989, p. 97; September, 1991, p. 106; March, 1993, Frances Bradburn, review of *The Harmony Arms,* p. 84.

L

LASS, Bonnie

Personal

Children: Jed. *Education:* University of Illinois, Ph.D.

Addresses

Home—30 Gibbs St., Brookline, MA 02446-6093.

Career

Children's textbook editor. Has also worked as a reading specialist and college professor, teaching at Boston University and Lesley College.

Writings

(With Beth G. Davis) *The Remedial Reading Handbook,* Prentice-Hall (Englewood Cliffs, NJ), 1985.
(With Beth G. Davis) *Elementary Reading: Strategies That Work,* Allyn and Bacon (Boston, MA), 1996.
(With Philemon Sturges) *Who Took the Cookies from the Cookie Jar?,* illustrated by Ashley Wolff, Little, Brown (Boston, MA), 2000.

Sidelights

Growing up in Brooklyn, Bonnie Lass fondly remembers time spent playing with other children after school, as she recalled on the *Time Warner Bookmark* Web site. Until it was time to go inside, she and the other neighborhood kids would play various games, including rhyming ones, on the doorsteps and in the local park. The author noted that in her first book for children, *Who Took the Cookies from the Cookie Jar?,* she "wanted to convey that sense of fun with rhythm and rhyme." In the book, coauthored by Philemon Sturges, everyone wants to know the answer to the question "Who Took the Cookies from the Cookie Jar?" Leading the investigation is Skunk, who baked the cookies, only to have them disappear from his cookie jar. Together with Lizard, the two question their fellow animals in the desert, trying to solve the mystery of the missing baked goods. By the story's end, the sleuths have tracked down the stolen cookies, but decide to share the sweets with the thieves and all of the other animals involved in the search. According to *School Library Journal* critic Tim Wadham, "Children will enjoy the challenge of solving the mystery." The authors also include instructions for playing the traditional childhood game "Who Took the Cookies from the Cookie Jar?," as well as provide the music to accompany the song.

Biographical and Critical Sources

BOOKS

Lass, Bonnie and Philemon Sturges, *Who Took the Cookies from the Cookie Jar?,* illustrated by Ashley Wolff, Little, Brown (Boston, MA), 2000.

PERIODICALS

Booklist, October 15, 2000, Todd Morning, review of *Who Took the Cookies from the Cookie Jar?,* p. 445.
Publishers Weekly, October 2, 2000, "All Together Now," p. 83.
Reading Teacher, March, 1986, Richard W, Burnett, review of *The Remedial Reading Handbook,* pp. 723-724.
School Library Journal, October, 2000, Tim Wadham, review of *Who Took the Cookies from the Cookie Jar?,* p. 128.

OTHER

Time Warner Bookmark, http://www.twbookmark.com/ (March 9, 2002), Bonnie Lass, "Stoop Time."*

* * *

LAVERT, Gwendolyn Battle 1951- (Gwendolyn Battle-Lavert)

Personal

Born September 28, 1951, in Paris, TX; daughter of Charles Edward and Ozie Mae (Dangerfield) Battle;

Gwendolyn Battle Lavert

married Donald Rae Lavert, February 24, 1975 (divorced, March 24, 1997); children: Leslie Lynn, Lance Lamont. *Education:* Paris Junior College, A.S. (elementary education), 1972; Texas A&M University, B.S. (elementary education), 1974, M.Ed. (reading), 1976. *Politics:* Democrat. *Religion:* Baptist.

Addresses

Home and office—842 Ross Dr., Marion, IN 46953. *E-mail*—glavert@aol.com.

Career

Texarkana Independent School District, Texarkana, TX, teacher and reading supervisor, 1974-90; Harcourt Publishing, Dallas, TX, consultant, 1990-95; DeSoto Independent School District, DeSoto, TX, assistant principal, 1995-97; Irving Independent School District, Irving, TX, principal, 1997-99; Indiana Wesleyan University, Marion, IN, assistant professor of education, 1999—. Writing consultant, 1999—. St. Paul Human Services, board member; St. Paul Missionary Baptist Church, guest soloist. *Member:* International Reading Association, KDP.

Awards, Honors

Off to School was named a notable book for children by *Smithsonian* magazine, 1995; Parents Choice Silver Honor, for *The Shaking Bag.*

Writings

AS GWENDOLYN BATTLE-LAVERT

The Barber's Cutting Edge, illustrated by Raymond Hilbert, Children's Book Press (San Francisco, CA), 1994.
Off to School, illustrated by Gershom Griffith, Holiday House (New York, NY), 1995.
The Flying Red Tails, The Wright Group/McGraw-Hill (Chicago, IL), 1999.
The Shaking Bag, illustrated by Aminah Brenda Lynn Robinson, Albert Whitman (Morton Grove, IL), 2000.
Not Yet, Uncle Skeet, The Wright Group/McGraw-Hill (Chicago, IL), 2000.
The Music in Derrick's Heart, illustrated by Colin Bootman, Holiday House (New York, NY), 2000.
Papa's Mark, illustrated by Colin Bootman, Holiday House (New York, NY), 2002.

Contributor of fiction to periodicals, including *Cricket, Ladybug,* and *Adoptive Families* magazine.

Adaptations

Off to School was recorded as an audiocassette by Talking Books, 1995.

Work in Progress

"D-Man and Beans Adventure" series for reluctant readers for The Wright Group/McGraw-Hill, beginning in 2002.

Sidelights

A former elementary school principal and a college professor of reading, Gwendolyn Battle Lavert believes in the importance of literacy. To promote reading and her African-American heritage, she has given dozens of presentations about Martin Luther King, Jr., as well as published picture books, fiction for reluctant readers, and magazine articles for children and adults. This enthusiasm for reading is a must for Lavert-the-writer, who told *SATA,* "Early in life, I learned that the key to writing is reading. Therefore, I read something every day. I collect ideas from reading. I listen to the things around me. When I'm walking, I listen to the trees, the wind whistling. Writing is letting the inner voice come out."

In her picture books Lavert presents appealing African-American children in realistic situations. She explained to *SATA:* "In my stories, characters are so important. I want my readers to fall in love with my characters. The feelings are so strong that the reader doesn't want the story to end." For example, this "likeable tale," as a *Publishers Weekly* critic described *The Barber's Cutting*

Edge, portrays the relationship of Rashaad and his barber, Mr. Bigalow, who is more than just a hair stylist. *Off to School* revolves around the efforts of Wezielee, a sharecropper's daughter, to be able to attend school. In the view of *Booklist*'s Susan Dove Lempke, despite some flaws in the telling and illustration, the story features a "likeable" main character and "warm family atmosphere," as well as details about a sharecropper's lifestyle. *The Music in Derrick's Heart* tells the story of how Derrick learns to play the harmonica with the help of his Uncle Booker. Although a *Publishers Weekly* critic called the work "little more than a one-note story," *Booklist*'s Shelle Rosenfeld described it as a "charming, uplifting story," with "easy-flowing, rhythmic prose [that] beautifully echoes and conveys the messages." In *School Library Journal,* Nancy Mendali-Scanlan noted a similarity between this work and Karen Ackerman's *Song and Dance Man* and predicted that *The Music in Derrick's Heart* would "radiate 'sweet, sweet music' to its listeners' ears."

In her award-winning original folktale *The Shaking Bag,* Lavert focuses on Annie Mae, a woman who is so generous, to her own detriment, that even the birds that visit her home never go hungry. Finally, she is reduced to having a little bird seed and three slices of bread for herself and her dog, when a stranger, called Raven Reed, appears on her doorstep. True to her generous spirit, Annie Mae shares her only food. In return, Raven Reed shakes her empty birdseed sack and out comes food, firewood, and furniture. The magical visitor promises that Annie Mae will never go hungry. Reviewing the work for *School Library Journal,* Donna L. Scanlon praised its "rhythmic language" and "straightforward manner that is elegant in its sheer simplicity," while in *Horn Book,* a critic called the tale a "well-honed narrative."

To ensnare reluctant readers, in 2000 Lavert began work on a ten-book series titled "D-Man and Beans." These books, to quote the author in *The Big Picture @ Indiana Wesleyan University,* "use inner-city adventure to help keep the reader's interest." For example, she wrote at the online site, "In the book I'm writing now, the main character Benita is wondering how she can pay for her dance classes. She is facing the possibility of having to quit dance classes because her mother lost her job."

"Finally," Lavert told *SATA,* "it is important for me to write everyday. Doodling causes ideas to formulate into a story. Writing is fun. Each time I write, I leave a little of myself to readers. Writing is forever."

Biographical and Critical Sources

PERIODICALS

American Visions, December-January, 1995, Yolanda Robinson Coles, review of *Off to School,* p. 39.
Booklist, October 15, 1995, Susan Dove Lempke, review of *Off to School,* p. 410; February 15, 2000, Shelle Rosenfeld, review of *The Music in Derrick's Heart,* p. 1104; April 1, 2000, Shelley Townsend-Hudson, review of *The Shaking Bag,* p. 1466.

Horn Book, July, 2000, review of *The Shaking Bag,* p. 432.
Publishers Weekly, November 14, 1994, review of *The Barber's Cutting Edge,* p. 68; January 24, 2000, review of *The Music in Derrick's Heart,* p. 310.
School Library Journal, January, 1995, Jan Shepherd Ross, review of *The Barber's Cutting Edge,* p. 81; January, 1999, Louise L. Sherman, review of *Off to School,* p. 76; March, 2000, Nancy Menaldi-Scanlan, review of *The Music in Derrick's Heart,* p. 178; April, 2000, Donna L. Scanlon, review of *The Shaking Bag,* p. 90.

OTHER

The Big Picture at Indiana Wesleyan University, http://www.indwes.edu/BigPicture/ (February 28, 2002), "Faculty Spotlight."

*   *   *

LEA, Joan
See NEUFELD, John Arthur

*   *   *

LEACOCK, Elspeth 1946-

Personal

Born November 5, 1946; daughter of Richard (a film maker) and Eleanor (an anthropologist; maiden name, Burk) Leacock; married Richard Timperio (an artist); children: Cheyenne, Willy. *Education:* Attended University of Wisconsin, 1964-66.

Addresses

Home—319 Bedford Ave., Brooklyn, NY 11211. *E-mail*—elleacock@aol.com.

Career

Worked in publishing industry, beginning in 1979.

Awards, Honors

Nebraska Book Award (Children/Young Adult category), 2001, for *Places in Time.*

Writings

Hands-On Geography, Scholastic (New York, NY), 1993.
Geography Brain Quest, Workman Publishing (New York, NY), 1997.
(With Susan Buckley) *Journeys in Time; A New Atlas of American History,* illustrated by Rodica Prato, Houghton Mifflin (Boston, MA), 2001.
(With Susan Buckley) *Places in Time: A New Atlas of American History,* illustrated by Randy Jones, Houghton Mifflin (Boston, MA), 2001.
The West, National Geographic Society (Washington, DC), 2002.
Journeys for Freedom: A New Atlas of American History, Houghton Mifflin (Boston, MA), 2002.

A combination atlas and storybook written by Elspeth Leacock and Susan Buckley, **Places** **in** **Time** *describes living in twenty different sites, such as Ellis Island, for one day in history. (Illustrated by Randy Jones.)*

Children in Time: A New Atlas of American History, Houghton Mifflin (Boston, MA), 2003.

Worked with the New York Labor History Association to create a poster map called *The History of Labor in New York State.*

Sidelights

History and geography specialist Elspeth Leacock is a writer and designer whose maps grace the pages of children's books. Since 1979 she has written, edited, and developed map programs for social studies text books. Her own children gave her special insight into the needs of students for appealing maps. "I always loved history, especially American history, but my children, Cheyenne and Willy, taught me two great lessons that brought me to these books," she told *SATA.* "I learned the first lesson when I pulled out a funny tourist map of the Southwest. Cheyenne and Willy both wanted to see it and even vied for the one nearby chair to get a better

view. After pulling over a second chair, I marveled as they excitedly poured over the map. The map was beautiful, but it was also rich with all kinds of information. Now, at that time, I worked designing maps for social studies text books. And I knew that no one would ever climb on a chair to get a better view of one of my text book maps! I decided right then and there to change the look of maps made for children.

"I learned my second lesson as I watched Cheyenne and Willy in school," she continued. "One was 'reading disabled' or 'challenged.' The other read well. So one found school easy, the other found it difficult. But I knew that one was not smarter than the other. I began to notice that many people who are 'reading disabled' are spatial/visual learners and can read maps well! People who are readers are often 'spatially disabled' and need help reading maps. So I learned how to make books that both spatially-abled and reading-abled people can enjoy."

Together with Susan Buckley, who wrote the stories, Leacock made two atlases of American history called *Journeys in Time: A New Atlas of American History* and *Places in Time: A New Atlas of American History*. In the first work, she presented twenty personages important in history through "a winning blend of facts, maps, and the drama of a well-written story," observed Pamela K. Bomboy of *School Library Journal*. The second book similarly presents twenty significant places. These volumes are, according to *Booklist* reviewer John Peters, "a great way to get readers interested in the U.S.'s past and people."

Biographical and Critical Sources

PERIODICALS

Booklist, June 1, 2001, John Peters, reviews of *Journeys in Time: A New Atlas of American History* and *Places in Time: A New Atlas of American History*, p. 1866.
Child Life, July, 2001, review of *Journeys in Time*, p. 24.
Horn Book, July, 2001, reviews of *Journeys in Time* and *Places in Time*, p. 471.
School Library Journal, November, 1997, John Peters, review of *Maps of the World*, p. 139; June, 2001, Pamela K. Bomboy, review of *Journeys in Time*, p. 176.*

*   *   *

LESTER, Mike 1955-

Personal

Born March 3, 1955, in Atlanta, GA; son of Bob (an automobile dealer) and Helen (a homemaker) Lester; married Cynthia Yancey (a teacher), November 20, 1982; children: Grady, Hope. *Education:* University of Georgia, B.A. (graphic design), 1977. *Hobbies and other interests:* Family, golf, cooking.

Addresses

Home—49 Bellemont Dr., Rome, GA 30165. *Office*—17 E. Third Ave., Rome, GA 30161. *E-mail*—MLESTER-101@aol.com.

Career

Freelance artist, 1985—. *Member:* National Cartoonists Society.

Awards, Honors

Best Book Award, National Cartoonists Society, 2000.

Writings

(Self-illustrated) *A Is for Salad*, Putnam & Grosset (New York, NY), 2000.

ILLUSTRATOR; FOR CHILDREN

Lisa Rojany-Buccieri, *Santa's New Suit!: A Dress-up and Fold-out Santa*, Penguin (New York, NY), 1993.

Katy Hall, *Really, Really, Really Bad Jokes*, Candlewick Press (Cambridge, MA), 1999.
Elizabeth Werley-Prieto, *Racing Through Time on a Flying Machine*, Raintree Steck-Vaughn (Austin, TX), 1999.
Rick Winter, *Dirty Birdy Feet*, Rising Moon (Flagstaff, AZ), 2000.
Cynthia Rothman, *Funny Bugs*, William H. Sadlier (New York, NY), 2000.
Natasha Wing, *The Night before the Night before Christmas*, Grosset & Dunlap (New York, NY), 2002.

ILLUSTRATOR; FOR ADULTS

Gary D. Christenson, *Fatherhood Is Not Pretty*, Peachtree Publishers (Atlanta, GA), 1986.
Lewis Grizzard, *Lewis Grizzard on Fear of Flying*, Longstreet Press (Atlanta, GA), 1989.
Lewis Grizzard, *Lewis Grizzard's Advice to the Newly Wed*, Longstreet Press (Atlanta, GA), 1989.
Rita Rudner, *Naked Beneath My Clothes: Tales of a Revealing Nature*, Viking (New York, NY), 1992.
Jim Minter, *Some Things I Wish We Wouldn't Forget*, Midtown Publishing (Atlanta, GA), 1998.

Also author and illustrator of *Mike Du Jour*, a daily animated cartoon.

Sidelights

For nearly two decades, Mike Lester has created images for children's books as well as advertising campaigns for major corporations and national magazines. Among his most recognizable creations are the yellow jacket logo used by the Georgia Institute of Technology and the alphabet picture book *A Is for Salad*. Not your typical alphabet book, *A Is for Salad* plays on the joke that follows this pattern: the "A is for salad" text is accompanied by an alligator eating a salad, all painted in bright acrylic colors. "B is for Viking" shows a beaver wearing a Viking helmet, and so on it goes, until X and Y are deemed unimportant and hauled to a trash bin. Reviewers gave *A Is for Salad* qualified praise. Several critics expressed reservations about confusing young children who do not yet know the alphabet; yet others focused on the book's humor. "More advanced readers will appreciate the book's tricky premise," wrote Peter D. Sieruta in *Horn Book*, while a *Publishers Weekly* contributor described the book as a "fun cavort through the 26 letters." Likening the work to the break-the-mold picture books by Jon Scieszka, *Booklist* reviewer Hazel Rochman wrote that Lester "makes parody into a hilarious farce that both mocks the original and creates its own wonderful silliness."

Biographical and Critical Sources

PERIODICALS

Booklist, June 1, 2000, Hazel Rochman, review of *A Is for Salad*, p. 1896.
Horn Book, March, 2000, Peter D. Sieruta, review of *A Is for Salad*, p. 188.
Instructor, August, 2001, Judy Freeman, review of *A Is for Salad*, p. 20.

Publishers Weekly, April 28, 1989, review of *Lewis Grizzard on Fear of Flying* and *Lewis Grizzard's Advice to the Newly Wed,* p. 71; May 11, 1992, review of *Naked Beneath My Clothes: Tales of a Revealing Nature,* p. 60; April 3, 2000, review of *A Is for Salad,* p. 79

School Library Journal, April, 2000, Grace Oliff, review of *A Is for Salad,* p. 108.

U.S. News & World Report, May 29, 2000, John Molinaro, review of *A Is for Salad,* p. 66.

OTHER

Mike Lester Web Site, http://www.mikedujour.com (April 20, 2002).*

* * *

LEVINE, Shar 1953-

Personal

Born August 29, 1953, in Edmonton, Alberta, Canada; daughter of Max and Dorothy Levine; married Paul Rosenberg (a litigation attorney), 1977; children: Shira (daughter), Joshua. *Education:* University of Alberta and University of Manitoba, B.A. (English and psychology), 1974; studied toward M.Sc. at University of British Columbia. *Religion:* Jewish. *Hobbies and other interests:* In-line skating, golfing, skiing, cooking.

Addresses

Home—Vancouver, British Columbia, Canada. *E-mail*—sharlevine@shaw.ca.

Career

Writer and businesswoman. City of Calgary, Calgary, Canada, member of Personnel Department; negotiator and representative for Canadian trade union; Einstein's: The Science Center (toy store), founder, 1987-93; Isolation Solutions (marketer of portable negative pressure isolation rooms), president; freelance writer and commercial marketing/design consultant. Television consumer expert for noon-hour news, VTV. *Member:* Children's Writers and Illustrators of British Columbia (president, 2001-02).

Awards, Honors

Merchandising Achievement Award of Merit for departmental design, Playthings, 1989; third prize for commercial presentation, Sea Festival Parade, 1989, for parade float; Our Choice Award, Canadian Children's Book Centre, 1993, for *Projects for a Heathy Planet,* 1994, for *The Paper Book and Paper Maker,* 1995, for *Everyday Science,* 1996, for *Science around the World,* 1997, for *The Microscope Book,* and 1998, for *The Magnets Book* and *Fun with Your Microscope;* National Parenting Publication Award, 1997, and Parent's Choice Bronze Award, 1998, both for *WormWorld.*

Writings

(With Alison Grafton) *Projects for a Healthy Planet: Simple Environmental Experiments for Kids,* illustrated by Terry Chui, John Wiley & Sons (New York, NY), 1992.

The Paper Book and Paper Maker, illustrated by Joe Weissmann, Hyperion (New York, NY), 1993.

(With Alison Grafton) *Einstein's Science Parties: Easy Parties for Curious Kids,* illustrations by Terry Chui, John Wiley & Sons (New York, NY), 1994.

(With Leslie Johnstone) *Silly Science: Strange and Startling Projects to Amaze Your Family and Friends,* John Wiley & Sons (New York, NY), 1995.

(With Leslie Johnstone) *Everyday Science,* John Wiley & Sons (New York, NY), 1995.

(With Leslie Johnstone) *The Microscope Book,* illustrated by David Sovka, Sterling Publishers (New York, NY), 1996.

(With Leslie Johnstone) *Science around the World: Travel through Time and Space with Fun Experiments and Projects,* illustrated by Laurel Aiello, John Wiley & Sons (New York, NY), 1996.

(With Vicki Scudamore) *The Chocolate Lover's Cookbook,* Sterling Publishers (New York, NY), 1997.

(With Leslie Johnstone) *The Magnet Book,* illustrated by Jason Coons, Sterling Publishers (New York, NY), 1997.

Shar Levine and Leslie Johnstone present thirty-five activities, such as a wave machine and a water cannon, in **Bathtub Science.** *(Illustrated by Dave Garbot.)*

Human Dynamo

Levine and Johnstone's **Shocking Science** *gives historical background and instructions for experiments with static electricity and electrical circuits.* *(Illustrated by Emily S. Edliq.)*

WormWorld: The Worm Book (includes worm habitat), illustrated by Louise Phillips, Andrews & McMeel (Kansas City, MO), 1997.

(With Leslie Johnstone) *Fun with Your Microscope,* illustrated by Jason Coons, Sterling Publishers (New York, NY), 1998.

(With Vicki Scudamore) *Marbles: A Players' Guide,* illustrated by Emily S. Edliq, Sterling Publishers (New York, NY), 1998.

(With Leslie Johnstone) *The Optics Book: Fun Experiments with Light, Vision, and Color,* illustrated by Jason Coons, Sterling Publishers (New York, NY), 1998.

(With Leslie Johnstone and Elaine Humphrey) *3-D Bees and Micro Fleas* (includes stereoscopic cards and 3-D viewer), Somerville House (Toronto, Canada), 1999.

(With Leslie Johnstone and Elaine Humphrey) *3-D Lungs and Micro Tongues* (includes stereoscopic cards and 3-D viewer), Somerville House (Toronto, Canada), 1999.

(With Leslie Johnstone) *Shocking Science: Fun and Fascinating Electrical Experiments,* illustrated by Emily S. Edliq, Sterling Publishers (New York, NY), 1999.

(With Bob Bowden) *Awesome Yo-Yo Tricks,* Sterling Publishers (New York, NY), 2000.

(With Leslie Johnstone) *Quick-but-Great Science Fair Projects,* illustrated by Emily S. Edliq, Sterling Publishers (New York, NY), 2000.

(With Leslie Johnstone) *Build Your Own Solar Oven* (with solar cooker), Scholastic (New York, NY), 2000.

(With Leslie Johnstone) *BLAST OFF: A Rocket Science Kit* (with kit), illustrated by Ty Pollard, Troll Communications (Mahwah, NJ), 2000.

(With Leslie Johnstone) *It's My World, You Just Live in It,* Scholastic (New York, NY), 2000.

(With Leslie Johnstone) *Bathtub Science,* illustrated by Dave Garbot, Sterling Publishers (New York, NY), 2000.

(With Leslie Johnstone) *The Science of Sound and Music,* Sterling Publishers (New York, NY), 2000.

(With Leslie Johnstone) *The Incredible Secret Formula Book: Make Your Own Rock Candy, Jelly Snakes, Face Paint, Slimy Putty, and Fifty-five More Awesome Things!,* illustrated by John Manders, Troll Communications (Mahwah, NJ), 2001.

(With Michael Ouchi) *The Ultimate Balloon Book: Forty-six Projects to Blow up, Bend, and Twist,* Sterling Publishers (New York, NY), 2001.

(With Leslie Johnstone) *Build Your Own Remote Control,* Becker & Mayer (Kirkland, WA), 2001.

The Amazing Ice Cream Maker, Becker & Mayer (Kirkland, WA), 2001.

Also author, with Leslie Johnstone, of booklets *The Mega Dome Chemistry Book* and *Gross Lab,* both for Wild Planet Toys, 1999.

Former columnist for *Business in Vancouver;* contributor of articles on business, science, and other topics to periodicals and newspapers. Also author of a screenplay, with coauthor Alison Wells.

Work in Progress

Four children's books for Sterling Publishers.

Sidelights

Shar Levine is a Canadian writer and science buff who, with several coauthors, has produced a wealth of books that help young readers recognize and gain interest in the physical and natural phenomena occurring around them every day. Ranging from such introductory books as *Everyday Science: Fun and Easy Projects for Making Practical Things* to the far-more-specialized *Worm-World: The Worm Book* and *The Science of Sound and Music,* Levine's books were praised by *Science Activities* contributor Frances B. Spuler as maintaining a "writing style and approach to scientific investigation [that] is engaging to teachers and students alike."

Everyday Science and the related volume *Silly Science: Strange and Startling Projects to Amaze Your Family and Friends* are geared to older elementary-grade students, and each volume contains over twenty experiments that require easily gathered materials and which demonstrate a useful scientific principle. *Everyday Science* focuses on light, heat, chemistry, electricity and magnetism, and earth science, and readers learn how to construct a kaleidoscope, bath salts, and even a burglar alarm, all from things found around the average home. "What Happened?" and "Did You Know?" sections further illuminate beginning scientists and provide suggestions for further inquiry. In *Silly Science,* humorously titled experiments include "Slam Dancing Spaghetti," "Spongesaurus," and "Smoke Gets in Your Ivy." *Appraisal* reviewer Andrea Williams, praising both books as "terrific for in-home use," added that *Everyday Science* and *Silly Science* "could lead a child to a real hands-on understanding of some important scientific principles."

Other books by Levine that include experiments in a general area of interest include *Bathtub Science, The Science of Sound and Music, Shocking Science: Fun and Fascinating Electrical Experiments,* and *Quick-but-Great Science Fair Projects.* In her tantalizingly titled *The Incredible Secret Formula Book: Make Your Own*

Rock Candy, Jelly Snakes, Face Paint, Slime Putty, and Fifty-five More Awesome Things, fans of secret potions can delight in creating dough, paint, disappearing ink, paper, and crystals, as well as slimes and even more disgusting concoctions, all in the average kitchen.

Optics come in for special attention in several of Levine's books. *The Optics Book: Fun Experiments with Light, Vision, and Color* contains thirty-seven experiments that cover concepts ranging from polarization to the speed of light. The inclusion of directions for making pinhole cameras and an explanation of how rainbows are created add to what *School Library Journal* contributor Carolyn Angus concluded was "a useful source of science activities for individuals and classes exploring optics." In *Kirkus Reviews,* a critic dubbed *The Optics Book* "clever and informative," and useful for "budding scientists." Microscope owners and operators get a comprehensive operating manual in *The Microscope Book,* in which Levine and coauthor Leslie Johnstone discuss how microscope lenses work, how to prepare slides, and how microscopes are used in a variety of areas of scientific inquiry. While noting that the book assumes the use of a relatively sophisticated microscope and that creating slides requires more patience than some readers may possess, *Science Books and Films* contributor Louis J. Gotlib found the work to be "well-organized" and "nicely illustrated," and praised the authors for "mixing a sense of fun with and interest in

The Ultimate Balloon Book, *written by Levine and Michael Ouchi, shows how to bend and twist balloons into forty-six different shapes. (Photo by Jeff Connery.)*

science with explanations of the various activities." Cynthia M. Sturgis commented in particular on the "numerous simple experiments" included in *The Microscope Book,* citing in her *School Library Journal* review "watching yeast grow, observing simple one-cell animals in water, and collecting and studying fingerprints." *Fun with Your Microscope* follows a format similar to that used in the *Microscope Book,* although its focus is on slightly younger students, enticing kids with investigations of "dust bunnies," four-leaf clovers, socks, sewing needles, and peach fuzz. "Colorful cartoons lighten the tone," noted *School Library Journal* reviewer Allison Trent Bernstein of the book's visual appeal for youngsters, "and almost every page includes a full-color photo of a slide of a particular substance."

Levine explores earth science in several of her general nonfiction books, but in *Projects for a Healthy Planet: Simple Environmental Projects for Kids* readers learn a great deal about their home planet and the potential problems facing the Earth. Phenomena such as acid rain, the disintegrating ozone layer, air pollution, oil spills, and other forms of water pollution are illustrated through experiments performed with readily found ingredients. Praising the book for containing "a good selection of creative activities that will help kids understand the causes of pollution," *Quill & Quire* reviewer Pamela Hickman noted the value of *Projects for a Healthy Planet,* particularly during science-fair season. Nature's multi-hearted mini-composters are the focus of Levine's 1997 book *WormWorld,* which includes a kit that allows children to create their very own worm habitat and which contains chapters such as "Worm Wiggles," "Can You Hear a Worm?," and "Take a Worm's Pulse." The only caveat Levine has toward worm-related activities was the result of demonstrating worm behavior to children in a group so large that she had to work with buckets of garden worms. As she suggested on her Web site: "Do not eat spaghetti and work with worms. Trust me." Noting that "it's easy to get hooked on … *WormWorld,*" *Quill & Quire* reviewer Etta Kaner explained that in Levine's book all worm secrets are revealed, including "the food, music, and color preferences of worms, how worms help plants grow, and how worms sound when they move."

Levine and her coauthors have also forayed into several very specialized areas of "kid science" in books such as *Marbles: A Player's Guide, Awesome Yo-Yo Tricks,* and *The Ultimate Balloon Book: Forty-six Projects to Blow up, Bend, and Twist.* In addition to writing books for young readers, she works as a freelance writer and has had a regular segment on a local television station. Levine is also the president of Isolation Solutions, a company which markets portable negative pressure isolation rooms. Levine once ran a toy and game store in Vancouver, Canada, called Einstein's: The Science Center, which attracted the budding scientists that inspired her to begin teaching hands-on science and eventually begin writing her popular science books for kids.

Biographical and Critical Sources

PERIODICALS

Appraisal, spring, 1995, Andrea Williams, review of *Everyday Science* and *Silly Science,* pp. 36-37; fall, 1996, Karen Sanders, review of *Science around the World,* p. 22.

Booklist, August, 1992, Sheilamae O'Hara, review of *Projects for a Healthy Planet: Simple Environmental Experiments for Kids,* p. 2006; February 1, 1998, Kay Weisman, review of *The Magnet Book,* p. 915; November 15, 1998, April Judge, review of *Fun with Your Microscope,* p. 583; March 1, 1999, Carolyn Phelan, review of *The Optics Book: Fun Experiments with Light, Vision, and Color,* p. 1209; March 15, 1999, Susan Dove Lempke, review of *Marbles: A Player's Guide,* p. 1326; April 1, 2000, Carolyn Phelan, review of *Shocking Science: Fun and Fascinating Electrical Experiments,* p. 1459; January 1, 2001, Carolyn Phelan, review of *The Science of Sound and Music,* p. 944; August, 2001, Carolyn Phelan, review of *The Ultimate Balloon Book,* p. 2110.

Children's Digest, October-November, 1997, review of *The Microscope Book,* p. 30; April, 1999, review of *The Optics Book,* p. 25.

Kirkus Reviews, January 15, 1999, review of *The Optics Book,* p. 147.

Maclean's, August 27, 2001, "Mixed Emotions: Having Parents of Two Races Can Be Rich in Traditions but Also Rife with Emotions," p. 22.

Publishers Weekly, June 18, 2001, review of *The Ultimate Balloon Book,* p. 82.

Quill & Quire, May, 1992, Pamela Hickman, review of *Projects for a Healthy Planet,* p. 92; August, 1997, Etta Kaner, review of *WormWorld,* p. 38.

School Library Journal, August, 1992, Meryl Silverstein, review of *Projects for a Healthy Planet,* pp. 169-170; August, 1995, Carolyn Angus, review of *Everyday Science* and *Silly Science,* pp. 148-149; July, 1996, Carolyn Angus, review of *Science around the World,* p. 108; July, 1997, Cynthia M. Sturgis, review of *The Microscope Book,* p. 108; December, 1998, Allison Trent Bernstein, review of *Fun with Your Microscope,* pp. 138-138; April, 1999, Edith Ching, review of *Marbles: A Player's Guide,* p. 150; July, 1999, Carolyn Angus, review of *The Optics Book,* p. 110; May, 2000, Kathryn Kosiorek, review of *Shocking Science,* p. 185; August, 2000, Kathryn Kosiorek, review of *Awesome Yo-Yo Tricks,* p. 202; March, 2001, Linda Beck, review of *The Science of Sound and Music,* p. 272; August, 2001, Blair Christolon, review of *Bathtub Science,* p. 170; October, 2001, Cynde Marcengill, review of *The Ultimate Balloon Book,* p. 188.

Science Activities, spring, 2001, Frances B. Spuler, review of *Shocking Science,* p. 47; summer, 2001, Leonard P. Rivard, review of *The Science of Sound and Music,* p. 47.

Science Books and Films, August, 1994, Cynthia A. Bradbury, review of *Einstein's Science Parties,* p. 180; October, 1996, Louis J. Gotlib, review of *The Microscope Book,* p. 207.

OTHER

Shar Levine—Science Lady, http://www.sciencelady.com (December 12, 2001).

* * *

LEVITIN, Sonia (Wolff) 1934- (Sonia Wolff)

Personal

Born August 18, 1934, in Berlin, Germany; immigrated to United States, 1938; daughter of Max (a manufacturer) and Helene (Goldstein) Wolff; married Lloyd Levitin (a business executive), December 27, 1953; children: Daniel Joseph, Shari Diane. *Education:* Attended University of California, Berkeley, 1952-54; University of Pennsylvania, B.S., 1956; San Francisco State College (now University), graduate study, 1957-60. *Avocational interests:* Hiking, piano, Judaic studies, travel, history, painting.

Addresses

Home—10178 Baywood Court, Los Angeles, CA 90077. *Agent*—Toni Mendez, Inc., 141 East 56th St., New York, NY 10022. *E-mail*—slevitin@ucla.edu.

Career

Writer and educator. Junior high school teacher in Mill Valley, CA, 1956-57; adult education teacher in Daly City, CA, 1962-64; Acalanes Adult Center, Lafayette, CA, teacher, 1965-72; teacher of creative writing, Palos Verdes Peninsula, CA, 1973-76, and University of California, Los Angeles Extension, 1978—; University of Judaism, instructor in American Jewish literature, 1989—. Founder of STEP (adult education organization) in Palos Verdes Peninsula. Performed volunteer work, including publicity, for various charities and educational institutions. *Member:* Authors League of America, Authors Guild, PEN, Society of Children's Book Writers and Illustrators, California Writer's Guild, Moraga Historical Society (founder and former president).

Awards, Honors

Junior Literary Guild selection, 1970, for *Journey to America,* and 1978, for *The No-Return Trail;* Charles and Bertie G. Schwartz Award for juvenile fiction, Jewish Book Council of America, 1970, and Notable Book citation, American Library Association, for *Journey to America;* Dorothy Canfield Fisher Award nomination, Georgia State Award nomination, and Mark Twain Award nomination, all for *Roanoke: A Novel of the Lost Colony;* Notable Book citation, American Library Association, 1973, for *Who Owns the Moon?;* California Young Reader Medal award nomination in the junior high category, 1976, and Southern California Council on Literature for Children and Young People Award for fiction, 1981, both for *The Mark of Conte;* Golden Spur Award, Western Writers of America, 1978, and Lewis Carroll Shelf Award, both for *The No-Return Trail;* Children's Choice award, 1980, for *Nobody Stole the Pie;* Southern California Council on Literature for Children and Young People award for a distinguished body of work, 1981; Notable Children's Trade Book, 1982, and Pick of the Lists, American Booksellers Association, both for *The Fisherman and the Bird;* Notable Children's Trade Book, 1982, for *All the Cats in the World;* Pick of the Lists, American Booksellers Association, 1982, for *The Year of Sweet Senior Insanity;* National Jewish Book Award in children's literature, 1987, and PEN Los Angeles Award for young adult fiction, Association of Jewish Libraries Sydney Taylor Award, Austrian Youth Prize, Catholic Children's Book Prize (Germany), Dorothy Canfield Fisher Award nomination, Parent's Choice Honor Book citation, and American Library Association Best Book for Young Adults award, all 1988, all for *The Return;* Edgar Allen Poe Award, Mystery Writers of America, 1988, and Dorothy Canfield Fisher Award nomination and Nevada State Award nomination, both 1989, all for *Incident at Loring Groves;* Honor Book citation, Sydney Taylor Book Award, Jewish Library Association, and Best Book for Young Adults, ALA-YASD, both 1989, nominee, Dorothy Canfield Fisher Award, and finalist, Jefferson Cup Award, all for *Silver Days;* Kansas State Reading Circle Selection, 1993, and Recommended Book for Reluctant Young Adult Readers, YALSA, both for *The Golem and the Dragon Girl;* Pick of the Lists, American Booksellers Association, Riverside County Author's Award, 1993, and nominee, Georgia State Award, all for *Annie's Promise;* Distinguished Body of Work Award, Southern California Council on Literature for Children and Young People, 1994; recommended list, National Conference of Christians and Jews, 1994, outstanding book citation, *Voice of Youth Advocates,* 1994, Editor's Choice, *Booklist,* Best Books for Young Adults, YALSA, 1995, Books for the Teen Age, New York Public Library, 1995, nominee, South Carolina Junior Book Award, and nominee Tennessee Book Award, YA category, 1998-99, all for *Escape from Egypt;* Honor Book, Parents' Choice, Books for the Teen Age, New York Public Library, and Best of the Best Fiction, Pennsylvania Librarians Association, all for *Evil Encounter;* finalist, California Young Reader Medal, Best Book, *School Library Journal,* 1996, and nominee, Show Me Readers Award, Missouri Association of School Librarians, all for *Nine for California;* finalist, Edgar Award, Mystery Writers of America, and Books for the Teen Age, New York Public Library, both for *Yesterday's Child;* nominee, Nebraska Golden Sower Award, for *Boom Town;* Best Books, Bank Street College, 1998, and Sydney Taylor Honor Book, both for *The Singing Mountain;* "Pick of the Lists" selection, American Booksellers Association, and "Books in the Middle: Outstanding Titles of 1999," *Voice of Youth Advocates,* both 1999, both for *The Cure;* notable book, *Smithsonian* Magazine, for *Dream Freedom. Journey to America* and *The No-Return Trail* were both Junior Literary Guild selections.

Writings

FOR YOUNG ADULTS

Roanoke: A Novel of the Lost Colony, illustrated by John Gretzer, Atheneum (New York, NY), 1973.

The Mark of Conte, illustrated by Bill Negron, Atheneum (New York, NY), 1976, published without illustrations, Collier Books (New York, NY), 1987.

Reigning Cats and Dogs (nonfiction), illustrated by Joan Berg Victor, Atheneum (New York, NY), 1976.

Beyond Another Door, Atheneum (New York, NY), 1977.

The No-Return Trail, Harcourt (New York, NY), 1978.

The Year of Sweet Senior Insanity, Atheneum (New York, NY), 1982.

Smile Like a Plastic Daisy, Atheneum (New York, NY), 1984.

A Season for Unicorns, Atheneum (New York, NY), 1986.

The Return, Atheneum (New York, NY), 1987.

Incident at Loring Groves, Dial (New York, NY), 1988.

The Golem and the Dragon Girl, Dial (New York, NY), 1993.

Escape from Egypt, Little, Brown (Boston, MA), 1994.

Evil Encounter, Simon & Schuster (New York, NY), 1996.

Yesterday's Child, Simon & Schuster (New York, NY), 1997.

The Singing Mountain, Simon & Schuster (New York, NY), 1998.

The Cure, Harcourt (New York, NY), 1999.

Dream Freedom, Silver Whistle (San Diego, CA), 2000.

Clem's Chances, Orchard Books (New York, NY), 2001.

Room in the Heart, Dutton (New York, NY), in press.

"PLATT FAMILY" TRILOGY

Journey to America, illustrated by Charles Robinson, Atheneum (New York, NY), 1970.

Silver Days, Atheneum (New York, NY), 1989.

Annie's Promise, Atheneum (New York, NY), 1993.

PICTURE BOOKS FOR CHILDREN

Who Owns the Moon?, illustrated by John Larrecq, Parnassus, 1973.

A Single Speckled Egg, illustrated by John Larrecq, Parnassus, 1976.

A Sound to Remember, illustrated by Gabriel Lisowski, Harcourt (New York, NY), 1979.

Nobody Stole the Pie, illustrated by Fernando Krahn, Harcourt (New York, NY), 1980.

All the Cats in the World, illustrated by Charles Robinson, Harcourt (New York, NY), 1982.

The Fisherman and the Bird, illustrated by Francis Livingston, Houghton Mifflin (Boston, MA), 1982.

The Man Who Kept His Heart in a Bucket, illustrated by Jerry Pinkney, Dial (New York, NY), 1991.

A Piece of Home, illustrated by Juan Wijngaard, Dial (New York, NY), 1996.

Nine for California, illustrated by Cat Bowman Smith, Orchard (New York, NY), 1996.

Boom Town (sequel to *Nine for California*), illustrated by Cat Bowman Smith, Orchard (New York, NY), 1998.

Taking Charge (sequel to *Boom Town*), illustrated by Cat Bowman Smith, Orchard (New York, NY), 1999.

When Elephant Goes to a Party, illustrated by Jeff Seaver, Rising Moon (Flagstaff, AZ), 2001.

When Kangaroo Goes to School, illustrated by Jeff Seaver, Rising Moon (Flagstaff, AZ), 2001.

OTHER

Rita, the Weekend Rat (fiction), illustrated by Leonard W. Shortall, Atheneum (New York, NY), 1971.

Jason and the Money Tree (fiction), illustrated by Pat Grant Porter, Harcourt (New York, NY), 1974.

(Under name Sonia Wolff) *What They Did to Miss Lily* (fiction for adults), Harper (New York, NY), 1981.

(Author of introduction) Yale Strom, *A Tree Still Stands: Jewish Youth in Eastern Europe Today,* Putnam (New York, NY), 1990.

Adam's War (for children), illustrated by Vincent Nasta, Dial (New York, NY), 1994.

Feature columnist for Sun Newspapers, Contra Costa, CA, and *Jewish Observer of the East Bay,* Oakland, CA. Contributor to periodicals, including *Christian Science Monitor, Ingenue, Parents', Reform Judaism, San Francisco, Scholastic, Smithsonian, Together, Woman's World,* and *Writer.*

Work in Progress

Room in the Heart, for Dutton, 2003.

Sidelights

Sonia Levitin survived a difficult childhood to thrive as an award-winning children's author. Born to Jewish parents in 1934 amid the anti-Semitism of Nazi Germany, she soon fled with her family to the United States. There she grew up in poverty but went on to gain a college education and fulfill her girlhood dream of becoming a writer. After being honored by the Jewish Book Council of America in 1971 for her autobiographical first novel, *Journey to America,* she earned further awards for a wide variety of books, including the Western *No-Return Trail* and the murder mystery *Incident at Loring Groves.*

In the years before Levitin was born her parents had become prosperous members of the German middle class. Her father, without benefit of higher education, had become a skillful tailor and businessman, able with a few hasty scribbles to prepare designs and budgets for his line of clothing. The family enjoyed such comforts as household servants and vacations at some of Germany's most popular resorts. All that changed dramatically after the Nazis took power in 1933 and began the campaign of anti-Jewish terror and murder now known as the Holocaust. To escape persecution, three-year-old Sonia and her family left their belongings and savings behind them and slipped into neighboring Switzerland. There she waited with her mother and two sisters for a year as refugees while her father went to America to arrange a home for them. Once the family settled in the United States, young Sonia's parents had to work mightily to recreate the family business; they were so busy that for several years she was raised largely by one of her sisters. Her mother, moreover, suffered terrible guilt from knowing that she had been unable to save several relatives from death at the hands of the Nazis.

"The Holocaust experience left its deep mark on me," Levitin once recalled. "It is agonizing for me as a Jew to realize that our people were almost exterminated; it is equally agonizing, as a human being, to have to admit to the evil that humans can do to one another." Although Levitin was forced to confront discrimination and suffering at an early age, she also learned the power of compassion, as her family was helped by a variety of non-Jews who sympathized with their plight. "To them I owe a great debt," Levitin wrote, "not the least of which is my optimistic belief that despite evil in the world, there is goodness in great measure, and that goodness knows no boundaries of religion or race."

For a few years Levitin's parents moved the family back and forth between New York City and Los Angeles in an effort to find a profitable living; finally they settled for good in southern California. Young Sonia became an avid reader and at age eleven wrote to Laura Ingalls Wilder, beloved author of the "Little House on the Prairie" novels, to confess that she wanted to become a writer. "To my great joy," she recalled, "[I] received a reply, which remains among my treasures to this day." As Levitin progressed through school she continued to be drawn to the arts, writing poems and short stories and learning how to paint and play the piano.

When Levitin was eighteen she enrolled at the Berkeley campus of the University of California, and almost immediately she met her future husband, a fellow student. They were married when she was nineteen. Once the couple completed their studies they settled in the San Francisco area, and after Levitin had taught school for a year she became pregnant and decided to stay home to raise her family. To make full use of her time she resolved to become a writer in earnest, and with encouragement from her husband she became a part-time writing student at nearby San Francisco State College. Her teacher was Walter Van Tilburg Clark, renowned for the moral insight of his Western novel *The Ox-Bow Incident.* Levitin fondly recalled the weekly meetings where Clark explained the strengths and weaknesses of her short stories: "Why had he accepted me [for his classes]? I asked him later, when we had become friends. Was my writing good? Not so much the writing style, he replied, but the subjects that I had chosen made him want me as a pupil. The subjects were thoughtful and serious, dealing with war, aging, love, sacrifice, freedom."

Levitin's career as a writer began modestly. To gain experience, she volunteered to do publicity for charities, including the writing of press releases. This work eased her into writing articles for magazines and columns for local newspapers. She also taught creative writing classes of her own. She remained frustrated, though, by her efforts to make an impact as a short-story writer. As an exercise, she started writing a longer narrative based on the tribulations that her family experienced when she was very young. This story, which she originally intended only for her own children, grew over the course of several years into *Journey to America,* a full-length novel for young people that was published to widespread praise in 1970. The book describes a year in the life of the fictional Platt family, Jewish refugees whose escape from Nazi Germany to the United States resembles Levitin's own. "With *Journey to America,*" Levitin once remarked, "I felt that my career was launched, and that I had found my niche. I loved writing for young people. I felt that in this genre I could be both gentle and serious, idealistic and pragmatic. I realized that I happen to possess a wonderful memory for the details of my own childhood, for smells and sights and sounds, how faces looked, how feelings felt, and what childhood was really all about."

Levitin went on to publish a new book almost every year, and she looked at growing up from many different points of view. Some of her books, including *Rita the Weekend Rat* and *The Mark of Conte,* are humorous stories loosely inspired by the antics of her own son and daughter. *Rita* is about a girl who thinks of her pet rat as her closest friend, and *The Mark of Conte* features an energetic high-school freshman who tries to outsmart the school computer and earn credit for two years of classes in one year's time. Other books, in the spirit of *Journey to America,* are more serious works in which young people confront major challenges. *The No-Return Trail,* which won the prestigious Golden Spur Award, is a Western novel that breaks with tradition by stressing the heroism of a woman: the main character is a seventeen-year-old wife and mother who became the first female settler to cross the continent to California. The tale is based on a real wagon-train expedition from the 1840s and was researched in part through a local history society in Moraga, California, that Levitin founded with her husband. *Incident at Loring Groves,* which won the coveted Edgar Award for mystery fiction, is a novel about the moral dilemmas that teenagers face in the uncertain modern world. The story, again based on fact, describes the difficult choices faced by a group of irresponsible high-schoolers who discover that one of their classmates has been murdered—and then try to avoid telling the police for fear that their own drug abuse and vandalism will be exposed as well. A reviewer for *Publishers Weekly* hailed the book as "a searingly honest portrayal of adolescent society." "In each book I try to do something quite different from the previous work," Levitin once observed. "Themes and characters might repeat themselves, but I believe that my growth as a writer and as a person depends on accepting new challenges, deepening my experience and my efforts."

One theme that recurs in Levitin's work is the importance of her Jewish heritage. Nearly two decades after she wrote *Journey to America,* Levitin wrote a sequel—*Silver Days*—that follows the immigrant Platt family as it adjusts to life in the United States. When the mother of the family collapses with grief at news of the continuing Holocaust, she and the others find solace in carrying on the traditions of Judaism in their new homeland. "Our future," the father declares, "must have room in it for the past." *The Return,* a novel that won major awards in both America and Europe, recounts the saga of an unusual group of refugees who arrived in Israel in the mid-1980s. They were the "black Jews" of Ethiopia, Africans who for centuries had observed Jewish religious traditions in almost complete isolation from fellow Jews and the rest of the world. Facing increasing discrimination in their native land, they were smuggled to their new home by the Israeli government through a secret military airlift. As a former refugee, Levitin was deeply moved by the operation and dropped her other writing projects to create a novel about it, journeying to Israel to interview the Ethiopians herself. Writing in the *New York Times Book Review,* Sheila Klass called the book "a remarkable fictional account," praised its evocation of Ethiopian Jewish culture, and declared: "'The Return' is crammed with history, as Sonia Levitin, the author of other distinguished books for young people about Jewish history, here tells the story of an entire people."

Levitin's intense study of the Torah is evident in her historical novel *Escape from Egypt,* about the Jews' exodus from Egypt as seen through the eyes of Jesse, an Israelite slave, and the half-Egyptian girl Jennat, with whom he falls in love. Questions of love, duty, and faith intermingle with the action of Moses freeing the Israelites from the recalcitrant Pharoah in what a *Publishers Weekly* contributor labeled a "startling and searching" exploration that would "spur her audience to fresh appraisals of sacred history." "Working on this book was one of the most exhilarating experiences in my career," Levitin once explained, "for it brought together my love of research, the delight of rendering powerful and brilliant episodes described in the Bible, and exploring the questions that have engrossed mankind from the beginning of consciousness."

Levitin continued to explore what it means to be Jewish in her young adult novel *The Singing Mountain.* Told in alternating chapters by California natives Mitch and his cousin Carlie, the narrative follows Mitch's decision to study at a yeshiva in Jerusalem instead of attending college in the United States. As part of a coming-of-age novel, Levitin objectively presents both Orthodox and Reform Jewish practices. Commentators found much to like about the work. "This plot-driven novel bristles with questions about faith, love, family, acceptance, and self-determination," remarked *Booklist* critic Karen Simonetti. A *Publishers Weekly* reviewer added that Levitin uses a light touch and "maintains a remarkable evenhandedness with all her characters ... as she presents conflicting points of view without favoring any one of them." *The Singing Mountain* "succeeds as a realistic and poignant portrayal of a young man's search for God and self, conveying both the struggle and joy of the continuous journey," concluded Lauren Adams in *Horn Book.*

The Cure, which a *Horn Book* contributor considered a "compelling interior tale of the little-known true horror that faced 'the other' during the Middle Ages," was likened to Lois Lowry's award-winning novel *The Giver* for its vision of a future society that limits freedoms to

ensure social stability. When citizen Gemm 16884 finds himself attracted to music in a society that disallows music, he is considered a deviant and sent into the distant past to be cured of his malady. In fourteenth-century Europe, Gemm witnesses the persecution of Jews, who were made scapegoats for the plague that was terrorizing Europe. A *Publishers Weekly* critic maintained that the novel "handily combines futuristic science fiction and late-medieval Jewish history," and *Booklist* contributor Ilene Cooper asserted that "Gemm's experience in Strasbourg is carefully crafted and emotionally evocative." Similarly, a critic for *Kirkus Reviews* praised Levitin's "unusual mix of science and historical fiction," saying that the novel "pulsates with energy and freshness" and is "packed with spine-tingling historical detail."

Levitin examined another serious topic in *Dream Freedom.* In this novel, a boy and his classmates learn about present-day slavery in Sudan, and work to raise money to buy some of the slaves their freedom. The slaves' own stories are told in alternate chapters. Praising Levitin's "evocative language" and realistic detail, *Booklist* reviewer Shelle Rosenfeld observed that the author "offers perspective on what really matters: compassion, freedom, and how individuals can make a difference." Kathleen Isaacs expressed similar praise in *School Library Journal,* hailing the novel as a "moving narrative" that offers an "intense portrayal of the complex patterns of Sudanese society today and the issues surrounding buying back slaves."

In addition to her acclaimed young adult novels, Levitin has written several picture books, including the historically-themed *Nine for California* and its sequels, *Boom Town* and *Taking Charge. When Elephant Goes to a Party* and *When Kangaroo Goes to School* use humorous situations to present basic manners and social skills.

Levitin once said: "As time goes by I discover, somewhat to my surprise, that writing does not get any easier. It is still demanding and difficult work; at times I find it frustrating. I have a recurring dream where I stand before a large, oddly shaped room full of students, called to lecture to them, but the configuration of the room is such that I cannot possibly retain eye contact or voice contact with everyone. This is my struggle: I want to call out, reach everyone; I want to speak to them and to be heard. This is my mission, this is my goal with my books, to be a mind-bridge between people, among peoples of various colors, types, persuasions. Why else do I possess this intense interest about people and their past, their present desires and goals, their inclinations to do good, or to do evil?

"My writing is changing—it should with time. I am working with the same topics and themes, but delving deeper, I think, into my own experiences and beliefs, using them and blending them with fact and imagination to create stories that I hope will have the power to live and to persuade. I admit it, persuasion is surely the aim of the writer. Mine is to persuade beautifully, with clarity and in honesty. This demands self-examination and self-knowledge, both of which are attained only through a lifetime of effort—and then one is ever doubtful.

"All this sounds very serious; writing must also be fun. This is what I convey to my students. It must flow, laugh, sing, and dance with you. One is a writer purely by choice and from the love of it. It is well to remember that, and to glory in the independence and the sheer pleasure of being able to think and create and call it 'work.'

"Ideas abound. Right now, six various projects fill my desk space, and several more whisper in my mind for later development. One needs time, self-discipline, and a quiet, contemplative spirit in order to separate the valuable from the dross. I do take time to be silent each day, to meditate and sort out what is important, and what I shall use, how it fits together, what the universe has to tell me. Mysterious? No—it is simply—prayer.

"I should add, and not in jest, that it is very important to choose the right mate if one wishes to be a creative writer. I have been endowed with wonderful luck in that area. My husband knows when to listen well and to encourage, when to stand aside and say nothing, when to commiserate, when to celebrate with me. He sees my work as an important link between what the present reality is for us, and what we may yet leave behind. He understands the value of ideas and ideals. I know he would love me as well if I never wrote another book; the pressure is all mine, from within, the way it should be."

Biographical and Critical Sources

BOOKS

Authors and Artists for Young Adults, Volume 13, Gale (Detroit, MI), 1994.

Children's Literature Review, Volume 53, Gale (Detroit, MI), 1999.

Contemporary Literary Criticism, Volume 17, Gale (Detroit, MI), 1981.

Something about the Author Autobiography Series, Volume 2, Gale (Detroit, MI), 1986.

St. James Guide to Young Adult Writers, second edition, St. James Press (Detroit, MI), 1999.

PERIODICALS

Booklist, May 1, 1994, Ilene Cooper, review of *Escape from Egypt,* p. 1595; July, 1994, Stephanie Zvirin, review of *Adam's War,* p. 1949; February 15, 1998, Lauren Peterson, review of *Boom Town,* p. 1020; September 15, 1998, Karen Simonetti, review of *The Singing Mountain,* p. 221; April 15, 1999, Carolyn Phelan, review of *Taking Charge,* p. 1536; June 1,

1999, Ilene Cooper, review of *The Cure,* p. 1814; May 1, 2001, Amy Brandt, review of *When Elephant Goes to a Party,* p. 1691; November 1, 2000, Shelle Rosenfeld, review of *Dream Freedom,* p. 526.

Book Report, September-October, 1999, Ron Marinucci, review of *The Cure,* p. 60; May, 2001, Ruie Chehak, review of *Dream Freedom,* p. 60.

Bulletin of the Center for Children's Books, February, 1971; January, 1999, Janice M. Del Negro, review of *The Singing Mountain,* p. 173; July-August, 1999, p. 393.

Commonweal, May 22, 1970.

English Journal, November, 1989, p. 82.

Horn Book, April, 1970; June, 1976; May, 1989; March-April, 1998, Margaret A. Bush, review of *Boom Town,* p. 215; November, 1998, Lauren Adams, review of *The Singing Mountain,* p. 734; March, 1999, Margaret A. Bush, review of *Taking Charge,* p. 196; May, 1999, review of *The Cure,* p. 332.

Kirkus Reviews, February 1, 1999, p. 223; March 15, 1999, review of *The Cure;* September 1, 2001, review of *Clem's Chances,* p. 1294.

Los Angeles Times, August 15, 1987.

New York Times Book Review, May 24, 1970; May 17, 1987, Sheila Klass, "Waiting for Operation Moses," p. 36; May 17, 1998, Anne Scott MacLeod, "And No Television Either," p. 23.

Publishers Weekly, May 13, 1988, review of *Incident at Loring Groves,* p. 278; April 19, 1993, review of *Annie's Promise,* p. 63; March 28, 1994, review of *Escape from Egypt,* p. 98; June 13, 1994, review of *Adam's War,* p. 65; September 9, 1996, review of *Nine for California,* p. 83; September 7, 1998, review of *The Singing Mountain,* p. 96; April 5, 1999, p. 241; April 12, 1999, review of *The Cure,* p. 76; November 6, 2000, review of *Dream Freedom,* p. 92.

Reading Today, October, 2000, Lynne T. Burke, review of *Dream Freedom,* p. 32.

School Library Journal, May, 1970; June, 1988; March, 1998, Steven Engelfried, review of *Boom Town,* p. 182; November, 1998, Elisabeth Palmer Abarbanel, review of *The Singing Mountain,* pp. 122-123; April, 1999, Beth Tegart, review of *Taking Charge,* p. 102; May, 1999, pp. 127-128; October, 2000, Kathleen Isaacs, review of *Dream Freedom,* p. 162; June, 2001, Patricia Pearl Dole, review of *When Elephant Goes to a Party,* p. 124.

Voice of Youth Advocates, February, 1999, p. 437; June, 1999, Beth Karpas, review of *The Cure,* p. 123.

Writer, August, 1972.

OTHER

Sonia Levitin Web site, http://www.bol.ucla.edu/~slevitin (April 15, 2002).

*   *   *

Autobiography Feature

Sonia Levitin

L ife is, among other things, strange and unpredictable. I begin writing this autobiography on the beach on the lush and beautiful island of Hawaii. It is my favorite place in all the world, warm and tropical, with pleasant people and gentle winds bringing a sense of peace. Here, my thoughts drift back to my parents and to my beginnings, so vastly different, for I was born in a severe time and into a way of life that was to end in destruction more savage and devastating than any before or since.

To be born a Jew in Germany in 1934 was to be born into crisis. From earliest childhood I knew that if Hitler had had his way, I would have been killed along with millions of other Jews. That knowledge has made me reverence life even more. I realize, too, that in many ways it has shaped my ideas about what is worthwhile, and how life is to be lived.

The actual story of my birth became one of my father's many humorous anecdotes. My father had a fine sense of drama, and told how he went to work as usual that morning, returning home to discover Frau Leuffelbein, the midwife, already in attendance. It was customary then to be born at home, and this midwife had performed her duties for my parents twice before. On that afternoon of August 18, 1934, Frau Leuffelbein met my father in the parlor, giggling and beaming, exclaiming, "Congratulations, Herr Wolff. This time you have a beautiful little boy!"

"I knew better," my father recounted. "What a sly one she was! I rushed into the bedroom to see for myself. Of course, it was a lie. Another girl. Three daughters! Ah, me. It would cost a fortune to get them all married off!"

Psychologists today might frown at the implication that is clear in this story. My father wanted a boy. Instead, he got another girl. Me.

So what? He told it with good humor, as a trick played on him by the fates. And while we were never really close, I suspect this was because of our particular personalities and also the culture of the times. Oh, he was proud of us, and in company he recited our accomplishments. Not the least of our so-called virtues was the fact that family friends all praised our looks. It was common in those days, at least among our crowd, for the grown-ups to talk about such things at length, and to speculate about which of us was the most attractive. Frankly, we loved it; we ate it up.

We three, like most siblings, were very different from each other. In many ways we still are, but time has a way of mellowing people, of grinding down the sharp edges of difference, so we get along despite them.

My oldest sister, Vera, is an intense person, devoted to work and system, orderly and emotionally sparing of herself. She is a nurse, presently an administrator; the job suits her.

My sister Eva, seven years my senior, played the role of "second mother" in those years when, as refugee strangers in America, my parents were forced to work nearly all day and night to support us. They left at dawn for jobs in the city, my father starting out as a peddler of neckties, my mother as a cleaning woman, and they

Sonia Levitin

returned after I was in bed, often using evening hours to learn English in adult school. (In later years I taught English to new waves of foreigners; I felt a great sense of continuity in this, and could sympathize with my adult students.) What a frightful change for my parents, just at middle age. They had grown accustomed to luxury and status in Berlin, considering themselves fortunate to be living in a cultured and sophisticated society. My parents had two hired servants, a housekeeper-cook and a "girl for the children." They took winter vacations in elegant resorts like Oberhof, and summers in Wiesbaden and Marienbad. I have photos of those idyllic times. In them my parents look young, radiant, and optimistic. How swiftly, and how crushingly it all ended!

When we left Germany (I should say "escaped," for we left in secret and had to steal away like thieves, clutching only a few possessions), Vera was thirteen, Eva eleven, and I was three. Even then, Eva was already a dancer. She had studied ballet in Germany, and as soon as my parents were able, they continued her training in the United States. Eva was graceful and lithe. She always loved fashion and expensive, pretty things. She actively sought (and tried to indoctrinate me with) ways to improve herself, to become acceptable among genteel people. I often frustrated her, being more of a tomboy in my youth.

I loved animals from the start, sought out stray cats and fed them. I still do. I rode horses, not for the ride, which actually terrified me, but to be near the smell and sight of their flesh, to see those noble heads and magnificent gleaming bodies. I climbed trees, loving both the climb and the vantage point, and I spent a great deal of time looking into other people's lives, going into their houses when I could, or imagining their lives if actual entry was blocked.

In our early years in the United States, when I was five and six and seven, I spent a great deal of time just tagging after my big sisters. Vera was usually self-absorbed and did not like to be bothered playing nursemaid. But Eva enjoyed the role and was a fine playmate-parent; we played dolls, danced, sang in harmony, cooked (fudge and chocolate pudding were our specialties), and occasionally went to the movies. It cost a dime to get in, and sometimes we had an extra nickel for candy.

Like all siblings, Eva and I had our battles. It was a strong relationship, both of love and envy. When she scolded or criticized me, I was devastated. When she got married and left home, I cried for days, feeling utterly abandoned. Yet we had our differences. We fought, hit, kicked, and scratched. I look back on that with a smile and with some appreciation; sibling rivalry can help to toughen you up for life. And, heaven knows, we need to be tough.

Vera and I fought less, communicated less. She was a good student and a great reader and used to subscribe to a book club. This was a great boon to me as I eventually filched the books and read them in a quiet corner, until I was discovered with a shrill cry: "Mother! do you know what that *child* is reading?"

Mother, weary from work and perhaps confident that words in books are more enlightening than dangerous, paid little heed. Nobody censored my reading, though sometimes it was suggested that I wait another year or so before getting into "that subject." Meaning, of course, sex or perversion. The admonition made me an even more avid reader.

Eva, Sonia, and Vera in Los Angeles, 1941

I learned to read with the ease of a newly hatched fish taking to water. It was in first grade. One day, or so it seemed, the symbols suddenly *became* language. I was entranced and overjoyed. At six or seven I got my first library card and was amazed at the riches there for me, and all of it free. (I confess, however, that I never managed to avoid library fines for overdue books, always selecting more than I could possible finish in the allotted time. This weakness still persists.) Since then, I think there have always been books on my bedside table. I cannot imagine a day without reading.

I read all the Alcott books, all of "Nancy Drew," "Bobbsey Twins," Laura Ingalls Wilder, and the "Anne" books by L. M. Montgomery. I owned a few books, *A Girl of the Limberlost* and *Robinson Crusoe,* Kipling's *Tales, Jane Eyre,* and my all-time favorite, *Little Women,* which I read again and again and again. When I was eleven and had finished reading all the Laura Ingalls Wilder books, I was dismayed to learn that there were no more. A kind librarian suggested that I write a letter to the author. The idea would never have occurred to me: I had thought all authors were dead. I wrote the letter, and to my great joy, received a reply, which remains among my treasures to this day. In my letter I stated my desire to become an author, too. It was the first time I ever voiced that goal to anyone.

My father had preceded us to America without any savings, quite literally with only the clothes on his back. My mother arrived in New York with the three of us a year later, penniless. We were indeed poor. However, my parents bought me the things I really needed. Among them were books, paper, and art supplies. Eventually, too, we got an upright piano and I was given lessons. But at the beginning there was simply no money for extras.

We lived in New York City for a year, then moved to Los Angeles, to a neighborhood racially and ethnically mixed, all united by poverty and the desire to get ahead. In kindergarten I promptly fell in love with my teacher, Mrs. Stevens, and with the whole idea of school. Perhaps even then I already imagined myself as a teacher. By fourth grade that idea had crystallized. But between those years I had to face a minor disaster. After two years in Los Angeles, my parents, just having accumulated a little cash, decided to return to New York, largely because my aunt, uncle, and cousin had settled there. Back we went, from warm weather and casual atmosphere to the cold city with its crowds and clatter. I was always frightened on the city streets and, worse, found no friends on the cement school yard and no sense of accomplishment in the classroom.

In California I had been known as a bright student. In New York, with its educational system ahead of the west, I was immediately put back half a year and classified as a dullard in math. I got an F on my report card.

My mother was called to school. At that time my parents were the working partners in a five-and-dime store; someone else put up the money and my parents did all the work, weekends and nights included. We rarely saw them. Eventually the store failed and we were again reduced to utter poverty, my father having spent his savings on relocating us in New York. We returned to L.A., not by train, as we'd left, but by bus, a grueling, exhausting trip of four or five days and nights. But before that, Eva came to school in place of Mother, and I stood there while my ineptitude was paraded before me in the form of those disgraceful math papers.

"But Sonia knows how to add," my sister objected.

"Show me, then," said the teacher.

Eva, Vera, and Sonia, 1975

She wrote down strings of numbers. Deftly I added them up in my head, told her the answer, and she wrote it down, filling in the first column, carrying to the next.

I was astounded, It was so simple! In a twinkling I learned the method, and to the teacher's amazement I completed an entire page of problems correctly then and there.

But it had taken many weeks of agony to reach this moment of recognition. And while I was known as the "dullard," something else happened. The effect of failure carried over to the other students, their opinion of me. I had no friends. Nor was I chosen for any other privileges, the small but exhilarating honors that can make a child's day at school a glory.

This experience served me well in later years when, as a teacher, I remembered that every child needs to be honored, singled out, respected. I took special care to rotate privileges and to give praise. I also realized that when a student fails the fault often lies equally with the teacher. It is the teacher's task to be meticulous about repeating step by step the method for any task, always soliciting questions from the students, always pausing to ask, "Do you

Sonia, age thirteen, with Skippy

understand?" and being able to recognize a look of puzzlement, then speedily to correct the dilemma. A teacher must be attuned to her students, not only what they say or ask, but what they need. All through my adult life, I have been engaged in some form of teaching. I have always loved it—but along with the joy of teaching I have always felt a heavy responsibility. I still teach, now in the Writer's Program for UCLA Extension.

Back in Los Angeles, I was deliciously happy with the sunshine, the lawns, and easy atmosphere. I returned to my old school and friends. But there were changes. World War Two had begun. The Japanese in our neighborhood all vanished abruptly, including my friend Setsu and her family. I learned that they had been sent to a Japanese internment camp, as all Japanese were considered potential spies. The cruelty of this act dawned on me much later; then, we children were only perplexed. Setsu's house was rented by a Latino family with six children. All of them routinely chased me home from school, throwing rocks and yelling, "Dirty Jew! Dirty Jew!"

I did not stop to fight. I ran. Six-to-one are impossible odds. I have always believed one must know when to fight and when to retreat with dignity. However, I did have a couple of fist fights in the yard, complete with cheering section and "seconds" who ascribed victory to each of us contenders.

The summer I was eight brought another experience which combined dread and joy. I was sent to a summer camp run by Quakers especially for refugee children. I suffered terribly from homesickness, which seized me the moment the bus rolled out of Los Angeles and was made more disturbing by a bout of nausea due to a two-hour truck ride into the mountains.

When we arrived at Quaker Meadow, however, I was enchanted by the landscape, and ever since I have found solace and the greatest pleasure in pine trees, little brooks, forest paths, and meadows. I love a campfire at night, and communal eating and singing in a log lodge. At Quaker Meadow I hovered between the pain of missing my mother and the joys of hiking, swimming in the icy lake, and acting in campfire plays. The counselors were uniformly kind and gentle people, taking us Jewish refugee children into their care with good humor and love. I have always respected the Friends since then. I read a great deal about their religion and might have adopted it, were I not so attuned to Judaism as I am.

After our escape from Germany, which became the subject of my first children's book, *Journey to America*, Mother and we three children waited in Switzerland for nearly a year until we could enter America. In Switzerland we were helped by many good people, non-Jews, who extended themselves through sheer kindness. To them I owe a great debt, not the least of which is my optimistic belief that despite evil in the world, there is goodness in great measure, and that goodness knows no boundaries of religion or race. At a time when both religious and racial hatred were deep and extreme, this was a vital lesson to learn. To this day I do not believe in either racial or religious exclusivity. I do not believe in a God who cares about form of worship or mere words, who accepts people by one label and rejects those of another.

Helene and Max Wolff, 1963

I returned to the Quaker camp for four summers. I learned a great deal there. Later I took among my first paying jobs that of being camp counselor.

At camp, everything one knows becomes useful, so at various camps I have taught pottery, music, crafts, newspaper writing, nature studies. I have also, along with my husband, done less exalted tasks like digging latrines and hauling garbage to the dump.

When Lloyd and I first met he was twenty, I was eighteen, and we had each attended exciting camps that preceding summer. I had been to an interracial leadership camp, Anytown U.S.A., and he had been to Brandeis, featuring total Jewish experience. As we talked we shared those deeply emotional experiences and ideals. We dated almost exclusively from that first night and were married a little over a year later. First, however, our union also had to be blessed by two very special people in his life, Mom and Pop Walton, owners of the camp Lloyd had attended as a child. It became a lifelong friendship for all of us. The Waltons were the first visitors to see our infant son, Daniel. They remain as larger-than-life figures in our memories, Pop for his humor and common sense, Mom, still alive and active, filled with spunk, attested by her eightieth birthday photograph which shows her riding atop an elephant in Egypt. Such are the people I have been fortunate to find as role models.

At the age of nine or ten I met another person who was to have a profound influence on me. Mary Pollack, English by birth and breeding, the wife of an Austrian surgeon, came into our lives as my mother's employer. Mother, who

Graduating from Los Angeles High School, 1952

had studied baby nursing in Europe, was hired first as the housemaid by Dr. and Mrs. Pollack, and soon was elevated to the position of "nurse" to baby Daphne and her older sister Serena. Soon the relationship became a deeper one. When the Pollacks traveled, Daphne, an adorable baby with red-golden curls, stayed at our house in my mother's devoted care. When my mother became ill and had to be hospitalized for a series of surgeries, the Pollacks reciprocated. I was invited to their house for several weeks at a time and often on weekends. For me, their home and way of life was a revelation.

They lived in the lovely Las Feliz district near Griffith Park in a home that was beautiful, immaculate, and spacious. Mary Pollack seemed the essence of serenity and gentle womanhood. Strong, composed, cultivated, and kind, she drew me into her orbit without fanfare, making me part of the daily activities that I found so gratifying. I was allowed to play the piano as long as I liked. (Later, after the doctor died a tragic, early death, and she and the girls moved to England, Mary gave that piano to me.) The doctor played accordion while we sang along. On weekends there were sometimes musicals in the living room, with friends playing various instruments. The Pollacks spoke both French and German, loved art, and owned a good-size library, the shelves lining an entire room. There I was left to browse and read to my heart's content, then to share my love of stories with Mary, who to this day maintains, "There is nothing more important in the world than art."

Now, Mary lives in London, where I visit her whenever I am abroad, and find her always vitally engrossed in books, theater, and art. When my son, Daniel, made her acquaintance, she was absolutely delighted to learn that he is a musician and questioned him at once about his opinion of the new David Bowie album. My son found in Mary, as I did, an attitude of acceptance and quiet grace. Where my family life was often erratic and highly charged with emotion, her home was serene, a haven. My parents had no time for the arts, nor money to pursue them. By the time they had established themselves in the United States, perhaps they had lost interest through the harsh demands of having to earn a living in a strange land. Whatever their reasons, I always felt a sad lack in my home. Books, paintings, classical music, drama were always important to me, but absent from my parents' lifestyle. Fortunately, they respected my need and provided what they could and allowed me to find the rest on my own.

When I expressed an interest in painting, my parents encouraged me to work with a friend of the family, an old-timer who taught me something about color and perspective and had me painting in oils. Alas, he died soon after we began. It was the only art training I had until, as an adult, I took several classes in drawing and painting. But at the age of twelve I had made half-a-dozen oil paintings, and my parents were pleased and impressed when I actually sold one for thirty-five dollars. They were accustomed to my entrepreneurship. At the age of ten I had written and distributed a "neighborhood newspaper," filled mostly with escapades of the various pets in the Wolff household. We had two rabbits that almost daily escaped from their pen and hopped across the boulevard to graze in the produce section at Vons Market. At various times we also had numerous dogs and cats, all brought home by me. The best loved was Skippy, a brown terrier who slept on our beds, ran beside me for hours when I roller-skated on the streets of L.A., and learned various tricks, among them walking a narrow plank which I braced between two wooden benches. My father was delighted with the tricks and took home movies.

He was a showman, my father, with a natural gift for mimicry and the dramatic buildup. He played piano by ear, loudly and with exuberance. He sketched the coats and suits that he manufactured. He was the most artistic one in my family, yet it never occurred to him to devote any time to the fine arts or to write anything down. By the time my first book was published, he had already died. I know he would have been very pleased. He often claimed me as the "smartie" of the family, attributing this to his side, as his mother had had advanced schooling, a rare thing for a girl in those times. Mother, on the other hand, pointed out that one of *her* relatives had been a physician to the Kaiser, a remarkable feat for a humble Jew.

In several important ways, my parents were mismatched. This of course affected us children, not only in our youth, but when as adults we chose husbands and tried to make things right.

My father was brash and outgoing, impulsive and flirtatious, and at times he flew into thunderous rages. He also worked long and hard at his business of designing and manufacturing ladies' coats and suits. He rose at dawn and worked until six—a farmer's day. He toiled. And he was good at his work. He could create a design with a few swift strokes of a pencil, usually on the back of an old envelope, figure cost, profit, and sales potential in a matter of minutes, all without any formal higher education. Later, this was a source of some surprise to my young husband, with his numerous college degrees in business. My father had been apprenticed to a tailoring establishment at the age of fourteen. He told me often how desperately lonely he was in that town far away from home. My father's coats were stylish, warm (100 percent wool), moderately priced, and made to last. He was proud of his product and I, looking back, share that pride. At the time, however, there was nothing remarkable about his production line of garments filling our closets, hanging from door knobs and makeshift rods all over our small rented house in L.A. The detached garage was completely devoted to business. From there Father did all the wrapping and shipping. Boxes of buttons, labels, pins, bundles of swatches, piles of fur collars, and all the paraphernalia of the garment trade filled my growing-up years. We all learned to sew. Father bought me a huge old-fashioned factory machine. On it I constructed numerous outfits, often without using a pattern. Nobody thought it the least bit unusual to make a dress from "scratch." My family took it for granted that one must be inventive and capable.

We were all paid by the piece for sewing satin linings into fur collars, and for hemstitching lapels or sewing the

Sonia with Lloyd Levitin in San Francisco, 1952, the year they met

labels "Max Wolff-100% wool" onto sleeves. Mother was already sewing when I got up in the morning. She would ask me to thread as many needles as I could before I left for school. She was fifty then, the same age I am now. Now I can appreciate her gratitude for ten threaded needles. She sewed efficiently and well, the way she did any manner of work.

Unlike Father, my mother was reticent and often too critical with people, puritanical in her outlook, and given to melancholy. She suffered terribly from guilt. Her mother was killed in a concentration camp. She had been unable to save her. Eva says Mother's depressions began then and changed her personality. I wouldn't know. I never knew her before the war took its toll in anxiety, suspicion, and fear. I do know that as a child she felt deprived and unloved, overshadowed by her brother and older sister. The brother was beaten to death by the Nazis in Belgium. His wife was shot in a forest as she tried to leap from a train packed with Jews being deported to a concentration camp. The grief and horror of those events cannot be fully described. From my earliest childhood I heard them being discussed by the grown-ups.

My mother, poor by American standards, still managed to send boxes of food and hand-knitted scarves to hapless friends and relatives left in Germany. When their letters of gratitude arrived many months later, tears streamed down my mother's face. She wept a great deal in those years.

My father, on the other hand, took a stern and uncompromising attitude toward the Nazi regime. In his opinion, the entire German nation ought to have been pulverized.

The Holocaust experience left its deep mark on me. It is agonizing for me as a Jew to realize that our people were almost exterminated; it is equally agonizing, as a human being, to have to admit to the evil that humans can do to one another. I have returned to Germany several times as a tourist, always with trepidation and anxiety, and with some hostility. I cannot feel warm toward that nation; I cannot forget. I do not forgive. I believe strongly that some things are unforgivable, that we have to stand up and say "No! Never again."

When recently I visited Israel, and saw the memorial Yad Vashem, that overwhelming feeling struck through me: No. Never again. The truth is, that the Holocaust did not hurt only its obvious victims; it left a stain on all humanity, and all of us must join against the forces of evil, not only in the external world, but especially within ourselves. I believe that one of the greatest evils is not the active desire to do wrong, but apathy. Several books of mine have stressed this idea, especially my adult novel, *What They Did to Miss Lily,* and most recently, a young-adult novel still in the works, *Incident at Loring Groves.*

As to the effect of the Holocaust on my father, he vowed to enjoy life if ever he got back on his feet again, and he did. Enjoy! More than anything else, this was the legacy he left us. Life is short, he always said, shortening his own life with rich foods, cigarettes, and a frantic pace. He loved to dance, travel, fly, go to parties. He never drank, only coffee by the gallon, and a small glass of Passover wine. In the temple, which we attended infrequently, he sang loudly, more from a sense of showmanship, I suspect, than from religious fervor. I believe he believed in God and was perplexed by His inaction at the cries of the beleaguered Jews; but my father was also a pragmatist. It was man, not God, who stoked those ovens.

My mother spoke about God matter-of-factly. She taught us our prayers. Neither of my parents dwelt on philosophical matters, though both greatly admired teachers, philosophers, rabbis, and intellectuals.

Was it a happy childhood? Yes and no. My parents were strict and my life was often insecure, but I knew that they loved me, and their pride in me helped me to aim high.

Most of my aims centered around the arts and school activities. I took piano lessons until I was eighteen, and learned to play well enough to entertain my family, but could never get over the terrible nervousness that made recitals an agony. I wrote poems and short stories, tried various arts and crafts, working with clay, crushed glass, and fabrics. For sport, I roller-skated, walked, and played tennis, activities that I still enjoy, except that I have added jogging to the list.

The desire for physical fitness came to me relatively late. When I turned forty, I came to understand that life is limited, but that one does have choices about its quality. So I gave up smoking, the most difficult feat of self-discipline, and I took up yoga and running. Like many Californians, I am extremely body-conscious now, eating mostly vegetables and fruits, and taking exercise seriously.

As a child I was never good at team sports, but was often chosen as captain. My skills were people skills, I guess. I always craved leadership and participated in student government. I had a great interest in social concerns, and occasionally tried to put my ideas into action, as when I attempted to integrate my social club in high school. I failed. I discovered through many similar ventures since then that if you want something done, it's best to act without too much reliance on others.

As a young woman I joined many causes and volunteer organizations. The experience usually left me frustrated. I like to get things done quickly and efficiently; I have no tolerance for lengthy discussions on trivial matters. When at last I began to sell my writings, I considered it more important to make my contribution in that way, and by taking a portion of my earnings and sending money to the causes I espoused.

Shari, almost two; Daniel, age six

While I tend to become impatient with organizations, because they often become unwieldy and stray from their purpose, still I have initiated several groups. In 1965 my husband and I founded the Moraga Historical Society. The group remains active; it won us many good friends, organizational experience, and fine memories. Some years later I founded and headed a nonprofit adult education organization in Palos Verdes, called STEP.

Most of my life is divided between family and friends or my work, writing. Being a writer, to me, is a continuous and full-time process. It means living fully, then trying to transcribe feelings into words. It is always very, very difficult. Every morning I must sternly put aside lazy or hedonistic inclinations and go down to my study and *sit there* for five to seven hours, and struggle to fill those pages with something that might be worth saving. Like every writer, I often fail, and my wastebasket is the only recipient of a day's labor. Or, worse, I send out a story in the mistaken belief that it is good, only to have it return to me like a homing pigeon. I still write and rewrite, laboring over some chapters as many as ten times. Others slide from mind to hand in a matter of hours; we all know those magical moments when the muse sits on our shoulder, whispering encouragement, and all our risks pay off, all our impulses work out. This has happened to me several times, once in a picture book, *Who Owns the Moon?,* which poured out of my mind in a single afternoon, and another time when I wrote a young-adult novel in only three weeks, *The Year of Sweet Senior Insanity.* Of course, that book had been brewing in my mind for two years before I ever set it down on paper—and much of it was grounded in life.

Young writers are often surprised to learn that "old-timers" still get rejections. They do. And every writer I know still has those bad days, those down-in-the-dumps periods when nothing works, and there is a lot of grumbling and growling and threatening to change careers, to do something else like editing, promotions, studying veterinary medicine, or working at the local bakery—anything but writing!

Then suddenly, sometimes after weeks of depression, a word, a phrase, or a mental image snaps into place, like a new clear vision suddenly emerging, and, presto! It's there again. Then the world is big and beautiful again, anything is possible again, writing is a joy, "success" for its own sake no longer matters; only the process, the feeling of creating, of being truly alive.

I am most alive when I have work to do, and when it is flowing. When the flow is there, I can work seven, eight, nine hours a day, and rise up in the morning eager and longing for more. The characters live with me then. The images and people that I created seem like another reality coexisting with my own daily life in a very real way. "They" are only waiting for me to get back to my typewriter, to share their lives, to give them flesh and a purpose. It is exhilarating. It is the real reason why I continue to write.

"But it must be so exciting to see your name in print," people say, thinking that is the main reason to write. It is exciting, but the *process* is the real prize and the reason why I will never stop. And the process includes discussions and exchanges with other writers, people whose lives are, like mine, devoted to discovery and to ideas. Most of my dearest friends are writers or artists, except for my husband.

He and I are different in many ways, except those that count the most. We share the same values, and we adore and respect each other.

We met in college, at the University of California at Berkeley, where in a way my "real life" first began. Everything else seems like mere preparation. First of all, I was thrilled to be going away to school, to be living more or less on my own, to be spending all my time with my peers. I loved the idea of living in a boardinghouse, sharing my room, meals, study time, and social life. Group living has always had a certain appeal to me. The *kibbutz* lifestyle in Israel fascinates me; sometimes I think that in such an environment of cooperation and camaraderie I could flourish. Paradoxically, perhaps, I also greatly value my independence. My first taste of it came in college.

When classes began, I was completely dazzled and elated. I felt as if I had been hibernating all my life, and that the world was just now opening up before me. I had always been curious and eager to learn; now I encountered teachers who were just as eager to teach, to engage in endless discussion about everything, abstract or concrete, to speculate, delve, argue, go deeper. I studied psychology, sociology, anthropology, history, philosophy, religion, music, literature, economics, and education. Notably missing from this list were the sciences; I took only those required, stressing the humanities with emphasis on education. I had decided to become a teacher of English and social studies. The only other careers I had considered were journalism and veterinary medicine. I rejected the former because it seemed too insecure a profession. I rejected the latter because of my weakness in science and mathematics, and because I was afraid to commit to such an "unfeminine" line of work. I'm not proud of my reasoning, or of my lack of determination. However, teaching seemed a good choice for me, and one I have not regretted. I still teach, have always done so, and count education among my strongest interests.

That first weekend at Berkeley, even before classes began, my friends and I went to a dance at Hillel House, and there I met Lloyd Levitin. I had smiled at him across the room in a way that must have suggested that I thought him quite the most attractive fellow there. We danced. We talked. After that we began dating just about every day, and by March we were engaged. I was eighteen. He was twenty. His parents urged us to wait before marrying, and we agreed.

That summer, instead of going back to Los Angeles, I remained in northern California, having convinced myself and my parents that I desperately needed to go to summer school. I did go to summer school, and so did Lloyd, during which time we lived with his parents in Marin County. It was a wonderful, beautiful summer. We took the ferry across the bay to Berkeley every morning. Afternoons we spent at his house in Fairfax, enjoying the beautiful garden, waiting for his father, Joe, to come home from his radiology practice in San Francisco. It was an idyllic time. My parents came to Fairfax to visit. They loved the place, as we all did, and my future in-laws and I came to know each other well. There was never any stiffness between us; they loved me and I loved them.

In many ways, Joe became a real father to me, granting me that parental closeness and guidance that my father was never able to give me. He was a brilliant man, well respected by his colleagues as by his family. He understood my need to make my own statement; he encouraged my involvement in the arts. However, he had a quite old-fashioned streak by which he insisted vehemently that I owed all my first efforts to husband and children. With any energy that remained, he said, I could indulge my interest in the arts.

Of course, I did agree with him: children cannot be left to a shabby upbringing by a mother so involved in her own needs that the youngsters are neglected. However, I did not like the emphasis he gave the matter, or the feeling that I had no choice. Through the years of my children's growth, I felt I was always playing the part of the juggler, trying desperately to meet their needs, to be there, to give close attention and concern—and yet to save something special and separate, something of myself, for myself.

It was not made easier by the fact that I behaved like a perfectionist. Years later my doctor pointed out his suspicion that this accounted for my occasional migraines. I wanted to be the perfect wife, the loving daughter, the wonderful mother, the active community leader, good entertainer, and so on and so on; I was no different from most caring and educated women of my generation. We all felt we had to be like some feature-film paragon, a combination Doris Day, Greer Garson, and Katharine Hepburn—cheerful, continually courageous, and wise. The movies gave us a hard act to follow. I still wonder why we were so gullible, so ready to swallow the whole notion, hook, line, and sinker. I know I was, at least during my twenties and thirties.

Before that, during the summer I was eighteen, Lloyd and I went up to Walton's Grizzly Lodge, where we'd been hired as counselors. It was the first of several camp experiences, a subsequent one being two years later, when we worked at a camp for underprivileged children in New York, and learned a great deal about ourselves and about social dilemmas. At Walton's, I became quite ill, was briefly hospitalized, and Lloyd brought me back to his parents' house and took care of me for a week. The experience served to convince his parents that this was "really love" and not just a brief summer romance. We were married that December.

The first summer after our marriage, we took our delayed honeymoon trip, two months in Europe, his parents' gift to us. We left with one suitcase apiece, like two vagabonding kids, with no reservations and only the merest framework of an itinerary, based mainly upon the usual tourist sights, highlighting the art and architecture that Lloyd had studied in his Western Civilization course at Pomona College. That trip was the experience of a lifetime. It whetted my appetite for travel, an appetite which has never been sated.

Returning from Europe, we moved to Philadelphia, where my husband went to graduate school and I completed my education at the University of Pennsylvania. It was difficult being away from California; we resented the cold climate and the formality of the people. And we were living on a shoestring, in dilapidated furnished apartments, counting pennies for gasoline, sharing a single dessert not

Shari and her grandmother Helene at home in Palos Verdes, California, 1978

because of the calories but because we could not afford two pieces of cake.

A little poverty, I believe, never hurts, especially when it is experienced at the start of your life. We learned to be very frugal and to summon our priorities.

Back in California, I took a teaching job and Lloyd worked as a public accountant. I loved my job in Mill Valley, a lovely town in Marin County, with bright, active students and cooperative parents. I taught seventh grade in a self-contained classroom that taxed all my powers; I even had to teach math.

By the end of that year I was pregnant with Daniel and decided instantly to give up full-time teaching. It never occurred to me not to stay home and raise the child myself. Lloyd decided to enroll in law school. He obtained a job as an assistant professor at San Francisco State College, and we embarked on four years of toil—he studying, teaching, attending classes at night, and I taking care of the home front, tutoring and teaching night school to earn some money on the side, and starting my new career, writing.

I began with a clear and conscious decision: it was time to write. All my life I had dreamed of becoming a writer. Now, with time at home and long, empty hours to fill, I would begin.

I plunged in, writing half-a-dozen short stories, submitting them to magazines, and getting them back with printed rejections. Amazed, I reconnoitered; something was obviously wrong. I had no idea what—after all, I'd been reading stories all my life. Why should I have so much trouble writing them?

It was Lloyd who suggested that I go back to school. I received the idea with trepidation and excitement. At San Francisco College, one of the teachers in the writing department was the well-known Walter Van Tilburg Clark (*The Ox-Bow Incident*). Why not study with him? my husband suggested. I was awe-struck at the idea. The next day I submitted several stories to Mr. Clark, as requisites for acceptance into the Directed Writing Program. A week later Mr. Clark telephoned me. Yes, he said, in that strong, deep voice, he would accept me into the program.

I remember weeping with joy.

Why had he accepted me? I asked him later, when we had become friends. Was my writing good? Not so much the writing style, he replied, but the subjects that I had chosen made him want me as a pupil. The subjects were thoughtful and serious, dealing with war, aging, love, sacrifice, freedom.

For the next two years the weekly meetings with Mr. Clark were my salvation. At a time when my husband was overwhelmed with his own commitments, and my only company was a small child, I was in desperate need of mental stimulation. We lived in Daly City, a stultifying suburb with its "little boxes" of homes, and while I tried to find outlets in volunteer work, and in visiting with other mothers of small children, what I really needed was

meaningful work of my own, work that would help me to grow, to find approval and worth.

Mr. Clark arranged to meet with his directed writing students whenever they had a new manuscript to present. I made it my business to have a new manuscript ready every week, thus finding reason to request a meeting. Those meetings lasted two, sometimes three hours. During them, I truly lived. We talked about literature; he picked apart my stories, suggesting alternatives, always asking for realism, for motive, for detail, for artistic resolution. The first story I wrote under his tutelage was rewritten ten times. Upon the tenth submission, he wrote on the top in his small tortured hand, "Now you've got it!" No approval, whether in the form of money or words, ever meant more to me than that. That story was published in a literary magazine a few years later, my first fiction piece.

While I studied with Mr. Clark I read books about creative writing, scrutinized stories and novels, and looked for writing jobs, however insignificant or unremunerative. I

Daniel and Lloyd at a Chanukah party, 1978

Lloyd and Sonia Levitin, 1985

began by offering my services as "publicity chairman" for various charitable and educational organizations. In this way I became familiar with newspaper work, writing publicity articles, getting them printed, meeting the editors. By the time we moved from Daly City to our new home in Moraga in the East Bay, I had several published articles to my credit and was working on breaking into the slick magazine field. I produced many articles for *Parents' Magazine, San Francisco Magazine, Together,* and numerous smaller publications, and one long historical piece for *Smithsonian,* among others. In East Bay, I presented myself

to the local newspaper and soon had two different columns with bylines; I was launched as a writer and decided to readapt my adult teaching career from social studies and English to creative writing. Correspondence courses gave me the necessary certification; the community of Moraga, with its host of potential students, gave me the impetus.

I taught creative writing at an old church, summoning sometimes as many as forty students. Those sessions became for all of us, I think, a joy and an education. Many of the group have remained together ever since as friends and associates; several eventually ended up publishing books and others found work in newspaper and magazine writing. It was a gratifying experience, and one that gained me several lifelong friends.

In 1962 our second child, Shari, was born. I had prayed for a daughter to round out the family. I was elated. By then, Lloyd had graduated from law school and was working for Kaiser Industries, and we were in every way the typical young couple with thoughts of upward mobility—except that I had an additional goal, now thoroughly defined and resolutely stated: I wanted to become a fiction writer.

I sold several stories to magazines, but none the big time that I hoped for. One day, on a lark, and with the intention of merely leaving my family memoirs for my children, I began to write about my family's experiences in emigrating from Germany. I told the story from the viewpoint of twelve-year-old Lisa, a fictionalization of my sister Eva.

For several years I worked on the book, between other writing assignments, and eventually showed the half-finished copy to my niece, who was visiting. She loved the book, asked to see the rest. It gave me the encouragement I needed to finish the story.

I submitted it, cold, to an editor, and subsequently to eleven more, meanwhile rewriting, until *Journey to America* took on a tighter shape and moved from third to first person. After five entire rewrites, I sold the book to Atheneum, the publisher that had seen it first. Jean Karl became my editor for this and seven subsequent books for young people. When the book went to press, it was with only one editorial change! Never since have I been so lucky.

With *Journey to America* I felt that my career was launched, and that I had found my niche. I loved writing for young people. I felt that in this genre I could be both gentle and serious, idealistic and pragmatic. I realized that I happen to possess a wonderful memory for the details of my own childhood, for smells and sights and sounds, how faces looked, how feelings felt, and what childhood was really all about.

Journey to America won the Jewish Book Council of America award for best juvenile fiction of 1970. I went to New York to claim my prize and to bask in the glory of seeing a dream come true. It had taken me five years to write the book. Before that, it took seven years to come to grips with the mysteries of putting words on paper. Twelve years! And each night I had gone to bed with visions, mentally conjuring up the image of my little book standing on a library shelf, my words being read, my message being understood. I have heard, since then, that the way to success is just by such envisioning; I don't know. I only know that the reality of that first publication was more pure and more joyous than any since then.

Journey to America was followed by *Rita the Weekend Rat,* the middle-grade tale of a tomboy in love with a rodent, inspired by my daughter, Shari, and my son, Dan. I used all the homey, very ordinary events that can cause hilarity and distress in a family with two lively kids; I enjoyed writing it, and Shari loved reading it.

The next book, *Roanoke: A Novel of the Lost Colony,* was another labor of love and anguish. My fascination with the Lost Colony had begun when I was twelve years old and in sixth grade, challenged and irritated by the fact that this mystery of the disappearance of an entire colony had never been solved.

It was my mother-in-law's practice to take the children to her house once a week when they were babies; it gave her full charge, and it gave me free time. Nearly always I used those free hours to browse in the University library. On one such afternoon, amid the dusty stacks, I came upon a large, darkly bound volume, titled *Raleigh's Roanoke Voyages.* From that moment I was hooked, and spent the next year researching the lives, the times, the possible fates of those colonists. I began by attempting to solve the mystery; I ended by deciding to write the most complete, exciting historical novel about that era that I possibly could.

It took ten years, about half-a-dozen rewrites, and a great deal of pleading on my part to get the book published. When it came out, however, it was nominated for three important state-wide prizes, and it held its own for many years as a book highly recommended in that genre. It is in many ways still my favorite book.

The next three books happened easily; two were picture books, *Who Owns the Moon* and *A Single Speckled Egg,* and one a middle-grade tale, about a boy named Jason, very similar to my Daniel in good sense, sensitivity, and derring-do. *Jason and the Money Tree,* written in six weeks, revised at leisure, was, for its author, a charmer.

Next came *The Mark of Conte,* also inspired by Daniel, older now and a good deal funnier and craftier. Conte is a high-school boy bent on outsmarting the high-school computer; his pranks and his frantic dealings spring from a mother's encouragement of tall tales (I listened each day to Dan's accounts of high-school chaos) combined with a writer's knack for exaggeration. There is no doubt in anybody's mind who Conte represents, and who his mom, a crazy artistic type, is intended to portray. I wrote that book for both of us. It won the Southern California Council of Literature for Children and Young People best fiction award for 1975, and was nominated for the California Young Readers Medal.

After *Conte* came a girls' book, a response to my interest in psychic phenomena. I have read widely on the subject, always with fascination guarded by a heavy dose of skepticism. In the story, a young girl discovers her own latent psychic abilities, and in the process she learns some hidden facts about her own past. I loved researching that book. It took me to the home of a professional medium in the San Fernando Valley, to dealings with a "past life reader," to lengthy discussions with a friend heavily involved in extrasensory perception and other psychic matters.

Many ideas opened up to me and many opportunities simply presented themselves in the progress of this book. I have always found this to be true; one receives that which one is ready to know. Everything we need is out there in the world; we have only to tap it, to zero in, to concentrate, and utilize it. In no other book was this more apparent than in my work on *Beyond Another Door.*

On a brief vacation trip to the old Western town of Virginia City, I happened to spot a decrepit old covered wagon standing beside a road. I poked around. I felt the boards. I climbed up onto the seat. I was hooked.

I had always been fascinated by the saga of the California Trail; I had always marveled at the courage, foresight, and stamina of those who endured the westward migration. Somewhere in my reading I had come upon the name of Nancy Kelsey, one of the thousands of unsung heroines of the Trail, the first white woman ever to cross the plains into California, a young mother of seventeen who walked nearly all the way from Missouri to California.

The more I read about Nancy, the more I studied the diaries of that expedition, known as the Bidwell Bartleson Expedition of 1848, the more I was convinced that this was my story. Never mind that even cursory research into the card catalogue in the library showed a surfeit of pioneering books for young people. I was determined to write my story. And I did.

One of my severest critics, husband Lloyd, loved this book, *The No-Return Trail,* better than any other. He has amended his opinion only recently, with the publication of *Smile Like a Plastic Daisy.* For me, Nancy Kelsey came alive. I researched everything, from recipes for corn pone and johnnycakes, to how to build a log cabin, how babies were swaddled, fevers controlled, horses tended, and marriages performed out on the trail. *The No-Return Trail* won the Western Writers of America award for the best juvenile western of 1978, and the Lewis Carroll Shelf Award.

While I was away in Boulder, Colorado, to meet with my fellow writers and to accept my prize, my husband was promoting appointments for my subsequent project, an adult book that I had been wanting to write for years. Several newspaper items convinced me that the time was right, and that this was my book to write—the story of a teacher who is raped in her classroom, and whose lover is the cop charged with finding the rapist.

I knew nothing about rape or law enforcement or the psychology of the victim. It was frightening to imagine such trauma, to have to feel it along with my character. But I decided to plunge in and do research, this time with school officials, security guards, police, rape crisis center counselors, a district attorney, and gang kids.

That book, *What They Did to Miss Lily,* was published in 1981 under my maiden name, Sonia Wolff. In financial terms it was a dismal failure. I was heartsick when my potential "best-seller" garnered a few good reviews and promptly died. I was catapulted into the agonizing awareness that the adult market is a very different medium from the children's market, with its sanctuary in repeated sales to libraries, schools, and young readers eager for more of "their" discovered author. Perhaps it had been a mistake to use my maiden name. Perhaps none of that mattered; I was devastated, then briefly revitalized as several film prospects opened up, only to lead ultimately to disappointment. Now, I see that the book had its special value: it moved me into a new challenge, writing adult novels, and it gained me many friends who not only liked the book but considered it important and valuable as the story of a woman who is raped and who must discover how to overcome her trauma and to love again. Writing the book also got me personally involved in the problems of sexual assault, and prompted me to initiate a program for high-school students about rape awareness. With several new friends in the law enforcement field, I now do an annual program at the local high

"Posing on my sixtieth birthday," 1994

school, and I have encouraged various other districts to do likewise.

Between *The No-Return Trail* and *What They Did to Miss Lily,* I did three other projects. One was the lighthearted and loving account of our pets, two dogs and two adopted abandoned kittens, which I called *Reigning Cats and Dogs.* It is my only nonfiction book, a series of vignettes that makes gentle fun of us all, and which has brought a very important facet of my life into perspective, for I have always lived with animals and always loved them, believing that they enrich us and are true gifts from God. The kittens came into my life at a time when I was first feeling the "empty nest," Dan just having gone off to college. With two tiny kittens to nurture, I grew into my new phase, ready to meet the truly empty nest of a few years later, when Shari, too, went away to school.

Two other picture books, *A Sound to Remember,* and *Nobody Stole the Pie,* were published, and then two others, *The Fisherman and the Bird* and *All the Cats in the World.* Of course, it's not as easy as it sounds to write a picture book, which must have strict economy, poetry, and a good story. Mine are in the nature of folk tales, with a moral and twist; they are my present answer to my aborted career as a short-story writer.

My latest book due for publication is another young-adult novel, *A Season for Unicorns,* with a heroine who rides in a hot-air balloon in an effort to overcome her fears and take control of her life.

After my recent travels to Israel, I feel myself entering a new phase. For many years, I have wanted to write a novel about the Babylonian Captivity of ancient time, and I began this project two years ago. In the midst of it an event of such heroic proportions occurred that I dropped everything else to pursue it. It is the true story of the rescue of 10,000 Ethiopian Jews in a fabulous, secret airlift called Operation Moses, in late 1984 and 1985. I returned to Israel to see and interview many of those black Jews, a devout and courageous people. They inspired me to write *The Return,* a YA novel due out in spring 1987.

As things stand now, I have enough writing plans to keep busy for the next four to five years; meanwhile new ideas pop up continually. I tend to write quickly, and must moderate my own enthusiasm, write, rewrite, think, rethink, keeping in mind that my goal is quality.

In writing one's autobiography, pinpointing the highlights and major decisions of a life, it may appear that the road was smooth and purposeful, that all decisions led irrevoca-

bly to a well-defined goal. I am always bemused when reading other people's autobiographies or biographies at how organized and cohesive those lives seem, compared to the rather helter-skelter, fragmented times that I have experienced. Naturally, with the help of some distance, some introspection, things do seem to fall into orderly place. The emphasis on my life as a *writer* is a consequence of the fact that it is in this category that this autobiography has been solicited. However, I have worn many different hats and still do, and whether my life as a writer holds any special significance, only time will tell. I am also very much the teacher, the mentor, the wife, the mother.

From the moment my first baby was born, I took parenthood very seriously, and I still do. Children are our greatest responsibility, our wings to immortality. No relationship is quite so complex or so challenging.

When the children were little, I enjoyed playing with them. We went on outings to the park and the zoo and to every nearby attraction. We sang and played games and made projects. Shari was always interested in sports and got us involved in soccer league, softball, and horses. Dan was the tinkerer, the photographer, the fixer of anything

Sonia on a school visit in costume as "Mama" from the Amanda series, 1999

broken. We were always planning things, making things, going places, it seems. We did Brownies and Boy Scouts, and got involved in all these activities, some entirely new to us, that the children discovered. On weekends, grandparents usually came to visit. We had some lovely garden parties, always a big birthday party, and family celebrations for Passover, Thanksgiving, and Chanukah.

In 1973 we moved from northern California to Los Angeles, which entailed a considerable adjustment for all of us. It was very hard to say goodbye to old friends and to a lovely, close-knit small town. In Moraga we had been very active in civic affairs; we had many friends and associates. Leaving meant sacrifice, which in turn led to new discoveries, friends, and opportunities. Once again I learned that there is no growth without pain.

Both the children went away to college, and both live away from home now. Dan is a musician; he composes, mixes, arranges, and plays. Nothing is more gratifying than hearing a tape that he has produced, knowing that this work comprises all his various talents and labors.

Shari now sells real estate, and we believe that sales is her innate talent. She relates wonderfully to people of all types, all ages. She is a terrific "idea" person, a born entrepreneur.

I take tremendous delight in my children's creativity, their kind and gentle manner toward others, their high degree of self-respect.

Our greatest pleasure, as parents, is the relatively recent discovery that our children are among the most interesting and exciting "friends" to spend time with. We try to vacation together at least once a year, away from home. I look forward to having the family grow; in my youth I always debated whether we ought to have only two children, or four, five, or six. I am very, very fond of children and count myself lucky to have several youngsters as personal friends. However, raising them has often filled me with anxiety and real terror; motherhood is among the hardest jobs on earth.

Marriage, too, in all its facets, is a relationship that makes great demands on both partners, and again, both Lloyd and I believe that a marriage must constantly be nurtured, and that the partnership it implies must continually be redefined and enriched.

We have been to several Marriage Encounter weekends, which we consider peak experiences and a great boon to our union. Many friends and acquaintances express astonishment that our marriage, begun so early, has lasted so long—thirty-two years. Our answer is that we both give it top priority; we never take it for granted. It has taken a lifetime together to learn to listen and to accept, to grow separately and yet not apart. Nor are we finished learning, I hope. Someday I would like to write a book about our marriage.

For me, the marriage is like a place, a shelter from which we can reach out to the world, take risks, make mistakes, and return with a feeling of confidence that love remains constant, independent of success or failure. Within the marriage relationship, we can be honest about our mistakes, our faults, our unmet goals, and still find love and acceptance.

All this is when the marriage is good, when the family relationship flows. A marriage and a family, like anything else, have their highs and lows. We've had our share of sorrows, strife, and of monotony. These we seem to have weathered. Nobody can expect to live on a constant high. I think work helps to moderate and organize one's daily life. I do not remember a time that our work lapsed, except temporarily, because of an emotional upheaval or a crisis.

Now, with only the two of us in a fairly large house, shared by two dogs, one cat, and various occasional strays (and guests!), we work every day that we are home, weekends included, saving time for long walks and talks in between, casual dinners with friends, and occasional weekends with one of the children. We travel frequently, both for business and pleasure, and a good part of our social life involves business connections, his or mine. We each have our role to play for the other—I as the "corporate wife," he as the "writer's husband." As I accompany Lloyd to many corporate functions, so, too, he appears with me at various author's events, banquets, and speeches.

Many writers hate public speaking. I suppose I am an anomaly. I love it. I have talked to many, many groups about writing and about particular areas of expertise involved in my various books. Best of all I like doing radio. Television is exciting, but I find that the camera is very critical and very perceptive. I do not like to see myself on camera; I enjoy hearing my voice on radio. One of my dreams is to do a weekly radio show about the creative person; I have thought of it for years. Typically, ideas like these will ruminate in my mind to emerge one day as if newly and completely hatched. Suddenly the time seems right. Then I plunge in all at once and with total involvement.

What I want to do with the rest of my life is to continue along this path: to write a truly wonderful book, to give and receive love, and to slowly and delectably unravel the meaning of it all.

Postscript

Sonia Levitin contributed the following update to *SATA* in 2002:

Some big and exciting changes have come into my life since the last publication of this autobiography. My husband has retired from corporate life and gone back to university teaching, a full schedule, but it allows more time for leisure, too. I am still teaching my one class a semester at UCLA Extension and writing more than ever. Two years ago our son was married to a wonderful woman, so our family is growing, and we are delighted.

Another change is that we have returned to Orthodox Judaism, observing the Sabbath and all the other festival days, studying Torah and the writings of the sages. This has brought a whole new dimension into our lives, and it continues to bring us great fulfillment. This new commitment began with my first trip to Israel in 1985. Since then I have made seven trips to Israel, some with my son and daughter.

Naturally, my writing had been affected by these new experiences. *The Singing Mountain* is about a teenage boy who, during a trip to Israel, becomes so involved in his Jewish heritage that he decides to stay there and learn about his religious roots. It creates a crisis in the family back in California; his parents fear he has been kidnapped by a cult or brainwashed. The story parallels my own journey to

The author speaking at an anti-slavery rally in Washington, D.C., with Barbara Vogel and her class, 2000

traditional Judaism, exploring many issues that people face whenever they search for the spiritual component in their lives. The book won the Sydney Taylor Honor Book Award and was very well received.

My explorations into Judaism also led to another book, *Escape from Egypt.* I awakened suddenly from a deep sleep one night with this startling thought; "The greatest story of all has not been told for Young Adults!" I felt compelled to tell the story of the biblical Exodus, not through the eyes of the prophets, but as it might have happened to ordinary people caught in this cataclysmic moment. By writing about these events, I could really immerse myself in them and re-live them. My husband and I went to the Sinai Peninsula and Israel. There we wandered, rode camels, saw the Mount of Moses, stood before the shrub that is said to be "the burning bush," and in general steeped ourselves in the past. It was a glorious trip. The book, told from two view points, one a Hebrew slave called Jesse, the other an Egyptian girl, Jennat, is also a love story. Both flee from Egypt, both experience the dramatic epiphany in the wilderness, both must deal with prejudice and the longing for a spiritual home.

Another book of strong Jewish interest is *The Cure,* which I wrote in 1999, based on a real incident in Strasbourg, Germany, during the time of the Black Death. *The Cure* combines much of what I have tackled before, a historical episode that involves prejudice and terror—but it also tells of a special group of people who were so rich in their faith that they went, singing and dancing, to their death rather than deny God. This was also a new venture for me, in that the beginning and ending chapters of the

book are science fiction. I love science fiction, but never found the right story to make the attempt. Now, because I wanted to express hope and the possibility of change, I decided to create these "book ends" of the future, inventing a society where all violence has been eliminated, but at a terrible cost in love and human relationships.

I consider *The Cure* one of my most important books. It says what I needed to say about matters so vital to me, that we must truly learn to cherish our diversity, to understand each other—or we will be doomed, either to extinction, or to a life that is loveless and without beauty. Research for *The Cure* took us to Strasbourg, where I walked from morning to night, visited every museum to acquaint myself with life in the Middle Ages. I love doing research, and I explore every aspect, including the food, music, clothing, religious practices, literature—everything.

In between these books, I wrote three mysteries, and I discovered that I enjoy the change of pace from history to mystery; from the past to contemporary times. *Incident at Loring Groves* won the Edgar Award for young adult fiction, and *Yesterday's Child* was a finalist for that same award. *Evil Encounter,* a murder mystery, is also a story of mother-daughter relationship. It delves into the workings of encounter groups and self-styled gurus, who want to run your life. I enjoyed writing all these stories, the plotting and the research, which took me to police headquarters on many occasions, to work with detectives and explore actual crimes.

Another change of pace from the more serious literature lies in picture books. People often ask me how I shape these different genres, whether I "dumb down" a book for young children, how I know my audience. It is difficult to describe this process, because I never consciously "write down" to anyone. What I do is keep the story in mind, creating characters that fit the action and the interests of the intended reader. I think young children enjoy the droll and the ridiculous. They have tender feelings toward animals, nature, anyone who needs help. They are willing to imagine and dream and see the world through new, hopeful eyes. These are the things I like to write about in picture book format.

I've done two in a series of books about animals that are taught (by their child) how to behave in various social situations. The pictures, by Jeff Seaver, are hilarious, and both books, *When You Take an Elephant to a Party* and *When Kangaroo Goes to School,* are finding eager readers among young children. We are planning two follow these with several more.

For the "Amanda" series, I was lucky to team up with Cat Bowman Smith, who did wonderfully creative cartoon-like pictures. Amanda is a spunky girl who, with her mama, three brothers and baby sister goes from Missouri to California in a stage coach, in response to Papa's plea, "Come to California, my dears. I am lonely without you." It is a lively adventure, based on reality, exaggerated for fun. Following this book are two others, *Boom Town,* where Amanda's persistence and ingenuity lead her into the pie business and help the town to develop. *Taking Charge* deals with the same town and characters, with one addition, baby Nathan, who is the vehicle for teaching Amanda that "sometimes we need to ask for help."

A more sophisticated western is my latest novel, *Clem's Chances,* told through the eyes of a fourteen-year-old boy whose father seems to have vanished. Left utterly alone when his mother and baby sister die, Clem ventures across the plains in search of his father, who went off to seek gold in California. He joins a company of bull whackers, spends time as a stock tender in forlorn Nebraska, and eventually becomes part of a Mormon train headed for Salt Lake City. As Clem moves from Missouri to California—penniless and friendless—he makes many friendships and learns to judge people and situations for himself. Clem is involved in some exciting escapades, from a river crossing in which he nearly drowns, to a buffalo hunt and a midnight ride for the Pony Express on a wild horse. Resourceful and good natured, Clem survives not only the physical hardships of the journey, but more important, he endures the shock of his father's abandonment and vows to be a person who keeps his commitments. Clem is really a terrific hero, the kind of person I'd like to be.

Aside from writing, I am active with the Simon Wiesenthal Center/Museum of Tolerance in Los Angeles. Its mission to promote tolerance and diversity are in tune with my own goals. To this end my family sponsors the Once Upon a World Book Award, and the Write to Tolerance program. I assist with these and other activities.

A symposium at the Museum of Tolerance led to another book, *Dream Freedom,* and to my participation in many activities to abolish slavery in Sudan. I was horrified to discover that as part of Sudan's long civil war the Northern-led government has encouraged murder, displacement, and the capture and enslavement of women and children of the Dinka and Nuba tribes. Following the symposium, I immediately began a most fascinating research into these cultures. I was able to interview two distinguished Dinka chiefs, who are now scholars in the United States. I read widely about the culture and formulated a story that involves young people from completely different worlds, but united in their quest for freedom. Writing this book led me to friendships with some very inspiring and dedicated people who are working to abolish slavery. I learned of a group of fourth and fifth grade children in Colorado who, with their teacher, started an abolitionist group called STOP. Teacher Barbara Vogel and I have become good friends; her story is part of *Dream Freedom,* and together we continue to try to promote awareness and enlist the help of others.

My activities include visiting schools and organizations to speak about my work. Sometimes I bring slides, as in my presentations about Sudan and Ethiopia. I've also had many opportunities to participate in panel discussions about writing and the various issues presented in my novels. In the past several years I've used the new technique of video conferencing to exchange ideas with large groups of readers.

My very latest book, *Room in the Heart,* took me to Denmark, to see the country and speak to the people who behaved so courageously during World War II. Although the country was occupied by Nazi forces, the Danes refused to cooperate with the Germans and, when their Jewish neighbors were threatened with deportation, rescued nearly all of them. Danish people hid Jews in their homes, in hospitals and summer houses and arranged for them to be transported, in secret and at night, to Sweden, where over 7,000 people were saved. This story is unique in the annals of war; it demonstrates how, when people focus on doing what is right, evil cannot win.

Sometimes my students ask me why I never seem to experience writer's block. And I answer, there is just too much to do, to think about, to learn. There is drama all around us. I continue to work on several projects at once, and I never know when a newspaper article or a personal experience will suddenly create that special feeling—a tingle along my spine, a sense of amazement and gratitude that here another story has fallen into my lap, and I *have* to tell it.

LIES, Brian 1963-

Personal

Name pronounced "Lees"; born 1963, in Princeton, NJ; children: a daughter. *Education:* Brown University, B.A., 1985; studied drawing and painting at School of the Museum of Fine Arts (Boston, MA). *Hobbies and other interests:* Building things, bicycling, gardening, reading.

Addresses

Home—108 King Phillips Path, Duxbury, MA 02332-3504. *E-mail*—blies@earthlink.net.

Career

Editorial illustrator, 1987—. Illustrator of children's books, 1989—. *Member:* Society of Children's Book Writers and Illustrators (SCBWI), Graphic Artist's Guild.

Awards, Honors

Society of Publication Designers Merit Award, 1987, 1988. Society of Children's Book Writers and Illustrators Magazine Merit Award for Illustration, 1998.

Writings

(Self-illustrated) *Hamlet and the Enormous Chinese Dragon Kite,* Houghton Mifflin (Boston, MA), 1994.

(Self-illustrated) *Hamlet and the Magnificent Sandcastle,* Moon Mountain Publisher (North Kingstown, RI), 2001.

ILLUSTRATOR

Eth Clifford, *Flatfoot Fox and the Case of the Missing Eye,* Houghton Mifflin (Boston, MA), 1990.

Dianne Snyder, *George and the Dragon Word,* Houghton Mifflin (Boston, MA), 1991.

Eth Clifford, *Flatfoot Fox and the Case of the Nosy Otter,* Houghton Mifflin (Boston, MA), 1992.

Eth Clifford, *Flatfoot Fox and the Case of the Missing Eye,* Houghton Mifflin (Boston, MA), 1992.

Eth Clifford, *Flatfoot Fox and the Case of the Missing Whoooo,* Houghton Mifflin (Boston, MA), 1993.

Betty Bonham Lies, *The Poet's Pen,* Teacher Ideas Press, 1993.

Eth Clifford, *Flatfoot Fox and the Case of the Bashful Beaver,* Houghton Mifflin (Boston, MA), 1995.

Eth Clifford, *Flatfoot Fox and the Case of the Missing Schoolhouse,* Houghton Mifflin (Boston, MA), 1997.

Eth Clifford, *Flatfoot Fox and the Case of the Missing Eye,* Houghton Mifflin (Boston, MA), 1997.

Bruce Glassman, *The Midnight Fridge,* Blackbirch Press (Woodbridge, CT), 1998.

Kay Winters, *Where Are the Bears?* Bantam Doubleday Dell (New York, NY), 1998.

Charles Ghigna, *See the Yak Yak,* Random House (New York, NY), 2000.

Elaine Landau, *Popcorn,* Charlesbridge (Watertown, MA), 2003.

Irene Livingston, *Finklehopper Frog,* Tricycle Press (Berkeley, CA), 2003.

Contributor of illustrations to children's magazines, including *Cricket, Spider, Ladybug,* and *Babybug,* and to adult publications, including *Boston Globe, Chicago Tribune, Hartford Courant, Christian Science Monitor, Harvard Magazine, Princeton Alumni Weekly, Brown Alumni Monthly, PC Week, Boston Business, Lotus Magazine, New England Business, Technology Review, Washingtonian Magazine,* and *Mutual Funds Magazine.*

Sidelights

Beginning in 1989, political illustrator Brian Lies branched out into illustrating children's books, including Eth Clifford's popular series of early readers featuring the detective Flatfoot Fox. Lies also wrote and illustrated with watercolors his own picture books about a pig named Hamlet, *Hamlet and the Enormous Chinese Dragon Kite* and *Hamlet and the Magnificent Sandcastle,* which were published to good reviews.

Born in Princeton, New Jersey, then a very quiet and rural place, Lies spent many childhood hours with a best friend, making forts and building dams in the nearby woods. He also liked to read, invent things, and write and illustrate stories with his older sister. He explained on his Web site, "My favorite book when I was very young was Richard Scarry's *Best Word Book Ever.* When I was a little older I loved Roald Dahl's *Charlie* and the Chocolate Factory, and Jean Craighead George's *My Side of the Mountain.*"

Then a school visit, by author-illustrator Harry Devlin, started Lies to dreaming. "In fifth grade, an author and illustrator visited my school, and I was amazed at the idea that this was actually a *job,*" he recalled on his Web site. "I wished it could be *my* job. But I didn't think I was good enough at either writing or drawing to even try." Even so, Lies kept on drawing, for the fun of it. While in high school he learned to paint with oils and make stained glass windows. Lies took a detour from art during his college years, studying psychology and British and American literature at Brown University. Afterward he moved to Boston, where he learned drawing and painting at the School of the Museum of Fine Arts. "At the Museum School, I started getting paintings in exhibitions and won a few prizes, including the prestigious Dana Pond Painting Award, and then started getting political illustrations published in the *Christian Science Monitor* and the *Boston Globe.*"

As an illustrator, Lies worked for the *Boston Globe* and *Chicago Tribune,* as well as a wide variety of magazines, winning several awards in the process. After two years of periodical work, he ventured into children's book illustrating with Eth Clifford's popular early-reader series about a furry sleuth named Flatfoot Fox. From the beginning, reviewers praised Lies's black-and-white drawings for their humor. Writing about *Flatfoot Fox and the Case of the Missing Eye,* a *Booklist* critic remarked that his "expressive black-line drawings perfectly complement Clifford's dry wit," and in *School Library Journal* a critic stated, "Lies's entertaining ... drawings add to the fun." In her review of *Flatfoot Fox and the Case of the Missing Whoooo, Booklist* reviewer Emily Melton called Lies's illustrations "comical and charming," and Stephanie Zvirin, also of *Booklist,* noted that they "capture the dry comedy," in her review of *Flatfoot Fox and the Case of the Bashful Beaver.* Writing for *School Library Journal* about *Flatfoot Fox and the Case of the Missing Schoolhouse,* Lauren Peterson concluded, "Clifford and Lies get everything just right."

In 1994, Lies published his first self-written picture book, *Hamlet and the Enormous Chinese Dragon Kite,* in which he introduced readers to the pig Hamlet and his best friend Quince, a porcupine. When Hamlet becomes enamored of kites and buys a large Chinese dragon kite, cautious Quince senses trouble. Indeed, the kite lifts Hamlet from the ground and he has to be rescued by an eagle. For this solo debut, Lies used watercolor illustrations, which several reviewers likened to the works of Bill Peet and Berkeley Breathed. A *Publishers Weekly* reviewer praised Lies for his "meticulously detailed images and ability to sustain narrative tension." According to *Booklist* reviewer Deborah Abbott, the "bright color drawings ... carry the sprightly story." Six years later, Lies returned to Hamlet and Quince with *Hamlet and the Magnificent Sandcastle.* This time, while vacationing at the beach, the ever-enthusiastic Hamlet makes a sand castle of grand proportions, under the not-so-watchful eyes of slumbering Quince. When a sudden storm brews, Hamlet and Quince are stranded at the castle, to be rescued by the smart use of a beach umbrella. The work elicited qualified praise. Judith Constantinides, writing in *School Library Journal*, predicted that the *Hamlet and the Magnificent Sandcastle* "will appeal immensely to most youngsters."

When asked how long it takes to write a book, Lies replied on his Web site: "It depends on the book. I've written a manuscript (and re-written it many times!) in as little as three months, but I've also been working on a story for over ten years and still can't figure out how to tell it!"

Biographical and Critical Sources

PERIODICALS

Booklist, December 15, 1990, review of *Flatfoot Fox and the Case of the Missing Eye;* September 1, 1992, Kay Weisman, review of *Flatfoot Fox and the Case of the Nosy Otter*, p. 52; December 15, 1993, Emily Melton, review of *Flatfoot Fox and the Case of the Missing Whoooo*, pp. 753-754; October 15, 1994, Deborah Abbott, review of *Hamlet and the Enormous Chinese Dragon Kite*, p. 437; March 1, 1995, Stephanie Zvirin, review of *Flatfoot Fox and the Case of the Bashful Beaver*, p. 1242; March 15, 1997, Lauren Peterson, review of *Flatfoot Fox and the Case of the Missing Schoolhouse*, p. 1241; January 1, 2002, Michael Cart, review of *Hamlet and the Magnificent Sandcastle*, p. 866.

Boston Sunday Herald, July 8, 2001, review of *Hamlet and the Magnificent Sandcastle*.

Children's Bookwatch, March, 2001, review of *Hamlet and the Magnificent Sandcastle*.

Family Fun Magazine, June, 1998, review of *The Midnight Fridge*.

Family Life, August, 2001, review of *Hamlet and the Magnificent Sandcastle*.

Kirkus Reviews, August 15, 1994, review of *Hamlet and the Enormous Chinese Dragon Kite*, p. 1133.

Publishers Weekly, October 18, 1991, review of *George and the Dragon Word*, p. 62; June 20, 1994, review of *Hamlet and the Enormous Chinese Dragon Kite*, p. 105; June 4, 2001, review of *Hamlet and the Magnificent Sandcastle*, p. 80.

School Library Journal, March, 1991, review of *Flatfoot Fox and the Case of the Missing Eye;* January, 1992, Dorothy Evans, review of *George and the Dragon Word*, p. 98; September, 1992, Marge Loch-Wouters, review of *Flatfoot Fox and the Case of the Nosy Otter*, p. 201; August, 1993, Sharron McElmeel, review of *Flatfoot Fox and the Case of the Missing Whoooo*, p. 140; August, 1994, Margaret A. Chang, review of *Hamlet and the Enormous Chinese Dragon Kite*, p. 140; April, 1995, Janet M. Bair, review of *Flatfoot Fox and the Case of the Bashful Beaver*, p. 100; August, 1998, Jane Marino, review of *The Midnight Fridge*, p. 139; June, 2001, Judith Constantinides, review of *Hamlet and the Magnificent Sandcastle*, p. 124.

OTHER

Brian Lies Web Site, http://www.brianlies.com/ (February 26, 2002).

* * *

LYNCH, Chris 1962-

Personal

Born July 2, 1962, in Boston, MA; son of Edward (a bus driver) and Dorothy (a receptionist; maiden name, O'Brien) Lynch; married Tina Coviello (a technical support manager), August 5, 1989; children: Sophia, Walker. *Education:* Suffolk University, B.A. (journalism), 1983; Emerson University, M.A. (professional writing and publishing), 1991. *Politics:* "Decidedly no affiliation." *Religion:* "Decidedly no affiliation." *Hobbies and other interests:* Running.

Addresses

Agent—Fran Lebowitz, Writers House, 21 West 26th St., New York, NY 10010.

Career

Writer. Teacher of writing at Emerson University, 1995, and Vermont College, 1997—. Proofreader of financial reports, 1985-89. Conducted a writing workshop at Boston Public Library, summer, 1994. *Member:* Authors Guild, Author's League of America.

Awards, Honors

American Library Association (ALA) Best Books for Young Adults and Quick Picks for Reluctant Young Adult Readers citations, 1993, for *Shadow Boxer*, 1994, for *Iceman* and *Gypsy Davey*, and 1996, for *Slot Machine;* Best Books of the Year list, *School Library Journal*, 1993, for *Shadow Boxer;* Blue Ribbon Award, *Bulletin of the Center for Children's Books*, 1994, for *Iceman* and *Gypsy Davey;* Editors' Choice award, *Booklist*, 1994, for *Gypsy Davey;* finalist, Dorothy Canfield Fisher Award, and Book of the Year award from *Hungry Mind Review*, both for *Slot Machine;* Young Adults' Choices for 1997 citation, International Reading Association, for *Slot Machine*.

Writings

Shadow Boxer, HarperCollins (New York, NY), 1993.
Iceman, HarperCollins (New York, NY), 1994.
Gypsy Davey, HarperCollins (New York, NY), 1994.
Slot Machine, HarperCollins (New York, NY), 1995.
Political Timber, HarperCollins (New York, NY), 1996.
Extreme Elvin, HarperCollins (New York, NY), 1999.
Whitechurch, HarperCollins (New York, NY), 1999.
Gold Dust, HarperCollins (New York, NY), 2000.
Freewill, HarperCollins (New York, NY), 2001.
All the Old Haunts (stories), HarperCollins (New York, NY), 2001.

Chris Lynch

Contributor of short stories to anthologies, including *Ultimate Sports,* edited by Donald Gallo, Delacorte, 1995, and *Night Terrors,* edited by Lois Duncan, Simon & Schuster, 1996. Contributor of stories and articles to periodicals, including *Signal, School Library Journal,* and *Boston Magazine.*

Lynch's books have been translated into Taiwanese and Italian.

"BLUE-EYED SON" SERIES

Mick, HarperCollins (New York, NY), 1996.
Blood Relations, HarperCollins (New York, NY), 1996.
Dog Eat Dog, HarperCollins (New York, NY), 1996.

*"HE-MAN WOMAN-HATERS CLUB" SERIES; FOR YOUNG
    READERS*

Johnny Chesthair, HarperCollins (New York, NY), 1997.
Babes in the Woods, HarperCollins (New York, NY), 1997.
Scratch and the Sniffs, HarperTrophy (New York, NY),
    1997.
Ladies' Choice, HarperTrophy (New York, NY), 1997.
The Wolf Gang, HarperCollins (New York, NY), 1998.

Sidelights

Author Chris Lynch "is less concerned with constructing plot-driven narratives than in creating impressionist portraits of confused and misunderstood teenagers," wrote a *Horn Book* contributor in a review of the author's 2001 story collection, *All the Old Haunts.* Indeed, creating such portraits of confused and misun-

derstood teens is what Lynch's work is all about; these youth populate the pages of his fiction, from his ground-breaking *Shadow Boxer* and *Iceman* to his later novels such as *Freewill* and those in his "Blue-Eyed Son" series.

Lynch writes tough and edgy streetwise fiction. Episodic and fast-paced, his stories and novels question the male stereotypes of macho identity and inarticulate violence. His youthful characters are often athletes, or wanna-be athletes, or kids who have been churned up and spit out by the system. Outsiders, Lynch's protagonists desperately want to just be themselves. Using irony and a searing honesty that cuts through adolescent facades, Lynch lays out a deck of impressionistic cards of what it means to be young and urban and male in America, warts and all.

If Lynch can speak so directly to young readers, it is because he has been there. "Growing up I listened way too much to the rules as they were handed down," he recalled in an interview for *Authors and Artists for Young Adults* (*AAYA*). Though his youth was a much more stable one than those of many of his fictional characters, he was no stranger to the urban melange that is the backdrop for most of his work. Fifth of seven children, he grew up in the Jamaica Plains district of Boston, one that was once an Irish stronghold, but which had become largely Hispanic by the time of Lynch's youth. His father died when Lynch was five, and the family was then brought up by a single mother. "She did a good job of covering it up, but things were pretty lean back then," Lynch remembered. "We were definitely a free cheese family, though I never felt deprived as a kid." A somewhat reclusive child, Lynch attended Catholic schools through primary and secondary levels.

While his grammar school experience was what the author called "nurturing," high school was a different matter for Lynch. "I hated high school—every minute. It was rigid, kind of a factory. An all-boys' football factory. Nothing like the arts was encouraged in any way." Though Lynch had participated in street hockey, football, and baseball as a younger kid, by high school he had stopped playing. "When it was fun I played," Lynch recalled. But the football-factory ethic ruined it for him, a sentiment echoed by protagonists in many of his novels. "I'm not against all athletics," Lynch said in his *AAYA* interview. "Sports has a tremendous potential for channeling energy. But instead it mostly encourages the macho ethos and schools let athletes run wild. This carries through life, and results in Mike Tysons. People who were never told what they could not do."

High school was discouraging enough for Lynch that he dropped out in his junior year and entered Boston University where he studied political science. A news-writing course at Boston University provided a stimulus for change, for discovering what he really wanted to be doing. "I transferred to Suffolk where I took more writing classes, finally majoring in journalism. But I was still hiding from myself."

After graduation, Lynch spent about six years trying to let himself admit that simple fact that he wanted to write. He took jobs as a house painter, a driver of a moving van, and for several years proofread financial reports. Finally, in 1989 Lynch enrolled in a master's program in professional writing and publishing at Boston's Emerson University. At Emerson Lynch found a new direction. Taking a children's writing class from Jack Gantos, he began what became his first published novel, *Shadow Boxer,* as a class assignment. "We were supposed to write five pages on a childhood incident," Lynch recalled. "I had a vague idea of writing about some things my brother and I had done in our youth, but as soon as I sat down with it, I was off to the races. The stuff just poured out." With the help of Gantos, he first tried to place his manuscript with various editors, then found an agent who quickly found a willing publisher.

Shadow Boxer is a story of two brothers learning to deal with life after the death of their father, a journeyman boxer. Fourteen-year-old George is left as the man of the house after his father dies from all the years of battering he has taken in the ring. George's mother is bitter, hating the sport which cost her husband his life, but George's younger brother, Monty, wants to follow in his father's footsteps. He begins to train at the local gym with his uncle, and George sets about to discourage him from this path, exacerbating their sibling rivalry. Told in brief, episodic vignettes with urban slang, the novel reaches its climax when Monty is shown a video of one of the brutal beatings his father took in the ring. In the end, Monty is finally convinced, and George gets the final lines: "We left the gloves there on the ground, where they could rot in the coming rain."

Reviewing *Shadow Boxer* in *Horn Book,* Peter D. Sieruta was particularly struck with the cast of characters Lynch captures "with unflinching honesty" in the working-class Boston neighborhood where George and Monty live. While Sieruta found that, for him, the episodic style weakened the plot, he noted that individual chapters "read like polished short stories and are stunning in their impact." Gary Young in *Booklist* commented that "this is a guy's book. It is also a tidy study of sibling rivalry." Other reviewers also noted how the novel transcended the usual sports story tag. Tom S. Hurlburt, writing in *School Library Journal,* pointed to the passages describing the problems of a single-parent family in an urban setting and concluded that "Lynch has written a gritty, streetwise novel that is much more than a sports story." John R. Lord also commented upon Lynch's episodic style in *Voice of Youth Advocates,* calling the book "a series of character sketches," and noting that it could serve well with "reading for the at-risk students."

Regarding his episodic style, Lynch asserted that it was a "critical leap" for him to start writing that way. "I don't see transitions in my life," Lynch noted. "I can see moments. So it was incredibly liberating for me to realize that I don't have to write 'and then ... and then' in my books any more than I have that in my life." Lynch's short, snappy paragraphs result in books that seem to grow organically. More than one critic has also noted that such writing—brief, hard-hitting vignettes that reveal character—makes it easier for reluctant readers to get into the material.

While *Shadow Boxer* was being prepared for publication, Lynch was already hard at work on his second novel, *Iceman,* the story of a troubled youth for whom violence on the ice is his only release. Lynch's protagonist is fourteen-year-old Eric, a great hockey player with a reputation as a fine shooter and a strong defensive player with a penchant for hitting. Known as the "Iceman" for his antics on the ice, Eric actually seems to enjoy hurting people. His only friends are his older brother Duane, whose act of trading his skates for a guitar impresses Eric, and the local embalmer, McLaughlin, who equally impresses Eric with his devotion to his work.

Lynch divides the novel into three sections, echoing the periods of a hockey game, and the novel follows Eric's conflict-laden life to a certain epiphany. The source of his rage comes from his own dysfunctional family—his mother, a former nun who continually spouts from the Bible, and a father who only comes alive when Eric is doing damage on the ice. Slamming out his frustrations on the hockey rink, he is soon shunned by even his own teammates. McLaughlin, at first, gives him some comfort in his world of death, and Eric for a time thinks he might want to go into mortuary science until he comes upon the embalmer entwined with one of the female corpses. This startling scene helps Eric to face some of his own worst demons and begin to control his anger, to stop working out his father's vicarious rage—to in fact, join the living. Randy Brough, writing in *Voice of Youth Advocates,* noted that he found "this novel of disaffected adolescence to be as satisfying as a hard, clean hip check," and Jack Forman in *School Library Journal,* while commenting that the book would appeal to hockey enthusiasts, also pointed out that "this novel is clearly about much more and is no advertisement for the sport." Forman concluded that *Iceman* "will leave readers smiling and feeling good." Stephanie Zvirin summed up the effect of the novel in *Booklist:* "This totally unpredictable novel ... is an unsettling, complicated portrayal of growing up in a dysfunctional family.... A thought-provoking book guaranteed to compel and touch a teenage audience."

"With my third book," Lynch noted in his *AAYA* interview, "I was trying to show the confusion of life, the cyclical nature of it rather than a linear portrayal. The victim is perpetrator is victim. To show that even crappy people have their sides to them. To depict hope in the midst of it all." That third book was *Gypsy Davey,* the story of a brain-damaged youth and his family who does not care, and of the tenement neighborhood surrounding the boy—cheap bars and drug dealers. Out of this bleak atmosphere, Lynch weaves a tale of hope, of young Davey who tries body and soul to break the cycle of parental neglect initiated by his parents and seemingly perpetuated by his older sister, Jo. Jo's dysfunctional family forms the centerpiece of this novel, and it is Davey's attempts to bring love to Jo's son, his nephew, that is one of the few bright spots. Jo and her child ultimately drive off with a stranger—a new lover? a social worker?—and Davey tells himself, in stream-of-consciousness exposition—that the kid will be okay, that there is hope. "I'm gonna have my own find somebody who's gonna love' me and we're gonna have some babies and I'm gonna love 'em to pieces like nobody ever loved babies before." W. Keith McCoy, writing in *Voice of Youth Advocates,* noted that in spite of the dreary atmosphere of the novel, "Lynch provokes empathy for this family and its situation, and perhaps that is the only positive outcome in the book." Also focusing on the bleakness of the theme, especially as perceived by adults, Elizabeth Bush in *Bulletin of the Center for Children's Books* concluded that "young adults will appreciate its honesty and fast pace.... Lynch ... paints characters who ... ring true every time."

Lynch's fourth book, *Slot Machine,* is something of a departure. On the surface it is a boys-at-summer-camp comedy about an overweight youth who resists attempts at turning him into a jock. Thirteen-year-old Elvin Bishop is attending a Christian Brothers summer camp with a heavy emphasis on sports as preparation for high school—the coaches literally 'slot' young athletes for upcoming sports. Friends with Mike, who seems to fit in anywhere, and Frank, who sells his soul to fit in, Elvin steers a middle course and finally finds a niche for himself with the help of an arts instructor, finally lets himself be himself, finally sees that it is okay to be a non-athlete. But before this happens, he suffers from all forms of physical torture in football, baseball, and wrestling. According to Stephanie Zvirin, writing in *Booklist, Slot Machine* is a "funny, poignant coming-of-age story." While noting Lynch's ability to write broad, physical comedy as well as dark humor, Zvirin concluded that "this wry, thoughtful book speaks with wisdom and heart to the victim and outsider in us all." Maeve Visser Knoth, writing in *Horn Book,* also noted the use of humor and sarcasm in this "biting, sometimes hilarious novel," as well as the serious purpose in back of it all: "Lynch writes a damning commentary on the costs of conformity and the power gained by standing up for oneself."

Lynch reprised this protagonist in 1999's *Extreme Elvin,* where readers find Elvin now in his first year at a Catholic all-boys high school. A contributor for *Publishers Weekly* felt that "the wisecracking, irrepressible" Elvin is "just as funny—and perhaps even more likable" in this new installment. The same writer noted that the "pudgy hero has one scatological misadventure after the next," including gaining a terrible reputation for his eternal hemorrhoids and being tricked into believing he has caught a sexually transmitted disease from holding hands. In the end, Elvin—newly attracted to girls—goes against the grain, having learned a new lesson in this outing. Instead of chasing after the slim girl his buddies tell him to, he opts to date the rather plump one he is truly attracted to. "Witty and knowing, this novel will

have readers hoping Lynch writes another Elvin Bishop story soon," concluded the *Publishers Weekly* reviewer.

Lynch continued in this lighter vein for his fifth novel. While Lynch's inspiration for his books usually comes from his own life or from life around him in Boston, *Political Timber* was inspired by newspaper accounts of a teenager who ran for mayor of his small town. What resulted is a novel about a high school senior, Gordon Foley, who runs for mayor at the insistence of his grandfather, who is an old machine politician serving time for fraud. While young Gordon thinks it is all great fun, his grandfather is actually using him as a political puppet. Less bleak than much of his fiction, *Political Timber* is also unique in that it is specifically written for teens. Reviewing the novel in *Horn Book,* Elizabeth S. Watson called the book "[f]resh, funny, and at times devastatingly frank," and felt that this book "is a great read that offers some discussion fodder as well." A reviewer for *Publishers Review* thought that Lynch's "fast-paced and characteristically wry narrative" provides ample "hilarious jabs at politicking." "The outrageous story line works delightfully as a punchy, timely satire of the political scene," wrote *Booklist*'s Anne O'Malley.

With his "Blue-Eyed Son" trilogy, Lynch returned to the grittier mean streets of Boston to explore latent and sometimes very overt racism. Lynch's microcosm involves fifteen-year-old Mick, who sees his once predominately Irish neighborhood changing into a racially-mixed one as blacks, Latinos, and Asians move in. Mick unwittingly becomes a neighborhood hero when he throws an egg at a Cambodian woman during a St. Patrick's Day Parade. Though Mick hates that his friends and older brother Terry have planned to disrupt the parade by harassing gay and Cambodian marchers, he is forced into throwing the egg, an action caught on television. A hero in the local bar, he becomes an outcast at school. Only Toy, a mysterious sort of character, remains his friend, and soon Mick begins to break off ties with his close-knit Irish family and neighborhood and hangs out with Latinos instead. His drunken, oafish older brother has Mick beaten for such treachery, ending the first book of the trilogy, *Mick.* The story is carried forward in *Blood Relations* where Mick struggles to find himself, forming a brief liaison with beautiful Evelyn, and finally ending up in the bed of Toy's mother. The series is concluded with *Dog Eat Dog* in which the brothers face off for a final showdown and Mick's friend Toy comes out of the closet. "With realistic street language and an in-your-face writing style ... Lynch immerses readers in Mick's world," Kelly Diller, reviewing *Mick,* noted in *School Library Journal.* According to Diller, Lynch has created a "noble anti-hero." Reviewing *Blood Relations* in *School Library Journal,* Kellie Flynn commented that "this story moves quickly, Mick's seriocomic edginess is endearing, and the racism theme is compelling." However, Flynn also noted that the series concept made the ending of the novel something of a let-down, a point Elizabeth Bush returned to in a *Bulletin of the Center for Children's Books* review of the three books: "When the finish finally arrives, the unrelenting brutalities of the earlier volumes will leave the audience virtually unshockable."

A further series from Lynch are the five novels in the "He-Man Woman-Haters Club," books that employ the broad humor of the "Elvin" books to poke fun at the stereotypes of adolescent boys. Lincoln, also known as Johnny Chesthair, decides to start a club in his uncle's garage, including in membership wimpy Jerome, wheelchair-bound Wolfgang, and huge Ling-Ling. Later members include a guitarist named Scratch and Cecil, "gentle and synaptically challenged," according to *Booklist* contributor Randy Meyer in a review of *Scratch and the Sniffs*. Each of the original members takes a turn narrating a book in the five-volume series, each title involving the humorous undoing of the would-be heroes. Reviewing the last novel in the series, *The Wolf Gang*, Shelle Rosenfeld concluded in her review for *Booklist* that "Lynch's presentation of the boys' seesawing view of girls as enemies or attractions is dead-on, as is his portrayal of the ties of friendship that bind—and survive even the toughest tests in the end."

Lynch returned to stand-alone titles with *Whitechurch, Gold Dust,* and the 2001 novel, *Freewill*. A reviewer for *Publishers Weekly* called *Whitechurch* an "unsettling, coolly polished novel" that again demonstrates Lynch's "profound understanding of society's casualties, misfits and losers." Three teens, Pauly, Oakley, and Lilly, must learn to navigate treacherous shoals in their dilapidated New England town in these interconnecting short stories. Seemingly trapped in the dead-end environment of Whitechurch, the trio finds differing ways to break out of this stagnant environment. A reviewer for *Horn Book* felt that the "sharply evoked characters and their complex relationship are the novel's greatest strengths."

Reviewing *Gold Dust,* Michael McCullough announced in *School Library Journal* that the "novel contains some of the best sports writing readers will ever find in a YA novel." Set in Boston during the 1975 school bus controversy, *Gold Dust* features seventh-grader Richard Moncrief, who dreams of transforming the new transfer student from Dominica into a first-rate baseball player; the two will team up to be the adolescent equivalents of the "Gold Dust Twins" from the 1975 Boston Red Sox team, Fred Lynn and Jim Rice. However, Richard does not anticipate the fact that Napoleon Charlie Ellis, the transfer student, proves a difficult friend, forcing the young white boy to deal with racial tensions in the city. Lauren Adams, writing in *Horn Book,* felt that "Lynch's provocative novel tells a piece of the city's history and the more intimate story of a transforming friendship." "This is a wonderful baseball book," declared *Booklist* contributor Debbie Carton, "but it's the awkward, intense friendship that drives the story." A reviewer for *Publishers Weekly* felt that the novel's denouement "is as honest as it is heartbreaking."

Lynch's *Freewill*—partly inspired by the Columbine school shooting and partly by the tragedy of teen suicide—is something of a departure dramatically, written in the form of a mystery and in the second person. Having lost his father and stepmother in a seeming accident, Will is sent to a special school where a sudden rash of suicides forces the reader to wonder if Will is not responsible. One of Will's wood carvings is found at the scene of each of these suicides, making the police suspicious of the boy and also attracting a weird group of hangers-on to Will. Finally, Will's grandfather helps to unravel the mystery of what is really going on. Dubbed an "unsettling narrative" by *Horn Book* reviewer Adams, *Freewill* is a "dark, rich young-adult novel that offers something to think about as well as an intriguing story," according to *Booklist* contributor Susan Dove Lempke.

With his 2001 collection of stories, *All the Old Haunts,* Lynch creates a melange of ten tales describing family ties, man-woman relationships, and friendship, among other themes. A reviewer for *Publishers Weekly* noted that Lynch "once again excels in describing family bonds," and concluded that "there's something here for everyone." Angela J. Reynolds, writing in *School Library Journal,* also praised the "fresh twist" Lynch puts on old themes, concluding, "Teens who enjoy deftly crafted tales with more than a hint of the dark side will appreciate this sophisticated prose." And a contributor for *Kirkus Reviews* also commented about this dark side, stating that "fans of [Lynch's] edgy novels will find [this collection] lit with the same wry, raw view of adolescence."

Lynch himself does not want to "examine the why's [of his fiction] too closely" before he writes, as he noted in an interview for *Teenreads.com,* fearful that he will set "an agenda" for his writing. "I want to tell realistic stories, which I think come with their own messages built into them without my having to preach. Specifically, the issue of substance abuse—like violence, or racism—is a fact of our lives, and the only way I can contribute anything is merely to chronicle the facts of lives as I see them."

Biographical and Critical Sources

BOOKS

Authors and Artists for Young Adults, Gale (Detroit, MI), Volume 19, 1996, Volume 44, 2002.
Children's Literature Review, Volume 58, Gale (Detroit, MI), 2000.
Lynch, Chris, *Shadow Boxer,* HarperCollins (New York, NY), 1993.
Lynch, Chris, *Gypsy Davey,* HarperCollins (New York, NY), 1994.
St. James Guide to Young Adult Writers, 2nd edition, St. James Press (Detroit, MI), 1999.
Seventh Book of Junior Authors and Illustrators, H. W. Wilson (New York, NY), 1996.

PERIODICALS

ALAN Review, winter, 1997.
Booklist, December 15, 1993, Gary Young, review of *Shadow Boxer,* p. 747; February 1, 1994, Stephanie Zvirin, review of *Iceman,* p. 1001; March 15, 1994, p. 1358; October 1, 1994, p. 318; January 15, 1995,

p. 860; September 1, 1995, Stephanie Zvirin, review of *Slot Machine,* p. 74; October 15, 1996, Anne O'Malley, review of *Political Timber,* p. 414l; February 15, 1997, p. 1023; April 15, 1997, Randy Meyer, review of *Scratch and the Sniffs,* pp. 1429-1430; December 15, 1997, p. 697; August, 1998, Shelle Rosenfeld, review of *The Wolf Gang,* pp. 2006-2007; February 1, 1999, p. 969; September 1, 2000, Debbie Carton, review of *Gold Dust,* p. 116; May 15, 2001, Susan Dove Lempke, review of *Freewill,* p. 1745; September 1, 2001, p. 101.

Bulletin of the Center for Children's Books, November, 1994, Elizabeth Bush, review of *Gypsy Davey,* p. 93; October, 1995, p. 1023; April, 1996, Elizabeth Bush, review of *Mick, Blood Relations,* and *Dog Eat Dog,* p. 270.

English Journal, November, 1994, p. 101; November, 1995, p. 96.

Horn Book, May-June, 1994, Patty Campbell, "The Sand in the Oyster," pp. 358-362; November-December, 1995, Maeve Visser Knoth, review of *Slot Machine,* pp. 746-747; November-December, 1995, Peter D. Sieruta, review of *Shadow Boxer,* pp. 745-746; September-October, 1996, pp. 72, 602-603; March-April, 1997, Elizabeth S. Watson, review of *Political Timber,* p. 201; May-June, 1997, pp. 325-326; July-August, 1999, review of *Whitechurch,* p. 469; November-December, 2000, Lauren Adams, review of *Gold Dust,* p. 758; July-August, 2001, Lauren Adams, review of *Freewill,* p. 457; September-October, 2001, review of *All the Old Haunts,* p. 588.

Kirkus Reviews, November 15, 1993, p. 1464; February 1, 1994, p. 146; October 1, 1995, p. 1433; October 15, 2001, review of *All the Old Haunts,* p. 1488.

Publishers Weekly, August 23, 1993, p. 73; September 12, 1994, p. 127; March 11, 1996, p. 66; October 21, 1996, review of *Political Timber,* p. 84; December 9, 1996, p. 68; January 11, 1999, review of *Extremely Elvin,* p. 73; May 10, 1999, review of *Whitechurch,* p. 69; May 15, 2000, p. 119; August 21, 2000, review of *Gold Dust,* p. 74; January 8, 2001, p. 69; January 29, 2001, p. 90; August 30, 2001, p. 82; October 29, 2001, review of *All the Old Haunts,* p. 65.

School Library Journal, April, 1993, p. 150; September, 1993, Tom S. Hurlburt, review of *Shadow Boxer,* p. 252; December, 1993, p. 26; March, 1994, Jack Forman, review of *Iceman,* p. 239; October, 1995, p. 156; March, 1996, Kelly Diller, review of *Mick,* pp. 220-221; March, 1996, Kellie Flynn, review of *Blood Relations,* p. 221; May, 1996, p. 1354; October, 2000, Michael McCullough, review of *Gold Dust,* p. 164; March, 2001, p. 252; November, 2001, Angela J. Reynolds, review of *All the Old Haunts,* p. 160.

Voice of Youth Advocates, December, 1993, John R. Lord, review of *Shadow Boxer,* p. 295; April, 1994, Randy Brough, review of *Iceman,* p. 28; December, 1994, Keith W. McCoy, review of *Gypsy Davey,* p. 277; August, 1996, pp. 157-158.

OTHER

HarperCollins Web Site, http://www.harperchildren.com/ (August 1, 2001), "Chris Lynch."

Teenreads.com, http://www.teenreads.com/ (February 18, 2002), "Author Profile—Chris Lynch."*

—*Sketch by J. Sydney Jones*

M

McCULLOUGH, Sharon Pierce 1943-
(Sharon Pierce)

Personal

Born December 3, 1943, in Granite City, IL; daughter of Herman Edwin and Mildred Maxine (Kramer) Miller; married Ryan O. Pierce, June 26, 1965 (divorced, 1992); married Michael A. McCullough (a photographer and designer), January 15, 1994; children: (all from first marriage) Kristin, Ryan, Randall, Christopher, Kira. *Education:* Mt. Aloysius Junior College, A.A., 1963. *Politics:* Democrat. *Religion:* Roman Catholic. *Hobbies and other interests:* Reading, kayaking, spending time at the beach.

Addresses

Home—P.O. Box 310, Cashtown, PA 17310. *E-mail*—alligatorart@cvn.net.

Career

Writer and illustrator. Virginia Craft Festivals, show organizer, 1986—; Alligator Artworks, Cashtown, PA, owner and designer, 1996—. *Member:* Society of Children's Book Writers and Illustrators, Graphics Artists Guild.

Awards, Honors

Parents' Choice Award, 2001, for *Bunbun, the Middle One.*

Writings

ILLUSTRATOR; FOR CHILDREN

Bunbun at Bedtime, Barefoot Books (Cambridge, MA), 2001.
Bunbun, the Middle One, Barefoot Books (Cambridge MA) 2001.
Bunbun at the Fair, Barefoot Books (Cambridge, MA), 2002.

Sharon Pierce McCullough

FOR ADULTS; AS SHARON PIERCE

Making Folk Toys and Weather Vanes, Sterling (New York, NY), 1984.
Making Whirligigs and Other Wind Toys, Sterling (New York, NY), 1985.
Making Old Time Folk Toys, Sterling, (New York, NY), 1986.

Making Holiday Folk Toys and Figures, Sterling (New York, NY), 1987.

(With Herb Surman) *Making Miniature Country Houses,* Sterling (New York, NY), 1990.

McCullough's images have been licensed to the New York Graphic Society for prints, the What On Earth catalog for clothing, First Impressions for greeting cards, and Regal Design for accent rugs, shower curtains, and bath accessories. Her "Fur & Feathered Friends" images appeared on totebags and note cards to benefit the American Library Association, and the Society of Children's Book Writers and Illustrators used her image "Bedtime Bunny" on its totebags. She has also designed Christmas and Halloween ornaments, as well as a line of plush animals for Commonwealth Toy & Novelty Company, including the "Goodie TwoShoes" doll line.

Sidelights

Sharon Pierce McCullough's brightly colored designs can be seen in a wide range of permutations, from children's books, to plush toys and dolls, totebags, stationery, and even a line of bathroom accessories. During the 1980s, as Sharon Pierce, she published a handful of how-to books that demonstrate procedures for making such items as whirligigs, toys, and weathervanes, all in a folk-art style. "I have been interested in drawing since childhood, and my passion for naive, unusual art led me to folk art," she is quoted as saying on the Barefoot Books Web site. About the same time she started writing fiction for children. "I first started writing children's stories in 1983, once all five of my children were in school. I have always loved children's picture books and I love designing and creating characters, mainly animal characters," McCullough told *SATA.*

Eventually McCullough found her artistic focus in animal stories for the youngest "readers." "Since that particular time, however, I have developed a recognizable art style and this led me to realize that the type of stories I was writing, originally, did not fit my very simple artwork," she recalled to *SATA.* "Since it is essential for artwork and text to mesh, I starting working towards a preschool audience. After submitting my first two dummy books for this age group, I signed my first children's book contract for what is becoming a wonderful little series"—a paper-over board, as well as trade edition hard back, series about Bunbun the rabbit and his siblings, Benny and Bibi. *Bunbun at Bedtime* shows how Bunbun is a nonconformist when it comes to going to bed, while *Bunbun, the Middle One* stresses that being "middle" or "average" is all right. Several reviewers of the "Bunbun" series found McCullough's colored-pencil drawings to be the books' strong point. Reviewing *Bunbun at Bedtime* for *Booklist,* Carolyn Phelan predicted that the illustrations would "appeal to children and adults alike."

When counseling others, the author told *SATA:* "My advice to aspiring writers and illustrators is 'never give up.' If you love what you are doing, the persistence and hard work will eventually pay off, but it does take time.

One of the most valuable resources you can have is the *Children's Writers & Illustrator's Market.*"

Biographical and Critical Sources

PERIODICALS

Booklist, October 1, 2001, Carolyn Phelan, review of *Bunbun at Bedtime,* p. 326.

Publishers Weekly, February 12, 2001, review of *Bunbun, the Middle One,* p. 209.

School Library Journal, April, 2001, Thomas Pitchford, review of *Bunbun, the Middle One,* p. 118; November, 2001, Maryann H. Owen, review of *Bunbun at Bedtime,* p. 129.

OTHER

Barefoot Books Web Site, http://www.barefoot-books.com/ (February 28, 2002), "Sharon Pierce McCullough."

*   *   *

MORROW, Betty
See BACON, Elizabeth

*   *   *

MOWRY, Jess 1960-

Personal

Born March 27, 1960, in Starkville, MS; son of Jessup Willys Mowry (a crane operator); partner of Markita Brown (a social worker); children: Jeremy, Weylen, Shara, Keeja. *Education:* Attended elementary and middle school in Oakland, CA. *Politics:* "Survival."

Addresses

Home—Oakland, CA. *Office*—c/o Ms. Amanda G. Wheeler, Attorney at Law, 4848 Lakeview Ave., Ste. 202-D, Yorba Linda, CA 92886-3454.

Career

Writer, 1988—. Works with inner-city street children at drop-in center. Has also worked as a mechanic, truck driver, tugboat engineer, cartoonist, and scrap metal collector.

Awards, Honors

PEN-Oakland Josephine Miles Award, 1990, for *Rats in the Trees;* Best Books for Young Adults Award, American Library Association (ALA), 1993, for *Way Past Cool;* Pushcart Anthology Prize, 1993; Quick Picks for Reluctant Young Adult Readers, ALA, 1997, for *Ghost Train.*

Writings

Rats in the Trees (story collection), John Daniel & Co. (Santa Barbara, CA), 1990.

Children of the Night, Holloway House (Los Angeles, CA), 1991.

Way Past Cool, Farrar, Straus and Giroux (New York, NY), 1992.

Six Out Seven, Farrar, Straus and Giroux (New York, NY), 1993.

Ghost Train, Henry Holt (New York, NY), 1996.

Babylon Boyz, illustrated by Eric Dinger, Simon & Schuster (New York, NY), 1996.

(With Yule Caise) *Way Past Cool* (screenplay based on novel of same name), Redeemable Features (New York, NY), 1996.

Skeleton Key (stage play), 1999.

Bones Become Flowers, Windstorm Creative (Port Orchard, WA), 1999.

Also contributor to periodicals, including *Writer's Digest, Alchemy, Obsidian, Sequoia, Santa Clara Review, Nation, Los Angeles Times, Might Magazine, Buzz Magazine,* and *San Francisco Examiner.* Contributor to various anthologies, including *In the Tradition,* Harlem River Press (New York, NY), 1992; *Cornerstones,* St. Martin's Press (New York, NY), 1996; *California Shorts,* Heyday Books (Berkeley, CA), 1999; and *I Believe in Water,* Harper (New York, NY), 2000. Mowry's books have been published in English, French, German, Italian, Dutch, Swedish, Finnish, Danish, and Japanese.

Adaptations

Way Past Cool has been made into a feature-length film by Redeemable Features (New York, NY), Adam Davidson, director, as well as a stage theatrical (opera for a new audience), Jeff Langley, composer, Kathleen Masterson, librettist; it has also been made into an audiocassette by HarperCollins.

Work in Progress

Burma Jeep, a novel "about kids exploited for 'kiddie porn'"; *The Black Gang,* a novel about "saving the world's children versus saving endangered animals"; a novel based on Mowry's stage play titled *Skeleton Key* about "a ghetto ghost story"; *Phat Acceptance,* a novel and a screenplay about "accepting overweight kids as well as kids of other races"; *Voodu Dawgz,* a novel about "kids using Voodu magic to overcome a violent street gang"; *Fat Free* (a novel); *Babylon Boyz,* a screenplay based on the novel.

Sidelights

Most people who have lived the kind of life that Jess Mowry did in his youth are in jail, dead, or are fated to a life of hardship and poverty. Yet Mowry has defied the odds to become both an accomplished author and a role model for the young black street kids with whom he works and about whom he writes. Mowry is such a powerful, visceral writer that the editor of one of his books has likened him to Charles Dickens. The comparison is not far-fetched, for Mowry's keen talent and his gift for articulating the searing rage and frustrations of

black youth has been noted by numerous critics. According to Cathi Dunn MacRae of the *Wilson Library Bulletin,* the writer's "own life is so solidly enmeshed in his work that perhaps we need a new word for it. Such social commentary is actually 'docufiction.'" In a *Nation* review of *Way Past Cool,* Mowry's novel about rival Oakland street gangs, Ishmael Reed echoed that idea, hailing Mowry as "the Homer of inner-city youth."

With numerous books, two movie screenplays, a stage play, and many short stories to his credit, Jess Mowry emerged during the 1990s as one of America's most original and important—yet relatively unheralded—black writers. His low profile is as much a matter of personal preference as of any lack of merit or of public interest in his writing. Mowry has declined to take "the easy way," refusing to be seduced by fame or money, or to play the role of "angry black man," which America's mainstream media seem intent on ascribing to him. Instead, Mowry remains socially committed and aware; he prefers doing things his way as he works to improve the lives and self-image of black street kids. To that end, Mowry continues to live in his old neighborhood, and to work at a youth drop-in center. He also tries to advise young writers of color and to encourage them to follow his lead in breaking down the stereotypes that he feels have become so harmful to young blacks in America's inner cities. Mowry is as frank about his own role in that process as he is realistic. "The 'powers that be'—in this case meaning the 'mainstream' publishing industry (also film, music, and American society in general) WANT to see these stereotypes," Mowry told Ken Cuthbertson in an interview for *Authors and Artists for Young Adults.* "Stereotypes are very reassuring to them (yes, these kids are not really 'human,' so we don't have to feel bad about how we're treating them), but I'm only one man. I can't 'save' the world, or all the kids in it; I can only do the best I can with what I've got."

Mowry likewise told *SATA,* "Publishers hate being questioned or challenged; they only want the stereotypes when it comes to stories of young black men, and just like cops they'll beat you down if you criticize or question them. As long as my characters stayed in the ghetto and acted like publishers thought they should, my books would sell (so the editors said). But, if kids began to question the System—like why they were being miseducated and taught to hate and kill each other, or worse, began to *help* each other—then fewer people would buy my books and it would be harder to get them published."

Everything that Jess Mowry has, he's worked hard for. His early life was a hardscrabble existence, filled with the kind of pain and struggle that breaks—or hopelessly embitters—most people. Mowry was born on March 27, 1960, near the town of Starkville, Mississippi, the product of an interracial relationship; his father is black, his mother white. "One has only to read about the social mores (or lack of same) in Mississippi in that era to know that this was 'not a good thing,'" Mowry told Cuthbertson. "My mother 'disappeared,' and has not been heard of to this day, though I haven't been interested enough . . . to try to find her. Nor do I care to." Mowry's father, Jessup, moved west with his infant son to Oakland, California, about three months later. Young Jess was raised there, learning the ways of the street early on. Yet Mowry recalls a childhood filled "with much love and fun," although he does point out that his upbringing was anything but conventional "by today's white middle-class American standards."

Mowry inherited his passion for words from his father. Jessup Mowry was "a voracious, eclectic reader," the author recalled. "When one grows up surrounded by books of all sorts—even if they be mostly junk-shop paperbacks—then reading is a very natural thing." Like his dad, Mowry read anything that was at hand. While the environment made it difficult for him to succeed in school, Mowry was precocious, which sometimes put him in conflict with "the system." He angered his fourth-grade teacher, for instance, by reading ahead in assigned books. Mowry read the Herman Melville classic *Moby Dick* when his teacher had criticized him by saying that someone his age could never understand such a serious novel. Mowry didn't stop with Melville; he went on to read books by John Steinbeck (whose 1947 novel *The Wayward Bus* remains Mowry's favorite book), by black novelist Ralph Ellison, and horror and fantasy writers such as H. P. Lovecraft and J. R. R. Tolkien, among others.

Despite his love of reading, the school system proved too tedious and restrictive for a thirteen-year-old who had been working in "the real world" since the age of eight, and Mowry dropped out of school in eighth grade. For a short time he worked as a drug dealer's bodyguard, but by age fourteen he had discovered that "crime doesn't pay. . . . At least in my case, not very much," and he and his partner, Markita Brown, joined Mowry's father in the Arizona desert near Tucson. In 1974, they welcomed the arrival of the first of their four children, Jeremy, followed over the next five years by Weylen, Shara, and Keeja. To support his family, Mowry worked by times as a heavy-equipment and aircraft mechanic, truck driver, tugboat engineer (in Alaska), and a scrap metal collector. In 1987, the family moved back to Oakland and Mowry, with some money put away, began reading to and working with kids at a neighborhood center. He soon found that there was a dearth of books and stories that young black children could relate to, so he set up a "studio" in an abandoned Greyhound bus, bought a 1923 Underwood typewriter for eight dollars, and began writing for the kids.

"I began writing stories for and about the kids at a West Oakland youth center in 1988," he told Cuthbertson. "I sent one of those stories to *Zyzzvya* (a San Francisco literary magazine). They published it. The rest, as they say, is history." To help dispel negative media stereotypes and to offer positive messages these same kids could relate to, he began writing down some of the stories he had been creating about street kids. The product of Mowry's efforts is *Rats in the Trees,* a collection of nine related stories about a thirteen-year-old Oakland street kid named Robby. "*Rats* reflects the inner-city conditions for kids during the late 1980s, . . . when crack-cocaine was starting to flood into U.S. 'ghettoes,'" Mowry explained in an essay about his writing, which appears on his Web page. The book, which is written in the gritty lingo of the streets, was published in paperback by a small Santa Barbara publisher, and distribution was limited. However, what little critical response there was to Mowry's literary debut in the United States was highly favorable, and the book was also published overseas in the United Kingdom, Germany, and Japan. A *Publishers Weekly* reviewer wrote that *Rats in the Trees* "at once saddens, overwhelms and charms as it explores a realm unto itself—urban gangs." Cathi Dunn MacRae of the *Wilson Library Journal* observed: "Rarely has street life been so encapsulated in its own language."

It is with no sense of satisfaction that Mowry points out on his Web page how the grim predictions he made in 1990 in *Rats in the Trees* have come to pass. "Sadly, all [of them] have come true. . .," he writes, "the ever-increasing and senseless Black-on-Black crime, the 'guns, gangs, drugs, and violence' in U.S. inner cities, the kids killing kids, and the decline in the quality of public education. . . . It was also predicted in *Rats* that 'guns, gangs, drugs and violence' would move into 'white suburbia,' too—as Chuck (an older white teenager in *Rats*) said: 'Coming soon to a neighborhood near YOU!'—and they have. Does anyone remember Columbine?"

Despite favorable reviews and positive word-of-mouth for *Rats in the Trees,* mainstream publishers failed to take note of Jess Mowry or of his writing. Mowry's second book, the novel *Children of the Night,* was published in 1991 by Holloway House, a small West Coast publisher. Once again, Mowry's work appeared as an inexpensive paperback. The book is the story of Ryo, a thirteen-year-old West Oakland youth and his "homey" Chipmunk, who go to work for a neighborhood crack dealer named Big Bird. When Chipmunk is killed in a drug run, Ryo reevaluates the life that he has chosen and then sets out to save himself and destroy Big Bird.

Children of the Night is gritty, vivid, and uncompromising in its condemnation of the parasitic drug lords and the systemic racism which confines young black street kids to lives of poverty, crime, and hardship. As Mowry points out, speaking through one of the characters in the book, Brownie, a big problem is "[white] people not believin' what's goin' on in places like this . . . as long as they can keep it in places like this." Despite Mowry's hopes, *Children of the Night* attracted little media attention. However, the few reviews there were again hailed Mowry as an important new black literary voice; for example, Cathi Dunn MacRae praised his novel as a "vibrant, mesmerizing evocation . . . of an underworld that the classes above ignore." Mowry's work, MacRae added, "captures that world with descriptions of ugly places and desperate people so lyrical that they force us to really see what we would rather not."

With two critically acclaimed books to his credit, in 1992 Mowry suddenly won the kind of literary success that he had never dared to dream about. The street-kid-turned-author's next book, another novel about black youth gangs—"Little Rascals with Uzis," he termed them—was published by Farrar, Straus and Giroux, a major New York-based national publisher. Farrar, Straus and Giroux made *Way Past Cool* its lead fiction title in its spring catalog. According to Bronwen Hruska, writing in *Voice Literary Supplement,* Mowry received a $30,000 advance. What's more, according to Hruska, the "Disney studios optioned the film rights to the book for another $75,000." That money, more than Mowry had ever earned before in his life, enabled him to move his family into an apartment. He spent what was left on worthwhile projects in his own neighborhood. Hruska explained, Mowry "didn't write *Cool* for profits.... He wrote it for the kids it's about—even though they won't be the ones laying down the $17 for the hardback edition." Daniel Max of the entertainment industry trade publication *Variety* later reported that Mowry turned down a request to write a screenplay based on the book. He eventually did so, however, for a company called Redeemable Features, the third company to option the rights. "The screenplay they had was such a mess I just basically said, 'Oh here, let me do the damn thing!'" Mowry told Cuthbertson.

"It seems as if many writers will have one book in their careers for which they will be remembered more than for any others they write," Mowry notes on his Web page. "It seems that for me the book I will probably be most 'remembered' (if at all) for is *Way Past Cool.*" This "has been both a blessing and a curse," he adds. "A 'blessing' in that I was able to tell the truth and to show the world a view of how the U.S. treats [black street kids] ... but a 'curse' in that I seem to be expected (by the 'mainstream' publishers) to write this kind of 'ghetto fiction' for evermore; and it has become clear to me ... that 'they' are not about to publish anything of mine outside of or beyond this type of work—and DEFINITELY not 'just stories.'"

Unlike Mowry's first two books, *Way Past Cool* grabbed the media's attention. Novelist Robert Ward, writing in *Los Angeles Times Book Review,* praised the work as "a gut-wrenching, heart-breaking suspense novel about black gang life in Oakland." However, reviewers for many mainstream publications were not quite as enthusiastic in their assessments. Nelson George of *New York Times* described *Way Past Cool* as "maddeningly uneven, occasionally poetic." Reviewer Nick Kimberley, writing in *New Statesman & Society,* mused that "there's tough urgency in its street ellipses, and a pulpy cheerfulness in its sudden switches of mood and scene.... But its very mobility eventually drains *Way Past Cool* of its purpose." Although Mowry concedes that he is disappointed by negative reviews, he says that he is not surprised by them. "Many are racist," he told Cuthbertson in his interview for *Authors and Artists for Young Adults.* "Often, it seems, without their (white) writers being aware of it; they really want to see the

stereotypes, and it angers and/or confuses them when they don't."

Undeterred, Mowry continued to write about issues that he felt were of vital concern to the black community. His next novel, *Six Out Seven* (which was actually written before *Way Past Cool,* but published after), is "basically a 'country-mouse, city-mouse,' kind of tale," according to Mowry's Web page. The story deals with Corbitt Wainwright, a thirteen-year-old black youth from rural Mississippi, who moves to Oakland to escape some trouble back home. In the novel's early chapters, Mowry juxtaposes details of Corbitt's life in the two locales. He then goes on to describe Corbitt's enforced coming of age after he joins a street gang called The Collectors; the boy becomes a foot soldier in the deadly turf war that's being fought on the streets of Oakland and other American cities—a war where to "kick" someone is to kill him, and "dirt nap" is a euphemism for death. Mowry explained on his Web site, "Unlike *Way Past Cool,* which presented a view of Black kids trapped in the inner city—knowing there was probably a way out but too caught up in day-to-day survival to try to find it—*Six Out Seven* dug deeper in to the reasons WHY these kids have to live as they do—the 'self-cleaning oven,' the fact that 'gang-violence,' and kids killing kids is actually encouraged by certain segments of white U.S. society, and that drugs are seldom if ever brought into the U.S. and poured into the 'ghettoes' by Black people."

In the words of Bob Sipchen of the *Los Angeles Times Book Review,* in *Six Out Seven* Jess Mowry "grapple[s] angrily and honestly with the forces killing young black men; with individual and societal responsibility; with the complexities of modern racism, including drive-by shooters whom, Mowry says, roam inner cities "like the KKK's Afro-American auxiliary." Sipchen went on to praise *Six Out Seven* as a "heartfelt, beautifully written book that will make readers see that the kids [Mowry] portrays are *everyone's* kids, and to let their dreams wither unnurtured is *everyone's* shame." Clarence Petersen, writing in the Chicago *Tribune Books,* echoed those comments when he wrote, "Mowry tells us things we need to hear with a raw eloquence that both touches and enrages."

Mowry's next book is decidedly lighter fare and a clear change of pace for him. *Ghost Train* is a supernatural mystery story aimed at young readers. The story is about Remi DuMont, a young Haitian immigrant, who with help from his new American friend Niya, sets out to solve a fifty-year-old murder mystery. Mowry spins a suspense-filled yarn about time travel, social issues, and Voodoo magic—the latter being a subject in which the author himself has a keen interest. Mowry says his main purpose in writing *Ghost Train* was to tell a good story, something he feels that not enough black male writers are doing—or being allowed to do—by a white-dominated publishing industry that insists on turning out books about stereotypical black characters living in a world of guns, drugs, gangs, and killing. The negative influence of black intellectuals who feel writing—or reading—escapist fiction is not a worthwhile pastime is also a hindrance to the development of black male writers, Mowry says. "Of course our young people should know their history and be aware of racism on all levels, and of social issues and concerns in the world around them," Mowry wrote on his Web page, "but they MUST also be entertained in positive ways," and offered valid, realistic role models.

Mowry apparently succeeded on all counts with *Ghost Train.* Although reviewer Ann C. Sparanese of the *Voice of Youth Advocates* faulted the "dialog['s] stilted quality" that interrupts the story's flow, she asserted that "the novel's strength is in its plot." From the start of the novel, "the suspense pulls the reader along to the climactic last chapter, where danger gives way to a satisfying resolution." Susan L. Rogers of *School Library Journal* praised *Ghost Train* as a "short, easy-to-read, and very successful mystery."

Mowry returned to familiar turf with *Babylon Boyz,* a 1996 novel about three teenage friends named Dante, Pook, and Wyatt, who live in a run-down inner-city Oakland neighborhood called Babylon. Mowry tells the story of what happens when the youths find a suitcase full of drugs, which has been discarded by a white drug dealer on the run. Dante, Pook, and Wyatt are suddenly confronted with gut-wrenching decisions about whether or not to try to sell the drugs. *Babylon Boyz* is a tough, hard-hitting story with earthy dialogue, violence, and some graphic sex scenes. "While it's sometimes difficult to read about this subject matter, toning it down would have sadly compromised the story's realism," maintained *Voice of Youth Advocates* contributor Florence Munat. "Instead, Mowry has delivered a realistic, tenacious tale of urban hopes and dreams." Bill Ott of *Booklist* similarly noted, "Each of the boys rises above the stereotypical aspects of his character to become, not emblems of hard life in the ghetto, but vivid reminders that we are all more than the sum of our situations." *School Library Journal* contributor Beth Wright observed that *Babylon Boyz* offers a view of "family, friendship, love, and ... kids living in poverty and victimized by drugs still trying to make the right choices in their lives."

In 1998, Mowry decided to pursue his dream of writing black adventure stories and produced the novel *Bones Become Flowers,* which is set in present-day Haiti. The protagonist is a thirty-three-year-old, self-made and wealthy black woman named Tracy who comes to Haiti to fund a children's refuge, but instead finds herself immersed in a culture of Voodoo and magic. Taking passage on a rusty Haitian freighter, crewed entirely by young boys, on a voyage to an island called Cayes Squellette, she falls in love with the ship's captain and discovers that material possessions mean nothing in the larger picture of life. Mowry commented to *SATA,* "Predictably, the novel was rejected by mainstream publishers on the grounds that 'black people don't read these kinds of books,'" even though he had gathered comments from several noted authors before submitting the work. Among these were Dr. Robert L. Allen, co-

editor of *Brotherman,* who wrote, "Jess Mowry's creativity shines brilliantly in *Bones Become Flowers,* his lyrical and richly descriptive new novel. Set in modern-day Haiti, it invites us into an unsettling and disturbing world of forgotten children—children who nonetheless teach us that love and human connection have a way of transcending despair and even death itself." Despite this and numerous other positive comments from fellow writers, mainstream rejections forced Mowry to again seek a smaller publisher as with his first books. The book was published in 1999 by Windstorm Creative of Port Orchard, Washington, and is now in its third printing, which, Mowry told *SATA,* "is proof enough that black people do, indeed, 'read these kinds of books.'"

In addition to his novels and short stories, Mowry has shown his versatility by writing a stage play called *Skeleton Key,* which was staged at a private school in Berkeley, and by collaborating on the screenplay for a film based on his novel *Way Past Cool.* Nonetheless, Mowry feels that he still faces an uphill struggle to succeed as a writer, even if he does concede that he is still learning, about writing and about life. "One radio talk-show host gave me a left-handed compliment on the air by saying how 'well I expressed myself, considering that I'd only completed seventh grade,'" Mowry said in his interview. "I replied that I'd always thought life was a learning process that never stopped, as opposed to those who had finished high school and perhaps college and so felt they had learned everything they needed to know."

Mowry's own independence of mind (he has been with four literary agents in his brief career and is now representing himself), which is one of his strengths, has also been one of the biggest obstacles he has had to overcome. However, he insists that an even greater difficulty is the racism that he—and other blacks—face on a daily basis in American society. "In the case of [black] writers, musicians, or filmmakers it's very hard because 'they' (and you should know who 'they' are) control everything," Mowry explained to Cuthbertson. "A 'black book' that does not please a white editor will not be published.... A white writer with my track record—ALL of my books still in print after almost ten years (in eight languages), a film, and a play—would have no problem finding a publisher for their next work. With me, it's a case of back to square-one every time and start all over again. It's very tiring to say the least."

Mowry feels strongly that every successful black man or woman has a duty to serve as a role model for young people in their communities. To that end, he continues to speak out against social injustice and to do all that he can to help smash the harmful black stereotypes that are perpetuated in the media. As he told Cuthbertson, "I'd be less than human if I didn't [get angry]. Although I try to temper my anger with the 'I used to be disgusted, now I'm just amused' philosophy."

Biographical and Critical Sources

BOOKS

Authors and Artists for Young Adults, Ken Cuthbertson interview with Jess Mowry, Volume 29, Gale (Detroit, MI), 1999.

Beacham's Guide to Literature for Young Adults, Volume 10, Gale (Detroit, MI), 2000, pp. 39-46, 113-118, 407-416.

Contemporary Black Biography, Volume 7, Gale (Detroit, MI), 1994.

St. James Guide to Young Adult Writers, 2nd edition, St. James Press (Detroit, MI), 1999.

PERIODICALS

Booklist, September 15, 1993, p. 128; February 15, 1997; February 15, 1997, Bill Ott, review of *Babylon Boyz,* p. 1020.

Kirkus Reviews, August 1, 1993, p. 960; April 15, 1997.

Knight-Ridder/Tribune News Service, November 1, 1993, Michalene Busico, "Author Jess Mowry Can Describe Himself, Thanks."

Los Angeles Times Book Review, April 19, 1992, Robert Ward, "Dispatch From the Hood," pp. 2, 7; November 7, 1993, Bob Sipchen, "What the Use in Dreamin?" pp. 2, 9.

Nation, September 21, 1992, Ishmael Reed, "The Activist Library: A Symposium," pp. 293-294.

New Statesman & Society, July 17, 1992, Nick Kimberley, "Unhappy Days," pp. 46-47.

New York Times, May 24, 1992, Nelson George, "Boyz Against the Hoods," p. 21.

New York Times Book Review, October 31, 1993, p. 9.

People, June 22, 1992, p. 66.

Publishers Weekly, March 2, 1990, review of *Rats in the Trees,* p. 78; February 3, 1997, p. 107.

San Francisco Chronicle, June 29, 1997, "Books Focus on Challenge of Youth/Gritty but Uplifting Stories about Black Males," p. 7.

School Library Journal, December, 1996, Susan L. Rogers, review of *Ghost Train,* p. 139; September, 1997, Beth Wright, review of *Babylon Boyz,* p. 222.

Tribune Books (Chicago, IL), September 18, 1994, Clarence Petersen, "Paperbacks," p. 8.

Variety, January 27, 1992, Daniel Max, "Will Hollywood Get Serious about Black Lit?" p. 68.

Voice Literary Supplement, May, 1992, Bronwen Hruska, "Goodbye, Cool World," p. 31.

Voice of Youth Advocates, February, 1997, Ann C. Sparanese, review of *Ghost Train,* p. 330; June, 1997, Florence Munat, review of *Babylon Boyz,* p. 112.

Washington Post Book World, November 2, 1993, p. E-2.

Wilson Library Bulletin, March, 1991, Cathi Dunn MacRae, "The Young Adult Perplex," pp. 112-113.

OTHER

Jess Mowry Web Site, http://members.tripod.com/~Timoun/index-2.html (January 16, 2002).

*   *   *

Autobiography Feature

Jess Mowry

It's raining tonight. I've always loved the patter of rain, a soothing, sleepy and shivery sound that seems to bring a peaceful feeling; a sound of dreams—at least for me.

The rhythm of rain is a comforting thing when you're warm and dry inside somewhere, but it's also cool to go out in the rain, maybe walking late at night when the empty streets and sidewalks glisten like rippling rivers beneath the lights, the power lines sputter and buzz overhead, and the rushing gutters and gurgling drains make you think of a wild mountain stream.

Sitting here now in this basement room with the trickling music of rain outside, I could almost forget being wet and cold, when my sodden clothes felt heavy as lead and my sneakers squished with every step as if my socks were soggy sponges wrapped around my frozen feet.

It's 3:00 a.m. as I write these words: I usually do my writing at night when the city sounds are most subdued and the streets outside are silent. The rainfall makes a shivery sound, but here I'm warm and dry. I suppose I should feel peaceful tonight, yet I know that for many blocks around there are people and kids who aren't so lucky, who curse this rain through chattering teeth with ghostly smoking breath.

There's a boy out there about thirteen who's trudging through those streets tonight in soggy shoes and sodden clothes and streaming beanie cap. He might recall a different time when rain was something comforting, a liquid lullaby at night beyond his bedroom window. The sound of water enhanced his dreams, becoming a song of splashing streams, the surge of surf on sandy shores, a sailboat cruising sunny seas in search of peaceful islands.

Jess Mowry, 2001

The boy read books and dreamed big dreams of sailing all around the world and walking sunny beaches.

This boy is in my mind tonight. He wears an Army field jacket, olive-drab and tattered. It might have clad an older youth who served in Vietnam, but it ended up in an old junk shop forgotten like its soldier. Battered sneaks are on his feet, concealed beneath the ragged cuffs of sagging Levis jeans. A black knit cap corrals his mop of curly midnight hair. These clothes were like a uniform in 1973: black kids wore those Army jackets in honor of the Panther Party, an organization of brave black men like Huey Newton and Bobby Seale who fought to build a better world. There were younger Panthers too, like little Bobby Hutton, killed at seventeen years old for dreaming daring dreams.

Hippies also wore these jackets: for some they represented peace, a kind of subtle irony in garments meant for war. For other kids these jackets were a street-survival kit, warm enough for winter wear, yet comfortable in summer. But, no matter who you were back then, those jackets stood for something.

Today, the boy might wear the cap beneath a ragged hoodie, while Nikes would replace the sneaks along with baggy gangstuh jeans. But, no matter how he's dressed tonight, I know this boy is wet and cold and wishing for a place to sleep.

It's raining a little harder now; water invades my window frame to trickle down the wall. I see two boys out there tonight, the present shadowed by the past. Neither boy can see the other with thirty years between them, and yet they might be twins except for what they dream about.

I know the boy in the Army jacket. I know the dreams inside his mind because they once were mine. A lot of my dreams have been fulfilled: I have climbed mountains,

explored some deserts, and driven an eighteen-wheeler truck. I've sailed sometimes to sandy shores, flown in ancient cargo planes, and had some "literary success." I've even had a film produced, based on one of my books.

To the boy who walks in the rain tonight, a shadow behind the hooded one, the age of twenty was ancient, man—pyramids and dinosaurs, rocking chairs and walking canes. Like most of his homies, drinking beer and smoking Camel cigarettes, he never believed he'd live that long. And reach the age of forty-one? That would *never* happen!

It's funny when talking to kids and teens, doing book readings, visiting schools—or the many youth-prisons this nation has built to prove how much it loves its kids—that I'll catch a glimpse of myself in a window and wonder who that "old guy" is.

I think there's a message in what I just said, especially if you're young yourself.... I *know* what it's like to be thirteen, but you don't have a clue about forty-one. And, whether you want to believe it or not, you're probably going to get here.

Where is "here" for me right now?

I rent the basement of an ancient house in Oakland, California. It was only supposed to be temporary until I got paid for *Way Past Cool,* a film based on my second novel. The film was finished two years ago but hasn't been released as yet, so naturally I haven't been paid. This happens a lot in the writing game—waiting to be paid. But, I guess I shouldn't complain too much; there's a roof above me, food to eat, and I'm doing what I want to do, which is more than a lot of people can say. And, I'm not out there in the rain tonight with all I own on my back.

But, you don't know much about me yet, except that I was thirteen once and now I'm forty-one.

I was born in northeast Mississippi on March 27, 1960. The place, I'm told, didn't have a name, but was near the town of Starkville. I've been back there exactly once in my life, and "stark" is the perfect description. There used to be a joke in the South that no matter how poor you thought you were, no matter how hard your life might seem, be thankful you weren't in Mississippi.

Even today, civil rights seem less than "civil" in Mississippi. I'm sure some white folks wouldn't agree, but most black residents would. The movie, *Mississippi Burning,* was based on something that happened near Starkville—the murder of civil rights activists by members of the Ku Klux Klan in the early 1960s. If you keep these frightening facts in mind, you'll get the point that a black boy—my father, age 16—and white girl of 18 falling in love was not the wisest thing to do.

Anyway, that's how I happened. I didn't burst upon the world as living proof that love unites: I'm sure it was just the opposite. I was born at home with a midwife's help, which was fortunate for my father—he'd of likely been hung from the nearest tree if a hospital birth had taken place. My mother's family packed up and left town, which was no doubt a wise move for her.

It's hard to miss people you never knew, and I don't think she had any choice about leaving. My father and mother were painfully poor as only the rural poor can be. They knew almost nothing about the world; though my dad was always a reader of books and collected a lot of useful knowledge. He didn't have a television, but I doubt if my mother did either; and it might be hard to imagine today but

TV news and even shows were racially censored then in the South (you wouldn't have seen Lieutenant Uhura kissing Captain Kirk). My mom may have dreamed about running away and raising her "golden child" in peace, but I'm sure that her chances of doing so were limited by her education and desperate lack of money. There's an old southern proverb which cynically says, "you can't get there from here," and I'm sure that must have been how it seemed to my mother in 1960.

My dad, however, was lucky enough to have picked up a lot of mechanical skills by working on trucks and farm equipment. Most blacks weren't allowed to learn such things, no doubt because they might "better themselves." For three months he kept my existence a secret with help from a kindly neighbor lady. He managed to scrape up fifty dollars and buy a battered old Reo truck—a 1946 flatbed—and in June of that year, at age seventeen, he set out for Oakland, California with me in a blanket beside him.

Why did he go to Oakland? That's a funny kind of tale. There weren't many book stores in Mississippi, even in the larger cities, and nearly none in smaller towns. There were paperbacks sold in variety stores—selected and radically censored like television—which gave you a choice of second-hand shops or browsing the public library. My father had gone to a black school, of course, where he'd earned a sixth-grade diploma, but they didn't have many up-to-date books. Word would have spread like wildfire if he'd bought any new books in town; and I don't imagine the library was actually "public" for blacks. This left him only the second-hand store; and the books he bought were all very old. He'd read about Oakland's industries and how they built big ships, and he'd always dreamed of going to sea like many landlocked country boys. There were also lots of black people there, and compared to the South they had their freedom to live their lives as they pleased.

At least there weren't any "valiant knights" who hid their faces behind white sheets while burning your house and stringing you up.

Naturally, he had no clue that Oakland's shipbuilding industry had dwindled to little more than nothing after the end of World War II. In fact, west Oakland in 1960 was a grimy sprawl of rust and soot, a place of clanking railroad trains and smoky, snorting trucks. Mountains of scrap metal shadowed the streets among the rows of Victorian houses, shoulder-to-shoulder with truck garages, iron works and wrecking yards where ships were often broken up.

My very first story was called "The Ship," but I'm getting ahead of myself.

The Reo's top speed was forty-five (I later learned how to drive in that truck) but my dad kept the pedal down to the metal until we were well out of Mississippi. Even then, he didn't relax until Arkansas, Oklahoma, and Texas had faded away in the mirrors. At last we were safely in New Mexico where the cowboys didn't discriminate much—as long as you weren't an Indian. He told me once how shocked he was when a white man washed the truck's windshield and checked the oil and water.

If this sounds more like a daring escape—or maybe Liza crossing the ice—than a drive across the "Land Of The Free," remember that here was a young black man with a baby who could have passed for white, in the year of 1960. As a matter of fact, he *had* escaped: incredible as it might seem today, a lot of racist southern whites hated black people who wanted to leave, as if we were being ungrateful to them after all the good they'd done for us!

I received a letter a few years ago from a Mississippi magazine, a very prestigious publication. They wanted to claim me as "one of their own"—a fellow Mississippian—and asked me to write them a story. I tried to imagine my dad in that state and how life must have been for him. I know it was bad before I was born, but then he lived in constant fear while working to make his get-away. I pictured that night in our battered old truck on those lonely country backroads: he must have checked the mirrors behind as much as watching the road ahead. Heaven knows what might have happened if he'd been stopped by a cop. But, what was his crime in America? Taking his son out of Mississippi and daring to dream of a better life.

I said, "No thanks," to the magazine.

I have a pretty good memory, but of course I can't recall that trip or finally arriving in Oakland. I'm told it took us about a week, and crossing the desert in early July was a hellish test of man and machine; but the truck never gave us a bit of trouble except for burning a lot of oil. No new ships were being built, and jobs were far from plentiful, but my dad found work at a wrecking yard within a couple of days. Those skills he'd learned on old farm trucks were as good as gold in Oakland. In less than a week we had a new home, a three-room flat on the second floor of an old Victorian house.

The house was owned by a kindly woman who'd lost her husband in World War II. Her name was Mrs. Hawker, and she was amazed by my father's escape—her family had come from Louisiana, where Mississippi was whispered about like the place of eternal punishment. She took immediate charge of me and soon became my adopted grandmother.

"My dad at age ten, with his cousin in Mississippi"

"Our 1946 Reo truck"

My memories start at around age four, though I seem to recall Mrs. Hawker's tears when President John F. Kennedy died, assassinated in 1963. That was also the year when the Ku Klux Klan, America's noble terrorists, had bombed a church in Birmingham and murdered four little girls. I also recall my father reading, often and aloud to me, but we'll get to that in a little while.

I'm sorry I missed our arrival in Oakland by being only a baby: I would have watched my father's face when he first sat down in the front of a bus or took any seat in a movie theater. He must have looked for a "WHITE ONLY" sign the first time he went to a restaurant. I imagine his shock when white folks smiled and even began conversations with him; and now he could meet a white man's eyes without being cursed as "uppity."

I'm not trying to say that Oakland was heaven or that he might have thought it was: even then there were neighborhood gangs, guns, drugs, and random violence. The Oakland police were brutal and racist: they practiced their own kind of terrorism upon the black community. Yet, to a man from Mississippi, it must have seemed like freedom and justice, words recited saluting the flag in a one-room school for colored kids, were a little bit closer to happening.

Our landlady's house was a haunted mansion, at least to me at four years old, a narrow and tottering three-stories tall and badly in need of a new coat of paint. Down below was a dirt-floored basement that somehow smelled like a grave to me—or how I imagined a grave would smell. The stairways squeaked, the door hinges creaked, and the light bulbs were feeble and dim. Even the stove in the kitchen was scary, crouching high on spidery legs and looking as if it would chase you. The floors and walls were dark old wood with mysterious carvings above the doors and "skeleton's keys" in all the locks. The rooms were small with lofty ceilings, shadowy corners and nooks and crannies where creepy creatures might have lurked. There were window seats with "coffin lids," and little clawed feet on the monster tub in a gloomy bathroom with a whispering toilet.

The house itself was spotless inside, but blackberry vines overgrew the back yard and all but buried a ramshackle shed, where sunlight shafted between the planks and dust motes danced in the golden beams. The berries provided sweet snacks in summer for birds, tree rats, and the neighborhood kids, who were all as wild as coyotes. Mrs. Hawker made blackberry pies, but she never tried to tame the brambles and so they almost ruled the place. She did her wash in a cranky Maytag, the kind with a wringer attachment on top, but hung out the laundry to dry on a line. It was one of those rope-and-pulley things that ran from the porch to a pole out back, so the clothes swung over the briar patch and fluttered like colorful ghosts in the breeze. If a shirt or a pair of my jeans fell off, my dad would manfully chop his way as if performing a jungle rescue.

My dad had a casual conception of clothes, and you sure wouldn't say that he dressed to impress. Being the youngest of three growing boys, he'd naturally gotten the hand-me-downs, which looked like scarecrow rags by then. For Mississippi country kids, underwear was a luxury, shirts were something you wore in the winter—and only if it was *really* cold—while jackets and coats were hoarded away and saved for howling blizzards. This also applied to shoes and socks. You've probably heard of somebody's father who walked barefoot through rain and snow for the privilege of getting an education? In the case of my dad it was true.

Like most people raised in poverty, he'd learned to stretch a dollar bill until it screamed for mercy. He soon discovered the Salvation Army, astonished at what people threw away. Socks were about the only things that couldn't be found at a second-hand store—at least without holes in the heels and toes—and only someone foolish and rich would buy new clothes for a growing boy.

I *was* a rapidly growing boy, thanks to Mrs. Hawker's cooking, which featured tons of beans and rice along with spicy Cajun food and other very filling fare. My tummy was round as a basketball by the time I reached the age of five, and I often displayed a lot of skin between my jeans and T-shirt tails, though jeans were usually all I wore. My dad had a simple philosophy when it came to dressing little boys—what isn't there doesn't wear out. My clothes from spring though summer and fall consisted of second-hand Levis jeans with ragged cuffs and shredded knees. My father favored the button-flys because of the extra wearing time—you simply left the buttons open, one by one as you got bigger, until there weren't any options left or secrets to conceal. Believe me, "saggers" are nothing new and hip-hoppers didn't invent them. But, I have to say I loved those jeans, softly faded and well broken-in; and even today I'll wash a new pair before I put them on.

I wasn't allowed to cross the street until I reached the age of five—the stop sign at the intersection was treated like a joke—so the only use I had for shoes was going uptown with my dad. The year was 1965, and thirty more would have to pass until boys my age had tons of shoes to coordinate their wardrobes. It's funny how growing up in a city, surrounded by concrete, brick and steel, by thundering trains and rumbling trucks, I knew the rain and sun on my skin and the feel of the earth—though usually paved— beneath the soles of my feet.

Those soles, as you can probably guess, were often darker than my dad's and tougher than a tennis shoe. I could dance on broken glass unharmed, strut through searing asphalt streets, and I loved the oily goo in puddles from leaking engines and diesel fuel. The major hazard was dog you-know.

I don't mean to say that my dad was cheap: most of his clothes were as ragged as mine and he often went shirtless in summer, but style was not his priority. Two of his passions were books and movies, things he taught me to love as well, and he always read to me out loud no matter what the story was. Some of my earliest memories are lying in bed on rainy nights while he read to me from *The Grapes Of Wrath, Invisible Man,* or *Lord of the Rings,* while I, half-asleep, absorbed the words, although I didn't know it.

Along with this was another concept which probably came from his own upbringing when boys learned early to act like men because there was no other choice: he talked to children like equals. Baby-talk, he told me once, is like a crime to force on kids. It's learning a language that has no future, a language the world doesn't recognize, and you have to abandon it later on because it holds you back. There weren't any "blankies" in my early years, no "doo-doo," no "wee-wee," no "doggies" or "kitties," no "chickie" for supper with "ikie" dessert. There was no such thing as an "owie toe," and a "boo-boo" was Yogi Bear's homie. The parts of my body were properly named—not always in terms a doctor might use. Their functions were also explained to me—at least the ones I needed back then. He also taught me how to count, along with teaching me the alphabet. By four-and-a-half I could print my name and spell a lot of simple words. He brought home tons of children's books, dusty and faded from second-hand stores, and I was so proud I could read like him. It's funny to think that my father's teaching would get me in trouble at school.

My dad loved ghost and horror movies as much as he loved a good scary book, and usually took me with him. One of the first I recall is *The Birds,* and neither of us liked the ending. I was treated to hundreds of nasty vampires, werewolves, ghosts and bony old things, maniacal monsters, men from Mars, and badly bandaged muttering mummies who tottered around with an attitude. The special-effects were primitive then, but *Screaming Skull* gave me creepy dreams, along with *House on Haunted Hill.* Most of those movies seem funny today, and it's hard to believe they scared me so much that I often ran out to the lobby. But, I guess it takes more to scare us now, which is probably not a good thing.

Movies had simple messages then—the bad guys got what they deserved and the good were always rewarded—but reading expanded my own horizons. Reading taught me how to dream and imagine myself anywhere in the world while doing adventurous things. Reading taught me there *was* a world out beyond those dirty streets with their rivers of rust in oily gutters that ran through canyons of crumbling brick.

In the summer of 1965, my world consisted of one city block, a random mix of Victorian houses, truck garages and welding shops. A scrap yard lay across the street with a towering mountain of jagged junk and a battered old crane like an iron dinosaur that clattered and smoked from dawn until dusk while feeding on unwanted things. Six other families lived on our street but they didn't have any kids my age, and by five years old I wanted a friend. I also wanted a bigger world: I knew all the cracks in my own sidewalk and every square inch of my yard.

There were several new things in 1965—besides the Beatles and Rolling Stones—the brave defiance of Malcolm X (assassinated in February) the soul-stirring speeches of Dr. King, the rising cry for Civil Rights, the ominous war in Vietnam, and a spooky feeling like smoke in the air that something was wrong in the U.S.A. I was dimly aware of all these events from overhearing grownups talk and watching the nightly TV news; but from my point of view what really mattered were Stingray bikes in candy colors with chopper bars, banana seats, and racing-slick rear tires. Naturally, these were out of my reach, though my dad had offered to build me a bike from corpses found in the wrecking yard. I'm sure it would have been kickin' cool, but then I discovered skateboards.

Of course, there weren't any skate shops yet, but I took my dad to a toy store and showed him my desire. He studied the board for a minute or two, then we drove to the Salvation Army and bought some rusty roller skates. By that afternoon I had my ride—steel wheels on a wooden plank. This might sound a little bit lame today, but the primitive boards they sold in stores weren't really much better back then.

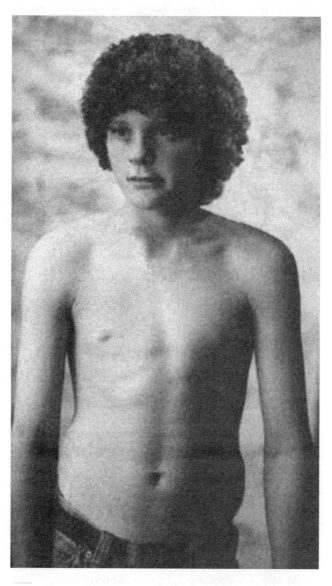

Jess at age thirteen in 1973

Even though "owies" didn't exist, I lost a lot of my blood and skin learning to ride that treacherous thing. Naturally, I was only in jeans, sagging so low that my bottom was bare while their cuffs completely covered my feet; but within a week my falls were few, though steel wheels were dangerous things and a chunk of gravel or broken glass were all it took for a tumble. Still, I was soon making sweaty speed runs from the welding shop at one end of our block to the truck garage on the other. My world began to seem very small. I felt like an airplane with too short a runway, trapped on the ground and longing to fly. I would skid to a stop at the corner curb, pull up my droopy jeans a bit, and wistfully gaze at the grimy horizon of new and undiscovered stuff.

Across the busy intersection was a shabby little neighborhood market. I went there daily with my dad, who bought two bottles of beer after work like "Doc" in the novel, *Cannery Row.* He held my hand as we crossed the street while raising his other to stop the trucks as if he was making a magic sign. The store was a black-owned family business where light bulbs dangled from dangerous wires and the aisles were only twisting trails through dimlit rows of sagging shelves that trembled whenever a train went by. Way in the back was a glass-fronted cooler that sounded like a locomotive. Racked within were sodas and beer, along with milk and orange juice—you didn't *buy* water in those ancient times; it just came out of a faucet. A lot of the brands weren't sold uptown and were cheaper than names like Pepsi or Coke. I especially liked the Shasta sodas, which only cost twelve cents a can. The cans were steel in those ancient days, and you punched the tops with an opener that hung on a chain at the counter. There were also lots of candy bars you didn't see in the bigger stores. One of these was called a "Zero"; its wrapper was blue with a polar bear, and it only cost a nickel. I was surprised the first time I got one because it was like a "reversed" candy bar, something you'd see in a picture negative, white on the outside and chocolate within.

I was finally allowed to cross the street in the summer of 1965, and now I could skate to the railroad yard, which gave me a whole new world to explore. I set out one morning in mid-July, dressed as always in jeans and my skin, with twenty-one cents and adventure ahead. I stopped at the store to stock up on supplies, and there I met my first real friend.

His name was Donny. You might have met him in some of my books. He was black as a panther at midnight, and maybe the fattest five-year-old this world has ever seen. He had more rolls than a bakery truck, and every step was an earthquake in Jell-O. Like me, he was barefoot and only in jeans, which sagged even lower than mine always did and often slipped completely off if he wasn't paying attention.

It's funny how often I get asked if growing up was hard for me because I don't "look very black," but it's mostly white people who ask me that. My meeting Donny should answer that question: I said "hi," he said "hi," and then we had a long discussion about the choice of candy. His parents had just moved onto my block, and he wasn't acquainted with Zero bars or the fabulous value of Shasta sodas. By pooling our resources, thirty-one cents, we were able to buy a pair of Zeros, a few Tootsie-rolls and a can of root beer. Did Donny mention the subject of color? Well, in

"My friend, Jeremy, at age thirteen"

a way. While we were eating our candy bars he pointed out that I looked like one, white on the outside but black underneath.

Donny was skating within a week. My father had built him a massive ride because he weighed about 200 pounds. He might have lacked a little in grace but once he got rolling he couldn't be stopped. We made two other good friends that summer, Jeremy, who was six years old but looked like a muscular lion cub, and Rick, a lean and wiry boy with oversize beaver-like teeth. You might have met them in *Rats in the Trees,* my first collection of published stories. Jerry became our commander, of course, and we kept my dad busy repairing our rides. Maybe you would have called us a "gang," but so were The Little Rascals.

In September we started kindergarten, except for Jerry who went to first grade. There were also two students in college that year whose names would go down in history: Huey Newton and Bobby Seale, who would found the Black Panthers the following fall.

I won't say much about going to school, except that trouble began right away. I could already count to a hundred by then, I knew my colors and alphabet, and I could spell a lot of words because my dad had taught me. But, far from getting praised for this, or being allowed to help other kids, I seemed to irritate my teacher. I remember my very first day at school: we were given pencils like telephone poles and told to draw letters twenty feet tall on pieces of paper resembling plywood. I asked for a pen and "regular paper," and the teacher told me to stop being smart. (Think about that for a minute.) I had never been talked to like a child, and I wasn't about to be treated like one, but logic was lost on this "educator."

Most of the teachers were white in those days and none of them lived in our neighborhood. They knew almost nothing about our lives, but seemed determined to make us fit their own conception of "little black kids"—and to make me *unlearn* what I already knew so they could teach me all over again. It's not that I was a gifted child or smarter than anyone else, it was just that I already *knew* this stuff. You can't teach kids by holding them back, but that's what my teacher was trying to do and I battled her and others like her all the way to seventh grade.

The "revolt of the four" was a good example: my father had taught me this kind of four (4), but my teacher demanded the open-top model. I thought that was stupid and promptly refused. Worse for me, so did Donny and Rick, who my father had also tutored a bit. Like, what did it matter *how* we made fours as long as we knew what they meant? It must have mattered a lot to the teacher because I was sent to the principal's office for being "rebellious" in class. That was the first of many such trips, but we didn't become the best of friends by seeing each other so often. Naturally, he backed the System, and only because it *was* the System. We finally arrived at an uneasy truce where I pretended to lose these fights and let my "superiors" think they had won—which was how my dad had survived in the South.

It also seemed to annoy my teachers whenever I read ahead in my books. I recall in fourth grade hearing, "Open your readers to page ninety-eight, but I'm sure Jess has already been there." My teacher also got very upset when I wanted to check out junior-high books that I "couldn't possibly read." (What did she think I was doing with them?) I remember taking home *Moby Dick* and how mad she got about two weeks later when I told her all about it.

A lot of kids read in the 1960s before computers and video games, so I wasn't very unusual: I just didn't want books with duckies and bunnies. It also upset my teachers a lot when I asked why there weren't any black kids' books in a school where most of the students were black.

You might think school was easy for me, but my grades were never impressive. If I turned in a well-written book report, I was always accused of copying. The same thing happened with story assignments—I must have stolen something. The best part of school was getting out, when me and the homies would strip off our shirts, mount up our skateboards and ride.

But, things were changing around us, and now you could almost smell the smoke and sometimes hear the sounds of battle as people began to stand up for their rights and question the powers oppressing them. All across America, long-haired kids in leather and beads were marching against the Vietnam War. College students in neighboring Berkeley began holding rallies for freedom and peace, but cops attacked them with tear gas and clubs. This was something we'd never seen; police assaulting and beating white people as brutally as they treated us.

In January of 1967 the Black Panther Party was born: Huey Newton and Bobby Seale opened their Oakland

Jess with cargo airplanes in the Caribbean, 1979

headquarters where education meant liberation. Peaceful protest had not been effective in winning black people their civil rights, and the Panthers believed we had to fight against the powers oppressing us. We began seeing young black men in the streets who were dressed like soldiers we saw on TV; but these young warriors were fighting for us. Black kids now had strong role-models, men who were out there changing things instead of just talking about them. Boys were recruited to pass out leaflets describing the Party's agenda and goals. The Panthers started a free breakfast program so kids could eat before going to school. Grocery stores and neighborhood markets were asked to donate food and clothes. Something good was going on, and we wanted a part of it. There didn't seem like a lot we could do at the ages of eight and nine, but we tried to help whenever we could by running errands or messages. Across the Bay in San Francisco the hippies were having their "summer of love," but here we had a war to fight.

Our hair was bushy and wild anyway, but now we let it grow longer. At first these styles were "naturals," though soon they became known as "Afros." Wearing your hair in an African way proved that you were proud of your ancestry and were fighting to build a better world for all the people in it. My own hair was only a little bit curly, but Mrs. Hawker gave me a perm (a nasty ordeal to suffer through) which showed where I stood in this battle.

The Panthers often followed police to watch what they did in our neighborhoods, so we started tailing them too. Naturally, they hated that—having observers to see what they did—and threatened or tried to scare us away. Sometimes they pointed their guns at us, or drew their clubs and chased us. We were hard to catch on skate boards, and that only made them madder. At eight years old I was beaten by cops, slammed on the sidewalk, kicked and clubbed, because I wouldn't go away when I saw them attacking an older boy. I wore my bruises like medals of honor; they showed that I knew what it meant to be black in the "Land of the Free and the Home of the Brave." These beatings began to happen more often—the cops wouldn't tolerate being watched or having their authority questioned. In February of 1968, the police declared war on the Panthers. In March, the F.B.I. joined in. The Panthers were getting too powerful: many black people were being inspired to stand up and fight for their rights. Anyone who looked like a Panther was questioned and often assaulted by cops; and this included any young kids suspected of helping or working with them. Jerry was beaten several times, and even Donny was kicked and clubbed.

On April 4th of 1968, Dr. Martin Luther King, Jr., was killed in Memphis, Tennessee—shot while giving a speech for peace. The government prepared for riots: it feared the Panthers more than ever, afraid our people would rally behind them and stage an armed revolt. Two days later, on April 6, the Oakland police attacked two Panthers, Eldridge Cleaver and Bobby Hutton. Little Bobby was seventeen. After wounding and capturing Eldridge Cleaver, the cops told Bobby to run away, then opened fire and murdered him.

The Panthers were hunted constantly now, and the organization began to crumble. The men we admired were being killed and the System was beating us down again. But, the Panthers survived for several more years, doing many good things for the neighborhood. Besides the

breakfasts for children each day, the Panthers set up free health clinics, gave shoes and clothing to needy kids, and free transportation to elderly people for shopping or seeing their doctors. The Panthers still exist today and publish a small community paper; but for me, Donny, Jerry and Rick, they died that night with Little Bobby, and so did a lot of our dreams.

I was thirteen in 1973, and had grown to a lanky, big-footed boy. I still had a bit of my little-kid tummy, but gone was the comical basketball. Donny now weighed about 300 pounds but skated as much as ever. Jerry was tall and beautifully muscled; but Rick had moved away that summer and things just weren't the same. The Vietnam War was almost over and so, it seemed, was our own. The 1960s had been a battle, but blacks had won many victories—at least on paper we now had rights. The hippies were rapidly vanishing too: we heard they were going to live on farms. A lot of young people still wore long hair, though now it was only a popular style and didn't stand for anything. But, there was something new in our 'hood—a virtual tidal wave of drugs.

Of course, there had always been things like that, especially during the 1960s, though our little gang had grown up drinking beer, which had been enough of a high for us: but now it was like an epidemic of drugs, addiction and rising crime. Some black leaders said it was government-sponsored—pouring in drugs to bring us down—but whether or not that was actually true, our people were turning against each other and neighborhood crime was increasing.

My dad began talking of moving away. He'd surrendered his dream of going to sea, but developed an interest in Arizona, which may have been sparked by our crossing the desert back in 1960. We still had our trusty old Reo truck: my father had rebuilt its engine twice and taught me how to drive. We now ran our own little family business, collecting scrap metal and cleaning up yards, which kept me strong and darkly tanned: but my father had read of abandoned mines in the wide-open desert around Tucson. There were tons of metal and worn-out equipment just laying around for the taking. He'd even checked up on a foundry in Phoenix that paid good prices for salvage iron and contracted people to haul it. But, I wasn't sure if I wanted to move: I'd spent my whole life in the neighborhood, and I didn't like leaving my friends.

Rick was already gone by then: his parents had wanted him out of the city, away from this plague of drugs and crime. My dad was also concerned about this; but there was another complication—I had a girlfriend. Her name was Markita, a beautiful, ebony, tomboyish girl whom I had met in seventh grade. She liked wearing Levis and tattered T-shirts, and I introduced her to skating. Even cooler from my point of view, she loved our truck, admired my driving and liked to go fishing down at the wharf. She often seemed more like a friend than a girl, though she certainly *looked* like a girl at thirteen, finely full-figured and charmingly cute.

Seventh grade had been hard for me; not the work but the atmosphere. In the real world I was doing a job, driving a truck and earning my money. I felt like a man in all respects, and yet at school I was only a child, forced to follow ridiculous rules and learn what it thought was best for me in a system I couldn't relate to. My grades were

"Chillin' with friends on the famous couch, 1988"

barely better than "Cs", though I did get an "A" in English class for writing a few short stories. But, school seemed stupid and boring to me. I could add, subtract, multiply, and divide. I could read a lot better than many adults and probably write better too. So, what was the point in going?

My father had only completed sixth grade, and now he ran his own business. We had never been rich but were seldom poor, and I thought he'd done all right for himself, so why should I try doing anything more? Naturally, we talked about this; he wanted me to stay in school and at least get my eighth grade diploma. We finally made an agreement: if I would go on and complete junior-high, then he would wait for my graduation to make the Arizona move.

Eighth grade turned out worse than seventh. We got a new crop of teachers that year, mostly young, completely clueless, but brimming with brand new ideas. Instead of being "rebellious," I now had a short attention span and was placed in "special education." Many kids there had learning problems: I'm sure I could have gotten straight "A's," but what was the point in trying to prove that I could do better than them? I often brought a book to class and secretly read while "studying." Each day was like prison sentence: the final bell was like parole, releasing me into the real world where people did things that mattered.

At the end of November Jerry was killed, shot in the back like Bobby Hutton for "running away" from a cop. Most of the details were never released and, of course, the cop was never punished. Apparently, a store had been robbed and the thief was a "young black male." Everyone knew it wasn't Jerry: he'd been a brave and adventurous boy who swore and spit and smoked cigarettes, but he'd never stolen a thing in his life, not even a Zero bar. (You would have probably run away too if you knew you'd get beaten and clubbed.) The day of his funeral was sunny and warm, but I thought it should have been raining. I dropped a handful of dirt on his coffin and said I would never forget him.

I took Jerry's death as a sign; a sign that school was a nowhere place and I was a fool to keep going. Jerry had been an excellent student, but what good were "As" and "Bs" (I thought) in a world where you could be murdered for nothing except the shade of your skin? Jerry was buried that sunny Sunday, and I never went back to school.

Of course, my dad was unhappy with that and tried his best to change my mind, but I wasn't having any. I started working with him full time, collecting scrap metal and loading the truck. I pushed myself as hard as I could, lifting things too heavy for me, cutting my hands on jagged junk, but trying to heal the empty place that Jerry's life had filled. Markita and Donny missed him too: we spent many evenings down at the wharf recalling our times together.

My father gave me space to mourn, but he was also a practical man and pointed out that now it was winter, the best time of year for a desert move. I told him I wasn't going. I'd already lost two lifelong friends and didn't want to leave the others. And, why would I want to live in the desert; a barren waste (or so I imagined) with nothing but sand and rattlesnakes? My feet had been toughened on city streets, on broken glass and rusty nails: I'd seen a dream die and my friend had been killed, so, what was the use of adventure (I thought), of going new places and seeing new things? I doubt if I was that poetic, but my father seemed to understand. I remember he said to let Jerry go, release his spirit to leave this place for something new and better, but I didn't know what he meant.

It's funny what some people want to know, especially when you're supposed to be famous. It's like that question I'm often asked: if growing up was hard for me? Twenty years later in 1993, after selling my third book, *Way Past Cool,* I was interviewed for an article in a San Francisco newspaper. I mentioned a ratty old couch in our house where the neighborhood kids would lounge all day to get off the streets and watch TV, or sometimes simply sleep in peace. The reporter asked where I'd gotten the couch—had I found it, she wanted to know, in a dumpster? A couch wouldn't fit in a dumpster, of course, and anyone raised in a city would know it; and yet she seemed determined to say that I'd salvaged it out of the trash. (It came from the Salvation Army.)

I've noticed since then that a lot of reporters have basically written their "interviews" before they actually meet you, and all they want are a few details to make their fiction seem more on the real. This reporter wanted that couch to make a "human interest story"—not the kids who came to our house because there was nowhere else to go. When the article finally appeared in the paper, it didn't surprise me at all to see that our couch had been "found in a dumpster." The rest of the story was slanted like that—nothing about the homeless kids or how we gave them a place to stay, only that I was "rich and famous" but still salvaged things from the trash.

I guess that doesn't apply to kids.

I was interviewed by a big magazine in 1994. They wanted to know about my life, especially growing up in Oakland. Of course, they wanted the "gritty stuff," the "gangs, guns, drugs and violence." They didn't care about skateboarding stories or how I'd admired the Panthers, and they didn't want any positive things like having a happy childhood. I mentioned I'd been a "bodyguard" to a neighborhood kid who sold pot. My "job" consisted of counting money, making change and occasional threats, and packing a rusty old .45 while watching the other kid's back. Naturally, the reporter loved this—another "couch in a dumpster" story—and when he wrote his piece he didn't explain that my life of crime had only lasted about two months in the winter of 1973. Nor did he say I was only thirteen and my "boss" was about a year older. I was now a "drug-dealer's bodyguard," so I fit his conception of young black males to make a "realistic" story.

In December of 1973, my dad packed up and left for Tucson, while I stayed behind to figure things out. I still had a room in our landlady's house—no point in keeping the whole apartment—which cost me a hundred dollars a month and included her wonderful cooking. My father had found me a wrecking yard job, which paid around fifty dollars a week. My "drug-dealing" got me about thirty more, which proved that crime doesn't pay—at least in my case not very much. I was often out on the rainy streets, and sometimes stranded away from home when the busses stopped running at night. I was that boy in the Army jacket, wet and cold with nowhere to sleep and slowly forgetting my dreams. My father was writing to me every week: he'd found a place way out in the desert and was hauling scrap metal to Phoenix. He wanted me to join him, of course, and offered to send me some money, but I was too proud to accept anything. I wanted to make it on my own, though I wasn't sure what "making it" was, or what I really wanted in life. But, tell you the truth, on those rainy nights, a hot sunny desert seemed pretty good.

In March of 1974, I found that I'd soon be a father myself: Markita and I would be having a child. There weren't many options back in those days, but we decided we wanted this life and to spend our own together. In April I bought two Greyhound tickets and said goodbye to Mrs. Hawker. Markita and I were both fourteen when we set out for Tucson, Arizona.

That part of my life was a healing experience: the desert was far from desolate, a stony land of grays and browns yet filled with a colorful life of its own. There were coyotes, of course, clever and quick, and as lean and wiry as Rick had been. There were lizards, snakes and horned-toads, tortoises and scorpions. There were wild pigs called Javalinas, hawks that soared in the clear blue sky, and buzzards that seemed to float in the air without ever flapping their wings. Naturally, there were lots of cactus, standing like dancers with upraised arms in various poses beneath the sun. There were little trees called Palo Verdes because their bark is emerald green, and tumbleweeds that rolled about to scatter their seeds in the wind.

We lived in a ramshackle tin-roofed house which had once been a copper mine office. The place was thirty miles from town, with no running water or power. I learned what being "quiet" was like, and how free it felt to step out the door and see for miles in every direction. At night we could hear only silence and coyotes. I learned many things in those desert years—a lot of new survival skills, and that life could be sweet without money and "things." Of course, a *little* money is nice, and we made enough hauling scrap.

In August of 1974, President Nixon resigned in disgrace. He'd kept the Vietnam War going on, and had been behind the policies causing civil unrest in America, including the war on the Black Panther Party. I wasn't sorry to see him go: in a way it was like a victory that my generation had finally won. In September of 1974, Markita gave birth to our first son. We named him Jeremy after our friend. He, too, was a brave and adventurous boy. Two more sons and a daughter would follow—Weylen, Keeja and Shara. Jeremy was "born with muscles," while Weylen seemed to take after Donny, cheerful, cute, and fantastically fat. Shara displayed a love for all creatures—including rats and rattlesnakes—and Keeja was always a dreamy boy who would sit in the shade reading books all day if there was nothing else to do. Of course, we encouraged them all to read, and their grandfather helped with that.

In April of 1975, the Vietnam War was officially over; a war that had never been declared, and a war America had finally lost, costing billions of dollars and thousands of lives, while back in my West Oakland neighborhood there were children who went to bed hungry at night and some with out any beds at all. I was fifteen in 1975, and it seemed that war had been going on for as long as I could remember. A smaller war *had* been declared back in the 1960s: it was called "The War On Poverty," and wouldn't have cost a lot to win, but it seemed as if the United States had given it up without a fight.

Our kids grew up wild and free in the desert, usually wearing next to nothing and often even less. There were mines to explore and a Jeep to drive as soon as their feet could reach the pedals. They were always finding desert treasures and hauling them back to the house—rusty lanterns, miner's lamps, ancient tools and pretty things like bottles turned blue in the sun. City folks collected this stuff so we took it to antique shops in town. They also wanted old mine carts, which people used for flower planters or placed in yards for decoration, so I started going down deep in the mines and salvaging whatever I could. It wasn't the safest thing to do; there was always the chance of a shaft caving in, and rattlesnakes were abundant. I remember one day when my light went out and I heard a rattlesnake buzz in the dark. It's one of the scariest sounds in the world.

The 1970s and 1980s were years of adventure and travel for me. With four growing children to feed and bring up (clothes were not a priority) I started taking different jobs to make a little more money. I learned to drive a semi-truck and hauled scrap iron for companies in Arizona, New Mexico, Utah, and Nevada. It was cool to travel and see new places while getting paid to drive. I also learned about diesel engines and how to operate heavy equipment like cranes, bulldozers, and quarry trucks. I learned how to weld and make repairs and became a good mechanic. I spent one summer up in Alaska as an engineer on a tugboat. We sailed past beautiful glittering glaciers and towering mountains with forested slopes. The water up there is a clear emerald green; and we often dodged icebergs known as "growlers," a sound they make in the lapping waves. The following year I worked on a freighter that struck a reef and sank—which might be a story all by itself. I also worked on cargo planes that carried Alaskan salmon in summer and then flew south like birds in winter to islands in the Caribbean. It might sound a little bit funny to you, but these airplanes often carried cement, a valuable thing in parts of this world; and sometimes they were loaded with lumber, exotic hardwoods for boat-building shops and the furniture-making industry.

Of course, these jobs kept me far from home, so I missed Markita and seeing our kids, but my father watched over and cared for them. These jobs paid well, being hazardous work with long and often exhausting hours.

You won't find the men I worked for in cities: most of them hated "civilization" and did their best to avoid it. Their lives were hard and dangerous, but they were mostly kind-hearted folks who'd developed a rugged sense of humor from all that life had thrown at them. I recall the Alaskan freighter captain after our ship hit the reef: I was working down in the engine room and was suddenly up to my waist in water! There was no way our pumps could handle all that, so I dashed up and told him the ship was sinking. "Well," he said, without batting an eye. "I guess we don t have time for supper." There were four other crewmen aboard the ship, and we spent a day in our little lifeboat while the captain kept us entertained by telling dirty jokes.

Then there was the airplane pilot who owned an ancient C-47. We were flying into a muddy airstrip to pick up a cargo of salmon, but a gust of wind hit the plane as we landed, slamming it sideways and off the runway so one of its wheels dropped into a ditch. The pilot throttled up the engines and got us back up in the air again, then circled around for another approach. I was "warming" the co-pilot's seat, and he told me to look out my right side window and see if the landing gear was still down. I did and it was. Then I asked about the gear on his side, the one that had dropped in the ditch. "Yep," he said, "It's down all right ... but there ain't no wheel on it now."

He brought us in for an expert landing on just the tail and right side wheels, dragging the left side gear through the mud, which spun us around like a top. "Not one of my best," he said when we stopped. "I guess we'd better go have us a beer, then figure out how to fix this thing before those fish begin to stink." We worked all night to install a "new" wheel, which came off an old Army truck.

The world might be a better place with a lot more people like him around who fix their problems, don't complain, and always find something to laugh about.

In the spring of 1987, Markita found out that her mother was ill and needed a lot of care at home, so we decided to move back to Oakland. We had some money put away, and our kids were eager to see the place where their mom and dad had grown up. Jeremy was thirteen then, a strong and lanky muscular boy with graceful hands and puppy feet. Weylen, twelve, was 200 pounds of rolly-poly chocolate-chub whose jeans would never stay on. Shara, ten, was as bold as her brothers and dressed about the same, while Keeja, nine, still loved his books and collected *Elfquest* comics. I'd kept in touch with Mrs. Hawker, writing at least a letter each month and often talking with her on the phone. She was in her eighties now, but still drove her car—a Studebaker—and lived in her old "haunted mansion." Our kids considered her "great-grandmom" although they'd never met her. She'd stopped renting rooms a few years before, but offered to let us move into her house for a very low rent plus "maintenance." It surely needed a lot of that, and the yard was a blackberry jungle.

There's a famous quote from Thomas Wolf that says "You can't go home again," and I'll leave it to you to decide what it means. My neighborhood had changed a lot, and the "Hawker Mansion" seemed to have shrunk to a modest and shabby Victorian house, still badly in need of a new coat of paint. Gone were most of the wrecking yards, though trucks still rumbled along the streets and freight trains clattered and clanked. A Korean family now owned the market. They were friendly, honest people but suffered a lot of disrespect for "coming in and taking over"—a concept I've never understood. The air was a little bit cleaner now, but everything I remembered was old.

Except for something called crack.

My first four books, *Rats in the Trees, Children of The Night, Way Past Cool,* and *Six Out Seven,* were all about kids who sold and used crack. Black leaders back in the 1970s had suspected that drugs were part of a plan to divide

The author in Marcus Books, Oakland, 1992

our people and hold them down, to keep us from getting together again the way we'd supported the Panthers: but, whether or not this was actually true, crack seemed custom-designed for kids, available cheap, and highly addictive. Once you got hooked you just wanted more and would do anything to get it. I'm not trying to say I believe in a "plan"; but looking around in the late 1980s, seeing kids as young as eight robbing, stealing, or begging for money, money to score them a bag of crack while throwing away their childhoods, I found it difficult not to believe. "Plan" or not, something was wrong: a lot of black kids felt no purpose in life. Few dared to dream of escaping the city or having adventures all over the world. Neighborhood gangs were packing steel and killing each other for childish things, like clothes and shoes or cheap bandanas. Even the music now carried a message to grab what you could in the inner city, to fight with, rob and kill each other because you were black and the world didn't care. To be a "gangstuh" was way past cool—as many rappers were saying. Black kids said what they "couldn't do" instead of what they wanted to do, as if some power had filled their minds with only negative things. They didn't dream of becoming ship captains, airplane pilots, or even truck drivers, and most didn't think about leaving the city or building a life in a better place.

Our own kids were stunned and confused by all this; but we'd brought them up like my father raised me—never talking down to them and respecting their words and ideas. They knew they were all entitled to dreams, and though some of those dreams might be harder for black kids, they'd work and fight to make them come true. Drugs are like substitutes for dreams, so maybe that's why our kids didn't want them.

Of course, most kids were not doing drugs—it only seemed like that sometimes—and our own began to make new friends, bringing them home to watch TV, stay for supper and spend the night. They told their new homies

about the desert, of driving our Jeep, exploring old mines, and dealing with snakes and scorpions. I often heard the other kids say that they "didn't know black kids could do those things." I wondered who had told them that, put limits upon their imaginations and walls around their hopes and dreams—the TV, movies, hip-hop music? I pictured myself as a space alien, orbiting high above the earth and trying to learn about young black people from what I saw on television or heard on the radio waves. I would probably think they all carried guns, lived in a ghetto, hated each other, and only dreamed of expensive cars, the latest clothes, and lots of money.

We still had some savings put away, so I didn't have to go right to work. I'd been working since I'd been eight years old when I'd helped my dad in the wrecking yard, and felt that now, at age twenty-seven, I'd earned a little vacation time. Donny and I had kept in touch—unlike me, he had finished high school and taken a few college courses. He had always been a cartoon artist (long before the days of tagging) and dreamed of drawing black cartoons with a positive lean for kids. He was working then at a children's center, a small and privately funded place. He was just as fat and cheerful as ever, and often drew cartoons of the kids.

I began coming in to read to the kids and encouraging them to read for themselves, but I found there weren't a lot of books that black kids could relate to, so I bought an ancient typewriter and started writing stories for them.

The first of these was called "The Ship", which would later be used in *Rats in the Trees*. There were ten of these tales, interrelated, about a gang called "The Animals." They were wily boys of thirteen and fourteen who rode battered skateboards and fought to stay free in a dirty world of drugs and guns.

These stories seemed very popular, and the kids were always improving on them while wanting to know what happened next. Donny did a few cartoons to illustrate the various tales, then brought me a copy of *Writer's Market,* a directory of publishers. I hadn't thought about selling my stories, but I sent "The Ship" to a small magazine across the bay in San Francisco. The editor rejected it but wanted to see another. I sent him "One Way," my second story, and was paid $300.00.

Was I onto something here, I wondered, or had it just been luck? I sent out "The Ship" again, and this time a magazine bought it. Within a few months I'd sold three stories. Then I sold the whole collection, and *Rats in the Trees* became a book. It was out on the shelves in 1990, and even won an award.

This seemed like a cool way to make a living—better than hauling scrap anyhow—so I wrote the novel, *Children of the Night,* published in 1991. Following that was *Way Past Cool.* It told about life for kids in the 'hood—the "guns, gangs, drugs and violence"—but really of kids only wanting to dream and live their childhoods peacefully. The book became a small success. It was published in 1992 and was also sold around the world in seven other languages. Disney Studios optioned the rights to possibly make a movie. Suddenly, I was "rich and famous": magazines wanted to interview me and I went on TV several times.

My fourth book, *Six Out Seven,* was about a Mississippi boy who runs away to Oakland. It was published in 1993, and took a slightly different approach to the problems faced by young black kids: instead of just showing them trapped in the cities, surrounded by violence, drugs and gangs, it searched for the reasons behind their plight—who had stolen away their dreams, who was bringing in the drugs, encouraging them to fight each other and telling them they had no hope?

I learned something then about writing black books; that publishers hate being questioned or challenged as much as the cops in our neighborhood. They only want the stereotypes when it comes to stories of young black men, and like those cops they'll beat you down if you criticize or question them. As long as my characters stayed in the ghetto and acted like publishers thought they should, my books would sell (so the editors said). But, if kids began to question the System—like why they were being miseducated and taught to hate and kill each other ... or, worse, began to *help* each other—then fewer people would buy my books and it would be harder to get them published.

Not only that, but I now I was called a "ghetto writer," and basically told by my editors that this was all I should write about. Here were white people saying to me that black kids shouldn't be given hope, informed they had alternatives, that they could go out and see the world, or read about ghosts and haunted houses.

Nevertheless, I wrote *Ghost Train,* a ghost story set in my neighborhood. It was published in 1995 and did pretty well for a "young adult" book, though a critic complained that it "mentioned a lot of social issues"—as if kids weren't supposed be told about things like homelessness and poverty!

I followed *Ghost Train* with *Babylon Boyz* in 1997. The characters in this book had dreams, but were seemingly trapped in the inner city by (you guessed it) "guns, gangs, drugs and violence." My editor really liked this book: it was published three times in hardcover format and then again in paperback, and is still selling very well today. But, the next book I wrote, called *Skeleton Key* (another ghost tale), was rejected by my editor. He said it would "feed the stereotypes," and black kids wouldn't read it. This seemed pretty stupid to me—in *Skeleton Key* there's a boy of thirteen whose life has been messed up by drugs. He's also a victim of violence at home. Yet, he manages to solve his problems in tough and realistic ways, but all without resorting to violence, and with the help of a gang-member's ghost. The kids who've read the manuscript seem to love this kind of tale, and yet in the words of the editor, it "feeds the stereotypes!" On the other hand, according to him, a book like *Babylon Boyz*—containing three murders, a brutal beating, guns, drugs and lots of violence—*doesn't* "feed the stereotypes!?!"

I learned this is what black writers face when trying to get their works into print—editors telling us what to write and what they *think* we want to read. Of course, they can't *make* us write what they want, but they simply don't publish any books that go against the stereotypes.

This editor feels insulted by me and won't publish anything else of mine, despite the fact that *Babylon Boyz* is still a pretty good selling book and kids of all colors enjoy it. Think about that for a minute—these are the people who chose the books that American kids are allowed to read.

My seventh book was *Bones Become Flowers.* It's an adventure and set in Haiti. It was published in 1999, and has done pretty well for a small-press book. I've written five more books since then, but none have found a publisher yet. Naturally, there's *Skeleton Key,* along with a book called *Voodu Dawgz,* which is set in mysterious New Orleans and about two boys who use Voodu magic to break up a violent young gang. Another book deals with overweight kids, another is set in the slavery days, and another takes place in Alaska. They're stories I hope might inspire black kids to dream big dreams and have adventures, and so they haven't been published.

Way Past Cool was made into a film, for which I co-wrote the screenplay, though it hasn't been released as yet. There is also a stage production of *Cool,* which is presently looking for funding. I've also written a lot of short stories, a stage play based on *Skeleton Key,* and a screenplay based on *Babylon Boyz.*

So that's how I've spent my vacation time since 1987.

Mrs. Hawker passed away in 1997. Her own grandmother had been a slave. My father still lives in Arizona and works as hard as ever. Markita is traveling in Africa now, a land she always wanted to see. Our children, all in their twenties today, completed high school and went on to adventures—Jeremy works in Haiti with kids, and Weylen is down in Louisiana, living aboard a houseboat. Shara is now a seventh-grade teacher, while Keeja has gotten his pilot's license and hopes to buy his own cargo plane. To me, this is proof of what can happen when children have dreams and books to read that open whole new worlds for them.

I still work with kids here in Oakland, and mentor a lot of young writers: one, Apollo, sold his first book at the age of only fourteen. I usually write every day myself—or actually late at night, like now. It's raining again I as finish this piece, a soothing, sleepy and shivery sound. A few hours ago, around four o'clock, I heard a shy knock at my door. There was a soaking-wet boy in a hoodie, who's now warm and dry, asleep on a cot, with the patter of rain for a lullaby.

I hope he's dreaming big dreams.

N

NANJI, Shenaaz 1954-

Personal

Born October 8, 1954, in Mombasa, Kenya; immigrated to Canada, 1981; daughter of Kasamally (a business man) and Roshan (a homemaker; maiden name, Mangalji) Zaver; married G. Mohamed Nanji (an anesthesiologist), October 8, 1977; children: Hussein, Shaira. *Education:* University of Nairobi (Kenya), B. Comm., 1976. *Religion:* Islam. *Hobbies and other interests:* Swimming, traveling, reading, daydreaming.

Addresses

Home—121 Patton Ct., Calgary, Alberta T2V 5G3, Canada. *E-mail*—s.nanji@home.com.

Career

Worked variously in computer programming and business administration. *Member:* Canadian Society of Authors, Illustrators, and Performers, Writers Union, Young Alberta Book Society, Canadian Children's Book Centre.

Awards, Honors

Brendon Donelly Children's Literature Award runner up, for *The Old Fisherman of Lamu,* 1994; Sunshine Sketches Award for Humor, Calgary Writers Association, 1996; First Novel Groundwood Books Twentieth Anniversary Contest, finalist, 1998.

Writings

Teeny Weeny Penny, illustrated by Rossitza Skortcheva Penney, TSAR Publications (Toronto, Canada), 1993.
Grandma's Heart, illustrated by Rossitza Skortcheva Penney, TSAR Publications (Toronto, Canada), 1993.
The Old Fisherman of Lamu, illustrated by Shahd Shaker, TSAR Publications (Toronto, Canada), 1995.

Shenaaz Nanji

Treasure for Lunch, illustrated by Yvonne Cathcart, Second Story Press (Toronto, Canada), 2000.

Work in Progress

Child of Dandelions, a young adult novel.

Sidelights

A cultural hybrid, Shenaaz Nanji lists African, Indian, and Canadian as her heritages. Thus it is not surprising that she should be the author of multicultural picture books, including *Teeny Weeny Penny, Grandma's Heart,* and *Treasure for Lunch,* which all feature Shaira, a young girl of Indian background. In the first-named book, Shaira finds a penny, claims it to be her lucky penny, and must decide despite the advice of others what to do with it. In *Grandma's Heart,* the young girl wonders if her Nani-ma's heart will be big enough to love all the members of the family, especially her. Reviewing *Teeny Weeny Penny* and *Grandma's Heart* for *Canadian Children's Literature,* Kerry Vincent noted the author's accurate portrayal of a child at a certain level of emotional development. Moreover, he found that "Nanji's books celebrate the family and the individual" and called them "welcome affirmations of basic values." "These picture books should engage young readers," predicted *Quill and Quire* contributor Fred Boer.

Lunch time at school can be a challenge, especially if a child's lunch seems strange to peers. In her picture book *Treasure for Lunch,* Nanji depicts Shaira's feelings about the school lunches of Indian food that her grandmother prepares for her. It is winter, and Shaira, rather than face ridicule, secretively buries her lunches in a snowbank on the playground. Eventually she is found out, however, and to her delight, her classmates find her lunches fascinating and want to try her ethnic food. In the view of Eva Wilson of *Resource Links, Treasure for Lunch* is "a timely and overdue book" that could lend itself to many applications in the classroom.

Nanji told *SATA:* "One fine day I found myself shipwrecked on a desolate island afflicted by the writer's bug. Over the years, I find myself still learning different strokes of this craft. I am a cultural hybrid sculpted and influenced by the three cultures that I grew up in—East Indian, African, and Canadian/American. I write multi-cultural stories about celebrating one's heritage. Today with shrinking geographical boundaries, the world seems to be a pot of melting cultures. I hope my stories will break cultural barriers and make people of different cultures understand each other.

"Writing for me is therapy and a process of self-discovery. I think of the strengths and weaknesses of my characters and it makes me reflect on my own. More and more, I see myself objectively as another person, an explorer, discovering truths about myself in this great 'safari' of writing."

Biographical and Critical Sources

PERIODICALS

Books in Canada, May, 1994, Phil Hall, review of *Teeny Weeny Penny,* pp. 57-58.

Canadian Children's Literature, spring, 1996, Kerry Vincent, reviews of *Teeny Weeny Penny* and *Grandma's Treasure,* pp. 44-45.

Quill and Quire, March, 1994, Fred Boer, reviews of *Teeny Weeny Penny* and *Grandma's Treasure,* p. 82.

Resource Links, April, 2001, Eva Wilson, review of *Treasure for Lunch,* p. 6.

School Library Journal, May, 2001, Bina Williams, review of *Treasure for Lunch,* p. 130.

*   *   *

NEUFELD, John (Arthur) 1938-
(Joan Lea)

Personal

Born December 14, 1938, in Chicago, IL; son of Leonard Carl (a manufacturer) and Rhoda (Padway) Neufeld. *Education:* Yale University, B.A., 1960.

Addresses

Agent—c/o Phyllis Fogelman Books, an imprint of Penguin Putnam Books for Young Readers, 345 Hudson St., New York, NY 10014.

Career

Editor, teacher, television scriptwriter, and author. Worked in New York, NY, for various publishing companies, 1962-69, including as an advertising copy writer for Harcourt, Brace, and World, as a publicist for Franklin Watts, George Braziller, McGraw-Hill, and Holt, Rinehart, & Winston, and as an editor for Western Publishing Company; taught English in a Los Angeles, CA, private school. *Military service:* U.S. Army, 1961-62.

Awards, Honors

Book of the Year citation, *Time* magazine, 1968, for *Edgar Allan;* Best Book of the Year citations, children's division, *New York Times,* and Notable Book citations, American Library Association, 1968, for *Edgar Allan,* and 1969, for *Lisa, Bright and Dark;* YASLA Quick Pick and New York Public Library's list of best books for young adults, 1999, for *Boys Lie;* MacDowell Colony fellowship.

Writings

Edgar Allan, S. G. Phillips (New York, NY), 1968.

Lisa, Bright and Dark, S. G. Phillips (New York, NY), 1969, Puffin Books (New York, NY), 1999.

Touching, S. G. Phillips (New York, NY), 1970, published as *Twink,* New American Library (New York, NY), 1971.

Sleep Two, Three, Four!, Harper (New York, NY), 1971.

You Think I'd Go around Making These Things Up?, Random House (New York, NY), 1973.

For All the Wrong Reasons, Norton (New York, NY), 1973.

Freddy's Book, Random House (New York, NY), 1973.

Sunday Father, New American Library (New York, NY), 1975.

(Under pseudonym Joan Lea) *Trading Up,* Atheneum (New York, NY), 1975.

The Fun of It, Putnam (New York, NY), 1977.

A Small Civil War, Fawcett/Ballantine (New York, NY), 1982.

Sharelle, New American Library (New York, NY), 1983.

Rolling the Stone, New American Library (New York, NY), 1984.

Family Fortunes, Atheneum (New York, NY), 1988.

Almost a Hero, Atheneum (New York, NY), 1995.

Gaps in Stone Walls, Atheneum (New York, NY), 1996.

Boys Lie, DK Ink/Jackson (New York, NY), 1999.

The Handle and the Key, Phyllis Fogelman Books (New York, NY), 2002.

OTHER

Lisa, Bright and Dark (teleplay; *Hallmark Hall of Fame* presentation), NBC-TV, 1973.

Death Sentence (teleplay), ABC-TV, 1974.

You Lie So Deep My Love (teleplay), ABC-TV, 1975.

Contributor of book reviews to national publications, including the *New York Times.*

Adaptations

Edgar Allan, Freddy's Book, For All the Wrong Reasons, The Fun of It, A Small Civil War, and *Sharelle* have all been optioned for television.

Sidelights

In his books for both young people and adults, John Neufeld tackles difficult issues with insight, humor, and strongly realized characters. Whether writing about mental illness, political oppression, prejudice, or teen pregnancy, Neufeld strives for honesty in his depictions. Many of his works feature young protagonists whose perceptiveness and capability are in sharp contrast to the general ineffectiveness of the adults around them. "I hadn't planned to write for children, or young adults," Neufeld admitted in an essay for *Something about the Author Autobiography Series* (*SAAS*). "The things that interest me are ideas and problems that face us all, but which we often face first when we're young. If writing about how imaginary young people meet and overcome certain problems helps real young people when *they* meet the same problems, then I was doing something useful as well as fun."

Born in Chicago and raised in Des Moines, Iowa, Neufeld had a childhood guaranteed to make, if not a writer, at least an avid reader. Neufeld's early interest in books was fostered by his mother, a former English teacher who encouraged her three children to read many types of literature. Neufeld told *SAAS:* "I was encouraged to read anything I could find in our house. There were worlds to choose. Classics; current best-sellers; series adventures suitable for boys; collections of plays (Ibsen, Coward, Maugham, Shaw); children's books." While still in junior high school, Neufeld began to write stories modeled on those he read in magazines such as the *Saturday Evening Post.* None of the stories sold,

however, and Neufeld soon became too busy with other things to write for pleasure.

By the time he reached Phillips Exeter, a prep school in New Hampshire, his writing had become confined to assignments, though his world of reading was growing to include such literary greats as Ernest Hemingway, Leo Tolstoy, Albert Camus, and Federico Garcia Lorca. From Exeter, Neufeld went on to Yale. "I did generally well in university, especially in English courses," Neufeld once recalled. "It was there I took my first creative writing course, and I began to think of myself as a writer—but one who would never be stuck in a groove. I would do one of each genre: novel, play, screenplay." After college, Neufeld went on an extended tour of England. Upon his return, he was drafted into the Army for a six-month tour of duty at Fort Leonard, Missouri. "I was assigned (no doubt only on the basis of my Yale diploma) to teach English to men who were to become clerk-typists for the Army. I liked the Army. (I seemed to have liked just about everything in those days.) I liked the food; I liked the people who served with me . . . and I was proud as hell to have weathered basic training as well as I did," Neufeld related in his essay.

Upon his release from the Army, Neufeld began to think seriously about his future plans. "It was time to grow up," he disclosed. "I had to find a job somewhere, doing something." Because he loved reading and writing, Neufeld decided that publishing was a good career choice. He spent three months looking for a job in New York and Boston. Eventually, Neufeld found work as an advertising copy editor. "I was fired from my first job as an advertising copy writer for Harcourt," Neufeld recalled, "largely because I was spending too much time writing my own plays and short stories on company time." From there he took a series of jobs in publicity and promotion for various publishers, experience that would later help him publish his own first juvenile novels because he had established links with book-buying committees and school libraries throughout the country. When not at work, Neufeld wrote television dramas (all unproduced), one-act plays, and a "terrible novel." He wrote in *SAAS:* "I was not unhappy. I *was* writing. I enjoyed it. I now know I was practicing, learning, copying, editing, and exploring. Of course I had no assurance that all this would . . . make me any better than I had been, but I had hope."

Neufeld's first novel, *Edgar Allan,* was inspired by a true story. "An editor for a small California publishing house . . . had a story she thought I could write and write well," he noted. "She told me the bare bones story of a family that had adopted a black child and, because of community pressures and their own fears, gave him up." While interested in the story, Neufeld did not want to use newspaper accounts. "I wanted the story to be my own. . . . I wanted to concentrate on the children in the family, the white children, and I wanted complete freedom to make them whatever I could," he wrote in *SAAS.* Thus was born Neufeld's first novel, *Edgar Allan,* a book that deals with racial issues in an uncompromising manner. Not originally intended as a juvenile title, the book was soon seen as such by editors who wanted the author to expand on the topic. Neufeld, however, disagreed with their recommendations to write a longer book. "I thought then, and do so now, that it is terrifically important for young people to be able to start and finish a book in a couple of sittings. That the book be small enough yet filled with enough ideas and emotion that they learn they can read and enjoy the act of reading."

Critical response to *Edgar Allan* was generally favorable. Richard Horchler, writing in the *New York Times Book Review,* called the novel "a serious work of art . . . about what it means to be human." He added: "Better than easy answers, *Edgar Allan* offers an experience in the growth of compassion and understanding." "This book about a family on trial is one to save and share and perhaps to discuss; certainly its reflection of reality will be noted and praised by the young people who read it," lauded Jean C. Thompson in *School Library Journal.* And Virginia Haviland praised the novel in *Horn Book,* noting that "issues and relationships more complex than those commonly found in literature for young readers are presented in depth and with conviction." Earning a spot on two "best books of the year" lists, Neufeld's premier work was a success that won him a place in the world of juvenile literature, and his second novel, *Lisa, Bright and Dark,* secured his position as a writer unafraid of dealing with strong issues.

The result of a dinner conversation with a New York psychiatrist who related the story of a young patient who was descending into madness, *Lisa, Bright and Dark* was another profound story for Neufeld. "Again, I instinctively knew I had an important story in Lisa," the author once commented. "I wrote the first draft in a very short time, but the publisher was a bit more nervous with this one. This was the first time in children's literature that mental health was being addressed, and the first time that almost all the adults came off looking shoddy. Nobody got off the hook." The story tells of a teenage girl who is losing her mind and realizes it, but whose parents refuse to recognize the problem. In the end, Lisa's only hope for help lies with three close friends—compassionate Betsy, uptight Mary Nell, and former psychiatric patient Elizabeth. Sada Fretz, writing in *School Library Journal,* termed the book "superior to most juvenile novels," adding that it is "skillfully constructed and more exciting than Neufeld's previous, highly praised *Edgar Allan.*" In addition to the positive reviews, *Lisa, Bright and Dark* also won a new audience of adults for Neufeld once it was aired as a television special. With the sale of television and film rights to the book, Neufeld was finally able to quit his desk job in New York and devote all his time to writing.

Neufeld moved to England in the late 1960s. While there, he completed a third novel, *Touching,* the story of Harry Walsh and his stepsister, Twink, who suffers from cerebral palsy. "I wrote the book about my own stepsister," Neufeld explained. "It was an attempt to make us all more tolerant and understanding of other persons' limitations." Twink's brave battle with cerebral palsy becomes the focus of her family's world—to the frequent disdain of her very popular stepbrother Harry. Much of the novel addresses Harry's emotional state as he tries to handle the myriad of feelings he has for his embattled sister—disgust, shame, revulsion, and ultimately, love and understanding. For some reviewers the treatment of Twink's ailment was all too realistic and graphic, and they voiced fears about the effect it would have on young readers. But *English Journal* contributor John W. Conner noted the book's "tightly structured style and sparse but brilliant language," and felt that adolescents would be intrigued by the main characters and the story of acceptance. Georgess McHargue, writing in the *New York Times Book Review,* found the book to be "quite effective."

Neufeld turned to politics in *Sleep, Two, Three, Four!,* an Orwellian look at America projected into the future with the villains named: Nixon and company. The story of a group of teenagers who escape their own programming by a totalitarian society and set out to rescue one of their friends from a detention center, the book proved to be Neufeld's first difficult experience. Reviews were lukewarm to savage, and the publisher, Harper and Row, "washed its hands" of the book, according to Neufeld. But the discouragement did not last long. By 1973, Neufeld had two more titles out. The first was *Freddy's Book,* the story of a young boy who tries to track down the meaning of the "F-word," which he has seen scrawled on a wall. "I wanted to do the book," Neufeld once commented, "because there were no other books like it for boys. There was just no place for them to go to learn about sex." Though the word is mentioned only a few times in the text, the publication of the book was still a risky venture, yet it paid off. "This is a charmingly personalized approach to sex education," a critic wrote in *Kirkus Reviews.*

Freddy's Book was followed quickly by *For All the Wrong Reasons,* the story of a teenage girl who becomes pregnant and decides to have the baby. "This was the first of the written-to-order-books that I did," Neufeld said in his interview. "I agreed to write a problem book about teen pregnancy, but I made sure the publishers knew how I would handle it. The girl would know how she got pregnant, she would enjoy sex, and there would be no falling off horses [and losing the baby] to save the day." In 1975, Neufeld's second written-to-order juvenile, *Sunday Father,* appeared. "This is the single book I regret having written," Neufeld recalled in *SAAS.* "It is, I think, my weakest—a mild enough story of a family in mid-divorce and coping therewith." Fourteen-year-old Tessa O'Connell tries to deal with the inevitable dissolution of her family. As her parents fight over the debris of their marriage, the young teen struggles with her own emotional burdens, including the pressure of conflicting loyalties and a sometimes overwhelming sense of loss. Writing in *Wilson Library Bulletin,* Michael McCue and Evie Wilson praised the characterization and "sensitivity" with which Neufeld treated his subject, and thought that the book "should enjoy a wide readership among YAs"—which it did.

By this time, Neufeld was leading a successful writer's life. Several of his novels had been optioned for movies. He was spending more and more time in Los Angeles and wrote an adult title, *Trading Up,* under the pseudonym of Joan Lea, which sold well. There followed another adult title under his own name, a *Love Story* look-alike, the 1978 novel, *The Fun of It.* For the time being, Neufeld seemed to have left the young adult audience behind. "It's usually a social issue that grabs me," Neufeld explained in his interview. "But by the mid-70s I was so stereotyped as that kind of writer, that I just got off the boat. The last straw was a call from a New York editor who wanted me to write to the following formula: a blind Hispanic in Harlem who is raped. Things had gotten out of control. Since the 1970s nothing has *not* been addressed in juvenile and young adult literature, and I need something new to really write meaningfully." A writing hiatus ensued, during which Neufeld enjoyed his success as Joan Lea. "I lived the life of a gentleman of leisure," Neufeld confessed. "My biggest regret about those five years is that I was not being productive."

Then in the early 1980s Neufeld again found themes that grabbed him. *A Small Civil War* looks at the censorship issue through the lens of an Iowa family torn over the issue of banning John Steinbeck's novel *The Grapes of Wrath; Voice of Youth Advocates* critic Mary K. Chelton praised the way the author "eloquently" presents all points of view. A year later, in 1983, Neufeld's *Sharelle* appeared, another book about teen pregnancy, but this time with a new twist. The fourteen-year-old heroine decides that there is more to her life than taking care of a child, no matter how much she loves it. While the novel is "written with candor," a *Bulletin of the Center for Children's Books* reviewer thought that "it is more a message than a narrative." A *Publishers Weekly* writer, however, found *Sharelle* "a profoundly moving story," told "compellingly" so that the reader "cares for the girl and her beloved daughter." In his interview, Neufeld said, "I think that book has more depth than any I've done for young adults."

After *Sharelle* there followed a stint of English instruction at a Los Angeles Catholic school, where he worked harder than he ever had before. "My focus everyday was on 240 children," Neufeld wrote for *SAAS,* "not on myself or my characters or my checkbook." Soon, however, the world of books drew him back. *Family Fortunes,* an adult title, appeared in 1988, and several years were spent on an unsuccessful movie biography which never saw publication. Finally, in the early 1990s, the author stumbled onto a social issue that once again needed to be explored. The writing was spurred on by real-life research, this time in a Santa Barbara, California, day care center for homeless children, where Neufeld worked as a volunteer. What resulted is *Almost a Hero,* a children's book about twelve-year-old Ben Derby, who volunteers in a similar center during his spring break. Returning to the younger audience he reached with *Edgar Allan* and *Freddy's Book,* Neufeld explained in his interview that "I needed to set out in a

new direction. I wanted to have my passport stamped in a different way now, with a mature children's book."

Other mature young adult books followed with *Gaps in Stone Walls* and *Boys Lie. Gaps in Stone Walls* is a historically accurate novel set in 1880 which tells the story of Merry, a deaf twelve-year-old living in a town on Martha's Vineyard. When a man no one in town likes is murdered, Merry is one of four suspects. Afraid of what might happen, she plots to flee the island. Ultimately, the reader discovers who the true murderer is though the characters in the novel do not. The story earned mixed reviews: Shelley Townsend-Hudson wrote in *Booklist,* "The novel excels in its sense of place and strong characterizations, but the story loses power and coherence when it oddly switches focus to the boyfriend of Merry's cousin," while a *Horn Book* reviewer noted that "the conclusion is unsatisfying, but the novel contains some of Neufeld's finest prose."

Boys Lie chronicles the difficulties of Gina, a fourteen-year-old who was assaulted at a public swimming pool by a group of boys. Hoping to put the past behind her, she and her mother move out of state. But when her secret is discovered, the problems begin again with a new set of boys. One of them attempts to rape her, and though she fights him off, he spreads the word that he was successful. Gina finally works up the courage to confront him publicly and turn the tables against him instead. "The story may be issue-heavy," wrote a *Kirkus Reviews* critic, "but everyone displays conflicting emotions, and both good judgment and bad."

Experimentation in life and art is Neufeld's hallmark. In fact, his youthful plan for the types of genres in which he would excel has become a reality for him. He has written at least one of each of an amazing variety of works. "The adult books I need for my ego," he once commented. "I'm an adult: I have adult concerns, and I want to see myself as an adult author as opposed to only a YA author. But the reason I continue to write books for children is simple. I firmly believe that if you put down a credible story about facing a fictional difficulty, and it is read by another person facing a similar *real* difficulty, then that person will be better prepared. You can reach readers at an early age, really move them and inform them. I'm not a do-gooder, but I think it's very important we give young people the tools to cope with the complex problems facing them."

Part of Neufeld's success lies in his understanding of his audience. He told *SAAS:* "Praise and encouragement are very important to any young person facing an obstacle of any sort. But learning to understand the *similarities* between you and other people is desperately important. Its what can pull you down if you let it (it needn't) but it's also what can make your work, as a writer, understandable and enjoyable.... It's what we all have in common—our humanity, our joys, our disappointments." According to the essayist for the *St. James Guide to Young Adult Writers,* "Neufeld creates teenage characters who are perceptive and make decisions to take action. They are willing to learn about and understand situations unfamiliar to them. Neufeld's reputation for portraying teens as more capable of facing complex problems than adults is an appealing affirmation for young adult readers."

Biographical and Critical Sources

BOOKS

Authors and Artists for Young Adults, Volume 11, Gale (Detroit, MI), 1993.
Contemporary Literary Criticism, Volume 27, Gale (Detroit, MI), 1981, pp. 307-311.
St. James Guide to Young Adult Writers, 2nd edition, Gale (Detroit, MI), 1999.
Something about the Author Autobiography Series, Volume 3, Gale (Detroit, MI), 1986, pp. 175-187.

PERIODICALS

Bulletin of the Center for Children's Books, February, 1970, p. 103; March, 1974, p. 116; December, 1983, review of *Sharelle,* p. 74.
English Journal, December, 1970, John W. Connor, review of *Touching,* pp. 1303-1304; February, 1972, John W. Connor, review of *Sleep, Two, Three, Four,* pp. 305-306.
Horn Book, April, 1969, Virginia Haviland, review of *Edgar Allan,* p. 172.
Kirkus Reviews, October 15, 1969, p. 1124; October 15, 1970, p. 1163; August 15, 1971, pp. 882-883; August

1, 1973, review of *Freddy's Book,* p. 817; February 1, 1978.
Library Journal, October 15, 1973.
Los Angeles Times Book Review, December 13, 1987, review of *Family Fortunes,* p. 11.
New York Times Book Review, November 3, 1968, Richard Horchler, "Stories for Ages 9 to 12: *Edgar Allan,*" p. 33; November 11, 1969; November 29, 1970, Georgess McHargue, review of *Touching,* p. 38; February 12, 1972.
Publishers Weekly, June 10, 1983, review of *Sharelle,* p. 64; May 29, 1995, review of *Almost a Hero,* p. 85; April 15, 1996, review of *Gaps in Stone Walls,* p. 69; February 15, 1999, review of *Boys Lie,* p. 108.
School Library Journal, December, 1968, Jean C. Thomson, review of *Edgar Allan,* p. 47; February, 1970, Sada Fretz, review of *Lisa, Bright and Dark,* p. 90; November, 1970, pp. 121-122; September, 1973, p. 98; February, 1974, pp. 21-25; November 15, 1979, Jean C. Thompson, review of *Touching,* p. 47; August, 1983, p. 79.
Times Literary Supplement, July 15, 1977; January 25, 1980.
Voice of Youth Advocates, October, 1982, Mary K. Chelton, review of *A Small Civil War,* p. 45.
Washington Post Book World, August 21, 1983.
Wilson Library Bulletin, April, 1977, Michael McCue and Evie Wilson, review of *Sunday Father,* pp. 674, 687.*

*   *   *

Autobiography Feature

John Neufeld

This is an opportunity. I am two years past forty-five, changing directions in what I choose to write about and how, and have absolutely no sense of security about the future.

Which is what the life of a writer provides.

(More of what a writer's life is, and how to try to understand whether it's something you yourself want, later.)

Details of how I got here and why are few and simple. I was lucky. In my parents, in my education, in the support and understanding I received and still receive from my family.

I was born in Chicago and grew up in Des Moines, Iowa, a lovely green and quiet spot in those days, the best possible place to be a child. The city was small enough then to know people on board an airplane, either one's own friends or the parents of a friend, and my own parents were successful enough within the community to have many.

My mother had been an English teacher before her marriage; during her lifetime she was a driven reader and for the three of us, Director of Studies. I can recall at the age of eleven sitting with her in our library, reading *Macbeth* or *The Merchant of Venice* aloud to each other—all the parts, delving into the mysteries of language, practicing how to read the meter that most find heavy going in a light and natural fashion.

I was encouraged and allowed to read anything I could find in our house. There were worlds to choose. Classics; current best-sellers; series adventures suitable for boys; collections of plays (Ibsen, Coward, Maugham, Shaw); children's books—although of these only a few are remembered: *Ferdinand the Bull, Bartholomew Cubbins,* horse stories, Grimms' and Andersen's fairy tales, and a story about two ducks—one black and one white, in a strawberry patch—which I adored and have long since lost.

I was an early and happy traveller. I was sent to camp in Minnesota at four-and-a-half, and loved it, even the early morning roustings when we had to run, wrapped only in towels, to the lake's edge and dive in—an instantaneous submersion on most days. A day's activity there might include practice on the rifle range, tennis, horseback riding, touch football, crafts, choir, Capture the Flag. Evenings brought campfires and sing-alongs. I was very happy and felt cherished both in the woods and in Des Moines.

I began to "write" while still in junior high school, perhaps at twelve or thirteen. One of the magazines that regularly arrived by mail at home was the *Saturday Evening Post,* long since vanished. In it I read weekly romances. Fame and fortune seemed only a matter of putting a blonde heroine in the path of a dark stranger. I wrote tens of stories then and bravely, or innocently, sent them off to the magazine. Each was returned, always with the identical note of rejection.

I don't think I had illusions about my abilities with pen and ink. After all, I was copying more than creating, changing a few details and offering a formula that seemed to be what the magazine and its readers wanted. While I wrote less as a teenager (there were simply too many other ideas and worlds to explore), usually there was a play or "novel" floating in my mind. "Novel" is put in quotes because this, too, seemed too easy a task. What, I ask you, is a novel but a longer story about a blonde and a dark stranger?

At Phillips Exeter, a boys prep school in New Hampshire, I wrote only what was requested of us all. But by the time I got to New Haven and Yale, I was reignited. My worlds, through reading, were expanding rapidly. As one should at that age, I read Salinger and Fitzgerald, Hemingway and Tolstoy, Dostoevsky and Dreiser. But also Anouilh, Mauriac, Lorca, Claudel, Gerard Manley Hopkins, Camus, Sterne, Addison and Steele, Richardson, Fielding, Voltaire. In fact, I read to escape. Any time I was faced with a major exam or a final, I went directly to Sterling Library and withdrew the five longest books I had always meant to read. Holed up in my room, I read until the last moment, usually the night before the test, and then crammed compulsively what I thought I should know before the next morning. This seemed to work although, as a method of learning, it wasn't satisfying or lasting.

We graduated. In those days (1960), there were four things people did on leaving university: (1) get a job in the City (New York or Boston) and marry; (2) go into the Army for a six-month term, followed by reserve duty for six years after; (3) go to graduate school; (4) go to Europe "to write short stories."

(1) I had no idea what sort of work I wanted, and my father assured me I could not afford to marry. (2) The idea of the Army was not appealing. (3) I would have felt terribly guilty taking someone else's place in graduate school, assuming I could get in, since I hadn't the faintest idea what it would be I might want to study. (4) I was fated.

I had been to Europe before, as a teenager, to ski. Now I planned a Grand Tour—starting in England, crossing the Channel to Scandinavia, down through central Europe (Germany, Austria) to Greece, back to Italy, Spain and Portugal, and finally to France.

I never left England. I was having too much fun. Furthermore, as I remember writing to one of the masters at

John Neufeld

Exeter, at every street corner in London there was history. There were endless associations to be made from my reading or studying. London seemed more like home than any place I'd ever been.

I was also fortunate in meeting and then living with a group of people my age who came from Canada, Australia, the United States. We were all poor, comparatively, but we had resources (our families and our own wits) and curiosity. It was a grand time, and better than this was the restriction placed on all our passports at that time: we were allowed to stay in England only for three months at a stretch. This meant every ninety days a weekend in France, in Paris especially. Egad, how unjust! (I also remember at this time a friend of mine, from both prep school and college, now a United States Senator, daily risking his life and mine in Paris. France then was in turmoil about its colony Algeria—whether to give it independence or to keep fighting to stay there as an imperial power. There were machine-gun emplacements on nearly every street corner of the Left Bank in Paris then, and Jack used to delight in coming out of the apartment where we were staying with another friend, looking up and down the street, raising his fist in the air and shouting in French, *"Algerie pour les—!"* He would never finish his battle cry. Guns would swivel instantly towards us and we would cower in the doorway, grinning sheepishly and waving that we really meant no harm, that we were just kidding around. Astonishingly stupid.)

It was a grand and simple time, and I fell in love, twice, which by no means was excessive.

But the following year I was drafted. I sailed back on the *Queen Mary* to begin a six-month tour of duty at Ft. Leonard Wood, Missouri, where, after learning how to kill people during basic training, I was assigned (no doubt only on the basis of my Yale diploma) to teach English to men who were eventually to become clerk-typists for the Army.

I liked the Army. (I seemed to have liked almost everything I was doing in those days.) I liked the food; I liked the people who served with me—largely other college types skipping through their duty as quickly as possible— and I was proud as hell to have weathered basic training as well as I did: angular, trim, fit, and more than anything else, alive, despite crawling under live tracer bullets on a muddy obstacle course in the middle of the night.

After this, it was time to grow up. I had to find a job somewhere, doing something. What? I loved reading and writing. OK, that led me directly to the publishing world: newspapers or book publishing. When you're a beginner, and for years afterwards, newspapers pay very little. My choice was even easier.

An additional inspiration was that, from my reading at Yale, I had discovered the fabled figure of Max Perkins, the editor of Hemingway, Fitzgerald, Thomas Wolfe. Since I thought I knew what good writing was, since I was more or less able to communicate ideas easily and simply, I decided to model myself after him. (This man has a lot to answer for. I am not the only person alive in America today who let the idea of Max Perkins guide his life. Actually, having thereafter entered the publishing world and staying locked within it for a dozen years, I am now free to announce to the world a long and closely guarded secret: there *was* no "Max Perkins." He was an ideal. Try today to find an editor whose word you trust, whose job is secure, whose only ambition is to improve your work.)

My decision was made. Now to find someone who would let me be "Max."

Not easy. I spent three months looking in Boston and New York. No one seemed to think I was seasoned enough to edit, or even to read manuscripts and report on them. But I could write quickly and clearly. Swell. I decided that the foot in the door was worth being able to discover later what was in that room. I began writing advertising copy for Harcourt, Brace and World in New York.

I was fired, after a year and a half, largely because writing was too easy for me, and I seemed to be spending too much of Harcourt's time in my office writing plays or short stories. I managed, with a friend's help, to find a position at Franklin Watts, Inc., another publisher, doing publicity and promotion—a slot that eventually held me captive until well after *Lisa, Bright and Dark* was published in 1969, although at a succession of other houses: McGraw-Hill, Holt, Braziller, Western.

Twice during those years I stopped working, convinced that surely by now I had enough experience of the industry as a whole to move into editing. I could understand the reasons publishers hesitated—I was good at publicity; why take a chance on my mucking up something new? Still I sought that fabled mahogany desk with manuscript pages (other people's) spread out on it, blue pencil in hand, an attentive ear across from me nodding and smiling at my perception and insight. I would even have bought a pipe.

I *had* been writing all this time, unsuccessfully. I had taken a summer's course at the American Academy of Dramatic Art in playwrighting. I had even applied (three times) to Yale's School of Drama to study the same thing. But each time I went back to New Haven, I could not escape the feeling that life there at the Drama School was too tightly controlled and academic; after all, I didn't want to write about my fellow students but about people "out there." While I was accepted three times, I never moved north.

So on my own I wrote a great number of television dramas, all unproduced. I wrote a terrible novel, full of self-exploration and revelation, which people do at that age, and which has been lost since. I hope. I wrote one-act plays, and with these seemed to have more success, largely because I joined with other aspiring writers in a group that rented a theatre in which to stage, listen, and learn. I was told that my skill lay in dialogue. I was happy enough to believe that. Meanwhile, I kept writing other things—in play form, a piece about my years in England; poetry (falling in love again did that); short stories using as locales places I visited either for work or on holiday, although not too many of them centered on delicious blondes and roguish strangers. None of this—I repeat, NONE—was any good.

But I was not unhappy. I *was* writing. I enjoyed it. I now know I was practicing, learning, copying, exploring, and experimenting. Of course I had no assurance all this would, in the end, make me any better than I had ever been, but I had that hope. And since no one would hire me as an editor, what else was I to do? I travelled the country constantly, publicizing and promoting other people's work, and I enjoyed that—the people, the adventures, the cities. People were kind to me, and I was grateful.

To illustrate how kind exactly, let's move now to *Edgar Allan.*

I was in Los Angeles, attending a publishing convention, when I had lunch one afternoon with Marjorie Thayer, an editor for a small California publishing house. She had a story she thought I could write and write well. I never asked her why she thought this; I wish I had. In any case, she told me the bare bones of a story of a family that adopted a black child and, because of community pressure and their own fears, gave him up. She told me that the details of the case could be found in the files of the *Los Angeles Times* if I were interested.

I was, desperately, but not in the real story. I knew almost immediately that if I went to the newspaper and read about this family, my story would in the end be theirs. I didn't want that. I wanted my story to be my own. Also, of course, I didn't want to be sued later. I wanted to concentrate on the children in the family, the white children, and I wanted complete freedom to make them whatever I could.

I began the book at a lunch counter on Sunset Boulevard ("This is a story about my father and about God. Neither is very easy to understand.") I returned to New York and continued. I finished perhaps thirty pages and sent them off to Marjorie, since after all the idea had been hers. She liked what I'd done, with reservations. I was pleased. I asked for a contract . . . not money, mind you, but a *contract,* something that would legitimize my efforts, would make me feel I was working finally and honestly at something worthwhile, something that could be taken home to be shown to my father as proof I hadn't been wasting my time all those years.

But Marjorie thought I was holding her up for loot. We quarreled long-distance. She couldn't see my position and wanted me to write more before committing herself. We parted, she in anger at my insistence on a contract of some sort, I in frustration. (I wrote her, when the book was later published, that I knew the book was hers and that I was enormously grateful to her for her initial faith and trust. I cannot recall what she wrote in reply, but it was gracious and forgiving.)

I was writing *Edgar Allan* in my spare time, slowly. After a few months (for while the story and its style are simple, its effort was not), I had one half of it completed, enough, I felt, to offer it to other publishers. I first offered it to Macmillan whose editor, Susan Hirschman, said she liked it but wanted a much longer book, more like one of the Cleavers' stories. I disagreed. I didn't want a long book. I knew from my years of publishing that many young people do not know the thrill of starting and *finishing* a book, ever. I wanted this book to break those habits. I wanted *Edgar Allan* not only to be as good as I could make it, but also to be an experience that young people could *happily* have. It could have been a longer book; it could have been an adult novel. But I wanted to reach the broadest possible audience with it because of its sentiments and my own. Finally, I said, thanks but no thanks to Susan and sent it to Sidney Phillips who, at that time, was operating a smaller, newer publishing house and for whom I had done some freelance publicity in the past.

Sidney telephoned me almost immediately and said he would buy it. I was thrilled. Also worried. I had only written half. What if I ruined it later? He assured me that he thought that impossible and we agreed to agree. The contract was for $750, half on signing and half on delivery, which just goes to show you how hard it was then, and still is today, to live on what you earn. If you began a book in January, having received $375, and completed it in December, receiving then the second sum, how could one pay for food, travel, rent, and a little amusement during that whole year? Not easily. (I took my $375 and flew to Des Moines to wave the contract under my father's nose. He, very sensibly, told me I could have mailed it to him for twelve cents and made the same impression.)

Edgar Allan was published at last in 1968 (one day before I turned thirty, the same day it was reviewed in *Time* ... the same magazine in which my father had once appeared and, therefore, one more important to me than was really rational). Due to my years of travelling throughout the country and knowing as many critics and reviewers as I did by then, the book was reviewed warmly and well. The first review I ever read of my own work, in the *New York Times,* has since become the one I keep trying to earn again, every time out: "a work of art."

Reviews and notices around the country, from *all* sources, were glowing. This was a wonderful way to begin—launched with figurative champagne and caviar.

But common sense prevailed. I didn't stop working nine-to-five. Favorable reviews are all well and good but they don't pay for your monthly utility bills. In fact, you

earn very little on a book, even a relatively successful one, for quite a period of time. You are paid an advance against royalties—which means, in effect, you are loaned money that will be deducted from your share of earnings on a book, should there be any. The amount of time it takes for this loan to be repaid can vary widely ... and sometimes a publisher never earns enough on a title to refill his pockets for his initial expenses. If the publisher doesn't, the writer doesn't. It's that simple. So, if your advance isn't huge—and mine wasn't, remember—no money materializes for at least six months. (Royalties generally are distributed in the spring and fall of each year, six months apart.)

While I stayed deskbound, then, I did take one week off to fly to Des Moines. A few weeks before my departure, I had dinner one evening with a New York City psychiatrist who told me, generally and with no identifying detail, of an interview he had had that day with a new patient. He felt certain that the young woman was in considerable trouble; he also felt fairly certain that her parents would never allow her to return for help or therapy. I listened and proverbial bells went off. I knew what my next book would be.

This girl's plight, translated as that of Lisa Shilling in *Lisa, Bright and Dark,* seemed (sadly enough) a natural story begging to be told. I arrived in Des Moines, set up an office in a corner of my parents' living room, and worked every day from nine in the morning until noon, and again from nine at night until midnight. One week later, the first draft was completed ... a feat unduplicated since because I came to realize just how special the circumstances surrounding this book were; and I learned eventually that writing a "novel" was a lot more difficult than putting a blonde (Lisa) in proximity to a dark stranger (Dr. Neil Donovan).

After several more months of rewriting, the text was ready, and set. Sidney paid me the same amount of money for an advance, meager certainly. What did I know? Actually, I knew a lot about publishing by that time but I put all of this aside for the pleasure of finally "being" a writer. Who cared about little things like money?

But then, without warning, Sidney had second thoughts. After the book was in page proofs, he telephoned me to ask worriedly if I were sure I wanted it published. I was certain I did. Why? Well, he said, it's not *Edgar Allan.* Of course it wasn't, I replied. It was entirely different. I didn't want to write the same book twice. I took a big breath. If he didn't want to publish it, all he had to do was say so.

(Bluffing, I was breathless, weak, my pulse astronomical and I quickly sat on the nearest chair in order not to keel over with light-headed nerves.)

I said firmly that I was certain I could sell the manuscript elsewhere if he felt the risk was unacceptable to him. Sidney relented and we published it. *Lisa, Bright and Dark* was the best-selling title on Sidney's list that year, and for many more to come.

(Initially, I had wanted to call the book, "I'll Always Love You, Paul Newman." The reasons are clear, obvious, and not very nice. Mr. Newman was at the peak of his appeal just then. I thought his name on the cover of a book would lift that title into the stratosphere. Besides, it was also appropriate, and he *was* a public figure. Further, I had met him years before when he was performing in *Sweet Bird of Youth,* a Tennessee Williams play, on Broadway. I wrote him a short letter, explaining what I wanted to do and why. He wrote back, declining the honor. He was right, of course, and I was wrong. The title eventually selected was Sidney's suggestion.)

When the film and television rights to *Lisa* were sold in California, I stopped working, at last, nine-to-five.

I also found myself being asked to review other people's books in the *New York Times*. I was flattered and eager. What fun to get to read in advance other people's work, think about it, make constructive criticisms if warranted; to praise or damn. The pay was nothing (twenty-five dollars a title) but the exposure was terrific.

This was during a time when the Federal Government was beginning to spend a good deal of money to support school and public libraries, as well as programs that served minorities and the disadvantaged. What this meant to the world of publishing for young people was a spate of novels, less than successful in most cases, with themes centering on disadvantaged minority children. These books were rushed out in order to qualify for Federal monies that became available to libraries to purchase them—i.e., for a quick buck.

Now, to be fair, some of these books *did* address useful, meaningful, often moving ideas and characters. But many did not. I recall in particular one title that pretended to be a story of a teenage girl whose heaviest cross was the presence at home of a retarded sister. Ostensibly, the crux of the book was how the girl managed to live a normal life while trying to take care of someone slightly less than normal. But in fact, what the book became was something else: would our heroine be able to ride in the horse show at the "club" if her friends found out about her sister? In other words, what we had here was another teenage horse story, tarted up with a set of trials and tribulations that belonged in a second, altogether different, story—all in order to qualify as a title about the disadvantaged, and to make libraries and schools spend their money faster.

I couldn't help myself. I nailed it.

Again, for the *New York Times,* the then-editor approached me one day at a meeting and asked me how I'd like to review a really terrible book. I was amused by the slanted invitation and said, Sure, send it to me. What arrived was a novel written by a Newbery Award-winning writer. I was curious. I read the book. It was not 100 percent successful, but I could see what the woman was trying to do, and also how close she came to doing it. I wrote a review indicating that the book was flawed, to be sure, but nonetheless worthwhile and perhaps even valuable in the long run.

The editor called me on the telephone. He disagreed. He thought the book was rotten. I felt equally that it wasn't. I went down to the *Times* offices where he and I slugged it out for eight hours. I won, I'm happy to report, and a review appeared of which the editor did not approve, but which was certainly a kinder and more helpful one than the writer might have gotten otherwise.

I wasn't crazy about this approach to reviewing, I decided then. If an editor approached a reviewer who was expected to knuckle down, and the reviewer *did,* then what claim to objectivity or thoughtfulness could a newspaper or magazine have? I soon stopped.

About this same time I began receiving invitations to travel around the country to speak to groups of teachers or librarians, or both together, about juvenile literature, about my own work, about anything I wanted to spout. It was flattering, of course, but more important, it made me stop to think about *why* I was writing, and *how.*

I hadn't planned to write for children, or young adults. That I was on the cutting edge of a movement in publishing and readership was clear and true, but why was I? Well, I thought then, and still do today, I'm not an intellectual giant. My prose style is simple and rarely convoluted. The things that interest me are ideas and problems that face us all, but which we often meet first when we're young. If by writing about how imaginary young people meet and overcome certain problems helps real young people when *they* meet the same problems, then I was doing something useful as well as fun. So I zipped back and forth across the nation, eating a lot of chicken and standing up at the conclusion of any number of meals to tell people what I thought. I took part in panels and workshops, and sat on committees and advisory groups.

Which, naturally enough, keeps one from writing. It's grand for ye olde ego, but it's not so healthy for one's pocketbook.

Despite the enormous amount of money that *Lisa* was making, I was spending almost as fast as the checks arrived. This is called improvidence. Some would also call it immaturity. Others, just stupid. I certainly didn't want to "retire" after only two books, to be enshrined as a lecturer and after-dinner speaker, dining out year after year on minimal successes.

Happily, or not, as one decides, Mr. Nixon was inaugurated about that time. *I* certainly was not happy, perhaps for the first time in my life. I thought then, and do so now, that he was contemptible. I looked ahead in my crystal ball and saw America sliding into totalitarianism under his regime, and decided that if America weren't smart enough to see this, then tough—I for one was getting out.

I flew to London. I knew what my next book was (*Touching*) and I had work to do. I could live happily and safely there, under a system I admired and loved for its traditions and history. Clearly America had much to learn. I didn't feel compelled to help her.

But while I was there, I began to have second thoughts. If I felt as strongly about Nixon and America as I did, what was I doing in England? If there *were* any hope for us all, shouldn't I be where I could make a difference? What difference could I make? I could write a book that would awaken America and save it! (Youthful idealism dies hard; also enormous conceit.)

I returned to New York, the manuscript of *Touching* completed and ready for Sidney. (In paperback this became *Twink* since three novels that season carried the same title; titles are not copyrightable.)

But I was being wooed by other publishers after *Edgar Allan* and *Lisa.* I was not cool to the approaches, being susceptible to flattery and thinking I *should* perhaps be making more money than Sidney was able to pay.

One afternoon I awoke from a short nap with "Sleep two, three, four, Sleep two, three, four," running through my mind. I knew what the next book was to be. I called Harper and Row. In particular I called Charlotte Zolotow who had been wining and dining me for months. She was enthusiastic. I called the William Morris Agency, my representatives, and they arranged the deal at what seemed then a huge increment over the first three books: $4,000, half on signing, half on delivery.

Sleep Two, Three, Four! is a story, written in 1970 and published the following year, in which the villains are, by name: Richard Nixon, Spiro Agnew, J. Edgar Hoover, and John Mitchell. These names may not be familiar to you now. In order: the President; the then-Vice-President, who later resigned under fire for taking kickbacks as governor of Maryland; the director of the FBI, who had been in place since the agency's founding; and the then-Attorney General of the United States, who was to be imprisoned over malfeasance following the Watergate scandal which forced Mr. Nixon's resignation.

The narrative told of a group of young people who, under a totalitarian regime (the story was set in "1983" . . . one year short of Mr. Orwell's "1984" and therefore a warning, of sorts), struggle cross-country to rescue a friend from a reconditioning camp—a euphemism for a concentration camp, in this case for the physically handicapped. Their exciting escapes and ultimate success, although not without hardship and loss, were set against conditions I felt certain would soon prevail throughout the United States.

The purpose of the book was, first, to alert readers to the Bill of Rights and its erosion under the then-current Republican administration of Mr. Nixon. Second, of course, the aim was to tell a rousing good story.

I loved the book. Charlotte seemed to like it, as well, and telephoned me one day in January of 1971 to say that she thought it was ready for the printer. I disagreed. I felt more work could be done to make it better. But I also wanted the book "out," its message abroad, and badly. I agreed finally and the manuscript was sent off to be typeset.

The history of the book is not a happy one. While it received a glowing review in *School Library Journal* and was "starred" (indicating exceptional merit), the *New York Times* was savage. (This might have had something to do with the fact that the editor of the *Times* had written *his* first young adult book and, when I was asked about it, I thoughtlessly said it was not very good. Who knows?)

While I could not be called innocent in the ways of publishing, apparently some naivete still existed because I hoped Harper would counter the bad notice (my first) with some small amount of space advertising carrying other, laudable, reviews. Harper washed its hands; Charlotte lost her nerve; I was miserable. I was due to go to Chicago and Detroit to promote the book, and I felt totally abandoned.

Eventually, the book became invisible. Harper did nothing for it, and Avon, who printed it in paperback, put it out in a black cover with nothing to indicate for example, that the *Saturday Review* had felt strongly enough about the story to review it—and favorably—as a book of general interest. It sank.

Perhaps because this has been my least successful effort to date, it is the one I remain fondest of. True enough, for the first time reviews split, and the one in the *Times* scarred me for life. (It also taught me never to reply honestly to a review editor's inquiry about his or her own work.)

There were other lessons learned from this experience. For one thing, I had a tendency to be didactic in print, which is to say that I concentrated overmuch on the message of a story to the detriment of its telling. Well, it *is* ideas that interest me, that make a story of any sort worth telling.

Also, this was my first less-than-happy editorial experience, based no doubt on two factors, if I am trying to be at all fair. One is that *because* I had a dozen years in publishing, on the "inside," I thought I knew what could and should be done with a book. This often makes me seem impatient and short-tempered—"difficult" in other words—because too often I feel I can do a better job promoting and publicizing than the people who are, in theory, trained and hired to do so for me, and for others. The other factor is that earlier disclosure I mentioned:—there is no "Max Perkins." Or at least in the early seventies there were none—no editors who followed an author's work through *every* phase and fought for it. Editors then (and perhaps now) were nervous, timid, worried about their own necks and longevity on the job, anxious to bring in a success but not brave enough to fight for one.

But then, after learning both these lessons, I turned around to have two other experiences diametrically opposed to the one at Harper and Row: *Freddy's Book,* published by Random House in 1973, and *For All the Wrong Reasons,* published by Norton and then by New American Library in the same year, in hardcover and then in paper.

Walter Retan, then the editor at Random House, *was* brave. *Freddy's Book* is the story of how a boy of nine or ten discovers what a certain four-letter Anglo-Saxon word ending in "k" actually means. It's a simple and funny story of a boy tracking down information that, in fact, he's too young to use when he finally does understand it. It was less a sex-education book than a story of looking briefly into the adult world and deciding one could wait, after all, to get there.

I used "the word" half-a-dozen times in the course of the story, always with care, caution, and as much good taste as I could muster. Walter and Random House stood behind me all the way. (Walter also reasoned me gently out of a second story line I wanted to use in the same tale . . . that of a child [the same child] who was becoming increasingly neurotic from watching the Vietnam War being shown nightly on his television set at home. Walter's approach was low-keyed and eminently correct: sex, sure, but not sex-and-violence in the same book; one is enough.) The book was well reviewed but, of course, its subject matter kept it from many schools and libraries for fear of public outrage. Nonetheless it was written, it was a good job, and it was a book that was, at that time (and perhaps even today), needed.

For All the Wrong Reasons grew from the success of Ann Head's *Mr. and Mrs. Bo Jo Jones,* a young-adult novel New American Library had published in paperback with considerable success. Mrs. Head had died, and NAL came to me to ask if I would be interested in trying to write something like it. I said I would, but only under certain conditions: that I could use whatever words I chose, within reason; that the heroine actually knew how she got pregnant, had had sex more than once and liked it; that she would have the baby—no accidents on horseback or stairways. The editor, Bob Haney, agreed and stood as good as his word. Norton published it first in hardcover, NAL in paperback, and it was a success.

By this time I was living the life of a writer, which is to say, I was living the way I thought successful writers should. I had my apartment in New York City; I had a rented summer home in East Hampton, near the edge of the Atlantic; I zipped back and forth from Los Angeles to New York whenever I felt like a change, and frequently went to Europe, as well. I was walking around with holes in my pockets, hot hands, and the conviction that this could last forever. Of course, I was wrong.

New American Library then asked if I could write a book around a particular title. Needing the loot and feeling confident of my power, I said I could—assuming the subject matter was neither technical nor scientific; math and science had been my worst subjects in school. They offered the title, *Sunday Father.* I said yes immediately. My checkbook needed a transfusion.

This is the single book I regret having written. It is, I think, my weakest—a mild enough story of a family in mid-divorce and coping therewith. Oddly enough, the book was well reviewed in surprising quarters; the *Sunday New York Times* reviewed it as a work of general fiction and praised it. I was then, and remain now, embarrassed. It had been agony to write and a continual source of pain to realize what I had produced.

The book was written necessarily under "crash" circumstances. I knew the moment I agreed to do it that I hated it. I needed, therefore, to get away in order to concentrate on the task at hand, and to complete it as quickly as I could. I applied to the MacDowell Colony in Peterborough, New Hampshire, for a fellowship, a stay in which to do it.

The MacDowell Colony is a lovely, quiet spot in the up-country of New England, endowed and run for artists of all kinds—writers, painters, musicians—so that their work can be done under ideal circumstances. You have a small cabin in which to work, or a studio. You are left undisturbed all day; lunch is delivered to your doorstep silently so as not to disturb your concentration; it is possible to work twenty-four hours a day there if you wish. I sat in my studio for four weeks, started and finished *Sunday Father,* and hated the book at the same time I loved the Colony, and was grateful to have been accepted there.

(I've never reapplied for a second stay because (a) the rules of acceptance have changed and (b) I feel that since I've had success already, to take someone else's studio, someone who had not yet had success, would be unfair. In those days, you applied by stating what you wished to do and by submitting *all* your already published work to a committee. At that time, admittance meant you could, if the need arose, reapply from time to time. But now you must go through the process of application each time you want a study grant, and to ship dozens of books to committee members for each application is just too much, it seems to me. Besides, I can work anywhere, as I've discovered, and often have had wonderful working conditions either of my own making or through others' generosities. I've never applied for a National Arts Endowment grant for the same reasons ... I've been fortunate enough to be able to fund my own work and therefore should.)

After *Sunday Father,* I went to California to watch (after four years of preparation and sweat) "Lisa, Bright and Dark" being filmed for *The Hallmark Hall of Fame* on NBC-TV. While there, I discovered that my agent from William Morris was switching companies, and cities as well, moving from New York to Los Angeles. I met with him and we decided that if he could find me work, I too might switch.

Gary was able to get me an assignment adapting a mystery novel into a television film for Aaron Spelling, who now produces "The Love Boat," "Dynasty," etc. I flew West again, thinking the job could be done in six weeks. It was, or rather my job was. But television and film are not overnight productions, and so I was kept waiting around for six months before we finally shot a foot of film. During this time, I realized that the days of flying a writer from one coast to another for work were long gone; there were ten thousand writers in Hollywood already. If I wanted to work in television, I had better be on the spot. So over Memorial Day that year I flew back to New York, closed up my apartment there and the house in East Hampton, and returned to Los Angeles, ready to set the film world on fire.

I did four or five television projects then, one after the other, all more or less forgettable. I was grateful for two things: the money, of course, but more important, the people with whom I was involved. For while one may enjoy writing (and most of the time I do), it is an entirely solitary existence. Writing for television is, alas, more often by committee than not—always keeping the networks' Programs and Practices Departments in mind (i.e., the censors)—but at least one is surrounded by other points of view, personalities, suggestions, and this can make it entertaining as well as educating.

At the end of 1974, however, I was dissatisfied. While I had success as a writer of books for young people, I was a little put out that the only people in the world who might recognize my name were all under thirteen. Further, the best-seller list was heavy with novels by Jacqueline Susann, Harold Robbins, Irving Wallace. I did not admire these efforts, although realistically and honestly one had to admit that the art of making people turn pages, no matter how silly the story, was a considerable one. Still, I was irate and jealous. Nuts, I thought, I can do that! So I did.

Trading Up was published by Atheneum (and later by Fawcett in paperback) in 1975. It was, and is, an incredibly dirty novel. The stories in it are exciting enough, but its major focus was sexual, its purpose to go everyone one better. If during a sex scene, Robbins-Susann-Wallace "panned" up and away to a night filled with exploding fireworks, symbolically indicating arousal and excitement, I decided that my work would go straight through and show it all. All. The *New York Times* called the book "slick, gossipy, and thoroughly tasteless," a review I couldn't have hoped to better. The paperback rights were bought for an incredible sum.

There were two flies in this ointment: (1) I had written under a pseudonym in order to protect my children's and young-adults' work from suffering; consequently no one in the world knew or cared who had written this book. (2) Because I had chosen to do this, there was no legitimate way of publicizing the effort. The book was about women, primarily for women, and in theory written by a woman. Those were my choices, perhaps all wrong; but short of fraud, there was, thus, no author to send out on the road to boost sales.

Afterwards, instead of being hungry to do this again and cash in, I decided that the effort had been gargantuan (which was true) and that I didn't want to be tied down to writing the same kind of book endlessly. Despite the fact that I then changed agencies (which eventually meant a long, *long* separation from working in television … admittedly an error) and was "hot," I hesitated. A contract was offered me to do another *Trading Up,* or rather three of them (one a year), and the money offered along with it was staggering. Sometimes I regret not taking the swag, but more often I don't. Reaching forty, I decided that apparently I was happy enough, after all, doing only those books I really cared about. If they made money, swell; if not, I'd survive anyway. Not necessarily the sagest point of view, but ultimately one I could live with.

Basically, then, I sat on my hands and stopped writing, spent the dough and saw the world. I convinced myself that, during the next few years, I was "learning," experiencing things I would later, when the time was ripe, write about. What I did in fact was have a good time and come, eventually, to be disappointed in myself for not being more productive. I bought a typical southern California "show business" home, complete with a pool and a studio in the back in which to work, and didn't work. But I was *tan* and my tennis had never been better.

In short, I wasn't happy. I had nothing of which to complain but myself. Here in paradise I did occasionally swing the switch "on" … on those few cloudy days when passing the swimming pool and deck wasn't impossible. This is not to say "Oh, poor me, having everything and enjoying nothing." But in fact my life then was a variation on that theme: I had everything and was doing nothing, not even anything to make certain I could keep everything.

I did one book for Putnam, a romance that was purposely gooey, intended for a popular readership whose idea of literature was a little tension and a happy ending. This was really, I suppose, the first time I had written about that blonde and the dark stranger. That it worked as well as it did by this time wasn't a surprise. I *had* paid my dues; I *had* been learning, and the technicalities of sculpting a decent-enough story were now in my satchel.

I wrote a heavy-handed but deeply felt warning about how technology in this country was killing us all prematurely. It never saw print or page. It may have been badly written, but the topic only made matters worse: had it been written as nonfiction, it would have been disturbing enough; as fiction, it was such a downer one could hardly wade through it.

I dabbled with another *Trading Up* kind of novel, but found that my instincts had been accurate: my heart wasn't in it, not even in the sex scenes. It languished and resides now in some filing cabinet in my office.

I didn't know it then, but I do now, looking back. I was vainly looking about for something that would validate my lifelong good fortune. It took me a few more years even to begin to understand this, and to act on the inspiration.

In the meantime, I was bored. I was boring myself. I took an apartment in New York City and spent three or four years flying back and forth whenever the urge took me.

While I loved the ease of living in California, I was going crazy. So off to New York I'd go for two or three weeks to be mentally "goosed" and juiced up with ideas and experiences that would, on my return to Los Angeles, carry me through another six or eight weeks. This was all expensive and silly, but the very motion of crossing the continent convinced me I wasn't idle or worthless. What I was fighting, of course, was the realization that despite being grateful for good fortune, I was profoundly dissatisfied and displeased with myself for the way I accepted and squandered it. (I am *trying* to be honest here.)

By 1980, I was beginning to pull myself out of this slough. Again, this was because of politics. Mr. Reagan had been elected and the Moral Majority, or New Right, was making a good deal of noise about its aims and ideals, most of which I disagreed with radically. A new book was born as one afternoon I listened to *All Things Considered,* the National Public Radio news hour. A small town in rural Iowa (where, after all, I had grown up) was up in arms over John Steinbeck's *The Grapes of Wrath.* That was all the news I needed. I devised a story of one family in a small Iowa town divided over the issue and let them go at it, hammer and tongs. This, too, occasional critics found didactic, preachy, but I was pleased with it and felt it aired important ideas. I was even more pleased, inwardly, that again I seemed to be able to focus clearly and write with anger and a purpose.

I say "occasional" critics because *A Small Civil War* is one of the unknown but, I suspect, common-enough horror stories of publishing.

I had had a good deal of difficulty with the editor on it, who admitted to me that she never felt comfortable working with me. I asked why but never received an answer. In any case, when the galleys were sent to me, I found she had rewritten whole chunks of the book, and badly. I went bananas, fixed everything back up and flew to New York, ready for a shoot-out. Instead, she calmly took the reworked manuscript from my trembling hands and said, "Let's give this to the copy editor." That was that. I was astonished. Worse, all my anger had no place to go. Why had she gone to all the trouble of messing around with the manuscript if it didn't mean anything? (The answer, I surmise, is that some editors cannot keep their hands off work, whether it needs help or not.)

But this sort of conflict could be forgotten in the face of a successful launching. Alas. The very day that *A Small Civil War* was published was also the day that Random House took possession of Fawcett Publishing. I was in New York at the time and, being the eager author I am, I called Random House to offer my help at getting the book off the ground, to find out what size printing had been ordered so I would have an idea of how much work I had to do.

What book?

I told them its title.

They looked once more. They could find neither record nor file; had no idea what size the printing had been; couldn't even tell me if the book had been officially published and sent out for review!

Bad timing is a simple explanation, and in time one accepts that. But at that moment, life was a conspiracy!

The book was never really announced or offered to the public at all. I persuaded Random House to send out a thousand letters announcing its existence, and to do a thousand dollars' worth of advertising in small journals, but that was as far as they would go. A definite disaster, whether or not the book was good. If I didn't like what I do, I'd have packed it in and taken a job selling shoes.

But I was already deep into planning a new book, *Sharelle,* and spending a lot of time in San Diego, at Washington High School, researching and talking with its students.

This was a new experience for me . . . not just writing, to which I was accustomed certainly and knew that ultimately it was a matter of me, my typewriter, and my ear; but more important, working for the first time with the intended readers of the book. The kids at Washington were warm and helpful, honest, and full of ideas—to which I listened and from which I learned. I sent down chunks of chapters for them to read, and then, a few days later, I'd arrive to discuss the work with them, to hear their complaints and to answer their questions as best I could.

There were aspects of this book—a story of a girl who, at fourteen, becomes a mother and decides ultimately that there is more ahead in her life than simply caretaking, no matter how charming and bright her daughter is—that were new to me: ideas and concerns that astonished me but with which I felt suddenly comfortable and capable. Its greatest success lay in an adult character, Sharelle's mother, Melba, and I knew from the moment she stepped onto a page that here was a creation who lived and breathed, could be surprising and dependable, too, and was a thorough enchantress despite her selfishness. I had to focus with extra attention on most of the younger characters because I was so taken by Melba. By the end of *Sharelle,* I had come to feel the book was really about two things: Melba . . . and faith.

"Faith" was a new vein explored in this book and, as I set out, I had no idea it would play a part in its development. I suppose, rather than use such an all-encompassing term, I should narrow this down a bit. There is a character in *Sharelle* unlike any other I'd ever created, called Patrick, who is a high school senior destined to become a priest. Now, there really aren't many young people today looking to the Church for a career, not to mention young people with the gift to enter a clergy and find satisfaction within giving, caring, listening, aiding, counseling, guiding.

Patrick doesn't play a major role in *Sharelle.* He's there from time to time, almost held in front of Sharelle herself as a possible romantic choice, but removed from that position not only by his own desires to serve, but also by Sharelle's understanding of what makes him tick. Their relationship is sad in a way, but also, I feel, joyful and healthy and full of respect for each other. For me, the presence of Patrick and his concerns, as well as the character of Melba—drunk, lazy, angry—lift *Sharelle* out of the run of books for young adults I've done. Further, when it was published in hardcover, it was published as a book of general fiction, not simply labelled for young readers. I was pleased.

More important, I was curious—about this new interest in religion. It had to be somewhere inside of me. These ideas reflect, after all, the writer as well as the characters in a book. The fact that I'd included these characters in a story of decision and hard-headedness indicated something important about them in my own mind.

I wasn't ready to preach, certainly. I wasn't ready to do anything, in fact, in public, except wonder at it all.

To try for continuing honesty, I must admit this new concern did not arise unheralded. I had met, in New York, a young fellow who had jumped the fence, so to speak. He had been slated to enter the priesthood and, as the time neared for his ordination as a deacon (the step that precedes the priesthood itself), he decided that outside life was more challenging than that in a cloister. He left the seminary in which he was studying, moved to New York and began working, very successfully, on Wall Street.

For all the success he was having in New York and in the stock market, however, he was still uneasy. What had kept him from final vows was outwardly simple: sex. He didn't feel that the Church's stand on celibacy was necessary in order to be either a good Christian or a good counselor of a flock. He wasn't a libertine. He was simply a thoughtful young man who wanted to "serve" and found that the restrictions laid out in one particular hierarchy of service were too severe for his personality.

Meeting him and talking with him about these matters was more than instructive; it was, in a way, confirming. We spent many hours discussing the Church, Vatican II, changes in church doctrine, the new forms of the mass, mysticism. I listened and learned, and also heard in his voice and his arguments the sounds of one who, I suspect, eventually *will* return to give service in the only complete way open to him.

As I wrote *Sharelle,* I recalled his youthful certainty and enthusiasm. They became "Patrick's." To have later written about the doubts and waverings, or even a return, would have been presumptuous. But from our talks together, I was instructed in many ways about a human heart's yearning, and the obstacles to its achievements.

When *Sharelle* was completed, I had already envisioned another novel, this time for older readers, adults, that dealt openly with a religious conversion—a man with four children, a widower, who has an "experience" through which he rediscovers his own sensations of God and the universe. That he will pass successively through phases of hope, then of certainty and tyranny, and finally to acceptance in a limited way, is the simple, straight line of the plot.

I decided to set the story in Washington, D.C., largely because of Mr. Reagan's born-again cabinet members and what I thought many of their statements and tenets were: tyrannical, too sure, unforgiving. In fact, they were (and are, for the book is yet unfinished) to act as a counterweight to the progress of the story's hero.

I flew to Washington to begin investigating the surroundings there—something that matters little to anyone but the author of a book striving for realism. I visited a number of church-sponsored elementary, junior high, and high schools, insofar as my "father" will have taken his children from public schools to place them in surroundings where he feels certain moral values will be instructed and maintained. I took an apartment in the city and went where I thought my father and his children would go.

Then, while I was driving back to the city from a day's outing in suburban Virginia, a thought came to me: by the standards of my own time, the education offered young people today was neither received as eagerly nor presented as effectively as I recalled. In short, I decided it wasn't that today's students were under-informed; rather, it might be that today's teachers were under-trained. I rushed ahead in my own mind. If I felt that teachers were not as entertaining or insightful or successful today as I had thought them in my own time. I had only to try to prove this by enlisting myself. As I drove over the Potomac to my apartment, I was on fire. *I* would throw myself into the fray. *I* could be as good a teacher as many I had audited in the past few weeks. I doubted not the sincerity of the men and women who had kindly allowed me to sit at the backs of their classrooms. I only felt that if I tried, perhaps I could do as well as they did, and probably better. This sounds egotistical, but I did think I should get in with both hands and try.

I decided that the children I wanted to teach were not children of privilege, as I myself had been. If advantaged youths couldn't make sense of their lives, that was their problem. What I wanted was disadvantaged young people, people whose horizons were more limited by economics, surroundings, habits. I wanted, in other words, to try to share some of the richness I had received at that age. I was on fire.

I also had no conception of the difficulties of my goal.

I returned to Los Angeles and began working on the new Washington novel. I also took time to inquire of the Archdiocese about teaching positions. Since I had no academic credential that would allow me to teach in a public school, I had to look to the private schools to find a place. I did not, as I said, want a prep school; I wanted an inner-city environment where what I felt I had to offer might not have been offered before.

I fell into a jam pot. The Archdiocese actually gambled on me, taking (I suppose) my eagerness and determination in place of experience. In the autumn of 1983 I began at St. Eugene School, teaching English to the fifth-, sixth-, seventh-, and eighth-grade classes, as well as reading (to one section of the eighth grade) and social studies (to the sixth grade).

I made a mistake. (One of hundreds that year, but this is perhaps the largest ... coloring the entire school year as it did.) I realized almost instantly when school began that I was up in front of those classes saying just one thing to them: "Love me."

They did.

Which meant discipline went down the tubes. Actually, it hardly had enough strength to resist swirling waters.

The kids at St. Eugene's and I adored each other. They were entertaining, quick, clever, lazy, sly, unused to success, unused to the English language in a clear, untinted accent that carried simple, direct meanings. Of course we worked on grammar, but we also worked to learn about history, about personalities and characters, both in fiction and in real life, who helped shape our world. We wrote ... pages and pages of short stories as well as daily theme assignments.

I had never, and to this date have never, worked harder. Preparation for six classes daily, more often than not at least four sets of papers or tests to see to each evening, special appearances at basketball games and school trips, holiday pageants and contests, parent-teacher conferences. My life was finally full. I was exhausted, and yet I never felt better physically ... simply because I had no time to be ill. My focus everyday was on 240 children, *not* on myself or my characters or my checkbook.

I had as my goal the results of a standardized test taken each year by the children in various parishes of the diocese. My intention was to raise those scores, if only by a fraction of a percentage point. This would, in my mind, have indicated a successful effort.

I failed.

The scores did not soar.

They hardly moved.

More—by the end of the year, in fact within the first few weeks of the first semester, my attitudes towards teaching and teachers had changed vividly. The line that runs, "Those that can't, teach," is specious beyond any I know. No one works harder to less external purpose than a teacher ... whose hopes rest entirely in and for the future of his/her students, and who will almost never see the fruits of such titanic labor. Other teachers, more experienced teachers, worked as hard as I or harder. Their dedication and care for their classes of individuals were extraordinary. I learned from the kids, of course. I certainly learned as much from the staff about giving and giving and giving.

I cannot think I was a successful teacher. But I regret not a moment of the effort. I might even try it again, a second time, better armed and prepared but equally determined with the same sort of almost unrealistic expectations I had when I began.

The point I think I'm making here is that during the years I did not write, during the months I sat on my hands or wheeled about the countryside telling myself I would soon be ready to do *something,* I was actually looking for something *outside* myself to concentrate on—a cause, a person, an ideal. I am not trying to say this is necessarily a religious notion. But it *is* an idea I had not previously felt within me as active; and now that I *have* experienced it, it is one I do not want to retire.

This is not a unique discovery. One of the sadnesses of life is that it can come so very late. My hope is that thousands of people younger than I, students and "yuppies" and people in their thirties who have been able to satisfy some of their early urges, already understand this and are *acting* on it in a way that I didn't. After one's first commercial successes, one's happy—even idyllically happy—marriage and children, one's Porsches and lakeside homes and trustfunds for college tuition, there is still time and energy (and need!) for more. *Unless* our lives contain focuses that are not personal but abstract, altruistic at some point, we all will become burdened by a feeling of dissatisfaction that too closely resembles guilt. Not only can this feeling make our days heavy and purposeless, it can, in short, kill the discovery and fun in them.

Let's take a glimpse of what it means to be a writer, and how to decide if it's something you want to be or have the talent to develop.

First, you work alone. That sounds foolishly simple but it's not. It means that only *you* can do the work ... you can depend on no one else for inspiration or accomplishment. It requires discipline ... something that *can* be developed, and it requires a certain amount of being comfortable with yourself, being able to spend hours each day with no other companion but your mind and its visions.

Second, while this kind of occupation may sound ideal—after all, you're your own boss—it may not be. You will have editors to deal with, agents, critics to withstand, producers to persuade, directors to stand up to, performers who "really would feel more comfortable" saying something else. Your bankbook will fluctuate rather wildly … one year you're golden and the next you're worried about paying the dentist, not to mention the rent. Often you will find yourself debating whether or not to do something you really aren't that keen on … of necessity. (There are, of course, men and women made of sterner stuff than I, who hold out for principles and artistic integrity. I have some of both, but also am blessed—or cursed—with a certain capacity for realism.)

Third, you will need a sizable ego. Projects will be turned down that you love; books will be reviewed horribly, and you'll be expected to write on, no matter what. Favorite ideas will be snapped up by other people (who had them at the same time) and emerge in print or on the screen *far* less successfully than if you yourself had been allowed to do the work. (If you work in television or film, you may find yourself replaced without reason … often because a director has a favorite set of writers he/she wants to use, or is more comfortable with; sometimes because the producers feel you've hit a dead-end and someone fresher would be an advantage. Rarely will you be given a chance to discuss these feelings, or your own freshness.)

Fourth, talent helps.

This cannot really, I think, be developed.

Either you have "it" or you don't. You can learn to write more precisely, more grammatically. But not more imaginatively. (You'll find, as you investigate, hundreds of Writers Workshops in progress throughout the country in all seasons. My own feelings about these are mixed. They're fun to go to. You often meet interesting people. Sometimes you'll even collect an idea that can pay out for you later. But no matter the intent of the gathering, or the amount of money required to attend, you really won't come out a better *writer* than when you enrolled. More knowledgeable about the marketplace, perhaps; about agents and magazine editors, or television in general. Or romance novels, children's books, whatever. But the writing part of life, the real part of the writing life, still depends on what you have *inside.* On guts and insight, "stick-to-it-iveness," the desire to make human emotions and experiences accessible to other people.

How does one know if one has an ability to write?

Discard the opinions that run like this: "You write such interesting letters, you'd make a terrific writer." These notions come from family and friends. Besides, a letter generally addresses the activities of the world's most fascinating individual—yourself. You can't really make a career out of this.

Here are a few clues to hidden literary "genius":

Do you find yourself "talking" to others in your own mind? Relating an experience or an idea? Good. You're practicing to present something to other people that will make them laugh or cry or understand or sympathize.

Do you find yourself sitting at a lunch counter imagining the lives and tribulations of people you see only from the outside? Good. You're honing your curiosity; eventually you'll be able to make use of the events and conversations you imagine this way.

Do you like reading? If not, forget the whole thing!

Do you like history? If not, ditto. If the idea of someone else's life in the past doesn't grab you—say Henry VIII, for example, a man with many wives and many appetites in sixteenth-century England—then the curiosity, imagination, and sympathy you need to be a writer isn't on hand.

(As a test, for fun, how many of these people and their accomplishments can you identify? Henri Matisse, Harry S. Truman, Marie Curie, Catherine the Great, Geoffrey Chaucer, Herbert Hoover, Antonio Vivaldi, Mary Shelley, Charles Dickens, Edward Teller. A score of ten means you *might* be on your way!)

Do you like our language? Do you like speaking it? Do you, when thinking, choose your words as carefully as you would in a conference with your school principal? Or an angry parent? If not, you're in deep trouble.

Do you make an effort to "keep up," sometimes even with things that seem unimportant? Of course you're "into" music and movies. What about science and astronomy, or politics and nuclear electricity? You'll have to sometime, and you may as well begin building your knowledge and understanding now while you have the time and while, incidentally, doing so will increase your opportunities for college and beyond.

Do you have a sense of humor? About yourself, or just about others? You need both.

Are there *ideas* you care deeply about? Political, personal, theological? If not, I'm sorry.

Finally, are you aware there is a chance that you may not be special? (This is a trick question.) Of course your family for years has assured you that you are, and you've believed them. This is not a bad thing. Praise and encouragement are very important to any young person facing obstacles of any sort. But learning to understand the *similarities* between you and other people is desperately important. It's what can pull you down emotionally if you let it (it needn't) but it's also what can make your work, as a writer, understandable and likable. People adore reading about ideas, emotions, experiences they've had themselves, or imagine that they could have. It's what we all have in common—our humanity, our joys, our disappointments. Being special is wonderful. Being human is more so.

Apparently, as I look back over the years, I was a "slow learner," a "reluctant" reader of my own abilities.

To find *now* that I'm not so damned special is one of the most exciting discoveries I've ever made.

I hope you make yours earlier.

Postscript

John Neufeld contributed the following update to *SATA* in 2002:

Unless one keeps a journal, the request to "update" one's biography is—or was, by me—met with mixed feelings. Of course, I'm happy still to be breathing, and also to be writing. But to actually sit down and think about what I've done in these past twenty years, and to think whether what I've done has been worth doing, is difficult.

When last we spoke, I was busy giving advice to would-be writers. My advice is exactly now what it was then.

With one or two additions.

First, if you're fortunate enough to be published as a young person or as an adult, my advice is simple: keep writing. Don't stop. Don't take a break.

Second, if the above happy situation turns out to be yours, think about writing a "theme" and "variations." Which is to say, stake your territory and mine it until you're absolutely certain there's nothing left worth extracting.

The value of these two suggestions will, I hope, be discovered in what follows.

When last we talked, I was just coming out of a teaching stint at St. Eugene's School in Inglewood, California. *Sharelle* had been published and I wasn't working on anything except trying to save the world. Careful readers will recall that that didn't work.

One afternoon, a friend called me (I was then living in Los Angeles) and invited me to Santa Barbara to see a particular daycare center at which she was working. As she explained the daily routine, and especially as she described the sorts of children she dealt with, I began to get that tiny, often-longed-for-but-not-often-enough-experienced tingle of a book in the air.

Her daycare center was fascinating to me, for it was intended only for children of the homeless. I had never considered that the people one saw on street corners and in vacant lots and bedding down for the night in doorways or under boxes even had children. And that was just the first of many surprises I received.

I applied for permission to work in the daycare center, too. And after a period of time, I knew I had indeed found my next book. *Almost a Hero* is the story of children who don't have homes, don't eat regularly, don't have clean clothes all the time. They also have huge responsibilities … some of them are even detailed to watch out for and care for their own parents who may be going off one deep end or another without warning.

What I loved best about the book, and still do, is that in it I used an extended metaphor for homelessless … the daily life of the daycare center's pet rat, named Buster. (The original title for the book was *Buster's World*—but the publisher thought this sounded too much like a recent comedy for the screen called "Wayne's World." I was not happy.)

Buster doesn't have a terrible life; what he has is a life that's impossibly difficult to change in any meaningful way.

In the story, Ben Derby is assigned to work at "Sidewalk's End" for a class project, and while at first it's not anything he's happy about, he comes to love the tiny kids who are his charges. He gets so involved in their lives that he almost makes a terrible mistake. In fact, he does make a mistake—identifying the wrong child in danger when in reality another child is in peril. *Almost a Hero* hasn't a happy ending; it has a wiser ending, which in my mind is just as good.

Wiser is what we are all supposed to be as we age. That hasn't been my experience. I still get too quickly enthusiastic and go overboard when a wiser head would

think first, and understand the value of caution and other people's advice.

Before I wrote *Almost a Hero,* I was hired to write the biography of a well-known film and television actress ("my-glamorous-life-as-I-lived-it-as-told-to"). I jumped at the chance. First, I liked her. Second, I thought this would add a string to my bow. If for whatever reason I couldn't find a book for young readers I wanted to write, someone "out there" might—after *this* book became a bestseller—say, "Get me that guy who did what's-her-name's book!" and there I'd be, busy working away in an entirely different genre. And since stars always need someone to write their exciting, fascinating lives, I'd be set for life.

Not so fast.

I made two telephone calls. One to a famous "ghost writer" who had done books for Nancy Reagan and Lee Iococa, and one to my father. Both of them said the same thing. "Is it too late to get out of it?"

Of course I didn't listen. How bad could this be?

Quick cut. The famous "star" and I hit it off wonderfully. We dined together, played tennis together, went to the movies together, spoke on the phone often three or four times a day. I had purchased a small tape recorder. She would tell me what she remembered and, more importantly, how she remembered it, and the tape machine captured it. At home, I transcribed what had been recorded and then sat down to "write" in her own style.

Later, I would show her what I had written.

That's where the rub was.

Everything really good and noteworthy about her life was being excised. I would say, "But weren't you single at the time?" "Yes." "And wasn't he?" "Yes." "Then what's the problem?" "Oh, I know his wife now, you see, and I wouldn't hurt her feelings for the world."

My "star" was a genuinely nice person. That was the trouble. She'd lived a colorful life, and met amazing people, but she wouldn't talk about them. And when we argued about this, of course, she had the last word: "It's *my* life!"

The bigger problem was that the publisher who had hired us to work together expected something for his money. What we wound up with was a six hundred page soufflé, wonderfully written (no false modesty; it was) but empty of nourishment.

Although the editor we worked with had kept telling us how wonderful the manuscript was, and how much better it was getting every day, eventually the publisher decided not to publish the book.

I had spent eighteen months and a lot of money on this project. When the publisher said he wanted his advance returned, I rebelled. I hired a lawyer and fought. I won. But of course that, too, cost money.

And the star? She wound up repaying her advance *and* lost the rights to her own life story, for that was one of the things I had fought for: if anyone were to tell her story but me, they would have to get my permission.

A miserable deal all around.

And before I forget, not the first (or probably the last).

Prior to this effort, I had been commissioned to write a modern *King Lear.* This, although I didn't know it, at the time that Jane Smiley was beginning to write her take on the same Shakespeare play, updated also, to be called *A Thousand Acres.*

I decided to tell an international tale of suspense and high fashion, using *Lear* as an outline, in some cases actually paraphrasing some of the more famous speeches from the play.

Family Fortunes came out, and sank. I understood. My heart hadn't been in the project really; it was a puzzle to be solved, a challenge, a job. I had needed the money. (N.B. Those projects one accepts for that reason, i.e., money, more often than not turn out to be far less accomplished and interesting when finished than if one had spent the time doing something one really desperately wanted to do. Another good lesson learned, and one I actually have learned. Finally.)

Jane Smiley's book won the Pulitzer Prize.

That was all before *Almost a Hero.* By the time I had finished that book, I was on fire with other projects. Every day I came up with ideas for new children's stories. To this date, I have more ideas than time to write them all, I'm sure.

What came next was *Gaps in Stone Walls,* a novel for young readers set on Martha's Vineyard in 1870. I had heard about a colony on the island that for years had had an extraordinarily high percentage of deaf people. I was fascinated, especially since, as I researched, I found that these people (whom we used to call "handicapped") were in no way treated differently from their neighbors.

I flew to the Vineyard four times, and found people there who were generous and helpful and enthusiastic. I researched everything! I mean it! I have notes about fascinating events and ideas and characters that were never included in the finished book. I have so much research still on hand, in fact, that to do a sequel, or even two, would be wonderful fun and fast.

Gaps in Stone Walls was my first attempt at writing a historical novel. I loved writing it almost more than any other book I've done. It required not just research, but a sense of what could legitimately be included without slowing down the story. And I had such vivid characters to deal with, some of them almost Dickensian in their attitudes and speech.

There was only one traumatic moment in this experience. At the end of the book, the final two chapters that exist now are not those I first wrote. I had been on fire that day at my computer, knowing I was reaching the climax of the book. I was so full of eagerness to finish that in my delirium I accidentally pushed the wrong key on my keyboard. Two whole chapters disappeared! There was no way that I could retrieve them. I sat stunned for a moment, and then shouted and stamped my feet and hit anything within distance.

Then I sat down again and rewrote those two chapters as quickly as I could, hoping against hope that I could remember enough to reconstruct not only the chapters themselves but the feelings within them.

I couldn't. And didn't.

Gaps in Stone Walls was nominated for an Edgar Allan Poe Mystery award. It didn't win but I didn't truly care. I was pleased by the recognition and by the reviews, and the awards party in New York was certainly fun.

I rushed ahead. *A Small Civil War,* a book for young readers I had written in 1981, had never, in my mind, been given the attention it deserved. It's a story about censorship, and since censorship still exists today, as it did in

1995 when I began to rewrite it, I thought the project timely and important. I "resold" the book and we republished it and at least now I think it's had its moment.

All of this was not done in a vacuum. I did have a life. In fact, I was changing that life as I wrote.

Living conditions in California were not improving, I thought. As I travelled about the country promoting one book or another, I developed a routine. I would arrive in a new city and call a realtor at random. I explained there was no money in my visit for him (or her), but that I had a budget for a house and I wanted to know what I could get in that community for it. Also, I wanted to get a sense of the "pulse" and flavor of the city as we toured.

I knew California. I began my search in Arizona. Eventually, I travelled all the way to Portland, Maine, asking the same questions and seeing dozens of houses.

I found a part of the country I loved. I rented a house nearby for six months in order to continue to search for a house I could afford. I looked in New York, Massachusetts, and Connecticut. Finally I made a decision: the northwest corner of Connecticut was green and rocky, quiet and lovely. And the town of Salisbury appealed to me in the way that, almost forty years before, East Hampton had. I thought that behind those hedges and trees might live people of accomplishment and value who would, if I made an effort, be generous and supportive.

I couldn't have been more right.

My long-held but never-tested theory was that if one knew just one person in a new town, one could make a happy life. I knew my realtor. That was a start. And wonder of wonders, she passed me on to other people who welcomed me and made me feel comfortable and valuable. I was, and remain, happy here.

Part of my enjoyment of Salisbury is that it is a small town. I had lived in New York and Los Angeles; I had been brought up in Des Moines. I had never really experienced this kind of life—one where you actually went to the post office and talked to people about politics on its front steps. Where the fellow who was painting your house knew where you were going to dinner and who else was likely to be there. Where, if one chose, one could actually have some input into daily living conditions and the progress of a community.

I hadn't realized, of course, how much fun this all could be. I dove immediately into the deep end of the pool. I've just finished a three-year term on my church's Vestry; I am about to become president of a community service club; I sit on the local ambulance service's board; I help organize the annual Salisbury Fall Festival; I sing barbershop and in my church choir; I write "op-ed" pieces for the local newspaper.

And somehow, every so often, I get to do some real work. (I think writers live to be interrupted ... by a telephone call, by a meeting, by a doctor's appointment. If I haven't mentioned this before, a writer has to learn how to live by him or herself for large portions of every day. "Company" always intrudes. I regret to say that these intrusions keep me going!)

After having moved eastwards and settling in a bit, my agent recommended that I send an outline on which I'd been working to a new editor, a person I would never have chosen for myself. As a matter of fact, this editor had once turned me down on another project. But this time he said yes, after challenging me to write a hard-hitting opening chapter. I did. *Boys Lie* is the result.

I had loved the characters I used in *Almost a Hero,* and I wanted to use them again (and I still want to). So I let Ben Derby grow a year and set this new story once more in Santa Barbara. *Boys Lie* is a fairly hard-hitting book about sexual harassment in junior high school. And its heroine, Gina, has some tough times. In this book, I thought a happy ending was appropriate.

As I travelled back to California to promote this book, I remember in particular visiting one small city with a terrific bookstore in which a girl who was probably thirteen or fourteen came on successive days to "audition" *Boys Lie.* She would arrive at mid-morning, go quietly to pick up a copy, and stand there reading. The list price on this book was $16.95, a lot of money for a young person. I didn't blame her a bit.

I'll be out on the road again this autumn (2002) promoting another story, *The Handle and the Key.* A fairly short, simple tale, this book is meant for younger readers than I usually address: eight to twelve years old. The story—about a foster child who has been adopted and struggles to fit into his new family—came from a conversation I had one night at a dinner party with the grandparents of the young man who eventually became the story's hero.

I discovered, as I wrote *The Handle and the Key,* that this story was almost a continuation of my very first published novel, *Edgar Allan.* That early effort is about a black child who is adopted by a white minister and his family. The story ends unhappily.

For all these years (almost thirty-five!), young people to whom I speak have wanted to know what happened later to Edgar Allan. I have always answered that I didn't know, that I didn't feel I could write about Edgar Allan as he grew. And yet, in *The Handle and the Key,* I have. Daniel Johnson Knox is older than Edgar Allan was when he was taken in by loving people, but really his story as a foster child could be Edgar Allan's, too.

What I find most strange about life is that ideas, plans, dreams often actually materialize. Our problem, as the dreamers in question, is to recognize when this happens and make ourselves comfortable with these events.

For example, as a teenager, I had visited friends who lived in Connecticut. I had never before been in this part of the country, and immediately I loved it. Actually, I had said to myself that someday this is where I'd like to live. And now, without realizing or remembering that inner conversation, here I am, living in Connecticut and happily.

While I had sworn never to write about Edgar Allan again, I have done so.

On the other hand, if the reader will go back to the beginning of this postscript, the two new bits of advice I gave there are reactions to events I wanted to have happen, and which did happen, but to which I was fairly insensate when they did.

I had always wanted to write. I was fortunate in finding wonderful stories to tell. I wrote them. But—and here's the kicker—I took time off from doing this. Sometimes several years might pass between projects. Part of this was because I hadn't found a topic that, in my mind, was either new enough or interesting enough to write. And part of this happened because I was so fortunate, having had early

success, earning money that enabled me to be idle, an existence I had imagined as being wonderful.

But idleness is not a happy state of affairs. Of course, one feels happy doing nothing for a while, until guilt seeps into your consciousness. Then, as one grows older, one regrets the wasted years of nonproduction, not only for the money one might today be earning from these unwritten books, but also for energy one may have lost but which one had in abundance earlier.

Therefore, if you can write, do. And never stop. Every newspaper, every conversation, every experience has, somewhere inside it, a story idea that is only waiting to be discovered. Not all are equally worthwhile, but one can pick and choose, and produce books that, even if not internationally important, may well have something of value embedded in them that can profit their readers.

The second addition to my series of caveats about becoming a writer is more practical, and a little less obvious.

I had longed to be a writer. And I had promised myself that what I wrote would never be the same . . . each book would be in a different style and about a different set of characters facing different problems.

To a large degree, I have fulfilled this promise. But now I find that because I have written about young people facing such a variety of problems, young readers (and critics) have found it difficult to understand what they're getting with one of my stories. If each story is different, it is more difficult for readers to identify a particular style, an individual sense of humor or commitment—and certainly more difficult to remember the author of these stories.

When I spoke about "mining" your field and extracting every last mineral of importance from it, I didn't mean to suggest writing "series" books. (Although I have to say that while *I* may not like the series themselves, I do admire their authors for being able to sit down every day and write about the same people, the same towns and events. What really impresses me is that these same writers actually believe in what they're doing—which is, after all, hugely necessary. In the field of adult fiction, for example, while I can't read Danielle Steele, I admire her for believing in herself and telling the same story over a hundred times. And profiting mightily from it.)

If I had been more closely tuned in to what publishing was all about, for example, I would have written more about Edgar Allan's travels and travails. I would have written more about Lisa and her friends as they grew older. What one accomplishes by doing this, first of all, is a lasting readership (if the books prove to be popular), readers who will follow you from one story to the next *because* they already know the characters and like them.

Additionally, readers come to remember one's name as the author of a life-long reading experience. This makes it easier for you, as an author, to continue writing what you may actually want later. With income assured, one can gamble and take chances and *then* write something entirely different. And because of the success of your earlier series, critics are likely to begin their reviews, good or bad, with: "The author of the popular XXXX series has taken a new step in his/her latest effort." Your series is thus once more brought to the mind of readers, giving you a greater currency not only in their eyes but also in the critics'.

This advice may seem selfish. It is. It is exactly what I have not done. Do I regret not mining my own fields? You betcha! I could have done so and still had time to write other stories, many of them. Would I be happier? I think I might have been.

But I chose to stick to my own promise of writing something different every time out. It was certainly more interesting for me, and is today. I may not have a gigantic fund of readers trailing me from story to story, but I believe I have a small, dedicated group of readers, and that certainly makes me return to the white page or space on a screen, eager still to see what happens if I put a blonde girl in a story with a dark-haired boy.

You see, I'm still doing what I did when I was twelve.

O–P

OUGHTON, Jerrie (Preston) 1937-

Personal

Born April 13, 1937, in Atlanta, GA; daughter of Edwin (a college president) and Mary Frances (an educational director and author; maiden name, Johnson) Preston; married William Paul Oughton (a business owner and college professor), November 28, 1963; children: Cher, Lisa, Shannon, Sean, Preston. *Education:* Meredith College, B.A. *Religion:* Disciples of Christ. *Hobbies and other interests:* "Writing, writing, writing."

Addresses

Home—1220 Gainesway Dr., Lexington, KY 40517. *Office*—c/o Publicity Director, Houghton Mifflin Co., 222 Berkeley St., Boston, MA 02116-3764. *E-mail*—JerriePOughton@cs.com.

Career

Writer. Teacher in Raleigh, NC, 1963-64; substitute teacher and teaching assistant, Washington, NC, 1974-85; secretary with Fayette County Public Schools, 1989-2000.

Awards, Honors

Notable Book selection, National Council for the Social Studies, California Children's Media Award for Excellence in Poetry, Music, and Legend, and Best Children's Books selection, *Smithsonian* magazine, all 1992, all for *How the Stars Fell into the Sky: A Navajo Legend;* Notable Book selection, National Council for the Social Studies, and Best Children's Books selection, *Smithsonian* magazine, both 1994, both for *The Magic Weaver of Rugs: A Tale of the Navajo;* Bank Street College Award, 1995, for *Music from a Place Called Half Moon;* Best Book for Young Adults selection, American Library Association (ALA), 1998, for *The War in Georgia;* Best Book for Young Adults selection, ALA, and Best Books

selection, Bank Street College, both 2001, both for *Perfect Family.*

Writings

How the Stars Fell into the Sky: A Navajo Legend, illustrated by Lisa Desimini, Houghton Mifflin (Boston, MA), 1992.

The Magic Weaver of Rugs: A Tale of the Navajo, illustrated by Lisa Desimini, Houghton Mifflin (Boston, MA), 1994.

Music from a Place Called Half Moon, Houghton Mifflin (Boston, MA), 1995.

The War in Georgia, Houghton Mifflin (Boston, MA), 1999.

Perfect Family, Houghton Mifflin (Boston, MA), 2000.

Contributor to periodicals, including *Catholic Digest* and denominational magazines. *The War in Georgia* has been translated into Italian, and *Music from a Place Called Half Moon* has been printed in Braille.

Sidelights

Critics commend Jerrie Oughton as a writer of young-adult books that tackle complex emotional situations, both in families and the larger community, with sensitivity and grace. A native of Atlanta, Oughton graduated from Meredith College, but postponed her career to raise five children. Her first book appeared in 1992, three years after she began working as a secretary for a public school system. She once commented: "There came a point which I really believe is a milestone most writers have to pass. I knew that I would be writing whether or not I ever had a book published. It is part of my make-up and if I tried to turn it off, it would be as futile as stemming a flood.

"It was at this point that I sent Houghton Mifflin Co. two manuscripts. One I discussed in the cover letter. A 'P.S.' stated that I was also enclosing a manuscript for a Navajo legend called *How the Stars Fell into the Sky.* This is the book they bought. My editor linked me up with Lisa Desimini, who is an extraordinary artist. When the first copy of the book came to me, I felt that I had written the words to a song and Lisa had written the music. I was astounded.

"Sometimes people ask me how I got interested in Native American lore. I admire the Navajo greatly and feel any honor and recognition that can be channeled their way is certainly richly deserved. So much of their literary heritage is oral history from their Medicine Men and others who told the stories. I was just fortunate enough to find mention of two oral legends and to be able to pass them on through my mind and soul."

Oughton's first book, *How the Stars Fell into the Sky: A Navajo Legend,* relates the Navajo story of why the stars in the night sky are arranged as humans see them. The text explains that First Woman wanted laws written in the sky for everyone to read. She arranges her jewelry in the night sky, and Coyote comes to help her, but is overeager to finish and knocks many of the sparkling gems about. The disarray is then permanent. "Oughton's text echoes First Woman's self-confidence and is sprinkled throughout with deft turns of phrase," remarked a *Publishers Weekly* reviewer.

Oughton and illustrator Desimini collaborated again on *The Magic Weaver of Rugs: A Tale of the Navajo.* This

Spider Woman teaches two Navajo women how to weave to help their cold, hungry people in Jerrie Oughton's **The Magic Weaver of Rugs,** *illustrated by Lisa Desimini.*

story recounts how the nation's famed rug craft originated. During a time of winter starvation two Navajo women leave the community to pray for aid. Spider Woman intercedes for them, building a loom on which she teaches the pair how to weave a patterned rug. Spider Woman cautions that they must think beautiful thoughts while doing so, but the women are hungry and worried about their families, and negative thoughts creep in. Spider Woman realizes this, becomes angry, and takes the rug—but the woman return to their community having learned the skill. They begin to weave rugs, and the community prospers. They wish to thank the Spider Woman properly and return to the spot where they learned their skill and call to her, but she never comes. "Oughton's fluid prose, studded with images," a *Publishers Weekly* contributor stated, possesses "a poetic intensity, mirrored by Desimini's lush if dark illustrations." *Booklist* reviewer Elizabeth Bush also liked *The Magic Weaver of Rugs,* calling it a "sober and sophisticated tale" and "another fine collaboration" from Oughton and Desimini.

Oughton won critical accolades for her debut novel for young-adult readers, *Music from a Place Called Half Moon.* The story centers on Edie Jo Houp, a thirteen-year-old in the small North Carolina town of Half Moon. Her liberal-minded father suggests one day that their congregation at the Vine Street Baptist Church should allow children from an impoverished Indian community to attend its Vacation Bible School. The bigoted community reacts unkindly to this, and the Houps are ostracized. Even Edie's grandmother sides with the conservative townspeople when arson destroys her house. Edie has befriended Cherokee Fish, a part-Indian classmate, but she begins to wonder if he was the one who set the fire. Then Edie overhears an argument between Cherokee and his brother Sierra, and realizes Sierra was the culprit. Despite its tragic aura, *Music from a Place Called Half Moon* was commended by reviewers for its message of tolerance and hope. "Poverty doesn't ennoble people: the Indian outsiders are as angry and alienated as the whites," noted *Booklist's* Hazel Rochman in her assessment of the book's strengths. A contributor to *Publishers Weekly* called it "understated and candid ... [a] first novel [that] will linger in the reader's memory." *Horn Book's* Maeve Visser Knoth praised it as a work that "takes on strong issues with an intensity and style that mirrors the tension in Half Moon," and described Oughton's creation of Edie Jo as "a carefully drawn heroine who takes small, realistic steps toward understanding" the reasons behind her community's deeply entrenched racism.

In her novel for teens *The War in Georgia,* Oughton recalled memories of her own Southern childhood for this novel, told in flashback, about a family during the final days of World War II. Shanta is thirteen years old in 1945, and an orphan. She lives in Atlanta with her grandmother and uncle Louis, who is prematurely disabled by arthritis. Shanta longs for a "real" family, and envies the one that moves in across the street. She befriends the girl near her own age, who has an older brother with a severe brain injury. After a terrible

In this work, set during the 1950s, pregnant fifteen-year-old Welcome is sent to live with her aunt and uncle until her baby is born. (Cover photo by Kamil Vojnar.)

incident, Shanta realizes the presence—and history—of horrific abuse in her new friend's family. Though the subject matter is a tough one, Oughton lightens the mood throughout with a cast of secondary characters like Uncle Louie's magician friends, who are innovative practical jokers. Often their stunts involve creative ways of leaving money around to help Shanta's grandmother survive and care for her charges on a fixed income. Shanta realizes that her own form of family, while a bit unconventional, provides her with the nurturing and support everyone needs. "This story makes you believe in the love and laughter and friendship that give you hope in the worst of times," suggested *Booklist*'s Rochman. A *Publishers Weekly* reviewer also praised Oughton's style, finding that her "graceful writing here clearly expresses the hope, laughter and sheer stubbornness bringing strength to a clan of survivors."

Oughton's next work recounted a more conservative era when premarital sex was a deeply taboo subject. *Perfect Family* is set in a small town in North Carolina in the 1950s. Welcome Marie O'Neal is fifteen and the youngest in her family, which appears outwardly "perfect." After a romance ends suddenly, a dalliance with a

friend results in an unexpected pregnancy for Welcome. She tells her parents, who send her off to live with relatives in Virginia. Oughton's tale hints at such strategies to conceal teen pregnancy at the time, when young women suddenly went away to "boarding school"; other times shady doctors were visited. Welcome is determined to keep her child, but she undergoes a difficult labor, and tries to return to school, work part time, and care for her son. In the end, she decides to give him to her childless aunt and uncle to adopt. The last page of the novel presents an invitation to Welcome's graduation ceremony from medical school. Some critics faulted the implicit message that a teen in such circumstances will find a pleasant solution to her dilemma, but *Booklist*'s Frances Bradburn noted that "though the story takes place years ago, it's still relevant to teens today."

Biographical and Critical Sources

PERIODICALS

Booklist, March 1, 1994, Elizabeth Bush, review of *The Magic Weaver of Rugs,* p. 1265; May 1, 1995, Hazel Rochman, review of *Music from a Place Called Half Moon,* p. 1563; April 1, 1997, Hazel Rochman, review of *The War in Georgia,* p. 1330; April 15, 2000, Frances Bradburn, review of *Perfect Family,* p. 1540.

Horn Book, July-August, 1995, Maeve Visser Knoth, review of *Music from a Place Called Half Moon,* p. 460.

Publishers Weekly, March 16, 1992, review of *How the Stars Fell into the Sky,* p. 78; February 21, 1994, review of *The Magic Weaver of Rugs,* p. 253; April 17, 1995, review of *Music from a Place Called Half Moon,* p. 61; February 10, 1997, review of *The War in Georgia,* p. 84; April 19, 1999, review of *The War in Georgia,* p. 75.

School Library Journal, April, 2000, Kim Harris, review of *Perfect Family,* p. 140.

OTHER

Author Illustrator Source, www.author-illustr-source.com/ (April 27, 2002).

*   *   *

PACE, Lorenzo 1943-

Personal

Born September 29, 1943, in Birmingham, AL; son of Eddie T. and Mary A. Pace; children: Shawn, Ezra, Jalani, Esperanza. *Education:* School of the Art Institute of Chicago, B.F.A., 1974, M.F.A., 1976; Illinois State University, Ed.D., 1978.

Addresses

Home—300 Morgan Ave., Brooklyn, NY 11211. *Office*—Montclair State University, 1 Normal Ave., Upper Montclair, NJ 07043.

Career

University of Illinois—Chicago Circle, Chicago, IL, assistant professor, 1979-82; Medger Evers College, New York, NY, adjunct assistant professor, 1983-88; Montclair State University, Upper Montclair, NJ, director of university art galleries, 1988—. Performance artist, 1983-90; commissioned art work includes the sculpture "Triumph of the Human Spirit," Outdoor Memorial, African Burial Ground, 2000; work represented in solo and group exhibitions, including shows at Smithsonian Institution, New Jersey Historical Society, Museum of Contemporary Art (Los Angeles, CA), Neuberger Museum of Art, Bronx River Gallery, and Tribes Gallery; represented in permanent collections at School of the Art Institute of Chicago, National Woodcarvers Museum, and DeSable Museum of Afro-American History.

Awards, Honors

Artist in residence, Jamaica Art Center, Jamaica, NY, 1986, and Bedford Stuyvesant Restoration Center, 1987; award for museum leadership, People to People Citizen Ambassador Program, Smithsonian Institution, 1992; award for excellence in design, Art Commission of the City of New York, 1997; key to the city of Birmingham, AL, 1998.

Writings

(Self-illustrated) *Jalani and the Lock,* PowerKids Press/ Rosen Publishing Group (New York, NY), 2001.

Work in Progress

The Making of the Monument, the history of the African Burial Ground in New York, NY.

Sidelights

African-American artist Lorenzo Pace is perhaps best known for his sculpture "Triumph of the Human Spirit," a massive granite structure located in New York City's Foley Square, site of an eighteenth-century burial ground for African slaves. Pace is also the author of a self-illustrated children's book, *Jalani and the Lock,* published in 2001. In the work, a young boy is taken from his forest home and, after being locked in chains, forced into slavery. Jalani eventually gains his freedom, and he passes on the locks to his children and grandchildren, so they will not forget their roots. In *Booklist,* Hazel Rochman stated that the work "tells the history of slavery for young children with a few simple words and big, childlike illustrations."

Biographical and Critical Sources

PERIODICALS

Booklist, February 15, 2001, Hazel Rochman, review of *Jalani and the Lock,* p. 1156.
Daily News (New York, NY), July 27, 2000, Stanley Crouch, "City Honors Black History beyond Slavery."
New York Arts, July-August, 2000, interview with Lorenzo Pace, p. 31.
New York Post, July 31, 2000, Maria Alvarez, "Slave Memorial Bound in Secrecy."
New York Times, September 16, 2000, Eun Lee Koh, "Shrouded for Months, Memorial to Be Unveiled;" September 27, 2000, Robin Finn, "With Memorial, a Monumental Predicament."
Publishers Weekly, January 15, 2001, review of *Jalani and the Lock,* p. 76.*

*   *   *

PERKINS, Lynne Rae

Personal

Children: two. *Education:* Pennsylvania State University, B.A., 1978; Wisconsin University, M.A., 1981.

Addresses

Home—Cedar, MI. *Agent*—c/o Greenwillow Books, 10 East 53rd St., New York, NY 10022.

Career

Author and illustrator.

Awards, Honors

100 Titles for Reading and Sharing, New York Public Library, *Booklist*'s Best Books, and Blue Ribbon for Fiction, *Bulletin of the Center for Children's Books,* all 1999, all for *All Alone in the Universe.*

Writings

Home Lovely, Greenwillow Books (New York, NY), 1995.
Clouds for Dinner, Greenwillow Books (New York, NY), 1997.
All Alone in the Universe, Greenwillow Books (New York, NY), 1999.
The Broken Cat, Greenwillow Books (New York, NY), 2002.
(Illustrator) Sharon Phillips Denslow, *Georgie Lee,* Greenwillow Books (New York, NY), 2002.

Sidelights

Lynne Rae Perkins creates worlds in her books that "are individual yet palpable, with people who could walk right into the real world without any adjustment," observed Deborah Stevenson in the *Bulletin of the Center for Children's Books.* Perkins's work is unusual because she uses illustrations in narratives that are geared towards older readers, an age group that usually is targeted with text alone. This combination of text and pictures, noted Stevenson, creates an "offhand verisimilitude of moments in text and image that catch readers, hooking them on for the ride to wherever Perkins wants to take them."

Home Lovely concerns Janelle and her young daughter, Tiffany, who combats her loneliness by planting a garden near their trailer home. As the plants grow, Tiffany imagines a garden full of trees and flowers, but she is devastated when their mailman, Bob, compliments her instead on the wonderful-looking tomatoes, melons, and other vegetables she has planted. A *Publishers Weekly* reviewer called *Home Lovely* "a spacious story that allows ordinary loneliness and unexpected kindness to assume their proper proportions." *Horn Book*'s Martha V. Parravano praised Perkins for the "rich" characterizations in the book, writing, "the book is especially welcome for its affirmation ... that a home does not have to be a palace to feel like one."

Perkins's next story, *Clouds for Dinner,* is also accompanied by pen-and-ink drawings, this time telling the story of Janet and her unorthodox parents. Living in a house that is eighty-seven steps up, spending time with parents who spend more time gazing at the sky than they do preparing dinner, Janet longs for an ordinary life. Her wish comes true when she is invited to stay with her suburban, traditional, and totally practical aunt. Janet immerses herself in the mundane events of life with her aunt, including regular dinner and even a carwash, until the first time she tries to describe the magic of nature to her aunt. In a "strong text" accompanied by pictures that "do justice to the beauty of the northern Michigan landscape," Perkins, stated *Horn Book*'s Martha V. Parravano, "once again celebrates the nontraditional."

In "a quiet story about growing up," wrote Roxanne Burg in *School Library Journal, All Alone in the Universe* tells of Debbie and Maureen, two best friends as they grow apart during a school year full of changes and growth. "The agony of change is depicted well" in this powerful telling of "the all-too-familiar experience," commented Deborah Stevenson in *Bulletin for the Center of Children's Books.*

Biographical and Critical Sources

PERIODICALS

Booklist, September 1, 1999, Hazel Rochman, review of *All Alone in the Universe,* p. 127.
Bulletin of the Center for Children's Books, October, 1999, Deborah Stevenson, review of *All Alone in the Universe,* pp. 65-66.
Horn Book, November, 1995, Martha V. Parravano, review of *Home Lovely,* p. 736; September, 1997, Martha V. Parravano, review of *Clouds for Dinner,* pp. 562-563.
Kirkus Reviews, June 15, 1997, review of *Clouds for Dinner,* p. 955.
Publishers Weekly, October 9, 1995, review of *Home Lovely,* p. 86; October 18, 1999, review of *All Alone in the Universe,* p. 84; December 20, 1999, Kate Pavao, "Writing from Experience," an interview with the author, p. 25; April 1, 2002, review of *The Broken Cat,* p. 81.
School Library Journal, October, 1999, Roxanne Burg, review of *All Alone in the Universe,* pp. 156-157.

OTHER

Bulletin of the Center for Children's Books, http://alexia.lis.uiuc.edu/puboff/bccb/ (February, 2000), Deborah Stevenson, "Rising Star: Lynn Rae Perkins."*

*   *   *

PEVSNER, Stella

Personal

Born in Lincoln, IL; married a surgeon (deceased); children: Barbara, Stuart, Charles, Marian. *Education:* Attended Illinois University and Northwestern University.

Addresses

Home—Chicago, IL. *Agent*—c/o Clarion/Houghton, 222 Berkeley St., Boston, MA 02116.

Career

Writer. Has worked as a teacher, as an advertising copywriter for a drugstore chain, and a copywriter for various advertising agencies; former promotion director, Dana Perfumes; freelance writer of articles, commercial filmstrips, and reading texts. *Member:* Authors Guild, Society of Children's Book Writers and Illustrators, Society of Midland Authors.

Awards, Honors

Chicago Women in Publishing first annual award for children's literature, 1973, for *Call Me Heller, That's My Name;* Dorothy Canfield Fisher Award, Vermont Congress of Parents and Teachers, 1977, and Junior Literary Guild Outstanding Book, both for *A Smart Kid Like You;* Golden Kite Award, Society of Children's Book Writers and Illustrators, and Clara Ingram Judson Award, Society of Midland Authors, both 1978, both for *And You Give Me a Pain, Elaine;* Carl Sandburg Award, Friends of the Chicago Public Library, 1980, for *Cute Is a Four-Letter Word;* ALA/YASD Best Books for Young Adults Award, 1989, and Virginia Young Readers Award, Virginia State Reading Association, 1994, both for *How Could You Do It, Diane?;* Honor Book, Charlie May Simon Award, Arkansas Department of Education, 1994, Rebecca Caudill Young Readers' Book Award List, 1994-95, Sunshine State master list of titles, and Sequoyah Children's Book Award master list, all for *The Night the Whole Class Slept Over.*

Writings

The Young Brontes (one-act play), Baker, 1967.
Break a Leg!, Crown, 1969, published as *New Girl,* Scholastic, 1983.
Footsteps on the Stairs, Crown, 1970.
Call Me Heller, That's My Name, Seabury, 1973.
A Smart Kid Like You, Seabury, 1975.
Keep Stompin' Till the Music Stops, Seabury, 1977.
And You Give Me a Pain, Elaine, Seabury, 1978.

Cute Is a Four-Letter Word, Clarion/Houghton, 1980.

I'll Always Remember You ... Maybe, Clarion/Houghton, 1981.

Lindsay, Lindsay, Fly Away Home, Clarion/Houghton, 1983.

Me, My Goat, and My Sister's Wedding, Clarion/Houghton, 1985.

Sister of the Quints (Junior Library Guild selection), Ticknor & Fields, 1987.

How Could You Do It, Diane?, Clarion/Houghton, 1989.

The Night the Whole Class Slept Over, Clarion/Houghton, 1991.

I'm Emma, I'm a Quint, Clarion/Houghton, 1993.

Jon, Flora, and the Odd-Eyed Cat (Junior Library Guild selection), Clarion/Houghton, 1994.

Would My Fortune Cookie Lie? (Junior Library Guild selection), Clarion/Houghton, 1996.

(With Fay Tang) *Sing for Your Father, Su Phan,* Clarion/Houghton, 1997.

Is Everyone Moonburned but Me?, Clarion/Houghton, 2000.

Adaptations

A Smart Kid Like You was made into an ABC-TV *Afterschool Special* in 1976, under the title "Me and Dad's New Wife."

Sidelights

"When I was a child growing up in the small town of Lincoln, Illinois, the career choices for a girl were pretty well limited to teacher, secretary, nurse," wrote award-winning children's book author Stella Pevsner in an essay in *Something About the Author Autobiography Series* (*SAAS*). For those reasons, Pevsner didn't spend much time pondering a career as an author as a young child—she simply didn't think it was a possibility. Years later she wrote for advertising agencies and a perfume company, then began writing freelance articles. It was not until one of her own children challenged her to write an entertaining book for kids that she decided to give it a try. That first book was published the following year. Since then, Pevsner has published many successful juvenile novels dealing with contemporary life.

Pevsner grew up in a large family in central Illinois. She had two older sisters whom she admired, and three brothers near her own age with whom she played. As a young girl she found herself acting like a tomboy to compete with her brothers, and at the same time admiring her sisters as they put on makeup and went out on dates. Her time off from school was filled with many of the traditional joys of childhood. She related in *SAAS*, "When I think of my childhood I often think of the summers. We would sit on the front porch and call out to the occasional acquaintance who walked by on the brick sidewalk. My three brothers and the neighborhood kids and I would play the childhood games of the era ... hide-and-seek, Red Rover ... and when it was dark, we'd dart around bushes, across stretches of grass, and capture lightning bugs to put into jars."

Stella Pevsner

Another one of Pevsner's early loves was reading. She quickly became known as a bookworm in her family. Her mother, an accomplished needlepointer, often tried to get her daughter interested in embroidery. But Pevsner tried hard to get out of the assignments. At one time, her talented mother became interested in quilting and encouraged Pevsner to work at it. "The first time I stuck my finger hard enough to draw blood," she wrote in *SAAS*. "I thought I'd be excused and allowed to go back to my book. Wrong. Adhesive tape around the fingers kept the blood in me and off the quilt. If mothers of today want to drive their children into doing more reading, my advice to them is to put a quilt in a frame."

Housework was often seen by Pevsner as an annoying distraction from her reading. Her assignment was dusting, which was made more complicated by her mother's crocheted doilies covering every piece of furniture. But Pevsner found a way to relieve the tedium of the chore. "Saturday it was my job to take everything off the piano and the living room tables, dust and wax, and put it all back," she told *SAAS*. "To make all this bearable, I propped open a book in a hidden corner, and went back and forth, reading a few sentences before sending more dust flying. What could have been a simple task took me forever."

After cleaning, however, Pevsner was allowed to do all the reading she wanted. She made regular trips to the public library and brought home stacks of books. "Choosing books at the library was the highlight of my week. So many to choose from! I can still recall being in the cool shaded room set aside for children's books," she wrote in *SAAS*. When she got home, she sat under a big tree in the front yard and read for hours. Even though she read extensively as a child, Pevsner had little inkling that she herself would one day be a writer. "If someone had tapped me on the shoulder and whispered, 'Someday books you have written yourself will be on these very shelves,' I would probably have thought there was a lunatic at large," she commented in *SAAS*.

Dolls were also an obsession that Pevsner carried from childhood into adulthood. When she wasn't reading books, Pevsner was often sewing clothing for her collection of dolls. She wrote in *SAAS* that "at Christmas I can remember looking at my older sisters' gifts, compacts, clothes, fancy comb sets ... and wishing I never had to grow up and get things like that and give up dolls. Well, I did, but I didn't." As an adult, with children in school, Pevsner once found herself attending an auction where many antique dolls were being offered for sale. Not being a connoisseur of dolls as collectibles, she bid on the ones that no one else wanted. Then she took them home and again sewed clothes for them. "Partly to make these dolls legitimate, I used them in a book. In the narrative, it was the mother who kept the dolls. Her daughter referred to them, as did mine, as the 'glassy-eyed goons,'" she stated in *SAAS*.

A high school English teacher helped push Pevsner toward her future career. He asked her to write a humor column for the school paper. "Although I had only a vague notion of what a humor column might be, I said sure, I would," she once commented in *SAAS*. "He gave me a collection of essays by [James] Thurber and other humorists of the period for inspiration and suggested I write something clever on the subject of babysitting. . . . When my column appeared in print, I was amazed that the world didn't stop while everyone gaped at me and gasped, 'She writes!' Yet the fact that no one seemed shaken or more than mildly impressed didn't affect the new perception I had of myself. Indeed, I was a writer."

Further classes in creative writing were fun for Pevsner, and she continued to take writing classes in college. But her immediate goal was to be a teacher. She did teach for two years, but a summer spent in Chicago changed that. While accompanying a friend who was signing up for a class in advertising, Pevsner decided to enroll also. She found out that she really loved the field. "It was such fun writing copy that didn't actually bend the truth, but certainly put the best possible view on the product," she wrote in *SAAS*. With the help of an employment agency, she landed that first crucial job in the field, working for a drugstore chain. She found the job challenging, but not very stimulating. She discovered ways to increase her duties when a coworker who wrote radio spots suddenly quit. Asked if she could write for radio, she said, "Certainly," and did it. Eventually she moved on to another job—writing copy for a department store. Then she began writing fashion copy for an advertising agency, moved on to agencies with varied products, and still later became the promotion director for a perfume house.

Pevsner's copywriting career came to an abrupt end when she got married. She quit her job and moved into a Chicago suburb that was an hour—and a world—away from the city. Her days were filled with the duties of a suburban housewife—cooking, cleaning, and taking care of her expanding family. However, she knew that she didn't quite fit in. While the other women were interested in home decor, she found herself thinking about her writing. Eventually, she began doing feature articles for a local paper. "I asked a friend to assess the general neighborhood opinion, and she said the women felt I was a bit eccentric, but generally okay," she explained in *SAAS*. Her house soon became the neighborhood play place, with her four children and their friends finding in Pevsner a permissive and fun mother. Pevsner got used to listening to dialogue and stories directly from the mouths of children that would be useful to her later in writing her stories. Still, writing novels for children was not in her plans. She continued to write for newspapers and finished a children's play and a reading program for children.

One of her sons first encouraged her to write for children. He had just written to his favorite author, asking her to write faster so he could have more books to read. When she politely answered that she was working as fast as she could, he informed his mother that she would have to write a book for children. She was dumbfounded at first, but soon decided that if her son had confidence in her abilities, she couldn't do anything but try. That summer she spent her time researching books that kids liked. She wanted to wait until the kids went back to school in the fall to actually begin writing. When the school bell rang again, she dove into writing *Break a Leg!*

"I'd never enjoyed writing so much," Pevsner declared in *SAAS*. "I was buoyed by my kids' interest in reading 'the next chapter' when they banged back into the house in what seemed to me just minutes after they'd left." *Break a Leg!* combines Pevsner's love of drama with her love of writing. The book centers around Fran, a sixth-grader who joins a summer drama program. With her best friend away at camp, she must deal with some new personalities. A critic for the *Bulletin of the Center for Children's Books* said that "the theatrical background is appealing."

No sooner was this book finished than Pevsner launched a new one. This time, she started writing a mystery story. In *Footsteps on the Stairs,* Chip's interest in ESP and the occult causes him to become especially concerned about the apparent haunting of his friend Maury's house. "The book is well written, particularly in its dialogue," wrote a critic in *Bulletin of the Center for Children's Books. Call Me Heller, That's My Name* was Pevsner's first novel set in a different time period. Published in 1973, the book is about a young, spunky, orphaned girl of the 1920s. Heller gets her Aunt Cornelia to come look after her, but she ends up feeling trapped by her aunt's control and her annoying habits, especially her insistence on calling Heller by her given name, Hildegarde. This book received the first annual

Chicago Women in Publishing Award in children's literature in 1973.

Pevsner delved in to deeper topics as she continued writing. *A Smart Kid Like You,* published in 1975, dealt with the issue of divorce. The main character, Nina, finds out that the teacher for her accelerated math class is her father's new wife. Not having adjusted to the divorce yet, she and her classmates try hazing the teacher. In the end, she learns to accept what has happened and begins dating. Carol R. McIver wrote in *School Library Journal* that "the topic is highly relevant to many of today's young people." The book was made into an ABC-TV *Afterschool Special* under the title "Me and Dad's New Wife." Dyslexia is the subject of *Keep Stompin' Till the Music Stops.* Historic Galena, Illinois, is the setting for this novel about Richard and his great-grandfather. The family tries to ship off the old man to a retirement village, but he manages to foil their plans. During this trauma, Richard accepts his learning disability and gains confidence.

And You Give Me a Pain, Elaine is one of Pevsner's most-loved books. It chronicles the adventures of Andrea, a girl who feels ignored by her parents because her rebellious older sister Elaine demands so much time and attention. Much of her angst is washed away by the tragic death of her beloved older brother. Critics noted how well this novel deals with the problems, both trivial and monumental, of the protagonist. Cyrisse Jaffee, writing in *School Library Journal,* indicated that teens may enjoy it owing to its "realistic dialogue, likable protagonist, [and] humor." Pevsner recognized the impact of the book, claiming that "there must be many Elaines around, because since that book was published several girls have written to ask, 'Do you know my sister?' One of my favorite letters is from a girl who said, 'Your book is like a movie in my mind.'"

Travel has been a passion of Pevsner's ever since she was a little girl. "I distinctly remember an art appreciation session in fifth grade where the painting was of Venice," Pevsner once stated in *SAAS.* "I told myself, *I'm going to go to Venice.* It didn't seem an extravagant notion, even though up to that age, the farthest away I'd ever been was Ohio. Through the years, I remembered that silent vow." As an adult, she has traveled quite frequently, to places as far away as Nepal, Iran, China, and India. These settings have helped her write some of her books, including *Lindsay, Lindsay, Fly Away Home,* a story about a young American girl who is raised in India and who must return to America during high school. A goat that Pevsner met in Katmandu helped inspire her to write *Me, My Goat, and My Sister's Wedding.* "When I asked my editor what he thought of my writing this book, he said cheerfully, 'Well, be sure the goat has an interesting personality,'" she once commented in *SAAS.* She drew upon her adventures with the faraway goat to liven up her narrative.

Once, when speaking before a group of eighth-graders, Pevsner was asked by one of the girls to write a book about suicide. At first, she demurred, saying it was too

Middle child Hannah remains dependable and steady when the rest of her family gets a little crazy as her divorced parents plan new marriages. (Cover illustration by Nancy Carpenter.)

sad a subject. However, finding that she couldn't forget the girl's request, she did write a book called *How Could You Do It, Diane?* The story is told from the viewpoint of Bethany, who painfully tries to find out why her stepsister, a seemingly fun-loving girl, chose to end her life. *Publishers Weekly* stated, "This book never answers that question [of why Diane committed suicide], which keeps the emotional bends of the story ringingly honest."

After the death of her husband, Pevsner spent a year helping to manage his medical clinic. After it was finally sold, she decided to leave the suburbs and move to Chicago. Having received many requests from readers to write a sequel to the popular *Sister of the Quints,* the story of a thirteen-year-old girl who loses her identity when her stepmother has quintuplets, Pevsner wrote *I'm Emma: I'm a Quint.* This story is told from the viewpoint of one of the Wentworth quintuplets, Emma, now an adolescent facing her own identity crisis. Matters are complicated when her older sister Natalie asks her to be maid of honor in her upcoming wedding and the girls' father angrily refuses to allow Emma to participate unless the other quints get a role in the wedding as well.

In his review for the *Bulletin of the Center for Children's Books,* Roger Sutton wrote that "Pevsner brings a practiced hand to blending the various subplots and secrets, and the book has an appealing balance of light moments and intense family argument." If episodes like this one highlight the unique rivalry among quintuplets, this sequel never fails to illustrate their special bond as well.

Making a change of scene from suburbia, Pevsner next wrote *Jon, Flora, and the Odd-Eyed Cat,* a story that takes place in the small South Carolina town of Leesville and centers on thirteen-year-old Jon—who is recovering from rheumatic fever—and his encounter with a mystical girl named Flora. Flora's father was granted custody of her when her parents divorced, and she has run away from him to return to Leesville, where she involves Jon in a strange summer solstice ceremony. Sutton wrote in the *Bulletin of the Center for Children's Books* that this book is "a satisfying summer mystery ... with supernatural overtones that are resolved on the side of reality in a dramatic conclusion." *Would My Fortune Cookie Lie?* is another story about a thirteen-year-old, a girl named Alexis who is upset by her father's departure and her mother's decision to move the family away from Chicago and back to the suburbs. There, a mysterious stranger with a threatening secret becomes more and more prominent in Alexis's life. *Booklist*'s Carolyn Phelan commented that in this page-turner Pevsner "brings to life a cast of original and convincing characters.... Even parents are portrayed as actual, multifaceted people."

The people that Pevsner encounters during her daily life are also a rich source of inspiration for her fiction. "Several years ago, in the grip of a sudden urge of altruism, I signed up as a volunteer at Literacy Chicago, to teach English as a second language," Pevsner told *SATA.* "The student assigned to me was a young Chinese woman who had been raised in North Vietnam during the war. (Incidentally, over there it's known as the *American War.*) Fay Tang was the mother of three middle-grade kids who were quickly becoming Americanized. She wanted her children to understand their heritage and to realize what a hard path she had taken to give them a home in the United States. As we became better acquainted, Fay began describing events of her childhood; how the war made life treacherous for the villagers, who moved deeper and deeper into the jungle to escape bombing raids. I began using her stories as a basis for language and writing exercises. Eventually we had quite a collection of stories. With Fay's permission, I wove these stories into a fictionalized account of her life. To the delight of both of us these stories were published in a book called *Sing for Your Father, Su Phan.* Now the once shy, uncertain student had a tangible record for her children. Her verbal and social abilities also increased. She took a course which led to her employment in a beauty salon and then, secure in business and communication skills, to the opening of her own salon. People tell me I helped change her life, but Fay and her family have given my world a richer texture as well."

The true story of Fay Tang's childhood "opens up an unfamiliar world, that of the North Vietnamese peasants in the years before and during the war," wrote a reviewer in *Kirkus Reviews.* "For US readers, it will be a compelling portrait of the life of a child for whom terrible hardship was an accepted part of reality, and it will linger in their minds." Julie Corsaro, writing in *Booklist,* observed that "Any number of the [book's] scenes would make a compelling book-talk." The emotional strength of the book, Corsaro remarked, ensures that "Readers will care about Su Phan and her family, and will be relieved to read the epilogue that talks about Su Phan's current life, and how she teamed up with coauthor Pevsner at the Literacy Center in Chicago."

For Pevsner, "It's impossible to know when a casual conversation may turn into a book idea," she remarked. "Once, chatting with a teacher before giving a speech at her school, she made a statement that stayed with me: 'Parents like to think they're impartial but still, they often have a favorite child or a least favorite,' she said. 'And the kids know it.' That was the genesis of *Is Everyone Moonburned But Me?* This is about the middle girl of three sisters whose divorced mother is most involved with her Miss Princess first-born and also the baby of the family, who makes the most of her allergies. Hannah was close to her father but now he's involved with a woman who has a precocious son Hannah's age. She begins to believe that everyone around her is moonburned; she's the only rational (dull) person in her little universe. Her life begins to change when she recognizes that her steadiness, rather than a handicap, is the very force that will ensure her eventual success."

"One of the reasons I find writing for children so satisfying is I know in advance my potential audience. Not personally, of course!" Pevsner once remarked. "Yet I'm reasonably aware of what will amuse, intrigue, delight, or create recognition in readers of a certain age range.... Although the lives of children today are a great deal different from earlier eras, emotions and feeling remain the same. Kids still hurt, they still struggle, and they still triumph." Pevsner's many books for adolescents are a testament to her ability to entertain and enlighten children. She says in conclusion, "I hope my books help by saying, 'Yes, life is like this sometimes. It's not always easy. But you can make it if you just keep trying ... and keep remembering to laugh.'"

Biographical and Critical Sources

BOOKS

Something about the Author Autobiography Series, Volume 14, Gale (Detroit, MI), 1992.
Speaking for Ourselves, National Council of Teachers of English (Urbana, IL), 1990.

PERIODICALS

Booklist, February 15, 1996, Carolyn Phelan, review of *Would My Fortune Cookie Lie?,* p. 1017; January 1, 1998, Julie Corsaro, review of *Sing for Your Father,*

Su Phan; May 1, 2000, Kay Weisman, review of *Is Everyone Moonburned but Me?*

Bulletin of the Center for Children's Books, February, 1970, review of *Break a Leg!*, p. 105; February, 1971, review of *Footsteps on the Stairs*, p. 96; November, 1993, Roger Sutton, review of *I'm Emma: I'm a Quint*, p. 94; October, 1994, Roger Sutton, review of *Jon, Flora, and the Odd-Eyed Cat*, p. 62; June, 2000, review of *Is Everyone Moonburned but Me?*

Kirkus Reviews, October 1, 1997, review of *Sing for Your Father, Su Phan*, p. 1536.

Publishers Weekly, June 30, 1989, review of *How Could You Do It, Diane?*

School Library Journal, May, 1975, Carol R. McIver, review of *A Smart Kind Like You*, p. 58; November, 1978, Cyrisse Jaffee, review of *And You Give Me a Pain, Elaine*, pp. 77-78; July, 2000, Jennifer Ralston, review of *Is Everyone Moonburned but Me?**

*　　*　　*

PIENKOWSKI, Jan (Michal) 1936-

Personal

Born August 8, 1936, in Warsaw, Poland; immigrated to England, 1946; son of Jerzy Dominik and Wanda Maria (a chemist; maiden name, Garlicka) Pienkowski. *Education:* King's College, Cambridge, B.A. (with second class honors), 1957, M.A., 1961. *Religion:* Catholic. *Hobbies and other interests:* Movies, gardening, painting.

Addresses

Home—Oakgates, 45 Lonsdale Rd., Barnes SW13 9JR, England. *Agent*—Angela Holder, Gallery Five Ltd., 121 King St., London W6 9JG, England.

Career

J. Walter Thompson (advertising agency), London, England, art director, 1957-59; William Collins Sons & Co. (publisher), London, art director in publicity, 1959-60; *Time and Tide,* London, art editor, 1960-61; Gallery Five Ltd. (publisher), London, co-founder and art director, 1961-78, consultant art director, 1978—; McCann Erickson (advertising agency), London, television producer, 1962-63; author and illustrator of children's books, 1967—. Graphic illustrator for *Watch!,* BBC-TV, 1969-71. Designed sets for stage productions of the *Meg and Mow Show,* 1981-88, and *Beauty and the Beast,* 1986. *Member:* Society of Authors, Polish Hearth.

Awards, Honors

Kate Greenaway Medal, British Library Association, 1971, for *The Golden Bird,* 1972, for *The Kingdom under the Sea and Other Stories,* and 1980, for *Haunted House;* Kurt Maschler Award (runner up), Book Trust, 1984, for *Christmas: The King James Version.*

Writings

JUVENILE; SELF-ILLUSTRATED

Numbers, Heinemann (London, England), 1973, Harvey House (New York, NY), 1975.

Colours, Heinemann (London, England), 1973, published as *Colors,* Harvey House (New York, NY), 1975.

Shapes, Heinemann (London, England), 1973, Harvey House (New York, NY), 1975.

Sizes, Heinemann (London, England), 1973, Harvey House (New York, NY), 1975.

Homes, Heinemann (London, England), 1979, Messner (New York, NY), 1983.

Weather, Heinemann (London, England), 1979, Messner (New York, NY), 1983.

ABC, Heinemann (London, England), 1980, Simon & Schuster (New York, NY), 1981.

Time, Heinemann (London, England), 1980, Messner (New York, NY), 1983.

(With Helen Nicoll) *Quest for the Gloop,* Heinemann (London, England), 1980.

Christmas: The King James Version, Puffin (New York, NY), 1984.

Farm, Heinemann (London, England), 1985.

Zoo, Heinemann (London, England), 1985.

Faces, Heinemann (London, England), 1986.

Food, Heinemann (London, England), 1986.

Easter: The King James Version, Random House (New York, NY), 1989.

Oh My! A Fly!, Price Stern Sloan, 1989.

Eggs for Tea, Doubleday (New York, NY), 1989.

Pet Food, Doubleday (New York, NY), 1989.

Home Sweet Home, Doubleday (New York, NY), 1989.

Race You!, Doubleday (New York, NY), 1989.

(With Joan Aiken) *A Foot in the Grave,* Puffin (New York, NY), 1989.

Wheels, Heinemann (London, England), 1991.

Pets, Heinemann (London, England), 1991.

Yes No, Heinemann (London, England), 1991.

Stop Go, Heinemann (London, England), 1991.

(With Russell Hoban) *M.O.L.E.,* Cape, 1993.

1001 Words, Heinemann (London, England), 1994.

Batto the Bat, Dorling Kindersley (London, England), 1997.

Big Machines, Dutton (New York, NY), 1997.

Boats, Dutton (New York, NY), 1997.

Froggo the Frog, Dorling Kindersley (London, England), 1997.

Legs the Spider, Andrews McMeel, 1997.

Octo the Octopus, Dorling Kindersley (London, England), 1997.

Planes and Other Things That Fly, Dutton (New York, NY), 1997.

Tickles the Octopus, Andrews McMeel, 1997.

Trucks and Other Working Wheels, Dutton (New York, NY), 1997.

Pets, Piggy Toes Press, 1998.

Sea, Piggy Toes Press, 1998.

The Monster Pet, Rigby Literacy, 2000.

POP-UP BOOKS; SELF-ILLUSTRATED

Haunted House, Dutton (New York, NY), 1979.

Readers hunt for characters from fifty-six masterpieces, such as Botticelli's Venus and Whistler's Mother, hidden in the ten rooms of an intricate, pop-up bed-and-breakfast. (Written and illustrated by Jan Pienkowski.)

(With Anne Carter) *Dinner Time,* Gallery Five, 1980, published as *Dinnertime,* Price Stern, 1981.

Robot, Delacorte (New York, NY), 1981.

Gossip, Price Stern, 1983, published as *Small Talk,* Orchard Books (New York, NY), 1985.

Little Monsters, Price Stern, 1986.

Fancy That!, Orchard Books (New York, NY), 1989.

Christmas Kingdom, Penguin (New York, NY), 1991.

Phone Book, Orchard Books (New York, NY), 1991.

Door Bell, Orchard Books (New York, NY), 1992.

ABC Dinosaurs: And Other Prehistoric Creatures, Heinemann (London, England), 1993.

Road Hog, Price Stern Sloan, 1993.

Toilet Book: Don't Forget to Flush!, Price Stern Sloan, 1994.

Botticelli's Bed and Breakfast, Simon & Schuster (New York, NY), 1996.

I'm Not Scared, Reed, 1997.

Goodnight, Candlewick Press, 1999.

Pizza!, Walker Books, 2001.

The Cat With 9 Lives, Mathew Price, 2002.

The Animals Went in 2 by 2, Walker Books, 2002.

CLOTH BOOKS

Animals, Heinemann (London, England), 1995.

Friends, Heinemann (London, England), 1995.

Fun, Heinemann (London, England), 1995.

Play, Heinemann (London, England), 1995.

"BEL AND BUB" SERIES; SELF-ILLUSTRATED

Bel and Bub and the Baby Bird, Dorling Kindersley (London, England), 2000.

Bel and Bub and the Bad Snowball, Dorling Kindersley (London, England), 2000.

Bel and Bub and the Big Brown Box, Dorling Kindersley (London, England), 2000.

Bel and Bub and the Black Hole, Dorling Kindersley (London, England), 2000.

"LOOK AT ME" BOOKS; SELF-ILLUSTRATED

I'm Cat, Simon & Schuster (New York, NY), 1986.

I'm Frog, Simon & Schuster (New York, NY), 1986.

I'm Mouse, Simon & Schuster (New York, NY), 1986.

I'm Panda, Simon & Schuster (New York, NY), 1986.

ILLUSTRATOR

Jessie Gertrude Townsend, *Annie, Bridget and Charlie: An ABC for Children of Rhymes,* Pantheon, 1967.

Joan Aiken, *A Necklace of Raindrops and Other Stories,* J. Cape, 1968; Doubleday (New York, NY), 1969; revised edition, 1972.

Nancy Langstaff and John Langstaff, compilers, *Jim Along, Josie: A Collection of Folk Songs and Singing Games for Young Children,* Harcourt (New York, NY), 1970, new edition published as *Sally Go round the Moon,* Revels, 1986.

Edith Brill, *The Golden Bird,* F. Watts (New York, NY), 1970.

Joan Aiken, *The Kingdom under the Sea and Other Stories,* J. Cape, 1971; revised edition, Penguin (New York, NY), 1986.

Agnes Szudek, *The Amber Mountain and Other Folk Stories,* Hutchinson, 1976.

Dinah Starkey, *Ghosts and Bogles,* Hutchinson, 1976.

Joan Aiken, *Tale of a One-Way Street and Other Stories,* J. Cape, 1978; Doubleday (New York, NY), 1980.

Joan Aiken, *Past Eight O'Clock* (stories), J. Cape, 1986; Viking Kestrel, 1987.

"MEG AND MOG" SERIES; WITH HELEN NICOLL

Meg and Mog, Heinemann (London, England), 1972; Atheneum, 1973; revised edition, Heinemann (London, England), 1977.

Meg's Eggs, Heinemann (London, England), 1972; Atheneum, 1973; revised edition, Heinemann (London, England), 1977.

Meg on the Moon, Heinemann (London, England), 1973; Penguin, 1978.

Meg at Sea, Heinemann (London, England), 1973; Penguin, 1978; revised edition, Heinemann (London, England), 1979.

Meg's Car, Heinemann (London, England), 1975; David & Charles, 1983.

Meg's Castle, Heinemann (London, England), 1975; David & Charles, 1983.

Mog's Mumps, Heinemann (London, England), 1976; David & Charles, 1983.

Meg's Veg, Heinemann (London, England), 1976; David & Charles, 1983.

Meg and Mog Birthday Book, Heinemann (London, England), 1979; David & Charles, 1984.

Mog at the Zoo, Heinemann (London, England), 1982; David & Charles, 1983.

Owl at School, Heinemann (London, England), 1984.

Mog in the Fog, Heinemann (London, England), 1984.

(With David Wood) *Meg and Mog Show,* Samuel French, 1984.

Mog's Box, Heinemann (London, England), 1987.

Owl at the Vet, Heinemann (London, England), 1990.

Meg and Mog (omnibus), Ted Smart, 1994.

Mog's Games, Heinemann (London, England), 1990.

Meg and Mog Colour In Book, Puffin (New York, NY), 1990.

(With David Wood) *Meg and Mog: 4 Plays for Children,* Puffin (New York, NY), 1994.

Meg Up the Creek, Puffin (New York, NY), 2002.

EDITOR AND ILLUSTRATOR; "JAN PIENKOWSKI'S FAIRY TALE LIBRARY" SERIES

Jacob Grimm and Wilhelm Grimm, *Jack and the Beanstalk,* Heinemann (London, England), 1977.

Jacob Grimm and Wilhelm Grimm, *Snow White,* Heinemann (London, England), 1977.

Jacob Grimm and Wilhelm Grimm, *Sleeping Beauty,* Heinemann (London, England), 1977.

Charles Perrault, *Puss in Boots,* Heinemann (London, England), 1977.

Charles Perrault, *Cinderella,* Heinemann (London, England), 1977.

Jacob Grimm and Wilhelm Grimm, *Hansel and Gretel,* Heinemann (London, England), 1977.

OTHER

Meg and Mog (play; first produced in London, England at the Unicorn Theatre, 1981), Samuel French, 1984.

Adaptations

Meg and Mog, Meg's Eggs, Meg at Sea, and *Meg on the Moon* have been recorded on audiocassette and released by Cover to Cover, 1985.

Sidelights

Jan Pienkowski is well known to young readers for his colorful picture books. Often citing both his Central European background and comic book art as inspirations, Pienkowski specializes in illustrations that feature heavy lines and flat hues. He is also credited with revitalizing the pop-up book with titles such as *Haunted House* and *Dinnertime.* Despite his success, Pienkowski still sees room for improvement in his work. "Sometimes, I think I'm a total failure," he commented in *Books for Keeps.* "When you show what you've done, every single thing you've got is there. And if you've had a little success it gets worse because there's more at stake.... I am driven from within by an energy that makes me try harder."

Although he had no formal art training, Pienkowski began designing plays, posters, and greeting cards while attending Cambridge University. After graduation, he held a number of jobs in advertising and publishing. Eventually disillusioned by the business world, Pienkowski started a Christmas card company in 1958. Over time, Pienkowski's card designs became very fashionable. In an interview with Cathy Courtney in *Something about the Author* (SATA), Pienkowski noted: "My designs were right for the moment: I did very bright paper bags, paper clothes were all the rage, and stickers."

Pienkowski became heavily involved in book design when he met Helen Nicoll, a director of children's programming for the British Broadcasting Company (BBC). At Nicoll's request, Pienkowski created the opening and closing credits for the television show *Watch!.* When Nicoll left the BBC to raise a family, she and Pienkowski began the "Meg and Mog" book series. Meg (a witch) and Mog (Meg's pet cat) were based on two very popular characters that Pienkowski had originally drawn as part of the opening and closing credits for *Watch!.* "What appealed to me enormously ... [in the] 'Meg and Mog' books is the idea that there is no essential difference between the drawing and the writing," Pienkowski told Courtney. "They both convey information and fight for supremacy. Sometimes the writing is important, sometimes the drawing."

Pienkowski produced his first pop-up books in 1979. One of the most popular of these works is *Haunted House,* in which the reader comes face to face with scary creatures and spooky scenes that shift and change. Because of their complex nature, the board books require a great deal of planning and effort. Pienkowski told Tony Bradman in *Publishing News* that "these mechanical books, although they may have my name in big, bold type or lettering on the cover, they're really a team effort, and they're the work of a ... lot of people."

When not working on new titles, Pienkowski likes to visit schools. Rather than giving prepared speeches, however, he tries to encourage student participation through group art projects. "I like working with other people," Pienkowski related in the *SATA* interview. "I get much better ideas when I do. I don't think I'm as good on my own as when I'm part of a group." Ultimately, Pienkowski is interested in doing one thing for his young audience: entertaining them. He noted for Courtney: "I never discuss my books with children and I don't believe in market research. The most important thing is that it must entertain me, then it's got a chance of entertaining someone else."

Biographical and Critical Sources

BOOKS

Courtney, Cathy, interview with Pienkowski in *Something about the Author,* Volume 58, Gale (Detroit, MI), 1990.

PERIODICALS

Author Zone, Volume 2, 2002.
Arts Review, January 29, 1988, p. 50.
Books for Keeps, November, 1981, interview with Jan Pienkowski.

New York Times Book Review, November 11, 1984; March 19, 1989, p. 24.
Publishing News, October 16, 1981, Tony Bradman, "How Girls with Nimble Fingers Have Helped a Publishing Success."
School Library Journal, September, 1983; September, 1987; October, 1987.

*   *   *

PIERCE, Sharon
See McCULLOUGH, Sharon Pierce

R–S

RIVERS, Karen 1970-

Personal

Born June 12, 1970; in Nanaimo, British Columbia, Canada; daughter of Norman (a physician) and Elizabeth (a nurse) Rivers. *Education:* Attended University of Victoria, 1987-89; University of British Columbia, B.A., 1991.

Addresses

Home—P.O. Box 8725, Victoria, British Columbia V8W 3S3, Canada. *Agent*—Carolyn Swayze, WRP.O. Box 39588, White Rock, British Columbia V4B 5L6, Canada. *Email*—karen@karenrivers.com.

Career

Writer. Also works for a telephone company. *Member:* Writers Union of Canada, Canadian Society of Authors, Illustrators, and Performers, Children's Writers and Illustrators of British Columbia.

Awards, Honors

British Columbia Book Award, 2000; Sheila Egoff Book Award nomination, 2000; Silver Birch Award nomination, 2002, for *Waiting to Dive.*

Writings

The Tree Tattoo, Cormorant (Dunvegan, Canada), 1999.
Dream Water, Orca (Custer, WA), 1999.
Waiting To Dive, Orca (Custer, WA), 2000.
Surviving Sam, Polestar (Vancouver, Canada), 2001.
The Gold Diggers Club, Orca (Custer, WA), 2002.

Contributor of short story, "The Skinny One," to *Nerves Out Loud,* edited by Susan Musgrave, Annick Press, 2001.

Sidelights

Images of water have played a central role in several works by Canadian writer Karen Rivers. In her novel

Ten-year-old Carly must overcome her grief and depression over her friend's diving accident to dive like a champion in Karen Rivers's novel for young readers. *(Cover illustration by Ljuba Levstek.)*

Dream Water, the main characters Cassie and Holden are deeply affected by the experience of seeing a group of captive orca whales drown their trainer when she accidentally falls into the aquarium after a show. Years later, the two are still held captive to these memories as they both struggle with the additional challenges posed by their dysfunctional families. The work garnered mixed reviews. While Pam Spencer in *School Library Journal* and Shelley Glantz of *Book Report* judged the plot to be too complex, which impeded clarity and character development, a *Resource Links* reviewer found the work overall to be "good, even great at times."

Rivers continued to hone her skills with *Waiting To Dive,* which revolves around friends Carly and Montana, who are diving at a beach while on vacation when disaster strikes. Montana suffers a crippling accident, and Carly must confront both her guilt and her fear. Reviewers found much to like about the novel, including Rivers's use of the first-person, present tense, which according to *Booklist* critic Hazel Rochman "will draw" readers. Rochman also praised the work for the "exhilarating" portrayal of diving and the realism of the relationships among the characters. Moreover, in *Resource Links,* a reviewer noted the effectiveness of Rivers's style, "Rivers writes in a very subtle style and the changes that take place in Carly's life happen quietly and slowly." With so much going for the work, "readers are sure to find something to enjoy here," predicted Debbie Whitbeck in her *School Library Journal* review.

Rivers told *SATA:* "I began writing because I've always been an avid reader and writing seemed a natural progression. More accurately, I began writing seriously after waffling for years between a career in law and one in medicine and ultimately deciding that neither were as much fun as writing. And both required many, many years of school. School loses its appeal after four or six years. The good thing is that I love to write. I didn't love those other things. My ultimate goal is to support myself through writing and not have to work at the phone company until I wither away and die. I write everything, but my main love is writing adult literary fiction. None of my books have been adapted or issued in a foreign language, but there's always hope. I feel kind of bad now that you've asked that question because you've reminded me now that I'm really a great flop. But I'm really just starting out.

"My advice to new writers: don't take reviews seriously, don't be afraid of rejection. Let's face it, writing as a career is fun! Don't let anyone ruin that for you. Besides, it could be worse. You could have to work at the phone company. I try to write every day for at least a couple of hours before I go earn my living. You should do that, too. Write your heart out and eventually you'll find an audience, and even if you don't, at least you'll give your mum some bragging rights. Oh, I have some more advice: try not to over-use certain words. For example, in this sidelight, I may or may not have abused the word 'fun.' I'm either trying to convince you that this is fun, or I'm trying to convince myself. Don't worry about it. Have fun!"

Biographical and Critical Sources

PERIODICALS

Booklist, March 1, 2001, Hazel Rochman, review of *Waiting to Dive,* p. 1281.
Book Report, May-June, 2000, Shelley Glantz, review of *Dream Water,* p. 64.
Quill & Quire, October, 1999, Maureen Garvie, review of *The Tree Tattoo,* pp. 37-38.
Resource Links, February, 2000, review of *Dream Water,* pp. 28-29; February, 2001, review of *Waiting to Dive,* pp. 18-19.
School Library Journal, April, 2000, Pam Spencer, review of *Dream Water,* p. 142; May, 2001, Debbie Whitbeck, review of *Waiting to Dive,* p. 159.

OTHER

Karen Rivers Web Site, http://www.karenrivers.com (April 17, 2002).

*   *   *

SAYRE, April Pulley 1966-

Personal

Born April 11, 1966, in Greenville, SC; daughter of David Clarence (a university professor) and Elizabeth Richardson (a science educator and businesswoman) Pulley; married Jeffrey Peter Sayre (an author and ecologist), 1989. *Education:* Duke University, B.A., 1987; Vermont College, M.F.A. (creative writing). *Hobbies and other interests:* Birdwatching, herb gardening, travel, scuba diving.

Addresses

Home and office—17912 Edgewood Walk, South Bend, IN 46635. *E-mail*—downy@aprilsayre.com.

Career

World magazine, National Geographic Society, intern, 1988; National Wildlife Federation, associate editor, school programs, 1988-91; author and video producer, 1991—. *Member:* Society of Children's Book Writers and Illustrators, National Audubon Society, Nature Conservancy, American Birding Association.

Awards, Honors

Best Books citation, *School Library Journal,* and Notable Books for Children citation, *Smithsonian,* both 1995, both for *If You Should Hear a Honeyguide;* Outstanding Science Trade Book for Children selection, National Science Teachers Association/Children's Book Council, for *Home at Last* and *Dig, Wait, Listen;* "Best Books for the Teen Age" selection, New York Public Library, for *Endangered Birds.*

April Pulley Sayre

Writings

If You Should Hear a Honeyguide, illustrated by S. D. Schindler, Houghton Mifflin (Boston, MA), 1995.

Endangered Birds of North America, Holt (New York, NY), 1996.

Hummingbirds: The Sun Catchers, NorthWord Press (Minocqua, WI), 1996.

Endangered Birds of North America, Twenty-First Century Books (Brookfield, CT), 1997.

Put on Some Antlers and Walk Like a Moose: How Scientists Find, Follow, and Study Wild Animals, Twenty-First Century Books (Brookfield, CT), 1997.

Home at Last: A Song of Migration, illustrations by Alix Berenzy, Holt (New York, NY), 1998.

El Niño and La Niña: Weather in the Headlines, Twenty-First Century Books (Brookfield, CT), 2000.

Turtle, Turtle, Watch Out!, illustrated by Lee Christiansen, Orchard Books (New York, NY), 2000.

Splish! Splash! Animal Baths, Millbrook Press (Brookfield, CT), 2000.

Crocodile Listens, pictures by JoEllen McAllister Stammen, Greenwillow Books (New York, NY), 2001.

It's My City!: A Singing Map, illustrated by Denis Roche, Greenwillow Books (New York, NY), 2001.

Dig, Wait, Listen: A Desert Toad's Tale, illustrated by Barbara Bash, Greenwillow Books (New York, NY), 2001.

The Hungry Hummingbird, illustrated by Gay W. Holland, Millbrook Press (Brookfield, CT), 2001.

Noodle Man: The Pasta Superhero, illustrated by Stephen Constanza, Orchard Books (New York, NY), 2001.

Rainforest, Scholastic (New York, NY), 2002.

Army Ant Parade, illustrated by Rick Chrustowski, Holt (New York, NY), 2002.

Shadows, illustrated by Harvey Stevenson, Holt (New York, NY), 2002.

Secrets of Sound: Studying the Calls and Songs of Whales, Elephants, and Birds, Houghton Mifflin (Boston, MA), 2002.

One Is a Snail: Ten Is a Crab, illustrated by Randy Cecil, Candlewick Press (Cambridge, MA), 2003.

Articles have appeared in *World, Ranger Rick, Earth Explorer Encyclopedia* (CD-ROM), and various educator's guides and scientific curricula.

"EXPLORING EARTH'S BIOMES" SERIES

Tropical Rain Forest, Twenty-First Century Books (Brookfield, CT), 1994.

Desert, Twenty-First Century Books (Brookfield, CT), 1994.

Grassland, Twenty-First Century Books (Brookfield, CT), 1994.

Temperate Deciduous Forest, Twenty-First Century Books (Brookfield, CT), 1994.

Taiga, Twenty-First Century Books (Brookfield, CT), 1994.

Tundra, Twenty-First Century Books (Brookfield, CT), 1994.

River and Stream, Twenty-First Century Books (Brookfield, CT), 1996.

Lake and Pond, Twenty-First Century Books (Brookfield, CT), 1996.

Wetland, Twenty-First Century Books (Brookfield, CT), 1996.

Seashore, Twenty-First Century Books (Brookfield, CT), 1996.

Coral Reef, Twenty-First Century Books (Brookfield, CT), 1996.

Ocean, Twenty-First Century Books (Brookfield, CT), 1996.

"SEVEN CONTINENTS" SERIES

North America, Twenty-First Century Books (Brookfield, CT), 1998.

Europe, Twenty-First Century Books (Brookfield, CT), 1998.

Antarctica, Twenty-First Century Books (Brookfield, CT), 1998.

Australia, Twenty-First Century Books (Brookfield, CT), 1998.

South America, Twenty-First Century Books (Brookfield, CT), 1999.

Africa, Twenty-First Century Books (Brookfield, CT), 1999.

Asia, Twenty-First Century Books (Brookfield, CT), 1999.

Sidelights

April Pulley Sayre is the author of dozens of science books for children, including books in series and stand-alone titles. In the "Exploring Earth's Biomes" series she presents young readers with information about the various habitats found on earth, and in the "Seven Continents" series she provides overviews on the geography, wildlife, and weather to be found on each continent. While a number of reviewers found the "Seven Continents" series to be of average quality and appeal, the "Earth's Biomes" series fared better with critics, who singled out the author's "lively and precise" writing style, to quote *Booklist*'s Carolyn Phelan in a review of *Wetland* and *Lake and Pond*. In a joint review of *Coral Reef* and *Ocean* for *Voice of Youth Advocates*, Mary Ojibway praised the "conversational style" in which Sayre presents "clear, accurate information."

Sayre is an avid bird watcher, and a handful of her books attest to her keen interest, including *If You Should Hear a Honeyguide, Hummingbirds: The Sun Catchers, The Hungry Hummingbird*, and *Endangered Birds of North America*. *If You Should Hear a Honeyguide* and *Hummingbirds*, both picture books, give glimpses into the life of the birds mentioned, followed up with an author's note to give more detailed information. According to Maryann H. Owen of *School Library Journal*, the artwork and easily accessible facts combine to make *The Hungry Hummingbird* "a winner" and a "pleasant, versatile book." Written for somewhat older juvenile readers, *Endangered Birds of North America* presents information on the snail kite, Kirtland's warbler, red-cockaded woodpecker, piping plover, and whooping crane, in what *Booklist* critic Stephanie Zvirin called "a stimulating fashion." Not only did Patricia Manning of *School Library Journal* praise the text as "clear" and "readable," she also remarked favorably on the photographs and maps.

Turtle, Turtle, Watch Out!, Crocodile Listens, and *Dig, Wait, Listen: A Desert Toad's Tale* number among Sayre's other picture book treatments of individual animal species. In *Turtle, Turtle, Watch Out!* she shows the life cycle of the sea turtle, "drawing readers into the turtle's story without anthropomorphism," wrote Carolyn Phelan of *Booklist*. Similarly, in *Crocodile Listens* she gives readers a glimpse of life in the habitat of this dangerous African reptile, which a *Kirkus Reviews* contributor called "playful without being precious." The only book for children presenting the life cycle of the desert-dwelling spadefoot toad, *Dig, Wait, Listen* is also, in the opinion of Phelan, writing in *Booklist*, "clear, precise, and poetic."

Sayre has also treated various topics from a wider point of view. For example, in *Put on Some Antlers and Walk Like a Moose: How Scientists Find, Follow, and Study Wild Animals*, she introduces some methods that biologists use in the field to track and study a variety of species. For balance she presents both the pros and cons of such work. Reviewing the work for *School Library Journal*, Arwen Marshall declared it a "lively and informative book" and an "excellent resource." *Splish! Splash! Animal Baths* and *Home at Last: A Song of Migration* are picture book treatments about how animals bathe and find their ways "home," respectively. In the former title, which *Booklist* critic Ellen Mandel called "wonderfully entertaining," readers learn about how elephants, birds, horses, and even fish groom themselves. Birds, sea turtles, and Monarch butterflies number among the animals discussed in *Home at Last*. With its combination of text and pastel illustrations, the work might "strike a chord in young readers," wrote a *Kirkus Reviews* commentator.

Sayre told *SATA:* "As a child, I spent hours picking flowers, watching insects and birds, reading books, and writing. Now I do the same thing, only as a career. My favorite part of the work is researching—reading books and magazines, calling people on the phone, and visiting museums, parks, and aquariums. The writing itself is difficult. But I write and rewrite until I'm satisfied with every paragraph. I try to communicate the excitement I feel about nature and my fascination with the way scientists discover how nature works. I also feel it's important to write about the environmental problems our planet faces and what's being done to solve those problems.

"My favorite activity is traveling. I have been fortunate to visit many of the grasslands, forests, seashores, rain forests, deserts, and other biomes I describe in my books. I scuba dive and snorkel over coral reefs. My husband and I spent a month in the rain forest of Madagascar, studying lemurs. But most of the time we tromp through wetlands, forests, and grasslands nearby, in order to watch birds.

"My advice to young writers/naturalists is to read a lot, write a lot, and grab a hand lens, go outdoors, and check out all the bizarre and beautiful insects and spiders that live on the plants in your neighborhood. Like me, you'll probably be amazed by what you find living close to home."

Biographical and Critical Sources

PERIODICALS

Appraisal: Science Books for Young People, winter-spring, 1996, p. 54.

Booklist, January 1, 1995, Mary Harris Veeder, reviews of *Temperate Deciduous Forest, Tropical Rain Forest*, and *Desert*, p. 821; September 1, 1995, Julie Corsaro, review of *If You Should Hear a Honeyguide*, p. 80; June 1, 1996, Carolyn Phelan, reviews of *Wetland*, and *Lake and Pond*, pp. 1712-1713; December 1, 1997, Susan Dove Lempke, review of *Put on Some Antlers and Walk Like a Moose: How Scientists Find, Follow, and Study Wild Animals*, p. 632; December 1, 1997, Stephanie Zvirin, review of *Endangered Birds of North America*, p. 632; December 1, 1998, Hazel Rochman, review of *Home at Last: A Song of Migration*, p. 682; February 1, 1999, Carolyn Phelan, review of *Antarctica*, p. 972; August, 1999, Hazel Rochman, review of *Asia*, p. 2055; April 1, 2000, Ellen Mandel, review of

Splish! Splash! Animal Baths, p. 1466; August, 2000, Carolyn Phelan, review of *Turtle, Turtle, Watch Out!,* p. 2150; September 15, 2000, Catherine Andronik, review of *El Niño and La Niña: Weather in the Headlines,* p. 238; December 1, 2000, Stephanie Zvirin, *Splish! Splash! Animal Baths,* p. 73; June 1, 2001, Carolyn Phelan, review of *Dig, Wait, Listen: A Desert Toad's Tale,* p. 1881; November 15, 2001, Gillian Engberg, review of *The Hungry Hummingbird,* p. 579; December 1, 2001, Stephanie Zvirin, review of *Dig, Wait, Listen,* p. 658; February 15, 2002, Kay Weisman, review of *Noodle Man: The Pasta Superhero,* p. 1021; March 1, 2002, Lauren Peterson, review of *Army Ant Parade,* p. 1138.

Horn Book, November-December, 2001, Lolly Robinson, review of *It's My City!: A Singing Map,* p. 738.

Horn Book Guide, spring, 1999, Peter D. Sieruta, review of *Europe,* p. 148, and review of *Australia,* p. 155; fall, 1999, Peter D. Sieruta, reviews of *Antarctica, North America,* and *South America,* p. 385.

Kirkus Reviews, October 1, 1998, review of *Home at Last,* p. 1464; August 15, 2001, review of *Crocodile Listens,* p. 1221.

Publishers Weekly, July 9, 2001, review of *It's My City: A Singing Map,* p. 67; February 11, 2002, review of *Shadows,* p. 184; April 8, 2002, review of *Noodle Man,* p. 226.

School Library Journal, January, 1995, Eva Elisabeth Von Ancken, reviews of *Tropical Rain Forest, Desert,* and *Temperate Deciduous Forest,* p. 131; February, 1995, Eva Elisabeth Von Ancken, reviews of *Tundra, Taiga,* and *Grassland,* p. 110; October, 1995, Susan Scheps, review of *If You Should Hear a Honeyguide,* p. 129; June, 1996, Lisa Wu Stowe, reviews of *Wetland, River and Stream,* and *Lake and Pond,* p. 148; January, 1997, Frances E. Millhouser, reviews of *Seashore, Ocean,* and *Coral Reef,* pp. 134-135; January, 1998, Patricia Manning, review of *Endangered Birds of North America,* pp. 130-131; February, 1998, Arwen Marshall, review of *Put on Some Antlers and Walk Like a Moose,* pp. 124-123; December, 1998, Patricia Manning, review of *Home at Last,* pp. 113-114; February, 1999, Jeanette Larson, reviews of *Australia* and *Europe,* p. 125; April, 1999, Mollie Bynum, review of *Antarctica,* p. 156; May, 2000, Blair Christolon, review of *Splish! Splash! Animal Baths,* p. 164; October, 2000, Susan Scheps, review of *Turtle, Turtle, Watch Out!,* p. 136; June, 2001, Ellen Heath, review of *Dig, Wait, Listen,* p. 129; October, 2001, Anne Knickerbocker, review of *It's My City,* p. 130; October, 2001, Kathleen Kelly MacMillan, review of *Crocodile Listens,* p. 130; November, 2001, Maryann H. Owen, review of *The Hungry Hummingbird,* p. 150.

Teacher Librarian, March, 1999, Shirley Lewis, review of *Home at Last,* p. 44.

Voice of Youth Advocates, April, 1997, Mary Ojibway, reviews of *Coral Reef* and *Ocean,* p. 60; February, 1998, Marilyn Brien, review of *Put on Some Antlers and Walk Like a Moose,* p. 404.

OTHER

April Pulley Sayre Web Site, http://www.aprilsayre.com (April 28, 2002).*

*   *   *

SCHWARTZ, Amy 1954-

Personal

Born April 2, 1954, in San Diego, CA; daughter of I. Henry (a writer) and Eva (a professor of chemistry; maiden name, Herzberg) Schwartz; married; children: Jacob Henry. *Education:* Attended Antioch College; California College of Arts and Crafts, B.F.A., 1976.

Addresses

Agent—c/o Jane Feder, 305 East 24th St., New York, NY 10010.

Career

Freelance illustrator, 1976—, and author of children's books. Windrush School, Berkeley, CA, art teacher, 1977-78; Simon & Schuster, Inc., New York, NY, production assistant, 1981.

Awards, Honors

Best Children's Books of 1982 citation, *School Library Journal,* and 100 Best Children's Books citation, New York Public Library, 1982, both for *Bea and Mr. Jones;* National Jewish Book Award for Illustrated Children's Books, and Association of Jewish Libraries Award for

Amy Schwartz

Finding her cherished Sabbath candlesticks after moving from her home to a small apartment cheers and inspires an older woman to make her new apartment her home and invite her family for Sabbath dinner. (From Mrs. Moskowitz and the Sabbath Candlesticks, *written and illustrated by Schwartz.)*

Best Picture Book, both 1984, and Sydney Taylor Book Award, 1985, all for *Mrs. Moskowitz and the Sabbath Candlesticks;* Parents' Choice Award, Parents' Choice Foundation, 100 Best Children's Books citation, New York Public Library, both 1984, and Children's Choice citation, International Reading Association-Children's Book Council (IRA-CBC), 1985, all for *The Crack-of-Dawn Walkers;* Children's Choice citation, IRA-CBC, 1985, for *Her Majesty, Aunt Essie;* Best Children's Books citation, *School Library Journal,* 1985, for *The Witch Who Lives Down the Hall;* Christopher Award, 1987, for *The Purple Coat;* Parents' Choice Awards, 1989, for *The Lady Who Put Salt in Her Coffee: From the Peterkin Papers,* and 1991, for *Magic Carpet; New York Times* Best Illustrated Children's Book and *Booklist* Editors' Choice, both 1995, both for *A Teeny Tiny Baby.*

Writings

SELF-ILLUSTRATED

Bea and Mr. Jones, Bradbury (Scarsdale, NY), 1982.
Begin at the Beginning, Harper (New York, NY), 1983.

Mrs. Moskowitz and the Sabbath Candlesticks, Jewish Publication Society, 1983.
Her Majesty, Aunt Essie, Bradbury (Scarsdale, NY), 1984.
Yossel Zissel and the Wisdom of Chelm, Jewish Publication Society, 1986.
Oma and Bobo, Bradbury (Scarsdale, NY), 1987.
Annabelle Swift, Kindergartner, Orchard (New York, NY), 1988.
(Adaptor) Lucretia Hale, *The Lady Who Put Salt in Her Coffee: From the Peterkin Papers,* Harcourt, 1989.
(Editor, with Leonard S. Marcus) *Mother Goose's Little Misfortunes,* Bradbury (Scarsdale, NY), 1990.
Camper of the Week, Orchard (New York, NY), 1991.
A Teeny Tiny Baby, Orchard (New York, NY), 1994.
(With father, Henry Schwartz) *Make a Face: A Book with a Mirror,* Scholastic (New York, NY), 1994.
Old MacDonald, Scholastic Press (New York, NY), 1997.
How to Catch an Elephant, Dorling Kindersley, (New York, NY), 1999.
Some Babies, Orchard (New York, NY), 2000.
The Boys Team, Atheneum Books for Young Readers (New York, NY), 2001.
What Do You Think James Likes Best?, Atheneum Books for Young Readers (New York, NY), in press.

ILLUSTRATOR

Elizabeth Metzger, *The Breakfast Book,* Chronicle, 1979.

Diana Saltoon, *The Common Book of Consciousness,* Chronicle, 1979.

Henry Schwartz, *Tales of Old Town,* Associated Creative Writers, 1980.

Amy Hest, *The Crack-of-Dawn Walkers,* Macmillan (New York, NY), 1984.

Eve Bunting, *Jane Martin, Dog Detective,* Harcourt (New York, NY), 1984.

Joanne Ryder, *The Night Flight,* Four Winds (New York, NY), 1985.

Donna Guthrie, *The Witch Who Lives Down the Hall,* Harcourt (New York, NY), 1985.

Amy Hest, *The Purple Coat,* Four Winds (New York, NY), 1986.

Mary Stolz, *The Scarecrows and Their Child,* Harper (New York, NY), 1987.

Elizabeth Lee O'Donnell, *Maggie Doesn't Want to Move,* Four Winds (New York, NY), 1987.

Larry L. King, *Because of Lozo Brown,* Viking (New York, NY), 1988.

Henry Schwartz, *How I Captured a Dinosaur,* Orchard (New York, NY), 1989.

Nancy White Carlstrom, *Blow Me a Kiss, Miss Lilly,* HarperCollins (New York, NY), 1990.

Amy Hest, *Fancy Aunt Jess,* Morrow (New York, NY), 1990.

Stephanie Calmenson, *Wanted: Warm, Furry Friend,* Macmillan (New York, NY), 1990.

Pat Brisson, *Magic Carpet,* Bradbury (Scarsdale, NY), 1991.

Henry Schwartz, *Albert Goes Hollywood,* Orchard (New York, NY), 1992.

A toddler asks for stories to avoid going to sleep in Schwartz's self-illustrated **Some Babies.**

David Gale, editor, *Funny You Should Ask: The Delacorte Book of Original Humorous Short Stories,* Delacorte (New York, NY), 1992.

Kathryn Lasky, *My Island Grandma,* Morrow (New York, NY), 1993.

Amy Hest, *Nana's Birthday Party,* Morrow (New York, NY), 1993.

Kathleen Krull, *Wish You Were Here: Emily Emerson's Guide to the Fifty States,* Doubleday (New York, NY), 1997.

Amy Hest, *Gabby Growing Up,* Simon & Schuster (New York, NY), 1998.

Adaptations

Bea and Mr. Jones was shown on PBS-TV's *Reading Rainbow,* 1983, and *The Purple Coat* was broadcast on the program in 1989.

Sidelights

Since the 1982 publication of her first picture book, *Bea and Mr. Jones,* Amy Schwartz has become known for the gently humorous tales she illustrates with a distinctive style. Her works, which include everyday situations such as starting kindergarten and attending sleepaway camp, "have been praised for accurately capturing a child's point of view," Maureen O'Brien summarized in *Publishers Weekly.* Schwartz explained her insight into childhood in a *Something about the Author Autobiography Series* (*SAAS*) essay: "All of my stories begin with something real and important to me, something that has struck an emotional chord in me. A specific incident or relationship may be my starting point, or some set of feelings about a situation in my current life, which melds with childhood memories to produce a story and a set of characters reflective of both past and present." The author then uses her trademark rounded and elongated drawings, rendered in pen-and-ink and watercolors, to add detail and atmosphere to her tales. "Characterized by her comically droll illustrations," wrote O'Brien, "virtually all of Schwartz's books include one overriding theme: that anything is achievable if you just put your mind to it."

Schwartz grew up in Southern California, the third of four sisters in a loving extended family which included her grandmother. Her parents, who had their own interests in writing and painting, fostered a love for tales by reading and storytelling. "Every summer my family took a long car trip," Schwartz recounted in *SAAS.* "I remember deliberating which parent to ask for a story during these lengthy drives. If I asked my mother I was sure to hear a long, comforting tale.... On the other hand, if I asked my father, the story would be short, but probably quite wild and preposterous." Books also played a vital part in her family's life. "We always had stacks of library books at home and my father could not go near a bookstore without making several purchases," Schwartz recalled. "Sometimes, for an evening's entertainment, we would all be given twenty minutes to decide on a literary selection, then reconvene in the living room to read aloud to each other. My parents also organized play readings with their friends now and then, and we children would be given small parts."

A quiet, studious child, Schwartz spent much of her time reading and drawing. "Some of my strongest memories from my childhood involve books . . . ," the author once told *Something about the Author (SATA).* "I remember attempting to read as I walked home from school every day, trying not to run into someone's hedge, or fall off the curb, or lose my place in my book when I crossed the street." A love for reading led to creative exploits of her own. "I wrote stories and plays in elementary school, and adapted my favorite picture books for school theater productions. I was very shy and awkward in real life, but I had a very active fantasy life. I was also a real ham on stage." Drawing also provided an outlet for her imagination, Schwartz told Leonard S. Marcus of *Horn Book.* "I liked making art, and I was considered good at it. I was a child who lived in her head a lot, and drawing, like reading, allowed me to do that. It also provided me with an identity. I was 'the artist in the family.'"

An excellent student, Schwartz graduated from high school early and attended Antioch College, a progressive school in Ohio, for a year and a half before returning home to California to study art. There, she recounted in *SAAS,* "I had to discover on my own that in illustration, or any other kind of art, one's own quirks and personality can become an artistic strength, rather than a liability. Somehow this wasn't communicated to me in school. In painting classes, for instance, I had tried to fit into an instructor's style rather than to develop my own. . . . In contrast to all that, I found the straightforwardness of my figure drawing classes a welcome relief." Schwartz decided to major in drawing, and following graduation she found occasional illustrating jobs. A friend introduced her to children's book illustration, and she began to consider the field as a possible career. After taking a class in illustration and compiling a portfolio, she travelled to New York City to look for work. Although she didn't obtain any offers, the encouragement she did receive motivated her to relocate to the city permanently to continue pursuing her goal. After several editors suggested she might have a better chance selling her illustrations if she wrote a story to accompany them, she took another class, this time in writing and illustration.

It was after two of these classes and a year of submissions that Schwartz published her first two books. *Bea and Mr. Jones* was published in 1982 and tells of a kindergartner who, tired of the childish activities in class, switches places with her father, a burned-out advertising executive. While a *Publishers Weekly* reviewer believed that Schwartz's "talent for satire" in her debut "goes overboard in burlesquing the characters," Kenneth Marantz found in *School Library Journal* that the "efficiently trimmed and noncondescending story" creates "a parable about the way we organize our lives." "Best of all are the pictures," Janice Prindle declared in *Village Voice.* "Full of chubby little dumpling people bearing purposive expressions, they form an extended cartoon satire." *Begin at the Beginning* similarly uses "a

refreshingly unique style" in portraying young Sara's frustration in trying to complete an art assignment, wrote Nancy Palmer in *School Library Journal.* The little girl's problems in starting her project and her family's bothersome attempts to help "will all strike a sympathetic chord," the critic added, "as will the lesson to bite off what you *can* chew."

Schwartz's Jewish upbringing informs her next book, *Mrs. Moskowitz and the Sabbath Candlesticks.* Asked by a publisher to write a book about the Jewish Sabbath, the author recalled her own experiences of the weekly day of rest and worship, in particular the welcoming feelings she got from observing the day at a friend's home after first moving to New York. Schwartz explores those feelings of "home" with the elderly Mrs. Moskowitz, who has just moved to a small apartment and believes it will never feel like "home" as her old house did. When her son arrives with a misplaced box of belongings, she discovers her Sabbath candlesticks and recalls the happy times her family shared around them. After she polishes the candle sticks, she begins to fix up her new quarters to match, until her new home is prepared for a family Sabbath dinner. The "warm story" is complemented by Schwartz's drawings of "the appealing characters and their neighborhood," wrote a *Publishers Weekly* critic. The illustrations are "full of emotion and humor," stated *Booklist's* Ilene Cooper; "even more than the text, they show that when one door is closed, another can be opened."

Family life is portrayed in a more lighthearted fashion in *Her Majesty, Aunt Essie.* Ruthie is so certain that her visiting Aunt Essie is of royal blood that she makes a bet with her best friend—with her beloved pet dog as the prize. Ruthie's attempts to prove Essie's royalty to Maisie make for "a funny story that will tickle American children who share the fantasy" of royal lineage, Lillian N. Gerhardt of *School Library Journal* remarked . While *Booklist's* Cooper felt the book's "premise is far too sophisticated" for its audience, she noted that "all ages will enjoy Schwartz' roundly shaped people, who manage to pack a good deal of emotion into their small features." British reviewer Colin Mills had similar praise for Schwartz's pictures, and added in *Books for Keeps* that the ending "has irony and pathos that is still too rare in books for the age group."

The multi-generational family is also featured in *Oma and Bobo,* Schwartz's tribute to her own grandmother. The story of Oma's growing acceptance for her granddaughter Alice's new dog Bobo "is a fresh portrait of an unlikely friendship that allows room for both humor and dignity," Roger Sutton of the *Bulletin of the Center for Children's Books* remarked. Calling the "vividly written" story "insightful as well as entertaining," Cooper also praised Schwartz's illustrations as "unusual in the best sense of the word." The critic cited details such as cross-hatching and patterns as things that "add to the visual interest." *Oma and Bobo* "has all of the elements that a picture book *should* have," Trev Jones concluded in *School Library Journal:* "A strong story, memorable characters, and pictures that are self-explanatory. Like Bobo, it deserves a blue ribbon."

The author's next two original stories follow young girls dealing with situations away from home. In *Annabelle Swift, Kindergartner,* Annabelle's first day at school is complicated by her big sister Lucy's bad advice—until Annabelle turns out to be the only one who can count the class's milk money, a skill also taught to her by Lucy. "This engaging story has tremendous appeal for young children" beginning school, Ellen Fader commented in *Horn Book,* and Schwartz's "ability to highlight Annabelle's eventual triumph makes the book exceptional." In addition, "Schwartz's well-designed, cartoonish illustrations are brightly colored and wonderfully expressive," a *Kirkus Reviews* critic noted, strengthening this "exceptionally perceptive look" at childhood concerns. "Her droll illustrations perfectly capture Annabelle's expressions," a *Publishers Weekly* reviewer concluded, making this "a sweetly endearing tale, told very much from a child's perspective."

Camper of the Week similarly shows a young girl trying to fit in with her peers. Rosie's good behavior has earned her the title of "Camper of the Week," so when she helps her friends get away with a prank against the camp bully, she feels guilty when they are caught and punished. "Schwartz once again shows her ability to evoke children's half-submerged fears, and readers will empathize," a *Publishers Weekly* critic observed. While some critics believed Rosie's feelings about her problem are unclear—does she feel guilty, or just left out?— Karen James of *School Library Journal* found Rosie's solution, as she volunteers to share in her friends' punishment, a "satisfying" ending. In addition, the critic praised Schwartz's illustrations which, while "showing minimal facial features," are "surprisingly expressive." Young readers "are likely to respond" to Rosie's dilemma and solution, Zena Sutherland concluded in the *Bulletin of the Center for Children's Books,* as well as to "the textual simplicity, and the brightness of the spacious line-and-wash pictures."

In addition to her original stories, Schwartz has also adapted several familiar stories for the picture book format. In *Yossel Zissel and the Wisdom of Chelm,* the author takes the foolish village of Chelm from Jewish folklore and retells the story of how Yossel Zissel spread their brand of wisdom all over the world. *Booklist*'s Cooper hailed Schwartz's "always pleasing illustrations" whose "highly distinctive style ... [is] one that is perfect for the story's humor." In *The Lady Who Put Salt in Her Coffee: From the Peterkin Papers,* Schwartz takes an episode from Lucretia Hale's classic *The Peterkin Papers* about a charming but foolish Victorian family. In adapting the story of how the family searches for a remedy to salty coffee, Schwartz "has succeeded brilliantly, showing respect for her material and appreciation for the time and place in which it is set," Mary M. Burns of *Horn Book* stated. *School Library Journal* contributor Susan Scheps likewise praised Schwartz's revision as "more accessible to today's children" and hailed the artist's "whimsical characters with wonderfully expres-

sive faces." And in questioning whether the collection of traditional rhymes in Schwartz's *Mother Goose's Little Misfortunes* is valuable, *Horn Book*'s Fader replied: "The answer can only be *yes* when the collection is as fresh, well-focused, and intelligently chosen as this." "In her best illustrations to date," wrote a *Kirkus Reviews* critic, "Schwartz swirls the beleaguered but cheerful characters across the page.... [This collection is] not to be missed."

With the birth of her son Jacob in 1992, Schwartz added another phase to her career. Inspired by the "overwhelming experience" of being a new parent, Schwartz quickly wrote the manuscript for *A Teeny Tiny Baby,* in which a two-week-old infant relates how he commands the family's attention and can "get anything I want." "At that time I found parenting to be so all-absorbing that it was difficult to imagine that I would be able to combine motherhood with my drawing and writing," the artist recounted in *SAAS.* "It felt wonderful to complete the manuscript of *A Teeny Tiny Baby.*" "Schwartz's pitch-perfect ear and her comedienne's timing find visual expression in her upbeat, inviting gouaches," a *Publishers Weekly* reviewer remarked, creating work "sure to be appreciated and enthusiastically revisited." Besides inspiring this work, Schwartz added in *SAAS,* "I feel sure that as Jacob grows and continues to delight and amaze us with new exploits and talents, he will have more stories for me, too."

Two of Schwartz's more recent works include *How to Catch an Elephant* and *Some Babies.* A *Publishers Weekly* reviewer noted that in *How to Catch an Elephant* "the author chronicles the capturing of a temperamental, brightly hued yellow pachyderm" and concluded, "Generous supplies of whimsy and understated humor turn out an engaging outlandish how-to." *Some Babies* is a companion book to Schwartz's *A Teeny Tiny Baby.* Writing in the *School Library Journal,* reviewer Joy Fleishhacker commented, "The soothing tone of the repetitive text balances nicely with the high-energy illustrations. An engaging choice for toddlers who like to look at other toddlers."

No matter what the inspiration for her stories, Schwartz tries to invest each work with a personal feeling. As she explained once in an interview, "I assume that my heroine's emotions are the same as my own, only the situations which provoke these emotions might be different for a child than for myself." Illustrating these story ideas is a creative art as well, she told Jim Roginski in *Parents' Choice.* "It's creative problem solving. It's not as simple as just fitting pictures to words, because you could make a very small book with stick figures or you could make a very large book with lush oil paintings. If you look at the same story—for example, a fairy tale—illustrated by two different artists, it becomes clear what power the illustrator has to present a specific viewpoint to the reader." The artist continued: "You do want your pictures to match the words in books, but it's so much more than that. You're creating a *world* for the reader."

The worlds Schwartz has helped to create include those written by other authors, including her father, Henry. To each she brings her distinctive drawing style with its humor and exacting detail. Her stories have common elements between them as well. The author's heroines "all want to be respected in their world, and sometimes they have to scramble to get there," Schwartz told Marcus. "They start by casting themselves in a difficult role, which they then have to live up to. So they share an odd combination of insecurity and worry, while also having a very strong sense of self." As a result, she concluded, "I want my readers to feel that they'll be able to find a way out of their own quandaries, too. And, most of all, I want them to have laughed and to have felt that they've heard a really good story."

Biographical and Critical Sources

BOOKS

Children's Literature Review, Volume 25, Gale (Detroit, MI), 1991, pp. 183-192.

Silvey, Anita, editor, *Children's Books and Their Creators,* Houghton (Boston, MA), 1995.

Something about the Author Autobiography Series, Volume 18, Gale (Detroit, MI), 1994, pp. 277-289.

PERIODICALS

Booklist, August, 1984, Ilene Cooper, review of *Mrs. Moskowitz and the Sabbath Candlesticks,* p. 1629; January 1, 1985, Ilene Cooper, review of *Her Majesty, Aunt Essie,* p. 643; January 1, 1987, Ilene Cooper, review of *Yossel Zissel and the Wisdom of Chelm,* p. 788; April 1, 1987, Ilene Cooper, review of *Oma and Bobo,* p. 1210; November 1, 1989, p. 558; July, 1994, p. 1945; June 1, 1997, April Judge, review of *Wish You Were Here: Emily's Guide to the Fifty States,* pp. 1692-1693; January 1, 1998, Ilene Cooper, review of *Gabby Growing Up,* pp. 822-823; May 15, 1999, Lauren Peterson, review of *Old MacDonald,* p. 1700; November 15, 1999, Shelle Rosenfeld, review of *How to Catch an Elephant,* p. 639; December 15, 2000, Ilene Cooper, review of *Some Babies,* p. 829.

Books for Keeps, November, 1986, Colin Mills, review of *Her Majesty, Aunt Essie,* p. 15.

Bulletin of the Center for Children's Books, June, 1987, Roger Sutton, review of *Oma and Bobo,* p. 196; July, 1991, Zena Sutherland, review of *Camper of the Week,* p. 274.

Horn Book, January-February, 1985, p. 48; March-April, 1988, Ellen Fader, review of *Annabelle Swift, Kindergartner,* pp. 194-195; January-February, 1990, Leonard S. Marcus, "An Interview with Amy Schwartz," pp. 36-45; January-February, 1990, Mary M. Burns, review of *The Lady Who Put Salt in Her Coffee: From the Peterkin Papers,* p. 51; November-December, 1990, Ellen Fader, review of *Mother Goose's Little Misfortunes,* p. 755; January-February, 1995, p. 53; March, 1999, Mary M. Burns, review of *Old MacDonald,* p. 200.

Kirkus Reviews, January 1, 1988, review of *Annabelle Swift, Kindergartner,* p. 59; June 15, 1990, review of *Mother Goose's Little Misfortunes,* p. 879.

Lion and the Unicorn, April, 1987, pp. 88-97.

New York Times Book Review, November 9, 1986, p. 60; May 17, 1987, p. 40; November 11, 1990, p. 31; November 13, 1994, p. 29; March, 1999, Mary M. Burns, review of *Old MacDonald,* p. 200.

Parents' Choice, Volume 12, number 1, 1989, Jim Roginski, "Interview with the Artist," p. 1.

Publishers Weekly, May 28, 1982, review of *Bea and Mr. Jones,* p. 71; May 11, 1984, review of *Mrs. Moskowitz and the Sabbath Candlesticks,* p. 272; January 15, 1988, review of *Annabelle Swift, Kindergartner,* p. 94; February 26, 1988, Maureen O'Brien, "*PW* Interviews: Amy Schwartz," pp. 176-177; July 12, 1991, review of *Camper of the Week,* p. 66; August 29, 1994, review of *A Teeny Tiny Baby,* p. 78; July 26, 1999, review of *How to Catch an Elephant,* p. 90.

School Library Journal, August, 1982, Kenneth Marantz, review of *Bea and Mr. Jones,* p. 105; August, 1983, Nancy Palmer, review of *Begin at the Beginning,* p. 58; November, 1984, Lillian Gerhardt, review of *Her Majesty, Aunt Essie,* pp. 117-118; March, 1987, Trev Jones, review of *Oma and Bobo,* p. 150; May, 1988, pp. 87-88; October, 1989, Susan Scheps, review of *The Lady Who Put Salt in Her Coffee,* pp. 85-86; September, 1991, Karen James, review of *Camper of the Week,* p. 241; September, 1994, p. 193; October, 2000, Joy Fleishhacker, review of *Some Babies,* p. 136.

Village Voice, December 14, 1982, Janice Prindle, review of *Bea and Mr. Jones,* p. 76.*

*　　　　*　　　　*

SCHWARTZ, Virginia Frances 1950-

Personal

Born December 14, 1950, in Stoney Creek, Ontario, Canada; parents' names, Frank and Frances; married Neil Eric Schwartz (an educator), January, 1978. *Education:* Waterloo Lutheran University (now Wilfrid Laurier University), B.A.; Pace University, M.S. *Politics:* Democrat.

Addresses

Agent—c/o Author Mail, Holiday House, Inc., 425 Madison Ave., New York, NY 10017. *E-mail*—neils@con2.com.

Career

Worked as a registered nurse in New York, NY, and in Canada, between 1975 and 1988; elementary school teacher in New York, NY, 1988-94; elementary school writing teacher in New York, NY, 1994—. *Member:* Society of Children's Book Writers and Illustrators.

Awards, Honors

Gold Award (fiction category), Parents' Choice, 2000, Best Book for Young Adults selection, American Library Association, Notable Book for a Global Society selection, International Reading Association, Top Shelf

Fiction for Middle School Readers selection, *Voice of Youth Advocates,* and Books for the Teen Age selection, New York Public Library, all 2001, all for *Send One Angel Down.*

Writings

YOUNG ADULT HISTORICAL FICTION

Send One Angel Down, Holiday House (New York, NY), 2000.

If I Just Had Two Wings, Stoddart Kids (Toronto, Canada), 2001.

Messenger, Holiday House (New York, NY), 2002.

Work in Progress

Salmon Wife, "a young adult historical novel about the Kwakiutls of Canada," for Stoddart; a historical novel for middle-grade readers about a conductor on the Underground Railroad in Indiana in the 1880s, "as seen through the eyes of a young girl."

Sidelights

Virginia Frances Schwartz told *SATA:* "I knew I wanted to be a writer by the time I went to school. School gave me the written word, but, long before that, the environment in which I was raised prepared me to write. It provided me with certain qualities: beauty, space, endless time to daydream, storytelling, and access to books.

"I grew up in Canada in the heart of the fruit belt that stretched across southern Ontario from Niagara Falls to Toronto. When I was young, it was completely rural, 'like a slice of heaven' as my grandfather says in my latest novel about my family, *Messenger.* My backyard was a twenty-acre orchard of blossoming fruit trees where I played, daydreamed, and read. My mind traveled to a million places as I dangled upside down, played dress-up, and spent every moment I could, even throughout the long, snowy winters, outside. Beauty and space were essential for me to become a writer.

"I lived in a multi-cultural neighborhood of immigrants who came from all areas of Europe—Croatia, Serbia, Italy, England, Scotland, Italy, Sicily, France, and Ireland. They spoke with strong accents, ate delicious foods, looked and dressed differently, all of which mesmerized me. Their traditions, like ours, were shared orally. Something in their voices sparked so many images in my mind about their characters and the countries they had left behind. In the afternoons, when our neighbors dropped over for a scone and tea, they spilled their stories into my ears. We had no television in our house until I was twelve, but we always had entertainment. On hot summer evenings, spread out on a blanket beneath the cherry trees and the Milky Way, my grandparents, aunts, uncles, and parents competed to tell the stories of their lives: spooky stories like my grandmother's, funny stories like my father's, and of course, great fishing stories and jokes from Uncle Phillip. I became a listener, a sponge, at an early age.

"Storytelling was the fuel. Reading provided the fire. By sheer luck, the one library in the whole county was built a block away from my house. I had a new place to explore then. When I read everything in the juvenile section, the librarian secretly allowed me access to that intermediary section, on a landing between the kids' books in the basement and the real adult books on the sunny upper floor. This was 'young adult,' for teenagers, a collection of historical fiction and mysteries that fed my imagination. I had reached a new land, and the best part was getting there while I was still a fourth-grader.

"Although I did write as a child, I did not take writing all that seriously. Perhaps that was because it came easily to me to write the required essays and assignments. But I didn't venture out on my own much. The stories were still locked in my head. It wasn't until I was an adult that I could finally focus on writing. I began a teaching career in the fourth and fifth grades. I loved teaching writing and reading the most. I used to say to my fellow teachers, 'If only I could just teach writing all day!' My wish came true. I was sent by my district to Columbia University to be trained as a teacher of 'The Writing Process.' Each day, I visited classrooms to inspire and train young writers from kindergarten to grade six. Side by side with the children, we read great stories from Cynthia Rylant, Gary Paulsen, Eloise Greenfield, and Donald Crews. We wrote in writers' notebooks every day and learned the steps of drafting, revision, editing, and proofreading. You can't imagine how lucky I felt working each day to transform children into writers. It fed something deep inside. I felt as if I was facing the child in me who dreamed of becoming a writer, but had no idea how to do it. It was during my tenure as a writing teacher that my first book was accepted for publication.

"My subject is always historical fiction for young adults, although I hope to write for middle-graders soon. In life, I always root for the underdog, the one who is left behind in some way, the one I recognize as having so much potential that is covered or perhaps crushed. They often sat in my classroom: girls so shy they never looked up, boys who stuttered, new immigrants lost without the words and friendships to make them feel at home, kids who stumbled over math, students who, at eight years of age, had dark worry-circles beneath their eyes. I wanted them to succeed and realize the tremendous power they had inside them. I wanted the other children to learn tolerance, to know that others can be different from you on the outside, but that inside we are all the same. It is no surprise to me that I write about slaves, immigrants, and Native Americans. These groups suffered tremendous hardships and injustices. In my novels I give them hope and a different life.

"One of the ways in which I have dealt with suffering in my own life was developing into a spiritual person. That means that I look to a higher place than just my own mind for everyday guidance. The songs and prayers of the slaves in *Send One Angel Down* and *If I Just Had Two Wings* mirror the spiritual belief that helped slaves endure centuries of degradations. In *Messenger,* the fatherless narrator is soothed by prayer, literature, poetry, and a belief in the afterlife. These books explore ways to nourish a spirit that has been crushed by abuse and overwhelming family or social problems. Spirituality, or thinking about God, helps us recognize our true selves and develop our potential.

"As a writer, I sit down at my desk, or lie in a field studying clouds in the sky, and listen carefully to the words in my head, the same way I did as a child. I try to get them down as fast as I can at first and do a lot of revision later. The words often come in a rush and my hand moves so fast that it hurts. I keep a notebook by my bedside because ideas often come just before I fall asleep. My characters seem to find me. I did not decide, for instance, to write about slavery. One evening, as I was falling asleep, a girl's face appeared in my mind. At once I knew she was a slave. What drew me into her was her extreme pain and urgency. She had a story to tell. All I had to do was listen. That character was Phoebe and her story became *If I Just Had Two Wings.* Slavery is obviously something that needs to be talked about in the new millennium. America needs racial healing.

"What I realize is that to be a children's author today is to take responsibility for the ways in which children think and grow. I'd like to help make the world a healing place for all races, religious, and cultures."

Biographical and Critical Sources

PERIODICALS

Booklist, June 1, 2000, Debbie Carton, review of *Send One Angel Down;* December 1, 2001, Michael Cart, review of *If I Just Had Two Wings,* p. 638.

Horn Book, July, 2000, review of *Send One Angel Down,* p. 465.

Publishers Weekly, May 1, 2000, review of *Send One Angel Down,* p. 71.

School Library Journal, August, 2000, Bruce Anne Shook, review of *Send One Angel Down,* p. 188; December, 2001, Farida S. Dowler, review of *If I Just Had Two Wings,* p. 143.*

*   *   *

SEIDLER, Ann (G.) 1925-

Personal

Born September 8, 1925, in Northampton, MA; daughter of William F. (a professor) and Anna (Hobbet) Ganong; married William D. Seidler (a lawyer), August 14, 1948; children: Jan, Karen, Bayard, Christopher. *Education:* Smith College, B.A., 1946; New York University, M.A., 1951, Ph.D., 1967. *Hobbies and other interests:* Music.

Addresses

Home—15 Undercliffe Rd., Montclair, NJ 07042.

With help from a clever little boy, the townspeople figure out what to feed a strange creature in **The Hungry Thing,** *written by Jan Slepian and Ann Seidler. (Illustrated by Richard Martin.)*

Career

Punahau School, Honolulu, HI, teacher of speech and drama, 1946-47; National Hospital for Speech Disorders, New York, NY, speech consultant, 1949-51; Mountainside Hospital, Montclair, NJ, speech consultant, 1953-54; Cedar Grove, NJ, Board of Education, speech consultant, 1954-62; Montclair State College, Upper Montclair, NJ, professor of speech, beginning 1967. Author of children's books and professional publications. *Member:* American Speech and Hearing Association, Authors League of America, Phi Beta Kappa.

Writings

WITH JANICE SLEPIAN, ILLUSTRATED BY RICHARD MARTIN

Alfie and the Dream Machine, Follett (Chicago, IL), 1964.
The Cock Who Couldn't Crow, Follett (Chicago, IL), 1964.
Lester and the Sea Monster, Follett (Chicago, IL), 1964.
Mr. Sipple and the Naughty Princess, Follett (Chicago, IL), 1964.
The Roaring Dragon of Redrose, Follett (Chicago, IL), 1964.
Magic Arthur and the Giant, Follett (Chicago, IL), 1964.
Ding-Dong; Bing Bong, Follett (Chicago, IL), 1967.
The Hungry Thing, Follett (Chicago, IL), 1967.
Listen Here Bendemolena, Follett (Chicago, IL), 1967.
Bendemolena, Follett (Chicago, IL), 1967.
An Ear Is to Hear, Follett (Chicago, IL), 1967.
The Silly Listening Book, Follett (Chicago, IL), 1967.

The Cat Who Wore a Pot on Her Head, Scholastic (New York, NY), 1981.

The Hungry Thing Returns, Scholastic (New York, NY), 1990.

OTHER

The Best Invention of All, illustrated by Joseph Veno, Cromwell-Collier (New York, NY), 1967.

(With Doris Balin Bianchi) *Voice and Diction Fitness: A Comprehensive Approach,* Harper & Row (New York, NY), 1988.

The Hungry Thing Goes to a Restaurant, pictures by Elroy Freem, Scholastic (New York, NY), 1992.

Contributor to *Make Yourself Clear,* Kendall/Hunt (Dubuque, IA), 1974. Coauthor of "Building Foundations for Better Listening, Speaking, and Reading," cassette tapes for I.D.I. Publications. Author of articles on young child's speech for Gesell Institute (New Haven, CT) and of a syndicated column, "Child Behavior." Editor, *Journal of New Jersey Speech and Hearing Association,* 1964-65.

Sidelights

During the 1960s, speech language specialist Ann Seidler created humorous beginning readers and picture books. In her books about a lizard-like monster known as the Hungry Thing, she portrayed problems caused by not speaking clearly. In the first monster book, *The Hungry Thing,* the monster comes to town and asks for "feetloaf" and other strange things, baffling the townspeople, who finally feed it. *The Hungry Thing* was popular, going through many reprints, and in the early 1990s Seidler published *The Hungry Thing Returns,* in which the monster and his daughter visit a school, asking for "flamburters, bellyjeans, and blownuts" to eat. In her subsequent *The Hungry Thing Goes to a Restaurant,* in which the monster took a different appearance with illustrations by Elroy Freem, the monster acts much the same. It asks for "bapple moose, spoonadish, and bench flies." After some confusion and effort by an anxious waiter, the monster, as always, leaves the restaurant satisfied.

Biographical and Critical Sources

PERIODICALS

Booklist, April 1, 1990, review of *The Hungry Thing Returns,* p. 1559.

Horn Book, January, 1990, review of *The Hungry Thing Returns,* p. 226.

Publishers Weekly, July 24, 1981, review of *The Cat Who Wore a Pot on Her Head,* pp. 148-149.

School Library Journal, April, 1990, Lori A. Janick, review of *The Hungry Thing Returns,* p. 97.*

SMITH, Lane 1959-

Personal

Born August 25, 1959, in Tulsa, OK; son of Lewis (an accountant) and Mildred Annette (a homemaker; maiden name, Enlow) Smith; married Molly Leach (a designer), 1996. *Education:* Art Center College of Design (Pasadena, CA), B.F.A., 1983.

Addresses

Home—12 West 18th Street #6W, New York, NY, 10011.

Career

Illustrator and author. Freelance illustrator, 1983—. Contributor of illustrations to periodicals, including *Rolling Stone, Time, Ms., Newsweek, New York Times, Atlantic,* and *Esquire.* Art director for film adaptation of *James and the Giant Peach,* Disney, 1996; contributed design work to *Monsters, Inc.,* Pixar, 2000. *Exhibitions:* Works have been exhibited at Master Eagle Gallery, New York City; Brockton Children's Museum, Brockton, MA; Joseloff Gallery, Hartford, CT; Bruce Museum; and in the AIGA touring show.

Awards, Honors

Ten Best Illustrated Books of the Year citation, *New York Times,* Best Book of the Year citation, *School Library Journal,* Honor List, *Horn Book,* Editor's Choice List, American Library Association (ALA) and

Lane Smith

Booklist, and Silver Buckeye Award, all 1987, all for *Halloween ABC;* Silver Medal, Society of Illustrators, Best Books of the Year citation, *New York Times,* Notable Children's Book citation, ALA, Maryland Black-Eyed Susan Picture Book Award, and Reading Magic Award, *Parenting,* all 1989, all for *The True Story of the Three Little Pigs!;* Golden Apple Award, Bratislava International Biennial of Illustrations, 1990, Silver Medal, Society of Illustrators, 1991, and first place, New York Book Show, all for *The Big Pets;* Award for Illustration, *Parent's Choice,* Best Books of the Year citation, *New York Times,* and Notable Children's Book citation, ALA, all 1991, for *Glasses—Who Needs 'Em?;* Caldecott Honor Book, ALA, Best Illustrated Books of the Year citation, *New York Times,* Best Books of the Year citation, *School Library Journal,* Children's Editors' "Top of the List" citation, *Booklist,* and Notable Children's Book citation, ALA, all 1992, all for *The Stinky Cheese Man and Other Fairly Stupid Tales;* Best Children's Book citation, *Publishers Weekly,* Blue Ribbon citation, *Bulletin of the Center for Children's Books,* Top of the List and Editors' Choice citations, *Booklist,* all 1995, Best Book for Young Adults citation, ALA, 1996, all for *Math Curse.*

Writings

SELF-ILLUSTRATED

Flying Jake, Macmillan (New York, NY), 1989.
The Big Pets, Viking (New York, NY), 1990.
Glasses—Who Needs 'Em?, Viking (New York, NY), 1991.
The Happy Hocky Family!, Viking (New York, NY), 1993.
Pinocchio, The Boy, Viking (New York, NY), 2002.
In the Country with the Hocky Family, Viking (New York, NY), 2002.

ILLUSTRATOR

Eve Merriam, *Halloween ABC,* Macmillan (New York, NY), 1987, revised edition published as *Spooky ABC,* Simon & Schuster (New York, NY), 2002.
Jon Scieszka, *The True Story of the Three Little Pigs!,* Viking (New York, NY), 1989.
Jon Scieszka, *The Stinky Cheese Man and Other Fairly Stupid Tales,* Viking (New York, NY), 1992.
Jon Scieszka, *Math Curse,* Viking (New York, NY), 1995.
Karey Kirkpatrick, *Disney's James and the Giant Peach,* Disney Press (New York, NY), 1996.
Roald Dahl, *James and the Giant Peach: A Children's Story,* Knopf (New York, NY), 1996.
Dr. Seuss and Jack Prelutsky, *Hooray for Diffendoofer Day!,* Knopf (New York, NY), 1998.
Jon Scieszka, *Squids Will Be Squids: Fresh Morals, Beastly Fables,* Viking (New York, NY), 1998.
George Saunders, *The Very Persistent Gappers of Frip,* Villard (New York, NY), 2000.
Jon Scieszka, *Baloney, (Henry P.),* Viking (New York, NY), 2001.

ILLUSTRATOR; "TIME WARP TRIO" SERIES; WRITTEN BY JON SCIESZKA

Knights of the Kitchen Table, Viking (New York, NY), 1991.

The Not-So-Jolly Roger, Viking (New York, NY), 1991.
The Good, the Bad, and the Goofy, Viking (New York, NY), 1992.
Your Mother Was a Neanderthal, Viking (New York, NY), 1993.
2095, Viking (New York, NY), 1995.
Tut, Tut, Viking (New York, NY), 1996.
Summer Reading Is Killing Me!, Viking (New York, NY), 1998.
It's All Greek to Me, Viking (New York, NY), 1999.

Sidelights

Young readers are well acquainted with the work of Lane Smith. In fact, college students and adults, too, enjoy his satirical illustrations, which have often been described as "goofy" and even "disturbing." Winner of numerous awards, Smith is best known for his collaboration with the writer Jon Scieszka (pronounced "shes-ka") on such popular children's books as *The True Story of the Three Little Pigs!, The Stinky Cheese Man and Other Fairly Stupid Tales,* and the "Time Warp Trio" series. Smith's illustrations have also appeared in magazines such as *Rolling Stone, Time,* and *Ms.,* and he designed the characters for the Disney film *James and the Giant Peach.*

Smith is noted for creating figures with large heads and small bodies, which he paints in dark oil colors that give them a distinctively strange, exaggerated quality, as if they stepped out of a dream—some might even say a nightmare. The artist traces his style directly back to his childhood interests and fantasies. In an essay for *Children's Books and Their Creators* he wrote that he is frequently asked by adults, "'Why *is* your art so dark?' I am not quite sure why myself," he continued. "All I can say is when I was a child, I *liked* dark things. I liked the night. I liked being inside with my family and listening to the sound the wind made outside. I liked the scratching of the clawlike branches against the roof. I liked thunderstorms. I liked building tents and castles out of blankets and chairs, then crawling under them. I liked telling ghost stories. I liked Halloween." Not surprisingly, he also loved watching monster movies and reading horror fiction.

While Smith's work can be unsettling, it also shows a zany sense of humor, which may be at least partly inherited. Born in Oklahoma, he grew up in Corona, California, with his parents and his brother Shane. Smith once commented about the rhyming names: "Shane and Lane. My mom thought that was funny. Yeah, a real hoot." He added that "*her* brothers were named Dub, Cubby, Leo, and Billy-Joe! My dad's brothers were Tom and Jerry (this is the truth)!" Smith developed an early fascination for the offbeat and the absurd. During summer trips back to Oklahoma on the old Route 66 highway, he enjoyed watching for unusual sights along the way. He stated, "I think that's where my bizarre sense of design comes from. Once you've seen a 100-foot cement buffalo on top of a doughnut stand in the middle of nowhere, you're never the same."

Smith's artistic talent became evident during his years in grade school and junior high school. He made the wry comment in *Talking with Artists* that his future career was determined by his lack of mathematical ability: "I guess I really knew I wanted to be an artist when my fourth-grade math test came back with a big 'D' on it." While Smith spent his time drawing and writing stories, he also read extensively. As he recalled in *Talking with Artists,* "I think one of my fondest memories is of lying stretched out on the library floor at Parkridge Elementary, reading Eleanor Cameron's *Wonderful Flight to the Mushroom Planet.* I loved the story and the art. To this day, whenever I smell hard-boiled eggs I think of how Chuck and David saved the planet with the sulfur-smelling eggs. From then on I drew only space stuff." As he grew older he became interested in cartoons, and he seriously thought about being a cartoonist.

After high school Smith enrolled at the Art Center College of Design in Pasadena, California, where he studied illustration. To earn money for tuition he worked as a janitor at Disneyland, cleaning out park attractions such as the Haunted Mansion and the Revolving Teacup at night. While in art school he developed an interest in Pop Art and European illustration, yet one of his teachers warned him he would never find a job in the United States. In 1984, a year after he earned his degree, he moved to New York City. Contrary to the teacher's prediction, Smith was soon a successful illustrator for some of the country's most popular magazines. He admitted in an essay in *Horn Book* that he had initially been worried about his employment prospects, but "the punk/new-wave movement came, and my work seemed to fit acceptably into that category."

Working on assignments from *Ms., Time, Rolling Stone,* and other magazines by day, Smith learned how to use oil paints at night. In college he had concentrated on drawing, so oil painting was a new medium for him. Smith's first real project was a series of thirty paintings, based on a Halloween theme, that illustrated the letters of the alphabet. He submitted the paintings to the children's book department at the Macmillan publishing house. Impressed by his work, the company hired children's author Eve Merriam to compose poems for each of the illustrations. Smith enjoyed his first experience in collaboration, finding that Merriam's poetry gave him new ideas. For instance, as he commented in his *Horn Book* essay, "I had *V* for 'Vampire,' and she came up with 'Viper,' which I liked a lot because I could use the *V* for the viper's open mouth." When their book, *Halloween ABC,* was published in 1987, reviewers responded positively to Smith's illustrations. Although the book was banned in some places because it was considered "satanic," it received several awards.

In the mid-1980s Smith met Scieszka, a teacher and aspiring children's author. They found they shared a wacky sense of humor, and they both enjoyed "Monty Python" movies and *Mad* magazine. Scieszka liked Smith's work, so they collaborated on a book titled *The True Story of the Three Little Pigs!* In their version of the traditional tale, which they tell from the wolf's point of view, Alexander T. Wolf is locked up in the Pig Pen for killing the three pigs. He says he has been misunderstood and victimized by the media, for he had called on the pigs only to borrow a cup of sugar to make a birthday cake for his grandmother. At the time he had a bad cold, and when he sneezed he blew their houses down. Alexander is quick to add that if the houses had not been so poorly constructed they would not have collapsed. Defending his decision to eat the pigs, he says, "It seemed like a shame to leave a perfectly good ham dinner lying there in the straw." In *Horn Book* Smith explained his approach to illustrating Scieszka's story: "I think Jon thought of the wolf as a con artist trying to talk his way out of a situation. But I really believed the wolf, so I portrayed him with glasses and a little bow tie and tried to make him a victim of circumstance."

At first Smith and Scieszka had little success in selling their manuscript, but when the book was finally published by Viking in 1989 it sold out within a few weeks. Children, teachers, and librarians all liked the contemporary twist to an old story. While Kimberly Olson Fakih and Diane Roback in *Publishers Weekly* thought some readers might find Smith's pictures "mystifyingly adult," many critics were delighted by his quirky style. In a review for *Wilson Library Bulletin,* Donnarae MacCann and Olga Richard observed, "Using minimal but subtly changing browns and ochres, he combines a great variety of creative modes: fanciful, realist, surreal, cartoonish." In an interview with Amanda Smith in *Publishers Weekly,* Smith expressed his surprise at the enthusiastic reception of the book, saying he was "stupefied when *The Three Little Pigs* took off."

In 1989 Smith also wrote and illustrated his own book, *Flying Jake.* He dedicated it to his high school art teacher, Mr. Baughman, who had taught him how to experiment with different media to express various moods. The following year Smith published *The Big Pets,* which he described in *Children's Books and Their Creators* as "a surreal nighttime journey of a little girl and her giant cat." They travel to the Milk Pool, where children swim and other cats happily lap up the milk. The story also features children and oversized pets in the Bone Garden and the Hampster Hole. In *Children's Books and Their Creators* Smith said, "When I wrote *Big Pets* . . . , I was expanding on my own childhood fantasies of slipping out into the night for fantastic adventures while knowing there was a home base of security to come back to." Reviewers were charmed by the illustrations, finding them to be less threatening than the pictures in *The Three Little Pigs.* A typical response came from Diane Roback and Richard Donahue in *Publishers Weekly,* who noted that the "enticing illustrations . . . provide the perfect landscape for this nocturnal romp."

Smith's third self-illustrated book, *Glasses—Who Needs 'Em?,* describes a boy's visit to an eye doctor to be fitted for glasses and is based on the author's own experience. Smith told interviewer Amanda Smith in *Publishers Weekly* that he had to get glasses in the fifth grade, but he rarely wore them because they made him look "too geeky." He said he wanted the character in the book to be "a little reluctant about [getting glasses] but still be kind of cool, so kids who wear glasses empathize and get some laughs out of the book, too, without its being heavy-handed." Writing in *Children's Books and Their Creators,* Smith credited designer Molly Leach with giving *Glasses—Who Needs 'Em?* the right visual effect by creating the opening lines of the story in the form of an eye examination chart. The words in the first line are in large letters, then they shrink down to the type size used in the rest of the book. "Not only did this device draw the reader into the story and establish the proper framework," Smith observed, "it also looked smashing!" Leach has designed several of Smith's other books.

While Smith was writing and illustrating his own works, he continued his collaboration with Scieszka. The success of *The Three Little Pigs* had made them popular guests in schools. During their visits to classrooms, they read the students other stories Scieszka had written. A particular favorite was "The Stinky Cheese Man," which, Smith said in his *Horn Book* essay, got "a huge reaction" from the children. They "would just roll in the aisles. And then for the rest of the day you wouldn't hear anything else.... they would raise their hand and say, 'How about "The Stinky Car"'? Or they would come up after class and say, 'How about "The Stinky Cat"'? Because you know you are not supposed to talk about things being stinky." These responses encouraged Smith and Scieszka to publish *The Stinky Cheese Man and Other Fairly Stupid Tales* in 1992.

The Stinky Cheese Man contains "updated" versions of such classic stories as "Chicken Little," "The Ugly Duckling," "The Princess and the Frog," and "The Princess and the Pea." Here, however, Chicken Little is renamed Chicken Licken, and the animals are indeed crushed—by the book's table of contents, not the sky. The ugly duckling grows up to be an ugly duck, not a lovely swan, and the frog prince is revealed to be just a frog. "The Princess and the Pea" is retitled "The Princess and the Bowling Ball." *The Stinky Cheese Man* was an immediate hit, receiving praise from readers and reviewers alike. Smith received a 1993 Caldecott Honor Book award as well as several other citations for his illustrations. A contributor in *Time* recommended *The Stinky Cheese Man* as "ideal kid stuff," and Mary M. Burns, writing in *Horn Book,* lauded it as "another masterpiece from the team that created *The True Story of the Three Little Pigs!*" *New York Times Book Review* contributor Signe Wilkinson claimed the book would appeal not only to children but to readers of all ages: "Kids, who rejoice in anything stinky, will no doubt enjoy the blithe, mean-spirited anarchy of these wildly spinning stories.... For those who are studying fairy tales at the college level, 'The Stinky Cheese Man' would be a perfect key to the genre.... Collectors of illustrated children's books won't want to miss it."

Smith and Scieszka launched their next project, the "Time Warp Trio" series, with the publication of *Knights of the Kitchen Table* and *The Not-So-Jolly*

Roger in 1991. *The Good, the Bad, and the Goofy* followed in 1992 and *Your Mother Was a Neanderthal* was released the next year. The "Time Warp Trio" stories feature three boys—Joe, Sam, and Fred—who travel back in time and, with the aid of a magical book, encounter fantastic adventures. When they are transported to medieval England in *Knights of the Kitchen Table,* they save King Arthur's Camelot. Using their magic power to read, they defeat an evil knight, a giant, and a dragon. On their second journey, in *The Not-So-Jolly Roger,* the boys meet Blackbeard and his band of pirates, who threaten to kill the trio and make them walk the plank. In *The Good, the Bad, and the Goofy* they travel to the nineteenth-century American wild west, where they again use their powers to survive an Indian attack, a cavalry charge, cattle stampedes, and a flash flood. The trio's fortunes change, however, in *Your Mother Was a Neanderthal.* After being transported back to the Stone Age, they find that not only are they naked, they also do not have their magic book. After Sam invents clothes, the boys embark on a series of escapades as they try to flee cavegirls, ultimately escaping to a happy ending.

The "Time Warp Trio" series received positive responses from reviewers who, like Smith-Scieszka fans,

Working from sketches and notes developed by the late Dr. Suess, Smith and poet Jack Prelutsky created the unusual teachers and classes of Diffendoofer School in **Hooray for Diffendoofer Day!**

looked forward to each new installment. Elizabeth-Ann Sachs observed in *New York Times Book Review* that *Knights of the Kitchen Table* is a "rollicking good story." Although she found *The Not-So-Jolly Roger* was "not nearly as much fun," she said "Time Warp Trio" enthusiasts would want to read it. Diane Roback and Richard Donahue expressed a similar reaction to *The Good, The Bad, and The Goofy* in *Publishers Weekly*. While they thought the story lacked the high-pitched "excitement of the trio's previous adventures," they expected readers to "gobble up this latest time-travel installment as they eagerly await the next one." Janice Del Negro, a contributor to *Booklist*, praised *Your Mother Was a Neanderthal*, especially Smith's illustrations: "Smith's pen-and-ink drawings add a rollicking, somewhat riotous air to the proceedings," she wrote. "This is the kind of book that kids tell one another to read—a surefire hit to the funny bone, whether read alone or aloud." Gale W. Sherman, in a review for *School Library Journal*, called it "Another great book from the dynamic duo!"

In 1993 Smith published his fourth independent work, *The Happy Hocky Family!*, a playful spoof on beginners' schoolbooks of the 1950s, which he described as his "favorite book to date." Smith created the seventeen-episode story of the Hocky family to help young readers understand the disappointments, mistakes, and accidents—as well as the positive experiences—that can happen in life. He used stick figures, basic outline shapes, and primary colors to depict the Hockys. In *New York Times Book Review* Edward Koren noted that "Mr. Smith's draftsmanship, wonderfully expressive, still manages to create a family that is general and unspecific, one that could be of any racial or ethnic group. So who wouldn't be happy to drop in on the Hocky family and visit awhile in their book home?"

In 1995 Smith and Scieszka published *Math Curse*, a picture book, and *2095*, the fifth installment in the "Time Warp Trio" series. *Math Curse* is the story of a girl who wakes up one morning to find every event during the day—getting dressed, eating breakfast, going to school—becomes a math problem that must be solved. She decides her teacher, Mrs. Fibonacci, has put a math curse on her, but that night she dreams of a way to get rid of the curse. Reviews of the book were glowing. Carolyn Phelan wrote in *Booklist*, "Bold in design and often bizarre in expression, Smith's paintings clearly express the child's feelings of bemusement, frustration, and panic as well as her eventual joy when she overcomes the math curse. Scieszka and Smith triumph, too, at the top of their class as artists and entertainers." Lucinda Snyder Whitehurst, a contributor to *School Library Journal*, liked the way the author and illustrator worked actual math problems into the story: "The questions, however, are not always typical workbook queries. For example, . . . How many yards in a neighborhood? How many inches in a pint? How many feet in my shoes?" She also observed that the book "can certainly be used as lighthearted relief in math class, but the story will be heartily enjoyed simply for its zany humor and nonstop sense of fun."

In *2095* Joe, Fred, and Sam are launched into the year 2095 by their magic book. Starting out in the 1920s room of the Natural History Museum, they eventually find themselves in the 1990s exhibition room at the museum. There they meet their great-grandchildren, who try to return them to the past. Julie Yates Walton, in a review for *Booklist*, noted that "the plot is a bit thin and meandering." However, she predicted that "readers will find sufficient distraction in the robots and levitation footwear of the future," and she praised Smith's black-pencil illustrations, which are "brimming with zany, adolescent hyperbole."

Smith and Scieszka have continued to add new titles to the "Time Warp Trio" series, including the 1998 contribution, *Summer Reading Is Killing Me!* In this vertiginous tale a 266-pound chicken ambles through the streets, Peter Rabbit pushes a wheelbarrow, and a one-legged pirate chases a duo of hippos about. When Joe forgetfully puts his summer reading list in The Book, these and other famous characters from children's literature are summoned forth to run amok. "The farce is as furious and silly as ever," announced *Booklist*'s Hazel Rochman.

Smith undertook a completely new venture in 1996 when he designed the characters for the Disney animated version of Roald Dahl's novel *James and the Giant Peach*. At first he was reluctant to become involved in the project, which used live action, animation, and computer effects. In a *New York* article Barbara Ensor quoted Smith as saying he knew it "could turn out to be a really bad thing where I'll commit for a year and I'll just keep getting stuff watered down." However, he thoroughly enjoyed the experience, and all of his work was used in the film. Commuting from New York City to San Francisco one week a month for nearly a year, Smith designed the animated bugs and insects that are the characters in the story. He made highly complex drawings, paying attention to even the smallest details such as pleated skirts and antennae.

Smith did have some difficulty designing the James character. A composite of live action and animation, James had to look like ten-year-old actor Paul Terry. Smith told Ensor, "In real life [Terry is] kind of cute." Because Smith has trouble creating "cute" figures, the director, Henry Selick, finally designed James. Dahl's widow, Liccy Dahl, was thrilled with the film. She told Ensor she would never forget "that first moment when the bugs all came to life on the screen. . . . [Roald] would so have loved that. Ladybug! You just want to hug her. And Grasshopper is pretty dear to my heart." And Liccy Dahl had only praise for Smith: "Lane has got something that's extraordinary, the way he is able to put into their faces every ounce of their character."

As a tie-in to the movie, Smith illustrated a picture-book version of *James and the Giant Peach*, which was written by Karey Kirkpatrick (one of the screenwriters of the film) and published as *Disney's James and the Giant Peach* in 1996. That year Smith also did pen-and-ink artwork for a reissue of the original novel by Knopf.

Ilene Cooper wrote in *Booklist,* "The art in both books is pure Smith, lots of Stinky Cheese Man-style faces. Kids new to the story or fresh from the movie won't mind a bit, but the contemporary artwork may cause a sigh among older readers who are fans of Nancy Burkert's [original] delicate and detailed illustrations." Apparently readers didn't mind a bit; the book became a *Publishers Weekly* number one bestseller.

As a result of his success with the animated *James and the Giant Peach,* Smith has been considering other Hollywood projects. He and Scieszka have reportedly discussed the possibility of making the Stinky Cheese Man a movie star. Smith told Ensor that in a screen version of *The Stinky Cheese Man,* "Stinky's role would be expanded. By virtue of his smell, he would create more and more havoc as the movie progressed, like a snowball that rolls down a hill and gets bigger and bigger. He starts out as a little stinky character that no one likes, but eventually he ends up sabotaging the whole fairy-tale land."

However, while waiting for screen adaptations, loyal fans will have to make do with further book collaborations from the duo, such as *Squids Will Be Squids.* In *Stinky Cheese Man* Smith and Scieszka tackled Mother Goose; with *Squids* the two deal with Aesop in eighteen contemporary wacky fables and tales. A reviewer for *Publishers Weekly* praised Smith's artwork which "ardently keeps pace with Scieszka's leaps of fancy," and concluded that "beneath this duo's playful eccentricity readers will discover some powerful insights into human nature." Again teaming up with Scieszka, Smith contributed artwork for the 2001 title, *Baloney (Henry P.),* the story of a little green alien of the same name who has to spin a wild tale for his teacher to explain why he was late for school. Using a partially made-up language (a lexicon is included), the book is "a hoot of a tall tale," according to Mary Ann Carich in *School Library Journal,* who further noted that *Baloney (Henry P.)* "continues the slightly subversive bent of other Scieszka and Smith collaborations," and also drew attention to Smith's "intricate illustrations/assemblages" which "work perfectly with bold white-on-black text blocks."

Smith has also provided illustrations for *Hooray for Diffendoofer Day!* by Dr. Seuss and Jack Prelutsky, and his artwork is "like translations," as *Horn Book*'s Joanna Ridge Long wrote: "satirical renditions, in his own distinctive, sophisticated style, of such zany folk and weirdly expressive settings as Seuss might have dreamed up to finish this book." And working with short story writer George Saunders, Smith also provided illustrations for *The Very Persistent Gappers of Frip,* "a delightful story, lavishly illustrated," as Susan Salpini commented in *School Library Journal.* Something of a departure for Smith, this book was targeted mainly for adults. Caitlin Dover, reviewing *Gappers* for *Print,* applauded Smith's "perceptive, eclectic paintings," and concluded, "This may be Smith's first foray into adult fiction, but we doubt it will be his last."

Biographical and Critical Sources

BOOKS

Authors and Artists for Young Adults, Volume 21, Gale (Detroit, MI), 1997.
Cummings, Pat, compiler and editor, *Talking with Artists,* Bradbury Press (New York, NY), 1992, pp. 72-75.
Silvey, Anita, editor, *Children's Books and Their Creators,* Houghton (Boston, MA), 1995.

PERIODICALS

Booklist, October 1, 1993, Janice Del Negro, review of *Your Mother Was a Neanderthal,* p. 346; July 1 & 15, 1995, Julie Yates Walton, review of *2095,* p. 1773; November 1, 1995, Carolyn Phelan, review of *Math Curse,* p. 472; May 1, 1996, Ilene Cooper, review of *Disney's James and the Giant Peach* and *James and the Giant Peach,* p. 1511; October 1, 1997, p. 352; May 1, 1998, p. 1522; June 1, 1998, Hazel Rochman, review of *Summer Reading Is Killing Me!* p. 1769; September 15, 1998, p. 232; January 1, 2000, p. 988.
Entertainment Weekly, November 19, 1999, p. 135.
Horn Book, November-December, 1992, Mary M. Burns, review of *The Stinky Cheese Man and Other Fairly Stupid Tales,* p. 720; January-February, 1993, Lane Smith, "The Artist at Work," pp. 64-70; November-December, 1995, p. 738; July-August, 1998, Joanna Ridge Long, review of *Hooray for Diffendoofer Day!,* pp. 479-481; May-June, 2001, p. 316.
New York, April 8, 1996, Barbara Ensor, "Mr. Smith Goes to Hollywood," pp. 50, 51-53.
New Yorker, December 25, 1995, pp. 45-46.
New York Times Book Review, October 6, 1991, Elizabeth-Ann Sachs, review of *Knights of the Kitchen Table* and *The Not-So-Jolly Roger,* p. 23; November 8, 1992, Signe Wilkinson, "No Princes, No White Horses, No Happy Endings," pp. 29, 59; November 14, 1993, Edward Koren, review of *The Happy Hocky Family!,* p. 44.
Print, November, 2000, Caitlin Dover, review of *The Very Persistent Gappers of Frip,* p. 16.
Publishers Weekly, July 28, 1989, Kimberly Olson Fakih, and Diane Roback, review of *The True Story of the Three Little Pigs!,* p. 218; December 21, 1990, Diane Roback, and Richard Donahue, review of *The Big Pets,* p. 55; July 26, 1991, Amanda Smith, "Jon Scieszka and Lane Smith," pp. 220-221; May 11, 1992, Diane Roback, and Richard Donahue, review of *The Good, The Bad, and The Goofy,* p. 72; February 9, 1998, p. 24; May 18, 1998, review of *Squids Will Be Squids,* p. 78; May 25, 1998, p. 28; July 10, 2000, p. 45; April 30, 2001, p. 76; July 16, 2001, p. 84.
School Library Journal, October, 1993, Gale W. Sherman, review of *Your Mother Was a Neanderthal,* p. 130; September, 1995, Lucinda Snyder Whitehurst, review of *Math Curse,* p. 215; June, 1998, pp. 121-122; August, 1998, p. 145; October, 1999, pp. 126-127; January, 2001, Susan Salpini, review of *The Very Persistent Gappers of Frip,* p. 160; May, 2001, Mary Ann Carich, review of *Baloney (Henry P.),* p. 134.
Time, December 21, 1992, "Kid-Lit Capers," pp. 69-70.

Wilson Library Bulletin, June, 1992, Donnarae MacCann, and Olga Richard, review of *The True Story of the Three Little Pigs!,* p. 118.

*   *   *

SOMMERDORF, Norma (Jean) 1926-

Personal

Born July 17, 1926, in Britt, IA; daughter of Carl (a minister) and Mabel (a schoolteacher; maiden name, Anderson) Seaquist; married Vernon L. Sommerdorf (a physician), December 31, 1946; children: Jean Sommerdorf Muirhead, Marianne Sommerdorf Dinwiddie, Delores Sommerdorf Corey, Philip. *Ethnicity:* "Swedish-American." *Education:* Bethel College, A.A., 1945; University of Minnesota, B.S., 1947. *Politics:* Democrat. *Religion:* American Baptist. *Hobbies and other interests:* Reading, photography.

Addresses

Agent—c/o Author Mail, Viking Children's Books, New York, NY. *E-mail*—nsommerd@mm.com.

Career

St. Paul Public Library, St. Paul, MN, clerk-librarian, 1943-46; State of Minnesota, St. Paul, MN, manager of governor's residence, 1969-76; U.S. Senate, Washington, DC, worked in a senator's office, 1976-77; Complete Traveler (travel agency), White Bear Lake, MN, owner, 1979-82; Travel Associates, St. Paul, MN, owner, 1982-93; writer, 1993—. Gateway and Step Group Homes, member of board of directors, 1969-99; American Baptist Homes of the Midwest, member of board of directors, 1970-96; St. Paul Heritage Preservation Commission, member, 1977-82. *Member:* Society of Children's Book Writers and Illustrators, Loft.

Writings

(Compiler) *A Church in Lowertown,* Mason, 1975.
An Elm Tree and Three Sisters, illustrated by Erika Weihs, Viking (New York, NY), 2001.

Contributor to books, including *Re-Membering and Re-Imagining,* Pilgrim Press, 1995; and *The Privilege for Which We Struggled: Leaders of the Woman Suffrage Movement in Minnesota,* Upper Midwest Women's History Center, 1999. Contributor to periodicals, including *Minnesota History* and *Ramsey County History.*

Work in Progress

Josette's Journey down the Red River Tail, a young adult novel; *My Uncle Ernie,* a picture book about building; *Tales from Kazakstan; My Gran's Haitian Feast; A Parade for San Patricio.*

Sidelights

Norma Sommerdorf told *SATA:* "People who have lived in other times and places have fascinated me ever since I learned to read. Learning about people who have been forgotten by the history books and the detective work of seeking obscure facts is challenging to me. The *National Geographic* brought glimpses of worlds unknown to me in rural Wisconsin and the prairies of Alberta. My father was a minister, and we moved to North Dakota just a few months before the attack on Pearl Harbor. I began keeping a journal and writing poetry during those lonely and frightening years of World War II, an exercise I recommend to would-be writers. By saving those notes it is possible to recapture feelings of long-ago events.

"For many years I wrote occasional articles while finishing college and working at a wonderful library. During those years I read many books for children and adults and dreamed that my name would someday be on one of them. During a long life of raising four adopted children, several foster children, and numerous international students, I never lost that dream. I researched the life of the first public schoolteacher in our state and wrote several articles about her. I have used that information to write a historical novel about a thirteen-year-old girl who comes down from Winnipeg to St. Paul on the Red River Trail in 1846 and becomes an interpreter for French and Ojibwe students at the teacher's new school. After visiting China and Haiti, I began writing about some of the places I have visited and the international students who have shared our home. *An Elm Tree and Three Sisters,* though, is a story I heard from my mother's cousin, when we stopped to visit her on the day her elm tree was being cut down. The emotion she felt about the tree prompted me to write her story. That story, like most everything we remember, is history too."

*   *   *

SONES, Sonya

Personal

Born in Boston, MA; married; two children. *Education:* Hampshire College, MA, B.A. *Hobbies and other interests:* Tending roses, dancing, reading, hunting for buried treasures at flea markets.

Addresses

Home—California. *Agent*—c/o Author Mail, 7th Floor, HarperCollins, 10 East 53rd St., New York, NY 10022.

Career

Film maker, film editor, animator, and writer.

Awards, Honors

Best Book for Young Adults citation, American Library Association, for *Stop Pretending: What Happened When My Big Sister Went Crazy.*

Writings

Stop Pretending: What Happened When My Big Sister Went Crazy, HarperCollins (New York, NY), 1999.
What My Mother Doesn't Know, Simon & Schuster (New York, NY), 2001.

Sidelights

Sonya Sones drew upon a real-life experience in her acclaimed 1999 debut as an author. Her young-adult novel, *Stop Pretending: What Happened When My Big Sister Went Crazy,* recounts in verse form one teen's impressions of her older sister's nervous breakdown and subsequent hospitalization for manic depression. Like Cookie, *Stop Pretending*'s thirteen-year-old narrator, Sones was an avid versifier and diarist as a teen. She later became a photographer and worked in the film industry as an animator and editor. In a creative writing class she took as an adult, Sones became known for her humorous stanzas. As she recalled in an interview published on the Internet site *ACHUKA,* one day her teacher "asked us to write a poem using dactyl and trochee rhythms which are very heavy and sombre rhythms. This poem just popped out about having to visit my sister in the hospital and about how scary it was. It really made a huge impact on me. I spent hours thinking should I show this to my teacher, should I read it aloud when it comes to my turn?" In the end, Sones said, she did not read it aloud, but did show it to her teacher later and was rewarded with a very positive response.

Thinking of expanding the topic into a book, Sones then applied for grant from the Society of Children's Book Writers and Illustrators, and was surprised to receive it. She attended the organization's annual conference, and made contacts there that led to publication. *Stop Pretending* was originally comprised of fifty poems, but then Sones's editor began asking other questions about the characters and the story. As Sones recalled in the *ACHUKA* interview, "Every question she asked me inspired me to write a new poem. It had taken me a year and a half to write the first fifty poems. The second fifty took just three months."

Stop Pretending recounts the events leading up to the Christmas Eve night when Cookie's beloved older sister runs out of the house in her nightgown, on her way to a Christian midnight service even though their family is Jewish. The story was drawn from Sones's own family, when her older sister, nineteen and much admired by the then-thirteen-year-old Sones, returned home from college and did the same thing. The next day she was taken to a psychiatric hospital by Sones's parents. In the book, Cookie recalls her sister's increasingly strange behavior before this, and the profound sense of shock that comes when her sister is hospitalized.

As Sones did, Cookie finds visiting her sister a distressing experience, and avoids going when she can. "When I tried to hug her, she recoiled," Sones recalled in an article she wrote for London, England's *Guardian* newspaper. "I realised then that she didn't even know who I was. It was as though my sister had gone away, leaving in her place someone who looked like her, but wasn't her at all." Sones's fictional stand-in, Cookie, confesses in her poems that she fears staying too long in her visits to the psychiatric ward because they might affect her own state of mind. In her everyday world, Cookie fears the reactions of her friends and schoolmates, and wonders if others will think she is susceptible to manic depression as well. Sometimes she is angry—at her parents for fighting, or at her sister, thinking that she may be "pretending." As Sones told *ACHUKA,* "when you visit someone with mental illness there's no feeling of satisfaction. It's just downright scary, a horrifying thing. So I would leave the hospital, feeling completely filled up with this horror, and I would go home and I found if I wrote down every detail of what she had done, what I had seen and everything that had been horrible about it, I felt emptied out of it."

As the poems in *Stop Pretending* move along, months pass, Cookie's sister improves, and Cookie discovers the hobby of photography as a way to help both herself and her sister. In an appendix Sones includes a list of resources for teens who might find themselves in similar circumstances. The work won overwhelmingly positive praise. A *Kirkus Reviews* contributor termed it "a compelling tale ... presenting a painful passage through young adolescence," and a reviewer for *Adolescence* described it as "an intense and brutally honest story." Sones's verse displays, according to *Booklist*'s Michael Cart, "a cumulative emotional power that creeps up on the reader, culminating in a moving, unexpected line or phrase."

Sones has been an avid diarist all her life, and told *ACHUKA* that her collection runs to 115 volumes now. Some of that she mined for her next book, *What My Mother Doesn't Know,* published in 2001. Here, free-verse poems mingle with straightforward narrative to help teen readers realize that all relationships change over time—and sometimes they change too quickly for comfort. The first-person narrator and poet is Sophie, aged fourteen, who falls in love for the first time with Dylan. She then begins another romance online with a "cyberboy," who turns out to be a dangerous character. A third teen, Zak, may be interested in Sophie, but she has a difficult time seeing this longtime friend, her playmate from childhood, in a romantic light. Meanwhile, Sophie's home life is unsupportive: her depressed mother watches television soap operas all afternoon, and when her father does come home, fights between them usually ensue. Sophie's friends Rachel and Grace provide good advice and add a bit of loyalty drama to the story as well. "Sophie's voice is colloquial and intimate, and the discoveries she makes are beyond formula," noted *Booklist* critic Hazel Rochman. Other reviews also praised Sones's style. "Sones is a bright, perceptive writer who digs deeply into her protagonist's soul," remarked *School Library Journal*'s Sharon Korbeck, who also noted that Sophie's dilemmas will resonate with the intended audience. "It could, after all, be readers' lives," Korbeck stated. The sentiment was echoed by a *Kirkus Reviews* contributor, who called the story "romantic and sexy" and commended its author for "a verse experience that will leave teenage readers sighing with recognition and satisfaction." A *Publishers Weekly* reviewer predicted that this "honest and earthy story feels destined to captivate a young female audience, avid and reluctant readers alike."

Sones has said that her sister was very supportive about the family history detailed in *Stop Pretending*, realizing that it was a way to help other teens. Sones wrote in the *Guardian* article that in the end, the experience so many years ago brought them closer together. "I still look up to her and I still admire her," Sones wrote, "but now it's for her strength, her courage, and her unfailing sense of humor in the face of all the difficulties that life has thrown her way."

Biographical and Critical Sources

PERIODICALS

Adolescence, spring, 2001, review of *Stop Pretending: What Happened When My Big Sister Went Crazy*, p. 182.
Booklist, November 15, 1999, Michael Cart, review of *Stop Pretending*, p. 612; November 15, 2001, Hazel Rochman, review of *What My Mother Doesn't Know*, p. 573.
Bulletin of the Center for Children's Books, October, 1999, Deborah Stevenson, review of *Stop Pretending*, p. 69.
Guardian (London, England), June 23, 2001, Sonya Sones, "When a Stranger Came Home," p. 74.
Kirkus Reviews, October 1, 1999, review of *Stop Pretending*, p. 1584; September 15, 2001, review of *What My Mother Doesn't Know*, p. 1368.
Publishers Weekly, October 15, 2001, review of *What My Mother Doesn't Know*, p. 72.
School Library Journal, October, 1999, Sharon Korbeck, review of *Stop Pretending*, p. 160; October, 2001, Sharon Korbeck, review of *What My Mother Doesn't Know*, p. 171.

OTHER

ACHUKA, http://www.achuka.co.uk/ (December 7, 2001), "Sonya Sones."
Teenreads, http://www.teenreads.com/ (April 27, 2002), interview with Sonya Sones.*

*   *   *

SUTTON, Margaret Beebe 1903-2001

OBITUARY NOTICE—See index for *SATA* sketch: Born Rachel Irene Beebe, January 22, 1903; died June 21, 2001, in Lock Haven, PA. Author. Sutton was the author of a thirty-eight-volume mystery series featuring heroine Judy Bolton. Sutton worked as a printer as a young woman and after marrying her first husband, William Sutton, began writing books, which had been her childhood dream. The first Bolton book, *The Vanishing Shadow*, came out in 1932. The last, *The Secret of the Sand Castle*, in 1967. Other Bolton titles include *The Mysterious Half Cat*, *The Haunted Apartment* and *The Trail of the Green Doll*. Sutton wrote several other children's books including *Lollypop: The Story of a Little Dog*, *Gail Gardner, Junior Cadet Nurse*, and *The Weed Walk*. Sutton also taught adult education classes and was a civil rights advocate.

OBITUARIES AND OTHER SOURCES:

PERIODICALS

Los Angeles Times, June 24, 2001, p. B13.
New York Times, June 25, 2001, p. A18.

*   *   *

SZEKERES, Cyndy 1933-

Personal

Surname is pronounced "*zeck*-er-es"; born October 31, 1933, in Bridgeport, CT; daughter of Stephen Paul (a toolmaker) and Anna (Ceplousky) Szekeres; married Gennaro Prozzo (an artist), September 20, 1958; children: Marco, Christopher. *Education:* Pratt Institute, certificate, 1954.

Addresses

Home—P.O. Box 280, RFD 3, Putney, VT O5346; 232 Rocky Rd., Putney, VT 05346. *Agent*—Marilyn Marlow, Curtis Brown Ltd., 10 Astor Pl., New York, NY. *E-mail*—mice@solver.net.

Career

Illustrator and writer.

Writings

FOR CHILDREN; SELF-ILLUSTRATED

Long Ago, McGraw (New York, NY), 1977.
A Child's First Book of Poems, Golden Books (New York, NY), 1981, published as *Cyndy Szekeres' ABC*, Golden Books (New York, NY), 1983.
Puppy Too Small, Golden Books (New York, NY), 1984.
Scaredy Cat!, Golden Books (New York, NY), 1984.
Thumpity Thump Gets Dressed, Golden Books (New York, NY), 1984.
Baby Bear's Surprise, Golden Books (New York, NY), 1984.
Cyndy Szekeres' Counting Book 1 to 10, Golden Books (New York, NY), 1984.
Suppertime for Frieda Fuzzypaws, Golden Books (New York, NY), 1985.
Hide-and-Seek Duck, Golden Books (New York, NY), 1985.

Nothing-to-Do Puppy, Golden Books (New York, NY), 1985.

Good Night, Sammy, Golden Books (New York, NY), 1986.

Puppy Lost, Golden Books (New York, NY), 1986.

Sammy's Special Day, Golden Books (New York, NY), 1986.

Little Bear Counts His Favorite Things, Golden Books (New York, NY), 1986.

Melanie Mouse's Moving Day, Golden Books (New York, NY), 1986.

(Compiler) *Cyndy Szekeres' Book of Poems,* Western Publishing (New York, NY), 1987.

(Compiler) *Cyndy Szekeres' Mother Goose Rhymes,* Golden Books (New York, NY), 1987.

(Compiler) *Cyndy Szekeres' Book of Fairy Tales,* Golden Books (New York, NY), 1988.

Good Night, Sweet Mouse, Golden Books (New York, NY), 1988.

Cyndy Szekeres' Favorite Two-Minute Stories, Golden Books (New York, NY), 1989.

Things Bunny Sees, Western Publishing (New York, NY), 1990.

What Bunny Loves, Western Publishing (New York, NY), 1990.

Cyndy Szekeres' Nice Animals, Western Publishing (New York, NY), 1990.

Cyndy Szekeres' Hugs, Western Publishing (New York, NY), 1990.

Puppy Learns to Share, Western Publishing (New York, NY), 1990.

Ladybug, Where Are You?, Western Publishing (New York, NY), 1991.

(Compiler) *Cyndy Szekeres' Favorite Fairy Tales,* Western Publishing (New York, NY), 1992.

(Compiler) *Cyndy Szekeres' Favorite Mother Goose Rhymes,* Western Publishing (New York, NY), 1992.

Fluffy Duckling, Western Publishing (New York, NY), 1992.

Teeny Mouse Counts Herself, Western Publishing (New York, NY), 1992.

Cyndy Szekeres' Colors, Western Publishing (New York, NY), 1992.

Kisses, Western Publishing (New York, NY), 1993.

Little Puppy Cleans His Room, Western Publishing (New York, NY), 1993.

Cindy Szekeres' Baby Animals, Western Publishing (New York, NY), 1994.

Cindy Szekeres' I Am a Puppy, Western Publishing (New York, NY), 1994.

Cindy Szekeres' Christmas Mouse, Western Publishing (New York, NY), 1995.

Cindy Szekeres' Giggles, Western Publishing (New York, NY), 1996.

Yes, Virginia, There Is a Santa Claus, Scholastic (New York, NY), 1997.

Cindy Szekeres' I Love My Busy Book, Western Publishing (New York, NY), 1997.

The Mouse That Jack Built, Scholastic (New York, NY), 1997.

The Deep Blue Sky Twinkles with Stars, Scholastic (New York, NY), 1998.

Young readers learn to count to ten by counting Wilbur Bunny's relatives as they arrive for a birthday party in Cyndy Szekeres's self-illustrated Learn to Count, Funny Bunnies.

I Can Count 100 Bunnies: And So Can You!, Scholastic (New York, NY), 1998.

Kisses, Golden Books (New York, NY), 1998.

A Very Merry Mouse Country Christmas: An Advent Calendar, Scholastic (New York, NY), 1998.

Learn to Count, Funny Bunnies, Scholastic (New York, NY), 2000.

Wilbur Bunny's Funny Friends A to Z, Scholastic (New York, NY), 2000.

"TINY PAW LIBRARY" SERIES; SELF-ILLUSTRATED

A Busy Day, Golden Books (New York, NY), 1989.

The New Baby, Golden Books (New York, NY), 1989.

Moving Day, Golden Books (New York, NY), 1989.

A Fine Mouse Band, Golden Books (New York, NY), 1989.

A Mouse Mess, Western Publishing (New York, NY), 1990.

"TOBY" SERIES; SELF-ILLUSTRATED

Toby!, Little Simon (New York, NY), 2000.

Toby's Alphabet Walk, Little Simon (New York, NY), 2000.

Toby's Rainbow Clothes, Little Simon (New York, NY), 2000.

Toby's Silly Faces, Little Simon (New York, NY), 2000.

Toby's New Brother, Little Simon (New York, NY), 2000.

Toby's Holiday Hugs and Kisses, Little Simon (New York, NY), 2000.

Toby's Flying Lesson, Little Simon (New York, NY), 2000.

Toby Counts His Marbles, Little Simon (New York, NY), 2000.

Toby's Please and Thank You, Little Simon (New York, NY), 2001.

Toby's Good Night, Little Simon (New York, NY), 2001.

Toby, I Can Do It, Little Simon (New York, NY), 2001.

Toby, Do You Love Me?, Little Simon (New York, NY), 2001.

Toby's Dinosaur Halloween, Little Simon (New York, NY), 2001.

Toby's Busy Christmas, Little Simon (New York, NY), 2001.

ILLUSTRATOR

Sam Vaughan, *New Shoes*, Doubleday (New York, NY), 1961.

Jean Latham and Bee Lewi, *When Homer Honked*, Macmillan (New York, NY), 1961.

Marjorie Flack, *Walter, the Lazy Mouse*, Doubleday (New York, NY), 1963.

Evelyn Sibley Lampman, *Mrs. Updaisy*, Doubleday (New York, NY), 1963.

Phyllis Krasilovsky, *Girl Who Was a Cowboy*, Doubleday (New York, NY), 1965.

(With others) Alvin Tresselt, editor, *Humpty Dumpty's Storybook*, Parents Magazine Press (New York, NY), 1966.

Edward Ormondroyd, *Michael, the Upstairs Dog*, Dial (New York, NY), 1967.

Nancy Faulkner, *Small Clown and Tiger*, Doubleday (New York, NY), 1968.

Kathleen Lombardo, *Macaroni*, Random House (New York, NY), 1968.

Peggy Parrish, *Jumper Goes to School*, Simon & Schuster (New York, NY), 1969.

Adelaide Holl, *Moon Mouse*, Random House (New York, NY), 1969.

Barbara Robinson, *Fattest Bear in the First Grade*, Random House (New York, NY), 1969.

John Peterson, *Mystery in the Night Woods*, Scholastic Book Services (New York, NY), 1969.

Joy Lonergan, *Brian's Secret Errand*, Doubleday (New York, NY), 1969.

Patsy Scarry, *Little Richard*, McGraw (New York, NY), 1970.

Scarry, *Waggy and His Friends*, McGraw (New York, NY), 1970.

Kathryn Hitte, *What Can You Do without a Place to Play?*, Parents Magazine Press (New York, NY), 1971.

Lois Myller, *No! No!*, Simon & Schuster (New York, NY), 1971.

Scarry, *Little Richard and Prickles*, McGraw (New York, NY), 1971.

Betty Jean Lifton, *Good Night, Orange Monster*, Atheneum (New York, NY), 1972.

Mary Lystad, *James, the Jaguar*, Putnam (New York, NY), 1972.

Betty Boegehold, *Pippa Mouse*, Knopf (New York, NY), 1973.

Holl, *Bedtime for Bears*, Garrard (Champaign, IL), 1973.

Scarry, *More about Waggy*, American Heritage Press, 1973.

Miriam Anne Bourne, *Four-Ring Three*, Coward (New York, NY), 1973.

Lystad, *The Halloween Parade*, Putnam (New York, NY), 1973.

Kathy Darling, *Little Bat's Secret*, Garrard (Champaign, IL), 1974.

Robert Welber, *Goodbye, Hello*, Pantheon (New York, NY), 1974.

Julia Cunningham, *Maybe, a Mole*, Pantheon (New York, NY), 1974.

Albert Bigelow Paine, *Snowed-in Book*, Avon (New York, NY), 1974.

Jan Wahl, *The Muffletumps' Christmas Party*, Follett, 1975.

Wahl, *The Muffletumps' Storybook*, Follett, 1975.

Carolyn S. Bailey, *A Christmas Party*, Pantheon (New York, NY), 1975.

Boegehold, *Here's Pippa Again!*, Knopf (New York, NY), 1975.

Wahl, *The Clumpets Go Sailing*, Parents Magazine Press (New York, NY), 1975.

Wahl, *The Muffletumps' Halloween Scare*, Follett, 1977.

Wahl, *Doctor Rabbit's Foundling*, Pantheon (New York, NY), 1977.

Tony Johnston, *Night Noises, and Other Mole and Troll Stories*, Putnam (New York, NY), 1977.

Mary D. Kwitz, *Little Chick's Story*, Harper (New York, NY), 1978.

Wahl, *Who Will Believe Tim Kitten?*, Pantheon (New York, NY), 1978.

Holl, *Small Bear Builds a Playhouse*, Garrard (Champaign, IL), 1978.

Judy Delton, *Brimhall Comes to Stay*, Lothrop (New York, NY), 1978.

Marjorie W. Sharmat, *The 329th Friend*, Four Winds Press (New York, NY), 1979.

Johnston, *Happy Birthday, Mole and Troll*, Putnam (New York, NY), 1979.

Catherine Hiller, *Argentaybee and the Boonie*, Coward (New York, NY), 1979.

Wahl, *Doctor Rabbit's Lost Scout*, Pantheon (New York, NY), 1979.

Boegehold, *Pippa Pops Out!*, Knopf (New York, NY), 1979.

Boegehold, *Hurray for Pippa!*, Knopf (New York, NY), 1980.

Scarry, *Patsy Scarry's Big Bedtime Storybook*, Random House (New York, NY), 1980.

Polly B. Berends, *Ladybug and Dog and the Night Walk*, Random House (New York, NY), 1980.

Marci Ridion, *Woodsey Log Library*, four volumes, Random House (New York, NY), 1981.

Margo Hopkins, *Honey Rabbit*, Golden Books (New York, NY), 1982.

Marci McGill, *The Six Little Possums: A Birthday ABC*, Golden Press, 1982.

McGill, *The Six Little Possums and the Baby Sitter*, Golden Press, 1982.

McGill, *The Six Little Possums at Home*, Golden Press, 1982.

McGill, *The Six Little Possums: Pepper's Good and Bad Day*, Golden Press, 1982.

Clement C. Moore, *The Night before Christmas*, Golden Books (New York, NY), 1982.

Selma Lanes, selector, *A Child's First Book of Nursery Tales*, Golden Books (New York, NY), 1983, published as *Cyndy Szekeres' Book of Nursery Tales*, 1987.

Johnston, *Five Little Foxes and the Snow,* HarperCollins (New York, NY), 1987.

Boegehold, *Here's Pippa!,* Knopf (New York, NY), 1989.

Margaret Wise Brown, *Whispering Rabbit,* Western Publishing (New York, NY), 1992.

Ole Risom, *I Am a Kitten,* Western Publishing (New York, NY), 1993.

Beatrix Potter, *The Tale of Peter Rabbit,* Western Publishing (New York, NY), 1993.

(Compiler) *A Small Child's Book of Cozy Poems,* Scholastic (New York, NY), 1999.

(Compiler) *A Small Child's Book of Prayers,* Scholastic (New York, NY), 1999.

Also illustrator of Albert Bigelow Paine's "Hollow Tree" series, three volumes, Avon (New York, NY), 1973.

OTHER

Also creator of calendars, including *Cyndy's Animal Calendar, 1973,* McGraw (New York, NY), 1973, *Cyndy's Animal Calendar, 1975,* McGraw (New York, NY), 1974, and *Long Ago,* McGraw (New York, NY), 1976; and of *My Workbook Diary, 1973,* McGraw (New York, NY), 1972, and *My Workbook Diary, 1975,* McGraw (New York, NY), 1974. Editor of *It's Time to Go to Bed,* by Joyce Segal, Doubleday (New York, NY), 1979.

Sidelights

Cyndy Szekeres is a well-known illustrator of both her own children's books and those of such writers as Betty Boegehold, Patsy Scarry, and Jan Wahl. Szekeres began drawing at an early age and soon showed promise. As she once commented: "I can't remember a time when I didn't draw. I was the artist in the family, an aptitude inherited from my father who never had a chance to develop his talent."

A child of the late-Depression era, Szekeres drew on paper bags flattened and trimmed by her father, a toolmaker. Although she continued drawing throughout adolescence and her young adult life, she harbored few illusions about actually working as an artist. "I assumed that I was headed for a job in a factory and probably marriage," she once recalled.

Before Szekeres graduated from high school, however, her father learned that advertising might prove a lucrative and fulfilling career for her. Though she did not plan to become a commercial artist, she enrolled at Pratt Institute at her father's urging. "I had no intention of embarking on a career in advertising," she once related. "I had my heart set on becoming an illustrator."

Szekeres won admittance to Pratt and studied there until earning her certificate in 1954. But upon leaving the school, she discovered that few career opportunities existed for budding illustrators. She eventually obtained commercial work as a designer at display houses serving prominent New York City department stores. "Then I did children's fashion illustration for the Saks Fifth Avenue department store, requiring overly well-groomed, coiffed children wearing perfectly fit clothing," Szekeres once said. "This interrupted the way I usually drew children and I didn't appreciate the influence. It caused me to focus more keenly on anthropomorphic animals and I eventually decided (later on, after several books) to illustrate these animals only."

Marriage to a fellow artist in 1958 changed Szekeres career plans. Writing in *Something about the Author Autobiography Series* (*SAAS*), Szekeres related that her husband "became the occasional boost that I needed, guiding and encouraging me" to become an illustrator. Gradually, Szekeres's luck began to turn for the better. In 1959, the publishing house Doubleday, which had been maintaining a file of Szekeres' department-store works, contacted her with a request that she produce illustrations for Sam Vaughan's *New Shoes,* a book for children. By this time Szekeres was pregnant with her first child, but she nonetheless accepted the Doubleday offer. The results were a success. As Szekeres wrote in *SAAS,* "I became a children's book illustrator and a mother at the same time."

In the ensuing years, though her family grew, Szekeres assumed a considerable pace illustrating various children's books. In 1969, for example, she provided drawings for five works, including Adelaide Holl's *Moon Mouse.* Within the next two years she illustrated five more books, including the Patsy Scarry volumes *Little Richard* (which was Szekeres's first full-color work), *Waggy and His Friends,* and *Little Richard and Pickles.*

From **Toby's Good Night,** *written and illustrated by Szekeres.*

During the early 1970s, Szekeres illustrated several calendars featuring her anthropomorphic animals. "In 1977 the most successful of these calendars was produced as a book, *Long Ago,*" Szekeres once noted. "Using research collected on what life was like a long time ago, this was the first book I both wrote and illustrated. I had never considered myself a writer, but with a lot of help from my friends, I overcame self-doubt."

In 1981 Szekeres signed an exclusive contract with Western Publishing, and as of 1996, more than fourteen million copies of her books had been sold. Her success has also been confirmed by reviewers, who have noted that her books, which often feature animals with childlike personalities, are illustrated with attractive, bright artwork brimming with ingenious details.

Working beyond the parameters of Western Publishing, Szekeres has continued to build a respected list of self-illustrated works while continuing to provide illustrations for the texts of others. Among popular books in the latter category are the 1999 publications, *A Small Child's Book of Prayers* and *A Small Child's Book of Cozy Poems.* Szekeres acted as editor and compiler of both of these books in addition to illustrating them. Reviewing *A Small Child's Book of Cozy Poems,* *Booklist*'s Hazel Rochman praised Szekeres's "gentle, domestic line-and-watercolor pictures of animals in old-fashioned dress," and indeed such animals have become something of a trademark of this author-illustrator.

Illustrating her own texts, such as *The Deep Blue Sky Twinkles with Stars,* Szekeres displays her full talents for anthropomorphic tales and warm, feel-good settings. "There is a very detailed, three dimensional anthropomorphic world, up there in my head," Szekeres told *SATA.* "It has been there since I could read. Now, characters rattle around in my brain, tumble out and run around my desk. When I am pleased with my work it is because I listened to them! When I am disappointed it is because I tried to please and accommodate others. There is a fine line between the two. An exceptional editor and art director can help one stay on the right side. It has been years and years since art school (Pratt Institute 1954) and I am still learning!

"Personally, I feel emotions sharp and clear," she continued. "[H]appiness, sadness, despair, delight, anger, glee. In the world in my head my characters exhibit these clearly. I draw them anatomically true (well almost!) But allow great liberties in face and gestures to get those feelings across to the reader."

Booklist's Ellen Mandel praised the world Szekeres created in *The Deep Blue Sky Twinkles with Stars,* commenting on the "sunny, spring colors of golden chicks, tawny bunnies, pink blossoms, and green grass" in this "inviting bedtime tale." A contributor for *Publishers Weekly* called the same book a "sprightly tale of a woodland bunny family getting ready to call it a day." More bunnies take center stage in the year 2000 *Learn to Count, Funny Bunnies,* a rhyming board book.

Kristina Aaronson, reviewing the title in *School Library Journal,* felt that "Children will love the rhythm of the story, the amusing illustrations, and the small size of the book."

An "energetic young mouse"—as a contributor for *Publishers Weekly* described the protagonist—is served up in Szekeres's "Toby" series, board books which also educate. Numbers, the alphabet, colors, feelings, and manners are just some of the topics covered in this "spunky series" of concept books, according to the *Publishers Weekly* critic, who further commented that the author's "spirited artwork offers winsome particulars."

Szekeres commented in *SAAS:* "Over the years, all of what [touches] me has found its way into my work ... the awareness of Nature's beauty in a tulip bed, the pride-and-pleasure work ethic that my grandmother enjoyed, the response of children as I sat and read to them, teachers, editors, and friends that kept me going ... most of all a loving family that continues to grow."

Among Szekeres's influences is another luminary of children's literature: Richard Scarry. "I am proud to have had Richard Scarry as my mentor," Szekeres told *SATA.* "I never met him," she said, but "we've exchanged letters that began with his encouragement. He said, 'If you're not having fun, you're not doing it right.' Sometimes, it is so hard. I was trained as a child to be obedient. It stuck! It takes discipline and conviction to be true to oneself and one's labors, to remember they should produce a smile! Encouragement is paramount. Mine, from special editors, art directors my ever-patient agent Marilyn Marlow and another most important mentor, my husband, Gennaro Prozzo (a fine artist) of 43 years."

For Szekeres, the process of creating is as important as the finished creation. "I have enjoyed illustrating because there is much to explore and share, and I am compelled to do this," Szekeres said in *SAAS.* "My few experiences with writing make the quest all the richer. Aspiring authors and illustrators should consider the purpose they wish to serve. A means to earn a living is not enough; find [conviction] and inspiration!"

Biographical and Critical Sources

BOOKS

Pendergast, Sara, and Tom Pendergast, *St. James Guide to Children's Writers,* 5th edition, St. James Press (Detroit, MI), 1999.

Szekeres, Cyndy, essay in *Something about the Author Autobiography Series,* Volume 13, Gale (Detroit, MI), 1992.

Ward, Martha E, and Dorothy A. Marquardt, *Illustrators of Books for Young People,* 2nd edition, Scarecrow Press (Metuchen, NJ), 1979.

PERIODICALS

Booklist, December 1, 1977, p. 616; January 1, 1985, p. 643; December 1, 1985, p. 577; March 1, 1992,

p. 1287; February 1, 1997, p. 949; February 15, 1998, Ellen Mandel, review of *The Deep Blue Sky Twinkles with Stars,* pp. 1020-1021; January 1, 1999, p. 891; February 1, 1999, Hazel Rochman, review of *A Small Child's Book of Cozy Poems,* p. 976.

Junior Literary Guild, April, 1973; September, 1974; March, 1975.

Publishers Weekly, September 26, 1977, p. 137; September 19, 1980; October 30, 1981, p. 63; March 26, 1982; June 22, 1984, p. 99; August 12, 1988, p. 455; June 15, 1992, p. 101; January 20, 1997, pp. 400-401; January 12, 1998, p. 58; January 12, 1998, review of *The Deep Blue Sky Twinkles with Stars,* p. 58; February 22, 1999, p. 97; June 5, 2000, review of *Toby!,* p. 92; May 14, 2001, p. 84.

School Library Journal, April, 1985, p. 83; March, 1986, p. 153; April, 1997, p. 118; October, 1997, p. 48; March, 1998, p. 188; February, 1999, p. 89; April, 1999, p. 126; May, 2000, Kristina Aaronson, review of *Learn to Count, Funny Bunnies,* p. 156.*

T

TALBOTT, Hudson 1949-

Personal

Born July 11, 1949, in Louisville, KY; son of Peyton (a mortgage loan officer) and Mildred (a dress shop manager; maiden name, Pence) Talbott; *Education:* Attended University of Cincinnati, 1967-69; Temple University, B.F.A., 1971. *Politics:* "Registered Democrat." *Religion:* Siddha yoga. *Hobbies and other interests:* Skiing, playing tennis, horse riding, gardening.

Addresses

Home and office—119 Fifth Ave., New York, NY 10003. *E-mail*—Hudsontal@aol.com.

Career

Freelance illustrator, New York, NY, 1974—. Clients include Metropolitan Museum of Art, Museum of Modern Art, Metropolitan Opera Guild, Bloomingdale's Department Store, and Easy Street, Inc. Member of board of directors of Art Awareness (a nonprofit arts-presenting organization), Lexington, NY. *Member:* Society of Children's Book Writers and Illustrators.

Awards, Honors

Book of the Year, Library of Congress, 1987; Notable Book selection, National Council for the Social Studies/Children's Book Council, 2000; Orbis Pictus Recommended Book, National Council of Teachers of English, 2002.

Writings

SELF-ILLUSTRATED

How to Show Grown-ups the Museum, Museum of Modern Art (New York, NY), 1986.
The Lady at Liberty, Ishihara, 1987.
We're Back! A Dinosaur's Story, Crown (New York, NY), 1987.

(Adaptor) *Into the Woods* (from Stephen Sondheim and James Lapine's play), Crown (New York, NY), 1988.
Going Hollywood: A Dinosaur's Dream, Crown (New York, NY), 1989.
King Arthur: The Sword in the Stone, Morrow (New York, NY), 1991.
Your Pet Dinosaur: An Owner's Manual, Morrow (New York, NY), 1992.
Excalibur, Morrow (New York, NY), 1996.
(With Mark Greenberg) *Amazon Diary: The Jungle Adventures of Alex Winters,* Puffin (New York, NY), 1997.
O'Sullivan Stew: A Tale Cooked Up in Ireland, Putnam (New York, NY), 1999.
Lancelot, Morrow (New York, NY), 1999.
Forging Freedom: The True Story of Heroism During the Holocaust, Putnam (New York, NY), 2000.
Safari Journal, Harcourt (San Diego, CA), 2002.

ILLUSTRATOR

Jean Fritz, *Leonardo's Horse,* Putnam (New York, NY), 2001.

Adaptations

We're Back! A Dinosaur's Story was adapted into a full-length animated feature film by Steven Spielberg for Universal, 1993.

Sidelights

Hudson Talbott is the author and illustrator of a number of children's books ranging in subject from dinosaurs to Renaissance art. A native of Louisville, Kentucky, Talbott earned a fine-arts degree from Temple University and began working as a freelance illustrator in New York City in 1974. His first book, 1986's *How to Show Grown-ups the Museum,* was written for young Museum of Modern Art visitors. Talbott found commercial success with *We're Back! A Dinosaur's Story,* a story premising the comical return of dinosaurs to live among humans in the modern age. The story's talking Tyrannosaurus Rex and his pals disrupt the New York City Thanksgiving Day parade and hide out at the Museum of

Natural History, among other adventures. The book's charms lured Steven Spielberg into making it the basis of a 1993 animated film.

Talbott has written two other dinosaur books, including a spoof on the household pet-care genre, *Your Pet Dinosaur: An Owner's Manual.* Humorous illustrations and text provide advice for the care, feeding, and training of various breeds of dinosaur. A contributor to *Publishers Weekly* liked the "dexterously drawn images of preppie families romping with their pets in immaculate suburban settings." In addition to his dinosaur books, Talbott has also penned several adaptations of the King Arthur legend for the publisher Morrow, and illustrated them as well. These include *King Arthur: The Sword in the Stone,* which recounts Arthur's boyhood times in early medieval London, and *Excalibur,* the story of young king Arthur and his reckless disregard of Merlin's advice. Ignoring his wizard's caution, he leads his army into battle and loses spectacularly. "Talbott's retelling of this celebrated story emphasizes Arthur's youthful hunger for adventure," noted *Booklist*'s Karen Morgan in a review of the second book. A *Publishers Weekly* reviewer found the artist/author "at his vivid best with animals: rearing horses, eager dogs and a miraculous Questing Beast."

Talbott, whose commercial-illustration clients have included the Metropolitan Museum of Art and Bloomingdale's department stores, has earned praise for the unique format of a few of his books. The first of these to attract attention was a project with Mark Greenberg, *Amazon Diary: The Jungle Adventures of Alex Winters,* which purported to be the scrapbook of a youngster who has accompanied his anthropologist parents to the South American rainforest. A plane crash leads them to the Yanomami, an indigenous people who have had almost no contact with the modern world. Alex is at first stunned by their primitive way of life, and the Yanomami are in turn fascinated by some of his gadgets, such as his Polaroid camera. As Alex adjusts he begins to appreciate the Yanomami way of life. A *Publishers Weekly* reviewer found that "the book's design and graphics are inventive," and particularly liked *Amazon Diary*'s text, which the writer described as "hand-lettered in a credible sixth-grade scrawl." *School Librarian*'s Angela Redfern also commended the book as "a wonderful mixture of photos, annotated sketches, drawings, and maps."

Talbott turned the famed Arabian Nights saga into an Irish fable for *O'Sullivan Stew: A Tale Cooked Up in Ireland.* The story is set in an Irish coastal town, Crookhaven, where residents live in fear of a local witch. When her horse is stolen one day by the king's army, her neighbors do nothing to help, and she retaliates by casting spells on the elements that wreak havoc on the local economy. Crookhaven's fishermen fail to bring back any fish, the cows have no milk to give, and famine seems imminent. Clever Kate O'Sullivan and her brothers decide to return the horse to the witch to save the town, but their plan goes awry, and they are arrested. Like Scheherazade of the 1,001

Arabian Nights, Kate saves herself by telling fantastical tales that captivate her listeners. Hers concern leprechauns, fairy folk, and serpents, and by her talent she saves each one of her brothers; then the king falls in love with her. "Several clever turns of plot add spice to this appetizing concoction," noted a contributor to *Publishers Weekly,* who also found it "visually and verbally inventive in its details and its broader storytelling." *Booklist*'s Kay Weisman also commended Talbott's effort, declaring that his "colorful illustrations complement the exaggerated text and add to the tall tale flavor."

Talbott was inspired by a true story from World War II to write and illustrate his next book. *Forging Freedom: The True Story of Heroism During the Holocaust* recounts the wartime heroics of Jaap Penraat, Talbott's friend. "The author's personal connection to and affection for Penraat is evident in the warmth of his descriptions," *School Library Journal*'s Kathleen Isaacs wrote, and she termed it a "compelling biography." Jaap was a young man in Amsterdam in the 1930s who had many Jewish neighbors; when Nazi Germany invaded the Netherlands in 1940, the climate became increasingly hostile, and Dutch Jews began to be deported to concentration camps. Jaap was a student of art and architecture, and he employed his artistic skills as a forger of identity and travel papers to help his Jewish friends and neighbors. In 1942, as *Forging Freedom* recounts, he launched an ingenious scheme: first, he created documents for a fictitious German construction company, and papers for himself as its official representative. He then applied for travel permits to take Dutch "workers" to an alleged construction site in France, from which his Jewish charges were then smuggled into Spain and out of Nazi jurisdiction. The clever two-year ruse helped more than 400 Dutch Jews escape to freedom.

Talbott's illustrations of Jaap's heroics included images of a teenage Jaap visiting his neighbors on the Shabbas, collages of the skillfully forged papers, and images of Amsterdam under Nazi rule. "Text and pictures both have a boyish enthusiasm that nevertheless acknowledges the real human cost of the war," stated a reviewer for *Horn Book.* A *Publishers Weekly* contributor praised the "freshly conceived and powerfully rendered paintings," and remarked that in his illustrations of crowd scenes depicting Nazi parades and Dutch sympathizers of fascism, "Talbott uses indistinct gray tones to imply the crowd mentality and reserves color for resisters like Jaap." *Booklist*'s Hazel Rochman also commended the book's images, singling out one that showed a barbed-wire bedecked map of Europe under Nazi occupation. "Always present is the horror of what the refugees are escaping, as well as the exciting action and the heroism of" Jaap, Rochman wrote.

Talbott's next project was another true story, this time in collaboration with noted juvenile biographer Jean Fritz. *Leonardo's Horse* recounted the long history of a massive bronze equine sculpture once sketched by famed Italian Renaissance artist Leonardo da Vinci. A commission for the Duke of Milan, the horse was modeled in clay in 1493, but before work in bronze could begin, French troops invaded this part of northern Italy and Leonardo's model was destroyed. The Duke was forced to use his store of bronze to make armaments instead. The never-realized project was said to have haunted Leonardo until his death. In 1977, American art collector Charles Dent decided to revive the project, and planned to have the sculpture completed by a contemporary artist and then presented to the people of Italy as a gift. Dent died in 1994, but "Leonardo's Horse" was unveiled in Milan in 1999. Fritz's story recounts this 506-year history with the help of Talbott's images. *Booklist*'s Carolyn Phelan commended his work, noting that "Talbott makes good use of the irregularly shaped pages in his pleasing and occasionally dramatic illustrations." A *Kirkus Reviews* contributor offered similar praise. Talbott's drawings, the reviewer noted, "range from utterly recognizable scenes of Florence to the ghostly horses at Leonardo's deathbed," and found that images depicting the contemporary part of the story of *Leonardo's Horse* are "drawn with as much spirit and vitality as the Renaissance ones."

Talbott once said: "I came into book authorship through my artwork. David Allender, an editor at Crown Publishers, saw my art on a calendar and called to ask if I would be interested in writing and illustrating a book. Although I'm still principally a visually-oriented person, I am very excited by the new challenge of exploring the verbal portion of my creativity."

Biographical and Critical Sources

PERIODICALS

Booklist, November 15, 1996, Karen Morgan, review of *Excalibur,* p. 585; February 1, 1999, Kay Weisman, review of *O'Sullivan Stew,* p. 983; July, 2000, Hazel Rochman, review of *Forging Freedom,* p. 2026; October 15, 2001, Carolyn Phelan, review of *Leonardo's Horse,* p. 394.

Books for Keeps, March, 1998, Clive Barnes, review of *Amazon Diary,* p. 23.

Entertainment Weekly, December 10, 1993, Steve Daly, "Going Hollywood: A Dinosaur's Dream," and "Your Pet Dinosaur: An Owner's Manual," p. 86.

Horn Book, January, 2001, review of *Forging Freedom,* p. 119; September, 2001, review of *Leonardo's Horse,* p. 609.

Kirkus Reviews, December 15, 1998, review of *O'Sullivan Stew,* p. 1804; September 15, 2001, review of *Leonardo's Horse,* p. 1357.

Publishers Weekly, October 18, 1991, review of *King Arthur,* p. 60; August 3, 1992, review of *Your Pet Dinosaur,* p. 72; July 22, 1996, review of *Excalibur,* p. 240; August 12, 1996, review of *Amazon Diary,* p. 83; January 11, 1999, review of *O'Sullivan Stew,* p. 72; October 23, 2000, review of *Forging Freedom,* p. 77.

School Librarian, summer, 1998, Angela Redfern, review of *Amazon Diary,* p. 96.

School Library Journal, October, 1999, Virginia Golodetz, review of *Lancelot,* p. 143; November, 2000, Kathleen Isaacs, review of *Forging Freedom,* p. 176.

OTHER

Hudson Talbott Web Site, http://www.hudsontalbott.com (April 24, 2002).

*   *   *

TROTTIER, Maxine 1950-

Personal

Born May 3, 1950, in Grosse Pointe Farms, MI; immigrated to Canada, 1960; became Canadian citizen, 1970; married William. *Education:* Graduated from the University of Western Ontario.

Addresses

Home—Ontario, Canada. *Agent*—Transatlantic Literary Agency, 72 Glengowan Rd., Toronto, Ontario M4N 1G4, Canada. *E-mail*—maxitrot@execulink.com.

Career

Writer. Former public-school teacher in Lambeth, Ontario, Canada.

Writings

Alison's House, illustrated by Michael Martchenko, Oxford University Press (New York, NY), 1993.

The Tiny Kite of Eddie Wing, illustrated by Art Van Mil, Kane/Miller Book Publishers (Brooklyn, NY), 1996.

Pavlova's Gift, illustrated by Victoria Berdichevsky, Stoddart (Toronto, Canada), 1996.

A Safe Place, illustrated by Judith Friedman, Albert Whitman (Morton Grove, IL), 1997.

Prairie Willow, illustrated by Laura Fernandez and Rick Jacobson, Stoddart (Toronto, Canada), 1998.

Claire's Gift, illustrated by Rajke Kupesic, North Winds Press (Markham, Canada), 1999.

Dreamstones, paintings by Stella East, Stoddart (Toronto, Canada), 1999.

Flags, illustrated by Paul Morin, Stoddart (Toronto, Canada), 1999.

One Is Canada, illustrated by Bill Slavin, HarperCollins (Toronto, Canada), 1999.

A Circle of Silver, Stoddart (Toronto, Canada), 1999.

The Walking Stick, illustrated by Annouchka Gravel Galouchko, Stoddart (Toronto, Canada), 1999.

By the Standing Stone, Stoddart (Toronto, Canada), 2000.

Laura: A Childhood Tale of Laura Second, illustrated by Karen Reczuch, North Winds Press (Markham, Canada), 2000.

Little Dog Moon, paintings by Laura Fernandez and Rick Jacobson, Stoddart (Toronto, Canada), 2000.

Storm at Batoche, illustrated by John Mantha, Stoddart (Toronto, Canada), 2000.

Native Crafts: Inspired by North America's First Peoples, illustrated by Esperanca Melo, Kids Can Press (Toronto, Canada), 2000.

There Have Always Been Foxes, paintings by Regolo Ricci, Stoddart (Toronto, Canada), 2001.

Under a Shooting Star, Stoddart (Toronto, Canada), 2001.

Also contributor to *Sherwood: Original Stories from the World of Robin Hood,* edited by Jane Yolen, illustrated by Dennis Nolan, Philomel (New York, NY), 2000.

Sidelights

Children's book author Maxine Trottier has written several works that draw upon Canadian history or illustrate themes borrowed from other cultures. Trottier draws on her own mixed heritage—Métis, descended from Indian and Canadian ancestors—for part of her inspiration. The author was born in the Detroit, Michigan, area in 1950, and attended elementary school in nearby St. Clair Shores, Michigan, before her family moved across the Detroit River to Windsor, Ontario. She later graduated from the University of Western Ontario, and began a long career as a public-school teacher in Ontario.

Trottier's first book was *Alison's House,* which appeared in 1993. Her second, *The Tiny Kite of Eddie Wing,* featured illustrations by Art Van Mil. Its story centers around Eddie, who comes from a poor family. Old Chan, a wealthy man in his neighborhood, hosts an annual kite-flying contest, and Eddie dreams of entering. Unfortunately, his family is so poor that he cannot afford even a simple paper kite. The contest's prize that year will be given to the smallest kite, and so Eddie creates an imaginary one for the contest. He does not win, but Old Chan gives him materials to make his own kite. "The story is sweet and moving," remarked *Booklist* critic Ilene Cooper.

Trottier moved from Asian culture to Russian for her next book, *Pavlova's Gift.* It presents a fictionalized event in the life of Russian ballerina Anna Pavlova, who died in 1931. Pavlova was considered the greatest ballerina of her era, and Trottier's story imagines the aging dancer balking when Imperial Russia's ruler, Czar Nicholas II, asks her to come out of retirement to give a special performance. In Trottier's tale, Pavlova meets a gypsy woman on her journey to the Czar's court, who tells her fortune and remarks that she has the gift of dance. The woman gives her a wooden heart necklace. Later, Pavlova sees a younger gypsy woman and gives her both her own cloak and the necklace. The ballerina tells her new protégée to go to St. Petersburg and impersonate her. Later Pavlova receives a letter from the Czar thanking her for her performance. "Trottier . . . has given a satisfying folktale shape to the story," noted a reviewer for *Quill & Quire,* who termed it "a quiet book that carries a sense of mystery muffled by the falling snow."

Trottier explored a more realistic subject in *A Safe Place.* It recounts the hardships of Emily and her mother, who flee an abusive household. They find comfort and safety at a domestic-violence shelter. Volunteers and professionals at the shelter help Emily's mother create a new, more positive life for herself and her daughter. "This useful book ends on a convincingly hopeful note," wrote *Booklist*'s Julie Corsaro. Susan Hepler, reviewing the book for *School Library Journal,*

Emily and her mother escape domestic abuse when they go to a women's shelter in Maxine Trottier's **A Safe Place,** *illustrated by Judith Friedman.*

found it a "reassuring" story, and liked the way Trottier showed readers that help is available, "that it is all right to be frightened, and that things work out."

In her first book to delve into the Canadian past, Trottier traced the life of a young protagonist named Emily. *Prairie Willow* depicts the hardships early pioneers faced in the provinces of Manitoba, Alberta, and Saskatchewan. Emily and her family live on the windswept prairie in a sod house, attempting to farm the barren, treeless landscape. After the first successful harvest, each member of the family is allowed to pick something extra from a seed and plant catalog. Emily chooses a weeping willow tree, which she carefully plants and nurtures into a symbol of their life there. The author's "rich, poetic language is well suited to the heartfelt emotions of this loving family," remarked *Booklist*'s Kay Weisman, while Carolyn Stacey, writing in *School Library Journal,* remarked that "Trottier creates some compelling images of a woman as deeply rooted to the prairie."

In *The Walking Stick,* Trottier borrows from Asian culture and spirituality. The story begins when a young boy named Van finds a branch from a famed teak tree on the ground near a Buddhist monastery and temple. He takes it to his uncle, a monk, who fashions a walking stick for Van from it. The uncle tells Van that the stick will always help him because it was found near the statue of Buddha, and so possesses the deity's guidance. Trottier's story recounts Van's eventful life, including a war in his homeland that he must flee. Later he tells his granddaughter the story of the walking stick, and she takes it back to Vietnam for him. She visits the now-deserted monastery and lays the stick at the statue of Buddha that remains there. *Magpies* reviewer Margaret Phillips commended "the simplicity of the telling and the absence of any bitterness," and called it "a fitting tribute" to the Vietnamese people and spirit.

Trottier drew upon the culture of Canada's first peoples for *Dreamstones*. The story tells about a young boy named David, who accompanies his father on an expedition to the Canadian Arctic. David's father is a naturalist, and his job is to sketch the region's flora and fauna. But their ship becomes ice-bound, and the expedition must remain during the long, cold winter. In this part of the globe, night lasts for months, and David longs for daylight and the freedom to roam. One night he sees foxes near and runs out to play with them. He becomes lost in the winter night, but a mysterious man rescues him and they make a fire. The man tells him stories about animals' secret dreams, and David is found by his father the next day wrapped in sealskin, near a dying fire. No one knows who his helper was, but David is found near an Inukshuk, or "sleeping stone" figure—

stone markers that the Inuit built in the Canadian Arctic to guide their way across the snowy, markerless landscape. *School Library Journal*'s Tali Balas called *Dreamstones* a "moving tale" with illustrations that depict "the beauty and silence of an ice-covered land without overshadowing the story." Trottier's book won praise from other reviewers as well. "In simple but poetic language she evokes the atmosphere of the Northern night, where the ordinary sense of time is altered," remarked Gwyneth Evans in *Quill & Quire,* while *Booklist*'s Cooper asserted that "this dreamy, evocative story will resonate most with children old enough to appreciate the mystery."

In 1999 Trottier began a trilogy about the MacNeil family and their experiences as eighteenth-century English immigrants to the Canadian wilderness. The story began with *A Circle of Silver,* which finds thirteen-year-old John MacNeil heading to North America with his father, an officer in the British Army. John is artistic, but his father hopes that the challenges of the new land will toughen him up. Instead, John's sketches of his experiences and encounters gain him fame and lead to his appointment as the colony's official artist. Letters from John's sister in England are interspersed into the

Emily and her family nurture a weeping willow tree for many years on the Canadian prairie in the poetic Prairie Willow, *written by Trottier and illustrated by Laura Fernandez and Rick Jacobson.*

Lost at night in the Far North, young David is aided by a mysterious man who gives him fire and tells him about the dreams of animals. (From Dreamstones, *illustrated by Stella East.)*

text recounting his adventures. *Quill & Quire*'s Laurie McNeill called *A Circle of Silver* "an excellent companion to any early Canadian history lesson. Trottier brings to this novel the depth and storytelling skill she has demonstrated in" earlier works. Carrie Schadle, writing in *School Library Journal,* found it "peppered with many fascinating characters, quite a few of them historical," and called it "a lively novel with elements of romance and adventure."

The MacNeil saga continued in Trottier's *By the Standing Stone.* John's younger sister, Mack, leaves England for Canada and is eagerly expecting many adventures. But hostilities are increasing and, while she finds freedom from the constraints of being a proper young lady in English society, there is also danger. The French and Indian War is going on, and anti-British sentiment, soon to incite the American Revolutionary War, is rife. Mack and her friend are kidnaped, and her brother John, now an Army officer himself, rescues them. "This is a story of adventure, intrigue, and suspense," stated Tina White in *Resource Links.*

Another Asian monastery serves as the setting for Trottier's *Little Dog Moon.* A monastery in Tibet houses

Moon, a Tibetan terrier, who keeps company with Tenzin, the youngest monk. One day two starving refugee children appear at the monastery's door. Tenzin sends the little dog Moon with them to guide them through the mountains. "This quietly provocative story of courage, faith, and kindness is sure to raise awareness regarding the reality of life in a restricted society," remarked *School Library Journal* critic Wendy Lukehart.

Trottier drew upon a legend surrounding Fortress Louisbourg on Cape Breton Island for *There Have Always Been Foxes.* The national historic site off the coast of Nova Scotia was built in 1713 by the French, then taken by the British. In Trottier's book, the Fort's long and storied history is recounted, as well as its famous legend: sometimes a fox can be seen dancing with a cat there. Trottier made a fox the narrator of the tale. "Young children will delight in this story told by a fox, while older readers will appreciate the historical aspect of the tale and hopefully be inspired to" read more on the subject, stated *Resource Links* reviewer Victoria Pennell.

Trottier lives on the shores of Lake Erie, and each summer she and her husband travel the Great Lakes on their boat. She began corresponding with students in her old elementary school when she began her writing career in the early 1990s, finding herself pulled to its memories. She described Ardmore Elementary in an article for the *Instructor* as the place "where I learned to cherish the written word, and where I was encouraged to be creative and let my imagination fly." An official visit was arranged, and Trottier spent a day there as a special guest. She conducted writers' workshops, spoke to classes, and was bestowed with several touching honors. "How I made it through this day without weeping I have no idea," she wrote in the *Instructor* article. "My experience that day had brought my journey full circle—from student to teacher to writer and, in a way, back to student again."

Biographical and Critical Sources

PERIODICALS

Booklist, November 15, 1996, Ilene Cooper, review of *The Tiny Kite of Eddie Wing,* p. 596; June 1, 1997, Julie Corsaro, review of *A Safe Place,* p. 1723; September 15, 1998, Kay Weisman, review of *Prairie Willow,* p. 241; July, 2000, Karen Hutt, review of *Native Crafts,* p. 2028; July, 2000, Ilene Cooper, review of *Dreamstones,* p. 2044.

Books in Canada, November, 1993, Janet McNaughton, review of *Alison's House,* p. 58; March, 1997, Rasa Mazeika, review of *Pavlova's Gift,* pp. 32-33.

Horn Book Guide, fall, 1997, Tanya Anger, review of *A Safe Place,* p. 283.

Instructor, March, 1994, "Coming Full Circle," p. 106.

Magpies, March, 1999, Margaret Phillips, review of *The Walking Stick,* p. 31.

Quill & Quire, August, 1996, review of *Pavlova's Gift,* pp. 43-44; January, 1999, Arlene Perly Rae, review of *One Is Canada,* p. 43; June, 1999, Bridget Donald, review of *Flags,* p. 64; September, 1999, Gwyneth Evans, review of *Dreamstones,* p. 68; November, 1999, Gwyneth Evans, review of *Claire's Gift,* p. 44-45; December, 1999, Laurie McNeill, review of *A Circle of Silver,* p. 37.

Resource Links, April 2001, "Picture Books for Older Readers," p. 49; June, 2001, Victoria Pennell, review of *There Have Always Been Foxes,* p. 6, Tina White, review of *By the Standing Stone,* p. 42;

School Library Journal, December, 1996, Christine A. Moesch, review of *The Tiny Kite of Eddie Wing,* p. 107; May, 1997, Susan Hepler, review of *A Safe Place,* p. 116; February, 1999, Carolyn Stacey, review of *Prairie Willow,* pp. 89-90; September, 1999, Diane S. Marton, review of *The Walking Stick,* p. 208; March, 2000, Lucinda Snyder Whitehurst, review of *Flags,* p. 218; June, 2000, Marion F. Gallivan, review of *Native Crafts,* p. 171; August, 2000, Tali Balas, review of *Dreamstones,* p. 166; September, 2000, Carrie Schadle, review of *A Circle of Silver,* p. 238; March, 2001, *Wendy Lukehart,* review of *Little Dog Moon,* p. 222; May, 2001, Susan Hepler, review of *Storm at Batoche,* p. 136.

OTHER

Maxine Trottier Web Site, http://www.execulink.com/ (April 20, 2002)*

W

WARNER, Sally 1946-

Personal

Born 1946, in New York, NY; daughter of Stuart and Mary Jane Warner; married Reynold Blight, 1968; children: Alex, Andrew. *Education:* Attended Scripps College, 1964-68; Otis Art Institute, M.F.A., 1971. *Hobbies and other interests:* Gardening, yoga, swimming.

Addresses

Home—Pasadena, California. *Agent*—Ginger Knowlton, Curtis Brown Ltd., 10 Astor Place, New York, NY 10003. *E-mail*—sallywarner@earthlink.net.

Career

Author. Pasadena City College, Pasadena, CA, teacher of art education for ten years. *Member:* Authors Guild, PEN.

Awards, Honors

Gold Crown Award in Visual Arts, 1996; Pasadena Arts Council artist residencies at Ragdale Foundation.

Writings

(Self-illustrated) *Dog Years,* Knopf (New York, NY), 1995.
Some Friend (sequel to *Dog Years*), Knopf (New York, NY), 1996.
Ellie and the Bunheads, Knopf (New York, NY), 1997.
Sort of Forever, Knopf (New York, NY), 1998.
Totally Confidential, HarperCollins (New York, NY), 2000.
Bad Girl Blues (sequel to *Totally Confidential*), HarperCollins (New York, NY), 2001.
Finding Hattie, HarperCollins (New York, NY), 2001.
(Self-illustrated) *How To Be a Real Person (in Just One Day),* Knopf (New York, NY), 2001.
Sister Split, American Girl (Middleton, WI), 2001.

First-grader Lily learns about friendship after a fight with her two best friends in Sally Warner's **Leftover Lily,** *illustrated by Jacqueline Rogers.*

This Isn't about the Money, Viking (New York, NY), 2002.

"LILY" SERIES

Sweet and Sour Lily, illustrated by Jacqueline Rogers, Knopf (New York, NY), 1998.
Private Lily, illustrated by Jacqueline Rogers, Knopf (New York, NY), 1998.

Accidental Lily, illustrated by Jacqueline Rogers, Knopf (New York, NY), 1999.

Leftover Lily, illustrated by Jacqueline Rogers, Knopf (New York, NY), 1999.

FOR ADULTS

(Self-illustrated) *Encouraging the Artist in Your Child (Even If You Can't Draw),* photographs by Claire Henze, St. Martin's Press (New York, NY), 1989.

(Self-illustrated) *Encouraging the Artist in Yourself: Even If It's Been a Long, Long Time,* photographs by Claire Henze, St. Martin's Press (New York, NY), 1991.

Making Room for Making Art: A Thoughtful and Practical Guide to Bringing the Pleasure of Artistic Expression Back into Your Life, Chicago Review Press (Chicago, IL), 1994.

Sidelights

Since the mid-1990s, Sally Warner has published a steady list of middle-grade novels that depict contemporary characters in a host of realistic situations, as well as her "Lily" quartet, geared to younger readers, and several books on creativity for adults. She first made her name as a novelist for children with *Dog Years* and its sequel *Some Friend.* In these works readers get to know sixth-grader Case, who has major challenges to contend with: his father is in prison for armed robbery, he lives with his mother and little sister in a tiny apartment with no privacy, and he has made only one friend, Ned, at his new school. Yet, things take a turn for the better when his English class starts a newspaper and he contributes a cartoon about a dog named Spotty. In the sequel, Case tries to help Ned, who has run away from the foster home in which he was placed after his grandmother/guardian was hospitalized. Both books garnered positive reviews. Discussing *Dog Years* in the *Bulletin of the Center for Children's Books,* Susan Dove Lempke praised Warner for her "light touch," "vivid characters," and "remarkable economy of words." *Booklist* contributor Mary Harris Veeder also praised Warner's portrayal of the consequences of lying and the tension among school groups. As in *Dog Years,* in *Some Friend* Warner balances the "hard-hitting, realistic edge" with "witty, lighthearted moments," according to a *Publishers Weekly* critic.

Warner's next preteen novel, *Ellie and the Bunheads,* tells the story of almost thirteen-year-old Ellie, a dance student who is pressured by her parents to pursue a ballet career. While *Booklist* reviewer Lauren Peterson found the end "anticlimactic and unconvincing," she judged the depiction of "preteen angst" to be "authentic." Despite calling Ellie's arguments with her mother "a bit repetitious," a *Publishers Weekly* reviewer thought that the book "consistently rings true, as does the dialogue that gives this narrative its fleet pace." A *Kirkus Reviews* critic applauded the work, saying that "Ellie's experiences and observations ring true, and the ways she solves her problems make for an admirable character."

Warner followed Ellie with two other memorable characters: Cady and Nana. They are best friends in *Sort of Forever,* which focuses on the girls' relationship as Nana is suffering from a fatal illness. This work fared better with reviewers. Calling the work a "piercing novel," a *Publishers Weekly* critic commented, "Warner is honest and convincing, writing without sentimentality." In *Bulletin of the Center for Children's Books,* Deborah Stevenson described the novel as "sometimes talky and awkward," but especially good at portraying the effect of Nana's illness on those around her. *Booklist*'s Chris Sherman felt that Warner "skillfully adds flashes of humor" to balance the "heartbreaking but satisfying story."

Warner reprised Lily, Case's six-year-old sister in *Dog Years* and *Some Friend,* for a four-book series of chapter books. Lily has her own take on many of the same problems as her brother. In *Sweet and Sour Lily* she tries to make friends at a new school, while in *Private Lily,* Lily tries to make a private space for herself in their crowded apartment. *Accidentally Lily* focuses on her bed-wetting problem, and *Leftover Lily* depicts what happens when she fights with her two best friends. Enthusiasts for the series often noted the books' humor. They included *Booklist* contributors Lauren Peterson, who called *Sweet and Sour Lily* a "charming chapter book" and Hazel Rochman, who called *Private Lily* a "tender, very funny chapter book."

Totally Confidential and its sequel *Bad Girl Blues* focus on middle-schooler Quinney. In the first novel she decides that her summer job is to become a professional listener, and finds out she needs some advice herself. In the latter book she is forced to deal with a friend who has taken a different path than she has chosen. Both books earned qualified praise. Writing about *Totally Confidential* for *Publishers Weekly,* a reviewer found the maturity of the main character to be implausible but praised Warner for a "tight and well-told story, full of empathy for kids' anxieties and concerns." The characters are "not developed deeply," in the opinion of Victoria Kidd of *School Library Journal,* but will elicit empathy. *Booklist* contributor Shelle Rosenfeld also liked the work, calling it a "lively, engaging novel [that] sympathetically portrays some familiar themes."

Warner departed from writing contemporary middle-grade fiction in *Finding Hattie,* a historical novel set in the early 1880s. After the deaths of her great-aunt and brother, Hattie is taken in by an aunt who lives in New York City and sent with her cousin to a boarding school. There Hattie must choose between friendship with the popular group or another girl, who, like Hattie herself, is of a different background. Because Warner modeled Hattie after her own great-grandmother and even used part of her journal entries in the text, it is not surprising that reviewers noticed the author's "scrupulous attention to period detail," to quote a *Horn Book* reviewer. Several critics noted the authenticity, including Kathryn Kosiorek, who called it a "well-written, carefully researched novel" in her *School Library Journal* review. A *Publish-

ers Weekly reviewer wrote that the author "seamlessly details Hattie's domestic and academic life" and keeps Hattie's "observations historically accurate."

In addition to *Finding Hattie,* the year 2001 saw the publication of three contemporary novels by Warner as well: *How To Be a Real Person (in Just One Day),* about a girl whose mother is mentally ill, *Sister Split,* about the effects of their parents' divorce on two sisters, and *Bad Girl Blues.* Warner sounded a right note with *How To Be a Real Person,* which was published to good reviews. In this novel, sixth-grader Kara has been hiding the truth from others: her father is gone and her mother is slipping into mental illness. By the end of this particular day, Kara realizes that she cannot hold her life together any longer and must seek help. Lauding Warner in *Booklist* for her accurate depiction of mental illness, Kelly Milner called the work a "brave, troubling novel" with a "riveting, well-crafted story." Likewise, Terrie Dorio, writing in *School Library Journal,* noted that the "descriptions of living with a manic-depressive hit the mark." A *Publishers Weekly* contributor summed up: "Warner has shaped a haunting, ultimately hopeful story, whose heroine is indisputably real."

Biographical and Critical Sources

PERIODICALS

Booklist, April 15, 1995, Mary Harris Veeder, review of *Dog Years,* p. 1501; June 1, 1996, Susan Dove Lempke, review of *Some Friend,* p. 1724; June 1, 1997, Lauren Peterson, review of *Ellie and the Bunheads,* p. 1707; June 1, 1998, Chris Sherman, review of *Sort of Forever,* p. 1769; August, 1998, Lauren Peterson, review of *Sweet & Sour Lily,* p. 2009; September 15, 1998, Hazel Rochman, review of *Private Lily,* p. 232; March 15, 1999, Stephanie Zvirin, review of *Accidental Lily,* p. 1330; July, 1999, Lauren Peterson, review of *Leftover Lily,* p. 1947; June 1, 2000, review of *Totally Confidential,* p. 1898; February 1, 2001, GraceAnne A. DeCandido, review of *Finding Hattie,* p. 1054; February 15, 2001, Kelly Milner, review of *How To Be a Real Person (in Just One Day),* p. 1138; July, 2001, Kay Weisman, review of *Bad Girl Blues,* p. 2007; January 1, 2002, Julie Cummins, review of *Sister Split,* p. 860.

Book Report, November-December, 1997, Allison Trent Bernstein, review of *Ellie and the Bunheads,* p. 43.

Bulletin of the Center for Children's Books, May 9, 1995, Susan Dove Lempke, review of *Dog Years,* pp. 325-326; May, 1998, Deborah Stevenson, review of *Sort of Forever,* pp. 342-343; September, 1998, Deborah Stevenson, review of *Private Lily,* p. 38.

Horn Book, May, 2001, review of *Finding Hattie,* p. 338.

Kirkus Reviews, April 15, 1997, review of *Ellie and the Bunheads,* pp. 651-652.

Publishers Weekly, March 6, 1995, review of *Dog Years,* p. 70; June 10, 1996, review of *Some Friend,* p. 100; April 14, 1997, review of *Ellie and the Bunheads,* p. 76; March 30, 1998, review of *Sort of Forever,* p. 83; June 7, 1999, review of *Leftover Lily,* p. 85; June 26, 2000, review of *Totally Confidential,* p. 75; January 1, 2001, review of *How To Be a Real Person (in Just One Day),* p. 93; January 1, 2001, review of *Finding Hattie,* p. 93.

School Library Journal, April, 1995, Connie Tyrrell Burns, review of *Dog Years,* p. 138; May, 1996, Carrie A. Guarria, review of *Some Friend,* p. 118; September, 1997, Amy Kellman, review of *Ellie and the Bunheads,* pp. 226-227; July, 1998, Carrie A. Guarria, review of *Sort of Forever,* p. 100; October, 1998, Mary M. Hopf, review of *Private Lily,* p. 117; October, 1998, Susan Helper, review of *Sweet & Sour Lily,* pp. 117-118; July, 1999, Faith Brautigam, review of *Accidental Lily,* pp. 82-83; July, 1999, Susan Helper, review of *Leftover Lily,* p. 83; June, 2000, Victoria Kidd, review of *Totally Confidential,* p. 155; February, 2001, Kathryn Kosiorek, review of *Finding Hattie,* p. 122; February, 2001, Terrie Dorio, review of *How To Be a Real Person (in Just One Day),* p. 123; July, 2001, Laura Glaser, review of *Bad Girl Blues,* p. 116.

OTHER

Sally Warner, http://www.sallywarner.com/ (January 23, 2002).

*   *   *

WATANABE, Shigeo 1928-

Personal

Born March 20, 1928, in Shizuoka, Japan; son of Yuzo (a photographer) and Seki (Imai) Watanabe; married Kazue Nagahara, June 29, 1958; children: Tetsuta, Mitsuya, Khota (sons). *Education:* Keio University, Tokyo, B.A., 1953; Case Western Reserve University, M.S.L.S., 1955.

Addresses

Home—2-40-8 Sakuragaoka, Tamashi, Tokyo 206, Japan.

Career

New York Public Library, New York City, children's librarian, 1955-57; Keio University, Tokyo, Japan, associate professor, 1957-69, professor of children's literature, 1970-75; author, translator, and critic of books for children. Vice-president, International Board on Books for Young People, 1976-78. Visiting lecturer at numerous institutions, including University of Illinois, Western Michigan University, Pratt Institute, Library of Congress, and Case Western Reserve University. *Member:* Japan Library Association.

Awards, Honors

Chosen as one of the outstanding storytellers for the Storytelling Festival at the American Library Association, Miami Beach conference, 1956; chosen May Hill

Arbuthnot Honor Lecturer by the Children's Services Division of the American Library Association, 1977; Fifteenth Mobil Children's Culture Award (Japan), 1980.

Writings

"I CAN DO IT ALL BY MYSELF" SERIES; ILLUSTRATED BY YASUO OHTOMO

Dosureba Iinokana, Fukuinkan (Tokyo, Japan), 1977, translated as *How Do I Put It On?: Getting Dressed,* Collins (London, England), 1979.

Kon'nichiwa, Fukuinkan (Tokyo, Japan), 1980, translated as *Hallo! How Are You?,* Bodley Head (London, England), 1980, published as *Where's My Daddy?,* Philomel (New York, NY), 1982.

Itadakimaasu, Fukuinkan (Tokyo, Japan), 1980, translated as *What a Good Lunch!: Eating,* Collins (London, England), 1980.

Yoi Don!, Fukuinkan (Tokyo, Japan), 1980, translated as *Get Set! Go!,* Philomel (New York, NY), 1981.

Doronko, Doronko, Fukuinkan (Tokyo, Japan), 1981, translated as *I'm the King of the Castle!: Playing Alone,* Philomel (New York, NY), 1982.

I Can Ride It: Setting Goals, Philomel (New York, NY), 1982.

Boku Ouchi o Tsukurunda, Fukuinkan (Tokyo, Japan), 1982, translated as *I Can Build a House!,* Philomel (New York, NY), 1983.

Itte Kimasu, 1983, translated as *I Can Take a Walk,* Philomel (New York, NY), 1984.

Otosan asobo, translated as *Daddy, Play with Me,* Putnam (New York, NY), 1985.

Ofuroda, Ofuroda, 1985, translated as *I Can Take a Bath,* Putnam (New York, NY), 1987.

"I LOVE SPECIAL DAYS" SERIES; ILLUSTRATED BY YASUO OHTOMO

Kumata-kun no tanjobi, translated as *It's My Birthday!,* Putnam (New York, NY), 1988.

Aisu kurimu ga futte kita, translated as *Ice Cream Is Falling!,* Putnam (New York, NY), 1989.

Boku oyogerunda, translated as *Let's Go Swimming!,* Putnam (New York, NY), 1990.

OTHER

Author of more than seventy additional children's books in Japanese. Translator of children's books from English into Japanese, including *A Visit from St. Nicholas* by Clement Moore, *A Wrinkle in Time* by Madeleine L'Engle, *The Moffats* by Eleanor Estes, and *Scrambled Eggs Super* by Dr. Seuss. Also translator of critical works such as *The Unreluctant Years: A Critical Approach to Children's Literature* by Lillian H. Smith. Contributor of articles on children's literature and library services to professional journals.

Sidelights

Shigeo Watanabe is a children's author and librarian who has written more than eighty books for young readers. Most of his work has appeared in Japanese, but some of his titles have been translated into English, especially the popular "I Can Do It All By Myself" series. In that series—aimed at a very young audience—an engaging little bear bungles his way through tasks such as eating, dressing, and playing by himself. In a review of the series for *School Library Journal,* Clarissa Erwin noted that the books "really encourage the young to 'go for it!' with bright vocabulary, illustration and concept."

Bear's enthusiasm and optimism are a reflection on the author, who has won awards for his oral storytelling. Shigeo Watanabe was born into a large family—twelve children in all—in Shizuoka City, Japan. His father was a photographer who made a scanty living, and his mother died when he was five. A stepmother raised him, but she had to work very hard to care for so many children. "I remember one night she fainted after she had done all the washing in the bathroom," Watanabe remembered in *Top of the News.* "She had, of course, no washing machine."

Watanabe's father was a pious believer in Buddhism. He enjoyed telling his children mystical stories about the Buddha, as well as folktales and legends of Japan. Sometimes a number of the neighborhood children would join Watanabe at his father's feet to hear fantastic tales from their native land and even from foreign countries. When Watanabe was still a young teen he began to tell stories himself, mimicking his father's dramatic style.

"It was a miracle how my parents had managed to keep the family surviving all through those years," Watanabe told *Top of the News.* "Our house was burnt down in a big fire which swept away the whole town when I was twelve years old. And toward the end of World War II, the whole city was burnt to ashes again. Twice in his life my father had to confront an impossible fate; a dozen children, no house in which to live, nothing to feed the children, and no work to earn his living."

Somehow Watanabe and his family endured, and the young man earned entry to Keio University in Tokyo. After earning his bachelor's degree there, he became an exchange student at Case Western Reserve University in Cleveland, Ohio, where he studied library science for a master's degree. In 1955 Watanabe took his first job, as the only male children's librarian in the New York City public library system. He soon gained recognition there as an outstanding storyteller. "As soon as I started working ... I became rather popular among my small patrons," Watanabe said in *Top of the News.* "I liked them very much. To my surprise, they were very friendly from the beginning. They were much more sociable and talkative than children I had known in Japan."

He added: "I still do remember very fondly all the children I came across while I worked as a children's librarian at St. George, Port Richmond, Harlem, Fordham, and a few other branches [of the city's public libraries]. And the books that I shared the pleasure of reading with these children mean so much to my life. *Harry, the Dirty Dog, My Father's Dragon, Make Way for Ducklings, The Moffats, The Twenty-One Balloons,* and many others gave me everlasting pleasure in working with books and children. These books I brought back to Japan and shared the pleasures once more with our children by translating them into Japanese. Most of them are still being widely read by Japanese children."

In 1957 Watanabe returned to Japan, where he became an associate professor at Keio University. He married and had three sons of his own. Watanabe became known in his native land and overseas as a specialist on children's literature and library services. He was promoted to full professor in 1970, and since then he has traveled to many countries to lecture on children's books. Watanabe is recognized as one of Japan's leading translators of children's stories—he has tackled such tough assignments as Clement Moore's *The Night Before Christmas* and Dr. Seuss's *Scrambled Eggs Super,* to name just a few.

Some of Watanabe's original work has found its way into English translation as well, including the two series "I Can Do It All By Myself" and "I Love Special Days." Both series are aimed at the very youngest children and are meant to be read aloud. The books show how crucial skills can be developed, even if first attempts are unsuccessful. Bear of the "I Can Do It All By Myself" series has proven a particular favorite with the critics. *Children's Book Review Service* contributor Maxine Kamin, for instance, called Bear an "amiable animal" whose amusing antics should encourage a child whose fear of failure keeps her or him from trying new things. Likewise, Betsy Hearne noted in *Booklist* that the series "serves young ones who are trying to get themselves coordinated—and maintain independence."

Watanabe told the *Sixth Book of Junior Authors:* "My childhood memories, studies in children's books, library and teaching experiences, and fortunate encounters with eminent authors and artists have helped me to write books for children. I have translated over a hundred American and English children's books into Japanese. While I am doing this I always enjoy a feeling of going back and forth between realms of different cultures, not only in terms of verbal symbols, but also of images, sounds, feelings, and emotions." Reflecting on his own work, the author added: "It is always a great joy to create a story. To do this my children and wife are everlasting sources of inspiration.... I am grateful to the family in which I was brought up and to the one my family is bringing up."

Biographical and Critical Sources

BOOKS

Chevalier, Tracy, editor, *Twentieth-Century Children's Writers,* 2nd edition, St. James Press (Chicago, IL), 1989.

Children's Literature Review, Volume 8, Gale (Detroit, MI), 1985.
Sixth Book of Junior Authors and Illustrators, Wilson, 1989, pp. 310-312.

PERIODICALS

Booklist, June 15, 1983, Betsy Hearne, review of *I Can Build a House!,* p. 1342.
Children's Book Review Service, June, 1981, Maxine Kamin, review of *Get Set! Go!,* p. 93.
Publishers Weekly, February 24, 1984.
School Librarian, March, 1981.
School Library Journal, December, 1982, Clarissa Erwin, review of *I Can Ride It!* and *I'm the King of the Castle!,* p. 61.
Top of the News, spring, 1977.*

*   *   *

WOLFF, Sonia
See LEVITIN, Sonia (Wolff)

*   *   *

WOOLSEY, Janette 1904-1989

OBITUARY NOTICE—See index for *SATA* sketch: Born December 11, 1904, in Livingston Manor, NY; died March 12, 1989, in York, PA. Librarian and children's writer. Woolsey received her A.B. degree in 1925 from Middlebury College, her B.S. degree in 1926 from the Pratt Institute, Brooklyn, and her M.S. degree in 1931 from Columbia University. She began her career as an assistant children's librarian at the Pratt Institute Library (1926-27), as a children's librarian for Ohio University Library, Athens, OH (1927-36), and as a children's librarian for Martin Memorial Library and an elementary school librarian for the York City School District, York, PA (1936-67). She published seven books during her career (all with Elizabeth Hough Sechrist), including *New Plays for Red-Letter Days* (1953), *It's Time to Give a Play* (1955), *It's Time for Thanksgiving* (1957), *It's Time for Christmas* (1959), *It's Time for Easter* (1961), *It's Time for Brotherhood* (1962; rev. ed., 1973), and *It's Time for Story Hour* (1964). She also compiled an anthology *Terribly Strange Tales* (1967). She was a member of the American Library Association, the Pennsylvania Library Association (chairman of children's, school, and young people's librarians, 1951), the Pennsylvania Parent Teachers Association (life member), the Pennsylvania Retired Public School Employees Association, the York League of Women Voters (vice-president, 1961), the Historical Society of York County, Delta Delta Delta, and the College Club of York. Several of her books have been made into Braille and Talking Books for the Blind versions, and *It's Time for Brotherhood* was selected by the United States Information Office to be adapted for its "Ladder Book" series for those for whom English is a second language. A Janette Woolsey Memorial Scholarship was established in her name by the York Chapter of the American

Association of University Women. The author commented in an interview before her death that "writing isn't an easy profession, especially when it is combined with another exacting full-time job. But to me, there has never been anything quite so rewarding and fulfilling."

OBITUARIES AND OTHER SOURCES:

OTHER

Obituary research by Robert Reginald.

Cumulative Indexes

Illustrations Index

(In the following index, the number of the *volume* in which an illustrator's work appears is given *before* the colon, and the *page number* on which it appears is given *after* the colon. For example, a drawing by Adams, Adrienne appears in Volume 2 on page 6, another drawing by her appears in Volume 3 on page 80, another drawing in Volume 8 on page 1, and so on and so on....)

YABC

Index references to *YABC* refer to listings appearing in the two-volume *Yesterday's Authors of Books for Children,* also published by The Gale Group. *YABC* covers prominent authors and illustrators who died prior to 1960.

Author Index

The following index gives the number of the volume in which an author's biographical sketch, Autobiography Feature, Brief Entry, or Obituary appears.

This index includes references to all entries in the following series, which are also published by The Gale Group.

YABC—*Yesterday's Authors of Books for Children: Facts and Pictures about Authors and Illustrators of Books for Young People from Early Times to 1960*
CLR—*Children's Literature Review: Excerpts from Reviews, Criticism, and Commentary on Books for Children*
SAAS—*Something about the Author Autobiography Series*

Author Index

Author Index

Author Index